Teacher, Student, One-Stop Internet Resources

Log on to fl6.msscience.com

STUDY TOOLS

JUST FOR FLORIDA

- Self-Check Quizzes
- Interactive Tutor
- Vocabulary PuzzleMaker
- Chapter Review Tests
- FCAT Practice

- Concepts in Motion
- Math Practice
- BrainPOP Movies
- Multilingual Glossary

EXTENSIONS

- WebQuest Projects
- Prescreened Web Links

- Unit Projects
- Internet Labs

INTERACTIVE STUDENT EDITION

- Complete Interactive Student Edition available at mhln.com

FOR TEACHERS

- Teacher Forum
- Teaching Today—Professional Development

SAFETY SYMBOLS

SAFETY SYMBOLS	HAZARD	EXAMPLES	PRECAUTION	REMEDY
DISPOSAL	Special disposal procedures need to be followed.	certain chemicals, living organisms	Do not dispose of these materials in the sink or trash can.	Dispose of wastes as directed by your teacher.
BIOLOGICAL	Organisms or other biological materials that might be harmful to humans	bacteria, fungi, blood, unpreserved tissues, plant materials	Avoid skin contact with these materials. Wear mask or gloves.	Notify your teacher if you suspect contact with material. Wash hands thoroughly.
EXTREME TEMPERATURE	Objects that can burn skin by being too cold or too hot	boiling liquids, hot plates, dry ice, liquid nitrogen	Use proper protection when handling.	Go to your teacher for first aid.
SHARP OBJECT	Use of tools or glassware that can easily puncture or slice skin	razor blades, pins, scalpels, pointed tools, dissecting probes, broken glass	Practice common-sense behavior and follow guidelines for use of the tool.	Go to your teacher for first aid.
FUME	Possible danger to respiratory tract from fumes	ammonia, acetone, nail polish remover, heated sulfur, moth balls	Make sure there is good ventilation. Never smell fumes directly. Wear a mask.	Leave foul area and notify your teacher immediately.
ELECTRICAL	Possible danger from electrical shock or burn	improper grounding, liquid spills, short circuits, exposed wires	Double-check setup with teacher. Check condition of wires and apparatus.	Do not attempt to fix electrical problems. Notify your teacher immediately.
IRRITANT	Substances that can irritate the skin or mucous membranes of the respiratory tract	pollen, moth balls, steel wool, fiberglass, potassium permanganate	Wear dust mask and gloves. Practice extra care when handling these materials.	Go to your teacher for first aid.
CHEMICAL	Chemicals can react with and destroy tissue and other materials	bleaches such as hydrogen peroxide; acids such as sulfuric acid, hydrochloric acid; bases such as ammonia, sodium hydroxide	Wear goggles, gloves, and an apron.	Immediately flush the affected area with water and notify your teacher.
TOXIC	Substance may be poisonous if touched, inhaled, or swallowed.	mercury, many metal compounds, iodine, poinsettia plant parts	Follow your teacher's instructions.	Always wash hands thoroughly after use. Go to your teacher for first aid.
FLAMMABLE	Flammable chemicals may be ignited by open flame, spark, or exposed heat.	alcohol, kerosene, potassium permanganate	Avoid open flames and heat when using flammable chemicals.	Notify your teacher immediately. Use fire safety equipment if applicable.
OPEN FLAME	Open flame in use, may cause fire.	hair, clothing, paper, synthetic materials	Tie back hair and loose clothing. Follow teacher's instruction on lighting and extinguishing flames.	Notify your teacher immediately. Use fire safety equipment if applicable.

 Eye Safety
Proper eye protection should be worn at all times by anyone performing or observing science activities.

 Clothing Protection
This symbol appears when substances could stain or burn clothing.

 Animal Safety
This symbol appears when safety of animals and students must be ensured.

 Handwashing
After the lab, wash hands with soap and water before removing goggles.

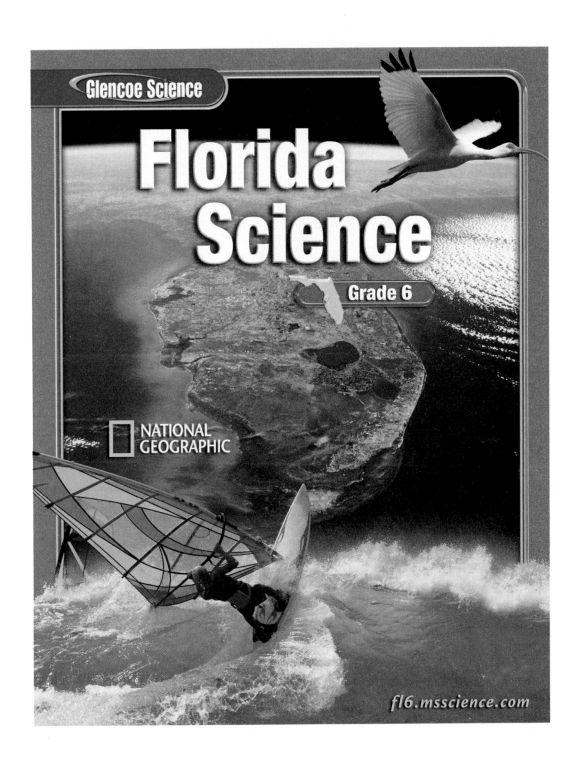

Glencoe Science

Florida Science

Grade 6

NATIONAL GEOGRAPHIC

fl6.msscience.com

Glencoe

New York, New York   Columbus, Ohio   Chicago, Illinois   Peoria, Illinois   Woodland Hills, California

Florida Science, Grade 6

The image of Florida was taken by satellite. Everglades National Park has a wide variety of plants and animals, like this white ibis. Windsurfing uses Bernoulli's principle to propel the surfer at greater speeds than the wind.

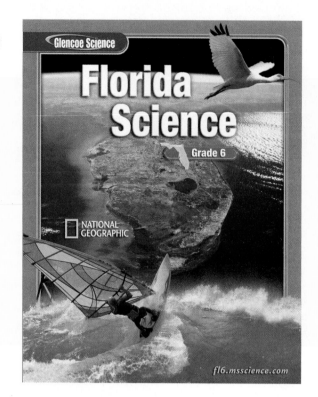

 **Glencoe**

The McGraw·Hill Companies

Send all inquiries to:
Glencoe/McGraw-Hill
8787 Orion Place
Columbus, OH 43240-4027
ISBN: 0-07-869387-X
Printed in the United States of America.
2 3 4 5 6 7 8 9 10 027/055 09 08 07 06

Contents In Brief

Acknowledgements

AUTHORS

NATIONAL GEOGRAPHIC
Education Division
Washington, D.C.

Alton Biggs
Retired Biology Teacher
Allen High School
Allen, TX

Lucy Daniel, PhD
Teacher/Consultant
Rutherford County Schools
Rutherfordton, NC

Ralph M. Feather Jr., PhD
Assistant Professor
Geoscience Department
Indiana University of Pennsylvania
Indiana, PA

Edward Ortleb
Science Consultant
St. Louis, MO

Peter Rillero, PhD
Professor of Science Education
Arizona State University West
Phoenix, AZ

Susan Leach Snyder
Retired Earth Science Teacher
Jones Middle School
Upper Arlington, OH

Dinah Zike
Educational Consultant
Dinah-Might Activities, Inc.
San Antonio, TX

SERIES CONSULTANTS

Content consultants reviewed chapters in their area of expertise and provided suggestions for improving the effectiveness of the science instruction.

Science Consultants

Jack Cooper
Ennis High School
Ennis, TX

Sandra K. Enger, PhD
Associate Director, Associate
    Professor
UAH Institute for Science Education
Huntsville, AL

Michael A. Hoggarth, PhD
Department of Life and Earth
    Sciences
Otterbein College
Westerville, OH

Jerome A. Jackson, PhD
Whitaker Eminent Scholar in
    Science
Program Director: Center for
    Science, Mathematics, and
    Technology Education
Florida Gulf Coast University
Fort Meyers, FL

William C. Keel, PhD
Department of Physics and
    Astronomy
University of Alabama
Tuscaloosa, AL

Linda McGaw
Science Program Coordinator
Advanced Placement Strategies, Inc.
Dallas, TX

Madelaine Meek
Physics Consultant Editor
Lebanon, OH

Robert Nierste
Science Department Head
Hendrick Middle School,
    Plano ISD
Plano, TX

Connie Rizzo, MD, PhD
Department of Science/Math
Marymount Manhattan College
New York, NY

Dominic Salinas, PhD
Middle School Science Supervisor
Caddo Parish Schools
Shreveport, LA

Carl Zorn, PhD
Staff Scientist
Jefferson Laboratory
Newport News, VA

Acknowledgements

Reading Consultants

Constance Cain, EdD
Literacy Coordinator
University of Central
    Florida
Orlando, FL

ReLeah Lent
Literacy Coordinator
University of Central
    Florida
Orlando, FL

Carol A. Senf, PhD
School of Literature,
    Communication,
    and Culture
Georgia Tech
Atlanta, GA

Math Consultants

Michael Hopper, DEng
Manager of Aircraft
    Certification
L-3 Communications
Greenville, TX

Teri Willard, EdD
Mathematics
    Curriculum Writer
Belgrade, MT

Safety Consultants

Jack A. Gerlovich, EdD
Professor Science
    Education/Safety
Drake University
Des Moines, IA

Dennis McElroy, PhD
Assistant Professor
Graceland University
Lamoni, IA

SERIES TEACHER REVIEWERS

Each Teacher Reviewer reviewed at least three chapters, providing feedback and suggestions for improving the effectiveness of the science instruction.

Deidre Adams
West Vigo Middle School
West Terre Haute, IN

John Barry
Seeger Jr.-Sr. High School
West Lebanon, IN

Tom Bright
Concord High School
Charlotte, NC

Marcia Chackan
Pine Crest School
Boca Raton, FL

Obioma Chukwu
J.H. Rose High School
Greenville, NC

Karen Curry
East Wake Middle School
Raleigh, NC

Joanne Davis
Murphy High School
Murphy, NC

Robin Dillon
Hanover Central High School
Cedar Lake, IN

Maria Grant
Hoover High School
San Diego, CA

Lynne Huskey
Chase Middle School
Forest City, NC

Nanette Kalis
Science Freelance Writer
Pomeroy, OH

Michelle Mazeika-Simmons
Whiting Middle School
Whiting, IN

Joe McConnell
Speedway Jr. High School
Indianapolis, IN

Mary Crowell Mills
Science Chairperson
Deerlake Middle School
Tallahassee, FL

Paola Ferreya Ortiz
Department Chairperson
Hammocks Middle School
Miami, FL

Darcy Vetro Ravndal
Director of Education
Center for Biological Defense
University of South Florida
Tampa, FL

Ava I. Rosales
District Curriculum Support
    Specialist
M-DCPS Division of Mathematics
    and Science
Miami, FL

Mark Sailer
Pioneer Jr.-Sr. High School
Royal Center, IN

Karen Watkins
Perry Meridian Middle School
Indianapolis, IN

Bonnie Weiler-Sagraves
Teacher of Gifted Science
Silver Sands Middle School
Port Orange, FL

Kate Ziegler
Durant Road Middle School
Raleigh, NC

Acknowledgements

SERIES LAB TESTERS

Lab Testers performed and evaluated the Student Edition labs and provided suggestions for improving the effectiveness of student instructions and teacher support.

Kevin Alligood
Science Department Chair
Silver Sands Middle School
Port Orange, FL

Marla Blair
Science Teacher
Belle Vue Middle School
Tallahassee, FL

Alan D'Aurora
Science Instructor
Arts Impact School
Columbus, OH

Theresa Goubeaux
Science Teacher
Sailorway Middle School
Vermilion, OH

Anetra Howard
Science Teacher
Sunbeam School
Cleveland, OH

Larry Howard
Science Coordinator
Ecole Kenwood
Columbus, OH

Deborah Howitt
Science Teacher
John F. Kennedy High School
Cleveland, OH

Lydia Hunter
Science Teacher
Warren School
Marietta, OH

Eugenia Johnson-Whitt
Health and Science Resource
    Specialist
Jewish Education Center of
    Cleveland
Cleveland, OH

Debra Krejci
Science Teacher
Patrick Henry Middle School
Cleveland, OH

Jill Leve
Science Teacher
Gross Schechter Day School
Cleveland, OH

Jason Mumaw
Science Coordinator
Rosemore Middle School
Whitehall, OH

Annette Potnick
Science Teacher
Rosemore Middle School
Whitehall, OH

Barbara Roberts
Science Teacher
Sailorway Middle School
Vermilion, OH

Glenn Rutland
Science Teacher
Holley-Navarre Middle School
Navarre, FL

Mary Sager
Science Teacher
Elgin Jr. High School
Green Camp, OH

Bob Smith
Science Teacher
Pleasant Middle School
Marion, OH

Jill A. Spires
Science Teacher
Buckeye Valley Middle School
Delaware, OH

Sheila Turkall
Science Teacher
St. Dominic School
Shaker Heights, OH

**Science Kit and Boreal
Laboratories**
Tonawanda, NY

FLORIDA SCIENCE ADVISORY BOARD

The Florida Science Advisory Board gave the editorial staff and design team feedback on the content and design of the Student Edition. They provided valuable input in the development of the 2006 edition of *Glencoe Florida Science.*

Jacqueline Amato
Science Subject Area Leader
Davidsen Middle School
Tampa, FL

Jacqua Ballas
Teacher on Assignment for
    Science, Curriculum, and
    Instruction
Marion County Public Schools
Ocala, FL

Dianna L. Bone
Science Department Head
Electa Lee Magnet Middle School
Bradenton, FL

Louise Chapman
Biology and Marine Science
    Teacher
Mainland High School
Daytona Beach, FL

Jan Gilliland
Biology Teacher
Braulio Alonso High School
Tampa, FL

Erick Hueck
Advanced Placement Coordinator
    and Science Dept. Chair
Miami Senior High School
Miami, FL

ReLeah Lent
Literacy Coordinator
University of Central Florida
Orlando, FL

Karen K. Lovett
Advanced Science Teacher, Science
    Department Chairperson
New Smyrna Beach Middle School
New Smyrna Beach, FL

Jim Nelson
Physics Teacher
University High School
Orlando, FL

Jane Nelson
Science Department Chairperson
University High School
Orlando, FL

Paula Nelson-Shokar
Science Curriculum Support
    Specialist
Miami-Dade County Public
    Schools
Miami, FL

Alicia K. Parker
Honors and Regular Biology
    Teacher
New Smyrna Beach High School
New Smyrna Beach, FL

Sharon S. Philyaw
Science Department Chairperson
Apalachicola High School
Apalachicola, FL

Leslie J. Pohley
Science Department Chairperson
Largo Middle School
Largo, FL

Chris Puchalla
Education Program Manager
G.WIZ—The Hands-On Science
    Museum
Sarasota, FL

Glenn Rutland
Regular and Gifted Science Teacher
Holley Navarre Middle School
Navarre, FL

Dana Sanner
National Board Certified
    Science Teacher and
    Department Head
Diplomat Middle School
Cape Coral, FL

Craig Seibert
K12 Coordinator for Science
Collier County Public Schools
Naples, FL

Jackie Speake
Curriculum and Instruction
    Specialist K12 Science,
    Health, and PE
Charlotte County Public Schools
Port Charlotte, FL

Ben Stofcheck
Program Specialist: Mathematics/
    Science K12
Citrus County Public Schools
Inverness, FL

Contents

 **FCAT practice is available in:**

- Section Reviews
- Chapter Reviews
- FCAT Practice Tests
- Annually Assessed Benchmark Checks
- Labs

Structure of Organisms—2

 chapter 1

Exploring and Classifying Life—4

chapter 2

The Living Cell—36

Florida Connections

Green Sea Turtle This reptile returns to the coast of Florida to lay its eggs. Find its classification on *page 23.*

chapter 3

The Role of Genes in Inheritance—66

Contents

Human Body Systems—92

Support, Movement, and Responses—94

Reading practice and help are available in:

- Section Vocabulary
- Section Summaries
- Chapter Summaries
- Science and Society
- Science and History
- Science and Language Arts

Digestion, Respiration, and Excretion—126

 Florida Connections

Sickle-Cell Disease In 2002, more than 10,156 Floridians were admitted with this abnormality of the red blood cells. Find out more about diseases of the blood on *page 166.*

Circulation and Immunity—160

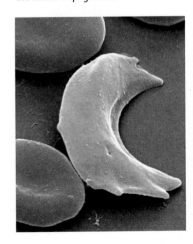

Contents

unit 3 Life and the Environment—194

Florida Connections

Coral Reefs Several coral reefs are located off the coasts of Florida. Coral reefs are homes to a variety of life. Find out about the relationships between the organisms in coral reefs and other environments on *page 208.*

 FCAT practice is available in:

- **Section Reviews**
- **Chapter Reviews**
- **FCAT Practice Tests**
- **Annually Assessed Benchmark Checks**
- **Labs**

Shaping Earth—286

The Atmosphere in Motion—288

Weathering and Soil—322

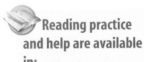

Reading practice
and help are available
in:

- **Section Vocabulary**
- **Section Summaries**
- **Chapter Summaries**
- **Science and Society**
- **Science and History**
- **Science and Language Arts**

Water Erosion and Deposition—350

Florida Connections

Hurricanes are becoming increasingly common on the Florida coasts. Find out about hurricanes and other severe weather on *pages 362–363*.

Contents

Diversity of Matter—410

Florida Connections

Tube Worms These giant tube worms live on the ocean floor near hot-water vents caused by seafloor spreading. Small submersibles and robots designed to help scientists study the ocean floor explore the Gulf of Mexico to find these and other creatures. Find out more about seafloor spreading on *page 389.*

FCAT practice is available in:

- **Section Reviews**
- **Chapter Reviews**
- **FCAT Practice Tests**
- **Annually Assessed Benchmark Checks**
- **Labs**

 **Reading practice and help are available in:**

- **Section Vocabulary**
- **Section Summaries**
- **Chapter Summaries**
- **Science and Society**
- **Science and History**
- **Science and Language Arts**

Florida Connections

Space shuttles, sent into space from Kennedy Space Center in Florida, are powered by a chemical reaction changing two elements into a compound. Find out more about compounds on *page 488.*

Contents

unit 7

Beyond Our Planet—620

Florida Connections

Lightning Strikes
According to the National Weather Service, from 1959–1994 there were more than twice as many deaths and casualties (1,523) caused by lightning in Florida than in any other state. Find out more about lightning on *pages 567–568*.

FCAT practice is available in:

- **Section Reviews**
- **Chapter Reviews**
- **FCAT Practice Tests**
- **Annually Assessed Benchmark Checks**
- **Labs**

Contents

Florida Connections

Space Flights This launch pad at Kennedy Space Center in Florida is where all space shuttles are launched. Find out more about past and future space missions on *page 665.*

Reading practice and help are available in:

- **Section Vocabulary**
- **Section Summaries**
- **Chapter Summaries**
- **Science and Society**
- **Science and History**
- **Science and Language Arts**

Cross-Curricular Readings

NATIONAL GEOGRAPHIC Unit Openers

NATIONAL GEOGRAPHIC VISUALIZING

Cross-Curricular Readings

Launch LAB

Mini LAB

Mini LAB *Try at Home*

LABS

available as a video lab on DVD or VHS

Traditional Labs

Design Your Own Labs

Model and Invent Labs

Use the Internet Labs

Activities

Applying Math

Applying Science

Activities

Astronomy: 21, 416, 650
Career: 57, 82, 244, 267, 339, 353, 399, 451, 478, 626, 668,
Chemistry: 41, 69, 111, 274, 333, 367, 389
Earth Science: 11, 178, 236, 244, 404, 491, 508, 579, 600
Health: 73, 132, 145, 292, 455, 567, 602, 659
History: 165, 209, 473, 548, 566
Language Arts: 97
Life Science: 257, 297, 451, 523, 512, 535, 551
Physics: 39, 108, 170, 214, 297, 353, 400, 389, 554, 598, 643, 646, 642
Social Studies: 16, 136, 301

8, 15, 23, 39, 49, 54, 69, 83, 105, 113, 134, 145, 163, 172, 200, 209, 227, 243, 261, 269, 298, 305, 309, 339, 356, 360, 385, 394, 428, 445, 459, 476, 481, 490, 521, 540, 567, 570, 603, 609, 628, 633, 670

Annually Assessed Benchmark Checks

10, 11, 17, 78, 111, 129, 181, 214, 215, 227, 235, 241, 264, 276, 340, 393, 417, 447, 448, 513, 516, 540, 541, 542, 595, 601, 633, 635, 676

FCAT Practice

34–35, 64–65, 90–91, 124–125, 158–159, 192–193, 222–223, 252–253, 284–285, 320–321, 348–349, 380–381, 408–409, 440–441, 468–469, 498–499, 530–531, 558–559, 590–591, 618–619, 654–655, 686–687

READING TO LEARN SCIENCE

Here are skills and strategies that can help you understand the words you read. *Reading and Succeeding* will help you build these skills and strategies. For example, the strategies you use depend on the purpose of your reading. You do not read a textbook or questions on the FCAT the same way you read a novel. You read a textbook for information. You read a novel for fun. To get the most out of your reading, you need to choose the right strategy to fit the purpose of your reading.

USE *READING AND SUCCEEDING* TO HELP YOU:

- identify new words and build your vocabulary,
- adjust the way you read to fit your reason for reading,
- use specific reading strategies to better understand what you read, and
- use critical-thinking strategies to think more deeply about what you read.

Identifying New Words and Building Vocabulary

What do you do when you come across a word you do not know as you read? Do you skip the word and keep reading? You might if you are reading for fun. But if you are reading for information, you might miss something important if you skip an unfamiliar word. When you come to a word you don't know, try the following strategies to figure out how to say the word and determine what the word means.

Sounding Out the Word

One way to figure out how to say a new word is to sound it out, syllable by syllable. Look carefully at the word's beginning, middle, and ending. Inside the word, do you see a word you already know how to pronounce? What vowels are in the syllables? Use the following tips when sounding out new words.

READING PRACTICE

- **What letters make up the beginning sound or beginning syllable of the word?**

  In the word *coagulate, co* rhymes with *so.*

- **What sounds do the letters in the middle part of the word make?**

  In the word *coagulate,* the syllable *ag* has the same sound as the *ag* in *bag,* and the syllable *u* is pronounced like the letter *u.*

- **What letters make up the ending sound or syllable?**

  In the word *coagulate, late* is a familiar word you already know how to pronounce.

- **Now try pronouncing the whole word: *co ag u late.***

- **Roots and Base Words** The main part of a word is called its root. When the root is a complete word, it may be called the base word. When you see a new word, identify its root or base word. It can help you pronounce the word and figure out the word's meaning. You will find a handbook of word origins in the Reference Handbook at the end of this book to help you figure out root words, prefixes, and suffixes.

- **Prefixes** A prefix is a word part added to the beginning of a root or base word. For example, the prefix *micro-* means "small," so *microorganism* means "small organism." Prefixes can change, or even reverse, the meaning of a word. For example, *non-* means "not," so nonvascular means "not vascular."

- **Suffixes** A suffix is a word part added to the end of a root or base word to change the word's meaning. Adding a suffix to a word also can change that word from one part of speech to another. For example, the word *human,* which is a noun, becomes an adjective when the suffix *-oid* (meaning "form") is added. *Humanoid* means "human form."

Reading and Succeeding

Using Syntax

Like all languages, English has rules for the way words are arranged in sentences. The way a sentence is organized is called its syntax. In a simple English sentence, someone or something (the subject) does something (the predicate or verb) to or with another person or thing (the object). In the sentence *"The rabbit ate the grass,"* *rabbit* is the subject, *ate* is the verb, and *grass* is the object.

READING PRACTICE

The blizzy kwarkles sminched the flerky fleans.

At first glance, you might think you can't determine anything about the meaning of this sentence. However, your experience with English syntax tells you that the action word, or verb, in this sentence is *sminched.*

• Who did the **sminching**? The **kwarkles.**

• Whom did they **sminch?** The **fleans.**

• What kind of **kwarkles** were they? **Blizzy.**

• What kind of **fleans?** Flerky.

Using Context Clues

You often can figure out the meaning of an unfamiliar word by looking at its context, or the words and sentences that surround it.

1. Look before and after the unfamiliar word for:
   • a definition or a synonym, another word that means the same as the unfamiliar word.
   • a general topic associated with the word.
   • a clue to what the word is similar to or different from.
   • an action or a description that has something to do with the word.
2. Connect what you already know with what the author has written.
3. Predict a possible meaning.
4. Use the meaning in the sentence.
5. Try again if your guess does not make sense.

Recognizing Word Meanings Across Subjects

Have you ever learned a new word in one class and then noticed it in your reading for other subjects? You can use what you know about the word's meaning to help you understand what it means in a different subject area.

READING PRACTICE

How can the meaning of the word *product* **in one subject help you understand its meaning in other subjects?**

Social studies: One *product* manufactured in the southern United States is cotton.

Math: After you multiply the two numbers, explain how you arrived at the *product.*

Science: One *product* of photosynthesis is oxygen.

Using Reference Materials

Dictionaries and other reference sources can help you learn new words.

- A **dictionary** gives the pronunciation and the meaning or meanings of words. A dictionary also might give other forms of words, their parts of speech, and synonyms. It also might provide the historical background of a word.

- A **glossary** is a word list that appears at the end—or appendix—of a book or other written work. It includes only words that are in that work. Like dictionaries, glossaries have the pronunciation and definitions of words.

- A **thesaurus** lists groups of words that have the same or similar meanings. Words with similar meanings are called synonyms.

Reading for a Reason

Why are you reading that paperback mystery? What do you hope to get from your science textbook? Do you read either of these books in the same way that you read a restaurant menu? How you read will depend on why you're reading.

Choosing Reading Materials

In school and in life, you will have many reasons for reading, and those reasons will lead you to a wide range of materials.

- **General Knowledge** To learn and understand new information, you might read news magazines, textbooks, news on the Internet, books about your favorite pastime, encyclopedia articles, primary and secondary sources for a school report, instructions on how to use a calling card, or directions for a standardized test.

- **Specific Information** To find specific information, you might read a Web page, a weather report, television listings, or the sports section of a newspaper.

- **Entertainment** To be entertained, you might read your favorite magazine, emails from friends, the Sunday comics, novels, or poems.

Adjusting How Fast You Read

How quickly or how carefully you should read depends on your purpose for reading it. Think about your purpose and choose a strategy that works best.

- **Scanning** means quickly running your eyes over the material, looking for key words or phrases that point to the information you're looking for. For example, you might scan a newspaper for movie show times.

- **Skimming** means quickly reading a piece of writing to find its main idea. You might skim the sports section of the daily newspaper to find out how your favorite teams are doing. You might skim a chapter in your textbook to prepare for a test.

- **Careful reading** involves reading slowly and paying attention with a purpose in mind. Read carefully when you're learning new concepts, following complicated directions, or preparing to explain information to someone else.

Understanding What You Read

Try using some of the following strategies before, during, and after reading to understand and remember what you read.

Previewing

When you preview a piece of writing, you are looking for a general idea of what to expect from the reading. Before you read, try the following.

- **Look at the title** and any illustrations that are included.
- **Read the headings,** subheadings, and anything in bold letters.
- **Skim** over the passage to see how it is organized. Is it divided into many parts? Is it a long poem or short story?
- **Look at the graphics**—pictures, maps, or diagrams.
- **Find** ✔ Reading Check **questions,** which will help you identify which ideas are most important in a paragraph.
- **Set a purpose** for your reading. Are you reading to learn something new? Are you reading to find specific information?

Using What You Know

Believe it or not, you already know quite a bit about what you are going to read. Your own knowledge and personal experience can help you create meaning in what you read. Before you read, ask yourself: *What do I already know about this topic?*

Predicting

A prediction is a guess about what will happen. You do not need any special knowledge to make predictions when you read. The predictions do not even have to be accurate. Try making predictions before and during your reading about what might happen in the story or article you are reading.

Visualizing

Creating pictures in your mind about what you are reading—called *visualizing*—will help you understand and remember it. As you read, picture the setting—city streets, the desert, or the surface of the Moon. Visualizing what you read can help you remember it for a longer time.

Identifying Sequence

When you discover the logical order of events or ideas, you are identifying sequence. Look for clues and signal words that will help you find how information is organized.

Determining the Main Idea

When you look for the main idea of a selection, you look for the most important idea. The examples, reasons, and details that further explain the main idea are called supporting details.

Questioning

Ask yourself questions as you read. *Why is this important? How does one event relate to another? Do I understand what I just read?* Asking and answering your questions helps you understand what you read.

Clarifying

As you read, you might find passages that you do not understand. Reread the passage using these techniques to help you clarify, or make the passage clear.

- **Reread** the confusing parts slowly and carefully.
- **Look up** unfamiliar words.
- **"Talk out"** the passage to yourself.

Reviewing

When you review in class, you go over what you learned the day before so that the information is clear in your mind. Reviewing when you read does the same thing. Take time now and then to pause and review what you have read. Think about the main ideas and organize them for yourself so you can recall them later. Filling in study aids such as graphic organizers can help you review.

Monitoring Your Comprehension

As you read, check your understanding by using the following strategies.

- **Summarize** When you read, pause from time to time and list for yourself the main ideas of what you have just read. Answer the questions *Who? What? Where? When? Why?* and *How?*

- **Paraphrase** Use paraphrasing to test whether you really got the point. Paraphrasing is retelling something in your own words. Try putting what you have just read into your own words. If you cannot explain it clearly, you should probably reread the text.

Thinking About Your Reading

Sometimes it is important to think more deeply about what you read so you can get the most out of what the author says. These critical thinking skills will help you go beyond what the words say and understand the meaning of your reading.

Interpreting

To interpret a text, first ask yourself: *What is the writer really saying here?* Then use what you know about the world to help answer that question.

Inferring

Writers sometimes suggest information or meaning without stating it directly. In reading, you infer when you use context clues and your own experience to figure out the author's meaning.

Drawing Conclusions

When you find connections between ideas and events, you are drawing conclusions. The process is like a detective solving a mystery. You combine information and evidence that the author provides to come up with a statement about the topic. This gives you a better understanding of what you are reading.

Analyzing

Analyzing, or looking at separate parts of something to understand the entire piece, is a way to think critically about written work. In analyzing informational text, you might look at how the ideas are organized to see what is most important.

Evaluating

When you form an opinion or make a judgment about something you are reading, you are evaluating. Ask yourself whether the author seems biased, whether the information is one-sided, and whether the argument that is presented is logical.

Synthesizing

When you synthesize, you combine ideas (maybe even from different sources) to come up with something new. For example, you might read a manual on coaching soccer, combine that information with your own experiences playing soccer, and come up with a winning plan for coaching your sister's team this spring.

Distinguishing Fact from Opinion

Distinguishing between fact and opinion is one of the most important reading skills you can learn. A fact is a statement that can be proved with supporting information. An opinion, on the other hand, is what a writer believes on the basis of his or her personal viewpoint.

As you examine information, always ask yourself, *Is this a fact or an opinion?* Opinions are important in many types of writing. You read editorials and essays for their authors' opinions. Reviews of books, movies, plays, and CDs can help you decide whether to spend your time and money on something. When opinions are based on faulty reasoning or prejudice or when they are stated as facts, they become troublesome.

READING PRACTICE

Look at the following examples of fact and opinion.

Fact: Spiders are arachnids.

Opinion: Spiders are scary.

You can prove that spiders are arachnids. However, not everyone thinks that spiders are scary. That is an opinion.

Understanding Text Structure

Good writers structure each piece of their writing in a specific way for a specific purpose. That pattern of organization is called text structure. When you know the text structure of a selection, you will find it easier to locate and recall an author's ideas. Here are four ways that writers organize text.

Compare and Contrast

Compare-and-contrast structure shows the similarities and differences between people, things, and ideas. When writers use compare-and-contrast structure, often they want to show you how things that seem alike are different, or how things that seem different are alike.

- **Signal words and phrases:** *similarly, on the other hand, in contrast to, however*

Cause and Effect

Just about everything that happens in life is the cause or the effect of some other event or action. Writers use cause-and-effect structure to explore the reasons for something happening and to examine the results of previous events. This structure helps answer the question that everybody is always asking: Why? Cause-and-effect structure is about explaining things.

- **Signal words and phrases:** *so, because, as a result, therefore*

Problem and Solution

How did scientists overcome the difficulty of getting a person to the Moon? How will I brush my teeth when I have forgotten my toothpaste? These questions may be very different in importance, but they have one thing in common: Each identifies a problem and asks how to solve it. Problems and solutions are part of what makes science interesting. Problems and solutions also occur in fiction and nonfiction writing.

- **Signal words and phrases:** *how, help, problem, obstruction, difficulty, need, attempt, have to, must*

Sequence

Take a look at three common types of sequences, or the order in which thoughts are arranged.

1. **Chronological order** refers to the order in which events take place. First you wake up; next you have breakfast; then you go to school. Those events don't make much sense in any other order.
   - **Signal words:** *first, next, then, later, finally*

2. **Spatial order** tells you the order in which to look at objects. For example, take a look at this description of an ice cream sundae: *At the bottom of the dish are two scoops of vanilla. The scoops are covered with fudge and topped with whipped cream and a cherry.* Your eyes follow the sundae from the bottom to the top. Spatial order is important in writing because it helps you as a reader to see an image the way the author does.
   - **Signal words:** *above, below, behind, next to*

3. **Order of importance** is going from most important to least important or the other way around. For example, a typical news article has a most-to-least-important structure.
   - **Signal words:** *principal, central, important, fundamental*

WHAT IS THE FCAT?

The **Florida Comprehensive Assessment Test (FCAT)** is part of Florida's effort to improve the teaching and learning of a higher level of standards. The primary purpose is to assess student mastery of the skills represented in the Sunshine State Standards (SSS) in reading, writing, mathematics, and science. The SSS portion of the FCAT is a criterion-referenced test.

A secondary purpose is to compare the performance of Florida students to the reading and mathematics performance of students across the nation using a norm-referenced test (NRT). All students in grades 3–10 take the Reading and Math FCAT in the spring of each year. All students in grades 4, 8, and 10 take the Writing FCAT. All students in grades 5, 8, and 11 take the Science FCAT.

Interpreting Benchmark Identifiers

The Sunshine State Standards are organized under eight major clusters called Strands:

A The Nature of Matter
B Energy
C Force and Motion
D Processes that Shape the Earth
E Earth and Space
F Processes of Life
G How Living Things Interact with Their Environment
H The Nature of Science

Major topics within each Strand are called Standards. Each Standard is divided into Benchmarks. Florida uses a special naming system to identify Strands, Standards, and Benchmarks. Here is how to interpret the Benchmark identifier **SC.B.1.3.1.**

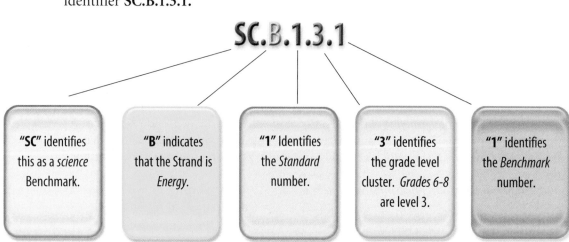

SC.B.1.3.1

| **"SC"** identifies this as a *science* Benchmark. | **"B"** indicates that the Strand is *Energy.* | **"1"** Identifies the *Standard* number. | **"3"** identifies the grade level cluster. *Grades 6–8* are level 3. | **"1"** identifies the *Benchmark* number. |

Preparing for the FCAT

Your *Glencoe Florida Science* text provides a wide variety of features to help you prepare for the FCAT.

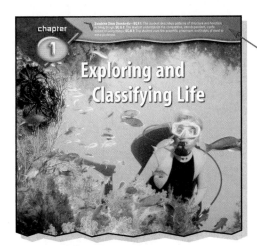

chapter
1
Exploring and Classifying Life

> **Every chapter** begins with a list of the Florida Standards covered in the chapter.

section
1

What is science?

as you read

What You'll Learn
■ Apply scientific methods to problem solving.
■ Demonstrate how to measure using scientific units.

Why It's Important
Learning to use scientific methods will help you solve ordinary problems in your life.

Review Vocabulary
✳ experiment: using controlled conditions to test a prediction

New Vocabulary
✳ scientific method
● hypothesis
● control
● variable
● theory
● law

✳ FCAT Vocabulary

The Work of Science

Movies and popcorn seem to go together. So before you and your friends watch a movie, sometimes you pop some corn in a microwave oven. When the popping stops, you take out the bag and open it carefully. You smell the mouthwatering, freshly popped corn and avoid hot steam that escapes from the bag. What makes the popcorn pop? How do microwaves work and make things hot? By the way, what are microwaves anyway?

Asking questions like these is one way scientists find out about anything in the world and the universe. Science is often described as an organized way of studying things and finding answers to questions.

Types of Science Many types of science exist. Each is given a name to describe what is being studied. For example, energy and matter have a relationship. That's a topic for physics. A physicist could answer most questions about microwaves.

On the other hand, a life scientist might study any of the millions of different animals, plants, and other living things on Earth. Look at the objects in **Figure 1**. What do they look like to you? A life scientist could tell you that some of the objects are living plants and some are rocks. Life scientists who study plants are botanists, and those who study animals are zoologists. What do you suppose a bacteriologist studies?

> **Every section** begins with a list of the Florida Benchmarks covered in the section.

> **Vocabulary** terms used on the FCAT are identified with a ✳.

Scientific Methods Help Answer Questions You can use scientific methods to answer all sorts of questions. Your questions may be as simple as "Where did I leave my house key?" or as complex as "Will global warming cause the polar ice caps to melt?" You probably have had to find the answer to the first question. Someday you might try to find the answer to the second question. Using these scientific methods does not guarantee that you will get an answer. Often scientific methods just lead to more questions and more experiments. That's what science is about—continuing to look for the best answers to your questions.

Annually Assessed Benchmark Check

SC.H.1.3.5 In the Applying Science activity below, why didn't the scientist use a different type of bacteria for each temperature?

Applying Science

Does temperature affect the rate of bacterial reproduction?

Some bacteria make you sick. Other bacteria, however, are used to produce foods like cheese and yogurt. Understanding how quickly bacteria reproduce can help you avoid harmful bacteria and use helpful bacteria. It's important to know things that affect how quickly bacteria reproduce. How do you think temperature will affect the rate of bacterial reproduction? A student makes the hypothesis that bacteria will reproduce more quickly as the temperature increases.

Identifying the Problem
The table below lists the reproduction-

Look at the table. What conclusions can you draw from the data?

> **Annually Assessed Benchmark Checks** located throughout your textbook highlight Benchmarks tested every year on the FCAT. The questions can help you identify which Benchmarks you have mastered and which you need to review.

Controls The technician separates the cats with sores from the other two cats. She puts each of the cats with sores in a cage by itself. One cat is called the experimental cat. This cat is given a litter box containing the cat litter without deodorant. The other cat is given a litter box that contains cat litter with deodorant. The cat with deodorant cat litter is the control.

A **control** is the standard to which the outcome of a test is compared. At the end of the experiment, the control cat will be compared with the experimental cat. Whether or not the cat litter contains deodorant is the variable. A **variable** is something in an experiment that can change. An experiment should have only one variable. Other than the difference in the cat litter, the technician treats both cats the same.

☑ **Reading Check** *How many variables should an experiment have?*

Analyze Data The veterinary technician observes both cats for one week. During this time, she collects data on how often and when the cats scratch or chew, as shown in **Figure 4.** These data are recorded in a journal. The data show that the control cat scratches and chews more often than the experimental cat does. The sores on the skin of the experimental cat begin to heal, but those on the control cat do not.

Draw Conclusions The technician then draws the conclusion—a logical answer to a question based on data and observation—that the deodorant in the cat litter probably irritated the skin of the two cats. To accept or reject the hypothesis is the next step. In this case, the technician accepts the hypothesis. If she had rejected it, new experiments would have been necessary.

Mini LAB

SC.H.1.3.5

Analyzing Data

Procedure
1. Obtain a **pan balance.** Follow your teacher's instructions for using it.
2. Record all data in your **Science Journal.**
3. Measure and record the mass of a **dry sponge.**
4. Soak this sponge in **water.** Measure and record its mass.
5. Calculate how much water your sponge absorbed.
6. Combine the class data and calculate the average amount of water absorbed.

Analysis
What other information about the sponges might be important when analyzing the data from the entire class?

Figure 4 Collecting and analyzing data is part of scientific methods.

> The Benchmarks practiced in the **MiniLABs** are listed above the MiniLAB.

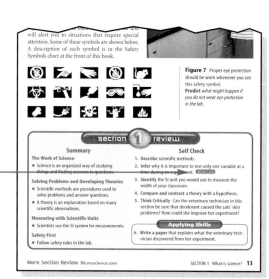

...will alert you to situations that require special attention. Some of these symbols are shown below. A description of each symbol is in the Safety Symbols chart at the front of this book.

Figure 7 Proper eye protection should be worn whenever you see this safety symbol.
Predict *what might happen if you do not wear eye protection in the lab.*

section 1 review

Summary	Self Check
The Work of Science ● Science is an organized way of studying things and finding answers to questions.	1. **Describe** scientific methods.
Solving Problems and Developing Theories ● Scientific methods are procedures used to solve problems and answer questions. ● A theory is an explanation based on many scientific observations.	2. **Infer** why it is important to test only one variable at a time during an experiment. SC.H.1.3.5 3. **Identify** the SI unit you would use to measure the width of your classroom. 4. **Compare and contrast** a theory with a hypothesis. 5. **Think Critically** Can the veterinary technician in this section be sure that deodorant caused the cats' skin problems? How could she improve her experiment?
Measuring with Scientific Units ● Scientists use the SI system for measurements.	
Safety First ● Follow safety rules in the lab.	**Applying Skills** 6. **Write** a paper that explains what the veterinary technician discovered from her experiment.

More Section Review fl6.msscience.com

SECTION 1 What is science? **13**

> **Section Review** questions that address a Benchmark are labeled with the Benchmark.

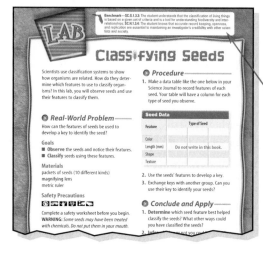

LAB

Benchmark—SC.G.1.3.2: The student understands that the classification of living things is based on a given set of criteria and is a tool for understanding biodiversity and interrelationships. **SC.H.1.3.4:** The student knows that accurate record keeping, openness, and replication are essential to maintaining an investigator's credibility with other scientists and society.

Classifying Seeds

Scientists use classification systems to show how organisms are related. How do they determine which features to use to classify organisms? In this lab, you will observe seeds and use their features to classify them.

● Real-World Problem

How can the features of seeds be used to develop a key to identify the seed?

Goals
■ **Observe** the seeds and notice their features.
■ **Classify** seeds using these features.

Materials
packets of seeds (10 different kinds)
magnifying lens
metric ruler

Safety Precautions

Complete a safety worksheet before you begin.
WARNING: Some seeds may have been treated with chemicals. Do not put them in your mouth.

● Procedure

1. Make a data table like the one below in your Science Journal to record features of each seed. Your table will have a column for each type of seed you observe.

Seed Data

Feature	Type of Seed
Color	
Length (mm)	Do not write in this book.
Shape	
Texture	

2. Use the seeds' features to develop a key.
3. Exchange keys with another group. Can you use their key to identify your seeds?

● Conclude and Apply

1. **Determine** which seed feature best helped classify the seeds? What other ways could you have classified the seeds?

> **Labs** give you hands-on practice of the Benchmark(s) listed at the beginning of the Lab.

Applying Math questions are correlated to the Mathematics Benchmarks.

FCAT Vocabulary terms are identified with a ✳.

Chapter Review questions that address a Benchmark are labeled with the Benchmark.

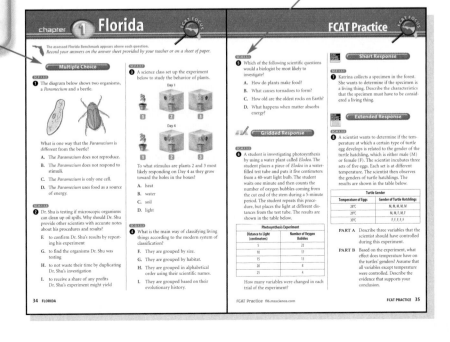

FCAT Practice provides you with multiple-choice, gridded-response, short-response, and extended-response questions.

Each question tests a Benchmark.

Guide to FCAT Success

How should I prepare for the FCAT?

Have you ever heard the saying "Practice makes perfect?" When preparing for the FCAT the best thing to do is practice. Solving example questions ahead of time will help you prepare and become more comfortable with the different types of question-and-answer formats that appear on the test. Depending on your grade and the subject matter of the test, questions have any of several different formats.

Multiple Choice

Multiple-choice items are worth 1 point each. These questions require you to choose the **best** answer from four possible choices. Answer choices are lettered with "A, B, C, D" or "F, G, H, I". Choose your answer by filling in the correct bubble.

1 A homeowner accidentally used a chemical treatment that eliminated the bacteria in the lawn. What would be the long-term effect of such an action?

A. an increase in nests in the lawn area

B. a need to pull more weeds from the lawn area

C. a need to fertilize the lawn area with plant nutrients

D. an increase in the number of rodents in the lawn area

FCAT TIPS section

FCAT TIPS

Read Carefully Be sure you understand the question before you read the answer choices. Make special note of words like NOT or EXCEPT. Read and consider all the answer choices before you mark your answer sheet.

When in Doubt If you don't know the answer to a multiple-choice question, try to eliminate as many incorrect answers as possible. Mark your best guess from the remaining answers before moving on to the next question.

Mark Your Answer Sheet Carefully Be sure to fill in the answer bubbles completely. Do not make any stray marks around answer spaces.

 ### Gridded Response

Each correct answer is worth 1 point. These questions require you to solve problems and then mark your numerical answer on an answer grid. You must fill in the bubbles accurately to receive credit for your answer.

Answer Grid Key

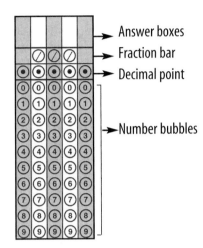

→ Answer boxes

→ Fraction bar

→ Decimal point

→ Number bubbles

Directions for Filling in Answer Grids

- Print your answer with the first digit in the first box **OR** the last digit in the last box.

- Print only one digit in each box. **DO NOT** leave a blank box in the middle of an answer.

- Include the decimal point or fraction bar if it is part of the answer.

- Fill in **ONLY** one bubble for each answer box. **DO NOT** fill in a bubble under an unused answer box.

- **DO NOT** write a mixed number such as $2\frac{1}{2}$. If this is your answer, you must first convert it to an improper fraction $\left(\frac{5}{2}\right)$ or a decimal (2.5).

 ## FCAT TIPS

Calculators When working with calculators, use careful and deliberate keystrokes. Calculators will display an incorrect answer if you press the wrong keys or press keys too quickly. Remember to check your answer to make sure that it is reasonable.

Be Careful For each question, double-check that you are filling in the correct answer bubble for the question number you are working on.

Be Prepared Bring at least two sharpened No. 2 pencils and a good eraser to the test. Before the test, check to make sure that your eraser erases completely.

Clear Your Calculator When using a calculator, always press clear before starting a new problem.

Gridded Response (continued)

1 The graph below shows the percentage of municipal wastes that were recycled between 1960 and 2000.

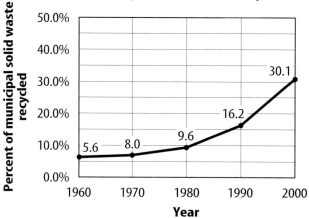

How much more waste, in percent, was recycled in 2000 than in 1960?

Each of the four grids below shows an acceptable response.

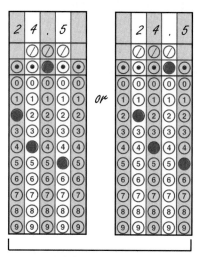

acceptable decimal answers

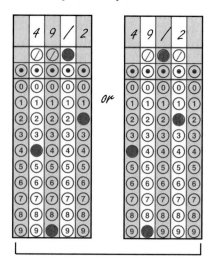

acceptable fraction answers

Short Response

Short-response items are worth 0-2 points depending on your answer. These questions ask you to respond in your own words or to show solutions in a concise manner. Spend about five minutes answering each short-response question.

1 Katrina collects a specimen in the forest. She wants to determine if the specimen is a living thing. Describe the characteristics the specimen must have to be considered a living thing.

The specimen must be organized into a cell or cells, respond to a stimulus, use energy, grow and develop, and reproduce.

FCAT TIPS

Show All Your Work For "Read, Inquire, Explain" questions, show all your work and any calculations on your answer sheet.

Write Clearly Write your explanations neatly in clear, concise language.

Double-Check Your Answer When you have answered each question, reread your answer to make sure it is reasonable and that it is the *best* answer to the question.

Practice Remember that test-taking skills can improve with practice. If possible, take at least one practice test to familiarize yourself with the test format and instructions.

Get Enough Sleep Do not "cram" the night before the test. It can confuse you and make you tired.

Pay Attention Listen carefully to the instructions from the teacher and carefully read the directions and each question.

Extended Response

Extended-response items are worth 0–4 points depending on your answer. These questions require you to provide a longer, more detailed response. Allow 10–15 minutes to answer each extended-response question.

Reanne investigated the effect of temperature on cultures of bacteria. She found that as the temperature increased, so did the population of the bacteria.

PART A Why is the temperature the independent variable in the experiment and the bacteria population the dependent variable?

Temperature is the independent variable because it is changed by the researcher during the experiment. The size of the bacteria population is the dependent variable because it responds to the change in temperature.

PART B Why must other factors of the experiment remain constant?

All other factors should be held constant because if they are not, Reanne will not be able to say for sure that temperature was the variable that caused the response in population size.

 FCAT TIPS

Keep Your Cool Stay focused during the test and don't rush, even if you notice that other students are finishing the test early.

List and Organize First For extended-response "Read, Inquire, Explain" questions, spend a few minutes listing and organizing the main points that you plan to discuss.

Keep Track of Time Allow about five minutes to answer short-response questions and about 10 to 15 minutes to answer extended-response questions.

SUNSHINE STATE STANDARDS CORRELATED TO
GLENCOE FLORIDA SCIENCE, GRADE 6

Bold page numbers indicate in-depth coverage of Benchmark.
AA: Benchmark is annually assessed or assessed as another Annually Assessed Benchmark.
CS: Benchmark is content sampled.

Strand A: The Nature of Matter

Standard 1—The student understands that all matter has observable, measurable properties.

Benchmark	Grade 6	Grade 7	Grade 8
SC.A.1.3.1: The student identifies various ways in which substances differ (e.g., mass, volume, shape, density, texture, and reaction to temperature and light). **AA**	**413–420, 444–453, 454–458** 434–435, 483–485, 487–489	41–44	**97, 99, 106–110, 112–117, 155, 169, 173, 175** 559–560
SC.A.1.3.2: The student understands the difference between weight and mass. **AA**	**419, 517**	421, 106	**225–226, 238–239**
SC.A.1.3.3: The student knows that temperature measures the average energy of motion of the particles that make up the substance. **CS**	**544–545, 550, 552–553** 296, 420	156	**157, 158, 160, 162–169, 278**
SC.A.1.3.4: The student knows that atoms in solids are close together and do not move around easily; in liquids, atoms tend to move farther apart; in gas, atoms are quite far apart and move around freely. **CS**	**449**	41	**156–158, 160, 162–168**
SC.A.1.3.5: The student knows the difference between a physical change in a substance (i.e., altering the shape, form, volume, or density) and a chemical change (i.e., producing new substances with different characteristics). **CS**	**444–453, 454–460**	40, 44, 46–55, 269–273	**128, 163** 102, 105, 106, 108, 110, 112–113

Guide to FCAT Success

Strand A: The Nature of Matter

Benchmark	Grade 6	Grade 7	Grade 8
SC.A.1.3.6: The student knows that equal volumes of different substances may have different masses. **AA**	**448** 290	 42	**175**

Standard 2—The Student understands the basic principles of atomic theory.

SC.A.2.3.1: The student describes and compares the properties of particles and waves. **CS**	**595–597, 611**	**185, 188–191**	137, 251
SC.A.2.3.2: The student knows the general properties of the atom (a massive nucleus of neutral neutrons and positive protons surrounded by a cloud of negative electrons) and accepts that single atoms are not visible. **CS**	**472–479, 483–484** 562	**66–75, 76–85, 269–273** .	**128–130, 134, 145–147**
SC.A.2.3.3: The student knows that radiation, light, and heat are forms of energy used to cook food, treat diseases, and provide energy. **AA**	**256, 263, 265, 266–271, 539–541** 52, 659	**201–202** 157, 161, 163–164, 171–173	**254–259** 582, 586, 587–594

Strand B: Energy

Standard 1—The student recognizes that energy may be changed in form with varying efficiency.

SC.B.1.3.1: The student identifies forms of energy and explains that they can be measured and compared. **AA**	**535–540, 543** 256–272, 266–271, 572–573	**155–158** 470–471, 482–483	**287, 289–291** 587–594
SC.B.1.3.2: The student knows that energy cannot be created or destroyed, but only changed from one form to another. **AA**	**541, 543**	**160–166** 382–387	 277, 287

Bold page numbers indicate in-depth coverage of Benchmark.
AA: Benchmark is annually assessed or assessed as another Annually Assessed Benchmark.
CS: Benchmark is content sampled.

Strand B: Energy

Benchmark	Grade 6	Grade 7	Grade 8
SC.B.1.3.3: The student knows the various forms in which energy comes to Earth from the sun (e.g., visible light, infrared, and microwave). **AA**	**598** 292–293	**202** 382	**247, 257** 559
SC.B.1.3.4: The student knows that energy conversions are never 100% efficient (i.e., some energy is transformed to heat and is unavailable for further useful work). **CS**	**542** 212, 572–574	**161, 165, 166, 485**	**277, 290–291, 539**
SC.B.1.3.5: The student knows the processes by which thermal energy tends to flow from a system of higher temperature to a system of lower temperature. **CS**	**296–299, 302–303, 548–551**	163	**283–284, 294–295** 162
SC.B.1.3.6: The student knows the properties of waves (e.g., frequency, wavelength, and amplitude); that each wave consists of a number of crests and troughs; and the effects of different media on waves. **AA**	**599–604, 611**	**188–191, 193, 195, 197, 199, 202**	**251, 252, 255, 262**
Standard 2—The student understands the interaction of matter and energy.			
SC.B.2.3.1: The student knows that most events in the universe (e.g., weather changes, moving cars, and the transfer of a nervous impulse in the human body) involve some form of energy transfer and that these changes almost always increase the total disorder of the system and its surroundings, reducing the amount of useful energy. **AA**	**542** 212, 297, 304–312	**154, 165**	**290–292** 536–539

Bold page numbers indicate in-depth coverage of Benchmark.
AA: Benchmark is annually assessed or assessed as another Annually Assessed Benchmark.
CS: Benchmark is content sampled.

Strand B: Energy			
Benchmark	Grade 6	Grade 7	Grade 8
SC.B.2.3.2: The student knows that most of the energy used today is derived from burning stored energy collected by organisms millions of years ago (i.e., nonrenewable fossil fuels). **CS**	**256–259**	168, 252	**582–583**

Strand C: Force and Motion			
Standard 1—The student understands that types of motion may be described, measured, and predicted.			
SC.C.1.3.1: The student knows that the motion of an object can be described by its position, direction of motion, and speed. **CS**	**505–510**	98–102	**190–195, 196–200**
SC.C.1.3.2: The student knows that vibrations in materials set up wave disturbances that spread away from the source (e.g., sound and earthquake waves). **AA**	597 611	186	42–43, 50, 251
Standard 2—The student understands that the types of force that act on an object and the effect of that force can be described, measured, and predicted.			
SC.C.2.3.1: The student knows that many forces (e.g., gravitational, electrical, and magnetic) act at a distance (i.e., without contact). **CS**	**515–516, 563–565, 578–579, 581**	105	220, 249–250, 251
SC.C.2.3.2: The student knows common contact forces. **AA**	514–515	106–109	**174, 178–179, 220–223, 228, 229–230**
SC.C.2.3.3: The student knows that if more than one force acts on an object, then the forces can reinforce or cancel each other, depending on their direction and magnitude. **AA**	512–513	104–105 423–424	219

Bold page numbers indicate in-depth coverage of Benchmark.
AA: Benchmark is annually assessed or assessed as another Annually Assessed Benchmark.
CS: Benchmark is content sampled.

Strand C: Force and Motion

Benchmark	Grade 6	Grade 7	Grade 8
SC.C.2.3.4: The student knows that simple machines can be used to change the direction or size of a force. **CS**	**519–523**	**125, 131, 132–134, 137–145**	221
SC.C.2.3.5: The student understands that an object in motion will continue at a constant speed and in a straight line until acted upon by a force and that an object at rest will remain at rest until acted upon by a force. **AA**	513, 667	**110–111**	**217, 220–221, 237** 208–209
SC.C.2.3.6: The student explains and shows the ways in which a net force (i.e., the sum of all acting forces) can act on an object (e.g., speeding up an object traveling in the same direction as the net force, slowing down an object traveling in the direction opposite of the net force). **AA**	513	**116–117** 423–424	**226–227**
SC.C.2.3.7: The student knows that gravity is a universal force that every mass exerts on every other mass. **CS**	**516**	**106** 285	**225, 238–239** 306

Strand D: Processes that Shape the Earth

Standard 1—The student recognizes that processes in the lithosphere, atmosphere, hydrosphere, and biosphere interact to shape the Earth.

Benchmark	Grade 6	Grade 7	Grade 8
SC.D.1.3.1: The student knows that mechanical and chemical activities shape and reshape the Earth's land surface by eroding rock and soil in some areas and depositing them in other areas, sometimes in seasonal layers. **CS**	**324–329, 338, 340, 352–362, 363–368, 369–372**	**231–233, 263** 218–223, 237–241, 250–252, 263	**69–74, 77–85**

Bold page numbers indicate in-depth coverage of Benchmark.
AA: Benchmark is annually assessed or assessed as another Annually Assessed Benchmark.
CS: Benchmark is content sampled.

Guide to FCAT Success

Strand D: Processes that Shape the Earth

Benchmark	Grade 6	Grade 7	Grade 8
SC.D.1.3.2: The student knows that over the whole Earth, organisms are growing, dying, and decaying as new organisms are produced by the old ones. **AA**	207, 384–387	250–256, 258–261, 272 233	556–557, 559 74–75, 536
SC.D.1.3.3: The student knows how conditions that exist in one system influence the conditions that exist in other systems. **CS**	**291, 296–303, 304–312, 385–386, 389–391, 392–403** 352–362, 363–368, 369–372	**228–233, 234–238, 249–257, 263–265, 273–275** 219, 223, 260, 476–481, 482–487	**74–75, 77–87, 554, 560–563, 567–571** 53–59
SC.D.1.3.4: The student knows the ways in which plants and animals reshape the landscape (e.g., bacteria, fungi, worms, rodents, and other organisms add organic matter to the soil, increasing soil fertility, encouraging plant growth, and strengthening resistance to erosion). **AA**	**227, 324–329, 330–336, 338–341** 52, 56–57, 202, 205, 213, 353	355, 470, 479, 528–529	**70–75, 85–87**
SC.D.1.3.5: The student understands concepts of time and size relating to the interaction of Earth's processes (e.g., lightning striking in a split second as opposed to the shifting of the Earth's plates altering the landscape; distance between atoms measured in Angstrom units as opposed to distance between stars measured in light-years). **CS**	**291–295, 296–303, 304–311, 352–362, 364–367, 369–372, 626, 633, 646** 324, 326, 328, 330, 334, 338–340, 384, 389, 401, 475, 567, 670	**250–257, 258–261, 262–268, 269–273** 300	**77–85, 88** 42–51, 53–59, 307, 343, 348–349, 358, 554–555

Standard 2—The student understands the need for protection of the natural systems on Earth.

Benchmark	Grade 6	Grade 7	Grade 8
SC.D.2.3.1: The student understands that quality of life is relevant to personal experience.	**205, 240, 241, 263–264, 266–271, 276–277**	502–507, 516, 524–527, 528–535, 536–542, 550–552, 554–558, 559–568	587–594, 596–599

Bold page numbers indicate in-depth coverage of Benchmark.
AA: Benchmark is annually assessed or assessed as another Annually Assessed Benchmark.
CS: Benchmark is content sampled.

Strand D: Processes that Shape the Earth

Benchmark	Grade 6	Grade 7	Grade 8
SC.D.2.3.2: The student knows the positive and negative consequences of human action on the Earth's systems. **AA**	**237, 240, 241, 263–264, 266–271, 276–277**	**502–507, 516, 524–527, 528–535, 536–542, 550–552, 554–558, 559–567** 168–170, 225–226	**567–573, 587–594, 596–599**

Strand E: Earth and Space

Standard 1—The student understands the interaction and organization in the Solar System and the universe and how this affects life on Earth.

	Grade 6	Grade 7	Grade 8
SC.E.1.3.1: The student understands the vast size of our Solar System and the relationship of the planets and their satellites. **AA**	**632, 634** 625–626, 631, 648, 670–671	**300, 305, 308** 287, 292	**307, 311** 312, 318, 320, 326, 330
SC.E.1.3.2: The student knows that available data from various satellite probes show the similarities and differences among planets and their moons in the Solar System. **AA**	**668** 634, 677, 680	304–305	**312** 318, 327
SC.E.1.3.3: The student understands that our sun is one of many stars in our galaxy. **CS**	**645**	301	**345** 308, 340, 357–358
SC.E.1.3.4: The student knows that stars appear to be made of similar chemical elements, although they differ in age, size, temperature, and distance. **CS**	**642**	300	**355** 344, 345

Standard 2—The student recognizes the vastness of the universe and the Earth's place in it.

	Grade 6	Grade 7	Grade 8
SC.E.2.3.1: The student knows that thousands of other galaxies appear to have the same elements, forces, and forms of energy found in our Solar System. **CS**	**643**	301	**340** 339, 358

Bold page numbers indicate in-depth coverage of Benchmark.
AA: Benchmark is annually assessed or assessed as another Annually Assessed Benchmark.
CS: Benchmark is content sampled.

Guide to FCAT Success

Strand F: Processes of Life

Benchmark	Grade 6	Grade 7	Grade 8
Standard 1—The student describes patterns of structure and function in living things.			
SC.F.1.3.1: The student understands that living things are composed of major systems that function in reproduction, growth, maintenance, and regulation. **AA**	**14–17, 97–98, 103, 104, 110–111, 128–132, 140–142, 147–149** 162, 167–169, 173–175	**354–356, 360–368** 417–428	**434–438** 374–380, 382, 404–407, 408–412, 413–420, 559–561
SC.F.1.3.2: The student knows that the structural basis of most organisms is the cell and most organisms are single cells, while some, including humans, are multicellular. **CS**	**14, 38–39, 50–57, 96, 102, 105** 163, 175	**320–321** 349, 361	 440–441
SC.F.1.3.3: The student knows that in multicellular organisms cells grow and divide to make more cells in order to form and repair various organs and tissues. **CS**	**70, 105, 163–164** 17, 96	**405** 363	**373–380** 405, 422–425
SC.F.1.3.4: The student knows that the levels of structural organization for function in living things include cells, tissues, organs, systems, and organisms. **CS**	**47–49, 96, 102, 105, 111–112** 141, 148, 162, 167, 169	**327** 363, 406–408, 409–416, 417–428	**436–437, 440–441**
SC.F.1.3.5: The student explains how the life functions of organisms are related to what occurs within the cell. **CS**	**42–44, 45, 111** 14, 135, 140, 143, 165	**322–327** 363, 380, 383–386	**372–374, 388–393**
SC.F.1.3.6: The student knows that the cells with similar functions have similar structures, whereas those with different structures have different functions. **CS**	**42–43, 45–46, 96, 102, 105, 111, 163, 174–176**	**320–326** 361, 381–382, 388	 440–441

Bold page numbers indicate in-depth coverage of Benchmark.
AA: Benchmark is annually assessed or assessed as another Annually Assessed Benchmark.
CS: Benchmark is content sampled.

Strand F: Processes of Life

Benchmark	Grade 6	Grade 7	Grade 8
SC.F.1.3.7: The student knows that behavior is a response to the environment and influences growth, development, maintenance, and reproduction. **CS**	**100, 110, 113–117** 15	**389–397, 440–445, 446–457**	**438, 442**

Standard 2—The student understands the process and importance of genetic diversity.

SC.F.2.3.1: The student knows the patterns and advantages of sexual and asexual reproduction in plants and animals. **CS**	**70–75**	**409–410, 412–413, 417–428**	**379–380, 382, 385, 404–407, 408–412, 413–420** 561
SC.F.2.3.2: The student knows that the variation in each species is due to the exchange and interaction of genetic information as it is passed from parent to offspring. **AA**	**77–83** 72	414–415	**464–471, 472–478, 482–483** 382, 393–395, 404, 409–411, 413–420, 492, 496
SC.F.2.3.3: The student knows that generally organisms in a population live long enough to reproduce because they have survival characteristics. **CS**	68	**441–442, 446–447, 449** 367, 406–408, 409–410, 417–428	**495–496, 500**
SC.F.2.3.4: The student knows that the fossil record provides evidence that changes in the kinds of plants and animals in the environment have been occurring over time. **CS**	21	**349, 357**	**501–505, 509–510**

Strand G: How Living Things Interact with Their Environment

Standard 1—The student understands the competitive, interdependent, cyclic nature of living things in the environment.

SC.G.1.3.1: The student knows that viruses depend on other living things. **AA**	**177–178, 180, 181** 38, 145	**334–337**	514

Bold page numbers indicate in-depth coverage of Benchmark.
AA: Benchmark is annually assessed or assessed as another Annually Assessed Benchmark.
CS: Benchmark is content sampled.

Guide to FCAT Success

Strand G: How Living Things Interact with Their Environment

Benchmark	Grade 6	Grade 7	Grade 8
SC.G.1.3.2: The student knows that biological adaptations include changes in structures, behaviors, or physiology that enhance reproductive success in a particular environment. **CS**	68, 228	**350–351, 406–408, 414–415, 428** 441–442, 446, 447, 449	**495–496** 413, 420
SC.G.1.3.3: The student understands that the classification of living things is based on a given set of criteria and is a tool for understanding biodiversity and interrelationships. **CS**	**22–27** 51, 53, 55–56	**352–353, 360** 406–408	508
SC.G.1.3.4: The student knows that the interactions of organisms with each other and with the non-living parts of their environments result in the flow of energy and the cycling of matter throughout the system. **AA**	**212–214** 205	**467–475, 476–481, 482–487**	**524–528, 531–535, 536–541** 108, 560
SC.G.1.3.5: The student knows that life is maintained by a continuous input of energy from the sun and by the recycling of the atoms that make up the molecules of living organisms. **AA**	**212–215** 15, 18	**481, 482–487**	**536** 560
Standard 2—The student understands the consequences of using limited natural resources.			
SC.G.2.3.1: The student knows that some resources are renewable and others are nonrenewable. **CS**	**256–265, 266–271, 277**	**168–175**	**582, 585–586, 587–594**
SC.G.2.3.2: The student knows that all biotic and abiotic factors are interrelated and that if one factor is changed or removed, it impacts the availability of other resources within the system. **CS**	**198–205** 54, 213, 237, 240, 241	**504–507** 467–475, 551, 561	**524–528** 560, 567–571

Bold page numbers indicate in-depth coverage of Benchmark.
AA: Benchmark is annually assessed or assessed as another Annually Assessed Benchmark.
CS: Benchmark is content sampled.

Strand G: How Living Things Interact with Their Environment

Benchmark	Grade 6	Grade 7	Grade 8
SC.G.2.3.3: The student knows that a brief change in the limited resources of an ecosystem may alter the size of a population or the average size of individual organisms and that long-term change may result in the elimination of animal and plant populations inhabiting the Earth. **CS**	**240, 241** 209	**502–507, 516** 481	**525, 538, 569–571**
SC.G.2.3.4: The student understands that humans are a part of an ecosystem and their activities may deliberately or inadvertently alter the equilibrium in ecosystems. **AA**	**263–264, 266–271, 276–277** 237, 240, 241	**502–507, 516, 524–527, 528–535, 536–542, 550–552, 554–558, 559–567** 481	**567–573, 587–594, 596–599**

Strand H: The Nature of Science

Standard 1—The student uses the scientific processes and habits of mind to solve problems.

Benchmark	Grade 6	Grade 7	Grade 8
SC.H.1.3.1: The student knows that scientific knowledge is subject to modification as new information challenges prevailing theories and as a new theory leads to looking at old observations in a new way. **AA**	**10, 19–20, 22, 31, 384–387, 473–479** 72, 165, 171, 238, 392–401, 464, 482, 625–626, 631	**6, 19, 66–75, 81, 88** 55, 276, 296–298, 310, 333, 340, 432, 488, 542	**7, 12, 14, 15, 16, 26, 306–307, 310** 31, 225, 329, 351, 465, 494–495, 574
SC.H.1.3.2: The student knows that the study of the events that led scientists to discoveries can provide information about the inquiry process and its effects. **CS**	**384–387** 10, 20, 120, 188, 392–401, 586	**8, 14–15, 67–72, 88** 208, 276, 340, 371, 432, 458, 488	**494** 172, 396, 465–466, 574
SC.H.1.3.3: The student knows that science disciplines differ from one another in topic, techniques, and outcomes, but that they share a common purpose, philosophy, and enterprise. **CS**	**679** 6, 82, 339, 668	**6, 333, 336, 340** 55, 66, 88, 208, 276, 310, 421, 432, 458, 508, 526, 568	**8–10, 12, 14** 28, 42, 514, 526, 574

Bold page numbers indicate in-depth coverage of Benchmark.
AA: Benchmark is annually assessed or assessed as another Annually Assessed Benchmark.
CS: Benchmark is content sampled.

Strand H: The Nature of Science

Benchmark	Grade 6	Grade 7	Grade 8
SC.H.1.3.4: The student knows that accurate record keeping, openness, and replication are essential to maintaining an investigator's credibility with other scientists and society. **AA**	**9–10, 631** 27–29, 44, 59, 76, 100, 118–119, 186–187, 238, 246–247, 314–315, 342–343, 373, 416, 426, 427, 434–435, 443, 518, 524–525, 543, 552–553, 577, 584–585, 612–613, 661, 681	**10–11, 19, 22, 23** 30–31, 45, 56, 85–87, 131, 166, 176–177, 193, 239–241, 268, 275, 299, 328, 332, 369–371, 388, 429, 456–457, 475, 486–487, 507, 514–515, 535, 540–541, 566–567	**17, 28–29** 70–75, 76, 118, 145, 208–209, 237, 238–239, 262, 268–269, 293–295, 311, 330, 394–395, 444, 468, 542–543, 572–573, 600, 606–607
SC.H.1.3.5: The student knows that a change in one or more variables may alter the outcome of an investigation. **AA**	**9–10** 20, 27–29, 71, 84–85, 100, 116, 118–119, 152–153, 185–187, 203, 216–217, 240, 246–247, 272, 289, 295, 314–315, 342–343, 361, 364, 374–375, 418, 428–429, 433, 448, 458, 471, 488, 503, 518, 524–525, 550, 552–553, 561, 577, 581, 584–585, 597, 604, 606, 648, 664	**5** 18, 21, 30–31, 56, 85–87, 97, 101, 107, 109, 116–117, 125, 129, 131, 144–145, 153, 156, 161, 193, 197, 202, 206–207, 223, 308, 328, 332, 338–339, 355, 361, 383, 388, 392, 396–397, 430, 449, 455, 495, 503, 507, 558, 566–567	**18** 5, 23, 31–33, 49, 75, 86–87, 60–61, 117, 169, 173, 189, 193, 198, 207, 208–209, 217, 228, 235, 237, 238–239, 255, 262, 268–269, 277, 283, 293–295, 305, 311, 362–363, 381, 424–425, 454–455, 482–483, 512–513, 542–543, 555, 592
SC.H.1.3.6: The student recognizes the scientific contributions that are made by individuals of diverse backgrounds, interests, talents, and motivations.	**280** 20, 22–23, 57, 82, 120, 154, 175, 177–179, 183, 188, 244, 267, 339, 344, 353, 384, 389, 399, 455, 464, 473–474, 566, 614, 626, 648, 668, 671–672, 674	**24, 26, 27, 28, 32, 67, 69, 74** 6, 16, 88, 128, 208, 222, 276, 302, 310, 332, 340, 350, 372, 381, 421, 432, 443, 450, 458, 488, 508, 526, 542, 554, 568	**560** 9, 10, 13, 25, 42, 98–99, 131, 132, 143, 202, 264, 270, 293–295, 306, 310, 312, 319, 326, 332, 375, 389, 396, 426, 439, 446, 465, 475, 478, 493, 501, 514, 526, 574

Bold page numbers indicate in-depth coverage of Benchmark.
AA: Benchmark is annually assessed or assessed as another Annually Assessed Benchmark.
CS: Benchmark is content sampled.

Strand H: The Nature of Science

Benchmark	Grade 6	Grade 7	Grade 8
SC.H.1.3.7: The student knows that when similar investigations give different results, the scientific challenge is to verify whether the differences are significant by further study. **AA**	**631** 84–85, 206, 217, 238, 314–315, 413, 443, 518, 524–525, 543, 552–553, 612–613, 648, 661	**22, 30–31, 69, 73, 74** 12, 45, 56, 176–177, 328, 388, 396–397, 488, 507, 514–515, 566–567	**29** 31–33, 52, 76, 86–87, 146–147, 237, 238–239, 262, 268–269, 330, 349, 394–395, 454–455, 472, 493, 512–513, 600

Standard 2—The student understands that most natural events occur in comprehensible, consistent patterns.

Benchmark	Grade 6	Grade 7	Grade 8
SC.H.2.3.1: The student recognizes that patterns exist within and across systems. **CS**	**47, 167–172, 197, 198–199, 207, 214, 226, 352–362, 384–386, 480–482, 484–485** 68–69, 79, 84–85, 102, 110–117, 128–132, 137, 147–149, 164, 175, 238, 294, 296–303, 304–315, 391, 402–403, 445–447, 451–452, 487, 594, 602, 609–610, 626–627, 641–644	**286, 321, 327, 335, 394, 405–408, 413–415, 441, 452, 453, 454, 467, 472, 474, 477–478, 480–481, 482–483, 484–485, 553** 26, 43, 139–141, 186, 188, 218, 220, 237–238, 240–241, 263–264, 270–271, 293–295, 303, 352, 363, 369, 380, 385, 387	**7–9, 26, 97–104, 130–132, 134, 307, 311, 404–407, 408–412, 417–420, 434–438, 439–443, 536–543** 12, 42–46, 54, 60–62, 69, 139, 142, 145–146, 157, 190, 205, 288, 290, 291, 330, 339–341, 346, 349, 358, 374–375, 380, 384, 466, 468, 474, 496–497, 506–507, 527, 531–532

Standard 3—The student understands that science, technology, and society are interwoven and interdependent.

Benchmark	Grade 6	Grade 7	Grade 8
SC.H.3.3.1: The student knows that science ethics demand that scientists must not knowingly subject coworkers, students, the neighborhood, or the community to health or property risks. **CS**	84–85, 98, 100	**81, 82** 532, 542, 554, 568	**19–20** 426
SC.H.3.3.2: The student knows that special care must be taken in using animals in scientific research. **CS**	6	**455** 430–431	**20** 542–543

Bold page numbers indicate in-depth coverage of Benchmark.
AA: Benchmark is annually assessed or assessed as another Annually Assessed Benchmark.
CS: Benchmark is content sampled.

Strand H: The Nature of Science

Benchmark	Grade 6	Grade 7	Grade 8
SC.H.3.3.3: The student knows that in research involving human subjects, the ethics of science require that potential subjects be fully informed about the risks and benefits associated with the research and of their right to refuse to participate. **CS**	339	**19** 443	**20** 493
SC.H.3.3.4: The student knows that technological design should require taking into account constraints such as natural laws, the properties of the materials used, and economic, political, social, ethical, and aesthetic values. **CS**	**264–265, 267–271, 274** 248, 314–315, 458, 474, 524–525, 648, 682	**27–29** 81, 82, 84, 118, 372, 532, 542, 554, 564–565	**11, 589–594** 11, 25, 180, 208–209, 240, 270, 315, 426, 481, 526
SC.H.3.3.5: The student understands that contributions to the advancement of science, mathematics, and technology have been made by different kinds of people, in different cultures, at different times and are an intrinsic part of the development of human culture.	**278, 280, 389, 459, 464, 630** 20, 28–29, 154, 177–179, 183, 188, 290, 384, 387, 482, 473–478, 482, 494, 586, 614, 645, 661, 671–672, 674	**66, 67, 69, 74, 329, 340** 6, 14, 20, 26, 28, 55, 88, 128, 208, 222, 273, 304, 350, 372, 443, 444, 458, 486–487	**306–307, 310, 319, 322, 326** 34, 98–99, 116, 131, 132, 143, 172, 210, 220, 221, 225, 270, 312–314, 340, 351, 354, 364, 389, 394, 465, 493, 514
SC.H.3.3.6: The student knows that no matter who does science and mathematics or invents things, or when or where they do it, the knowledge and technology that result can eventually become available to everyone. **CS**	**280, 679** 165, 664, 669	**24, 25, 27** 88, 198, 201, 202, 204, 208, 225, 228, 372, 450, 458, 510	**306, 310** 11, 180, 210, 270, 426, 574
SC.H.3.3.7: The student knows that computers speed up and extend people's ability to collect, sort, and analyze data; prepare research reports; and share data and ideas with others. **CS**	25	9 83, 176–177, 198	25 394–395, 572–573

Bold page numbers indicate in-depth coverage of Benchmark.
AA: Benchmark is annually assessed or assessed as another Annually Assessed Benchmark.
CS: Benchmark is content sampled.

SUNSHINE STATE STANDARDS FOR LANGUAGE ARTS IN *GLENCOE FLORIDA SCIENCE, GRADE 6*

Reading

Standard 1: The student uses the reading process effectively.

LA.A.1.3.4: uses strategies to clarify meaning, such as rereading, note taking, summarizing, outlining, and writing a grade level-appropriate report.

Standard 2: The student constructs meaning from a wide range of texts.

LA.A.2.3.1: determines the main idea or essential message in a text and identifies relevant details and facts and patterns of organization.

LA.A.2.3.5: locates, organizes, and interprets written information for a variety of purposes, including classroom research, collaborative decision making, and performing a school or real-world task.

LA.A.2.3.6: uses a variety of reference materials, including indexes, magazines, newspapers, and journals; and tools, including card catalogs and computer catalogs, to gather information for research topics.

LA.A.2.3.7: synthesizes and separates collected information into useful components using a variety of techniques, such as source cards, note cards, spreadsheets, and outlines.

Writing

Standard 2: The student writes to communicate ideas and information effectively.

LA.B.2.3.1: writes text, notes, outlines, comments, and observations that demonstrate comprehension of content and experiences from a variety of media.

▼ **South Beach, Miami**

LA.B.2.3.2: organizes information using alphabetical, chronological, and numerical systems.

LA.B.2.3.3: selects and uses appropriate formats for writing, including narrative, persuasive, and expository formats, according to the intended audience, purpose, and occasion.

LA.B.2.3.4: uses electronic technology including databases and software to gather information and communicate new knowledge.

Listening, Viewing, and Speaking

Standard 1: The student uses listening strategies effectively.

LA.C.1.3.1: listens and uses information gained for a variety of purposes, such as gaining information from interviews, following directions, and pursuing a personal interest.

Standard 3: The student uses speaking strategies effectively.

LA.C.3.3.3: speaks for various occasions, audiences, and purposes, including conversations, discussions, projects, and informational, persuasive, or technical presentations.

Language

Standard 2: The student understands the power of language.

LA.D.2.3.5: incorporates audiovisual aids in presentations.

Literature

Standard 1: The student understands the common features of a variety of literary forms.

LA.E.1.3.3: understands various elements of authors' craft appropriate at this grade level, including word choice, symbolism, figurative language, mood, irony, foreshadowing, flashback, persuasion techniques, and point of view in both fiction and nonfiction.

SUNSHINE STATE STANDARDS FOR MATHEMATICS IN *GLENCOE FLORIDA SCIENCE, GRADE 6*

Number Sense, Concepts, and Operations

Standard 3: The student understands the effects of operations on numbers and the relationships among these operations, selects appropriate operations, and computes for problem solving.

MA.A.3.3.1: understands and explains the effects of addition, subtraction, multiplication, and division on whole numbers, fractions, including mixed numbers, and decimals, including the inverse relationships of positive and negative numbers.

MA.A.3.3.2: selects the appropriate operation to solve problems involving addition, subtraction, multiplication, and division of rational numbers, ratios, proportions, and percents, including the appropriate application of the algebraic order of operations.

Measurement

Standard 2: The student compares, contrasts, and converts within systems of measurement (both standard/nonstandard and metric/customary).

MA.B.2.3.2: solves problems involving units of measure and converts answers to a larger or smaller unit within either the metric or customary system.

Standard 3: The student estimates measurements in real-world problem situations.

MA.B.3.3.1: solves real-world and mathematical problems involving estimates of measurements including length, time, weight/mass, temperature, money, perimeter, area, and volume, in either customary or metric units.

▼ a Florida orange grove

Algebraic Thinking

Standard 2: The student uses expressions, equations, inequalities, graphs, and formulas to represent and interpret situations.

MA.D.2.3.1: represents and solves real-world problems graphically, with algebraic expressions, equations, and inequalities.

Data Analysis and Probability

Standard 1: The student understands and uses the tools of data analysis for managing information.

MA.E.1.3.1: collects, organizes, and displays data in a variety of forms, including tables, line graphs, charts, bar graphs, to determine how different ways of presenting data can lead to different interpretations.

Standard 2: The student identifies patterns and makes predictions from an orderly display of data using concepts of probability and statistics.

MA.E.2.3.1: compares experimental results with mathematical expectations of probabilities.

▼ **the Everglades**

HOW TO...
Use Your Science Book

Before You Read

- **Starting a Chapter** Science is occurring all around you, and the opening photo will preview the science you will be learning about. The **chapter preview** will give you an idea of what you will be learning about, and you can try the **Launch Lab** to help get your brain headed in the right direction. The **Foldables™** exercise is a fun way to get you organized.

- **Starting a Section** Chapters are divided into two to four sections. The **As You Read** in the margin of the first page will let you know what is most important in the section. It is divided into four parts. **What You'll Learn** will tell you the major topics you will be covering. **Why It's Important** will remind you why you are studying this in the first place! The **Review Vocabulary** word is a word you already know, either through your science studies or your prior knowledge. The **New Vocabulary** words are words that you need to learn to understand this section. These words will be in **boldfaced** print and highlighted in the section. Make a note to yourself to recognize these words as you are reading the section.

Why do I need my science book?

Have you ever been in class and not understood all of what was presented? Or, you understood everything in class, but at home, got stuck on how to answer a question? Maybe you just wondered when you were ever going to use this stuff?

These next few pages are designed to help you understand everything your science book can be used for ... besides a paperweight!

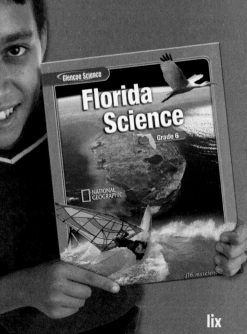

Science Vocabulary Make the following Foldable to help you understand the vocabulary terms in this chapter.

STEP 1 Fold a vertical sheet of notebook paper from side to side.

STEP 2 Cut along every third line of only the top layer to form tabs.

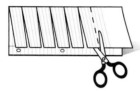

STEP 3 Label each tab with a vocabulary word from the chapter.

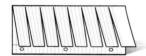

Build Vocabulary As you read the chapter, list the vocabulary words on the tabs. As you learn the definitions, write them under the tab for each vocabulary word.

Look For...

FOLDABLES™

at the beginning of every section.

As You Read

- **Headings** Each section has a title in large red letters, and is divided into blue titles and small red titles at the beginning of a paragraph. A good study tip may be to make an outline of the headings and sub-headings of a section.

- **Margins** In the margins of your text, you will find many helpful resources. The **Science Online** exercises and **Integrate** activities help you explore the topics you are studying. **MiniLABs** are chances to reinforce the science concepts you have learned, and are typically activities that can be done outside of the class-room in a short amount of time.

- **Building Skills** You will also find an **Applying Math** or **Applying Science** activity in each chapter. This will give you extra practice using your new knowledge, which comes in handy when preparing for standardized tests.

- **Student Resources** At the end of the book you will find **Student Resources** to help you throughout your studies. These include **Science, Technology,** and **Math Skill Handbooks.** You also will find an **English/Spanish Glossary** and **Index.** You can use this whenever you have questions about a math problem, or if you don't remember how to do a concept map.

In the Lab

Working in the laboratory is one of the best ways to understand the concepts you are studying. Your book will be your guide through your laboratory experiences, and help you begin to think like a scientist. In it, you not only will find the steps necessary to follow the investigations, but also helpful tips to make the most of your time.

- Each lab provides you with a **Real-World Problem** to remind you that science is something you use every day, not just in class. This may lead to many more questions about how things happen in your world. Congratulations—this is the start of thinking like a scientist!

- Remember, experiments do not always produce the result you expect. Scientists have made many discoveries based on investigations with unexpected results. You can try the experiment again to make sure your results were accurate, or perhaps even form a new hypothesis to test.

- Keeping a **Science Journal** is how scientists keep accurate records of observations and data. In your journal, you also can write any questions that may arise during your investigation. This is a great method of reminding yourself to find the answers later.

Look For...

- **Launch Labs** of the start of every chapter.
- **MiniLABs** in the margin of each chapter.
- **Two Full-Period Labs** in every chapter.
- EXTRA Try at Home Labs at the end of your book.
- The **Web site** with **laboratory demonstrations**.

Before a Test

Admit it! You don't like to take tests! However, there *are* ways to review that make them less painful. Your book will help you be more successful taking tests if you use the resources provided to you.

- Review all of the **New Vocabulary** words and be sure you understand their definitions.

- Review the notes you've taken on your **Foldables,** in class, and in lab. Write down any question that you still need answered.

- Study the concepts presented in the chapter by reading the **Study Guide** and answering the questions in the **Review.**

- Review the **Summaries** and **Self Check** questions at the end of each section.

Look For...

- **Reading Checks** and **caption questions** throughout the text.
- The **Summaries** and **Self Check questions** at the end of each section.
- The **Study Guide** and **Review** at the end of each chapter.
- The **FCAT Practice** after each chapter.

Let's Get Started

To help you find the information you need quickly, use the Scavenger Hunt below to learn where things are located in Chapter 1.

1. What is the title of this chapter?

2. How can you tell what you'll learn in Section 1?

3. Sometimes you may ask, "Why am I learning this?" Name a reason why the concepts from Section 2 are important.

4. What benchmark does the first Annually Assessed Benchmark Check cover?

5. How many reading checks are in Section 1?

6. What is the Web address where you could find extra information?

7. What is the main heading above the sixth paragraph in Section 2?

8. There is an integration with another subject mentioned in one of the margins of the chapter. What type is it?

9. List the new vocabulary words that are presented in Section 2.

10. List the safety symbols that are presented in the first Lab.

11. Where would you find a Self Check to be sure you understand the section?

12. Suppose you're doing the Self Check and you get stuck. Where could you find help?

13. Which Benchmarks are assessed in the Chapter Review?

14. Where would you find the Benchmarks that are covered in a section?

15. You complete the Chapter Review to study for your chapter test. Where could you find another quiz for more practice?

How Are
Seaweed &
Cell Cultures
Connected?

In the 1800s, many biologists were interested in studying one-celled microorganisms. But to study them, the researchers needed to grow, or culture, large numbers of these cells. And to culture them properly, they needed a solid substance on which the cells could grow. One scientist tried using nutrient-enriched gelatin, but the gelatin had drawbacks. It melted at relatively low temperatures—and some microorganisms digested it. Fannie Eilshemius Hesse came up with a better option. She had been solidifying her homemade jellies using a substance called agar, which is derived from red seaweed (such as the one seen in the background here). It turned out that nutrient-enriched agar worked perfectly as a substance on which to culture cells. On the two types of agar in the dishes below, so many cells have grown that, together, they form dots and lines.

unit ⚡ projects

Visit unit projects at **fl6.msscience.com** for project ideas and resources. Projects include:

- **Career** Brainstorm a list of questions for a health professional about cell reproduction, or bacteria and virus resistance to drugs.
- **Technology** Design both a chart and a graph that present information on cell reproduction rates during specific time intervals.
- **Model** Construct a thumb flip book that models mitosis. Complete a second book for meiosis to analyze and compare the two processes.

Web Quest *Classifying and Comparing Worms* investigates three different phyla of worms. Complete the *Worm Comparison* worksheet to compare and contrast worms.

Sunshine State Standards—SC.F.1: The student describes patterns of structure and function in living things; **SC.G.1:** The student understands the competitive, interdependent, cyclic nature of living things in the environment; **SC.H.1:** The student uses the scientific processes and habits of mind to solve problems.

Exploring and Classifying Life

chapter preview

Life Under the Sea

This picture contains many living things—including living coral. These living things have both common characteristics and differences. Scientists classify life according to similarities.

Science Journal List three characteristics that you would use to classify underwater life.

Start-Up Activities

SC.G.1.3.3

Classify Organisms

Life scientists discover, describe, and name hundreds of organisms every year. How do they decide if a certain plant belongs to the iris or orchid family of plants or if an insect is more like a grasshopper or a beetle?

1. Complete a safety worksheet.
2. Observe the organisms on the opposite page or in an insect collection in your class.
3. Decide which feature could be used to separate the organisms into two groups, then sort the organisms into the two groups.
4. Continue to make new groups using different features until each organism is in a category by itself.
5. **Think Critically** How do you think scientists classify living things? List your ideas in your Science Journal.

 **Preview this chapter's content and activities at** fl6.msscience.com

Vocabulary Make the following Foldable to help you understand the vocabulary terms in this chapter.

LA.A.1.3.4

STEP 1 Fold a sheet of notebook paper vertically from side to side.

STEP 2 Cut along every third line of only the top layer to form tabs.

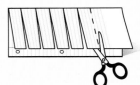

STEP 3 Label each tab.

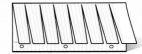

Build Vocabulary As you read the chapter, write the vocabulary words on the tabs. As you learn the definitions, write them under the tab for each vocabulary word.

Benchmarks—SC.H.1.3.1 Annually Assessed (p. 10): The student knows that scientific knowledge is subject to modification as new information challenges prevailing theories and as a new theory leads to looking at old observations in a new way; SC.H.1.3.5 Annually Assessed (pp. 9–10): The student knows that a change in one or more variables may alter the outcome of an investigation.

Also covers: SC.H.1.3.2 (p. 10); SC.H.1.3.3 (p. 6), SC.H.1.3.4 Annually Assessed (pp. 9–10), SC.H.3.3.2 (p. 6)

section 1

What is science?

as you read

What You'll Learn

- **Apply** scientific methods to problem solving.
- **Demonstrate** how to measure using scientific units.

Why It's Important

Learning to use scientific methods will help you solve ordinary problems in your life.

Review Vocabulary

✹ **experiment:** using controlled conditions to test a prediction

New Vocabulary

✹ **scientific method**
- **hypothesis**
- **control**
- **variable**
- **theory**
- **law**

✹ FCAT Vocabulary

The Work of Science

Movies and popcorn seem to go together. So before you and your friends watch a movie, sometimes you pop some corn in a microwave oven. When the popping stops, you take out the bag and open it carefully. You smell the mouthwatering, freshly popped corn and avoid hot steam that escapes from the bag. What makes the popcorn pop? How do microwaves work and make things hot? By the way, what are microwaves anyway?

Asking questions like these is one way scientists find out about anything in the world and the universe. Science is often described as an organized way of studying things and finding answers to questions.

Types of Science Many types of science exist. Each is given a name to describe what is being studied. For example, energy and matter have a relationship. That's a topic for physics. A physicist could answer most questions about microwaves.

On the other hand, a life scientist might study any of the millions of different animals, plants, and other living things on Earth. Look at the objects in **Figure 1.** What do they look like to you? A life scientist could tell you that some of the objects are living plants and some are rocks. Life scientists who study plants are botanists, and those who study animals are zoologists. What do you suppose a bacteriologist studies?

Figure 1 Some of the objects in this photo are *Lithops* plants. They commonly are called stone plants and are native to deserts in South Africa.

Critical Thinking

Whether or not you become a trained scientist, you are going to solve problems all your life. You probably solve many problems every day when you sort out ideas about what will or won't work. Suppose your CD player stops playing music. To figure out what happened, you have to think about it. That's called critical thinking, and it's the way you use skills to solve problems.

If you know that the CD player does not run on batteries and must be plugged in to work, that's the first thing you check to solve the problem. You check and the player is plugged in so you eliminate that possible solution. You separate important information from unimportant information—that's a skill. Could there be something wrong with the first outlet? You plug the player into a different outlet, and your CD starts playing. You now know that it's the first outlet that doesn't work. Identifying the problem is another skill you have.

Solving Problems

Scientists use the same types of skills that you do to solve problems and answer questions. Although scientists don't always find the answers to their questions, they always use critical thinking in their search. Besides critical thinking, solving a problem requires organization. In science, this organization often takes the form of a series of procedures called **scientific methods. Figure 2** shows one way that scientific methods might be used to solve a problem.

State the Problem Suppose a veterinary technician wanted to find out whether different types of cat litter cause irritation to cats' skin. What would she do first? The technician begins by observing something she cannot explain. A pet owner brings his four cats to the clinic to be boarded while he travels. He leaves his cell phone number so he can be contacted if any problems arise. When they first arrive, the four cats seem healthy. The next day, however, the technician notices that two of the cats are scratching and chewing at their skin. By the third day, these same two cats have bare patches of skin with red sores. The technician decides that something in the cats' surroundings or their food might be irritating their skin.

Figure 2 The series of procedures shown below is one way to use scientific methods to solve a problem.

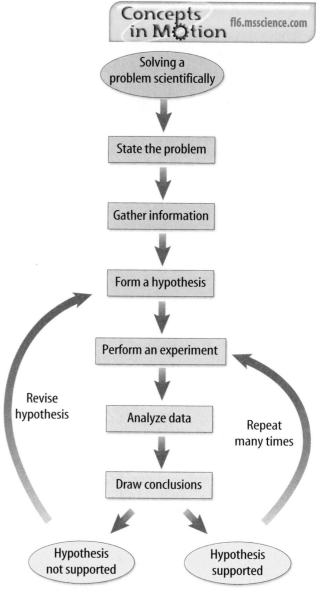

Laboratory investigations

Computer models

Fieldwork

Figure 3 Observations can be made in many different settings. **List** *three other places where scientific observations can be made.*

LA.B.2.3.4

Science online

Topic: Controlled Experiments
Visit fl6.msscience.com for Web links to information about how scientists use controlled experiments.

Activity List the problem, hypothesis, and how the hypothesis was tested for a recently performed controlled experiment.

Gather Information Laboratory observations and experiments are ways to collect information. Some data also are gathered from fieldwork. Fieldwork includes observations or experiments that are done outside of the laboratory. For example, the best way to find out how a bird builds a nest is to go outside and watch the bird. **Figure 3** shows some ways data can be gathered.

The technician gathers information about the problem by watching the cats closely for the next two days. She knows that cats sometimes change their behavior when they are in a new place. She wants to see if the behavior of the cats with the skin sores seems different from that of the other two cats. Other than the scratching and chewing at their skin, all four cats' behavior seems to be the same.

The technician calls the owner and tells him about the problem. She asks him what brand of cat food he feeds his cats. Because his brand is the same one used at the clinic, she decides that food is not the cause of the skin irritation. She decides that the cats probably are reacting to something in their surroundings. There are many things in the clinic that the cats might react to. How does she decide what it is?

During her observations she notices that the cats seem to scratch and chew themselves most after using their litter boxes. The cat litter used by the clinic contains a deodorant. The technician calls the owner and finds out that the cat litter he buys does not contain a deodorant.

Form a Hypothesis Based on this information, the next thing the veterinary technician does is form a hypothesis. A **hypothesis** is an explanation that can be tested. After discussing her observations with the clinic veterinarian, she hypothesizes that something in the cat litter is irritating the cats' skin.

Test the Hypothesis with an Experiment The technician gets the owner's permission to test her hypothesis by performing an experiment. In an experiment, the hypothesis is tested using controlled conditions. The technician reads the labels on two brands of cat litter and finds that the ingredients of each are the same except that one contains a deodorant.

Controls The technician separates the cats with sores from the other two cats. She puts each of the cats with sores in a cage by itself. One cat is called the experimental cat. This cat is given a litter box containing the cat litter without deodorant. The other cat is given a litter box that contains cat litter with deodorant. The cat with deodorant cat litter is the control.

A **control** is the standard to which the outcome of a test is compared. At the end of the experiment, the control cat will be compared with the experimental cat. Whether or not the cat litter contains deodorant is the variable. A **variable** is something in an experiment that can change. An experiment should have only one variable. Other than the difference in the cat litter, the technician treats both cats the same.

Reading Check *How many variables should an experiment have?*

Analyze Data The veterinary technician observes both cats for one week. During this time, she collects data on how often and when the cats scratch or chew, as shown in **Figure 4.** These data are recorded in a journal. The data show that the control cat scratches and chews more often than the experimental cat does. The sores on the skin of the experimental cat begin to heal, but those on the control cat do not.

Draw Conclusions The technician then draws the conclusion—a logical answer to a question based on data and observation—that the deodorant in the cat litter probably irritated the skin of the two cats. To accept or reject the hypothesis is the next step. In this case, the technician accepts the hypothesis. If she had rejected it, new experiments would have been necessary.

Although the technician decides to accept her hypothesis, she realizes that to be surer of her results she should continue her experiment. She should switch the experimental cat with the control cat to see what the results are a second time. If she did this, the healed cat might develop new sores. She makes an ethical decision and chooses not to continue the experiment. Ethical decisions, like this one, are important in deciding what science should be done.

Mini LAB

Analyzing Data

Procedure
1. Obtain a **pan balance.** Follow your teacher's instructions for using it.
2. Record all data in your **Science Journal.**
3. Measure and record the mass of a **dry sponge.**
4. Soak this sponge in **water.** Measure and record its mass.
5. Calculate how much water your sponge absorbed.
6. Combine the class data and calculate the average amount of water absorbed.

Analysis
What other information about the sponges might be important when analyzing the data from the entire class?

Figure 4 Collecting and analyzing data is part of scientific methods.

Annually Assessed Benchmark Check

SC.H.1.3.4 Why might a scientist report experimental procedures to other scientists?

Report Results When using scientific methods, it is important to share information. The veterinary technician calls the cats' owner and tells him the results of her experiment. She tells him she has stopped using the deodorant cat litter.

The technician also writes a story for the clinic's newsletter that describes her experiment and shares her conclusions. She reports the limits of her experiment and explains that her results are not final. In science it is important to explain how an experiment can be made better if it is done again.

Developing Theories

After scientists report the results of experiments supporting their hypotheses, the results can be used to propose a scientific theory. When you watch a magician do a trick, you might decide you have an idea or "theory" about how the trick works. Is your idea just a hunch or a scientific theory? A scientific **theory** is an explanation of things or events based on scientific knowledge that is the result of many observations and experiments. It is not a guess or someone's opinion. Many scientists repeat the experiment. If the results always support the hypothesis, as shown in **Figure 5,** the hypothesis can be called a theory.

Reading Check *On what is a theory based?*

A theory usually explains many hypotheses. For example, an important theory in life science is the cell theory. Scientists made observations of cells and experimented for more than 100 years before enough information was collected to propose a theory. Hypotheses about cells in plants and animals are combined in the cell theory.

A valid theory raises many new questions. Data or information from new experiments might change conclusions, and theories can change. Later in this chapter, you will read about the theory of spontaneous generation and how this theory changed as scientists used experiments to study new hypotheses.

Laws A scientific **law** is a statement about how things work in nature that seems to be true all the time. Although laws can be modified as more information becomes known, they are less likely to change than theories. Laws tell you what will happen under certain conditions, but do not necessarily explain why it happened. For example, in life science you might learn about laws of heredity. These laws explain how genes are inherited but do not explain how genes work. Due to the great variety of living things, laws that describe them are few. It is unlikely that a law about how all cells work will ever be developed.

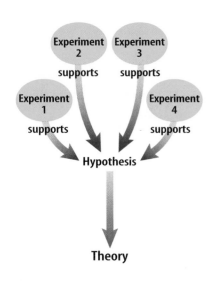

Figure 5 If data collected from many experiments over a period of time all support the hypothesis, it finally can be called a theory.

Scientific Methods Help Answer Questions You can use scientific methods to answer all sorts of questions. Your questions may be as simple as "Where did I leave my house key?" or as complex as "Will global warming cause the polar ice caps to melt?" You probably have had to find the answer to the first question. Someday you might try to find the answer to the second question. Using these scientific methods does not guarantee that you will get an answer. Often scientific methods just lead to more questions and more experiments. That's what science is about—continuing to look for the best answers to your questions.

Annually Assessed Benchmark Check

SC.H.1.3.5 In the Applying Science activity below, why didn't the scientist use a different type of bacteria for each temperature?

Applying Science

Does temperature affect the rate of bacterial reproduction?

Some bacteria make you sick. Other bacteria, however, are used to produce foods like cheese and yogurt. Understanding how quickly bacteria reproduce can help you avoid harmful bacteria and use helpful bacteria. It's important to know things that affect how quickly bacteria reproduce. How do you think temperature will affect the rate of bacterial reproduction? A student makes the hypothesis that bacteria will reproduce more quickly as the temperature increases.

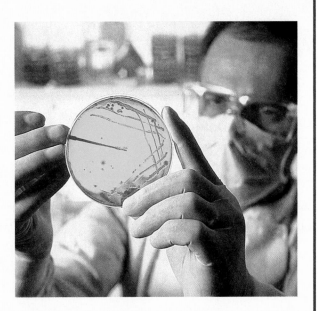

Identifying the Problem

The table below lists the reproduction-doubling rates at specific temperatures for one type of bacteria. A rate of 2.0 means that the number of bacteria doubled two times that hour (e.g., 100 to 200 to 400).

Bacterial Reproductive Rates	
Temperature (°C)	**Doubling Rate per Hour**
20.5	2.0
30.5	3.0
36.0	2.5
39.2	1.2

Look at the table. What conclusions can you draw from the data?

Solving the Problem

1. Do the data in the table support the student's hypothesis?
2. How would you write a hypothesis about the relationship between bacterial reproduction and temperature?
3. Make a list of other factors that might have influenced the results in the table.
4. Are you satisfied with these data? List other things that you wish you knew.
5. Describe an experiment that would help you test these other ideas.

Nutrition Facts
Serv. Size 8 fl oz (240 mL)
Servings 2

Amount Per Serving

Calories 110

% Daily Value*

Total Fat 0g	0%
Sodium 25mg	1%
Potassium 480mg	14%
Total Carb 27g	9%
Sugars 24g	
Protein 0g	

Vitamin C 100% • Thiamin 8%

Not a significant source of fat cal., sat. fat, cholest., fiber, vitamin A, calcium and iron.

*Percent Daily Values are based on a 2,000 calorie diet.

Figure 6 Your food often is measured in metric units. Nutritional information on the label is listed in grams or milligrams.

REGULAR ORANG

473mL

The label of this juice bottle shows you that it contains 473 mL of juice.

Measuring with Scientific Units

An important part of most scientific investigations is making accurate measurements. Think about things you use every day that are measured. Ingredients in your hamburger sandwich, cereal, frozen dinner, or soft drink are measured in units such as grams and milliliters, as shown in **Figure 6.** The water you drink, the gas the family car uses, and the electricity needed for a CD player are measured, too.

✓ **Reading Check** *Why is it important to make accurate measurements?*

In your classroom or laboratory this year, you will use the same standard system of measurement scientists use to communicate and understand each other's research and results. This system is called the International System of Units, or SI. For example, you may need to calculate the distance a bird flies in kilometers. Perhaps you will be asked to measure the amount of air your lungs can hold in liters or the mass of an automobile in kilograms. Some of the SI units are shown in **Table 1.**

Table 1 Common SI Measurements			
Measurement	**Unit**	**Symbol**	**Equal to**
Length	1 millimeter	mm	0.001 (1/1,000) m
	1 centimeter	cm	0.01 (1/100) m
	1 meter	m	100 cm
	1 kilometer	km	1,000 m
Volume	1 milliliter	mL	0.001 (1/1,000) L
	1 liter	L	1,000 mL
Mass	1 gram	g	1,000 mg
	1 kilogram	kg	1,000 g
	1 tonne	t	1,000 kg = 1 metric ton

Safety First

Doing science is usually much more interesting than just reading about it. Some of the scientific equipment that you will use in your classroom or laboratory is the same as what scientists use. Laboratory safety is important. In many states, a student can participate in a laboratory class only when wearing proper eye protection. Don't forget to wash your hands after handling materials. Following safety rules, as shown in **Figure 7,** will protect you and others from injury during your lab experiences. Symbols used throughout your text will alert you to situations that require special attention. Some of these symbols are shown below. A description of each symbol is in the Safety Symbols chart at the front of this book.

Figure 7 Proper eye protection should be worn whenever you see this safety symbol.
Predict *what might happen if you do not wear eye protection in the lab.*

section 1 review

Summary

The Work of Science

- Science is an organized way of studying things and finding answers to questions.

Solving Problems and Developing Theories

- Scientific methods are procedures used to solve problems and answer questions.
- A theory is an explanation based on many scientific observations.

Measuring with Scientific Units

- Scientists use the SI system for measurements.

Safety First

- Follow safety rules in the lab.

Self Check

1. **Describe** scientific methods.
2. **Infer** why it is important to test only one variable at a time during an experiment. `SC.H.1.3.5`
3. **Identify** the SI unit you would use to measure the width of your classroom.
4. **Compare and contrast** a theory with a hypothesis.
5. **Think Critically** Can the veterinary technician in this section be sure that deodorant caused the cats' skin problems? How could she improve her experiment?

Applying Skills

6. **Write a paper** that explains what the veterinary technician discovered from her experiment.

Benchmarks—SC.F.1.3.1 Annually Assessed (pp. 14–17): The student understands that living things are composed of major systems that function in reproduction, growth, maintenance, and regulation; SC.F.1.3.2 (p. 14): knows that the structural basis of most organisms is the cell and most organisms are single cells, while some, including humans, are multicellular.

Also covers: SC.F.1.3.3 (p. 17), SC.F.1.3.5 (p. 14), SC.F.1.3.7 (p. 15), SC.G.1.3.5 Annually Assessed (pp. 15, 18)

section 2

Living Things

as you read

What You'll Learn

- **Distinguish** between living and nonliving things.
- **Identify** what living things need to survive.

Why It's Important

All living things, including you, have many of the same traits.

Review Vocabulary

raw materials: substances needed by organisms to make other necessary substances

New Vocabulary

- ✳ **organism**
- ● cell
- ● homeostasis

✳ FCAT Vocabulary

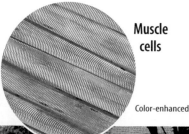

Muscle cells

Color-enhanced LM Magnification: 106×

What are living things like?

What does it mean to be alive? If you walked down your street after a thunderstorm, you'd probably see earthworms on the sidewalk, birds flying, clouds moving across the sky, and puddles of water. You'd see living and nonliving things that are alike in some ways. For example, birds and clouds move. Earthworms and water feel wet when they are touched. Yet, clouds and water are nonliving things, and birds and earthworms are living things. Any living thing is called an **organism.**

Organisms vary in size from the microscopic bacteria in mud puddles to gigantic oak trees and are found just about everywhere. They have different behaviors and food needs. In spite of these differences, all organisms have similar traits. These traits determine what it means to be alive.

Living Things Are Organized If you were to look at almost any part of an organism, like a plant leaf or your skin, under a microscope, you would see that it is made up of small units called cells. A **cell** is the smallest unit of an organism that carries on the functions of life. Most organisms are just one cell but some have many cells organized into systems. Cells take in materials from their surroundings and use them in complex ways. Each cell has an orderly structure and contains hereditary material. The hereditary material contains instructions for cellular organization and function. **Figure 8** shows some many-celled organisms. All the things that these organisms can do are possible because of what their cells can do.

Nerve cells

Figure 8 Your body is organized into many different types of cells. Two types are shown here.

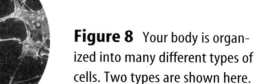

Color-enhanced SEM Magnification: 2500×

Living Things Respond Living things interact with their surroundings. Watch your cat when you use your electric can opener. Does your cat come running to find out what's happening even when you're not opening a can of cat food? The cat in **Figure 9** ran in response to a stimulus—the sound of the can opener. Anything that causes some change in an organism is a stimulus (plural, *stimuli*). The reaction to a stimulus is a response. Often that response results in movement, such as when the cat runs toward the sound of the can opener. To carry on its daily activity and to survive, an organism must respond to stimuli.

Living things also respond to stimuli that occur inside them. For example, water or food levels in organisms' cells can increase or decrease. The organisms then make internal changes to keep the right amounts of water and food in their cells. Their temperature also must be within a certain range. An organism's ability to keep the proper conditions inside no matter what is going on outside the organism is called **homeostasis.** Homeostasis is a trait of all living things.

Figure 9 Some cats respond to a food stimulus even when they are not hungry.
Infer *why a cat comes running when it hears a can opener.*

 **Reading Check** *What are some internal stimuli to which living things respond?*

Living Things Use Energy Organized living systems that carry on activities like homeostasis require energy. The energy used by most organisms comes either directly or indirectly from the Sun. Plants and some other organisms use the Sun's energy and the raw materials carbon dioxide and water to make food. You and most other organisms can't use the energy of sunlight directly. Instead, you take in and use food as a source of energy. Your food is plants, plant products, or other organisms that ate plants. Most organisms, including plants, also must take in oxygen in order to release the energy in foods.

Some bacteria live at the bottom of the oceans and in other areas where sunlight cannot reach. They can't use the Sun's energy to produce food. Instead, the bacteria use energy stored in some chemical compounds and the raw material carbon dioxide to make food. Unlike most other organisms, many of these bacteria do not need oxygen to release the energy that is found in their food.

LA.B.2.3.1

LA.B.2.3.4

Science nline

Topic: Homeostasis
Visit fl6.msscience.com for Web links to information about homeostasis.

Activity Describe the external stimuli and the corresponding internal changes for three different situations.

INTEGRATE Social Studies

Social Development Human infants quickly develop during their first year of life. Research to find out how infants interact socially at different stages of development. Make a chart that shows changes from birth to one year old.

Figure 10 The pictures below show the development of a dog, a human, a pea plant, and a butterfly.
Infer which of these organisms has the longest life span.

Living Things Grow and Develop When a puppy is born, it might be small enough to hold in one hand. After the same dog is fully grown, you might not be able to hold it at all. How does this happen? The puppy grows by taking in raw materials, like milk from its female parent, and making more cells. Growth of many-celled organisms, such as the puppy, is mostly due to an increase in the number of cells. In one-celled organisms, growth is due to an increase in the size of the cell.

Organisms change as they grow. Puppies can't see or walk when they are born. In eight or nine days, their eyes open, and their legs become strong enough to hold them up. All of the changes that take place during the life of an organism are called development. **Figure 10** shows how four different organisms changed as they grew.

The length of time an organism is expected to live is its life span. A dog can live for 20 years and a cat for 25 years. Some organisms have a short life span. Mayflies live only one day, but a land tortoise can live for more than 180 years. Some bristlecone pine trees have been alive for more than 4,600 years. Your life span is about 80 years.

Figure 11 Living things reproduce in many ways. A *Paramecium* reproduces by dividing into two new organisms. Beetles, like most insects, reproduce by laying eggs. Every spore released by a puffball fungus can grow into a new fungus.

Beetle

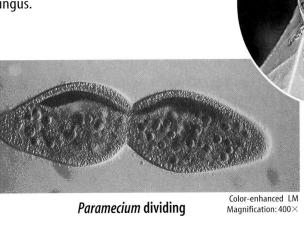

Paramecium **dividing**

Color-enhanced LM
Magnification: 400×

Puffballs

Living Things Reproduce Cats, dogs, alligators, fish, birds, bees, and trees eventually reproduce. They make more of their own kind. Some bacteria reproduce every 20 minutes, while it might take a pine tree two years to produce seeds. **Figure 11** shows some ways organisms reproduce.

Without reproduction, living things would not exist to replace those individuals that die. An individual cat can live its entire life without reproducing. However, if cats never reproduced, all cats soon would disappear.

✔ **Reading Check** *Why is reproduction important?*

What do living things need?

What do you need to live? Do you have any needs that are different from those of other living things? To survive, all living things need a place to live and raw materials. The raw materials that they require and the exact place where they live can vary.

A Place to Live The environment limits where organisms can live. Not many kinds of organisms can live in extremely hot or extremely cold environments. Most cannot live at the bottom of the ocean or on the tops of mountains. All organisms also need living space in their surroundings. For example, white ibises build their nests in trees or thickets two feet to 15 feet above the ground or water. If a nesting colony becomes too crowded, ibises will steal nesting materials from other nests. An organism's surroundings must provide for all of its needs.

Raw Materials Water is important for all living things. Plants and animals take in and give off large amounts of water each day, as shown in **Figure 12.** Organisms use homeostasis to balance the amounts of water lost with the amounts taken in. Most organisms are composed of more than 50 percent water. You are made of 60 to 70 percent water. Organisms use water for many things. For example, blood, which is about 90 percent water, transports digested food and wastes in animals. Plants have a watery sap that transports materials between roots and leaves.

Living things are made of substances such as proteins, fats, and sugars. Animals take in most of these substances from the foods they eat. Plants and some bacteria make them using raw materials from their surroundings. These important substances are used over and over again. When organisms die, substances in their bodies are broken down and released into the soil or air. The substances then can be used again by other living organisms. Some of the substances in your body might once have been part of a butterfly or an apple tree.

At the beginning of this section, you learned that things such as clouds, sidewalks, and puddles of water are not living things. Now do you understand why? Clouds, sidewalks, and water do not reproduce, use energy, or have other traits of living things.

Figure 12 You and a corn plant each take in and give off about 2 L of water in a day. Most of the water you take in is from water you drink or from foods you eat. **Infer** *where plants get water to transport materials.*

section 2 review

Summary

What are living things like?

- A cell is the smallest unit of an organism that carries on the functions of life.
- Anything that causes some change in an organism is a stimulus.
- Organisms use energy to stay organized and perform activities like homeostasis.
- All of the changes that take place during an organism's life are called development.

What do living things need?

- Living things need a place to live, water, and food.

Self Check

SC.G.1.3.5

1. **Identify** the source of energy for most organisms.
2. **List** five traits that most organisms have.
3. **Infer** why you would expect to see cells if you looked at a section of a mushroom cap under a microscope. SC.F.1.3.2
4. **Determine** what most organisms need to survive.
5. **Think Critically** Why is homeostasis important to organisms?

Applying Skills

6. **Use a Data Table** Use references to find the life span of ten animals. Use your computer to make a data table. Then, graph the life spans from shortest to longest.

section 3

Where does life come from?

Life Comes from Life

You've probably seen a fish tank, like the one in **Figure 13,** that is full of algae. How did the algae get there? Before the seventeenth century, some people thought that insects and fish came from mud, that earthworms fell from the sky when it rained, and that mice came from grain. These were logical conclusions at that time, based on repeated personal experiences. The idea that living things come from nonliving things is known as **spontaneous generation.** This idea became a theory that was accepted for several hundred years. When scientists began to use controlled experiments to test this theory, the theory changed.

Reading Check *Why did the theory of spontaneous generation change?*

Spontaneous Generation and Biogenesis From the late seventeenth century through the middle of the eighteenth century, experiments were done to test the theory of spontaneous generation. Although these experiments showed that spontaneous generation did not occur in most cases, they did not disprove it entirely.

It was not until the mid-1800s that the work of Louis Pasteur, a French chemist, provided enough evidence to disprove the theory of spontaneous generation. It was replaced with **biogenesis** (bi oh JE nuh suss), which is the theory that living things come only from other living things.

as you read

What **You'll Learn**

- **Describe** experiments about spontaneous generation.
- **Explain** how scientific methods led to the idea of biogenesis.

Why **It's Important**

You can use scientific methods to try to find out about events that happened long ago or just last week. You even can use them to predict how something will behave in the future.

Review Vocabulary
contaminate: to make impure by coming into contact with an unwanted substance

New Vocabulary
- spontaneous generation
- biogenesis

Figure 13 The sides of this tank were clean and the water was clear when the aquarium was set up. Algal cells, which were not visible on plants and fish, reproduced in the tank. So many algal cells are present now that the water is cloudy.

Figure 14

For centuries scientists have theorized about the origins of life. As shown on this timeline, some examined spontaneous generation—the idea that nonliving material can produce life. More recently, scientists have proposed theories about the origins of life on Earth by testing hypotheses about conditions on early Earth.

1668 Francesco Redi put decaying meat in some jars, then covered half of them. When fly maggots appeared only on the uncovered meat (see below, left), Redi concluded that they had hatched from fly eggs and had not come from the meat.

1745 John Needham heated broth in sealed flasks. When the broth became cloudy with microorganisms, he mistakenly concluded that they developed spontaneously from the broth.

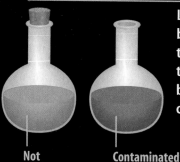

1768 Lazzaro Spallanzani boiled broth in sealed flasks for a longer time than Needham did. Only the ones he opened became cloudy with contamination.

Not contaminated   Contaminated

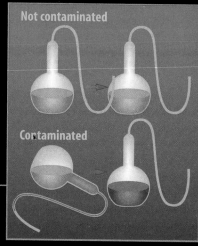

Not contaminated

Contaminated

1859 Louis Pasteur disproved spontaneous generation by boiling broth in S-necked flasks that were open to the air. The broth became cloudy (see above, bottom right) only when a flask was tilted and the broth was exposed to dust in the S-neck.

Gases of Earth's early atmosphere

Electric current

Oceanlike mixture forms

Cools

Materials in present-day cells

1924 Alexander Oparin hypothesized that energy from the Sun, lightning, and Earth's heat triggered chemical reactions early in Earth's history. The newly-formed molecules washed into Earth's ancient oceans and became a part of what is often called the primordial soup.

1953 Stanley Miller and Harold Urey sent electric currents through a mixture of gases like those thought to be in Earth's early atmosphere. When the gases cooled, they condensed to form an oceanlike liquid that contained materials such as amino acids, found in present-day cells.

Life's Origins

If living things can come only from other living things, how did life on Earth begin? Some scientists hypothesize that about 5 billion years ago, Earth's solar system was a whirling mass of gas and dust. They hypothesize that the Sun and planets were formed from this mass. It is estimated that Earth is about 4.6 billion years old. Rocks found in Australia that are more than 3.5 billion years old contain fossils of once-living organisms. Where did these living organisms come from?

Oparin's Hypothesis In 1924, a Russian scientist named Alexander I. Oparin suggested that Earth's early atmosphere had no oxygen but was made up of the gases ammonia, hydrogen, methane, and water vapor. Oparin hypothesized that these gases could have combined to form the more complex compounds found in living things.

Using gases and conditions that Oparin described, American scientists Stanley L. Miller and Harold Urey set up an experiment to test Oparin's hypothesis in 1953. Although the Miller-Urey experiment showed that chemicals found in living things could be produced, it did not prove that life began in this way.

For many centuries, scientists have tried to find the origins of life, as shown in **Figure 14.** Although questions about spontaneous generation have been answered, some scientists still are investigating ideas about life's origins.

Oceans Scientists hypothesize that Earth's oceans originally formed when water vapor was released into the atmosphere from many volcanic eruptions. Once it cooled, rain fell and filled Earth's lowland areas. Identify five lowland areas on Earth that are now filled with water. Record your answer in your Science Journal.

---

section 3 review

Summary

Life Comes from Life

- Spontaneous generation is the idea that living things come from nonliving things.
- The work of Louis Pasteur in 1859 disproved the theory of spontaneous generation.
- Biogenesis is the theory that living things come only from other living things.

Life's Origins

- Alexander I. Oparin hypothesized about the origin of life.
- The Miller-Urey experiment did not prove that Oparin's hypothesis was correct.

Self Check

1. **Discuss** how the idea of spontaneous generation developed. SC.H.1.3.1
2. **Describe** three controlled experiments that helped disprove the theory of spontaneous generation and led to the theory of biogenesis. SC.H.1.3.1   SC.H.1.3.1
3. **Summarize** the results of the Miller-Urey experiment.
4. **Think Critically** How do you think life on Earth began?

Applying Skills

5. **Draw Conclusions** Where could the organisms have come from in the 1768 broth experiment described in **Figure 14?**

---

section

4

Benchmarks—SC.G.1.3.3 (pp. 22–27): The student understands that the classification of living things ... set of criteria ... tool for understanding biodiversity and interrelationships. **SC.H.1.3.1 Annually Assessed** (pp. 22, 31): knows that scientific knowledge is subject to modification as new information challenges prevailing theories and as a new theory leads to looking at old observations in a new way.

Also covers: **SC.H.1.3.4 Annually Assessed** (pp. 27–29), **SC.H.1.3.5 Annually Assessed** (pp. 27–29), **SC.H.1.3.6** (pp. 22–23), **SC.H.3.3.5** (pp. 28–29)

How are living things classified?

as you read

What You'll Learn

- **Describe** how early scientists classified living things.
- **Explain** how similarities are used to classify organisms.
- **Explain** the system of binomial nomenclature.
- **Demonstrate** how to use a dichotomous key.

Why It's Important

Knowing how living things are classified will help you understand the relationships that exist among all living things.

Review Vocabulary

common name: a nonscientific term that may vary from region to region

New Vocabulary

- phylogeny
- kingdom
- binomial nomenclature
- genus

Classification

If you go to a library to find a book about the life of Louis Pasteur, where do you look? Do you look for it among the mystery or sports books? You expect to find a book about Pasteur's life with other biography books. Libraries group similar types of books together. When you place similar items together, you classify them. Organisms also are classified into groups.

History of Classification When did people begin to group similar organisms together? Early classifications included grouping plants that were used in medicines. Animals were often classified by human traits such as courage—for lions—or wisdom—for owls.

More than 2,000 years ago, a Greek named Aristotle observed living things. He decided that any organism could be classified as either a plant or an animal. Then he broke these two groups into smaller groups. For example, animal categories included hair or no hair, four legs or fewer legs, and blood or no blood. **Figure 15** shows some of the organisms Aristotle would have grouped together. For hundreds of years after Aristotle, no one way of classifying was accepted by everyone.

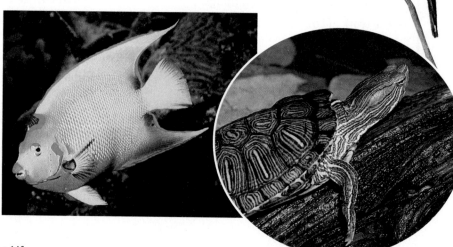

Figure 15 Using Aristotle's classification system, all animals without hair would be grouped together.
List *other animals without hair that Aristotle would have put in this group.*

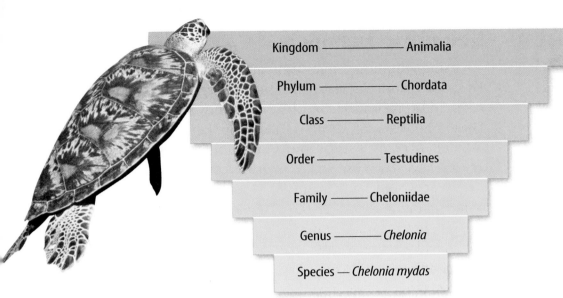

Figure 16 The classification of the green sea turtle shows that it is in the order Testudines. This order includes tortoises and snapping turtles.

Kingdom	Animalia
Phylum	Chordata
Class	Reptilia
Order	Testudines
Family	Cheloniidae
Genus	*Chelonia*
Species	*Chelonia mydas*

Linnaeus In the late eighteenth century, Carolus Linnaeus, a Swedish naturalist, developed a new system of grouping organisms. His classification system was based on looking for organisms with similar structures. For example, plants that had similar flower structure were grouped together. Linnaeus's system eventually was accepted and used by most other scientists.

Modern Classification Like Linnaeus, modern scientists use similarities in structure to classify organisms. They also use similarities in both external and internal features. Specific characteristics at the cellular level, such as the number of chromosomes, can be used to infer the degree of relatedness among organisms. In addition, scientists study fossils, hereditary information, and early stages of development. They use all of this information to determine an organism's phylogeny. **Phylogeny** (fi LAH juh nee) is the evolutionary history of an organism, or how it has changed over time. Today, it is the basis for the classification of many organisms.

 *What information would a scientist use to determine an organism's phylogeny?*

Science Online

LA.B.2.3.4

Topic: Domains
Visit fl6.msscience.com for Web links to information about domains.

Activity List all the domains and give examples of organisms that are grouped in each domain.

Six Kingdoms A classification system commonly used today groups organisms into six kingdoms. A **kingdom** is the first and largest category. Organisms are placed into kingdoms based on various characteristics. Kingdoms can be divided into smaller groups. The smallest classification category is a species. Organisms that belong to the same species can mate and produce fertile offspring. To understand how an organism is classified, look at the classification of the green sea turtle in **Figure 16.** Some scientists propose that before organisms are grouped into kingdoms, they should be placed in larger groups called domains. One proposed system groups all organisms into three domains.

SC.G.1.3.3

Mini LAB

Classifying Footwear

Procedure

1. Observe the **footwear** of students in your class or a group of friends. Form groups based on the types of footwear.
2. Each group is a genus. Brainstorm a name for your genus with others in the group.
3. Each person gives a species name to his or her footwear and records it on a **3-in × 5-in index card.**
4. Exchange cards with another group and match species name to the correct footwear.
5. Record the number of correct and incorrect responses in your Science Journal.

Analysis

1. What percentage of footwear was correctly identified by its species name?
2. How do scientific names make communication among scientists easier?

Try at Home

Scientific Names

Using common names can cause confusion. Suppose that Diego is visiting Jamaal. Jamaal asks Diego if he would like a soda. Diego is confused until Jamaal hands him a soft drink. At Diego's house, a soft drink is called pop. Jamaal's grandmother, listening from the living room, thought that Jamaal was offering Diego an ice-cream soda.

What would happen if life scientists used only common names of organisms when they communicated with other scientists? Many misunderstandings would occur, and sometimes health and safety would be involved. In **Figure 17,** you see examples of animals with common names that can be misleading. A naming system developed by Linnaeus helped solve this problem. It gave each species a unique, two-word scientific name.

Binomial Nomenclature The two-word naming system that Linnaeus used to name the various species is called **binomial nomenclature** (bi NOH mee ul • NOH mun klay chur). It is the system used by modern scientists to name organisms. The first word of the two-word name identifies the genus of the organism. A **genus** is a group of similar species. The second word of the name might tell you something about the organism—what it looks like, where it is found, or who discovered it.

In this system, the tree species commonly known as red maple has been given the name *Acer rubrum*. The maple genus is *Acer*. The word *rubrum* is Latin for red, which is the color of a red maple's leaves in the fall. The scientific name of another maple is *Acer saccharum*. The Latin word for sugar is *saccharum*. In the spring, the sap of this tree is sweet.

Figure 17 Common names can be misleading. Sea lions are more closely related to seals than to lions. **Identify** *another misleading common name.*

A jellyfish is not made of jelly.

Figure 18 These two lizards have the same common name, iguana, but are two different species.

Uses of Scientific Names Two-word scientific names are used for four reasons. First, they help avoid mistakes. Both of the lizards shown in **Figure 18** have the name *iguana*. Using binomial nomenclature, the green iguana is named *Iguana iguana*. Someone who studied this *iguana,* shown in the left photo, would not be confused by information he or she read about *Dispsosaurus dorsalis,* the desert iguana, shown in the right photo. Second, organisms with similar evolutionary histories are classified together. Because of this, you know that organisms in the same genus are related. Third, scientific names give descriptive information about the species, like the maples mentioned earlier. Fourth, scientific names allow information about organisms to be organized easily and efficiently. Such information may be found in a book or a pamphlet that lists related organisms and gives their scientific names.

✔ **Reading Check** *What are four functions of scientific names?*

Tools for Identifying Organisms

Tools used to identify organisms include field guides and dichotomous (di KAH tuh mus) keys. Using these tools is one way you and scientists solve problems scientifically.

Many different field guides are available. Most have illustrations or photographs of organisms, information about where each organism lives, and a general description of each organism's species. You can identify species from around the world by using the appropriate field guide.

INTEGRATE Earth Science

Computer Models
Meteorology has changed greatly due to computer modeling. Using special computer programs, meteorologists now are able to more accurately predict disastrous weather. In your Science Journal, describe how computer models might help save lives.

Dichotomous Keys A dichotomous key is a detailed list of identifying characteristics that includes scientific names. Dichotomous keys are arranged in steps with two descriptive statements at each step. If you learn how to use a dichotomous key, you can identify and name a species.

Do you know many types of mice exist? You can use **Table 2** to find out what type of mouse is pictured to the left. Start by choosing between the first pair of descriptions. The mouse has hair on its tail, so you go to 2. The ears of the mouse are small, so you go on to 3. The tail of the mouse is less that 25 mm. What is the name of this mouse according to the key?

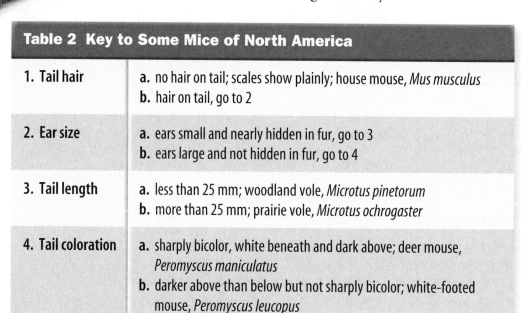

Table 2 Key to Some Mice of North America	
1. Tail hair	**a.** no hair on tail; scales show plainly; house mouse, *Mus musculus* **b.** hair on tail, go to 2
2. Ear size	**a.** ears small and nearly hidden in fur, go to 3 **b.** ears large and not hidden in fur, go to 4
3. Tail length	**a.** less than 25 mm; woodland vole, *Microtus pinetorum* **b.** more than 25 mm; prairie vole, *Microtus ochrogaster*
4. Tail coloration	**a.** sharply bicolor, white beneath and dark above; deer mouse, *Peromyscus maniculatus* **b.** darker above than below but not sharply bicolor; white-footed mouse, *Peromyscus leucopus*

section 4 review

Summary

Classification
- Organisms are classified into groups based on their similarities.
- Scientists today classify organisms into six kingdoms.
- Species is the smallest classification category.

Scientific Names
- Binomial nomenclature is the two-word naming system that gives organisms their scientific names.

Tools for Identifying Organisms
- Field guides and dichotomous keys are used to identify organisms.

Self Check

1. **State** Aristotle's and Linnaeus's contributions to classifying living things. SC.H.1.3.1 SC.H.1.3.6 SC.G.1.3.3
2. **Identify** a specific characteristic used to classify organisms.
3. **Explain** what each of the two words in a scientific name represent.
4. **Think Critically** Would you expect a field guide to have common names as well as scientific names? Why or why not?

Applying Skills

5. **Classify** Create a dichotomous key that identifies types of cars.

Benchmark—SC.G.1.3.3: The student understands that the classification of living things is based on a given set of criteria and is a tool for understanding biodiversity and inter-relationships; **SC.H.1.3.4:** The student knows that accurate record keeping, openness, and replication are essential to maintaining an investigator's credibility with other scientists and society.

Classifying Seeds

Scientists use classification systems to show how organisms are related. How do they determine which features to use to classify organisms? In this lab, you will observe seeds and use their features to classify them.

◉ Real-World Problem

How can the features of seeds be used to develop a key to identify the seed?

Goals
- **Observe** the seeds and notice their features.
- **Classify** seeds using these features.

Materials
packets of seeds (10 different kinds)
magnifying lens
metric ruler

Safety Precautions

Complete a safety worksheet before you begin.
WARNING: *Some seeds may have been treated with chemicals. Do not put them in your mouth.*

◉ Procedure

1. Make a data table like the one below in your Science Journal to record features of each seed. Your table will have a column for each type of seed you observe.

Seed Data			
Feature	**Type of Seed**		
Color			
Length (mm)	Do not write in this book.		
Shape			
Texture			

2. Use the seeds' features to develop a key.

3. Exchange keys with another group. Can you use their key to identify your seeds?

◉ Conclude and Apply

1. **Determine** which seed feature best helped classify the seeds? What other ways could you have classified the seeds?

2. **Infer** whether or not you could use your key to identify other seeds. Explain.

3. **Explain** why a standardized system to classify organisms is an advantage for scientists. Which of your observations support your answer?

𝒞ommunicating Your Data

Compare your conclusions with those of other students in your class. **For more help, refer to the** Science Skill Handbook.

Benchmark—**SC.H.1.3.4:** The student knows that accurate record keeping, openness, and replication are essential to maintaining an investigator's credibility with other scientists and society; **SC.H.1.3.5:** The student knows that a change in one or more variables may alter the outcome of an investigation; **SC.H.3.3.2:** The student knows that special care must be taken in using animals in scientific research.

Design Your Own

Using Scientific Methods *Inquiry*

Goals

- **Design** and carry out an experiment using scientific methods to infer why brine shrimp live in the ocean.
- **Observe** the jars for one week and notice whether the brine shrimp eggs hatch.

Possible Materials

500-mL, widemouthed containers (3)
brine shrimp eggs
small, plastic spoon
distilled water (500 mL)
salt
labels (3)
magnifying lens

Safety Precautions

Complete a safety worksheet before you begin. **WARNING:** *Protect eyes and clothing. Be careful when working with live organisms.*

▶ Real-World Problem

Brine shrimp are relatives of lobsters, crabs, crayfish, and the shrimp eaten by humans. They can hatch from eggs that have been stored in a dry condition for many years. However, your brine shrimp eggs are not hatching. Determine why they are not hatching by researching the conditions of their natural environment and testing the conditions of the water for your brine shrimp eggs. Then, create conditions in the lab that will allow your brine shrimp eggs to hatch.

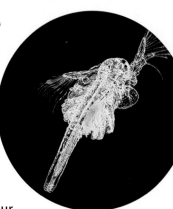

Brine shrimp

▶ Form a Hypothesis

Based on your literature research and observations, form a hypothesis to explain why your brine shrimp are not hatching.

▶ Test Your Hypothesis

Make a Plan

1. As a group, agree upon a hypothesis and decide how you will test it. Identify what results will confirm the hypothesis.

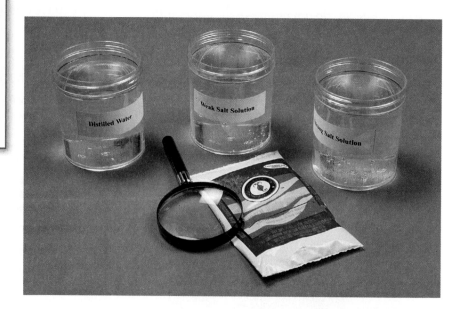

2. **List** steps that you need to test your hypothesis. Be specific. Describe exactly what you will do at each step.

3. **List** your materials.

4. **Prepare** a data table in your Science Journal to record your data.

5. Read over your entire experiment to make sure that all planned steps are in logical order.

6. **Identify** any constants, variables, and controls of the experiment.

Follow Your Plan

1. Make sure your teacher approves your plan before you start.

2. Carry out the experiment as planned by your group.

3. While doing the experiment, record any observations and complete the data table in your Science Journal.

▶ Analyze Your Data

1. **Describe** the contents of each jar after one week.

2. Use a bar graph to plot your results.

▶ Conclude and Apply

1. **Explain** whether or not the results support your hypothesis.

2. **Predict** the effect that increasing the amount of salt in the water would have on the brine shrimp eggs.

3. **Compare** your results with those of other groups.

4. **Determine** where possible sources of error were in your experiment and how it may have affected your results.

5. **Explain** how doing multiple trials of this experiment could affect your results.

6. **Describe** how you could apply your results or what other questions you could ask next.

Communicating Your Data

Prepare a set of instructions on how to hatch brine shrimp to use to feed fish. Include diagrams and a step-by-step procedure.

Monkey

Manicore marmoset

Acari marmoset

BUSINESS

In 2000, a scientist from Brazil's Amazon National Research Institute came across two squirrel-sized monkeys in a remote and isolated corner of the rain forest, about 2,575 km from Rio de Janeiro.

It turns out that the monkeys had never been seen before or even known to exist.

New Species

The new species were spotted by a scientist who named them after two nearby rivers the Manicore and the Acari, where the animals were discovered. Both animals are marmosets, which is a type of monkey found only in Central and South America. Marmosets have claws instead of nails, live in trees, and use their extraordinarily long tail like an extra arm or leg. Small and light,

both marmosets measure about 23 cm in length with a 38 cm tail and weigh no more than 0.4 kg.

The Manicore marmoset has a silvery-white upper body, a light-gray cap on its head, a yellow-orange underbody, and a black tail.

The Acari marmoset's upper body is snowy white, its gray back sports a stripe running to the knee, and its black tail flashes a bright-orange tip.

Amazin' Amazon

The Amazon Basin is a treasure trove of unique species. The Amazon River is Earth's largest body of freshwater, with 1,100 smaller tributaries. And more than half of the world's plant and animal species live in its rain forest ecosystems.

LA.A.2.3.5   LA.B.2.3.1

Research and Report Working in small groups, find out more about the Amazon rain forest. Which plants and animals live there? What products come from the rain forest? How does what happens in the Amazon rain forest affect you? Prepare a multimedia presentation.

TIME

For more information, visit fl6.msscience.com

Reviewing Main Ideas

Section 1 **What is science?**

1. Scientists use problem-solving methods to investigate observations about living and nonliving things.

2. Scientists use SI measurements to gather measurable data.

3. Safe laboratory practices help you learn more about science.

Section 2 **Living Things**

1. Organisms are made of cells, use energy, reproduce, respond, grow, and develop.

2. Organisms need energy, water, food, and a place to live.

Section 3 **Where does life come from?**

1. Controlled experiments finally disproved the theory of spontaneous generation.

2. Pasteur's experiment proved biogenesis.

Section 4 **How are living things classified?**

1. Classification is the grouping of ideas, information, or objects based on their similar characteristics.

2. Scientists today use phylogeny to group organisms into six kingdoms.

3. All organisms are given a two-word scientific name using binomial nomenclature.

Visualizing Main Ideas

Copy and complete this events-chain concept map that shows the order in which you might use a scientific method. Use these terms: analyze data, perform an experiment, *and* form a hypothesis.

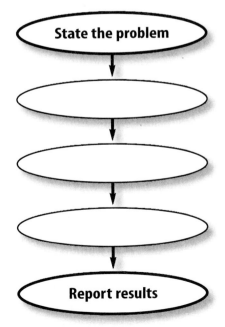

State the problem

⬇

( )

⬇

( )

⬇

( )

⬇

Report results

Using Vocabulary

binomial nomenclature p. 24	law p. 10
biogenesis p. 19	✹ organism p. 14
cell p. 14	phylogeny p. 23
control p. 9	✹ scientific methods p. 7
genus p. 24	spontaneous
homeostasis p. 15	generation p. 19
hypothesis p. 8	theory p. 10
kingdom p. 23	variable p. 9

✹ FCAT Vocabulary

Explain the differences in the vocabulary words in each pair below. Then explain how they are related.

1. control—variable **SC.H.1.3.5**

2. law—theory

3. biogenesis—spontaneous generation

4. binomial nomenclature—phylogeny

5. organism—cell **SC.F.1.3.4**

6. kingdom—phylogeny

7. hypothesis—scientific methods

8. organism—homeostasis

9. kingdom—genus

10. theory—hypothesis

Checking Concepts

Choose the word or phrase that best answers the question.

11. What category of organisms can mate and produce fertile offspring?
    A) family   C) genus
    B) class   D) species

12. What is the closest relative of *Canis lupus*?
    A) *Quercus alba*   C) *Felis tigris* **SC.F.1.3.3**
    B) *Equus zebra*   D) *Canis familiaris*

13. What is the source of energy for plants?
    A) the Sun   C) water **SC.G.1.3.5**
    B) carbon dioxide   D) oxygen

14. What makes up more than 50 percent of all living things?
    A) oxygen   C) minerals
    B) carbon dioxide   D) water

15. Who finally disproved the theory of spontaneous generation? **SC.H.1.3.6**
    A) Oparin   C) Pasteur
    B) Aristotle   D) Miller

16. What gas do some scientists think was missing from Earth's early atmosphere?
    A) ammonia   C) methane
    B) hydrogen   D) oxygen

17. What is the length of time called that an organism is expected to live?
    A) life span   C) homeostasis
    B) stimulus   D) theory

18. What is the part of an experiment that can be changed called? **SC.H.1.3.5**
    A) conclusion   C) control
    B) variable   D) data

19. What does the first word in a two-word name of an organism identify?
    A) kingdom   C) phylum
    B) species   D) genus

Use the photo below to answer question 20.

20. What SI unit is used to measure the volume of soda shown above?
    A) meter   C) gram
    B) liter   D) degree

Vocabulary PuzzleMaker fl6.msscience.com

Thinking Critically

21. Predict what *Lathyrus odoratus,* the scientific name for a sweet pea plant, tells you about one of its characteristics. `SC.F.1.3.3`

Use the photo below to answer question 22.

22. Determine what problem-solving techniques this scientist would use to find how dolphins learn.

Use the graph below to answer question 23.

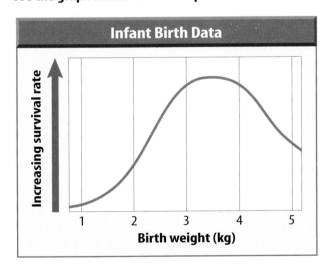

Infant Birth Data

Increasing survival rate

Birth weight (kg)

23. Interpret Data Do the data in the graph above support the hypothesis that babies with a birth weight of 2.5 kg have the best chance of survival? Explain.

24. List advantages of using SI units.

25. Form a Hypothesis A lima bean plant is placed under green light, another is placed under red light, and a third under blue light. Their growth is measured for four weeks to determine which light is best for plant growth. What are the variables in this experiment? State a hypothesis for this experiment. `SC.H.1.3.5`

Performance Activities

26. Bulletin Board Interview people in your community whose jobs require a knowledge of life science. Make a Life Science Careers bulletin board. Summarize each person's job and what he or she had to study to prepare for that job. `SC.H.1.3.6`

Applying Math

27. Body Temperature Normal human body temperature is 98.6°F. What is this temperature in degrees Celsius? Use the following expression, $5/9(°F-32)$, to find degrees Celsius. `MA.B.2.3.2`

Use the graph below to answer question 28.

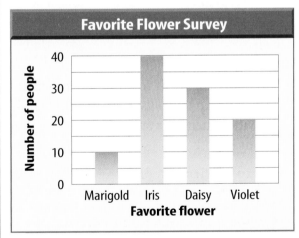

Favorite Flower Survey

Number of people

Favorite flower

28. Favorite Flower The graph above shows how many people selected a certain type of flower as their favorite. According to the graph, what percentage of the people picked daisy as their favorite? `MA.E.1.3.1`

The assessed Florida Benchmark appears above each question.
Record your answers on the answer sheet provided by your teacher or on a sheet of paper.

Multiple Choice

SC.F.1.3.2

1 The diagram below shows two organisms, a *Paramecium* and a beetle.

What is one way that the *Paramecium* is different from the beetle?

A. The *Paramecium* does not reproduce.

B. The *Paramecium* does not respond to stimuli.

C. The *Paramecium* is only one cell.

D. The *Paramecium* uses food as a source of energy.

SC.H.1.3.4

2 Dr. Shu is testing if microscopic organisms can clean up oil spills. Why should Dr. Shu provide other scientists with accurate notes about his procedures and results?

F. to confirm Dr. Shu's results by repeating his experiment

G. to find the organisms Dr. Shu was testing

H. to not waste their time by duplicating Dr. Shu's investigation

I. to receive a share of any profits Dr. Shu's experiment might yield

SC.F.1.3.7

3 A science class set up the experiment below to study the behavior of plants.

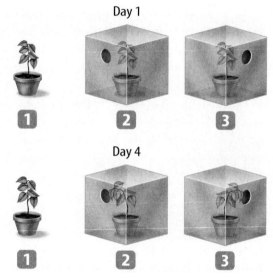

To what stimulus are plants 2 and 3 most likely responding on Day 4 as they grow toward the holes in the boxes?

A. heat

B. water

C. soil

D. light

SC.G.1.3.3

4 What is the main way of classifying living things according to the modern system of classification?

F. They are grouped by size.

G. They are grouped by habitat.

H. They are grouped in alphabetical order using their scientific names.

I. They are grouped based on their evolutionary history.

SC.H.1.3.1

5 Which of the following scientific questions would a biologist be most likely to investigate?

A. How do plants make food?

B. What causes tornadoes to form?

C. How old are the oldest rocks on Earth?

D. What happens when matter absorbs energy?

Gridded Response

SC.H.1.3.5

6 A student is investigating photosynthesis by using a water plant called *Elodea*. The student places a piece of *Elodea* in a water-filled test tube and puts it five centimeters from a 40-watt light bulb. The student waits one minute and then counts the number of oxygen bubbles coming from the cut end of the stem during a 5-minute period. The student repeats this procedure, but places the light at different distances from the test tube. The results are shown in the table below.

Photosynthesis Experiment	
Distance to Light (centimeters)	Number of Oxygen Bubbles
5	22
10	17
15	13
20	8
25	4

How many variables were changed in each trial of the experiment?

Short Response

SC.F.1.3.1

7 Katrina collects a specimen in the forest. She wants to determine if the specimen is a living thing. Describe the characteristics that the specimen must have to be considered a living thing.

Extended Response

SC.H.1.3.5

8 A scientist wants to determine if the temperature at which a certain type of turtle egg develops is related to the gender of the turtle hatchling, which is either male (M) or female (F). The scientist incubates three sets of five eggs. Each set is at different temperature. The scientist then observes the genders of turtle hatchlings. The results are shown in the table below.

Turtle Gender	
Temperature of Eggs	Gender of Turtle Hatchlings
28°C	M, M, M, M, M
29°C	M, M, F, M, F
30°C	F, F, F, F, F

PART A Describe three variables that the scientist should have controlled during this experiment.

PART B Based on the experiment, what effect does temperature have on the turtles' genders? Assume that all variables except temperature were controlled. Describe the evidence that supports your conclusion.

Sunshine State Standards—**SC.F.1:** The student describes patterns of structure and function in living things; **SC.H.2:** The student understands that most natural events occur in comprehensible, consistent patterns.

The Living Cell

Life's Building Blocks

If you look closely, you can see that these frogs and crocodiles are made up of small, plastic building blocks. Similarly, living organisms also are made of small building blocks. The building block of all living things is the cell.

Science Journal   List features common to small, plastic building blocks. Predict whether plastic building blocks or cells have the greater number of features in common.

Start-Up Activities

SC.F.1.3.2

Observe Onion Cells

An active, organized world is inside you and in all other living things. Yet it is a world that you usually can't see with just your eyes. Make the magnifier in the lab below to help you see how living things are organized.

1. Complete a safety worksheet.

2. Cut a 2-cm hole in the middle of an index card. Tape a piece of plastic wrap over the hole.

3. Turn down about 1 cm of the two shorter sides of the card, then stand it up.

4. Place a piece of onion skin on a microscope slide, then put it directly under the hole in the card.

5. Put a drop of water on the plastic wrap. Look through the water drop and observe the piece of onion. Draw what you see.

6. **Think Critically** In your Science Journal, describe how the onion skin looked when viewed with your magnifier.

FOLDABLES™
Study Organizer

Compare Cells Make the following Foldable to help you see how plant and animal cells are similar and different.

LA.A.1.3.4

STEP 1 Fold a vertical sheet of paper in half from top to bottom.

STEP 2 Fold in half from side to side with the fold at the top.

STEP 3 Unfold the paper once. Cut only the fold of the top flap to make two tabs. Turn the paper vertically and draw on the front tabs as shown.

Plant Cell

Animal Cell

Read and Write Before you read the chapter, write what you know about each of these cells. As you read the chapter, add to or correct what you have written under the tabs. Compare and contrast the two types of cells.

 **Preview this chapter's content and activities at** fl6.msscience.com

Benchmarks—**SC.F.1.3.2 (pp. 38–39):** The student knows that the structural basis of most organisms is the cell and most organisms are single cells, while some, including humans, are multicellular; **SC.F.1.3.6 (pp. 42–43):** The student knows that the cells with similar functions have similar structures, whereas those with different structures have different functions.

Also covers: **SC.F.1.3.5 (pp. 42–44); SC.G.1.3.1 Annually Assessed (p. 38); SC.H.1.3.4 Annually Assessed (p. 44)**

The World of Cells

as you read

What **You'll Learn**

- **Discuss** the cell theory.
- **Identify** some of the parts of animal and plant cells.
- **Explain** the functions of different cell parts.

Why **It's Important**

Cells carry out the activities of life.

Review Vocabulary
theory: an explanation of things or events based on scientific knowledge that is the result of many observations and experiments

New Vocabulary
- bacteria
- cell membrane
- cell wall
- cytoplasm
- organelle
- ✹ nucleus
- vacuole
- mitochondria
- ✹ photosynthesis
- chloroplast

✹ FCAT Vocabulary

Importance of Cells

A cell is the smallest unit of life in all living things. Cells are important because they are organized structures that help living things carry on the activities of life, such as the breakdown of food, movement, growth, and reproduction. Different cells have different jobs in living things. Some plant cells help move water and other substances throughout the plant. White blood cells, found in humans and many other animals, help fight diseases. Plant cells, white blood cells, and all other cells are alike in many ways.

Cell Theory Because most cells are small, they were not observed until microscopes were invented. In 1665, scientist Robert Hooke, using a microscope that he made, observed tiny, boxlike things in a thin slice of cork, as shown in **Figure 1.** He called them cells because they reminded him of the small, boxlike rooms called cells, where monks lived.

Throughout the seventeenth and eighteenth centuries, scientists observed many living things under microscopes. Their observations led to the development of the cell theory. The three main ideas of the cell theory are:

1. All living things are made of one or more cells.

2. The cell is the basic unit of life in which the activities of life occur.

3. All cells come from cells that already exist.

Figure 1 Robert Hooke designed this microscope and drew the cork cells he observed.

The Microscopic Cell All the living things pictured in **Figure 2** are made up of cells. The smallest organisms and greatest number of organisms on Earth are **bacteria.** They are one-celled organisms, which means each is only one cell.

> ✔ **Reading Check** *How many cells does each bacterium have?*

Larger organisms are made of many cells. These cells work together to complete all of the organism's life activities. The living things that you see every day—trees, dogs, insects, people—are many-celled organisms. Your body contains more than 10 trillion (10,000,000,000,000) cells.

Microscopes Scientists have viewed and studied cells for about 350 years. In that time, they have learned a lot about cells. Better microscopes have helped scientists learn about the differences among cells. Some modern microscopes allow scientists to study the small features that are inside cells and viruses.

INTEGRATE Physics The microscope used in most classrooms is called a compound light microscope. In this type of microscope, light passes through the object you are looking at and then through two or more lenses. The lenses enlarge the image of the object. How much an image is enlarged depends on the powers of the eyepiece and the objective lens. The power—a number followed by an ✕—is found on each lens. For example, a power of 10✕ means that the lens can magnify something to ten times its actual size. The magnification of a microscope is found by multiplying the powers of the eyepiece and the objective lens.

LA.B.2.3.1
LA.B.2.3.4

Science nline

Topic: Viruses
Viruses could not be seen until the electron microscope (EM) was invented. Visit **fl6.msscience.com** for Web links to information about electron microscopes and viruses.

Activity Make a pamphlet describing one virus and how it depends on a living organism.

Figure 2 All living things are made up of cells.

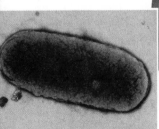

Magnification: 67500✕

E. coli—a bacterium—is a one-celled organism.

Plant cells are different from animal cells.
Infer *how the cells in this rose plant differ.*

Human cells are similar to other animal cells, like those in cats and turtles.

What are cells made of?

As small as cells are, they are made of even smaller parts, each doing a different job. A cell can be compared to a bakery. The activities of a bakery are inside a building. Electricity is used to run the ovens and other equipment, power the lights, and heat the building. The bakery's products require ingredients such as dough, sugar, and fillings, that must be stored, assembled, and baked. The bakery's products are packaged and shipped to different locations. A manager is in charge of the entire operation. The manager makes a plan for every employee of the bakery and a plan for every step of making and selling the baked goods.

A living cell operates in a similar way. Like the walls of the bakery, a cell has a boundary. Inside this boundary, the cell's life activities take place. These activities must be managed. Smaller parts inside the cell can act as storage areas. A cell also has parts that use ingredients such as oxygen, water, minerals, and other nutrients. Some cell parts can release energy or make substances that are necessary for maintaining life. Some substances leave the cell and are used elsewhere in the organism.

Figure 3 These are some of the parts of an animal cell that perform the activities necessary for life. **Identify** *the cell part that converts energy.*

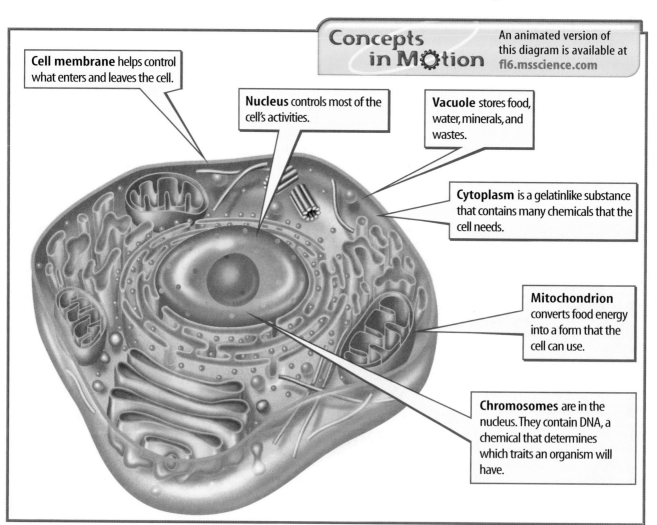

Concepts in Motion An animated version of this diagram is available at fl6.msscience.com

Cell membrane helps control what enters and leaves the cell.

Nucleus controls most of the cell's activities.

Vacuole stores food, water, minerals, and wastes.

Cytoplasm is a gelatinlike substance that contains many chemicals that the cell needs.

Mitochondrion converts food energy into a form that the cell can use.

Chromosomes are in the nucleus. They contain DNA, a chemical that determines which traits an organism will have.

Outside a Cell The **cell membrane,** shown in **Figure 3,** is a flexible structure that holds a cell together, similar to the walls of the bakery. The cell membrane forms a boundary between a cell and its environment. It also helps control what goes into and comes out of a cell. Some cells, like those in plants, algae, fungi, and many types of bacteria, also have a structure outside the cell membrane called a **cell wall,** shown in **Figure 4.** A cell wall helps support and protect these cells.

Inside a Cell The inside of a cell is filled with a gelatinlike substance called **cytoplasm** (SI tuh pla zum). Approximately two-thirds of the cytoplasm is water, but it also contains many chemicals that are needed by a cell. Like the work area inside the bakery, the cytoplasm is where a cell's activities take place.

Organelles Except for bacterial cells, cells contain **organelles** (or guh NELZ) like those in **Figure 3** and **Figure 4.** These specialized cell parts can move around in the cytoplasm and perform activities that are necessary for life. You could think of these organelles as the employees of a cell because each type of organelle does a different job. In bacteria, most cell activities occur in the cytoplasm.

LA.A.2.3.5

INTEGRATE Chemistry

Phospholipids The cell membrane is a double layer of complex molecules called phospholipids (fahs foh LIH pudz). Research to find the elements that are in these molecules. Find those elements on the periodic table at the back of this book.

Figure 4 Most plant cells contain the same types of organelles as in animal cells. A plant cell also can have a cell wall and chloroplasts.

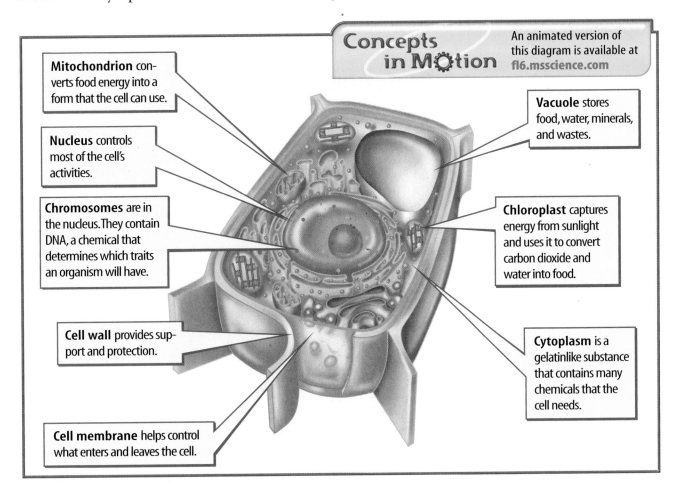

Concepts in Motion An animated version of this diagram is available at fl6.msscience.com

Mitochondrion converts food energy into a form that the cell can use.

Nucleus controls most of the cell's activities.

Chromosomes are in the nucleus. They contain DNA, a chemical that determines which traits an organism will have.

Cell wall provides support and protection.

Cell membrane helps control what enters and leaves the cell.

Vacuole stores food, water, minerals, and wastes.

Chloroplast captures energy from sunlight and uses it to convert carbon dioxide and water into food.

Cytoplasm is a gelatinlike substance that contains many chemicals that the cell needs.

Mini LAB

Modeling a Cell

Procedure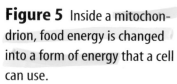

1. Collect **household materials such as clay, cardboard, yarn, buttons, dry macaroni,** or other objects.
2. Using the objects that you collected and **glue,** make a three-dimensional model of an animal or a plant cell.
3. On a separate sheet of **paper,** make a key to the materials in your cell model.

Analysis

1. What does each part of your cell model do?
2. Have someone look at your model. Which of the cell parts could they identify without using the key?
3. How could you improve your model?

Try at Home

The Nucleus A bakery's manager follows a business plan so that the business runs smoothly. A business plan describes how the business should operate. These plans could include how many donuts are made and what kinds of pies are baked.

A cell's hereditary material is like a bakery's business plan because it controls a cell's makeup and activities. Most of the hereditary material is a chemical called DNA. DNA contains instructions for an organism's traits, such as the shape of a plant's leaves or the color of your eyes. Hereditary material is found in one or many structures called chromosomes (KROH muh zohmz). In a cell with organelles, the hereditary material is in the **nucleus.** In a cell without a nucleus, like a bacterium, the hereditary material is in the cytoplasm.

Reading Check *Which important chemical determines the traits of an organism?*

Storage Pantries, closets, refrigerators, and freezers store food and other supplies that a bakery needs. Trash cans hold garbage until it can be picked up. In cells, food, water, and other substances are stored in balloonlike organelles in the cytoplasm called **vacuoles** (VA kyuh wohlz). Some vacuoles store wastes until the cell is ready to get rid of them. Plant cells usually have a large vacuole that stores water and other substances.

Energy and the Cell

Electrical energy or the energy in natural gas is converted to heat energy by the bakery's ovens. The heat then is used to bake the breads and other bakery products. Cells need energy, too. Cells, except bacteria, have organelles called **mitochondria** (mi tuh KAHN dree uh)(singular, *mitochondrion*). An important process called cellular respiration (SEL yuh lur • res puh RAY shun) takes place inside a mitochondrion as shown in **Figure 5.** Cellular respiration is a series of chemical reactions in which energy stored in food is converted to a form of energy that a cell can use. This energy is released as food and oxygen combine. Waste products of this process are carbon dioxide and water. Cells with mitochondria use the energy from cellular respiration to do most of their work.

Figure 5 Inside a mitochondrion, food energy is changed into a form of energy that a cell can use.
Infer *what happens to the water and carbon dioxide produced by mitochondria in human cells.*

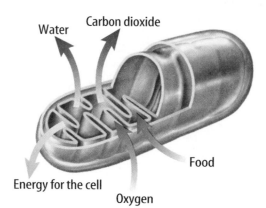

Water
Carbon dioxide
Energy for the cell
Oxygen
Food

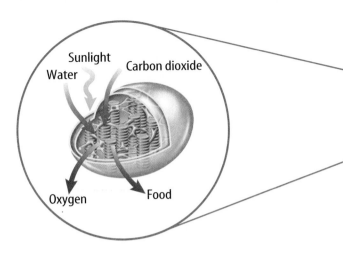

Nature's Solar Energy Factories Animals obtain food from their surroundings. A cow grazes in a pasture. A bird pecks at worms, and a dog eats from a bowl. Have you ever seen a plant eat anything? How do plants get energy-rich food?

Plants, algae, and many types of bacteria make food through a process called **photosynthesis** (foh toh SIHN thuh sus). Most photosynthesis in plants occurs in leaf cells. Inside these cells are green organelles called **chloroplasts** (KLOR uh plasts). Most leaves are green because their cells contain so many chloroplasts. During plant photosynthesis, as shown in **Figure 6,** chloroplasts capture light energy and combine carbon dioxide from the air with water to make food. Energy is stored in food. As the plant needs energy, its mitochondria release the food's energy. The captured light energy is passed to other organisms when they eat organisms that carry on photosynthesis.

Figure 6 Photosynthesis can take place inside the chloroplasts of plant cells.

section 1 review

Summary

Importance of Cells

- Cells are organized structures that help living things carry on the activities of life.
- The main ideas about cells are described in the cell theory.
- Microscopes help scientists study cells.

What are cells made of?

- Different cell parts do different jobs.

Energy and the Cell

- Cells need energy to function. This energy comes mainly from cellular respiration.
- Plants, algae, and some bacteria make food through photosynthesis.

Self Check

1. **List** the three main ideas of the cell theory.
2. **Explain** why the nucleus is so important to the living cell. `SC.F.1.3.5`
3. **Describe** how cells get the energy they need to carry on their activities.
4. **State** the purpose of a cell membrane. `SC.F.1.3.5`
5. **Think Critically** Suppose your teacher gave you a slide of an unknown cell. How would you tell whether the cell was from an animal or from a plant? `SC.F.1.3.6`

Applying Skills

6. **Compare and contrast** the parts of animal cells and plant cells and the jobs that they do.

Benchmark—SC.F.1.3.2: The student knows that the structural basis of most organisms is the cell and most organisms are single cells, while some, including humans, are multi-cellular; **SC.F.1.3.5:** The student explains how the life functions of organisms are related to what occurs within the cell.

Observing Algae

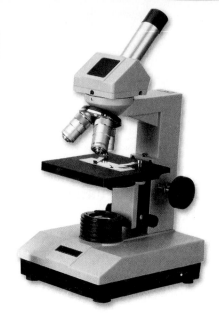

You might have noticed mats of green algae growing on a pond or clinging to the walls of the aquarium in your classroom. Why are algae green? Like plants, algae contain organelles called chloroplasts. Chloroplasts contain a green pigment called chlorophyll. It captures light energy that is needed to make food. In this lab, you'll describe chloroplasts and other organelles in algal cells.

▶ Real-World Problem

What organelles can be seen when viewing algal cells under a microscope?

Goals
■ **Observe** algal cells under a microscope.
■ **Identify** cell organelles.

Materials

microscope	pond water
microscope slides	algae
coverslips	dropper
large jars	colored pencils

Safety Precautions

Complete a safety worksheet before you begin.

WARNING: *Thoroughly wash your hands after you have finished this lab.*

▶ Procedure

1. Fill the tip of a dropper with pond water and thin strands of algae. Use the dropper to place the algae and a drop of water on a microscope slide.

2. Place a coverslip over the water drop and then place the slide on the stage of a microscope.

3. Using the microscope's lowest power objective, focus on the algal strands.

4. Once the algal strands are in focus, switch to a higher power objective and observe several algal cells.

5. **Draw** a colored picture of one of the algal cells, identifying the different organelles in the cell. Label on your drawing the cell wall, chloroplasts, and other organelles you can see.

▶ Conclude and Apply

1. **List** the organelles you found in each cell.
2. **Explain** the function of chloroplasts.
3. **Infer** why algal cells are essential to all pond organisms.

ℂommunicating Your Data

Work with three other students to create a collage of algal-cell pictures complete with labeled organelles. Create a bulletin board display about algal cells.

Benchmarks—SC.F.1.3.4 (pp. 47–49): The student knows that the levels of structural organization for function in living things include cells, tissues, organs, systems, and organisms; SC.F.1.3.6 (pp. 45–46): The student knows that the cells with similar functions have similar structures, whereas those with different structures have different functions.

Also covers: SC.F.1.3.5 (p. 45); SC.H.2.3.1 (p. 47)

section 2

The Different Jobs of Cells

Special Cells for Special Jobs

Choose the right tool for the right job. You might have heard this common expression. The best tool for a job is one that has been designed for that job. For example, you wouldn't use a hammer to saw a board in half, and you wouldn't use a saw to pound in a nail. You can think of your body's cells in a similar way.

Cells that make up many-celled organisms, like you, are specialized. Different kinds of specialized cells work as a team to perform the life activities of a many-celled organism.

Types of Human Cells Your body is made up of many types of specialized cells. The same is true for other animals. **Figure 7** shows some human cell types. Notice the variety of sizes and shapes. A cell's shape and size can be related to its function.

as you read

What You'll Learn
- **Discuss** how different cells have different jobs.
- **Explain** the differences among tissues, organs, and organ systems.

Why It's Important
You will understand how different types of cells work together to keep you healthy.

Review Vocabulary
☀ **organism:** anything that possesses all the characteristics of life

New Vocabulary
☀ **tissue**   ● organ system
☀ **organ**

☀ FCAT Vocabulary

Figure 7 Human cells come in different shapes and sizes.

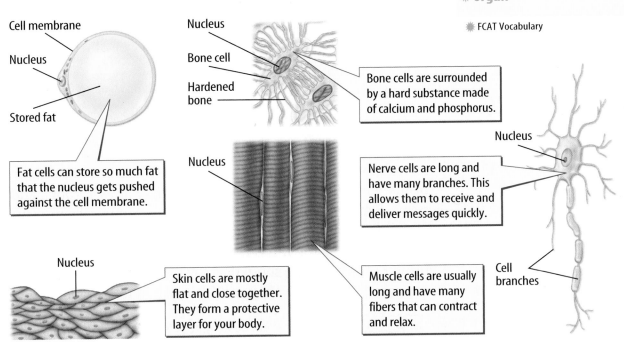

Cell membrane
Nucleus
Stored fat

Fat cells can store so much fat that the nucleus gets pushed against the cell membrane.

Nucleus
Bone cell
Hardened bone

Bone cells are surrounded by a hard substance made of calcium and phosphorus.

Nucleus

Nerve cells are long and have many branches. This allows them to receive and deliver messages quickly.

Nucleus
Cell branches

Nucleus

Skin cells are mostly flat and close together. They form a protective layer for your body.

Muscle cells are usually long and have many fibers that can contract and relax.

Figure 8 Plants, like animals, have specialized cells.
Infer *what process can occur in leaf cells but not in root cells.*

Some leaf cells are brick shaped and contain many chloroplasts.

LM, Magnification: 900×

Many of the cells in stems are long and tube-shaped. They move water and other materials through the plant.

SEM Magnification: 1500×

Most root cells are block shaped and do not contain chloroplasts.

Magnification: 450×

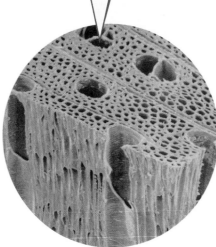

SC.F.1.3.6

Mini LAB

Analyzing Cells

Procedure
1. Complete a safety worksheet.
2. Examine **prepared slides of human cells.**
3. Draw each type of cell that you observe in your **Science Journal.** Label cell parts that you can see.

Analysis
1. In what ways were the cells that you observed similar? How were they different?
2. Hypothesize how the cells' shapes relate to their jobs.

Types of Plant Cells Like animals, plants also are made of several different cell types, as shown in **Figure 8.** For instance, plants have different types of cells in their leaves, roots, and stems. Each type of cell has a specific job. Some cells in plant stems are long and tubelike. Together they form a system through which water, food, and other materials move in the plant. Other cells, like those that cover the outside of the stem, are smaller or thicker. They provide strength to the stem.

✔ **Reading Check** *What do long, tubelike cells do in plants?*

Cell Organization

How well do you think your body would work if all the different cell types were mixed together in no particular pattern? Could you walk if your leg muscle cells were scattered here and there, each doing its own thing, instead of being grouped together in your legs? How could you think if your brain cells weren't close enough together to communicate with each other? Many-celled organisms are not just mixed-up collections of different types of cells. Cells are organized into systems that, together, perform functions that keep the organism healthy and alive.

Applying Math | Solve One-Step Equations

RED BLOOD CELLS Each milliliter of blood contains 5 million red blood cells (RBCs). On average, an adolescent has about 3.5 L of blood. On average, how many RBCs are in an adolescent's body?

Solution

1 *This is what you know:*
- number of RBCs per 1 mL = 5,000,000
- 1,000 mL = 1 L
- average volume of blood in an adolescent's body = 3.5 L

2 *This is what you need to find out:*
On average, how many RBCs are in an adolescent's body, N?

3 *This is the procedure you need to use:*
- Use the following equation:
  N = (number of RBCs/1mL) (1,000 mL/1 L) (3.5 L of blood)
- Substitute the known values
  N = (5,000,000 RBCs/1 mL) (1,000 mL/1 L) (3.5 L of blood)
  N = 17,500,000,000 RBCs
- On average, there are 17.5 billion red blood cells in an adolescent's body.

4 *Check your answer:*
Divide 17,500,000,000 RBCs by 1,000 mL/1 L then divide that answer by 3.5 L, and you should get 5,000,000 RBCs/1 mL.

Practice Problems

1. Each milliliter of blood contains approximately 7,500 white blood cells. How many white blood cells are in the average adolescent's body? **MA.A.3.3.2**

2. There are approximately 250,000 platelets in each milliliter of blood. How many platelets are in the average adolescent's body? **MA.A.3.3.2**

Math Practice | For more practice, visit fl6.msscience.com

NATIONAL GEOGRAPHIC VISUALIZING LIFE'S ORGANIZATION

Figure 9

Organs are two or more tissue types that work together. An organ performs a task that no other organ performs.

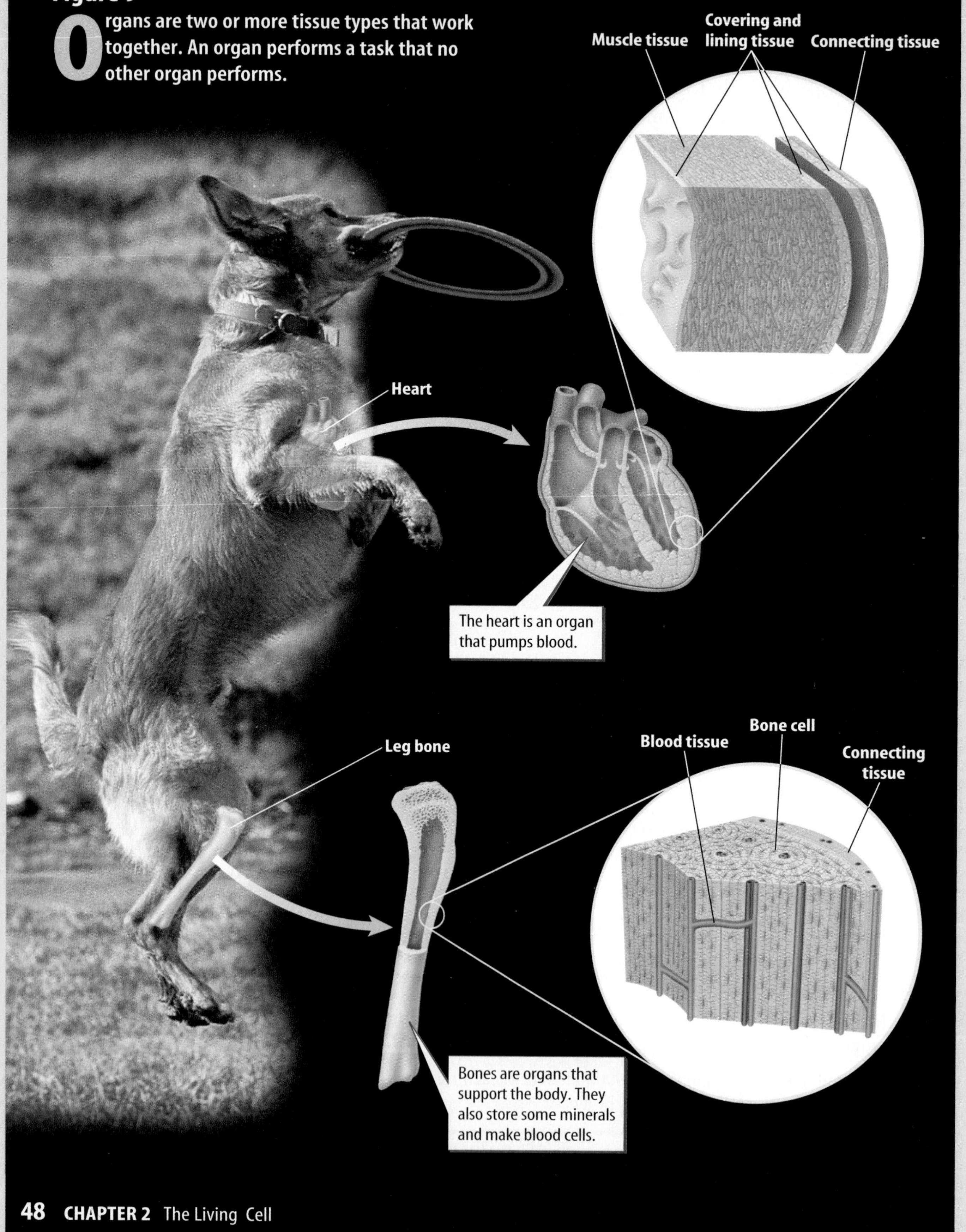

Muscle tissue
Covering and lining tissue
Connecting tissue
Heart
The heart is an organ that pumps blood.
Leg bone
Blood tissue
Bone cell
Connecting tissue
Bones are organs that support the body. They also store some minerals and make blood cells.

Tissues and Organs Cells that are alike are organized into tissues (TIH shewz). **Tissues** are groups of similar cells that all do the same sort of work. For example, bone tissue is made of bone cells, and nerve tissue is made of nerve cells. Blood, a liquid tissue, includes different types of blood cells.

As important as individual tissues are, they do not work alone. Different types of tissues working together can form a structure called an **organ** (OR gun). For example, the stomach is an organ that includes muscle tissue, nerve tissue, and blood tissue. All of these tissues work together and enable the stomach to perform its digestive functions. Other human organs include the heart and the kidneys.

LA.B.2.3.4

Science Online

Topic: One-Celled Organisms
Visit fl6.msscience.com for Web links to information about what types of organisms are made of only one cell.

Activity Create a table that includes images and information about five of these organisms.

✓ **Reading Check** *Which term means "two or more tissue types that work together"?*

Organ Systems A group of organs that work together to do a certain job is called an **organ system.** The stomach, mouth, intestines, and liver are involved in digestion. Together, these and several other organs make up the digestive system. Other organ systems found in your body include the respiratory system, the circulatory system, the reproductive system, and the nervous system.

Organ systems also work together, as shown in **Figure 9.** For example, the muscular system has more than 600 muscles that are attached to bones. The contracting cells of muscle tissue cause your bones, which are part of the skeletal system, to move.

section 2 review

Summary

Special Cells for Special Jobs

- Plant and animal cells come in a variety of sizes and shapes.
- The function of an animal cell can be related to its shape and size.
- The leaves, roots, and stems of plants are made of different types of cells to perform different functions.

Cell Organization

- Many-celled organisms are organized into tissues, organs, and organ systems.
- Each organ system performs a specific function that, together with other systems, keeps an organism healthy and alive.

Self Check

1. **Describe** three types of cells that are found in the human body. SC.F.1.3.6
2. **Compare and contrast** the cells found in a plant's roots, stems, and leaves. SC.F.1.3.6
3. **Explain** the difference between a cell and a tissue and between a tissue and an organ. SC.F.1.3.4
4. **Think Critically** Why must specialized cells work together as a team? SC.F.1.3.5

Applying Skills

5. **Concept Map** Make an events-chain concept map of the different levels of cell organization from cell to organ system. Provide an example for each level of organization. SC.F.1.3.4

section

3

Also covers: **SC.A.2.3.3** Annually Assessed (p. 52); **SC.D.1.3.4** Annually Assessed (pp. 52, 56–57); **SC.G.1.3.3** (pp. 51, 53, 55–56); **SC.G.2.3.2** (p. 54); **SC.H.1.3.4** Annually Assessed (p. 59); **SC.H.1.3.6** (p. 57)

Bacteria, Protists, and Fungi

as you read

What You'll Learn

- **Explain** that most organisms are single cells and that there is great diversity among one-celled organisms.
- **Compare and contrast** the basic characteristics of bacteria, protists, and fungi.
- **Discuss** the overall importance of these organisms.

Why It's Important

More one-celled organisms exist on Earth than any other type of organism. Some of these organisms are helpful to humans, while some others can cause disease.

Review Vocabulary

✹ life cycle: the entire sequence of events in an organism's growth and development

New Vocabulary

- antibiotic
- pasteurization
- ✹ protist
- protozoan
- algae
- lichen

✹ FCAT Vocabulary

Figure 10 Even though their cellular structure is simple, bacteria may be considered the most successful organisms living on Earth.

One-Celled Organisms

Every organism on Earth is made of cells. Some organisms, such as humans, are made of many cells that work together. Most organisms are made of only one cell. These one-celled organisms are found everywhere—in the air you breathe, in the food you eat, in the water you drink, and even in the deep ocean. It may be hard to imagine, but you have huge populations of them living in and on your body that are helpful to you.

For thousands of years people did not know that these one-celled organisms existed. Toward the end of the 17th century, Antonie van Leeuwenhoek, a Dutch merchant, used his simple microscope to look at scrapings from his teeth. His drawings were made about 200 years before it was proven that the tiny organisms he observed were living cells.

Bacteria

All bacteria, like the one shown in **Figure 10,** are one-celled organisms. They usually are smaller than plant and animal cells and contain no membrane-bound organelles. Some bacteria are found as individual cells. Others grow in groups or in long chains of cells. More bacteria exist on Earth than all other organisms combined. Evidence shows that one type of bacteria has existed for billions of years. Cyanobacteria make their own food from sunlight using chlorophyll.

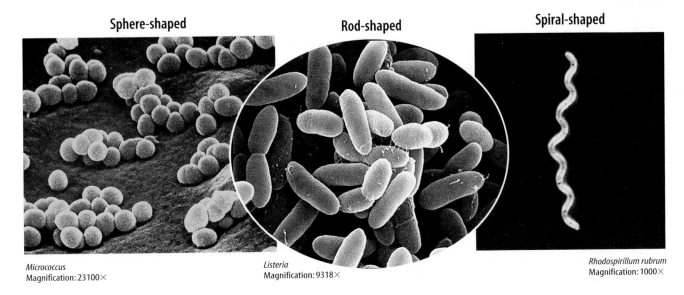

Sphere-shaped

Rod-shaped

Spiral-shaped

Micrococcus
Magnification: 23100×

Listeria
Magnification: 9318×

Rhodospirillum rubrum
Magnification: 1000×

Obtaining Food Bacteria obtain food in many ways. Some bacteria use energy from sunlight or chemicals to make their own food. Other bacteria must get food from other sources, such as absorbing it from other organisms. Bacteria that absorb nutrients from dead organisms are called decomposers. These bacteria return nutrients to the soil and are important in soil fertility and encouraging plant growth. Some bacteria absorb energy from other living organisms. If the organisms are harmed, the bacteria are parasites.

Structure and Function A bacterium contains cytoplasm surrounded by a cell membrane and a cell wall. Bacterial hereditary material is found in the cytoplasm. Some bacteria have a thick, gel-like capsule around the cell wall. This helps protect the bacterium. Many bacteria that live in moist conditions have whiplike tails that help them move. Some produce a thick wall around themselves in unfavorable conditions. The bacterium can survive for hundreds of years this way. The bacterium that normally inhabit your home and body have three basic shapes— spheres, rods, and spirals—as shown in **Figure 11.**

✓ **Reading Check** *What makes the cell of a bacterium different from an animal cell?*

Types of Bacteria There are two main groups of bacteria. Archaebacteria (ar kee bak TIHR ee uh) live in harsh environments where few other organisms can live, such as areas with high levels of salt and hot and acidic environments. These bacteria are classified by the environment that they live in. Eubacteria live in less harsh conditions. They can be classified by the condition that they grow in, composition of the cell wall, how they obtain food, and the wastes they produce.

Figure 11 Most bacteria can be identified as having one of these three shapes.
Classify *the shape of the bacterium* Streptococcus *by looking at the names of the bacteria pictured.*

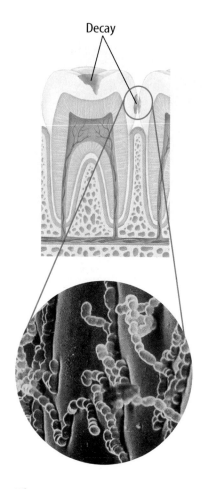

Figure 12 One important bacteria that has been found to cause tooth decay is *Streptococcus mutans*.

Harmful Bacteria Some bacteria are pathogens—organisms that cause disease. Bacteria that normally grow in your mouth can cause tooth decay. As shown in **Figure 12,** these bacteria grow on the surface of your teeth and use sugar as food. As they break down the sugar, an acid is produced that damages the enamel of your teeth. Bacteria then decay the softer parts of your teeth.

Many bacteria produce poisons called toxins as they grow in your body or in the food you eat. Botulism, a type of food poisoning, is caused by a bacterium that survives in canned food.

Helpful Bacteria Some bacteria produce chemicals called **antibiotics** that limit the growth of or kill other bacteria. Millions of bacteria live on your skin and in all other parts of your body. Many of these bacteria are harmless, and they limit the growth of harmful bacteria. Some bacteria help your body produce vitamins needed for survival.

Bacteria help to produce many of the foods you eat, such as yogurt, cheese, chocolate, vinegar, and sauerkraut. All foods contain some bacteria until the food is sterilized by heating it to high temperatures to kill harmful bacteria. **Pasteurization** is the process used to kill harmful bacteria with the minimum effect on the flavor of the product, as shown in **Figure 13.** Milk, fruit juices, and many other foods are pasteurized.

✔ Reading Check *Why are some foods pasteurized?*

Other uses in industry are to make medicines, vitamins, alcohol, cleansers, adhesives and food thickeners. In some landfills, bacteria are used to break down wastes into simpler, harmless substances. These bacteria are also used in sewage-treatment plants, septic systems, and to clean up oil spills.

Nitrogen is needed by every organism, but the nitrogen in Earth's atmosphere is not usable. Certain bacteria that live on the roots of some plants can combine nitrogen with other chemicals so it can be used by organisms.

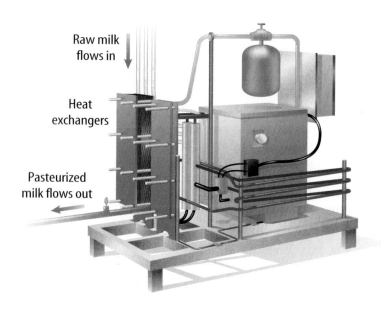

Figure 13 Most milk is pasteurized by heating it to at least 71.6°C for only 15 s. In the process, milk flows continuously past a heat exchanger. **Identify** *the type of energy commonly used to sterilize food.*

Protists

A **protist** is a one- or many-celled organism that lives in moist or wet surroundings. Unlike bacteria, protists' cells have a membrane-bound nucleus and other membrane-bound structures in their cytoplasm.

Funguslike Protists Many funguslike protists spend part of their lives as one-celled organisms and part of their lives as many-celled organisms. Slime molds, water molds, and downy mildews are examples of funguslike protists. They are all decomposers or parasites. The decomposers return nutrients and add organic matter to the soil.

Animal-like Protists One-celled, animal-like protists are called **protozoans.** They often are separated into groups based on how they move from place to place. Many use one or more whiplike tails. Others have short, threadlike structures that extend from the cell membrane. Still others move by using a temporary extension of their cytoplasm.

Plantlike Protists Some protists share many traits with plants. These plantlike protists are known as **algae.** Algae can be one-celled or many-celled. An example of many-celled algae is seaweed. Algae usually are grouped by their structure and the pigments that they contain. All algae can make their own food and produce oxygen because they contain chlorophyll. **Table 1** lists the characteristics of each group. In which group would you place the protist pictured below?

Table 1 Characteristics of Protist Groups		
Funguslike	**Animal-like**	**Plantlike**
Decomposers or parasites	Obtain food from the environment	Produce own food; contain chlorophyll
Spend part of their lives as one-celled organisms, part as many-celled organisms	Like animals, most do not have cell walls.	Many have cell walls like plants.
	Most can move from place to place.	Many-celled forms remain attached to surfaces with rootlike structures.

Harmful Protists Some protists harm crops, wildlife, or cause disease. Probably the most well-known disease caused by a protozoan is malaria. **Figure 14** shows how the protozoan is carried by mosquitoes and transferred to humans. Malaria kills more than one million people each year. More than a million people in Ireland died from the potato famine caused by a water mold. Other funguslike protists cause disease in fish and other plants and animals.

Algae are a food source for many organisms. However, sometimes algae grow uncontrolled, called an algal bloom. As the bacteria break down the wastes of the algae, the oxygen in the water is used up. This causes fish and other organisms to die. The toxins in the water also can cause humans who drink the water or swim in it to become sick.

Helpful Protists You probably have used a protist or its product today and not even realized it. Algae or their products are used in toothpaste, ice cream, and pudding. Some are used to make fertilizers, and some produce the sparkle that makes road lines visible at night.

Protists, such as algae and protozoans, are important as food for animals. Algae also produce oxygen, making it possible for animals to live in the water. Termites have protozoans in their digestive system that contain bacteria. These bacteria produce substances that help the termite digest wood. Some funguslike protists are important for enriching the soil, enabling plants to grow.

✔ **Reading Check** *What are some impacts of protists?*

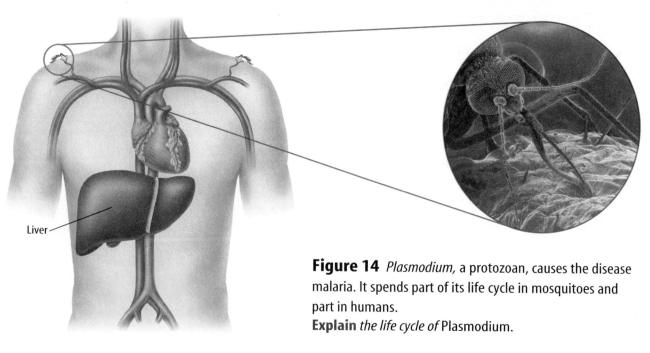

Liver

Figure 14 *Plasmodium,* a protozoan, causes the disease malaria. It spends part of its life cycle in mosquitoes and part in humans.
Explain *the life cycle of* Plasmodium.

Most club fungi are mushrooms. Although many mushrooms are edible, some are poisonous.

An example of sac fungi, many morels are edible and appear in early spring.

The mold growing on these strawberries is a zygospore fungus.

Figure 15 These are all examples of fungi.
Explain *the differences in the reproductive structures of these fungi.*

Fungi

Do you like fungi on your pizza? You do if you like mushrooms. Fungi were once considered plants. Their cells have cell walls, and some fungi are anchored to the soil. Unlike plants, fungi cells do not contain chlorophyll and cannot produce their own food. Most fungi are decomposers, but some are parasites. Most species of fungi are many-celled. Their cells have at least one nucleus and other organelles. Fungi reproduce using structures called spores. These spores spread from place to place and grow a new fungus. Fungi are very common in warm, humid places, such as tropical forests, on your shower curtain, or between your toes. Fungi are classified using several methods, but the structure and type of its reproductive structures are a good starting point. There are three main types of fungi, as shown in **Figure 15.**

✔ Reading Check *What are the characteristics of fungi?*

Club Fungi Mushrooms, shelf fungi, puffballs, and toadstools are all examples of club fungi. The spores of these fungi are produced in a club-shaped part found on the reproductive structure. On the bottom of the cap of a mushroom, you will see structures called gills. If you use a microscope to look at a gill, you will see spores hanging from these club-shaped parts.

Sac Fungi Yeasts, molds, morels, and truffles are all types of sac fungi. The spores are produced in little saclike parts of the reproductive structure. This group also includes examples of one-celled fungi, the yeasts.

Figure 16 Lichens can grow upright, appear leafy, or look like a crust on bare rocks.
Classify *How might lichens be classified?*

Zygospore Fungi The fuzzy, black mold that you sometimes find growing on old bread or a piece of fruit is a zygospore fungus. Spores are produced in large, round, reproductive structures growing from the body of the fungus. As the reproductive structures split open, hundreds of spores are released into the air. They will grow into new fungi if the conditions are right.

Other Fungi Some fungi have never been observed undergoing reproduction, or don't go through sexual reproduction. These fungi are called imperfect. They have an imperfect life cycle. Several diseases in humans, including athlete's foot, are caused by fungi in this group.

Lichens Some fungi live in close associations with other organisms. A **lichen** (LI kun) is formed when a fungus and either a green alga or a cyanobacterium live together. The alga or cyanobacterium gets a warm, moist, protected place to live, and the fungus gets the food made by the alga or cyanobacterium. The colorful organisms in **Figure 16** are lichens.

Lichens that grow in the surface cracks of a rock play an important role in the formation of soil. As lichens grow, they release acids as part of their metabolism. The acids help break down the rock. As bits of rock accumulate and lichens die and decay, soil is formed. Lichens also are indicators of the quality of the environment because they are sensitive to pollutants present in rain and air.

Reading Check *How do lichens help form soil?*

Fungi and Plants An association exists between certain plants and fungi. The fungi form a web around the roots of the plants. The plants provide the fungi with food, helping the plant roots absorb water and nutrients. Scientists have found these webs around the roots of about 90 percent of the plants they have studied. Some plants cannot grow unless these webs are present.

Harmful Fungi Fungi can cause diseases in plants and animals. Dutch Elm disease and chestnut blight are caused by sac fungi, and they wiped out hundreds of millions of these trees in the twentieth century. Many other crops are destroyed by rusts and smuts each year. Fungi can spoil food, as you might have noticed on food in the back of the refrigerator. Fungi also can cause disease in humans, such as athlete's foot and ringworm.

Helpful Fungi Fungi are important in the environment because they break down organic matter and return useful chemicals to the soil to be used by plants. They are nature's recyclers. Many fungi are eaten, and they also are important in producing foods. Yeasts and other fungi are used to produce bread and some cheeses. Another important use of fungi is in the production of antibiotics. Fungi naturally produce antibiotics to prevent bacteria from growing near them. These are used in medicines, such as penicillin.

INTEGRATE Career

Air Quality Engineer To help assess air quality, some air quality engineers observe lichens. Lichens are called bioindicators because sulfur dioxide, fluorides, heavy metals, and radioactive fallout can affect them. Air quality engineers can monitor changes in the air by studying how lichens react to pollutants. Research to learn what other jobs might be held by an air quality engineer.

section 3 review

Summary

Bacteria
- Bacteria are prokaryotic, one-celled organisms.
- Archaebacteria can survive in extreme conditions; eubacteria grows in less harsh environments.

Protists
- Protists are eukaryotic. They can be one- or many-celled.
- Protists can be funguslike, animal-like, or plantlike.

Fungi
- Fungi are eukaryotic. Most are many-celled, but some are one-celled.
- Club fungi, sac fungi, and zygospore fungi are some types of fungi.

Self Check

1. **Explain** why bacteria, protists, and fungi are classified separately. SC.F.1.3.2
2. **Identify** why bacteria, protists, and fungi are important to the environment.
3. **Compare and contrast** the ways that bacteria, protists, and fungi obtain food.
4. **List** two ways each that bacteria, protists, and fungi are harmful.
5. **Think Critically** If an imperfect fungus were found to produce spores on clublike structures, how would the fungus be reclassified? SC.G.1.3.3

Applying Skills

6. **Solve One-Step Equations** Air may have more than 3,500 bacteria per cubic meter. Use this number to estimate the number of bacteria in the air in your classroom.

LAB

Design Your Own

Water Movement in Plants

Goals

■ **Design** an investigation to show where water moves in a plant.

■ **Observe** how long it takes water to move in a plant.

Possible Materials

fresh stalk of celery with leaves

clear drinking glass

scissors

red food coloring

water

Safety Precautions

Complete a safety worksheet before you begin.

WARNING: *Use care when handling sharp objects such as scissors. Avoid getting red food coloring on your clothing.*

▶ Real-World Problem

When you are thirsty, you can sip water from a glass or drink from a fountain. Plants must get their water in other ways. In most plants, water moves from the soil into cells in the roots. Where does water travel in a plant?

▶ Form a Hypothesis

Based on what you already know about how a plant functions, state a hypothesis that explains where water travels in a plant.

▶ Test Your Hypothesis

Make a Plan

1. As a group, agree upon a hypothesis and decide how you will test it. Identify which results will support the hypothesis.

2. **List** the steps you will need to take to test your hypothesis. Be specific. Describe exactly what you will do in each step. List your materials.

3. Prepare a data table in your Science Journal to record your observations.

4. **Read** the entire investigation to make sure all steps are in logical order.

5. **Identify** all constants, variables, and controls of the investigation.

Follow Your Plan

1. Make sure your teacher approves your plan before you start.

2. Carry out the investigation according to the approved plan.

3. While doing the investigation, record your observations and complete the data tables in your Science Journal.

▶ Analyze Your Data

1. **Compare** the color of the celery stalk before, during, and after the investigation.

2. **Compare** your results with those of other groups.

3. Make a drawing of the cut stalk. Label your drawing.

4. What was your control in this investigation? What were your variables?

▶ Conclude and Apply

1. **Explain** whether the results of this investigation supported your hypothesis.

2. **Infer** why only some of the plant tissue is red.

3. **Explain** what you would do to improve this investigation.

4. **Predict** if other plants have tissues that move water.

▶ Inquiry Extension

Certain kinds of plants can be used to clean up soil contaminated with toxic waste. Infer how this process might work and draw a diagram showing what happens to the contaminants in the soil.

Communicating Your Data

Write a report about your investigation. Include illustrations to show how the investigation was performed. Present your report to your class.

TEST-TUBE TISSUE

Thanks to advances in science, skin tissue is being "grown" in laboratories

In Chicago, a young woman named Kelly is cooking pasta on her stove. Her clothes catch fire from the gas flame and, in the blink of an eye, 80 percent of her body is severely burned. Will she survive?

Just 20 years ago, the answer to this question probably would have been "no." Fortunately for Kelly, science has come a long way in recent years. Today, there's a very good chance that Kelly might lead a long and healthy life.

Like the brain or the heart, the skin is an organ. In fact, it is the body's largest organ, about 1/12 of your total body weight. Composed of protective layers, skin keeps your internal structure safe from damage, infection, and temperature changes.

Today, just as farmers can grow crops of corn and wheat, scientists can grow human skin. How?

A piece of test skin is removed from its culture.

Tissue Engineers

Scientists, called tissue engineers, take a piece of skin (no bigger than a quarter) from an undamaged part of the burn victim's body. The skin cells are isolated, mixed with special nutrients, and then they multiply in a culture dish.

After about two to three months, the tissue engineers can harvest sheets of new, smooth skin. These sheets, as large as postcards, are grafted onto the victim's damaged body and promote additional skin growth.

By grafting Kelly's own skin on her body rather than using donor skin—skin from another person or from an animal—doctors avoid at least three potential complications. First, donor skin may not even be available. Second, Kelly's body might perceive the new skin cells from another source to be a danger, and her immune system might reject—or destroy—the transplant. Finally, even if the skin produced from a foreign source is accepted, it may leave extensive scarring.

Tissue Testing

What else can tissue engineers grow? They produce test skin—skin made in the lab and used to test the effects of cosmetics and chemicals on humans. This skin is eliminating the use of animals for such tests. Also, tissue engineers are working on ways to replace other body parts such as livers, heart valves, and ears, that don't grow back on their own.

LA.A.2.3.5 LA.B.2.3.1

Safety List Visit the link shown to the right or your media center to learn about fire safety tips, including kitchen safety and escape routes in your home. Make a list and share it with your family.

TIME

For more information, visit fl6.msscience.com

Reviewing Main Ideas

Section 1 The World of Cells

1. The cell theory states that all living things are made of one or more cells, the cell is the basic unit of life, and all cells come from other cells.

2. The microscope is an instrument that enlarges the image of an object.

3. All cells are surrounded by a cell membrane and contain hereditary material and cytoplasm. Plant cells have a cell wall outside the cell membrane. Cells, except bacteria, contain organelles.

4. The nucleus directs the cell's activities. Chromosomes contain DNA that determines what kinds of traits an organism will have. Vacuoles store substances.

5. In mitochondria, the process of cellular respiration combines food molecules with oxygen. This series of chemical reactions releases energy for the cell's activities.

6. The energy in light is captured and stored in food molecules during the process of photosynthesis. Plants, algae, and some bacteria make their own food by photosynthesis.

Section 2 The Different Jobs of Cells

1. Many-celled organisms are made up of different kinds of cells that perform different tasks.

2. Many-celled organisms are organized into tissues, organs, and organ systems that perform specific jobs to keep an organism alive.

Section 3 Bacteria, Protists, and Fungi

1. Most organisms are one-celled.

2. There is great diversity among one-celled organisms.

3. Some bacteria, protists, and fungi are helpful in the environment and to humans, and some are harmful.

Visualizing Main Ideas

Copy and complete the following concept map on the parts of a plant cell.

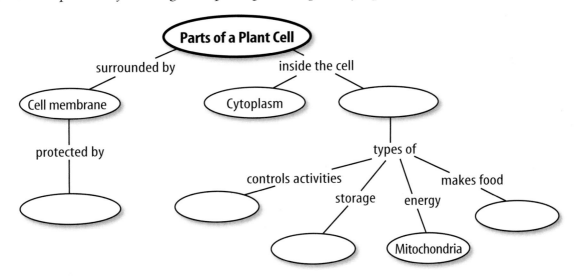

Using Vocabulary

algae p. 53
antibiotic p. 52
bacteria p. 39
cell membrane p. 41
cell wall p. 41
chloroplast p. 43
cytoplasm p. 41
lichen p. 56
mitochondria p. 42
✳ nucleus p. 42

✳ organ p. 49
organ system p. 49
organelle p. 41
pasteurization p. 52
✳ photosynthesis p. 43
✳ protist p. 53
protozoan p. 53
✳ tissue p. 49
vacuole p. 42

✳ FCAT Vocabulary

Explain the difference between the terms in the following sets.

1. mitochondria—chloroplast `SC.F.1.3.5`

2. tissue—organ `SC.F.1.3.4`

3. cell membrane—nucleus `SC.F.1.3.5`

4. nucleus—organelle

5. cytoplasm—nucleus `SC.F.1.3.5`

6. vacuole—mitochondria `SC.F.1.3.5`

7. organelle—organ `SC.F.1.3.4`

8. cell wall—cell membrane

9. protist—algae `SC.G.1.3.3`

10. antibiotic—pasteurization

11. bacteria—protist

12. potosynthesis—algae

Checking Concepts

Choose the word or phrase that best answers the question.

13. Which controls what enters and leaves the cell? `SC.F.1.3.5`
    A) mitochondrion
    B) cell membrane
    C) vacuole
    D) nucleus

Use the illustration below to answer question 14.

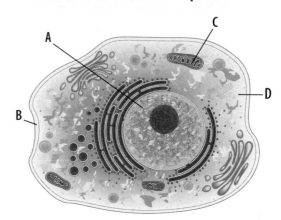

14. Which letter is the gelatinlike substance in a cell that contains water and chemicals?
    A) A   C) C
    B) B   D) D

15. Which organisms can be plantlike, animal-like, or funguslike? `SC.G.1.3.3` `SC.F.1.3.2`
    A) bacteria   C) protists
    B) fungi   D) lichens

16. Which term accurately describes the stomach? `SC.F.1.3.4`
    A) organelle   C) organ
    B) organ system   D) tissue

17. What does photosynthesis make for a plant?
    A) food   C) water
    B) organs   D) tissues

18. What does DNA do?
    A) makes food
    B) determines traits
    C) converts food to energy
    D) stores substances

19. Decomposition of organic materials is an important role of which organisms? `SC.D.1.3.4`
    A) protozoans   C) plants
    B) algae   D) fungi

20. What cell structure helps support plants?
    A) cell membrane   C) vacuole `SC.F.1.3.6`
    B) cell wall   D) nucleus

Thinking Critically

21. Predict what would happen to a cell if the cell membrane were solid and waterproof.

22. Describe what might happen to a cell if all its mitochondria were removed. `SC.F.1.3.5`

23. Explain why cells are called the units of life.

24. Infer what kinds of animal cells might have many mitochondria present. `SC.F.1.3.6`

25. Distinguish between a bacterium and a plant cell. `SC.F.1.3.2`

26. Compare and contrast photosynthesis and cellular respiration.

27. Make and Use Tables Copy and complete this table about the functions of the following cell parts: *nucleus, cell membrane, mitochondrion, chloroplast,* and *vacuole.* `SC.F.1.3.5`

Functions of Cell Parts

Cell Part	Function
Do not write in this book.	

28. Concept Map Make an events-chain concept map of the following from simple to complex: *small intestine, circular muscle cell, human,* and *digestive system.* `SC.F.1.3.4`

29. Identify and Manipulate Variables and Controls Describe an experiment you might do to determine whether water moves into and out of cells.

30. Recognize Cause and Effect Why is the brick-like shape of some plant cells important?

31. Infer why brushing and flossing your teeth help prevent tooth decay.

Performance Activities

32. Skit Working with three or four classmates, develop a short skit about how a living cell works. Have each group member play the role of a different cell part. `SC.F.1.3.5`

33. Make a Poster Find or draw pictures on a poster to show the importance of bacteria, protists, or fungi to life on Earth. Be sure to include helpful and harmful examples.

Applying Math

34. Magnification A microscope has an eyepiece with a power of 10× and an objective lens with a power of 40×. What is the magnification of the microscope? `MA.A.3.3.1`

35. Viruses Use a computer to make a line graph of the following data. At 37°C there are 1.0 million viruses; at 37.5°C, 0.5 milllion; at 37.8°C, 0.25 million; at 38.3°C, 0.1 million; and at 38.9°C, 0.05 million. `MA.E.1.3.1`

Use the graph below to answer question 36.

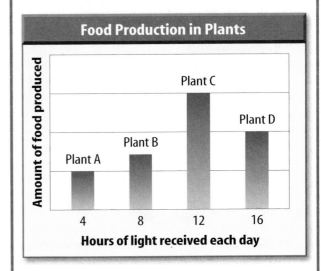

Food Production in Plants

36. Plant Food Production Light is necessary for plants to make food. Using the graph above, determine which plant produced the most food. How much light was needed by the plant every day to produce the most food? `MA.E.1.3.1`

The assessed Florida Benchmark appears above each question.
Record your answers on the answer sheet provided by your teacher or on a sheet of paper.

Multiple Choice

SC.A.2.3.3

1 A newly discovered type of bacteria is a producer. How does it most likely obtain energy?

A. It uses light energy to make food.

B. It uses light energy to make nitrogen.

C. It uses dead organisms as a source of chemical energy.

D. It uses living organisms as a source of chemical energy.

SC.F.1.3.4

2 The diagram below shows an animal cell.

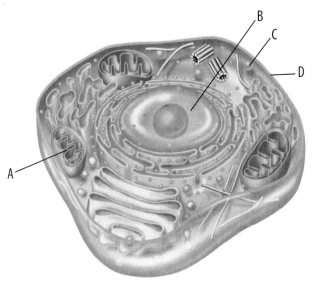

Which letter represents where most of the cell's hereditary material is found?

F. A

G. B

H. C

I. D

SC.F.1.3.4

3 Which choice shows the levels of organization in the human body from simplest to most complex?

A. muscle tissue → muscle cell → stomach → digestive system

B. muscle cell → stomach → digestive system → muscle tissue

C. digestive system → muscle cell → muscle tissue → stomach

D. muscle cell → muscle tissue → stomach → digestive system

SC.F.1.3.6

4 The diagram below shows cells in two types of tissue taken from the same person.

Skin cells  Muscle cells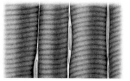

Which best explains why these cells look different?

F. They have different functions.

G. They get energy in different ways.

H. They were formed at different times.

I. They contain different sets of chromosomes.

SC.D.1.3.4

5 A certain type of bacteria is able to combine nitrogen from the air with other chemicals. What is the main way in which this activity benefits other types of organisms?

   A. It removes harmful pollutants from the atmosphere.

   B. It produces substances that slow the growth of pathogens.

   C. It converts an important nutrient into a form that plants can use.

   D. It breaks down dead material and removes it from the environment.

Gridded Response

SC.G.2.3.2

6 The table below shows the number of hours it takes a population of a certain type of bacteria to double at various temperatures.

Temperature (°C)	Number of Hours Required for Population to Double
5.0	15.6
10.0	5.9
35.0	0.7

One test tube containing a sample of 100 of the bacteria is kept at 5.0°C. A second test tube containing a sample of 100 of the bacteria is kept at 35.0°C. How many hours sooner will the population in the second test tube reach 200 bacteria than the population in the first test tube?

READ INQUIRE EXPLAIN

Short Response

SC.F.1.3.2

7 Describe the main ideas of the cell theory.

READ INQUIRE EXPLAIN

Extended Response

SC.H.2.3.1

8 The diagram below shows an organelle from a cell.

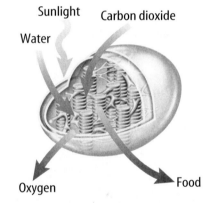

Sunlight Carbon dioxide

Water

Oxygen   Food

   PART A Name this organelle and describe its function.

   PART B Name an organism that would have this type of organelle in at least some of its cells. Explain how you know that the organism you chose has this type of organelle.

FCAT Tip

Get Enough Sleep Do not "cram" the night before the test. It can confuse you and make you tired.

chapter

3

Sunshine State Standards—SC.F.1: The student describes patterns of structure and function in living things; SC.F.2: The student understands the process and importance of genetic diversity.

The Role of Genes in Inheritance

Why do these horses look different from each other?

All living things obtain different characteristics from their parents. Knowing how organisms reproduce and what determines traits will help you understand why all horses in a herd of wild mustangs do not look exactly alike.

Science Journal Write three traits of horses that you could trace from parents to offspring.

Start-Up Activities

Why are seeds formed?

When you peel a banana or bite into an apple, you're probably only thinking about the taste and sweet smell of the fruit. You usually don't think about how the fruit was formed. Oranges, and most of the fruits you eat, contain seeds. Making seeds is one way that reproduction is carried out by living things. For life to continue, all living things must pass characteristics to their offspring.

WARNING: *Do not eat the orange.*

1. Complete a safety worksheet.

2. Obtain half of an orange from your teacher. Peel the orange and remove all of the seeds.

3. Examine, count, and measure the length of each seed. Record these data in your Science Journal.

4. When you finish, dispose of your orange half as instructed by your teacher. Wash your hands.

5. **Think Critically** Write a paragraph in your Science Journal describing why you think the seeds are different from one another.

Inheritance Make the following Foldable to help identify what you already know, what you want to know, and what you learned about the role of genes in inheritance.

LA.A.1.3.4

STEP 1 **Fold** a sheet of paper vertically from side to side. Make the front edge about 1.25 cm shorter than the back edge.

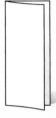

STEP 2 **Turn** lengthwise and **fold** into thirds.

STEP 3 **Unfold and cut** only the top layer along both folds to make three tabs. **Label** each tab as shown.

Identify Questions Before you read the chapter, write what you already know about the role of genes in inheritance under the left tab of your Foldable, and write questions about what you'd like to know under the center tab. After you read the chapter, list what you learned under the right tab.

Preview this chapter's content and activities at
fl6.msscience.com

section

1

Continuing Life

as you read

What You'll Learn

- **Describe** how cells divide.
- **Identify** the importance of reproduction for living things.
- **Compare and contrast** sexual and asexual reproduction.
- **Describe** the structure and function of DNA.

Why It's Important

All living things, including you, inherit characteristics from their parents.

Review Vocabulary

chromosome: structure in a cell's nucleus that contains genetic material

New Vocabulary

- DNA
- ✳ mitosis
- ✳ asexual reproduction
- cloning
- ✳ sexual reproduction
- sex cell
- ✳ meiosis
- fertilization

✳ FCAT Vocabulary

Reproduction

If you look carefully in a pond in the spring, you may see frog or toad eggs. Frogs reproduce by laying hundreds of eggs in gooey clumps. Tadpoles can hatch from these eggs and mature into adult frogs, as shown in **Figure 1.** Some other kinds of organisms, including humans, usually produce only one offspring at a time. How do frogs and all of the other living things on Earth produce offspring that are similar to themselves?

The Importance of Reproduction Organisms produce offspring through the process of reproduction. Reproduction is important to all living things. Without reproduction, species could not continue. Hereditary material is passed from parent to offspring during reproduction. This material is found inside cells. It contains the chemical deoxyribonucleic (dee AHK sih ri boh noo klay ihk) acid, called DNA. **DNA** controls how offspring will look and how they will function by controlling what proteins each cell will make. Although organisms have different adaptations for reproduction, such as laying eggs in water or in a nest, reproduction always involves the transfer of hereditary information.

Figure 1 When frogs reproduce, they continue their species.

Adult frogs reproduce by laying and then fertilizing eggs.

These frog eggs can hatch into tadpoles.

These tadpoles can develop into adult frogs.

**INTEGRATE Chemistry**

Life's Code You've probably seen or heard about science fiction movies in which DNA is used to grow prehistoric animals. What makes up DNA? How does it work?

DNA is found in all cells in one or many structures called chromosomes. All of the information that is in your DNA is called your genetic information. You can think of DNA as a genetic blueprint. It contains all of the instructions for making an organism what it is. Your DNA controls the texture of your hair, the shape of your ears, your blood type, and even how you digest the food that you eat every day.

DNA can be described as a twisted ladder. This structure, shown in **Figure 2,** is the key to how DNA works. The two sides of the ladder form the backbone of DNA. Just like a normal ladder, the rungs connect the sides together. It is the rungs of DNA that hold all the genetic information. Each rung is made up of a pair of chemicals called bases. There are just four kinds of bases and they only form two types of pairs. A DNA ladder can have hundreds of millions of rungs, and the bases can be arranged in thousands of different orders. The key to understanding DNA is the order or sequence of bases. The sequence forms a code. From this DNA code, a cell gets instructions about what substances to make, how to make them, and when to make them.

LA.B.2.3.1

LA.B.2.3.4

Science nline

Topic: Human Genome Project
Visit fl6.msscience.com for Web links to information about the Human Genome Project.

Activity List three genetic disorders and explain how the Human Genome project may help researchers who study these disorders.

Concepts in Motion fl6.msscience.com

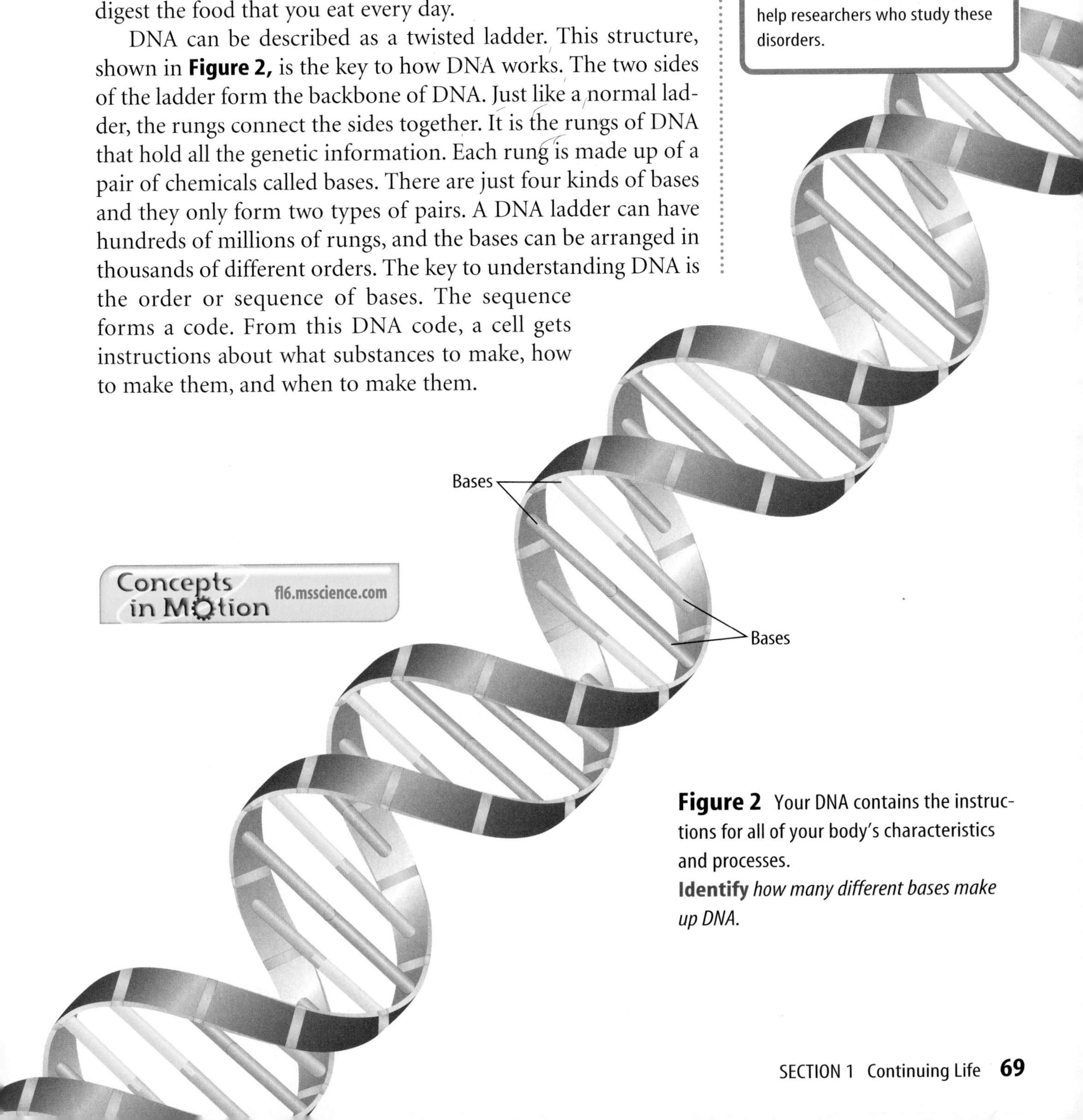

Bases

Bases

Figure 2 Your DNA contains the instructions for all of your body's characteristics and processes.
Identify *how many different bases make up DNA.*

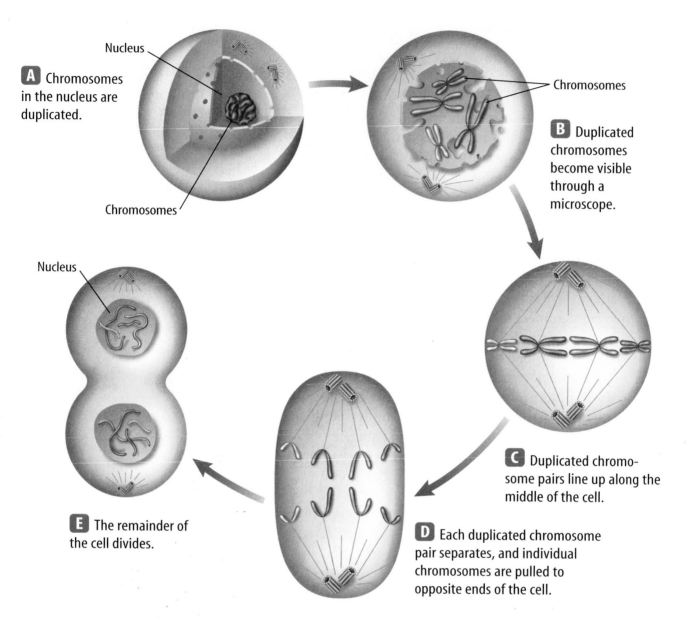

A Chromosomes in the nucleus are duplicated.

Nucleus

Chromosomes

Chromosomes

B Duplicated chromosomes become visible through a microscope.

Nucleus

C Duplicated chromosome pairs line up along the middle of the cell.

D Each duplicated chromosome pair separates, and individual chromosomes are pulled to opposite ends of the cell.

E The remainder of the cell divides.

Figure 3 During cell division, cells go through several steps to produce two cells with identical nuclei.

Infer *what cell types undergo mitosis.*

Cell Division

How did you become the size you are now? The cells of your body are formed by cell division. Cell division includes two important events. First, DNA in the nucleus is copied. Second, the nucleus divides into two identical nuclei. Each new nucleus receives a copy of the DNA. Division of the nucleus is called **mitosis** (mi TOH sus). Mitosis is the process that results in two nuclei, each with the same genetic information. You can follow the process of mitosis in **Figure 3.** After mitosis has taken place, the rest of the cell divides into two cells of about equal size. Almost all the cells in any plant or animal undergo mitosis. Whether it occurs in a plant or an animal, cell division forms, repairs, or replaces various cells, tissues, and organs.

☑ **Reading Check** *During cell division, why must the DNA be duplicated before the nucleus divides?*

Reproduction by One Organism

Shoots growing from the eyes of a potato are a form of reproduction. Reproduction in which a new organism is produced from a part of another organism by cell division is called **asexual** (ay SEK shoo ul) **reproduction.** In asexual reproduction, all the DNA in the new organism comes from one other organism. The DNA of the growing potato eye is the same as the DNA in the rest of the potato.

Some one-celled organisms, such as bacteria, divide in half, forming two cells. Before the one-celled organism divides, its DNA copies itself. After it has divided, each new organism has a copy of the first organism's DNA. The two new cells are alike. The first organism no longer exists.

Budding and Regeneration Many plants and species of mushroom, and even a few animals reproduce asexually. **Figure 4** shows asexual reproduction in hydra, a relative of jellyfish and corals. When a hydra reproduces asexually, a new individual grows from it by a process called budding. As shown below, the hydra bud has the same shape and characteristics as the parent organism. The bud matures and eventually breaks away to live on its own.

By a process called regeneration (rih je nuh RAY shun) that also uses cell division, some organisms are able to replace body parts or form two new organisms. Sea stars, for example, can grow one or more new arms when they are damaged or lost to a predator. Some organisms, like the flatworm *Planaria,* can separate their bodies into two pieces and regenerate all the missing parts of each piece to form two new organisms.

Mini LAB

SC.H.1.3.5

Observing Yeast Budding

Procedure
1. Complete a safety worksheet.
2. Use a **dropper** to place a drop of a **prepared yeast** and **sugar mixture** onto a **microscope slide.** Place a **coverslip** on the slide.
3. Examine the slide with a **microscope** under low power, then high power.
4. Record your observations in your **Science Journal.**
5. Make a new slide after 5 min. Examine the slide under low power, then under high power.
6. Record your observations in your Science Journal.

Analysis
1. What did you observe on the first slide?
2. What might account for any differences between what you observed on the first slide and the second slide?

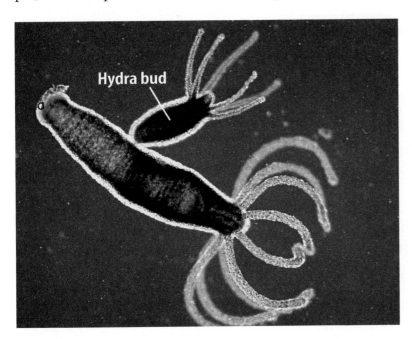

Hydra bud

Figure 4 Cell division can result in asexual reproduction. A hydra can reproduce asexually by a process called budding.

Cloning What would it be like if humans or other animals were exact copies of each other? Making copies of organisms is called **cloning.** The new organism produced is called a clone. The clone receives DNA from just one parent cell. It has the same DNA as the parent cell. In many ways, cloning is not a new technology. In the past, most cloning was done with plants. Gardeners can clone plants, like those in **Figure 5,** when they take cuttings of a plant's stems, leaves, or roots. They can grow many identical plants from one.

Only since the 1990s has cloning large animals become possible. In 1997, the birth of the first successfully cloned mammal, a sheep, was announced. The real value of this sheep's birth is that scientists now have a better understanding of how cells reproduce.

Figure 5 These African violets are clones.
Infer *whether or not the plants all came from one plant. Explain.*

Sex Cells and Reproduction

Does a human baby look exactly like its father or its mother? Usually, the baby has features of both of its parents. The baby might have her dad's hair color and her mom's eye color. However, the baby probably doesn't look exactly like either of her parents. That's because humans, as well as many other organisms, are the products of sexual (SEK shoo ul) reproduction. In **sexual reproduction** a new organism is produced from the DNA of two cells. **Sex cells,** as shown in **Figure 6,** are the specialized cells that carry DNA and join in sexual reproduction. During this process, DNA from each sex cell contributes to the formation of a new individual and that individual's traits.

Figure 6 A female sex cell usually is called an egg and a male sex cell is usually called a sperm. Each type of human sex cell contains 23 chromosomes.

✓ **Reading Check** *What results from sexual reproduction?*

A human egg cell

Magnification: 700×

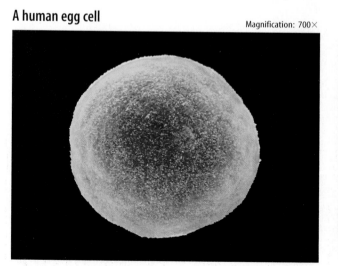

Human sperm cells

Magnification: 4500×

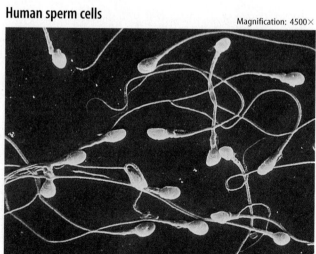

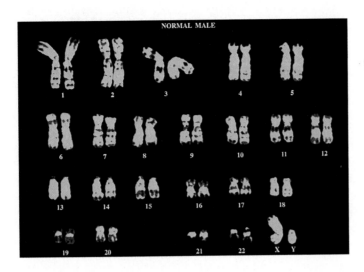

NORMAL MALE

Figure 7 Each chromosome in a human body is made of DNA. All 23 pairs of chromosomes of one person are shown in this photograph. The chromosomes were photographed after the DNA had duplicated.

Production of Sex Cells

Recall that your body is made up of different types of cells, most of which were formed by mitosis. When a skin cell, a bone cell, or another body cell divides, it produces two new cells by cell division. Each cell has DNA that is identical to the original cell. Recall that DNA can be found in structures called chromosomes. A human body cell has 46 chromosomes arranged in 23 pairs, as shown in **Figure 7.** Each chromosome of a pair has genetic information about the same things. For example, if one chromosome has information about hair color, its mate also will have information about hair color.

Sex cells are different. Instead of being formed by cell division like body cells are, sex cells are formed by **meiosis** (mi OH sus). **Table 1** compares cell division and sex cell formation. Only certain cells in reproductive organs undergo the process of meiosis. Before meiosis begins, DNA is duplicated. During meiosis, the nucleus divides twice. Four sex cells form, each with half the number of chromosomes of the original cell. Human eggs and sperm contain only 23 chromosomes each—one chromosome from each pair of chromosomes. That way, when a human egg and sperm join in a process called **fertilization,** the result is a new individual with a full set of 46 chromosomes. **Figure 8** shows sex cells that join to form a new cell that can develop into a new human being.

INTEGRATE Health

Cigarette Smoking In humans, sex cell production and fertilization can be affected by cigarette smoking. It can decrease the number of sperm produced. Also, some of the sperm produced by a male cigarette smoker may be deformed and unable to fertilize an egg.

Table 1 Cell Division and Sex Cell Formation in Humans		
	Cell Division	**Sex Cell Formation**
Process used	Mitosis	Meiosis
DNA duplicated?	Yes	Yes
Nucleus divides	Once	Twice
Number of cells formed	2	4
Chromosome number of beginning cell	46	46
Chromosomes in each new cell	46	23

Figure 8

Humans, like most animals and plants, reproduce sexually. In sexual reproduction, a new and genetically unique individual is produced when a female sex cell and a male sex cell join in a process called fertilization.

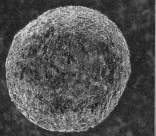

▲ A female's sex cell, an egg, has only 23 chromosomes—half the amount contained in human body cells.

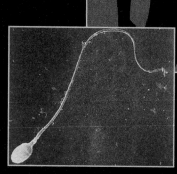

◄ A male's sex cell, a sperm, also contains only 23 chromosomes.

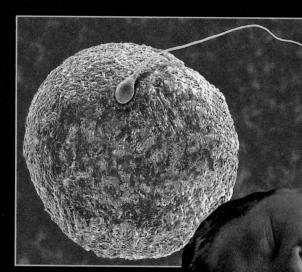

◄ When an egg and a sperm unite during fertilization, a new cell results that has a full set of 46 chromosomes.

▶ This new cell divides again and again, developing over time into a fully formed baby.

Sex Cells in Plants

Plants can reproduce sexually. How this occurs is different for each plant group. But in every case, a sperm and an egg join to create a new cell that eventually becomes a plant.

It may seem that flowers are just a decoration for many plants, but flowers contain structures for reproducing. Male flower parts produce pollen, which contains sperm cells. Female flower parts produce eggs. When a sperm and an egg join, a new cell forms. In most flowers, rapid changes begin soon after fertilization. The cell divides many times and becomes enclosed in a protective seed. The petals and most other flower parts fall off. A fruit that contains seeds soon develops, as shown in **Figure 9.**

Figure 9 An apple containing seeds will form if the eggs in the female reproductive structure of an apple blossom are fertilized.

section 1 review

Summary

Reproduction
- Reproduction always involves the transfer of hereditary information.

Cell Division
- Mitosis results in two nuclei, each with the same genetic information.

Reproduction by One Organism
- Two types of asexual reproduction are budding and regeneration.

Sex Cells and Reproduction
- DNA from each sex cell contributes to the formation of a new individual.

Production of Sex Cells
- Human eggs and sperm each contain only 23 chromosomes.

Sex Cells in Plants
- Flowers contain structures for reproduction.

Self Check

1. **Compare and contrast** the outcome of meiosis and the outcome of mitosis. SC.F.1.3.3
2. **Infer** why reproduction is an important process. SC.F.1.3.1 SC.F.2.3.2
3. **Explain** why offspring produced by asexual reproduction are usually identical to the parent that produced them.
4. **Describe** how DNA controls how an organism looks and functions.
5. **Think Critically** For a species, what are some advantages of reproducing asexually? Of reproducing sexually? Of having the ability to do either? SC.F.2.3.1

Applying Math

6. **Calculate** A female bullfrog produces 350 eggs. All of the eggs are fertilized and hatch in one season. Assume that half of the tadpoles are male and half are female. If all the female tadpoles survive and, one year later, produce 350 eggs each, how many eggs would be produced? MA.E.2.3.1

Benchmark—SC.H.1.3.4: The student knows that accurate record keeping, openness, and replication are essential to maintaining an investigator's credibility with other scientists and society.

Getting DNA from Onion Cells

DNA contains the instructions for the processes that occur in a cell. In this lab, you will see the actual DNA of one living thing—an onion.

▶ Real-World Problem

How is DNA taken out of cells?

Goals
- **Separate** DNA from onion cells.
- **Practice** laboratory skills.

Materials

prepared onion mixture (30 mL)
rubbing alcohol (30 mL)
toothpicks
50-mL graduated cylinder
50-mL beaker
magnifying lens
*measuring cup
*microscope
*Alternate materials

Safety Precautions

Complete a safety worksheet before you begin. Be sure to wear an apron and goggles throughout this lab. Keep hands away from face.

▶ Procedure

1. Obtain 30 mL of prepared onion mixture from your teacher. Empty it into the beaker or measuring cup.

2. Measure and then slowly pour 30 mL of rubbing alcohol down the side of the beaker onto the mixture. The alcohol should form a layer on top of the onion mixture.

3. **Observe** a milky substance gradually floating into the alcohol. This is DNA.

4. Use a toothpick to gently stir the alcohol layer. Use another toothpick to remove the DNA.

5. **Observe** DNA with a magnifying lens or a microscope. Record your observations in your Science Journal.

6. When you're finished, pour all liquids into containers provided by your teacher.

▶ Conclude and Apply

1. Based on what you know about DNA, predict whether onion DNA is different from the DNA of other types of plants.

2. **Infer** whether this method of taking DNA out of cells could be used to compare the amount of DNA between different organisms. Explain your answer.

Communicating Your Data

Compare and contrast your findings with those of other students in your class. Explain in your Science Journal why your findings were the same or different from those of other students. **For more help, refer to the** Science Skill Handbook.

Benchmarks—SC.F.2.3.2 Annually Assessed (pp. 77–83): The student knows that the variation in each species is due to the exchange and interaction of genetic information as it is passed from parent to offspring.

Also covers: SC.H.1.3.3 (p. 82), SC.H.1.3.5 Annually Assessed (pp. 84–85), SC.H.1.3.6 (p. 82), SC.H.1.3.7 Annually Assessed (pp. 84–85), SC.H.2.3.1 (pp. 79, 84–85), SC.H.3.3.1 (pp. 84–85)

Genetics—The Study of Inheritance

Heredity

When you go to a family reunion or browse through family pictures, like the one in **Figure 10,** you can't help but notice similarities and differences among your relatives. You notice that your mother's eyes look just like your grandmother's, and one uncle is tall while his brothers are short. These similarities and differences are the result of the way traits are passed from one generation to the next. **Heredity** (huh REH duh tee) is the passing of traits from parents to offspring. Solving the mystery of heredity has been one of the great success stories of biology.

Look around at the students in your classroom. What makes each person an individual? Is it hair or eye color? Is it the shape of a nose or the arch in a person's eyebrows? Eye color, hair color, skin color, nose shape, and many other features, including those inside an individual that can't be seen, are traits that are inherited from a person's parents. A trait is a physical characteristic of an organism. Every organism, including yourself, is made up of many traits. The study of how traits are passed from parents to offspring is called **genetics** (juh NE tihks).

Reading Check *What traits could you pass to your offspring?*

as you read

What You'll Learn

- **Explain** how traits are inherited.
- **Relate** chromosomes, genes, and DNA to one another.
- **Discuss** how mutations add variation to a population.

Why It's Important

You will understand why you have certain traits.

Review Vocabulary
genotype: the genetic makeup of an organism

New Vocabulary
- heredity
- genetics
- ✳ gene
- variation
- mutation

✳ FCAT Vocabulary

Figure 10 Family members often share similar physical features. These traits can be something obvious, like curly hair, or less obvious, such as color blindness.

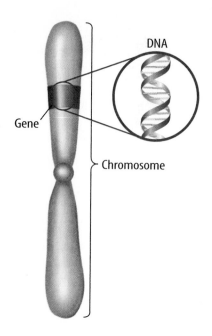

Gene

DNA

Chromosome

Figure 11 Hundreds of genes are located on each chromosome.

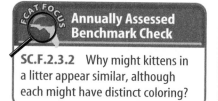

Annually Assessed Benchmark Check

SC.F.2.3.2 Why might kittens in a litter appear similar, although each might have distinct coloring?

Genes Half of your genetic information came from your father, and half came from your mother. This information was contained in the chromosomes of the egg and sperm that joined and formed the cell that eventually became you. Your chromosomes carry all the information that you need for life.

All chromosomes, like the one shown in **Figure 11,** contain genes (JEENZ). A **gene** is a small section of DNA that has information about a trait. Humans have thousands of different genes arranged on 23 pairs of chromosomes.

Genes control traits of organisms. Even traits that can't be seen, such as the shape of your stomach and your blood type, are controlled by genes. A trait that results from the presence of one or more genes is called an inherited trait. Some traits or skills, such as manners or juggling objects, are developed or learned and do not result directly from genes. Such traits are called acquired skills and are not inherited.

What determines traits?

Recall that in body cells, such as skin cells or muscle cells, chromosomes are in pairs. One pair of chromosomes can have genes that control many traits. Each gene on one chromosome of the pair has a similar gene on the other chromosome of the pair. Each gene of a gene pair is called an allele (uh LEEL), as shown in **Figure 12.** The alleles that make up a gene pair might or might not contain the same information about a trait. For example, the alleles for the flower color trait in some pea plants might be purple or white. If a pair of chromosomes contains different alleles for a trait, that trait is called a hybrid (HI brud). When a trait has two identical alleles, it's called pure.

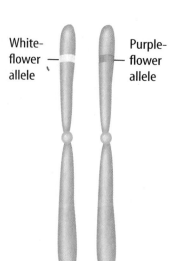

White-flower allele

Purple-flower allele

Chromosome pair

Figure 12 Pea flowers can be purple or white. The chromosome pair from a pea plant shows that both chromosomes have an allele for the flower color trait. A pea plant with this chromosome pair would have purple flowers.

Figure 13 When a person's hairline forms a vee on his or her forehead, it is called widow's peak hairline.
Infer *how many alleles for widow's peak this person might have.*

Dominant and Recessive Alleles The combination of alleles in a gene pair determines how a trait will be shown, or expressed, in an organism. In pea plants and other organisms, that depends on something called dominance (DAH muh nunts). Dominance means that one allele covers over or masks another allele of the trait. For instance, if a pea plant has one purple-flower allele and one white-flower allele or two purple-flower alleles, its flowers will be purple. Purple is the dominant flower color in pea plants. The dominant allele is expressed when the trait is hybrid or dominant pure. White flowers, the masked allele, are said to be recessive. Recessive alleles are expressed only when a trait is recessive pure.

There are human traits that are controlled by dominant and recessive alleles, just as some plant traits are controlled by dominant and recessive alleles. When a person inherits one or two dominant alleles for a trait, the dominant allele is expressed. In humans, a widow's peak hairline, as shown in **Figure 13,** is controlled by a dominant allele. Recessive alleles are expressed only when a person inherits a recessive allele for a trait from each parent.

Expression of Traits The traits of an organism are coded in the organism's DNA. However, the environment can play an important role in the way that a trait is shown, or expressed. You may know a person whose dark hair lightens when exposed to sunlight, or a person whose light skin darkens in sunlight. Human hair color and skin color are traits that are coded for by genes, but the environment can change the way that the traits appear. The environment can affect the expression of traits in every kind of organism, including bacteria, fungi, plants, and animals.

Sometimes the effects of the environment result in adaptations that help a species survive. For example, the arctic fox's fur color depends on the temperature of the environment. In cold winter months, the arctic fox does not produce fur pigment, and its fur appears white. The fox blends with the snow, helping it to avoid predators. In warmer months, the fox produces brown pigment, and it blends with the tundra.

SC.H.1.3.5
SC.H.2.3.1

Modeling Probability

Procedure

1. Flip a **coin** ten times. Count the number of heads and the number of tails.
2. Record these data in a data table in your **Science Journal.**
3. Now flip the coin twenty times. Count the number of heads and tails.
4. Record these data in a data table in your Science Journal.

Analysis

1. What results did you expect when you flipped the coin ten times? Twenty times?
2. Were your observed results closer to your expected results when you flipped the coin more times?
3. How is the pattern of coin flipping similar to the joining of egg and sperm at fertilization?

Try at Home

Passing Traits to Offspring

How are traits passed from parents to offspring during fertilization? The flower color trait in pea plants can be used as an example. Suppose a hybrid purple-flowered pea plant (one with two different alleles for flower color) is mated with a white-flowered pea plant. What color flowers will the offspring have?

The traits that a new pea plant will inherit depend upon which genes are carried in each plant's sex cells. Remember that sex cells are produced during meiosis. In sex cell formation, pairs of chromosomes duplicate, then separate as the four sex cells form. Therefore, gene pairs also separate. As a result, each sex cell contains one allele for each trait. Because the purple-flowered plant in **Figure 14** is a hybrid, half of its sex cells contain the purple-flower allele and half contain the white-flower allele. On the other hand, the white-flowered plant is recessive pure. The gene pair for flower color has two white alleles. All of the sex cells that it makes contain only the white-flower allele.

In fertilization, one sperm will join with one egg. Many events, such as flipping a coin and getting either heads or tails, are a matter of chance. In the same way, chance is involved in heredity. In the case of the pea plants, the chance was equal that the new pea plant would receive either the purple-flower allele or the white-flower allele from the hybrid plant.

Figure 14 The traits an organism has depends upon which genes were carried in its parents' sex cells. This diagram shows how the flower color trait is passed in pea plants.

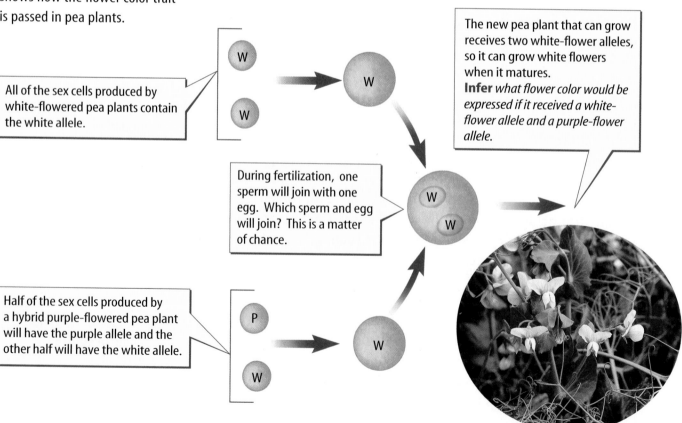

All of the sex cells produced by white-flowered pea plants contain the white allele.

During fertilization, one sperm will join with one egg. Which sperm and egg will join? This is a matter of chance.

Half of the sex cells produced by a hybrid purple-flowered pea plant will have the purple allele and the other half will have the white allele.

The new pea plant that can grow receives two white-flower alleles, so it can grow white flowers when it matures.
Infer what flower color would be expressed if it received a white-flower allele and a purple-flower allele.

Differences in Organisms

Now you know why a baby can have characteristics of either of its parents. The inherited genes from his or her parents determine hair color, skin color, eye color, and other traits. But what accounts for the differences, or variations (vayr ee AY shuns), in a family? **Variations** are the different ways that a certain trait appears, and they result from permanent changes in an organism's genes. Some gene changes produce small variations, and others produce large variations.

Applying Math | Find a Percentage

ALLELES IN SEX CELLS When sex cells form, each allele separates from its partner. Each sex cell will contain only one allele for each trait. Assume that a parent is a hybrid for a certain trait. That means that the parent has a dominant and a recessive allele for that trait. What percent of the parent's sex cells will contain the dominant allele?

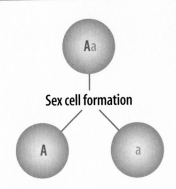

Sex cell formation

Solution

1 *This is what you know:* there are two possible alleles for the trait from the parent

2 *This is what you need to find out:* percent of sex cells with the dominant allele

3 *This is the procedure you need to use:*
- Use the following equation:

$$\frac{100\%}{\text{number of possible alleles from the parent}} = x$$

- Substitute in the known value and solve.

$$\frac{100\%}{2} = x \qquad x = 50\%$$

4 *Check your answer:* Multiply the number of possible alleles from the parent by the percent of sex cells with the dominant allele. You should get 100%.

Practice Problems

1. The attached-earlobes trait in humans is a recessive trait. What percent of the sex cells produced by a parent with attached earlobes would have an allele for this trait? (MA.E.2.3.1)

2. Assume one parent is a hybrid for a trait, and the other parent has two dominant alleles for the same trait. When the sex cells from the parents join, what is the percent chance that the offspring will have the recessive trait? (MA.E.2.3.1)

Math Practice | For more practice, visit fl6.msscience.com

Figure 15 Traits in humans that show great variation usually are controlled by more than one gene pair.

The members of this family have different hair color.

Height is a trait that has many variations.

INTEGRATE
Career

Genetic Counselor A genetic counselor is a medical professional who can help determine the chances of having a child with a genetic disorder. Genetic counselors test for genetic disorders and can provide help with treatment options. Investigate genetic disorders that can be tested for by a genetic counselor. In your Science Journal, write about one of the disorders.

Multiple Alleles and Multiple Genes Earlier, you learned how the flower color trait in pea plants is passed from parent to offspring. Flower color in pea plants shows a simple pattern of inheritance. Sometimes, though, the pattern of inheritance of a trait is not so simple. Many traits in organisms are controlled by more than two alleles. For example, in humans, multiple alleles A, B, and O control blood types A, B, AB, or O.

Traits also can be controlled by more than one gene pair. For humans, hair color, as shown in **Figure 15,** height, also shown in **Figure 15,** weight, eye color, and skin color, are traits that are controlled by several gene pairs. This type of inheritance is one of the reasons for the differences, or variations, in a species.

Mutations—The Source of New Variation If you've searched successfully through a patch of clover for a leaf with four parts instead of three, you've come face-to-face with a mutation (myew TAY shun). A four-leaf clover is the result of a mutation. The word *mutate* simply means "to change." In genetics, a **mutation** is a change in a gene or chromosome. This can happen because of an error during meiosis or mitosis or because of something in the environment. Many mutations happen by chance.

✔ **Reading Check** *What is a mutation?*

What are the effects of mutations? Sometimes mutations affect the way cells grow, repair, and maintain themselves. This type of mutation is usually harmful to the organism. Many mutations, such as a four-leaf clover, have a neutral effect. Whether a mutation is beneficial, harmful, or neutral, all mutations add variation to the genes of a species.

Figure 16 Dairy cattle are bred selectively for the amount of milk that they can produce.

Selective Breeding Sometimes, a mutation produces a new version of a trait that some people think is better than the original trait. To continue this trait, selective breeding is practiced.

Nearly all breeding of animals is based on their observable traits and is controlled, instead of being random. For many years, cattle, like the one in **Figure 16,** have been bred on the basis of how much milk they can produce. Racehorses are bred according to how fast they run. It eventually was learned that in a few generations, breeding closely related animals produced an increased percentage of offspring with the desired traits.

Science nline

LA.B.2.3.4

Topic: Selective Breeding
Visit fl6.msscience.com for Web links to information about selective breeding.

Activity List one type of plant and one type of animal that are bred selectively. Include the specific traits for which each is bred.

section 2 review

Summary

Heredity

- Genetics is the study of how traits are passed from parents to offspring.
- Genes control all the inheritable traits of organisms.

What determines traits?

- The expression of a trait is determined by the combination of alleles in a gene pair.
- A hybrid has a pair of chromosomes with different alleles for a trait.

Passing Traits to Offspring

- Traits of an offspring are determined by which genes are carried by its parents' sex cells.

Differences in Organisms

- Many traits are controlled by more than two alleles.
- More than one gene pair can control a certain trait.
- Mutations can happen by chance.

Self Check

1. **Define** the term *heredity*.
2. **State** which alleles for a trait must be present for a recessive allele to be expressed. SC.F.2.3.2
3. **Describe** how the chromosomes in human body cells are arranged.
4. **Explain** how mutations add variation to the genes of a species. SC.F.2.3.2
5. **Think Critically** What might happen if two hybrid purple-flowered pea plants are mated? What possible flower colors could the offspring have? Explain.

Applying Skills

6. **Concept Map** Make a concept map that shows the relationships between the following concepts: *genetics, genes, chromosomes, DNA, variation,* and *mutation.*
7. **Communicate** Research to find what a transgenic organism is, then find books or articles about these organisms. In your Science Journal, write a paragraph summary of your findings.

Benchmark—**SC.H.1.3.5:** The student knows that a change in one or more variables may alter the outcome of an investigation; **SC.H.1.3.7:** The student knows ... to verify whether the differences are significant by further study; **SC.H.2.3.1:** The student recognizes that patterns exist within and across systems; **SC.H.3.3.1**

Use the Internet

Genetic Traits: The Unique You

Goals

- **Identify** genetic traits.
- **Collect** data about three specific human genetic traits.
- **Investigate** what are dominant and recessive alleles.
- **Graph** your results and then communicate them to other students.

Data Source

Internet Lab

Visit **fl6.msscience.com** to get more information about human genetic traits and for data collected by other students.

Real-World Problem

What makes you unique? Unless you have an identical twin, no other person has the same combination of genes as you do. To learn more about three human genetic traits, you will collect data about your classmates. When you compare the data you collected with data from other students, you'll see that patterns develop in the frequency of types of traits that are present within a group of people. How are three genetic traits expressed among your classmates? Genetic traits can be dominant or recessive. Form a hypothesis about which trait, dominant or recessive, will be expressed by more people.

Make a Plan

1. **Research** general information about human genetic traits.
2. **Search** reference sources to find out which form of each characteristic being studied is dominant and which form is recessive.
3. **Survey** the students in your class to collect data about the three genetic traits being studied.

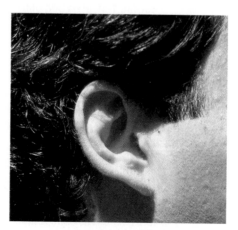

Attached earlobe

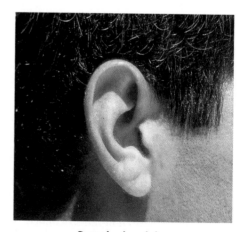

Detached earlobe

▶ Follow Your Plan

1. Make sure your teacher approves your plan before you start.

2. **Record** your data in your Science Journal. Use frequency data tables to organize your data.

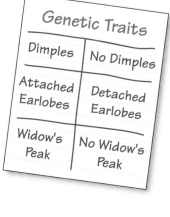

Genetic Traits	
Dimples	No Dimples
Attached Earlobes	Detached Earlobes
Widow's Peak	No Widow's Peak

▶ Analyze Your Data

1. **Record** the total number of people included in your survey.

2. **Calculate** the number of people who show each form of each of the three traits that are being studied. Record each of these numbers in your Science Journal.

3. **Graph** the data you collected on a bar graph. Bars should represent the numbers of students exhibiting each of the different genetic traits you investigated.

4. **Compare** the data among each of the three genetic traits you explored.

▶ Conclude and Apply

1. **Determine** Think about the genetic traits you investigated. Which traits were most common in the people you surveyed?

2. **Infer** Might surveying a larger group of people give different results?

3. **Analyze Results** Which genetic traits are least commonly found?

4. **Interpret Data** In the people you surveyed, were dominant alleles present more often than recessive alleles?

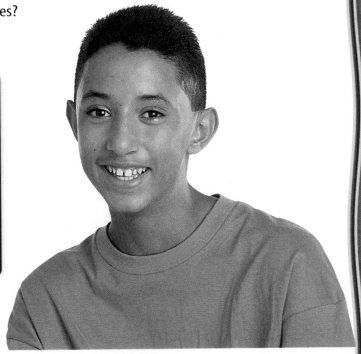

𝒞ommunicating
Your Data

Find this lab using the link below. **Post** your data in the table provided. **Compare** your data to that of other students. Combine your data with that of other students and **graph** the combined data on a bar graph.

Internet Lab
fl6.msscience.com

SEPARATED AT BIRTH

Are genes or the people who raised you important in determining personality?

These twins, separated at birth and reunited as adults, had the same kind of job, drove the same kind of car, and had the same hobbies.

When Barbara Herbert was about 40, she met her long lost twin sister, Daphne Goodship. She had not seen her since infancy. The two grew up in separate homes with separate families. Because they are identical twins, it makes sense that they look alike. What was shocking, however, was the number of coincidences in their lives. Although they were not in contact while growing up, they shared identical experiences. Both women:

• dropped out of school at age 14,
• got jobs working for the local government,
• met their future husbands at age 16,
• gave birth to two boys and one girl,
• are squeamish about blood and heights, and
• drink their coffee cold.

In the genes?

Barbara and Daphne are part of an ongoing scientific study at Minnesota's Center for Twin and Adoption Research, which examines twins who were separated at birth. This research is helping scientists to understand better what is stronger in a person's development—genetic makeup, or how and by whom twins are raised.

Identical twins make ideal subjects for this research because their genetic makeups are identical. First, a psychological assessment is made, using personality tests, job interest questions, mental ability, and I.Q. Tests. Then scientists analyze the twins' backgrounds, including where they were raised, what their parents were like, and what schools they attended. These help determine whether a person's habits and personality are based on genetic makeup or social interactions.

Recently, a pair of twins were reunited after more than 30 years. Both twins said they felt like they have known each other all their lives. And, perhaps, thanks to their genes, they have!

Interview Find a pair of identical twins that go to your school or live in your community. Make a list of ten questions and interview each of the twins separately. Write down their answers, or tape-record them. Compare the responses, then share your findings with the class. LA.C.1.3.1

TIME

For more information, visit fl6.msscience.com

Reviewing Main Ideas

Section 1 Continuing Life

1. Reproduction is an important process for all living things.

2. During reproduction, information stored in DNA is passed from parent to offspring.

3. Mitosis is the process that results in two nuclei with the same genetic information.

4. Organisms can reproduce sexually or asexually.

5. DNA is shaped like a twisted ladder. An organism's DNA contains all of the information about how it will look and function.

Section 2 Genetics—The Study of Inheritance

1. Genetics is the study of how traits are passed from parent to offspring.

2. Genes are small sections of DNA on chromosomes. Each gene has information about a specific trait.

3. Chromosomes are found in pairs. For each gene on a particular chromosome, a gene with information about the same trait can be found on the other chromosome of the chromosome pair. Each gene of a gene pair is called an allele.

4. The way a trait is expressed depends on the combination of dominant and recessive alleles carried on the chromosome pair.

5. Mutations are changes in a gene or chromosome. Mutations are a source of variation in populations.

6. Selective breeding allows favorable traits of organisms to be passed from one generation to the next.

Visualizing Main Ideas

Copy and complete the following concept map on reproduction.

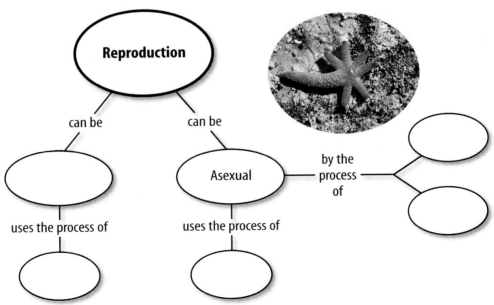

Using Vocabulary

* asexual reproduction p. 76
cloning p. 72
DNA p. 68
fertilization p. 73
* gene p. 78
genetics p. 77
heredity p. 77

* meiosis p. 73
* mitosis p. 70
mutation p. 82
sex cell p. 72
* sexual reproduction p. 72
variation p. 81

* FCAT Vocabulary

Explain the differences between the vocabulary words in each of the following sets.

1. mitosis—meiosis `SC.F.2.3.2`

2. asexual reproduction—sexual reproduction `SC.F.2.3.1`

3. cloning—variation

4. fertilization—sexual reproduction

5. mutation—variation

6. gene—DNA

7. asexual reproduction—mitosis

8. sex cells—meiosis `SC.F.2.3.1`

9. genetics—gene

10. DNA—mutation

Checking Concepts

Choose the word or phrase that best answers the question.

11. Which is reproduction that requires male and female sex cells? `SC.F.2.3.1`
    A) asexual reproduction
    B) sexual reproduction
    C) mitosis
    D) heredity

12. What is any change in the DNA of a gene or chromosome called?
    A) an embryo   C) a clone
    B) sex cells   D) a mutation

13. What is the small section of DNA that contains the code for a trait?
    A) a gene   C) a variation
    B) heredity   D) a cell

14. Which is another name for an observable feature or characteristic of an organism?
    A) sex cell   C) trait
    B) embryo   D) gene

15. How are specialized breeds of dogs, cats, horses, and other animals produced? `SC.F.2.3.2`
    A) regeneration
    B) asexual reproduction
    C) selective breeding
    D) budding

16. What is the passing of traits from parent to offspring called? `SC.F.2.3.2`
    A) genetics   C) heredity
    B) variation   D) meiosis

17. What are sperm and eggs?
    A) variations   C) mutations
    B) sex cells   D) genes

18. What is formed during meiosis?
    A) heredity   C) clones
    B) sex cells   D) fertilization

Use the photo below to answer question 19.

19. What flower color trait(s) would be in the sex cells of the above pea plant?
    A) purple only   C) purple and white
    B) white only   D) pink only

Thinking Critically

20. Explain the relationship among DNA, genes, and chromosomes.

21. Communicate Two brown-eyed parents have a baby with blue eyes. Explain the genetics of the baby. SC.F.2.3.2

22. Describe how the process of meiosis is important in sexual reproduction. SC.F.2.3.1

23. Explain how a mutation in a gene could be beneficial to an organism.

24. Draw Conclusions Some mutations are harmful to organisms. Others are beneficial, and some have no effect at all. Which mutation would be least likely to be passed on to future generations? SC.F.2.3.2

25. Compare and contrast sexual and asexual reproduction. SC.F.2.3.1

26. Recognize Cause and Effect What is the role of meiosis and mitosis in the fertilization and development that results in a human baby? SC.F.1.3.3 SC.F.1.3.3

Use the photo below to answer question 27.

SC.F.2.3.1

27. Infer why this plant is an example of asexual reproduction. How could the plant reproduce through sexual reproduction?

Performance Activities

28. Scientific Drawing Use your imagination and make illustrations for each of the following vocabulary words: *asexual reproduction*, *genetics*, and *mutation*.

29. Newspaper Article Many scientists have reported that it is possible to get DNA from prehistoric creatures. Visit the library and find a newspaper article that describes the discovery of ancient DNA. Write a summary of the article in your Science Journal.

Applying Math

30. Cell Division If a cell undergoes cell division every 20 minutes, how many cells will there be after 24 hours? MA.E.2.3.1

31. Meiosis Five cells undergo meiosis to form sex cells. How many sex cells are formed? MA.E.2.3.1

32. Human Genome Assume the human genome is three billion base pairs. If one million base pairs of DNA take up one megabyte of storage space on a computer, how many gigabytes (1,024 megabytes) would the whole human genome fill? MA.E.2.3.1

Use the illustration below to answer question 33.

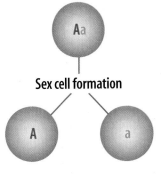

Aa

Sex cell formation

A   a

33. Wrinkled Seeds In pea plants, wrinkled seeds are recessive to round seeds. If two hybrid pea plants are crossed, what is the percent chance that the offspring will have the wrinkled-seed trait? MA.E.2.3.1

 The assessed Florida Benchmark appears above each question.
Record your answers on the answer sheet provided by your teacher or on a sheet of paper.

Multiple Choice

SC.F.1.3.3

1 The diagram below shows a chromosome.

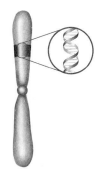

What does this diagram show about the structure of chromosomes?

A. A chromosome is a small section of a gene.

B. Chromosomes carry genetic material in DNA.

C. Both genes of a gene pair are on the same chromosome.

D. Chromosomes have a dominant half and a recessive half.

SC.F.2.3.1

2 Which is an example of regeneration?

F. A bacterium divides into two identical cells.

G. A spider sperm and egg join to form a cell with a complete set of chromosomes.

H. A lobster grows back a leg after it loses one to a predator.

I. A change in a chromosome causes a squirrel to be born with white fur instead of brown.

SC.F.1.3.3

3 What is the main purpose of mitosis?

A. to produce a new sex cell

B. to pair up the chromosomes of a cell

C. to reduce the number of chromosomes in a cell by half

D. to make a copy of the genetic material in a cell's nucleus

SC.F.1.3.3

4 The figure below shows a cell reproducing.

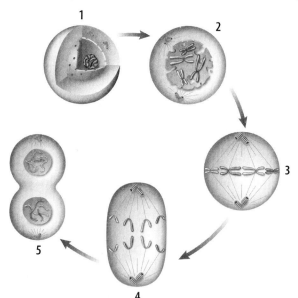

Which best describes what happens during Step 4?

F. Each duplicated chromosome pair separates.

G. The genetic material in the cell is duplicated.

H. The two sides of the DNA ladder pull apart.

I. A membrane forms around each identical nucleus.

SC.F.2.3.1

5 Which best describes what happens to a fertilized cell in a flowering plant?

   A. It undergoes meiosis.

   B. It matures into a flower.

   C. It becomes enclosed in a seed.

   D. It produces grains of pollen.

Gridded Response

SC.F.2.3.2

6 In fruit flies, the allele for red eyes (R) is dominant over the allele for white eyes (r). The diagram below shows the eye-color alleles of two fruit flies.

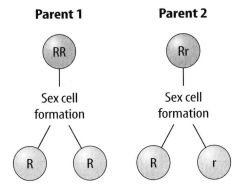

When the sex cells from these two fruit flies join, what is the percent chance that the offspring will have red eyes?

Short Response

SC.F.2.3.2

7 In rabbits, the allele for black fur is dominant over the allele for brown fur. Is it possible for two brown rabbits to produce offspring with black fur? Explain your answer.

Extended Response

SC.F.2.3.2

8 There are two alleles for pea color, green and yellow. The offspring from a pea plant with two green alleles and a pea plant with two yellow alleles are shown below. All of these offspring produce green peas.

Parent 1	Parent 2
Green peas Alleles: green, green	Yellow peas Alleles: yellow, yellow

Offspring

Green peas Alleles: ?, ?

   PART A What pair of alleles for pea color do the offspring have? Explain your answer.

   PART B Is the allele for green pea color dominant or recessive? Explain your answer in terms of hybrid, dominant pure, and recessive pure traits.

FCAT Tip

Pay Attention Listen carefully to the instructions from the teacher and carefully read the directions and each question.

How are
Chickens & Rice
Connected?

NATIONAL GEOGRAPHIC

Back in the 1800s, a mysterious disease called beriberi affected people in certain parts of Asia. One day, a doctor in Indonesia noticed some chickens staggering around, a symptom often seen in people with beriberi. It turned out that the chickens had been eating white rice—the same kind of rice that was being eaten by human beriberi sufferers. White rice has had the outer layers, including the bran, removed. When the sick chickens were fed rice that still had its bran, they quickly recovered. It turned out that the same treatment worked for people with beriberi! Research eventually showed that rice bran contains a vitamin, B_1, which is essential for good health. Today, white rice usually is "vitamin-enriched" to replace B_1 and other nutrients lost in processing.

unit ⚡ projects

Visit unit projects at **fl6.msscience.com** for project ideas and resources.
Projects include:

- **History** Contribute to a class "remedy journal" with interesting, out-dated medical treatments, and how techniques have improved.
- **Technology** Investigate rare and interesting medical conditions, including their history, characteristics, and treatments. Present a colorful poster with photos and information for class display.
- **Model** Research and create a menu that includes vitamin-rich foods. Prepare a sample and a recipe card for a class food fair.

 Learn about *Investigating Disease and Prevention,* and how science has progressed through history. Become acquainted with famous scientists and learn how healthy lifestyles prevent disease.

chapter

4

Sunshine State Standards—**SC.F.1:** The student describes patterns of structure and function in living things.

Support, Movement, and Responses

How are you like a building?

Buildings are supported and protected by internal and external structures. Your body is supported by your skeleton and protected by your skin. In this chapter, you also will learn how your body senses and responds to the world around you.

Science Journal Imagine for a moment that your body does not have a support system. How will you perform your daily activities? Explain your reasoning.

Start-Up Activities

 **SC.H.3.3.1**

Effect of Muscles on Movement

The expression "Many hands make light work" is also true when it comes to muscles in your body. In fact, hundreds of muscles and bones work together to bring about smooth, easy movement. Muscle interactions enable you to pick up a penny or lift a 10-kg weight.

1. Complete a safety worksheet.
2. Sit on a chair at an empty table and place the palm of one hand under the edge of the table.
3. Push your hand up against the table. Do not push too hard.
4. Use your other hand to feel the muscles located on both sides of your upper arm, as shown in the photo.
5. Next, place your palm on top of the table and push down. Again, feel the muscles in your upper arm.
6. **Think Critically** Describe in your Science Journal how the different muscles in your upper arm were working during each movement.

 **FOLDABLES™**
Study Organizer

Support, Movement, and Responses Make the following Foldable to help you understand the functions of skin, muscles, bones, and nerves.

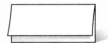 **LA.A.1.3.4**

STEP 1 **Fold** a sheet of paper in half lengthwise. Make the back edge about 1.25 cm longer than the front edge.

STEP 2 **Fold** the paper in half widthwise, twice.

STEP 3 **Unfold and cut** only the top layer along the three folds to make four tabs. **Label** the tabs as shown.

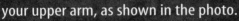
Skin | Muscles | Bones | Nerves

Read and Write As you read this chapter, list the functions that skin, muscles, bones, and nerves have in support, movement, and responses.

 **Science online**

Preview this chapter's content and activities at fl6.msscience.com

Benchmarks—SC.F.1.3.1 Annually Assessed (pp. 97–98): The student understands that living things are composed of major systems that function in reproduction, growth, maintenance, and regulation; SC.F.1.3.6 (p. 96): The student knows that the cells with similar functions have similar structures, whereas those with different structures have different functions.

Also covers: SC.F.1.3.2 (p. 96), SC.F.1.3.3 (p. 96), SC.F.1.3.4 (p. 96), SC.F.1.3.7 (p. 100), SC.H.1.3.4 Annually Assessed (p. 100), SC.H.1.3.5 (p. 100), SC.H.3.3.1 (pp. 98, 100)

section 1

The Skin

as you read

What You'll Learn

- **Distinguish** between the epidermis and dermis of the skin.
- **Identify** the functions of the skin.
- **Explain** how skin protects the body from disease and how it heals itself.

Why It's Important

Skin plays a vital role in protecting your body against injury and disease.

Review Vocabulary

☀ **organ:** a structure, such as the heart, made up different types of tissues that work together

New Vocabulary

- ● epidermis
- ● dermis
- ● melanin

☀ FCAT Vocabulary

Skin Structures

Your skin is the largest organ of your body. Much of the information you receive about your environment comes through your skin. You can think of your skin as your largest sense organ.

Skin is made up of three layers of tissue—the epidermis, the dermis, and a fatty layer—as shown in **Figure 1.** Each layer is made of different cell types. The **epidermis** is the outer, thinnest layer. The epidermis's outermost cells are dead and water repellent. Thousands of epidermal cells rub off every time you take a shower, shake hands, or scratch your elbow. New cells are produced constantly at the base of the epidermis. These new cells move up and eventually replace those that are rubbed off. The **dermis** is the layer of cells directly below the epidermis. This layer is thicker than the epidermis and contains blood vessels, nerves, muscles, oil and sweat glands, and other structures. Below the dermis is a fatty region that insulates the body. This is where much of the fat is deposited when a person gains weight.

Figure 1 Hair, sweat glands, and oil glands are part of your body's largest organ.

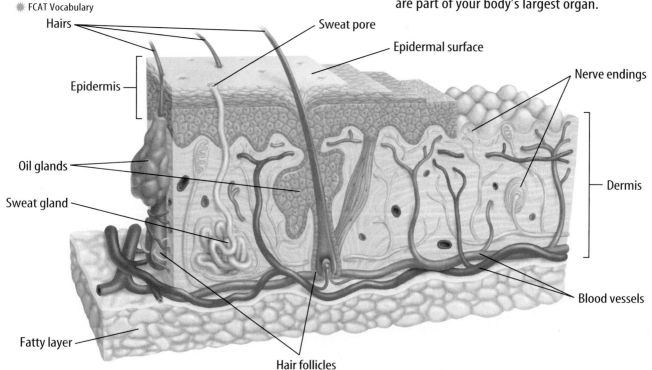

Hairs · Sweat pore · Epidermal surface · Nerve endings · Epidermis · Oil glands · Sweat gland · Dermis · Blood vessels · Fatty layer · Hair follicles

Melanin Cells in the epidermis produce the chemical **melanin** (ME luh nun), a pigment that protects your skin and gives it color. The different amounts of melanin produced by cells result in differences in skin color, as shown in **Figure 2.** When your skin is exposed to ultraviolet rays, melanin production increases and your skin becomes darker. Lighter skin tones have less protection. Such skin burns more easily and can be more susceptible to skin cancer.

Skin Functions

Your skin carries out several major functions, including protection, sensory response, formation of vitamin D, regulation of body temperature, and ridding the body of wastes. The most important function of the skin is protection. The skin forms a protective covering over the body that prevents physical and chemical injury. Some bacteria and other disease-causing organisms cannot pass through skin as long as it is unbroken. Glands in the skin secrete fluids that can damage or destroy some bacteria. The skin also slows water loss from body tissues.

Specialized nerve cells in the skin detect and relay information to the brain. Because of these cells, you are able to sense the softness of a cat, the sharpness of a pin, or the heat of a frying pan.

Another important function of skin is the formation of vitamin D. Small amounts of this vitamin are produced in the presence of ultraviolet light from a fatlike molecule in your epidermis. Vitamin D is essential for good health because it helps your body absorb calcium into your blood from food in your digestive tract.

LA.A.2.3.5

INTEGRATE
Language Arts

High Altitude and Skin
There have been many books written about mountain climbing. Search the library for a book about mountain climbing. Find references in the book about the effects of sunlight and weather on the skin at high altitudes. In your Science Journal, list the book title and author and summarize the passage that describes the effects of sunlight and weather on the skin.

Figure 2 Melanin gives skin and eyes their color.
Infer *which person has the least amount of melanin in his or her skin.*

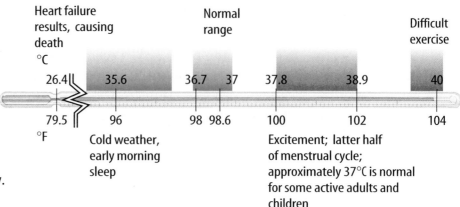

Figure 3 Normal human body temperature is about 37°C but can vary throughout the day. The highest is reached at about 11 A.M. and the lowest at around 4 A.M. At 43°C (109.5°F), fatal bleeding results, causing death.

Recognizing Why You Sweat

Procedure

1. Complete a safety worksheet.
2. Examine the epidermis and the pores of your skin using a **magnifying lens.**
3. Place a **clear-plastic sandwich bag** on your hand. Use **tape** to seal the bag around your wrist. **WARNING:** *Do not wrap the tape too tightly.*
4. Quietly study your text for 10 min, then remove the bag and look at your hand.
5. Wash your hands, then describe what happened to your hand while it was inside the bag.

Analysis

1. Identify what formed inside the bag. Where did this substance come from?
2. Why does this substance form even when you are not active?

Heat and Waste Exchange Humans can withstand a limited range of body temperatures, as shown in **Figure 3.** Your skin plays an important role in regulating your body temperature. Blood vessels in the skin can help release or hold heat. If the blood vessels expand, or dilate, blood flow increases and heat is released. In contrast, less heat is released when the blood vessels constrict. Think of yourself after running—are you flushed red or pale and shivering?

An adult human's dermis has about 3 million sweat glands that help regulate the body's temperature and excrete wastes. When blood vessels dilate, pores open in the skin that lead to the sweat glands. Perspiration, or sweat, moves out onto the skin. Heat transfers from the body to the sweat on the skin. Eventually, this sweat evaporates, removing the heat and cooling the skin. This process eliminates excess heat produced by muscle contractions.

Reading Check *What are two functions of sweat glands?*

Wastes are produced when nutrients are broken down in cells. Such wastes, if not removed, can act as poisons. In addition to helping regulate your body's temperature, sweat glands release waste products, such as water and salt. If too much water and salt are released during periods of extreme heat or physical exertion, you might feel light-headed or even faint.

Skin Injuries and Repair

Your skin often can be bruised, scratched, burned, ripped, or exposed to harsh conditions like cold, dry air. In response, the epidermis produces new cells and the dermis repairs tears. When the skin is injured, disease-causing organisms can enter the body rapidly. An infection often results.

Bruises When tiny blood vessels burst under unbroken skin, a bruise results. Red blood cells from these broken blood vessels leak into the surrounding tissue. These blood cells then break down, releasing a chemical called hemoglobin that gradually breaks down into substances called pigments. The colors of these pigments cause the bruised area to turn shades of blue, red, and purple, as shown in **Figure 4.** Swelling also may occur with a bruise. As the injury heals, the bruise eventually turns yellow as the pigment in the red blood cells is broken down even more and reenters the bloodstream. After all of the pigment is absorbed into the bloodstream, the bruise disappears and the skin appears normal again.

✓ **Reading Check** *What is the source of the yellow color of a bruise that is healing?*

The body usually can repair bruises and small cuts. What happens when severe burns, some diseases, and surgeries result in injury to large areas of skin? Sometimes there are not enough skin cells left to produce new skin. If not treated, this can lead to rapid water loss from skin and muscle tissues, leading to infection and possibly death. Skin grafts can prevent this. Pieces of skin are cut from one part of a person's body and moved to the injured or burned area where there is no skin. This new graft is kept alive by nearby blood vessels and soon becomes part of the surrounding skin.

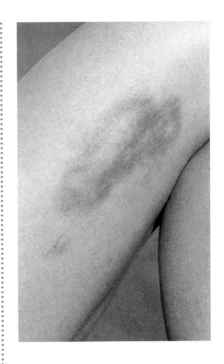

Figure 4 This leg bruise formed when tiny blood vessels beneath the skin burst, but the skin did not tear.
Infer *whether this bruise is new or is already healing.*

---

section 1 review

Summary

Skin Structures

- Skin is the largest organ in your body.
- There are three layers of tissue in skin and each layer is made of different cell types.
- Melanin protects your skin and gives it color.

Skin Functions

- The most important function of skin is protection.
- Specialized nerve cells in the skin detect and relay information to the brain.

Skin Injuries and Repair

- When skin is injured, disease-causing organisms can enter the body rapidly.
- When skin is damaged, the epidermis produces new cells and the dermis repairs tears.

Self Check

1. **Compare and contrast** the epidermis and dermis.
2. **Identify** the major functions of the skin. SC.F.1.3.4
3. **Describe** the role that your skin plays in regulating body temperature. SC.F.1.3.1   SC.F.1.3.4
4. **Explain** how skin helps prevent disease in the body.
5. **Describe** one way doctors are able to repair severe skin damage from burns, injuries, or surgeries. SC.F.1.3.3
6. **Think Critically** Why is a person who has been severely burned in danger of dying from loss of water? SC.F.1.3.1

Applying Math

7. **Solve One-Step Equations** The skin of eyelids is 0.5 mm thick. On the soles of your feet, skin is up to 0.4 cm thick. How many times thicker is the skin on the soles of your feet compared to your eyelids?
MA.D.2.3.1

Benchmark—SC.H.1.3.4: The student knows that accurate record keeping, openness, and replication are essential to maintaining an investigator's credibility with other scientists and society; **SC.H.1.3.5:** The student knows that a change in one or more variables may alter the outcome of an investigation; **SC.H.1.3.7:** The student knows that when similar investigations give different results, the scientific challenge is to verify whether the differences are significant by further study; **SC.H.3.3.1:** The student knows that science ethics demand that scientists must not knowingly subject coworkers, students, the neighborhood, or the community to health or property risks.

Measuring Skin Surface

Skin covers the surface of your body and is your body's largest organ. Skin cells make up a layer of skin about 2 mm thick. How big is this organ?

▶ Real-World Problem

How much skin covers your body?

Goals

■ **Estimate** the surface area of skin that covers the body of a middle-school student.

Materials

10 large sheets of newspaper
scissors
tape
meterstick or ruler

Safety Precautions

Complete a safety worksheet before you begin.

▶ Procedure

1. Form groups of three or four, either all female or all male. Select one person from your group to measure the surface area of his or her skin.

2. **Estimate** how much skin covers the average student in your classroom. In your Science Journal, record your estimation.

3. Wrap newspaper snugly around each part of your classmate's body. Overlapping the sheets of paper, use tape to secure the paper. Small body parts, such as fingers and toes, do not need to be wrapped individually. Cover entire hands and feet. Do not cover the face.

4. After your classmate is completely covered with paper, carefully cut the newspaper off his or her body. **WARNING:** *Do not cut any clothing or skin.*

5. Lay all of the overlapping sheets of newspaper on the floor. Using scissors and more tape, cut and piece the paper suit together to form a rectangle.

6. Using a meterstick, measure the length and width of the resulting rectangle. Multiply these two measurements for an estimate of the surface area of your classmate's skin.

▶ Conclude and Apply

1. Was your estimation correct? Explain.

2. How accurate are your measurements of your classmate's skin surface area? How could your measurements be improved?

3. **Calculate** the volume of your classmate's skin, using 2 mm as the average thickness and your calculated surface area from this activity.

Communicating Your Data

Using a table, record the estimated skin surface area from all the groups in your class. Find the average surface areas for both males and females. Discuss any differences in these two averages.

Benchmarks—**SC.F.1.3.1 Annually Assessed (p. 103):** The student understands that living things are composed of major systems that function in reproduction, growth, maintenance, and regulation; **SC.F.1.3.6 (p. 102):** The student knows that the cells with similar functions have similar structures, whereas those with different structures have different functions.

Also covers: **SC.F.1.3.2 (p. 102), SC.F.1.3.4 (p. 102), SC.H.2.3.1 (p. 102)**

section 2

The Muscular System

Movement of the Human Body

Muscles help make all of your daily movements possible. In the process of relaxing, contracting, and providing the force for movements, energy is used and work is done. Imagine how much energy the more than 600 muscles in your body use each day. No matter how still you might try to be, some muscles in your body are always moving. You're breathing, your heart is beating, and your digestive system is working.

Muscle Control Your hand, arm, and leg muscles are voluntary. So are the muscles of your face, as shown in **Figure 5.** You can choose to move them or not to move them. Muscles that you are able to control are called **voluntary muscles.** Muscles that you can't control consciously are **involuntary muscles.** They work all day long, all your life. Blood is pumped through blood vessels, and food is moved through your digestive system by the action of involuntary muscles.

Reading Check *What is another body activity that is controlled by involuntary muscles?*

Figure 5 Facial expressions generally are controlled by voluntary muscles. It takes only 13 muscles to smile, but 43 muscles to frown.

as you read

What You'll Learn
- **Identify** the major function of the muscular system.
- **Compare and contrast** the three types of muscles.
- **Explain** how muscle action results in the movement of body parts.

Why It's Important

The muscular system is responsible for how you move and the production of heat in your body. Muscles also give your body its shape.

Review Vocabulary
muscle: an organ that can relax, contract, and provide the force to move bones and body parts

New Vocabulary
- voluntary muscle
- involuntary muscle
- tendon

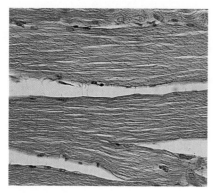

Skeletal muscles move bones. The muscle tissue appears striped, or striated, and is attached to bone.

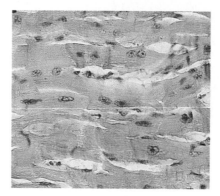

Cardiac muscle is found only in the heart. The muscle tissue has striations.

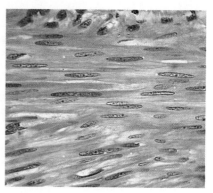

Smooth muscle is found in many of your internal organs, such as the digestive tract. This muscle tissue is nonstriated.

Figure 6 The structure of muscle tissue varies with the type and function.

Infer *what type of muscle tissue makes up the walls of veins, which carry blood.*

Classification of Muscle Tissue

Humans have three types of muscle tissue: skeletal, smooth, and cardiac. Skeletal muscles are voluntary muscles that move bones. They are more common than other muscle types, and are attached to bones by thick bands of tissue called **tendons.** Skeletal muscle cells are striated (STRI ay tud), and when viewed under a microscope, appear striped. You can see the striations in **Figure 6.**

The remaining two types of muscles also are shown in **Figure 6.** Cardiac muscle is found only in the heart. Like skeletal muscle, cardiac muscle is striated. This type of muscle contracts about 70 times per minute every day of your life. Smooth muscles are nonstriated involuntary muscles and are found in your intestines, bladder, blood vessels, and other internal organs.

 *Which muscles, voluntary or involuntary, can become tired because of daily use?*

Working Muscles

How do muscles allow you to move your body? You move because pairs of skeletal muscles work together. When one muscle of a pair of muscles contracts, the other muscle relaxes or returns to its original length. Muscles always pull; they never push. When the muscles on the back of your upper leg contract, as shown in **Figure 7,** they shorten and pull your lower leg back and up. When you straighten your leg, the back muscles relax and lengthen, and the muscles on the front of your upper leg contract. Compare how your leg muscles work with how the muscles of your arms work.

Changes in Muscles Over time, skeletal muscles can become larger or smaller, depending on whether or not they are used. Most of this change in muscle size is because individual muscle cells become larger. Some of this change is because the number of muscle cells increases. For example, Jin bicycles regularly and has large, strong leg muscles. In contrast, if he only participated in non-active pastimes, such as watching television or playing computer games, he likely would have smaller, weaker leg muscles. Muscles that aren't exercised become smaller in size. Paralyzed muscles also become smaller because they cannot be moved or have limited movement.

How Muscles Move Your muscles need energy to contract and relax. Blood carries energy-rich molecules to muscle cells, where the chemical energy stored in these molecules is released. As a muscle contracts, this released energy changes to mechanical energy (movement) and thermal energy (heat). The heat produced by muscle contractions helps keep your body temperature constant. A muscle becomes tired and needs to rest when the supply of energy-rich molecules is used up. During the resting period, blood supplies more energy-rich molecules to muscle cells.

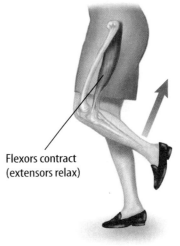

Flexors contract (extensors relax)

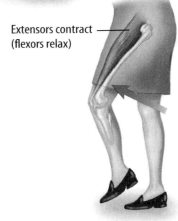

Extensors contract (flexors relax)

Figure 7 Leg muscles, like all skeletal muscles, work in pairs.

---

section 2 review

Summary

Movement of the Human Body

- Muscles contract to move bones and body parts.
- You can control voluntary muscles, but you cannot consciously control involuntary muscles.

Classification of Muscle Tissue

- Skeletal muscles are voluntary, smooth muscles control movement of internal organs, and cardiac muscle is striated and involuntary.

Working Muscles

- Muscles always pull, and when one muscle of a pair contracts, the other relaxes.
- Chemical energy is needed for muscle activity.

Self Check

1. **Describe** the function of muscles. `SC.F.1.3.4` `SC.F.1.3.6`
2. **Compare and contrast** the three types of muscle tissue.
3. **Identify** and describe the appearance of the type of muscle tissue found in your heart. `SC.F.1.3.6`
4. **Explain** how your muscles and bones work together to move your body. `SC.F.1.3.1`
5. **Describe** how a muscle attaches to a bone.
6. **Think Critically** What happens to your upper arm muscles when you bend your arm at the elbow to eat your favorite sandwich?

Applying Skills

7. **Concept Map** Using a concept map, sequence the activities that take place when you bend your leg at the knee.

Benchmarks—SC.F.1.3.1 Annually Assessed (p. 104): The student understands that living things are composed of major systems that function in reproduction, growth, maintenance, and regulation; SC.F.1.3.3 (p. 105): The student knows that in multicellular organisms cells grow and divide to make more cells in order to form and repair various organs and tissues.

Also covers: SC.F.1.3.2 (p. 105), SC.F.1.3.4 (p. 105), SC.F.1.3.6 (p. 105)

section 3

The Skeletal System

as you read

What You'll Learn

- **Identify** five functions of the skeletal system.
- **Compare and contrast** movable and immovable joints.

Why It's Important

You'll begin to understand how each of your body parts moves and what happens that allows you to move them.

Review Vocabulary

skeleton: a framework of living bones that supports your body

New Vocabulary

- periosteum
- cartilage
- joint
- ligament

Functions of Your Skeletal System

The skeletal system includes all the bones in your body and has five major functions.

1. The skeleton gives shape and support to your body.
2. Bones protect your internal organs.
3. Major muscles are attached to bones and help them move.
4. Blood cells form in the red marrow of many bones.
5. Major quantities of calcium and phosphorous compounds are stored in the skeleton for later use. Calcium and phosphorus make bones hard.

Bone Structure

Looking at bone through a magnifying lens will show you that it isn't smooth. Bones have bumps, edges, round ends, rough spots, and many pits and holes. Muscles and ligaments attach to some of the bumps and pits. In your body, blood vessels and nerves enter and leave through the holes in bones. How a bone looks from the inside and the outside is shown in **Figure 8.**

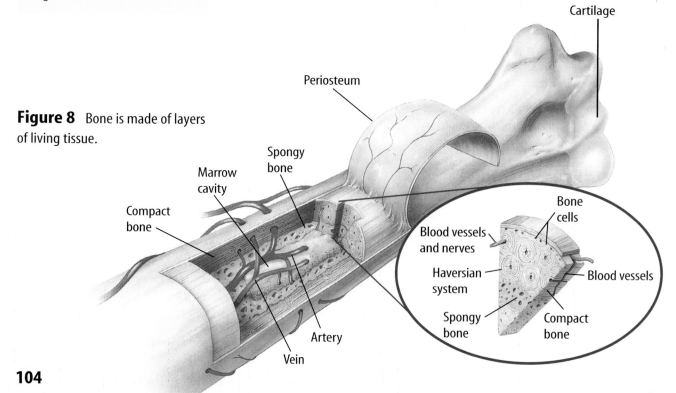

Figure 8 Bone is made of layers of living tissue.

104

Bone Tissue Living bone is an organ made of several different tissues. A living bone's surface is covered with a tough, tight-fitting membrane called the **periosteum** (pur ee AHS tee um). Small blood vessels in the periosteum carry nutrients into the bone and its nerves signal pain. Under the periosteum are compact bone and spongy bone.

Compact bone gives bones strength. It has a framework containing deposits of calcium phosphate that make the bone hard. Spongy bone is located toward the ends of long bones, such as those in your thigh and upper arm. Spongy bone has many small, open spaces that make bones lightweight.

In the centers of long bones are large openings called cavities. These cavities and the spaces in spongy bone are filled with a substance called marrow. Some marrow is yellow and is composed of fat cells. Red marrow produces red blood cells at a rate of 2 million to 3 million cells per second.

Cartilage The ends of bones are covered with a smooth, slippery, thick layer of tissue called **cartilage.** Cartilage does not contain blood vessels or minerals. It is flexible and important in joints because it acts as a shock absorber. It also makes movement easier by reducing friction that would be caused by bones rubbing together.

✔ Reading Check *What is cartilage?*

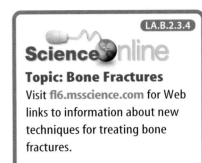

Science Online

LA.B.2.3.4

Topic: Bone Fractures
Visit fl6.msscience.com for Web links to information about new techniques for treating bone fractures.

Activity Using captions, illustrate one technique in your Science Journal.

Figure 9 Cartilage is replaced slowly by bone as solid tissue grows outward. Over time, the bone reshapes to include blood vessels, nerves, and marrow. **Name** *the type of bone cell that builds up bone.*

Bone Formation

Your bones have not always been as hard as they are now. Months before your birth, your skeleton was made of cartilage. Gradually, the cartilage broke down and was replaced by bone. This process is shown in **Figure 9.** Bone-forming cells called osteoblasts (AHS tee oh blasts) deposit calcium and phosphorus in bones, making the bone tissue hard. At birth, your skeleton was made up of more than 300 bones. As you developed, some bones fused, or grew together, so that now you have only 206 bones.

Healthy bone tissue is always being formed and re-formed. Osteoblasts build up bone. Another type of bone cell, called an osteoclast, breaks down bone tissue in other areas of the bone. This is a normal process in a healthy person. When osteoclasts break bone down, they release calcium and phosphorus into the bloodstream. These elements are necessary for the working of your body, including the movement of your muscles.

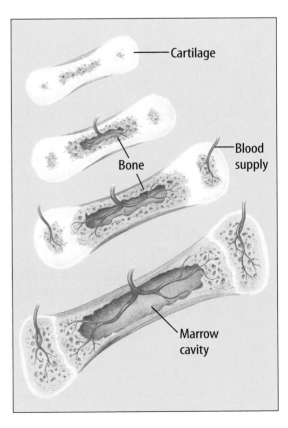

Cartilage

Bone

Blood supply

Marrow cavity

Joints

What will you do at school today? You might sit at a table, chew and swallow your lunch, or walk to class. All of these motions are possible because your skeleton has joints.

Any place where two or more bones come together is a **joint.** Bones are held in place at joints by tough bands of tissue called **ligaments.** Muscles move bones by moving joints. The bones in healthy joints are separated by a thin layer of cartilage so that they do not rub against each other as they move.

✔ Reading Check *What holds bones in place at joints?*

Applying Math Estimate

VOLUME OF BONES Although bones are not perfectly shaped, many of them are cylindrical. This cylindrical shape allows your bones to withstand great pressure. Estimate the volume of a bone that is 36 cm long and 7 cm in diameter.

Solution

1 *This is what you know:*

The bone has a shape of a cylinder whose height, h, measures 36 cm and whose diameter is 7.0 cm.

2 *This is what you want to find out:*

Volume of the cylinder

3 *This is the procedure you need to use:*

- Use this equation:
  Volume = π × (radius)^2 × height, or $V = \pi \times r^2 \times h$
- A radius is one-half the diameter $\left(\frac{1}{2} \times 7 \text{ cm}\right)$, so $r = 3.5$ cm, $h = 36$ cm, and π = 3.14.
- $V = 3.14 \times (3.5 \text{ cm})^2 \times 36 \text{ cm}$
  $V = 1{,}384.74 \text{ cm}^3$
- The volume of the bone is approximately 1,384.74 cm^3.

4 *Check your answer:*

Divide your answer by 3.14 and then divide that number by (3.5)^2. This number should be the height of the bone.

Practice Problems

1. Estimate the volume of a bone that has a height of 12 cm and a diameter of 2.4 cm. `MA.B.3.3.1`
2. If the volume of a bone is 62.8 cm^3 and its height is 20 cm, what is its diameter? `MA.B.3.3.1`

Math Practice | For more practice, visit fl6.msscience.com

Moving Smoothly When you rub two pieces of chalk together, their surfaces wear and get reshaped. Without the protection of the cartilage at the end of your bones, they also would wear away at the joints. Cartilage cushions your joints and helps make movement easier. It also reduces friction and allows bones to slide more easily over each other. Cartilage can be damaged or wear away. If this happens, joints become painful.

Movable Joints All movements, including somersaulting and working the controls of a video game, require movable joints, such as those in **Figure 10.** A movable joint allows the body to make a wide range of motions. There are several types of movable joints—pivot, ball and socket, hinge, and gliding.

In a pivot joint, one bone rotates in a ring of another bone that does not move. Turning your head is an example of a pivot movement. A ball-and-socket joint consists of a bone with a rounded end that fits into a cuplike cavity on another bone. A ball-and-socket joint provides a wider range of motion than a pivot joint does. That's why your legs and arms can swing in almost any direction.

A third type of joint is a hinge joint, which has a back-and-forth movement like hinges on a door. Elbows, knees, and fingers have hinge joints. Hinge joints have a smaller range of motion than the ball-and-socket joint. They are not dislocated, or pulled apart, as easily as a ball-and-socket joint can be.

A fourth type of joint is a gliding joint, in which one part of a bone slides over another bone. Gliding joints also move in a back-and-forth motion and are found in your wrists and ankles and between vertebrae. Gliding joints are used the most in your body. You can't write a word, use a joy stick, or take a step without using one of your gliding joints.

Figure 10 When a basketball player shoots a ball, several types of joints are in action.
Name *other activities that use several types of joints.*

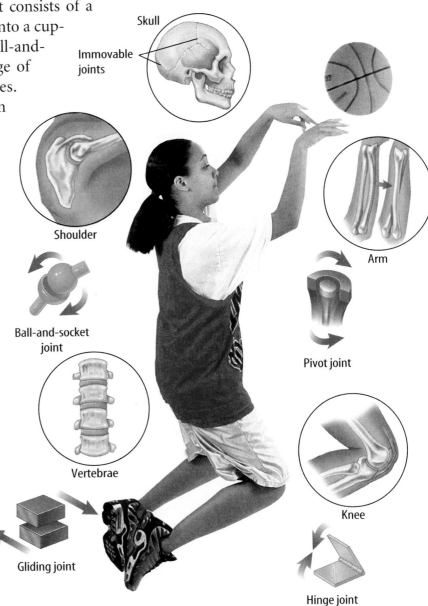

Skull

Immovable joints

Shoulder

Ball-and-socket joint

Vertebrae

Gliding joint

Arm

Pivot joint

Knee

Hinge joint

Immovable Joints Some joints are classified as immovable. An immovable joint allows little or no movement. It protects internal organs and provides a firm place for other bones to attach. The joints of the bones in your skull and pelvis are classified as immovable joints.

Your Body's Simple Machines—Levers

INTEGRATE Physics Your skeletal system and muscular system work together when you move, like a machine. A machine is any device that makes work easier. Some machines are called simple machines because they work with only one movement. One type of simple machine is a lever. It is a rod or plank that pivots or turns about a point called a fulcrum. Skeletal muscles, bones, and joints working together are like levers. In your body, bones are rods, and joints are fulcrums. Contracting and relaxing muscles provide the force to move body parts. Examples of levers found in the human body are shown in **Figure 11**.

section 3 review

Summary

Functions of Your Skeletal System

- The skeletal system includes all the bones in your body and is your body's framework.

Bone Structure

- Bones are living organs that need nutrients.
- Compact bone is hard and strong, and spongy bone is lightweight.
- Cartilage covers the ends of bones.

Bone Formation

- Bone-forming cells deposit calcium and phosphorus, making bone tissue hard.
- Healthy bone tissue is always being formed and reformed.

Joints

- Immovable joints allow little or no movement, and movable joints allow greater movement.
- Cartilage helps make joint movement easier.
- Your muscles, bones, and joints work together like levers to move your body.

Self Check

1. **List** the five major functions of the human skeletal system. `SC.F.1.3.4`
2. **Describe** and give an example of an immovable joint.
3. **Explain** the functions of cartilage in your skeletal system. `SC.F.1.3.4`
4. **Describe** ligaments and their function in the skeletal system. `SC.F.1.3.4`
5. **Think Critically** A thick band of bone forms around a broken bone as it heals. In time, the thickened band disappears. Explain how this extra bone material can disappear over time. `SC.F.1.3.3`

Applying Skills

6. **Make and Use Tables** Use a table to classify the bones of the human body as follows: *long, short, flat,* and *irregular.*
7. **Use graphics software** to make a graph that shows how an adult's bones are distributed: *29 skull bones, 26 vertebrae, 25 ribs, four shoulder bones, 60 arm and hand bones, two hip bones, and 60 leg and feet bones.*

Figure 11

All three types of levers—first class, second class, and third class—are found in the human body. In the photo below, a tennis player prepares to serve a ball. As shown in the accompanying diagrams, the tennis player's stance demonstrates the operation of all three classes of levers in the human body.

▲ Fulcrum
▼ Effort force
■ Load

FIRST-CLASS LEVER
The fulcrum lies between the effort force and the load. This happens when the tennis player uses his neck muscles to tilt his head back.

THIRD-CLASS LEVER
The effort force is between the fulcrum and the load. This happens when the tennis player flexes the muscles in his arm and shoulder.

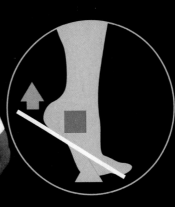

SECOND-CLASS LEVER
The load lies between the fulcrum and the effort force. This happens when the tennis player's calf muscles lift the weight of his body up on his toes.

section

4

Benchmarks—SC.F.1.3.1 Annually Assessed (pp. 110–111): The student understands that living things are composed of major systems that function in reproduction, growth, maintenance, and regulation; SC.F.1.3.7 (pp. 110, 113–117): The student knows that behavior is a response to the environment and influences growth, development, maintenance, and reproduction.

Also covers: SC.F.1.3.4 (pp. 111–112), SC.F.1.3.5 (p. 111), SC.F.1.3.6 (p. 111), SC.H.1.3.2 (p. 120), SC.H.1.3.4 Annually Assessed (pp. 118–119), SC.H.1.3.5 Annually Assessed (pp. 116, 118–119), SC.H.1.3.6 (p. 120), SC.H.2.3.1 (pp. 110–117)

The Nervous System

as you read

What You'll Learn

- **Describe** the basic structure of a neuron and how an impulse moves across a synapse.
- **Compare and contrast** the central and peripheral nervous systems.
- **List** the sensory receptors in each sense organ.
- **Explain** what type of stimulus each sense organ responds to and how.
- **Explain** how drugs affect the body.

Why It's Important

Your body reacts to your environment because of your nervous system.

Review Vocabulary

homeostasis: regulation of an organism's internal, life-maintaining conditions despite changes in its environment

New Vocabulary

- neuron
- synapse
- central nervous system
- peripheral nervous system

How the Nervous System Works

After doing the dishes and finishing your homework, you settle down in your favorite chair and pick up that mystery novel you've been trying to finish. Only three pages to go. . . Who did it? Why did she do it? Crash! You scream. What made that unearthly noise? You turn around to find that your dog's wagging tail has just swept the lamp off the table. Suddenly, you're aware that your heart is racing and your hands are shaking. After a few minutes, your breathing returns to normal and your heartbeat is back to its regular rate. What's going on?

Responding to Stimuli The scene described above is an example of how your body responds to changes in its environment. Any internal or external change that brings about a response is called a stimulus (STIHM yuh lus). Each day, you're bombarded by thousands of stimuli, like those shown in **Figure 12.** Noise, light, the smell of food, and the temperature of the air are all stimuli from outside your body. Chemical substances such as hormones are examples of stimuli from inside your body. Your body adjusts to changing stimuli with the help of your nervous system.

Figure 12 Stimuli are found everywhere and all the time, even when you're enjoying being with your friends.
List *the types of stimuli that are present at this party.*

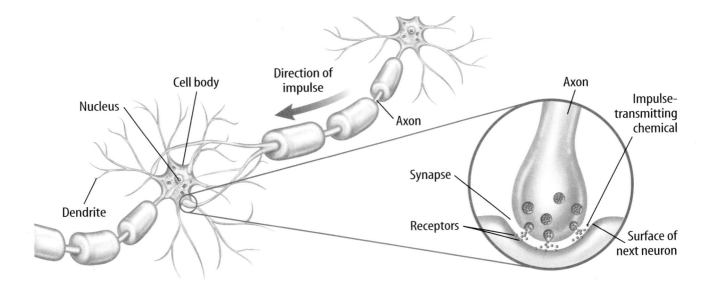

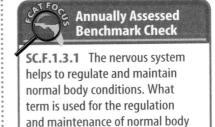

Homeostasis It's amazing how your body handles all these stimuli. Control systems maintain homeostasis. They keep steady, life-maintaining conditions inside your body, despite changes around or inside of you. Examples of homeostasis are the regulation of your breathing, heartbeat, and digestion. Your nervous system is one of several control systems used by your body to maintain homeostasis.

Nerve Cells

The basic working units of the nervous system are nerve cells, or **neurons** (NOO rahnz). As shown in **Figure 13,** a neuron is made up of a cell body, branches called dendrites, and axons (AK sahns). Any message carried by a neuron is called an impulse. Your neurons are adapted in such a way that impulses move in only one direction. Dendrites receive impulses from other neurons and send them to the cell body. Axons carry impulses away from the cell body. The end of the axon branches. This allows the impulses to move to many other muscles, neurons, or glands.

Three types of neurons—sensory neurons, motor neurons, and interneurons—transport impulses. Sensory neurons receive information and send impulses to the brain or spinal cord, where interneurons relay these impulses to motor neurons. Motor neurons then conduct impulses from the brain or spinal cord to muscles or glands throughout your body.

Synapses Neurons don't touch each other. As an impulse moves from one neuron to another it crosses a small space called a **synapse** (SIH naps). In **Figure 13,** note that when an impulse reaches the end of an axon, the axon releases a chemical. This chemical flows across the synapse and stimulates the impulse in the dendrite of the next neuron.

Figure 13 An impulse-transmitting chemical moves an impulse from an axon across a synapse. Receptors on the next neuron pick up the impulse.

Annually Assessed Benchmark Check

SC.F.1.3.1 The nervous system helps to regulate and maintain normal body conditions. What term is used for the regulation and maintenance of normal body conditions?

LA.B.2.3.1

Neuron Chemical
Acetylcholine (uh see tul KOH leen) is the chemical that carries an impulse across a synapse. After the impulse is started, acetylcholine breaks down rapidly. In your Science Journal, make an inference about why the rapid breakdown of acetylcholine is important.

The Divisions of the Nervous System

Figure 14 shows how organs of the nervous system are grouped into two major divisions—the central nervous system (CNS) and the peripheral (puh RIH fuh rul) nervous system (PNS). The **central nervous system** includes the brain and spinal cord. The brain is the control center for all activities in the body. It is made of billions of neurons. The spinal cord is made up of bundles of neurons. An adult's spinal cord is about the width of a thumb and about 43 cm long. Sensory neurons send impulses to the brain or spinal cord.

The Peripheral Nervous System All the nerves outside the CNS that connect the brain and spinal cord to other body parts are part of the **peripheral nervous system.** The PNS includes 12 pairs of nerves from your brain called cranial nerves, and 31 pairs of nerves from your spinal cord called spinal nerves. Spinal nerves are made up of bundles of sensory and motor neurons bound together by connective tissue. They carry impulses from all parts of the body to the brain and from the brain to all parts of your body. A single spinal nerve can have impulses going to and from the brain at the same time. Some nerves contain only sensory neurons, and some contain only motor neurons, but most nerves contain both types of neurons.

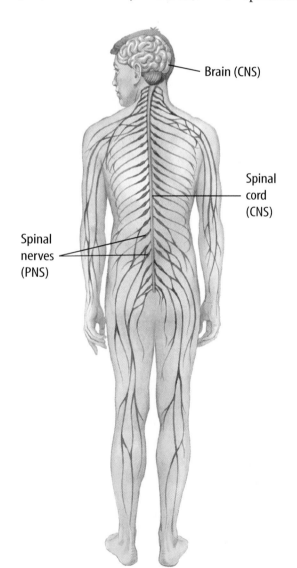

Figure 14 The brain and spinal cord (yellow) form the central nervous system (CNS). All other nerves (green) are part of the peripheral nervous system (PNS).

Brain (CNS)

Spinal cord (CNS)

Spinal nerves (PNS)

Safety and the Nervous System

Every mental process and physical action of the body involves structures of the central and peripheral nervous systems. Therefore, any injury to them can be serious. A severe blow to the head can bruise the brain and cause temporary or permanent loss of mental and physical abilities. For example, an injury to the back of the brain could result in the loss of vision.

Although the spinal cord is surrounded by the vertebrae of your spine, spinal cord injuries do occur. They can be just as dangerous as a brain injury. Injury to the spine can bring about damage to nerve pathways and result in paralysis (puh RAH luh suhs), which is the loss of muscle movement. Major causes of head and spinal injuries include automobile, motorcycle, and bicycle accidents, as well as sports injuries. Just like wearing seat belts in automobiles, it is important to wear the appropriate safety gear while playing sports and riding on bicycles and skateboards.

Reflexes You experience a reflex if you accidentally touch something sharp, something extremely hot or cold, or when you cough or vomit. A reflex is an involuntary, automatic response to a stimulus. You can't control reflexes because they occur before you know what has happened. A reflex involves a simple nerve pathway called a reflex arc, as illustrated in **Figure 15.**

A reflex allows the body to respond without having to think about what action to take. Reflex responses are controlled in your spinal cord, not in your brain. Your brain acts after the reflex to help you figure out what to do to make the pain stop.

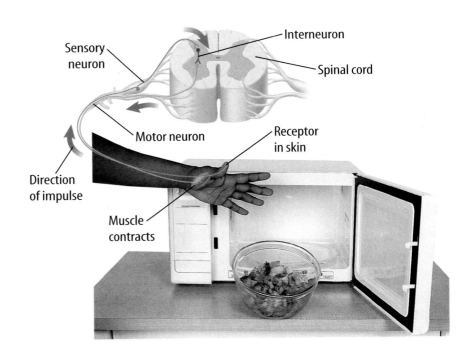

Sensory neuron — Interneuron — Spinal cord — Motor neuron — Receptor in skin — Direction of impulse — Muscle contracts

Figure 15 Your response in a reflex is controlled in your spinal cord, not your brain.

 **Reading Check** *Why are reflexes important?*

The Senses

Sense organs are adapted for intercepting stimuli, such as light rays, sound waves, heat, chemicals, or pressure, and converting them into impulses for the nervous system. Your skin and internal organs have sensory receptors that respond to touch, pressure, pain, and temperature and transmit impulses to the brain or spinal cord. In turn, your body responds to this new information. All of your body's senses work together to maintain homeostasis.

Smell How can you smell your favorite food? You can smell food because molecules from the food move into the air. If they enter your nasal passages, these molecules stimulate sensitive nerve cells, called olfactory (ohl FAK tree) cells. Olfactory cells are kept moist by mucus. When molecules in the air dissolve in this moisture, the cells become stimulated. If enough molecules are present, an impulse starts in these cells, then travels to the brain where the stimulus is interpreted. If the stimulus is recognized from a previous experience, you can identify the odor. If you don't recognize a particular odor, it is remembered and may be identified the next time you encounter it.

LA.B.2.3.1

LA.B.2.3.4

Science nline

Topic: Nervous System
Visit fl6.msscience.com for Web links to information about the nervous system.

Activity Make a brochure outlining recent medical advances.

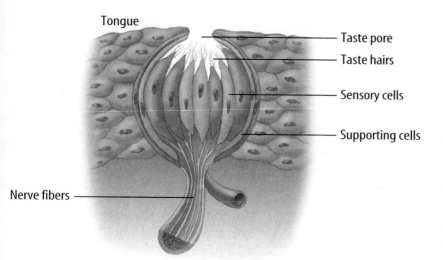

Tongue

Taste pore

Taste hairs

Sensory cells

Supporting cells

Nerve fibers

Figure 16 Taste buds are made up of a group of sensory cells with tiny taste hairs projecting from them. Food dissolved in saliva stimulates receptor sites on the taste hairs, and an impulse is sent to the brain.

Taste A taste bud, as shown in **Figure 16,** responds to chemical stimuli. In order to taste something, it has to be dissolved in water. Saliva begins this process. When a solution of saliva and food washes over taste buds, impulses are sent to your brain. The brain interprets the impulses, and you identify the tastes.

Sometimes when you taste a new food with the tip of your tongue, it tastes sweet. Then when you chew it, it tastes bitter. About 10,000 taste buds all over your tongue enable you to tell one taste from another. Most taste buds respond to several taste sensations. However, certain areas of the tongue are more receptive to one taste than another. The five taste sensations are sweet, salty, sour, bitter, and the taste of MSG (monosodium glutamate).

Reading Check *What needs to happen to food before you are able to taste it?*

Smell and Taste The sense of smell is needed to identify some foods such as chocolate. When saliva in your mouth mixes with chocolate, odors travel up the nasal passage in the back of your throat. Olfactory cells in the nose are stimulated, and the taste and smell of chocolate are sensed. When you have a stuffy nose, foods can seem tasteless because the food's molecules are blocked from contacting the olfactory cells in your nasal passages.

Vision The eye, shown in **Figure 17,** is a sense organ. Your eyes have unique adaptations that usually enable you to see shapes of objects, shadows, and color. It's amazing that at one glance you might see the words on this page, the color illustrations, and your classmate sitting next to you.

How do you see? Light travels in a straight line unless something causes it to refract or change direction. Your eyes have structures that refract light. Two of these structures are the cornea and the lens. As light enters the eye, it passes through the transparent cornea and is refracted. Then light passes through a lens and is refracted again. The lens directs the light onto the retina (RET nuh). It is a tissue at the back of the eye that is sensitive to light energy. Two types of cells called rods and cones are found in the retina. Cones respond to bright light and color. Rods respond to dim light. They are used to help you detect shape and movement.

Images Light energy stimulates impulses in rods and cones. These impulses pass to the optic nerve and are carried to the vision area of the brain. The image sent to the brain is upside down and reversed. The brain interprets the image correctly, and you see what you are looking at. The brain also interprets the images received by both eyes. It blends them into one image, and you can tell how close or how far away something is.

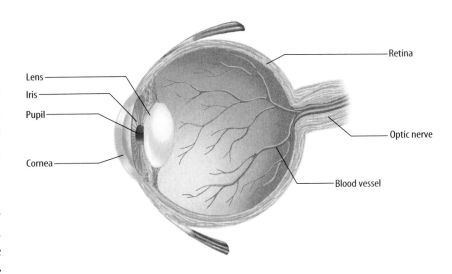

Figure 17 Light moves through the cornea and the lens—before striking the retina.
Name *the structures that enable you to see light.*

Hearing Whether it's the roar of a rocket launch or the song of a robin in a tree, sound waves are necessary for hearing. When an object vibrates, sound waves are produced. Sound waves can travel through solids, liquids, and gases. When sound waves reach your ear, they usually stimulate nerve cells deep within your ear. These cells send impulses to the brain. When the sound impulse reaches the hearing area of the brain, it responds and you hear a sound.

Figure 18 shows the parts of your ear. Your outer ear intercepts sound waves and funnels them down the ear canal to the middle ear. The sound waves cause the eardrum to vibrate much like the membrane on a musical drum vibrates when you tap it. These vibrations then move through three tiny bones called the hammer, anvil, and stirrup. The stirrup bone rests against a second membrane on an opening to the inner ear.

The inner ear includes the cochlea (KOH klee uh) and the semicircular canals. When the stirrup vibrates the membrane to the inner ear, fluids in the cochlea begin to vibrate. This bends sensory hair cells in the cochlea and causes impulses to be sent by a nerve to the brain. What you hear depends on how the nerve endings are stimulated.

Figure 18 Your ear responds to sound waves and to changes in the position of your head.

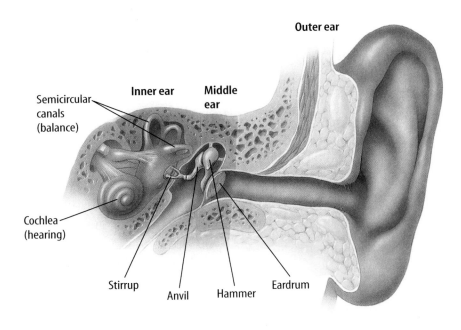

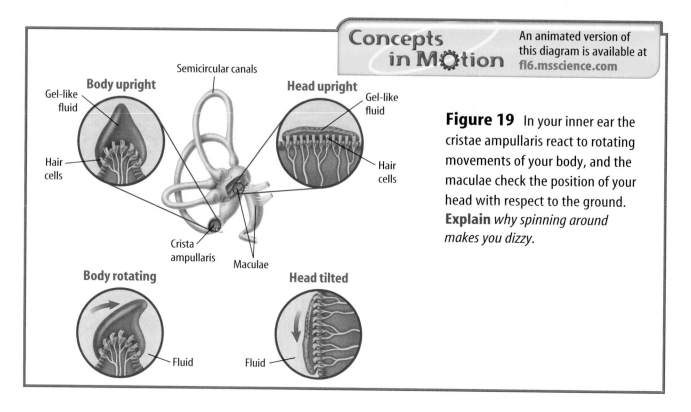

Concepts in Motion
An animated version of this diagram is available at fl6.msscience.com

Figure 19 In your inner ear the cristae ampullaris react to rotating movements of your body, and the maculae check the position of your head with respect to the ground. **Explain** *why spinning around makes you dizzy.*

Mini LAB

Observing Balance Control

Procedure
1. Place two narrow strips of **paper** on the wall to form two parallel, vertical lines 20–25 cm apart. Have a person stand between them for 3 min, without leaning on the wall.
2. Observe how well balance is maintained.
3. Have the person close his or her eyes, then stand within the lines for 3 min.

Analysis
1. When was balance more difficult to maintain? Why?
2. What other factors might cause a person to lose his or her sense of balance?

Try at Home

Balance Structures in your inner ear also control your body's balance. Structures called the cristae ampullaris (KRIHS tee • am pyew LEER ihs) and the maculae (MA kyah lee), illustrated in **Figure 19,** sense body movement. The cristae ampullaris react to rotating body movements, and the maculae respond to the tilt of your head. Both structures contain tiny hair cells. As your body moves, gel-like fluid surrounding the hair cells moves and stimulates the nerve cells at the base of the hair cells. This produces nerve impulses that are sent to the brain, which interprets the body movements. The brain, in turn, sends impulses to skeletal muscles, resulting in other body movements that maintain balance.

Reading Check *What produces nerve impulses that interpret body movement?*

Drugs Affect the Nervous System

Many drugs, such as alcohol and caffeine, directly affect your nervous system. When swallowed, alcohol directly passes into cells of the stomach and small intestine then into the circulatory system. After it is in the circulatory system, it can travel throughout your body. Upon reaching neurons, alcohol moves through their cell membranes and disrupts their normal cell functions. As a result, this drug slows the activities of the central nervous system and is classified as a depressant. Muscle control, judgment, reasoning, memory, and concentration also are impaired. Heavy alcohol use destroys brain and liver cells.

Stimulants Any substance that speeds up the activity of the central nervous system is called a stimulant. Caffeine is a stimulant found in coffee, tea, cocoa, and many soft drinks, like those shown in **Figure 20.** Too much caffeine can increase heart rate and aggravates restlessness, tremors, and insomnia in some people. It also can stimulate the kidneys to produce more urine.

Do you remember reading at the beginning of this section about being frightened after a lamp was broken? Think again about that scare. The organs of your nervous system control and coordinate responses to maintain homeostasis within your body. This task might be more difficult when your body must cope with the effects of drugs.

Figure 20 Caffeine, a substance found in colas, coffee, chocolate, and some teas, can cause excitability and sleeplessness.

section 4 review

Summary

How the Nervous System Works

- The nervous system responds to stimuli to maintain homeostasis.

Nerve Cells

- Neurons are the basic functioning units of the nervous system.
- To move from one neuron to another, an impulse crosses a synapse.

The Divisions of the Nervous System

- The central nervous system (CNS) includes the brain and spinal cord.
- The peripheral nervous system (PNS) includes all nerves outside the CNS.

Safety and the Nervous System

- Reflex responses are automatic and are controlled by the spinal cord.

The Senses

- Sense organs respond to stimuli and work together to maintain homeostasis.

Drugs Affect the Nervous System

- Drugs can slow or stimulate your nervous system.

Self Check

1. **Draw and label** the parts of a neuron and describe the function of each part. SC.F.1.3.2
2. **Name** the sensory receptors for the eyes, ears, and nose. SC.F.1.3.4
3. **Discuss** how the central and peripheral nervous systems work together. SC.F.1.3.1
4. **Explain** why you have trouble falling asleep after drinking several cups of hot cocoa. SC.F.1.3.7
5. **Identify** the role of saliva in tasting.
6. **Explain** why it is important to have sensory receptors for pain and pressure in your internal organs.
7. **Think Critically** Explain why many medications caution the consumer not to operate heavy machinery. SC.F.1.3.7

Applying Skills

8. **Communicate** Write a paragraph in your Science Journal that describes what each of the following objects would feel like: ice cube, snake, silk blouse, sandpaper, jelly, and smooth rock.
9. **Make and Use Tables** Organize the information on senses in a table that names the sense organs and which stimuli they respond to.

Benchmark—**SC.H.1.3.4:** The student knows that accurate record keeping, ... maintaining an investigator's credibility with other scientists and society; **SC.H.1.3.5:** The student knows that a change in one or more variables may alter the outcome of an investigation; **SC.H.1.3.7:** The student knows ... investigations give different results, ... verify whether the differences are significant by further study.

Design Your Own

Skin Sensitivity

Inquiry

Goals

■ **Observe** the sensitivity to touch on specific areas of the body.

■ **Design** an experiment that tests the effects of a variable, such as how close the contact points are, to determine which body areas can distinguish which stimuli are closest to one another.

Possible Materials

3-in × 5-in index card
toothpicks
tape
*glue
metric ruler
*Alternate materials

Safety Precautions

Complete a safety worksheet before you begin. **WARNING:** *Do not apply heavy pressure when touching the toothpicks to the skin of your classmates.*

◉ Real-World Problem

Your body responds to touch, pressure, temperature, and other stimuli. Not all parts of your body are equally sensitive to stimuli. Some areas are more sensitive than others are. For example, your lips are sensitive to heat. This protects you from burning your mouth and tongue. Now think about touch. How sensitive to touch is the skin on various parts of your body ? Which areas can distinguish the smallest amount of distance between stimuli?

◉ Form a Hypothesis

Based on your experiences, state a hypothesis about which of the following five areas of the body—fingertip, forearm, back of the neck, palm, and back of the hand—you believe to be most sensitive. Rank the areas from 5 (the most sensitive) to 1 (the least sensitive).

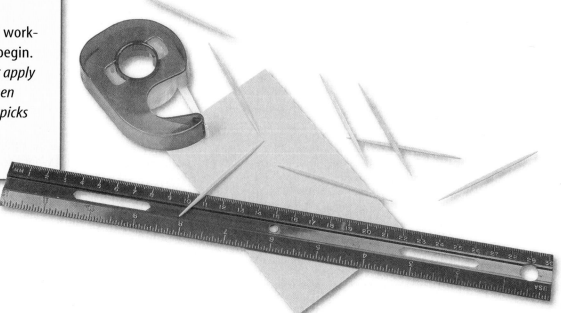

⊙ Test Your Hypothesis

Make a Plan

1. As a group, agree upon and write the hypothesis statement.

2. As a group, list the steps you need to test your hypothesis. Describe exactly what you will do at each step. Consider the following as you list the steps. How will you know that sight is not a factor? How will you use the card shown on the right to determine sensitivity to touch? How will you determine that one or both points are sensed?

3. Design a data table in your Science Journal to record your observations.

4. Reread your entire experiment to make sure that all steps are in the correct order.

5. Identify constants, variables, and controls of the experiment.

Follow Your Plan

1. Make sure your teacher approves your plan before you start.

2. Carry out the experiment as planned.

3. While the experiment is going on, write down any observations that you make and complete the data table in your Science Journal.

⊙ Analyze Your Data

1. **Identify** which part of the body tested can distinguish between the closest stimuli.

2. **Compare** your results with those of other groups.

3. Rank body parts tested from most to least sensitive. Did your results from this investigation support your hypothesis? Explain.

⊙ Conclude and Apply

1. **Infer** Based on the results of your investigation, what can you infer about the distribution of touch receptors on the skin?

2. **Predict** what other parts of your body would be less sensitive? Explain your predictions.

Communicating
Your Data

Write a report to share with your class about body parts of animals that are sensitive to touch.

First Aid Dolls

A fashion doll helps improve the lives of people

A fashion doll is doing her part for medical science! It turns out that the plastic joints that make it possible for one type of doll's legs to bend make good joints in prosthetic (artificial) fingers for humans.

Jane Bahor works at Duke University Medical Center in Durham, North Carolina. She makes lifelike body parts for people who have lost legs, arms, or fingers. A few years ago, she met a patient named Jennifer Jordan, an engineering student who'd lost a finger. The artificial finger that Bahor made looked real, but it couldn't bend. She and Jordan began to discuss the problem.

The engineer went home and borrowed one of her sister's dolls. Returning with it to Bahor's office, she and Bahor operated on the fashion doll's legs and removed the knee joints.

"It turns out that the doll's knee joints flexed the same way that human finger joints do," says Bahor. "We could see that using these joints would allow patients more use and flexibility with their 'new' fingers." Because these new prosthetic fingers can bend, the wearers can hold a pen, pick up a cup, or grab a steering wheel.

Bahor called the company that makes the fashion doll and shared the surprising discovery. The toymaker was so impressed that Bahor now has a ten-year supply of plastic knee joints—free of charge! But supplies come from other sources, too. "A Girl Scout troop in New Jersey just sent me a big box of donated dolls for the cause," reports Bahor. "It's really great to have kids' support in this effort."

Invent Choose a "problem" you can solve. Need a better place to store your notebooks in your locker, for instance? Use what Bahor calls "commonly found materials" to solve the problem. Then, make a model or a drawing of the problem-solving device.

Oops! For more information, visit fl6.msscience.com

Reviewing Main Ideas

Section 1 The Skin

1. The epidermis produces melanin. Cells at the base of the epidermis produce new skin cells. The dermis contains nerves, sweat and oil glands, and blood vessels.

2. The skin protects the body, reduces water loss, produces vitamin D, and helps to maintain body temperature.

3. Severe skin damage can lead to infection and death if left untreated.

Section 2 The Muscular System

1. Skeletal muscle is voluntary and moves bones. Smooth muscle is involuntary and controls movement of internal organs. Cardiac muscle is involuntary and located only in the heart.

2. Muscles only can contract. When one skeletal muscle contracts, the other relaxes.

Section 3 The Skeletal System

1. Bones are living structures that protect, support, make blood, store minerals, and provide for muscle attachment.

2. Joints are either movable or immovable.

Section 4 The Nervous System

1. The nervous system responds to stimuli to maintain homeostasis.

2. A neuron is the basic unit of structure and function of the nervous system.

3. A reflex is an automatic response.

4. The central nervous system is the brain and spinal cord. The peripheral nervous system includes cranial and spinal nerves.

5. Your senses enable you to react to your environment.

6. Many drugs affect your nervous system.

Visualizing Main Ideas

Copy and complete the following concept map on body movement.

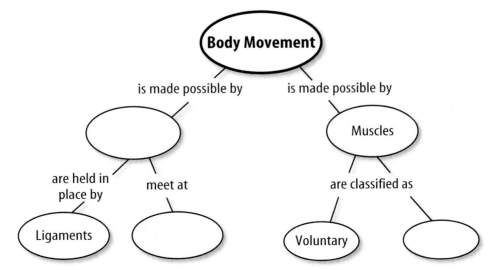

Using Vocabulary

cartilage p. 105	melanin p. 97
central nervous system p. 112	neuron p. 111
	periosteum p. 105
dermis p. 96	peripheral nervous system p. 112
epidermis p. 96	
involuntary muscle p. 101	synapse p. 111
joint p. 106	tendon p. 102
ligament p. 106	voluntary muscle p. 101

Match the definitions with the correct vocabulary word.

1. outer layer of skin

2. thick band of tissue that attaches a muscle to a bone

3. a muscle that you control

4. basic working unit of the nervous system

5. small space across which an impulse moves

6. tough outer covering of bone

7. a tough band of tissue that holds two bones together

Checking Concepts

Choose the word or phrase that best answers the question.

8. Where are blood cells made? SC.F.1.3.3
   A) compact bone **C)** cartilage
   B) periosteum **D)** marrow

9. What covers the ends of bones?
   A) cartilage **C)** ligaments
   B) tendons **D)** muscle

10. Where are human immovable joints found?
    A) at the elbow **C)** in the wrist
    B) at the neck **D)** in the skull

11. Which vitamin is made in the skin?
    A) A **C)** D
    B) B **D)** K

12. Which structure helps retain fluids in the body? SC.F.1.3.1
    A) bone **C)** skin
    B) muscle **D)** joint

13. How do impulses cross synapses between neurons?
    A) by osmosis
    B) through interneurons
    C) through a cell body
    D) by a chemical

14. What are the neurons called that detect stimuli in the skin and eyes? SC.F.1.3.7
    A) interneurons **C)** motor neurons
    B) synapses **D)** sensory neurons

15. Which is part of the central nervous system? SC.F.1.3.4
    A) brain **C)** cranial nerves
    B) motor neuron **D)** sensory neuron

16. What part of the eye is light finally focused on?
    A) lens **C)** pupil
    B) retina **D)** cornea

17. Which is in the inner ear?
    A) anvil **C)** eardrum
    B) hammer **D)** cochlea

Use the illustration below to answer question 18.

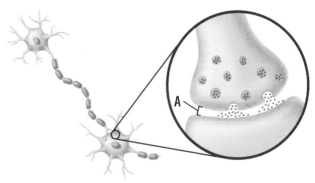

18. What is the name given to A?
    A) axon **C)** synapse
    B) dendrite **D)** nucleus

Thinking Critically

19. **Infer** why an infant's skull joints are flexible, but those of a teenager have fused together and are immovable.

20. **Predict** what would happen if a person's sweat glands didn't produce sweat. `SC.F.1.3.1`

21. **Compare and contrast** the functions of ligaments and tendons. `SC.F.1.3.4`

22. **Form a Hypothesis** Your body has about 3 million sweat glands. Make a hypothesis about where these sweat glands are on your body. Are they distributed evenly throughout your body?

23. **Draw Conclusions** If an impulse traveled down one neuron but failed to move on to the next neuron, what might you conclude about the first neuron? `SC.F.1.3.5`

24. **Concept Map** Copy and complete this events-chain concept map to show the correct sequence of the structures through which light passes in the eye.

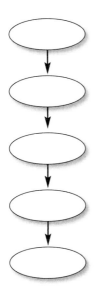

25. **List** what factors a doctor might consider before choosing a method of skin repair for a severe burn victim. `SC.F.1.3.3`

26. **Explain** why skin might not be able to produce enough vitamin D.

Performance Activities

27. **Illustrate** While walking on a sandy beach, a pain suddenly shoots through your foot. You look down and see that you stepped on the sharp edge of a broken shell. Draw and label the reflex arc that results from this stimulus. `SC.F.1.3.7`

Applying Math

Use the graph below to answer question 28.

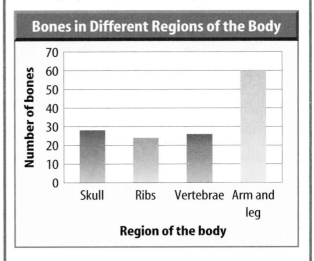

Bones in Different Regions of the Body

28. **Bone Tally** The total number of bones in the human body is 206. Calculate the percentage of bones in an arm and a leg.

29. **Skull Bones** The skull contains 28 bones. Fifty percent are part of the face. How many bones make up the face?

30. **Fireworks** You see the flash of fireworks and then four seconds later, you hear the boom. Light travels so fast that you see far away things instantaneously. Sound, on the other hand, travels at 340 m/s. How far away are you from the fireworks?

 The assessed Florida Benchmark appears above each question.
Record your answers on the answer sheet provided by your teacher or on a sheet of paper.

Multiple Choice

SC.F.1.3.1

1 The diagram below shows several types of joints.

Ball-and-socket joint

Pivot joint

Gliding joint

Hinge joint

Which type of joint connects an arm to the shoulder?

A. ball-and-socket

B. gliding

C. hinge

D. pivot

SC.F.1.3.1

2 The skin contains many blood vessels and sweat glands. What function do these structures help the skin perform?

F. defending against agents of disease

G. preventing the body from drying out

H. regulating body temperature

I. storing excess nutrients

SC.F.1.3.6

3 What is the **most** important difference between striated muscle and smooth muscle?

A. Their cells contain different materials.

B. Their cells have different shapes.

C. They have different sizes of cells.

D. They have different functions.

SC.F.1.3.6

4 A neuron's dendrites receive information, and the axon transmits nerve impulses. The following diagram shows the shape of an axon.

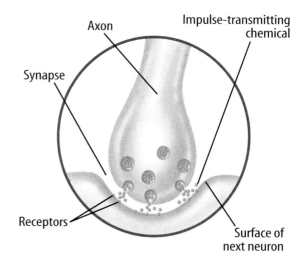

How does an axon's structure help it to perform its function?

F. It enables it to receive information from a large number of cells.

G. It enables it to receive messages directly without going between other neurons.

H. It enables it to transmit messages to one area at a time.

I. It enables it to transmit messages to several areas at the same time.

5 The iris of the eye has tiny muscles that enable the widening and narrowing of the pupil. Which is **most** likely the function of the iris of the eye?

A. It blends images to create a sense of distance.

B. It controls the amount of light entering the eye.

C. It receives information from the light that enters the eye.

D. It transmits images to the brain.

Gridded Response

6 In Florida, the legal blood-alcohol level is 0.08 percent for adults and only 0.02 percent for underage drivers. The table below shows how body weight and the number of alcoholic drinks affect the blood-alcohol level of adult men.

Approximate Blood-Alcohol Percentage for Men								
Drinks	**Body Weight in Kilograms**							
	45.4	**54.4**	**63.5**	**72.6**	**81.6**	**90.7**	**99.8**	**108.9**
1	0.04	0.03	0.03	0.02	0.02	0.02	0.02	0.02
2	0.08	0.06	0.05	0.05	0.04	0.04	0.03	0.03
3	0.11	0.09	0.08	0.07	0.06	0.06	0.05	0.05
4	0.15	0.12	0.11	0.09	0.08	0.08	0.07	0.06
5	0.19	0.16	0.13	0.12	0.11	0.09	0.09	0.08

Subtract 0.01% for each 40 min of drinking. One drink is 40 mL of 80-proof liquor, 355 mL of beer, or 148 mL of table wine.

What will be the approximate blood-alcohol level of a 54-kg (120-lb) man after having three drinks?

Short Response

7 A reflex is an automatic response to information from the environment. Reflexes happen very quickly because they do not go through the brain. How is this adaptation of value to humans?

Extended Response

8 Jake is testing the effect of listening to different types of music on the ability to complete mathematical problems. He has made the table below to organize the data from his investigation.

The Effects of Music Type on Math Ability			
Music Type	**Volume (decibels)**	**Task**	**Time to Finish Correctly (minutes)**
Classical	50	5 long-division problems	
R & B	65	5 long-division problems	
Top 40	70	5 long-division problems	
Rap	80	5 long-division problems	

PART A Are all of the variables controlled in Jake's investigation? Explain your answer.

PART B What affect might this have on the results of Jake's experiment?

FCAT Tip

Keep Your Cool Stay focused during the test and don't rush, even if you notice that other students are finishing the test early.

chapter

5

Sunshine State Standards—SC.F.1: The student describes patterns of structure and function in living things.

Digestion, Respiration, and Excretion

Playing soccer is hard work.

If you're like most people, when you play an active game like soccer you probably breathe hard and perspire. You need a constant supply of oxygen and energy to keep your body cells functioning. Your body is adapted to meet that need.

Science Journal Write a paragraph describing what you do to help your body recover after an active game.

Start-Up Activities

 SC.H.1.3.5

Breathing Rate

Your body can store food and water, but it cannot store much oxygen. Breathing brings oxygen into your body. In the following lab, find out about one factor that can change your breathing rate.

1. Complete a safety worksheet.
2. Put your hand on the side of your rib cage. Using a watch or clock with a second hand, count the number of breaths you take for 15 s. Multiply this number by four to calculate your normal breathing rate for one minute.
3. Repeat step 1 two more times, then calculate your average breathing rate.
4. Do a physical activity described by your teacher for one minute and repeat step 1 to determine your breathing rate now.
5. Time how long it takes for your breathing rate to return to normal.
6. **Think Critically** In your Science Journal, write a paragraph explaining how breathing rate appears to be related to physical activity.

Respiration Make the following Foldable to help identify what you already know, what you want to know, and what you learn about respiration.

LA.A.1.3.4

STEP 1 Fold a vertical sheet of paper from side to side. Make the front edge about 1.25 cm shorter than the back edge.

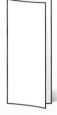

STEP 2 Turn lengthwise and fold into thirds.

STEP 3 Unfold and cut only the top layer along both folds to make three tabs. Label each tab.

Know   Want   Learn

Identify Questions Before you read the chapter, write *I breathe* under the left tab, and write *Why do I breathe?* under the center tab. As you read the chapter, write the answer you learn under the right tab.

Preview this chapter's content and activities at fl6.msscience.com

Benchmarks—SC.F.1.3.1 Annually Assessed (pp. 128–132): The student understands that living things are composed of major systems that function in reproduction, growth, maintenance, and regulation.

Also covers: SC.H.2.3.1 (pp. 128–132)

The Digestive System

as you read

What **You'll Learn**

- **Distinguish** the differences between mechanical digestion and chemical digestion.
- **Identify** the organs of the digestive system and what takes place in each.
- **Explain** how homeostasis is maintained in digestion.

Why **It's Important**

The processes of the digestive system make the food you eat available to your cells.

Review Vocabulary

bacteria: one-celled organisms without membrane-bound organelles

New Vocabulary

- nutrient
- enzyme
- peristalsis
- chyme
- villi

Functions of the Digestive System

Food is processed in your body in four stages—ingestion, digestion, absorption, and elimination. Whether it is a piece of fruit or an entire meal, all the food you eat is treated to the same processes in your body. As soon as food enters your mouth, or is ingested, digestion begins. Digestion breaks down food so that nutrients (NEW tree unts) can be absorbed and moved into blood. **Nutrients** are substances in food that provide energy and materials for cell development, growth, and repair. From blood, these nutrients can move through a cell membrane to be used by a cell. Unused substances pass out of your body as wastes.

Digestion is mechanical and chemical. Mechanical digestion takes place when food is chewed, mixed, and churned. Chemical digestion occurs when chemical reactions break down food.

Enzymes

Chemical digestion is possible only because of enzymes (EN zimez). An **enzyme** is a type of protein that speeds up the rate of a chemical reaction in your body. One way enzymes speed up reactions is by reducing the amount of energy necessary for a chemical reaction to begin. If enzymes weren't there to help, the rate of chemical reactions would be too slow. Some reactions might not even happen at all. As shown in **Figure 1,** enzymes work without being changed or used up.

Figure 1 Enzymes speed up the rate of certain body reactions.

Explain *what happens to the enzyme after it separates from the new molecule.*

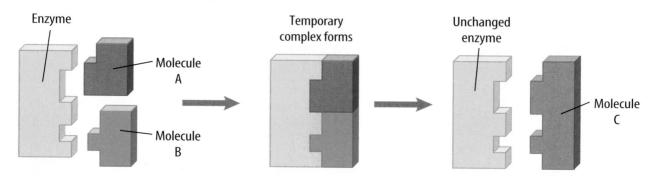

Enzyme · Molecule A · Molecule B · Temporary complex forms · Unchanged enzyme · Molecule C

Enzymes in Digestion Many enzymes help you digest the food that you eat. These enzymes are produced in some of the organs of your digestive system.

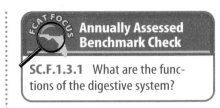
Annually Assessed Benchmark Check

SC.F.1.3.1 What are the functions of the digestive system?

 **Reading Check** *What is the role of enzymes in the chemical digestion of food?*

Other Enzyme Actions Enzyme-aided reactions are not limited to the digestive process. Enzymes also help speed up chemical reactions responsible for building your body. They are involved in the energy-releasing activities of your muscle and nerve cells. Enzymes also help the blood-clotting process. Without enzymes, the chemical reactions in your body would happen too slowly for you to exist.

Organs of the Digestive System

Your digestive system has two parts—the digestive tract and the accessory organs. The major organs of your digestive tract—mouth, esophagus (ih SAH fuh gus), stomach, small intestine, large intestine, rectum, and anus—are shown in **Figure 2.** Food passes through all of these organs. The tongue, teeth, salivary glands, liver, gallbladder, and pancreas, also shown in **Figure 2,** are the accessory organs. Although food doesn't pass through them, they are important in mechanical and chemical digestion. Your liver, gallbladder, and pancreas produce or store enzymes and other chemicals that help break down food as it passes through the digestive tract.

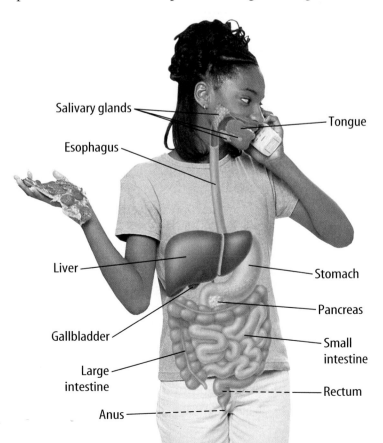

Figure 2 The human digestive system can be described as a tube divided into several specialized sections. If stretched out, an adult's digestive system is 6 m to 9 m long.

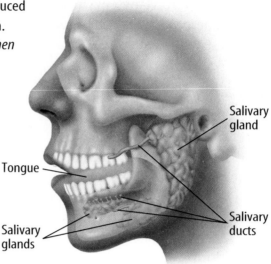

Figure 3 About 1.5 L of saliva are produced each day by salivary glands in your mouth. **Describe** *what happens in your mouth when you think about a food you like.*

Salivary gland

Tongue

Salivary glands

Salivary ducts

The Mouth Mechanical and chemical digestion begin in your mouth. Mechanical digestion happens when you chew your food with your teeth and mix it with your tongue. Chemical digestion begins with the addition of a watery substance called saliva (suh LI vuh), which contains water, mucus, and an enzyme that helps break down starch into sugar. Saliva is produced by three sets of glands near your mouth, shown in **Figure 3.** Food mixed with saliva becomes a soft mass and is moved to the back of your mouth by your tongue. It is swallowed and passes into your esophagus. Now ingestion is complete, but the process of digestion continues.

The Esophagus Food moving into the esophagus passes over a flap of tissue called the epiglottis (eh puh GLAH tus). This structure automatically covers the opening to the windpipe to prevent food from entering it, otherwise you would choke. Your esophagus is a muscular tube about 25 cm long. No digestion takes place in the esophagus. Smooth muscles in the wall of the esophagus move food downward with a squeezing action. These waves of muscle contractions, called **peristalsis** (per uh STAHL sus), move food through the entire digestive tract. Secretions from the mucous glands in the wall of the esophagus keep food moist.

The Stomach The stomach is a muscular bag. When empty, it is somewhat sausage shaped with folds on the inside. As food enters from the esophagus, the stomach expands and the folds smooth out. Mechanical and chemical digestion take place here. Mechanically, food is mixed in the stomach by peristalsis. Chemically, food is mixed with enzymes and strong digestive solutions, such as hydrochloric acid solution, to help break it down.

Specialized cells in the stomach's walls release about two liters of hydrochloric acid solution each day. This solution, with the enzyme pepsin, digests protein, such as meat, and destroys bacteria that are present in food. The stomach also produces mucus, which makes food more slippery and protects the stomach from the strong, digestive solutions. Food is changed in the stomach into a thin, watery liquid called **chyme** (KIME). Slowly, chyme moves out of your stomach and into your small intestine.

Reading Check *Why isn't your stomach digested by the acidic digestive solution?*

The Small Intestine Your small intestine, shown in **Figure 4,** is small in diameter, but it measures 4 m to 7 m in length. As chyme leaves your stomach, it enters the first part of your small intestine, called the duodenum (doo AH duh num). Most digestion takes place in your duodenum. Here, bile—a greenish fluid from the liver—is added. The acidic solution from the stomach makes large fat particles float to the top of the chyme. Bile breaks up the large fat particles, similar to the way detergent breaks up grease.

Chemical digestion of food occurs when a digestive solution from the pancreas is mixed in. This solution contains enzymes and chemicals that help neutralize the stomach acid that is mixed with chyme. Your pancreas also makes insulin that allows glucose to pass from the bloodstream into your cells.

Absorption of broken down food takes place in the small intestine. The wall of the small intestine, as shown in **Figure 4,** has many ridges and folds. These folds are covered with finger-like projections called **villi** (VIH li). Villi increase the surface area of the small intestine, which allows more places for nutrients to be absorbed. Nutrients move into blood vessels within the villi. From here, blood transports the nutrients to all cells of your body. Peristalsis continues to force the remaining undigested and unabsorbed materials slowly into the large intestine.

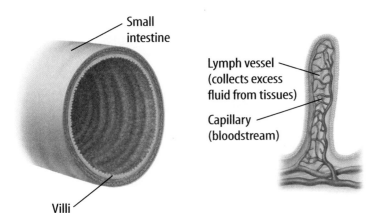

Small intestine

Lymph vessel (collects excess fluid from tissues)

Capillary (bloodstream)

Villi

Figure 4 Hundreds of thousands of densely packed villi give the impression of a velvet cloth surface. If the surface area of your villi could be stretched out, it would cover an area the size of a tennis court.
Infer *what would happen to a person's weight if the number of villi were drastically reduced. Why?*

Large Intestine Bacteria
The species of bacteria that live in your large intestine are adapted to their habitat. What do you think would happen to the bacteria if their environment were to change? How would this affect your large intestine? Discuss your ideas with a classmate and write your answers in your Science Journal.

The Large Intestine When the chyme enters the large intestine, it is still a thin, watery mixture. The large intestine absorbs water from the undigested mass, which helps maintain homeostasis (hoh mee oh STAY sus). Peristalsis usually slows down in the large intestine. After the excess water is absorbed, the remaining undigested materials become more solid. Muscles in the rectum, which is the last section of the large intestine, and the anus control the release of semisolid wastes from the body in the form of feces (FEE seez).

Bacteria Are Important

Many types of bacteria live in your body. Some bacteria live in many of the organs of your digestive tract including your mouth and large intestine. Some of these bacteria live in a relationship that is beneficial to the bacteria and to your body. The bacteria in your large intestine feed on some undigested material and make vitamins you need—vitamin K and two B vitamins. Vitamin K is needed for blood clotting. The two B vitamins, niacin and thiamine, are important for your nervous system and for other body functions. Bacterial action also converts bile pigments into new compounds. The breakdown of intestinal materials by bacteria produces gas.

section 1 review

Summary

Functions of the Digestive System

- Food is processed in four stages—ingestion, digestion, absorption, and elimination.

Enzymes

- Enzymes make chemical digestion possible.
- Enzymes are used in other chemical reactions, including blood clotting.

Organs of the Digestive System

- In the digestive system, food passes through the mouth, esophagus, stomach, small intestine, large intestine, rectum, and anus.
- Accessory digestive organs help in mechanical and chemical digestion.

Bacteria Are Important

- Some bacteria that live in the organs of the digestive tract are helpful to your body.

Self Check

1. **Compare and contrast** mechanical digestion and chemical digestion.

2. **Describe** the function of each organ through which food passes as it moves through the digestive tract. SC.F.1.3.1

3. **Explain** how activities in the large intestine help maintain homeostasis. SC.F.1.3.1

4. **Describe** how the accessory organs help digestion.

5. **Think Critically** Crackers contain starch. Explain why a cracker begins to taste sweet after it is in your mouth for five minutes without being chewed.

Applying Skills

6. **Recognize Cause and Effect** What would happen to some of the nutrients in chyme if the pancreas did not secrete its solution into the small intestine?

7. **Communicate** Write a paragraph in your Science Journal explaining what would happen to the mechanical and chemical digestion in a person missing a large portion of his or her stomach.

section 2

Nutrition

Why do you eat?

You might choose a food because of its taste, because it's readily available, or quickly prepared. However, as much as you don't want to admit it, the nutritional value of and Calories in foods are more important. A Calorie is a measurement of the amount of energy available in food. The amount of food energy a person requires varies with activity level, body weight, age, sex, and natural body efficiency. A chocolate donut might be tasty, quick to eat, and provide plenty of Calories, but it has only some of the nutrients that your body needs.

Classes of Nutrients

Six kinds of nutrients are available in food—proteins, carbohydrates, fats, vitamins, minerals, and water. Proteins, carbohydrates, vitamins, and fats all contain carbon and are called organic nutrients. Inorganic nutrients, such as water and minerals, do not contain carbon. Foods containing carbohydrates, fats, and proteins need to be digested or broken down before your body can use them. Water, vitamins, and minerals don't require digestion and are absorbed directly into your bloodstream.

Proteins Your body uses proteins for replacement and repair of body cells and for growth. Proteins are large molecules that contain carbon, hydrogen, oxygen, nitrogen, and sometimes sulfur. A molecule of protein is made up of a large number of smaller units, or building blocks, called **amino acids.** You can see some sources of proteins in **Figure 5.**

Figure 5 Meats, poultry, eggs, fish, peas, beans, and nuts are all rich in protein.

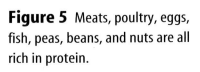

LA.B.2.3.4

Science nline

Topic: Fiber
Visit fl6.msscience.com for Web links to recent news or magazine articles about the importance of fiber in your diet.

Activity In your Science Journal, classify your favorite foods into two groups—*Good source of fiber* and *Little or no fiber.*

Protein Building Blocks Your body needs only 20 amino acids in various combinations to make the thousands of proteins used in your cells. Most of these amino acids can be made in your body's cells, but eight of them cannot. These eight are called essential amino acids. They have to be supplied by the foods you eat. Complete proteins provide all of the essential amino acids. Eggs, milk, cheese, and meat contain complete proteins. Incomplete proteins are missing one or more of the essential amino acids. If you are a vegetarian, you can get all of the essential amino acids by eating a wide variety of protein-rich vegetables, fruits, and grains.

Carbohydrates Study the nutrition label on several boxes of cereal. You'll notice that the number of grams of carbohydrates found in a typical serving of cereal is higher than the amounts of the other nutrients. **Carbohydrates** (kar boh HI drayts) usually are the main sources of energy for your body.

Three types of carbohydrates are sugar, starch, and fiber. Sugars are called simple carbohydrates. You're probably most familiar with table sugar. However, fruits, honey, and milk also contain forms of sugar. Your cells break down glucose, a simple sugar.

The other two types of carbohydrates—starch and fiber— are called complex carbohydrates. Starch is found in potatoes and foods made from grains such as pasta. Starches are made up of many simple sugars. Fiber, such as cellulose, is found in the cell walls of plant cells. Foods like whole-grain breads and cereals, beans, peas, and other vegetables and fruits, like those in **Figure 6,** are good sources of fiber. Because different types of fiber are found in foods, you should eat a variety of fiber-rich plant foods. You cannot digest fiber, but it is needed to keep your digestive system running smoothly.

Fats The term *fat* has developed a negative meaning for some people. However, fats, also called lipids, are necessary because they provide energy and help your body absorb vitamins. Fat tissue cushions your internal organs. A major part of every cell membrane is made up of a type of fat.

Figure 6 These foods contain carbohydrates that provide energy for all the things that you do. **Describe** *the role of carbohydrates in your body.*

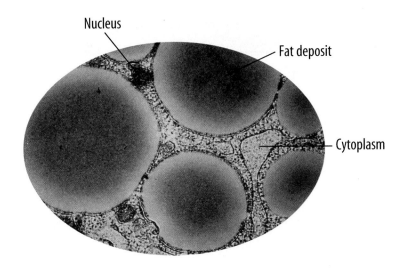

Nucleus

Fat deposit

Cytoplasm

Figure 7 Fat deposits in certain cells push the cytoplasm and nucleus to the edge of the cell.

A gram of fat can release more than twice as much energy as a gram of carbohydrate can. Excess energy from the foods you eat is converted to fat and stored in certain cells for later use, as shown in **Figure 7.**

Reading Check *Why is fat a good storage unit for energy?*

Fats are classified as unsaturated or saturated based on their chemical structure. Unsaturated fats are usually liquid at room temperature. Vegetable oils as well as fats found in seeds are unsaturated fats. Saturated fats are found in meats, animal products, and some plants and are usually solid at room temperature. Saturated fats have been associated with high levels of blood cholesterol. However, your body makes cholesterol in your liver. Cholesterol is part of the cell membrane in all of your cells. But, a diet high in cholesterol may result in deposits forming on the inside walls of blood vessels. These deposits can block the blood supply to organs and increase blood pressure. This can lead to heart disease and strokes.

Vitamins Your bone cells need vitamin D to use calcium, and your blood needs vitamin K in order to clot. **Vitamins** are organic nutrients needed in small quantities for growth, regulating body functions, and preventing some diseases.

Vitamins are classified into two groups. Some vitamins dissolve easily in water and are called water-soluble vitamins. They are not stored by your body so you have to consume them daily. Other vitamins dissolve only in fat and are called fat-soluble vitamins. These vitamins are stored by your body. Although you eat or drink most vitamins, some are made by your body. Vitamin D is made when your skin is exposed to sunlight. Recall that vitamin K and two of the B vitamins are made in your large intestine with the help of bacteria that live there.

SC.H.1.3.5

Comparing the Fat Content of Foods

Procedure

1. Complete a safety worksheet.
2. Collect three pieces of each of the following foods: **potato chips, pretzels, peanuts,** and **small cubes of fruits, cheese, vegetables,** and **meat.**
3. Place the food items on a piece of **brown grocery bag.** Label the paper with the name of each food. Do not taste the foods.
4. Allow foods to sit for 30 min.
5. Remove the items, properly dispose of them, and observe the paper.

Analysis

1. Which items left a translucent (greasy) mark? Which left a wet mark?
2. How are the foods that left a greasy mark on the paper alike?
3. Use this test to determine which other foods contain fats.

Table 1 Minerals		
Mineral	**Health Effect**	**Food Sources**
Calcium	strong bones and teeth, blood clotting, muscle and nerve activity	dairy products, eggs, green leafy vegetables, soy
Phosphorus	strong bones and teeth, muscle contraction, stores energy	cheese, meat, cereal
Potassium	balance of water in cells, nerve impulse conduction, muscle contraction	bananas, potatoes, nuts, meat, oranges
Sodium	fluid balance in tissues, nerve impulse conduction	meat, milk, cheese, salt, beets, carrots, nearly all foods
Iron	oxygen is transported in hemoglobin by red blood cells	red meat, raisins, beans, spinach, eggs
Iodine (trace)	thyroid activity, metabolic stimulation	seafood, iodized salt

Minerals Inorganic nutrients—nutrients that lack carbon and regulate many chemical reactions in your body—are called **minerals.** Of about 14 minerals that your body uses, calcium and phosphorus are used in the largest amounts for a variety of body functions. One of these functions is the formation and maintenance of bone. Some minerals, called trace minerals, are required only in small amounts. Copper and iodine usually are listed as trace minerals. Minerals are not used by the body as a source of energy. However, they do serve many different functions. Several minerals, their health effects, and some food sources for them are listed in **Table 1.**

Reading Check *Why is copper considered a trace mineral?*

Water Next to oxygen, water is the most important factor for survival. Different organisms need different amounts of water to survive. You could live for a few weeks without food but for only a few days without water because your cells need water to carry out their work. Most of the nutrients you have studied in this chapter can't be used by your body unless they are carried in a solution. This means that they have to be dissolved in water. In cells, chemical reactions take place in solutions.

LA.A.2.3.5

INTEGRATE
Social Studies

Salt Mines The mineral halite is processed to make table salt. In the United States, most salt comes from underground mines. Research to find the location of these mines, then label them on a map.

The human body is about 60 percent water by mass. About two-thirds of your body water is located in your body cells. Water also is found around cells and in body fluids such as blood. **Table 2** shows how your body loses water every day. To replace water lost each day, you need to drink about 2 L of liquids. However, drinking liquids isn't the only way to supply cells with water. Most foods have more water than you realize. An apple is about 80 percent water, and many meats are 90 percent water.

Why do you get thirsty? Your body is made up of systems that operate together. When your body needs to replace lost water, messages are sent to your brain that result in a feeling of thirst. Drinking water satisfies your thirst and usually restores the body's homeostasis. When homeostasis is restored, the signal to the brain stops and you no longer feel thirsty.

Food Groups

Because no naturally occurring food has every nutrient, you need to eat a variety of foods. Nutritionists have developed a simple system, called the food pyramid, shown in **Figure 8,** to help people select foods that supply all the nutrients needed for energy and growth. The recommended daily amount for each food group will supply your body with the nutrients it needs for good health.

Table 2 Water Loss	
Method of Loss	**Amount (mL/day)**
Exhaled air	350
Feces	150
Skin (mostly as sweat)	500
Urine	1,500

Figure 8 The pyramid shape reminds you that you should consume more servings from the bread and cereal group than from other groups.
Analyze *Where should the least number of servings come from?*

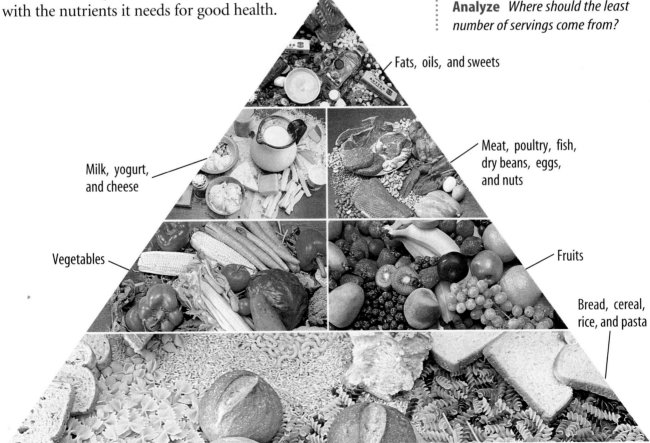

Fats, oils, and sweets

Milk, yogurt, and cheese

Meat, poultry, fish, dry beans, eggs, and nuts

Vegetables

Fruits

Bread, cereal, rice, and pasta

Figure 9 The information on a food label can help you decide what to eat.

Nutrition Facts
Serving Size 1 Meal

Amount Per Serving

Calories 330	Calories from Fat 60

% Daily Value*

Total Fat 7g	**10%**
Saturated Fat 3.5g	**17%**
Polyunsaturated Fat 1g	
Monounsaturated Fat 2.5g	
Cholesterol 35mg	**12%**
Sodium 460mg	**19%**
Total Carbohydrate 52g	**18%**
Dietary Fiber 6g	**24%**
Sugars 17g	
Protein 15g	

Vitamin A 15%	•	Vitamin C 70%	
Calcium 4%	•	Iron 10%	

* Percent Daily Values are based on a 2,000 calorie diet. Your daily values may be higher or lower depending on your calorie needs.

		Calories	2,000	2,500
Total Fat	Less than		65g	80g
Sat Fat	Less than		20g	25g
Cholesterol	Less than		300mg	300mg
Sodium	Less than		2,400mg	2,400mg
Total Carbohydrate			300g	375g
Dietary Fiber			25g	30g

Daily Servings Depending on your Calorie needs, each day you should eat six to eleven servings from the bread and cereal group, three to five servings from the vegetable group, two to four servings from the fruit group, two to three servings from the milk group, and two to three servings from the meat and beans group. Only small amounts of fats, oils, and sweets should be consumed.

The size of a serving is different for different foods. For example, a slice of bread or one ounce of ready-to-eat cereal is a bread and cereal group serving. One cup of raw leafy vegetables or one-half cup of cooked or chopped raw vegetables is a serving from the vegetable group. One medium apple, banana, or orange, one-half cup of canned fruit, or three-quarter cup of fruit juice is a fruit serving. A serving from the milk group can be one cup of milk or yogurt. Two ounces of cooked lean meat, one-half cup of cooked dry beans, one egg, or two tablespoons of peanut butter counts as a meat and beans group serving.

Food Labels The nutritional facts on all packaged foods make it easier to make healthful food choices. These labels, like the one in **Figure 9,** can help you plan meals that supply the daily recommended amounts of nutrients and meet special dietary requirements (for example, a low-fat diet).

section 2 review

Summary

Why do you eat?

- Nutrients in food provide energy and materials for cell development, growth, and repair.

Classes of Nutrients

- Six kinds of nutrients are found in food—proteins, carbohydrates, fats, vitamins, minerals, and water.

- Proteins are used for growth and repair, carbohydrates provide energy, and fats store energy and cushion organs.

- Vitamins and minerals regulate body functions.

- Next to oxygen, water is the most important factor for your survival.

Food Groups

- The food pyramid and nutritional labels can help you choose foods that supply all the nutrients you need for energy and growth.

Self Check

1. **List** one example of a food source for each of the six classes of nutrients.
2. **Explain** how your body uses each class of nutrients.
3. **Discuss** how food choices can positively and negatively affect your health.
4. **Explain** the importance of water in the body.
5. **Think Critically** What foods from each food group would provide a balanced breakfast? Explain.

Applying Skills

6. **Interpret Data** Nutritional information can be found on the labels of most foods. Interpret the labels found on three different types of food products.

7. **Use a Spreadsheet** Make a spreadsheet of the minerals listed in **Table 1.** Use reference books to gather information about minerals and add these to the table: *sulfur, magnesium, copper, manganese, cobalt,* and *zinc.*

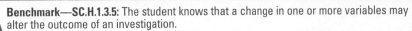

Nutrients in Food

Different foods contain different nutrients. It's important to eat a variety of foods to get the nutrients needed to maintain your health. Remember that there's truth in the saying "You are what you eat."

▶ Real-World Problem

What nutrients are in foods?

Goals

■ **Analyze** common foods for presence of nutrients.

■ **Infer** which tested food is a good source of energy.

Materials

water	1-cm³ pieces of apple (2)
skim milk	1-cm³ pieces of bread (2)
droppers (2)	1-cm³ pieces of cheese (2)
stirring rods (3)	10-mL graduated cylinder
test tubes (5)	brown paper
test-tube rack	iodine in dropper bottle

Safety Precautions

Complete a safety worksheet before you begin.

WARNING: *Iodine is toxic. It can irritate skin and stain skin and clothing.*

▶ Procedure

1. Copy the data table below into your Science Journal.

2. Using a pencil, mark five 3-cm × 3-cm areas on the brown paper and label them *Water, Bread, Apple, Milk,* and *Cheese.*

3. Rub the apple, cheese, and bread onto their areas. Place five drops of water and five drops of milk onto their areas. Allow the paper to dry as you complete this lab.

4. Place the apple, bread, cheese, 1 mL of water, and 1 mL of milk in five different test tubes. Place each test tube in the test-tube rack. Rinse the graduated cylinder.

5. Add 1 mL water to the apple, bread, and cheese test tubes. Use a different stirring rod to mix each test tube's contents.

6. Add two drops of iodine to each test tube. Iodine turns blue-black in the presence of starch. Record your results in the data table.

7. Observe the brown paper after it dries. A shiny, translucent area indicates the presence of fat. Record your results in the data table.

▶ Conclude and Apply

1. Which foods contain starch? Fat?

2. Infer the purpose in this lab of the water area on the brown paper and water test tube?

3. Which food contains the most energy? How do you know?

4. If you were on a low-carbohydrate diet, which tested food(s) could you eat?

Communicating Your Data

How many daily servings of the tested foods should be eaten? Create a menu for a meal that includes the tested food items.

Nutrient Data					
Nutrient	Water	Apple	Milk	Bread	Cheese
Starch yes or no					
Fat yes or no					

section 3

Also covers: SC.F.1.3.4 (p. 141), SC.F.1.3.5 (pp. 140, 143), SC.G.1.3.1 Annually Assessed (p. 145)

The Respiratory System

as you read

What You'll Learn

- **Describe** the functions of the respiratory system.
- **Explain** how oxygen and carbon dioxide are exchanged in the lungs and in tissues.
- **Identify** the pathway of air in and out of the lungs.
- **Explain** the effects of smoking on the respiratory system.

Why It's Important

Your body's cells depend on your respiratory system to supply oxygen and remove carbon dioxide.

Review Vocabulary

diaphragm: muscle beneath the lungs that contracts and relaxes to move gases in and out of the body

New Vocabulary

- larynx
- bronchi
- trachea
- alveoli

Functions of the Respiratory System

Can you imagine an astronaut walking on the Moon without a space suit or a diver exploring the ocean without scuba gear? Of course not. They couldn't survive in either location under those conditions because humans need to breathe air.

People often confuse the terms *breathing* and *respiration*. Breathing is the movement of the chest that brings air into the lungs and removes waste gases. The air entering the lungs contains oxygen. It passes from the lungs into the circulatory system because there is less oxygen in blood when it enters the lungs than in cells of the lungs.

Blood carries oxygen and glucose from digested food to individual cells. The oxygen delivered to the cells is used to release energy from glucose. This chemical reaction is called cellular respiration. Without oxygen, this reaction would not take place. Carbon dioxide and water molecules are waste products of cellular respiration. They are carried back to the lungs in the blood. Exhaling, or breathing out, eliminates waste carbon dioxide and some water molecules as shown in **Figure 10**.

✓ **Reading Check** *What is cellular respiration?*

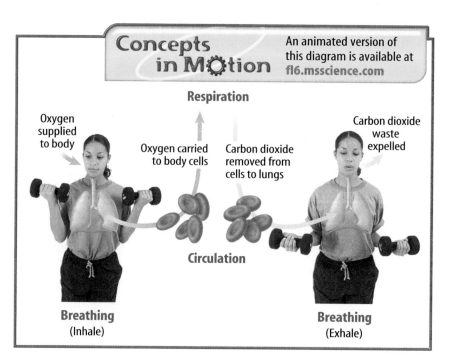

Concepts in Motion An animated version of this diagram is available at fl6.msscience.com

Figure 10 Several processes are involved in how the body obtains, transports, and uses oxygen.

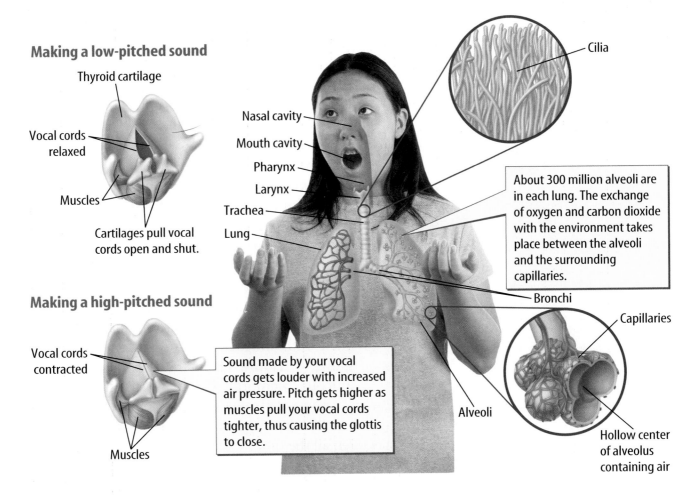

Making a low-pitched sound

Thyroid cartilage

Vocal cords relaxed

Muscles

Cartilages pull vocal cords open and shut.

Making a high-pitched sound

Vocal cords contracted

Muscles

Cilia

Nasal cavity
Mouth cavity
Pharynx
Larynx
Trachea
Lung

About 300 million alveoli are in each lung. The exchange of oxygen and carbon dioxide with the environment takes place between the alveoli and the surrounding capillaries.

Sound made by your vocal cords gets louder with increased air pressure. Pitch gets higher as muscles pull your vocal cords tighter, thus causing the glottis to close.

Bronchi

Capillaries

Alveoli

Hollow center of alveolus containing air

Figure 11 Air can enter the body through the nostrils and the mouth.

Explain *an advantage of having air enter through the nostrils.*

Organs of the Respiratory System

The respiratory system, as shown in **Figure 11,** is made up of structures and organs that help move oxygen into the body and waste gases out of the body. Air enters your body through two openings in your nose called nostrils or through the mouth. Fine hairs inside the nostrils trap particles from the air. Air then passes through the nasal cavity, where it gets moistened and warmed by the body's heat. Glands that produce sticky mucus line the nasal cavity. The mucus traps particles that were not trapped by nasal hairs. This process helps filter and clean the air you breathe. Tiny, hairlike structures, called cilia (SIH lee uh), sweep mucus and trapped material to the back of the throat where it can be swallowed.

.**Pharynx** Warmed, moist air then enters the pharynx (FER ingks), which is a tubelike passageway for food, liquids, and air. At the lower end of the pharynx is the epiglottis. When you swallow, your epiglottis folds down, which allows food or liquids to enter your esophagus instead of your airway. What do you think has happened if you begin to choke?

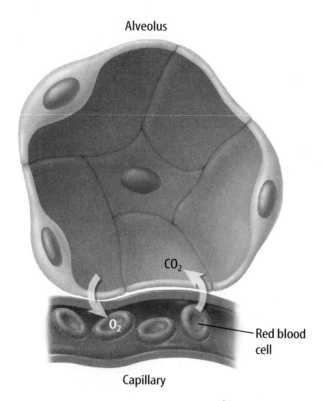

Alveolus

CO₂

O₂

Red blood cell

Capillary

Figure 12 The thin capillary walls allow gases to be exchanged easily between the alveoli and the capillaries.
Name *the two gases that are exchanged by the capillaries and alveoli.*

Larynx and Trachea Next, the air moves into your larynx (LER ingks). The **larynx** is the airway to which two pairs of horizontal folds of tissue, called vocal cords, are attached, as shown in **Figure 11** on the previous page. Forcing air between the cords causes them to vibrate and produce sounds. When you speak, muscles tighten or loosen your vocal cords, resulting in different sounds. Your brain coordinates the movement of the muscles in your throat, tongue, cheeks, and lips when you talk, sing, or just make noise. Your teeth also are involved in forming letter sounds and words.

From the larynx, air moves into the **trachea** (TRAY kee uh). Strong, C-shaped rings of cartilage prevent the trachea from collapsing. It is lined with mucous membranes and cilia, also shown in **Figure 11** on the previous page. The mucous membranes trap dust, bacteria, and pollen. The cilia move the mucus upward, where it is either swallowed or expelled from the nose or mouth. Why must the trachea stay open all the time?

Bronchi and the Lungs Air is carried into your lungs by two short tubes called **bronchi** (BRAHN ki) (singular, *bronchus*) at the lower end of the trachea. Within the lungs, the bronchi branch into smaller and smaller tubes. The smallest tubes are called bronchioles (BRAHN kee ohlz). At the end of each bronchiole are clusters of tiny, thin-walled sacs called **alveoli** (al VEE uh li) (singular, *alveolus*). Air passes into the bronchi, then into the bronchioles, and finally into the alveoli. Lungs are masses of alveoli, like the one shown in **Figure 12,** arranged in grapelike clusters. The capillaries surround the alveoli like a net.

The exchange of oxygen and carbon dioxide takes place between the alveoli and capillaries. The walls of the alveoli and capillaries are only one cell thick, as shown in **Figure 12.** Oxygen moves through the cell membranes of alveoli and through cell membranes of the capillaries into the blood. In blood, oxygen is picked up by hemoglobin (HEE muh gloh bun), a molecule in red blood cells, and carried to all body cells. At the same time, carbon dioxide and other cellular wastes leave the body cells and move into capillaries. Then they are carried by the blood to the lungs. In the lungs, waste gases move through cell membranes from capillaries into alveoli. Then waste gases leave the body when you exhale.

Why do you breathe?

Signals from your brain tell the muscles in your chest and abdomen to contract and relax. You don't have to think about breathing to breathe, just like your heart beats without you telling it to beat. Your brain can change your breathing rate depending on the amount of carbon dioxide present in your blood. If a lot of carbon dioxide is present, your breathing rate increases. It decreases if less carbon dioxide is in your blood. You do have some control over your breathing—you can hold your breath if you want to. Eventually, your brain will respond to the buildup of carbon dioxide in your blood and signal your chest and abdomen muscles to work automatically. You will breathe whether you want to or not.

Inhaling and Exhaling Breathing is partly the result of changes in volume and resulting air pressure. Under normal conditions, a gas moves from an area of higher pressure to an area of lower pressure. When you squeeze an empty, soft-plastic bottle, air is pushed out. This happens because air pressure outside the top of the bottle is less than the pressure you create inside the bottle when you changed its volume. As you release your grip on the bottle, the air pressure inside the bottle becomes less than it is outside the bottle because the bottle's volume changed. Air rushes back in, and the bottle returns to its original shape.

Your lungs work in a way similar to the squeezed bottle. Your diaphragm (DI uh fram) contracts and relaxes, changing the volume of the chest, which helps move gases into and out of your lungs. **Figure 13** illustrates breathing.

> ✔ **Reading Check** *How does your diaphragm help you breathe?*

When a person's airway is blocked, a rescuer can use abdominal thrusts, as shown in **Figure 14,** to save the life of the choking victim.

SC.H.1.3.4

Mini LAB

Comparing Surface Area

Procedure 🐊
1. Stand a **bathroom-tissue cardboard tube** in an **empty bowl.**
2. Fill the tube with **marbles** of equal size. Count the marbles used.
3. Repeat step 2 two more times. Calculate the average number of marbles needed to fill the tube.
4. Each marble has a surface area of approximately 8.06 cm². Calculate the surface area of the average number of marbles.

Analysis
1. Compare the inside surface area of the tube (approximately 161.29 cm²) with the surface area calculated in Step 4.
2. If the tube represents a bronchus, what do the marbles represent?
3. Using this model, explain what makes gas exchange in the lungs efficient.

Try at Home

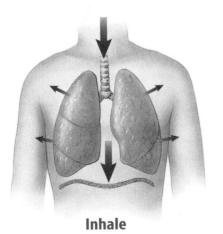

Inhale

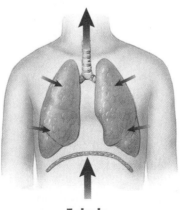

Exhale

Figure 13 Your lungs inhale and exhale about 500 mL of air with an average breath. This can increase to 2,000 mL of air per breath when you do strenuous activity.

NATIONAL GEOGRAPHIC

VISUALIZING ABDOMINAL THRUSTS

Figure 14

When food or other objects become lodged in the trachea, airflow between the lungs and the mouth and nasal cavity is blocked. Death can occur in minutes. However, prompt action by someone can save the life of a choking victim. The rescuer uses abdominal thrusts to force the victim's diaphragm up. This decreases the volume of the chest cavity and forces air up in the trachea. The result is a rush of air that dislodges and expels the food or other object. The victim can breathe again. This technique is shown at right and should only be performed in emergency situations.

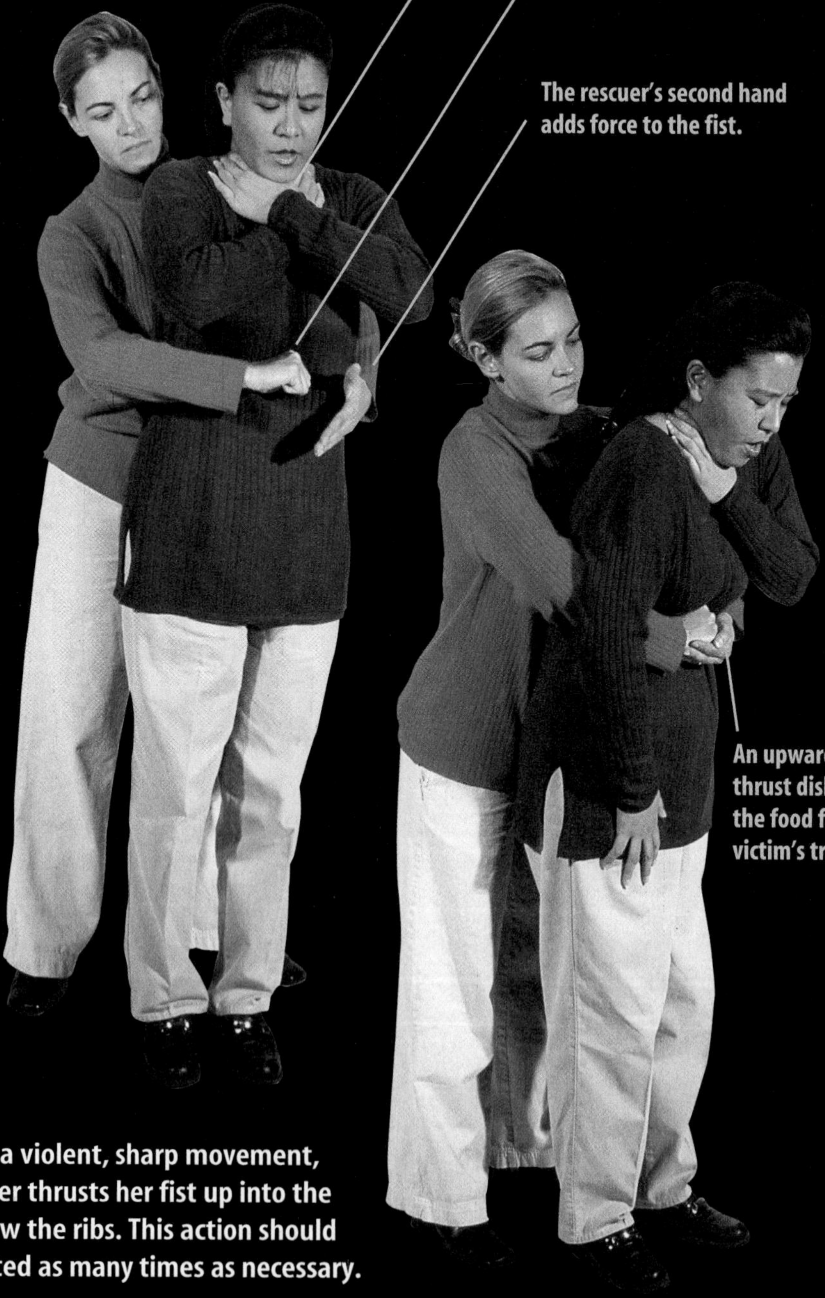

Food is lodged in the victim's trachea.

The rescuer places her fist against the victim's stomach.

The rescuer's second hand adds force to the fist.

An upward thrust dislodges the food from victim's trachea.

A The rescuer stands behind the choking victim and wraps her arms around the victim's upper abdomen. She places a fist (thumb side in) against the victim's stomach. The fist should be below the ribs and above the navel.

B With a violent, sharp movement, the rescuer thrusts her fist up into the area below the ribs. This action should be repeated as many times as necessary.

Diseases and Disorders of the Respiratory System

Table 3 Smokers' Risk of Death from Disease

Disease	Smokers' Risk Compared to Nonsmokers' Risk
Lung cancer	23 times higher for males; 11 times higher for females
Chronic bronchitis and emphysema	5 times higher
Heart disease	2 times higher

INTEGRATE Health If you were asked to make a list of some things that can harm your respiratory system, you probably would put smoking at the top. As you can see in **Table 3,** many serious diseases are related to smoking. The chemical substances in tobacco—nicotine and tars—are poisons and can destroy cells. The high temperatures, smoke, and carbon monoxide produced when tobacco burns also can injure a smoker's cells. Even if you are a nonsmoker, inhaling smoke from tobacco products—called secondhand smoke—is unhealthy and has the potential to harm your respiratory system. Smoking, polluted air, coal dust, and asbestos (as BES tus) have been related to respiratory problems such as asthma (AZ muh), bronchitis (brahn KI tus), emphysema (em fuh SEE muh), and cancer.

Respiratory Infections Bacteria and other micro-organisms and viruses can cause infections that affect any of the organs of the respiratory system. The common cold usually affects the upper part of the respiratory system—from the nose to the pharynx. The cold virus also can cause irritation and swelling in the larynx, trachea, and bronchi. The cilia that line the trachea and bronchi can be damaged. However, cilia usually heal rapidly.

Chronic Bronchitis When bronchial tubes are irritated and swell and too much mucus is produced, a disease called bronchitis develops. Many cases of bronchitis clear up within a few weeks, but the disease sometimes lasts for a long time. When this happens, it is called chronic (KRAH nihk) bronchitis.

Emphysema A disease in which the alveoli in the lungs enlarge is called emphysema. When cells in the alveoli are reddened and swollen, an enzyme is released that causes the walls of the alveoli to break down. As a result, alveoli can't push air out of the lungs, so less oxygen moves into the bloodstream from the alveoli. When blood becomes low in oxygen and high in carbon dioxide, shortness of breath occurs.

LA.B.2.3.1

Science Online

Topic: Secondhand Smoke
Visit fl6.msscience.com for Web links to information about the health aspects of secondhand smoke.

Activity Write a paragraph in your Science Journal summarizing the possible effects of secondhand smoke on your health.

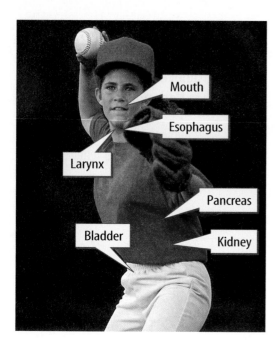

Lung Cancer The third leading cause of death in men and women in the United States is lung cancer. Inhaling the tar in cigarette smoke is the greatest contributing factor to lung cancer. In the body, tar and other ingredients found in smoke act as carcinogens (kar SIH nuh junz). Carcinogens are substances that can cause an uncontrolled growth of cells. In the lungs, this is called lung cancer. Lung cancer is not easy to detect in its early stages. As indicated in **Figure 15,** smoking also has been linked to the development of cancers of the mouth, esophagus, larynx, pancreas, kidney, and bladder.

Figure 15 More than 85 percent of all lung cancer is related to smoking. Smoking also can play a part in the development of cancer in other body organs indicated above.

Asthma Shortness of breath, wheezing, or coughing can occur in a lung disorder called asthma. When a person has an asthma attack, the bronchial tubes contract quickly. Inhaling medicine that relaxes the bronchial tubes is the usual treatment for an asthma attack. Asthma can be an allergic reaction. An allergic reaction occurs when the body overreacts to a foreign substance. An asthma attack can result from breathing certain substances such as cigarette smoke or certain plant pollen, eating certain foods, or stress in a person's life.

section 3 review

Summary

Functions of the Respiratory System

- Breathing moves the chest to bring air into and remove wastes from the lungs.
- Cellular respiration uses oxygen and releases energy from glucose.

Organs of the Respiratory System

- Air flows from your nostrils or mouth through the pharynx, larynx, trachea, bronchi, and into the alveoli of your lungs.
- Alveoli and capillaries exchange oxygen and carbon dioxide.

Why do you breathe?

- Your brain sends signals to your chest and abdominal muscles to contract and relax, which controls breathing rate.

Diseases of the Respiratory System

- Problems of the respiratory system include chronic bronchitis, emphysema, and lung cancer.

Self Check

1. **State** the main function of the respiratory system. `SC.F.1.3.1`
2. **Describe** the exchange of oxygen, carbon dioxide, and other waste gases in the lungs and body tissues. `SC.F.1.3.4`
3. **Explain** how air moves into and out of the lungs.
4. **Describe** the effects of smoking on the respiratory and circulatory systems.
5. **Think Critically** How is the work of the digestive and circulatory systems related to the respiratory system? `SC.H.2.3.1`

Applying Skills

6. **Research Information** Nicotine in tobacco is a poison. Using library references, find out how nicotine affects the body.
7. **Communicate** Use references to find out about lung disease common among coal miners, stonecutters, and sandblasters. Find out what safety measures are required now for these trades. In your Science Journal, write a paragraph about these safety measures.

More Section Review fl6.msscience.com

Benchmarks—SC.F.1.3.1 Annually Assessed (pp. 147–149): The student understands that living things are composed of major systems that function in reproduction, growth, maintenance, and regulation.

section

4

Also covers: SC.F.1.3.4 (p. 148), SC.H.1.3.5 Annually Assessed (pp. 152–153), SC.H.1.3.6 (p. 154), SC.H.3.3.5 (p. 154), SC.H.2.3.1 (pp. 147–149)

The Excretory System

Functions of the Excretory System

It's your turn to take out the trash. You carry the bag outside and put it in the trash can. The next day, you bring out another bag of trash, but the trash can is full. When trash isn't collected, it piles up. Just as trash needs to be removed from your home to keep it livable, your body must eliminate wastes to remain healthy. Undigested material is eliminated by your large intestine. Waste gases are eliminated through the combined efforts of your circulatory and respiratory systems. Some salts are eliminated when you sweat. These systems function together as parts of your excretory system. If wastes aren't eliminated, toxic substances can build up and damage organs. If not corrected, serious illness or death occurs.

The Urinary System

Figure 16 shows the role of the urinary system in the excretory system. The urinary system rids the blood of liquid wastes produced by the cells. It controls blood volume by removing excess water produced by body cells as a result of cellular respiration. The urinary system also balances the amounts of certain salts and water that must be present in cells for all cellular activities.

as you read

What You'll Learn

- **Distinguish** between the excretory and urinary systems.
- **Describe** how the kidneys work.
- **Explain** what happens when urinary organs don't work.

Why It's Important

The urinary system helps clean your blood of cellular wastes.

Review Vocabulary
capillary: blood vessel that connects arteries and veins

New Vocabulary
- nephron
- bladder
- ureter

Figure 16 The urinary, digestive, and respiratory systems, and the skin, make up the excretory system.

Digestive System
Food and liquid in

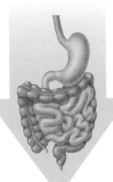

Water and
undigested food out

Respiratory System
Oxygen in

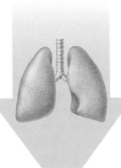

Carbon dioxide
and water out

Skin

Salt and some
organic substances out

Urinary System
Water and salts in

Excess water, metabolic
wastes, and salts out

Excretion

Regulating Fluid Levels To stay in good health, the fluid levels within the body must be balanced and normal blood pressure must be maintained. An area in the brain, the hypothalamus (hi poh THA luh mus), constantly monitors the amount of water in the blood. When the brain detects too much water in the blood, the hypothalamus releases a lesser amount of a specific hormone. This signals the kidneys to return less water to the blood and increase the amount of urine that is excreted.

✔ Reading Check *How does the brain control the volume of water in the blood?*

Organs of the Urinary System Excretory organs is another name for the organs of the urinary system. The main organs of the urinary system are two bean-shaped kidneys. Kidneys are located on the back wall of the abdomen at about waist level. The kidneys filter blood that contains wastes collected from cells. In approximately five minutes, all of the blood in your body passes through the kidneys. The red-brown color of the kidneys is due to their enormous blood supply. In **Figure 17,** you can see that blood enters the kidneys through a large artery and leaves through a large vein.

Figure 17 The urinary system removes wastes from the blood. The urinary system includes the kidneys, the bladder, and the connecting tubes.
Explain *how the kidneys help the body balance its fluid levels.*

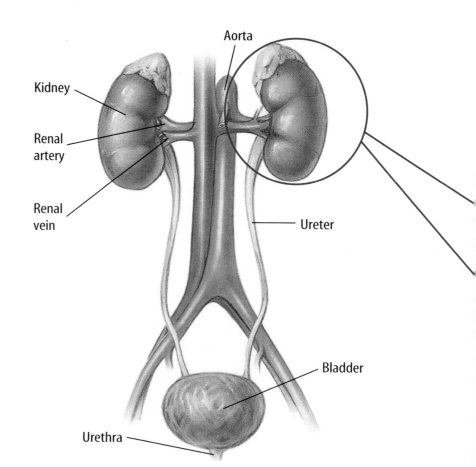

Aorta

Kidney

Renal artery

Renal vein

Ureter

Bladder

Urethra

Filtration in the Kidney A two-stage filtration system is an accurate description of a kidney, shown in **Figure 18.** It is made up of about one million tiny filtering units called **nephrons** (NE frahnz), also shown in **Figure 18.** Each nephron has a cuplike structure and a tubelike structure called a tubule. Blood moves from a renal artery to capillaries in the cuplike structure. The first filtration occurs when water and dissolved sugar, salt, and wastes move from the blood into the cuplike structure. Left behind in the blood are the red blood cells and proteins. Next, the liquid in the cuplike structure is squeezed into a tubule.

Capillaries that surround the tubule perform the second filtration. Most of the water and dissolved sugar and salt move from the nephron to the blood. These capillaries merge to form small veins, which merge to form a renal vein in each kidney. Purified blood is returned to the main circulatory system. The waste liquid left behind flows into collecting tubules in each kidney. This waste liquid, or urine, contains excess water and other wastes that are not reabsorbed by the body. An average-sized person produces about one liter of urine per day.

Urine Collection and Release The urine in each collecting tubule drains into a funnel-shaped area of each kidney that leads to the **ureter** (YOO ruh tur). Ureters are tubes that lead from each kidney to the bladder. The **bladder** is an elastic, muscular organ that can hold about one-half a liter of urine. When full, the bladder looks like an inflated balloon and the cells lining the bladder are stretched and thin. When empty, the bladder looks wrinkled and the cells lining the bladder are thick. A tube called the urethra (yoo REE thruh) carries urine from the bladder to the outside of the body.

Figure 18 The nephron is a complex structure.
Describe *the main function of a nephron.*

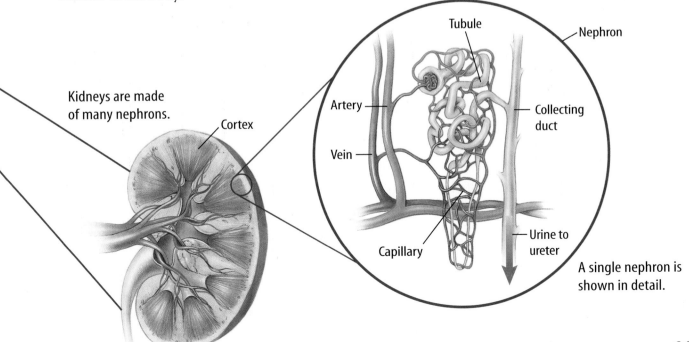

Kidneys are made of many nephrons.

Cortex

Tubule

Nephron

Artery

Vein

Collecting duct

Capillary

Urine to ureter

A single nephron is shown in detail.

Urinary Diseases and Disorders

What happens when someone's kidneys don't work properly or stop working? Waste products that are not removed build up and act as poisons in body cells. Without excretion, an imbalance of salts occurs. The body responds by trying to restore this balance. If the balance isn't restored, the kidneys and other organs can be damaged. Kidney failure occurs when the kidneys don't work as they should. This is always a serious problem because the kidneys' job is so important to the rest of the body.

Applying Science

How does your body gain and lose water?

Your body depends on water. Without water, your cells could not carry out their activities and body systems could not function. Water is so important to your body that your brain and other body systems are involved in balancing water gain and water loss.

Identifying the Problem

Table A shows the major sources by which your body gains water. Oxidation of nutrients occurs when energy is released from nutrients by your body's cells. Water is a waste product of these reactions. **Table B** lists the major sources by which your body loses water. The data show you how daily gain and loss of water are related.

Solving the Problem

1. What is the greatest source of water gained by your body? What is the greatest source of water lost by your body?
2. How would the percentages of water gained and lost change in a person who was working in extremely warm temperatures? In this case, what organ of the body would be the greatest contributor to water loss?

Table A Major Sources by Which Body Water Is Gained		
Source	Amount (mL)	Percent
Oxidation of nutrients	250	10
Foods	750	30
Liquids	1,500	60
Total	2,500	100

Table B Major Sources by Which Body Water Is Lost		
Source	Amount (mL)	Percent
Urine	1,500	60
Skin	500	20
Lungs	350	14
Feces	150	6
Total	2,500	100

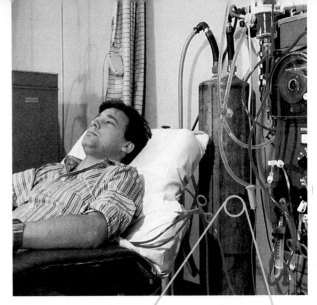

Blockage Because the ureters and urethra are narrow tubes, they can be blocked easily in some disorders. A blockage can cause serious problems because urine cannot flow out of the body properly. If the blockage is not corrected, the kidneys can be damaged.

Reading Check *Why is a blocked ureter or urethra a serious problem?*

Dialysis A person who has only one kidney still can live normally. The remaining kidney increases in size and works harder to make up for the loss of the other kidney. However, if both kidneys fail, the person will need to have his or her blood filtered by an artificial kidney machine in a process called dialysis (di AH luh sus), as shown in **Figure 19.**

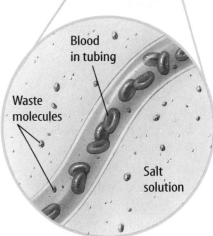

Figure 19 A dialysis machine can replace or help with some of the activities of the kidneys in a person with kidney failure. Like the kidney, the dialysis machine removes wastes from the blood.

---

section 4 review

Summary

Functions of the Excretory System

- The excretory system removes wastes from your body.
- The digestive, respiratory, and urinary systems and skin make up your excretory system.

The Urinary System

- The kidneys, which filter wastes from the blood, are the major organs of the urinary system.
- Urine moves from the kidneys through the ureters, into the bladder, then leaves the body through the urethra.

Urinary Diseases and Disorders

- Kidney failure can lead to a buildup of waste products in the body.
- An artificial kidney can be used to filter the blood in a process called dialysis.

Self Check

1. **List** the functions of a person's urinary system. `SC.F.1.3.1`
2. **Explain** how the kidneys remove wastes and keep fluids and salts in balance. `SC.F.1.3.1`
3. **Describe** what happens when the urinary system does not function properly.
4. **Compare** the excretory system and urinary system. `SC.H.2.3.1`
5. **Concept Map** Using a network-tree concept map, compare the excretory functions of the kidneys and the lungs. `SC.F.1.3.1`
6. **Think Critically** Explain why reabsorption of certain materials in the kidneys is important to your health. `SC.F.1.3.1`

Applying Math

7. **Make and Use Graphs** Make a circle graph of major sources by which body water is gained. Use the data in **Table A** of the Applying Science activity. `MA.E.1.3.1`

Benchmark—**SC.H.1.3.4:** The student knows that accurate record keeping, openness, and replication are essential to maintaining an investigator's credibility with other scientists and society; **SC.H.1.3.5:** The student knows that a change in one or more variables may alter the outcome of an investigation.

Particle Size and Absorption

Goals

- **Compare and contrast** the dissolving rates of different sized particles.
- **Predict** the dissolving rate of sugar particles larger than sugar cubes.
- **Predict** the dissolving rate of sugar particles smaller than particles of ground sugar.
- **Infer,** using the lab results, why the body must break down and dissolve food particles.

Materials

beakers or jars (3)
thermometers (3)
sugar granules
mortar and pestle
triple-beam balance
stirring rod
sugar cubes
weighing paper
warm water
stopwatch

Safety Precautions

Complete a safety worksheet before you begin.

WARNING: *Never taste, eat, or drink any materials used in the lab.*

◉ *Real-World Problem*

Before food reaches the small intestine, it is digested mechanically in the mouth and the stomach. The food mass is reduced to small particles. You can chew an apple into small pieces, but you would feed applesauce to a small child who didn't have teeth. What is the advantage of reducing the size of the food material? Does reducing the size of food particles aid the process of digestion?

◉ *Procedure*

1. Copy the data table below into your Science Journal.

Dissolving Times of Sugar Particles		
Size of Sugar Particles	Mass	Time Until Dissolved
Sugar cube		
Sugar granules	Do not write in this book.	
Ground sugar particles		

2. Place a sugar cube into your mortar and grind up the cube with the pestle until the sugar becomes powder.

3. Using the triple-beam balance and weighing paper, measure the mass of the powdered sugar from your mortar. Using separate sheets of weighing paper, measure the mass of a sugar cube and the mass of a sample of the granular sugar. The masses of the powdered sugar, sugar cube, and granular sugar should be approximately equal to each other. Record the three masses in your data table.

4. Place warm water into the three beakers. Use the thermometers to be certain the water in each beaker is the same temperature.

5. Place the sugar cube in a beaker, the powdered sugar in a second beaker, and the granular sugar in a third beaker. Place all the sugar samples in the beakers at the same time and start the stopwatch when you put the sugar samples in the beaker.

6. Stir each sample equally.

7. Measure the time it takes each sugar sample to dissolve and record the times in your data table.

◉ Analyze Your Data

1. **Identify** the experiment's constants and variables.

2. **Compare** the rates at which the sugar samples dissolved. What type of sugar dissolved most rapidly? Which was the slowest to dissolve?

3. **Identify** possible sources of error in this lab.

◉ Conclude and Apply

1. **Predict** how long it would take sugar particles larger than the sugar cubes to dissolve. Predict how long it would take sugar particles smaller than the powdered sugar to dissolve.

2. **Infer** and explain the reason why small particles dissolve more rapidly than large particles.

3. **Infer** why you should thoroughly chew your food.

4. **Explain** how reducing the size of food particles aids the process of digestion.

Communicating Your Data

Write a news column for a health magazine explaining to health-conscious people what they can do to digest their food better.

Eating Well

Does the same diet work for everyone?

Growing up in India in the first half of the twentieth century, R. Rajalakshmi (RAH jah lok shmee) saw many people around her who did not get enough food. Breakfast for a poor child might have been a cup of tea. Lunch might have consisted of a slice of bread. For dinner, a child might have eaten a serving of rice with a small piece of fish. This type of diet, low in calories and nutrients, resulted in children who were often sick and died young.

In the 1960s, R. Rajalakshmi was asked to help manage a program to improve nutrition in her country. North American and European nutritionists suggested foods that were common and worked well for people who lived in these areas. But Rajalakshmi knew this advice was useless in a country such as India.

The Proper Diet for India

Rajalakshmi knew that for a nutrition program to work, it had to fit Indian culture. First, she found out what healthy middle-class people in India ate. She took note of the nutrients available in those foods. Then she looked for cheap, easy-to-find foods that would provide the same nutrients. Rajalakshmi created a balanced diet of locally grown fruits, vegetables, and grains.

Rajalakshmi's ideas were thought unusual in the 1960s. For example, she insisted that a diet without meat could provide all major nutrients. It took persistence to get others to accept her ideas. Because of Rajalakshmi's program, Indian children almost doubled their food intake. Many children who would have been hungry and ill, grew healthy and strong.

Thanks to R. Rajalakshmi and other nutritionists, many children in India are eating well and staying healthy.

Report Choose a continent and research what foods are native to that area. As a class, compile a list of the foods and where they originated. Using the class list, create a world map on a bulletin board that shows the origins of the different foods. LA.A.2.3.4

TIME

For more information, visit fl6.msscience.com

Reviewing Main Ideas

Section 1 The Digestive System

1. Mechanical digestion breaks down food through chewing and churning. Enzymes and other chemicals aid chemical digestion.

2. Food passes through the mouth, esophagus, stomach, small intestine, large intestine, and rectum and then out the anus.

3. The large intestine absorbs water, which helps the body maintain homeostasis.

Section 2 Nutrition

1. Proteins, carbohydrates, fats, vitamins, minerals, and water are the six nutrients found in foods.

2. Health is affected by the combination of foods that make up a diet.

Section 3 The Respiratory System

1. The respiratory system brings oxygen into the body and removes carbon dioxide.

2. Breathing is the movement of the chest that allows air to move into the lungs and waste gases to leave the lungs.

3. The chemical reaction in cells that uses oxygen, releases energy, and produces carbon dioxide and water as wastes is called cellular respiration.

4. Smoking causes many respiratory problems, including chronic bronchitis, emphysema, and lung cancer.

Section 4 The Excretory System

1. The urinary system is part of the excretory system. The skin, lungs, liver, and large intestine also are excretory organs.

2. The kidneys are the major organs of the urinary system and have a two-stage filtration system that removes wastes.

3. When kidneys fail to work, an artificial kidney can be used to filter the blood in a process called dialysis.

Visualizing Main Ideas

LA.A.2.3.7

Copy and complete the following table on the respiratory and excretory systems.

Human Body Systems		
	Respiratory System	Excretory System
Major organs		
Wastes eliminated	Do not write in this book.	
Disorders		

Using Vocabulary

alveoli p. 142	mineral p. 136
amino acid p. 133	nephron p. 149
bladder p. 149	nutrient p. 128
bronchi p. 142	peristalsis p. 130
carbohydrate p. 134	trachea p. 142
chyme p. 131	ureter p. 149
enzyme p. 128	villi p. 131
larynx p. 142	vitamin p. 135

Write the vocabulary term that matches each definition given below.

1. muscular contractions of the esophagus

2. the building blocks of proteins

3. liquid product of digestion

4. inorganic nutrient

5. the filtering unit of the kidney   **SC.F.1.3.5**

6. thin-walled sacs in the lungs

7. elastic muscular organ that holds urine

8. a type of protein that speeds up the rate of a chemical reaction in your body

9. nutrient that is the main source of energy for your body

10. fingerlike projections covering the folds in the small intestine

Checking Concepts

Choose the word or phrase that best answers the question.

11. Where in humans does most chemical digestion occur?
    A) duodenum   **C)** liver
    B) stomach   **D)** large intestine

12. In which organ is water absorbed?
    A) liver   **C)** small intestine
    B) esophagus   **D)** large intestine

13. Which is an accessory organ?
    A) mouth   **C)** small intestine
    B) stomach   **D)** liver

14. What beneficial substances are produced by bacteria in the large intestine?
    A) fats   **C)** vitamins
    B) minerals   **D)** proteins

15. Which food group contains yogurt and cheese?
    A) dairy   **C)** meat
    B) grain   **D)** fruit

16. When you inhale, which organ contracts and moves down?
    A) bronchioles **C)** nephrons
    B) diaphragm   **D)** kidneys

17. Exchange of gases occurs between capillaries and which of the following structures?
    A) alveoli   **C)** bronchioles **SC.F.1.3.5**
    B) bronchi   **D)** trachea

18. Which condition does smoking make worse?
    A) arthritis   **C)** excretion
    B) respiration **D)** emphysema

19. Urine is held temporarily in which structure?

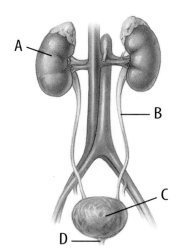

20. Which substance does not move into the blood after it passes through the kidneys?
    A) salt   **C)** waste liquid
    B) sugar   **D)** water

Thinking Critically

21. **Make and use a table** to sequence the order of organs in the digestive system through which food passes. Indicate whether ingestion, digestion, absorption, or elimination takes place in each. SC.F.1.3.1

22. **Compare and contrast** the three types of carbohydrates—sugar, starch, and fiber.

23. **Classify** the parts of your favorite sandwich into three of the nutrient categories—carbohydrates, proteins, and fats.

24. **Recognize cause and effect** by discussing how lack of oxygen is related to lack of energy.

25. **Form a hypothesis** about the number of breaths a person might take per minute in each of these situations: asleep, exercising, and on top of Mount Everest. Give a reason for each hypothesis.

26. **Concept Map** Make an events-chain concept map showing how urine forms in the kidneys. Begin with, "In the nephron …"

Use the table below to answer question 27.

Materials Filtered by the Kidneys

Substance Filtered in Urine	Amount Moving Through Kidney	Amount Excreted
Water	125 L	1 L
Salt	350 g	10 g
Urea	1 g	1 g
Glucose	50 g	0 g

27. **Interpret Data** Study the data above. How much of each substance is reabsorbed into the blood in the kidneys? What substance is excreted completely in the urine?

28. **Describe** how bile aids the digestive process.

29. **Explain** how the bacteria that live in your large intestine help your body.

Performance Activities

30. **Questionnaire and Interview** Prepare a questionnaire that can be used to interview a health specialist who works with lung cancer patients. Include questions on reasons for choosing the career, new methods of treatment, and the most encouraging or discouraging part of the job.

Applying Math

31. **Kidney Blood Flow** In approximately 5 min, all 5 L of blood in the body pass through the kidneys. Calculate the average rate of flow through the kidneys in liters per minute. MA.A.3.3.1

Use the graph below to answer question 32.

Total Lung Capacity

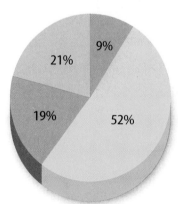

Total Lung Capacity = 5,800 mL

- Volume of air normally inhaled or exhaled
- Volume of additional air that can be inhaled forcefully
- Volume of additional air that can be exhaled forcefully
- Volume of air left in lungs after forcefully exhaling

32. **Total Lung Capacity** What volume of air (mL) is left in the lungs after forcefully exhaling? MA.E.1.3.1

The assessed Florida Benchmark appears above each question.
Record your answers on the answer sheet provided by your teacher or on a sheet of paper.

Multiple Choice

SC.F.1.3.1

1 The diagram below shows the interaction between an alveolus and a capillary. The labels A and B indicate the gases that are exchanged between these structures.

Alveolus

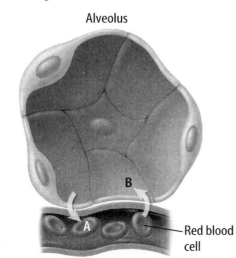

Red blood cell

Capillary

Which gases do the labels A and B represent?

A. A is oxygen, and B is carbon dioxide.

B. A is carbon dioxide, and B is water.

C. A is water, and B is carbon dioxide.

D. A is carbon dioxide, and B is oxygen.

SC.F.1.3.1

2 Many of the body's systems work together to perform vital functions. Which systems work together to maintain the proper balance of fluids in the body?

F. respiratory and excretory

G. respiratory and digestive

H. digestive and endocrine

I. endocrine and excretory

SC.G.1.3.4

3 Which is a benefit of the relationship between humans and intestinal bacteria?

A. Bacteria produce gases in the intestine.

B. Bacteria increase water absorption.

C. Bacteria can infect other body tissues.

D. Bacteria break down some of the indigestible material.

SC.F.1.3.1

4 The table below lists the nutrition facts for vanilla ice cream.

Nutrition Facts of Vanilla Ice Cream		
Item	**Amount**	**DV (Daily Values)**
Serving size	112 g	n/a
Calories	208	n/a
Total fat	19 g	29%
Saturated fat	11 g	55%
Cholesterol	0.125 g	42%
Sodium	0.90 g	4%
Total carbohydrates	22 g	7%
Fiber	0 g	0%
Sugars	22 g	n/a
Protein	5 g	n/a
Calcium	0.117 g	15%
Iron	n/a	0%

According to the information, which mineral has the greatest daily value (DV) percentage?

F. calcium

G. cholesterol

H. iron

I. sodium

SC.F.1.3.6

5 The walls of the small intestine are covered with millions of villi, which increase the surface area of the walls. What is most likely the advantage of these structures?

   A. They speed the release of digestive enzymes into the large intestine.

   B. They help break down food by mechanical digestion.

   C. They make the absorption of nutrients more efficient.

   D. They sweep nutrients into the bloodstream.

Gridded Response

SC.G.2.3.2

6 For one week, research scientists collected and accurately measured the amount of body water lost and gained per day for four different patients. The table below lists the data the scientists collected.

Body Water Gained (+) and Lost (−)				
Patient	**Day 1 (L)**	**Day 2 (L)**	**Day 3 (L)**	**Day 4 (L)**
Mr. Stoler	+0.15	+0.15	−0.35	+0.12
Mr. Jemma	−0.01	0.00	−0.20	−0.01
Mr. Lowe	0.00	+0.20	−0.28	+0.01
Mr. Cheng	−0.50	−0.50	−0.55	−0.32

In liters, what was the total body water gained by Mr. Stoler from Day 1 to Day 4?

Short Response

SC.G.1.3.4

7 Some people take in more calories than they can use. What is the possible outcome of this behavior? Does this outcome benefit or harm a person?

Extended Response

SC.H.1.3.5

8 Leo is investigating the effect of varying amounts of the enzyme amylase on the breakdown of starch. The table below shows how he set up his investigation.

Effect of Amylase of One Brand-X Cracker				
Volume of Amylase (mL)	**Temperature of Enzyme Solution**	**Fraction of Cracker Left**		
		1 min	**5 min**	**10 min**
2	17°C			
5	20°C			
10	21°C			

PART A According to the table, which variable has not been properly controlled?

PART B How might this affect the results of Leo's study?

FCAT Tip

Answer Every Question Never leave any answer blank. There is no penalty for guessing.

Sunshine State Standards—**SC.F.1:** The student describes patterns of structure and function in living things; **SC.G.1:** understands the competitive, interdependent, cyclic nature of living things; **SC.H.2:** understands that most natural events occur in comprehensible, consistent patterns.

Circulation and Immunity

chapter preview

sections

The Flow of Traffic

This highway interchange is simple compared to how blood travels within your body. In this chapter, you will discover how complex your circulatory system is—from parts of your blood to how it travels through your body and fights disease.

Science Journal Write three questions that you have about blood, circulation, or how diseases are spread.

Start-Up Activities

SC.H.2.3.1

Transportation by Road and Vessel

Your circulatory system is like a road system. Just as roads are used to transport goods to homes and factories, your blood vessels transport substances throughout your body. You'll find out how similar roads and blood vessels are in this lab.

1. Observe a map of your city, county, or state.
2. Identify roads that are interstates, as well as state and county roads, using the map key.
3. Plan a route to a destination that your teacher describes. Then plan a different return trip.
4. Draw a diagram in your Science Journal showing your routes to and from the destination.
5. **Think Critically** If the destination represents your heart, what do the routes represent? In your Science Journal, draw a comparison between a blocked road on your map and a clogged artery in your body.

Study Organizer

LA.A.1.3.4
LA.B.2.3.1

Circulation Make the following Foldable to help you organize information and diagram ideas about circulation.

STEP 1 Fold a sheet of paper in half lengthwise. Make the back edge about 5 cm longer than the front edge.

STEP 2 Turn the paper so the fold is on the bottom. Then fold it into thirds.

STEP 3 Unfold and cut only the top layer along both folds to make three tabs.

STEP 4 Label the Foldable as shown.

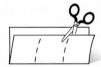

Read and Write As you read the chapter, write information about each circulatory system under the appropriate tab.

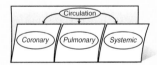

Preview this chapter's content and activities at fl6.msscience.com

Benchmarks—**SC.F.1.3.3 (pp. 163–164):** The student knows that in multicellular organisms cells grow and divide to make more cells in order to form and repair various organs and tissues; **SC.F.1.3.6 (p. 163):** The student knows that the cells with similar functions have similar structures, whereas those with different structures have different functions.

Also covers: **SC.F.1.3.1** Annually Assessed (p. 162), **SC.F.1.3.2** (p. 163), **SC.F.1.3.4** (p. 162), **SC.F.1.3.5** (p. 165), **SC.H.1.3.1** Annually Assessed (p. 165), **SC.H.2.3.1** (p. 164), **SC.H.3.3.6** (p. 165)

Blood

as you read

What **You'll Learn**

- **Identify** the parts and functions of blood.
- **Explain** why blood types are checked before a transfusion.
- **Give examples** of diseases of blood.

Why **It's Important**

Blood plays a part in every major activity of your body.

Review Vocabulary

diffusion: a type of passive transport within cells in which molecules move from areas where there are more of them to areas where there are fewer of them

New Vocabulary

- plasma
- platelet
- hemoglobin

Functions of Blood

You take a last, deep, calming breath before plunging into a dark, vessel-like tube. Water is everywhere. You take a hard right turn, then left as you streak through a narrow tunnel of twists and turns. The water transports you down the slide much like the way blood carries substances to all parts of your body. Blood has four important functions.

1. Blood carries oxygen from your lungs to all your body cells. Carbon dioxide diffuses from your body cells into your blood. Your blood carries carbon dioxide to your lungs to be exhaled.

2. Blood carries waste products from your cells to your kidneys to be removed.

3. Blood transports nutrients and other substances to your body cells.

4. Cells and molecules in blood fight infections and help heal wounds.

Anything that disrupts or changes these functions affects all the tissues of your body. Can you understand why blood is sometimes called the tissue of life?

Parts of Blood

A close look at blood tells you that blood is not just a red-colored liquid. Blood is a tissue made of plasma (PLAZ muh), red and white blood cells, and platelets (PLAYT luts), as shown in **Figure 1.** Blood makes up about eight percent of your body's total mass. If you weigh 45 kg, you have about 3.6 kg of blood moving throughout your body.

Plasma The liquid part of blood, which is made mostly of water, is called **plasma.** It makes up more than half the volume of blood. Nutrients, minerals, and oxygen are dissolved in plasma so that they can be carried to body cells. Wastes from body cells also are carried in plasma.

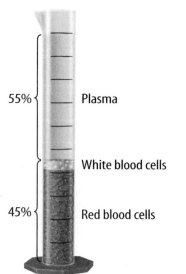

55%   Plasma

White blood cells

45%   Red blood cells

Figure 1 The blood in this graduated cylinder has separated into its parts. Each part plays a key role in body functions.

Blood Cells Disk-shaped red blood cells, shown in **Figure 2,** are different from other cells in your body because they have no nuclei when they mature. They contain **hemoglobin** (HEE muh gloh bun), which is a molecule that carries oxygen and carbon dioxide. Hemoglobin carries oxygen from your lungs to your body cells. Then it carries some of the carbon dioxide from your body cells back to your lungs. The rest of the carbon dioxide is carried in the cytoplasm of red blood cells and in plasma.

Red blood cells have a life span of about 120 days. They are made at a rate of 2 million to 3 million per second in the center of long bones, like the femur in your thigh. Red blood cells wear out and are destroyed at about the same rate.

A cubic millimeter of blood, about the size of a grain of rice, has about 5 million red blood cells. In contrast, a cubic millimeter of blood has about 5,000 to 10,000 white blood cells. White blood cells fight bacteria, viruses, and other invaders of your body. Your body reacts to invaders by increasing the number of white blood cells. These cells leave the blood through capillary walls and go into the tissues that have been invaded. Here, they destroy bacteria and viruses and absorb dead cells. The life span of white blood cells varies from a few days to many months.

Circulating with the red and white blood cells are platelets. **Platelets** are irregularly shaped cell fragments that help clot blood. A cubic millimeter of blood can contain as many as 400,000 platelets. Platelets have a life span of five to nine days.

LA.A.2.3.7

LA.B.2.3.4

Science Online

Topic: Human White Blood Cells
Visit fl6.msscience.com for Web links to information about the types of human white blood cells and their functions.

Activity Make a table showing the functions of the various types of white blood cells.

Figure 2 Red blood cells supply your body with oxygen, and white blood cells and platelets have protective roles.
Identify *the part of a cell found in white blood cells but not in red blood cells.*

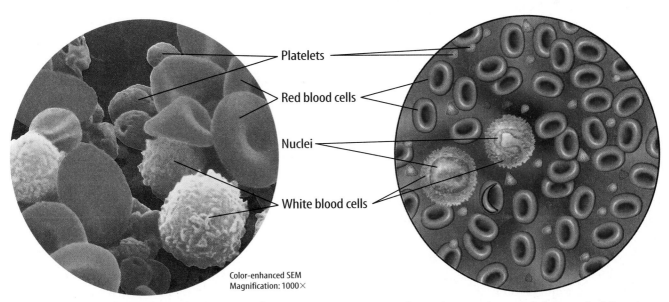

Platelets

Red blood cells

Nuclei

White blood cells

Color-enhanced SEM
Magnification: 1000×

Platelets help stop bleeding. Platelets not only plug holes in small vessels, they also release chemicals that help form filaments of fibrin.

Several types, sizes, and shapes of white blood cells exist. These cells destroy bacteria, viruses, and foreign substances.

Figure 3 When the skin is damaged, a sticky blood clot seals the leaking blood vessel. Eventually, a scab forms to protect the wound from further damage and allow it to heal.

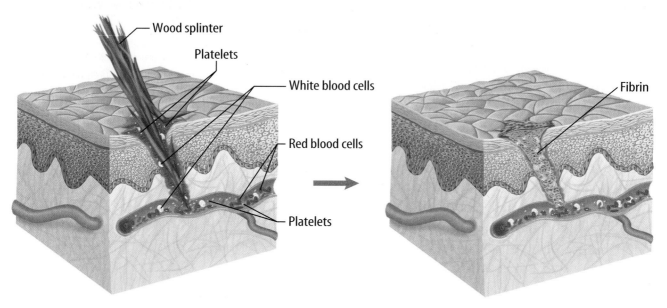

Wood splinter
Platelets
White blood cells
Fibrin
Red blood cells
Platelets

Mini LAB

Modeling Scab Formation

Procedure

1. Complete a safety worksheet.
2. Place a 5-cm × 5-cm square of **gauze** on a piece of **aluminum foil.**
3. Place drops of a **liquid bandage solution** onto the gauze and let it dry. Keep the liquid bandage away from eyes and mouth.
4. Use a **dropper** to place one drop of **water** onto the dried liquid bandage. Place another drop in another area of the gauze.

Analysis

1. Compare the drops of water in both areas.
2. Describe how the treated area of the gauze is like a scab.

Blood Clotting

You're running with your dog in a park, when suddenly you trip and fall down. Your knee starts to bleed, but the bleeding stops quickly. Already the wounded area has begun to heal. Bleeding stops because platelets and clotting factors in your blood make a blood clot that plugs the wounded blood vessels.

A blood clot also acts somewhat like a bandage. When you cut yourself, platelets stick to the wound and release chemicals. Then substances, called clotting factors, carry out a series of chemical reactions. These reactions cause threadlike fibers called fibrin (FI brun) to form a sticky net, as shown in **Figure 3.** This net traps escaping blood cells and plasma and forms a clot. The clot helps stop more blood from escaping. After the clot is in place and becomes hard, skin cells begin the repair process under the scab. Eventually, the scab is lifted off. Bacteria that get into the wound during the healing process usually are destroyed by white blood cells.

Reading Check *What blood components help form blood clots?*

Most people will not bleed to death from a minor wound, such as a cut or scrape. However, some people have a genetic condition called hemophilia (hee muh FIH lee uh). Their plasma lacks one of the clotting factors that begins the clotting process. A minor injury can be a life-threatening problem for a person with hemophilia.

Blood Types

Blood clots stop blood loss quickly in a minor wound, but with a serious wound a person may lose a lot of blood. A blood transfusion may be necessary. During a blood transfusion, a person receives donated blood or parts of blood. The medical provider must be sure that the right type of blood is given. If the wrong type is given, the red blood cells will clump together. Then, clots form in the blood vessels, and the person could die.

The ABO Identification System People can inherit one of four types of blood: A, B, AB, or O. Types A, B, and AB have chemical identification tags called antigens (AN tih junz) on their red blood cells. Type O red blood cells have no antigens.

Each blood type also has specific antibodies in its plasma. Antibodies are proteins that destroy or neutralize substances that do not belong in or are not part of your body. Because of these antibodies, certain blood types cannot be mixed. This limits blood transfusion possibilities, as shown in **Table 1.** If type A blood is mixed with type B blood, the antibodies in type A blood determine that type B blood does not belong there. The antibodies in type A blood cause the type B red blood cells to clump. In the same way, type B blood antibodies cause type A blood to clump. Type AB blood has no antibodies, so people with this blood type can receive blood from A, B, AB, and O types. Type O blood has both A and B antibodies.

> ✓ **Reading Check** *Why are people with type O blood called universal donors?*

The Rh Factor Another inherited chemical identification tag in blood is the Rh factor. If the Rh factor is on red blood cells, the person has Rh-positive (Rh+) blood. If it is not present, the person has Rh-negative (Rh−) blood. If an Rh− person receives a blood transfusion from an Rh+ person, he or she will produce antibodies against the Rh factor. These antibodies can cause Rh+ cells to clump. Clots then form in the blood vessels and the person could die. In the same way, an Rh− mother can make antibodies against her Rh+ baby during pregnancy. If the antibodies pass into the baby's blood, they can destroy the baby's red blood cells. To prevent deadly results, blood groups and Rh factor are checked before transfusions and during pregnancies.

LA.A.2.3.5
LA.B.2.3.1

INTEGRATE History

Blood Transfusions In 1665, the first successful blood transfusion was performed between two dogs. The first successful human-to-human blood transfusion was performed in 1818. However, many failures followed. The different blood types and the problems that result when they are mixed were unknown at that time. Research the discovery of the four types of blood and write a summary in your Science Journal.

Table 1 Blood Transfusion Possibilities		
Type	**Can Receive**	**Can Donate To**
A	O, A	A, AB
B	O, B	B, AB
AB	all	AB
O	O	all

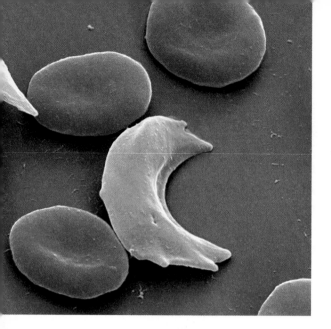

Diseases of Blood

Because blood circulates to all parts of your body and performs so many important functions, any disease of the blood is a cause for concern. One common disease of the blood is anemia (uh NEE mee uh). In this disease of red blood cells, body tissues can't get enough oxygen and are unable to carry on their usual activities. Anemia has many causes. Sometimes, anemia is caused by the loss of large amounts of blood. A diet lacking iron or certain vitamins also might cause anemia. Still other types of anemia are inherited problems related to the structure of the red blood cells. Cells from one such type of anemia, sickle-cell disease, are shown in **Figure 4.**

Leukemia (lew KEE mee uh) is a disease in which one or more types of white blood cells are made in excessive numbers. These cells are immature and do not fight infections well. These immature cells fill the bone marrow and crowd out the normal, mature cells. Then not enough red blood cells, normal white blood cells, and platelets can be made. Some types of leukemia affect children. Other kinds are more common in adults. Medicines, blood transfusions, and bone marrow transplants are used to treat this disease. If the treatments are not successful, the person will eventually die from related complications.

Figure 4 Persons with sickle-cell disease have misshapened red blood cells. The sickle-shaped cells clog the capillaries of a person with this disease. Oxygen cannot reach tissues served by the capillaries, and wastes cannot be removed. **Explain** *how this damages the affected tissues.*

section 1 review

Summary

Functions and Parts of Blood

- Blood carries oxygen, carbon dioxide, wastes, and nutrients.

- Blood contains cells that help fight infections and heal wounds.

- Blood is a tissue made of plasma, red and white blood cells, and platelets.

Blood Clotting and Blood Types

- Platelets and clotting factors form blood clots to stop bleeding from a wound.

- Blood type—A, B, AB, or O—must be identified before a person receives a transfusion.

Diseases of Blood

- Anemia affects red blood cells, while leukemia affects white blood cells.

Self Check

1. **List** the four functions of blood in the body. `SC.F.1.3.1`

2. **Compare and contrast** red blood cells, white blood cells, and platelets. `SC.F.1.3.2` `SC.F.1.3.5`

3. **Describe** how anemia and leukemia affect the blood.

4. **Explain** why blood type and Rh factor are checked before a transfusion.

5. **Think Critically** Think about the main job of your red blood cells. If red blood cells couldn't deliver oxygen to your cells, what would be the condition of your body tissues? `SC.F.1.3.5`

Applying Skills

6. **Interpret Data** Look at the data in **Table 1** about blood group interactions. To which group(s) can people with blood type AB donate blood?

section 2

Circulation

The Body's Delivery System

It's time to get ready for school, but your younger sister is taking a long time in the shower. "Don't use all the hot water," you shout. Water is carried throughout your house in pipes that are part of the plumbing system. It supplies water for your needs and carries away wastes. Just as you expect water to flow when you turn on the faucet, your body needs a continuous supply of oxygen and nutrients and a way to remove wastes. In a similar way, materials are moved throughout your body by your circulatory system, which is also known as your cardiovascular (kar dee oh VAS kyuh lur) system. It includes your heart, kilometers of blood vessels, and blood. Blood vessels carry the blood to every part of your body, as shown in **Figure 5.** Recall that blood moves oxygen and nutrients to cells and carries carbon dioxide and other wastes away from the cells.

The Heart

Your heart is an organ mostly made of cardiac muscle tissue. It is located behind your breastbone, called the sternum, and between your lungs. Your heart has four compartments called chambers. The two upper chambers are called the right and left atriums (AY tree umz). The two lower chambers are called the right and left ventricles (VEN trih kulz). A one-way valve separates each atrium from the ventricle below it. The blood flows from an atrium to a ventricle, then from a ventricle into a blood vessel. A wall between the two atriums or the two ventricles keeps blood rich in oxygen separate from blood low in oxygen.

as you read

What You'll Learn

- **Compare and contrast** arteries, veins, and capillaries.
- **Explain** how blood moves through the heart.
- **Identify** the functions of the pulmonary and systemic circulation systems.
- **Describe** functions of the lymphatic system.

Why It's Important

Your body's cells depend on blood vessels to deliver nutrients and remove wastes. The lymphatic system helps protect you from infections and disease.

Review Vocabulary

☀ **tissue:** group of similar cells that work together to do one job

New Vocabulary

- capillary
- artery
- vein
- lymph

☀ FCAT Vocabulary

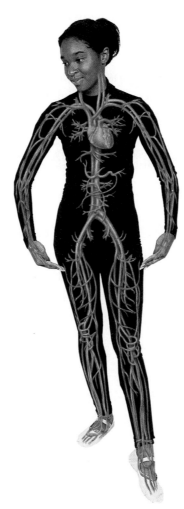

Figure 5 The blood is pumped by the heart to all the cells of the body and then back to the heart through a network of blood vessels.

Blood Vessels

In the middle 1600s, scientists discovered that blood moves by the pumping of the heart and flows in one direction from arteries to veins. But they couldn't explain how blood gets from arteries to veins. Using a new invention of that time, the microscope, scientists discovered **capillaries** (KA puh ler eez), the blood vessels that connect arteries and veins.

Capillaries The walls of capillaries are only one cell thick. Generally, nutrients and oxygen diffuse into body cells from capillaries. Waste materials and carbon dioxide diffuse from body cells into the capillaries. But in the lungs, waste gases including carbon dioxide diffuse from the blood into the lungs, and oxygen from lung cells diffuses into the blood.

Arteries As blood is pumped out of the heart, it travels through arteries, capillaries, and then veins. **Arteries,** shown in **Figure 6,** are blood vessels that carry blood away from the heart. They have thick, elastic walls made of connective tissue and smooth muscle tissue.

Veins The blood vessels that carry blood back to the heart are called **veins.** Veins have one-way valves, also shown in **Figure 6,** that help keep blood moving toward the heart. If blood flows backward, the pressure of the blood against the valves causes them to close. Blood flow in veins also is helped by your skeletal muscles. When skeletal muscles contract, this action squeezes veins and helps move blood toward the heart.

Reading Check *What are the similarities and differences between arteries and veins?*

Types of Circulation

Scientists have divided the circulatory system into three sections—coronary (KOR uh ner ee) circulation, pulmonary (PUL muh ner ee) circulation, and systemic circulation. The beating of your heart controls blood flow through each section.

Coronary Circulation Your heart has its own blood vessels that supply it with nutrients and oxygen and remove wastes. Coronary circulation is the flow of blood to and from the tissues of the heart. When the coronary circulation is blocked, oxygen and nutrients cannot reach all the cells of the heart. This can result in a heart attack.

Figure 6 The structures and functions of arteries, veins, and capillaries are different.

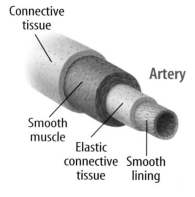

Connective tissue
Artery
Smooth muscle
Elastic connective tissue
Smooth lining

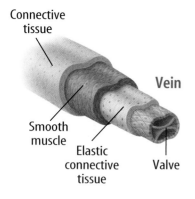

Connective tissue
Vein
Smooth muscle
Elastic connective tissue
Valve

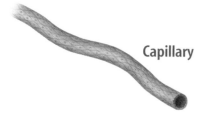

Capillary

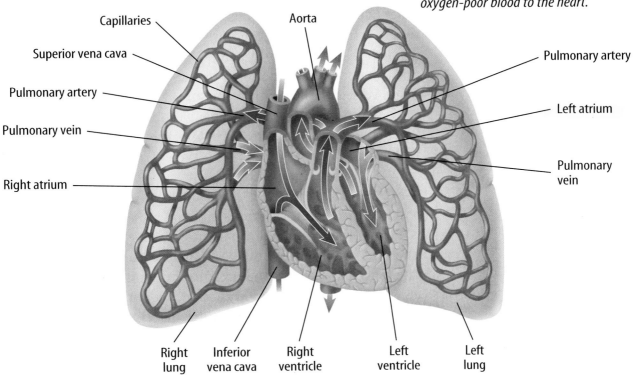

Figure 7 Pulmonary circulation moves blood between the heart and lungs. **Identify** *the blood vessels that return oxygen-poor blood to the heart.*

Capillaries

Superior vena cava

Pulmonary artery

Pulmonary vein

Right atrium

Aorta

Pulmonary artery

Left atrium

Pulmonary vein

Right lung   Inferior vena cava   Right ventricle   Left ventricle   Left lung

Pulmonary Circulation The flow of blood through the heart to the lungs and back to the heart is called pulmonary circulation. Use **Figure 7** to trace the path blood takes through this part of the circulatory system. The blood returning from the body through the right side of the heart and to the lungs contains cellular wastes. The wastes include molecules of carbon dioxide and other substances. In the lungs, gaseous wastes diffuse out of the blood, and oxygen diffuses into the blood. Then the blood returns to the left side of the heart. In the final step of pulmonary circulation, the oxygen-rich blood is pumped from the left ventricle into the aorta (ay OR tuh), the largest artery in your body. From there, the oxygen-rich blood flows to all parts of your body.

Systemic Circulation Oxygen-rich blood moves to all of your organs and body tissues, except the heart and lungs, and oxygen-poor blood returns to the heart by a process called systemic circulation. Systemic circulation is the largest of the three sections of your circulatory system. Oxygen-rich blood flows from your heart in the arteries of this system. Then nutrients and oxygen are delivered by blood to your body cells and exchanged for carbon dioxide and wastes. Finally, this blood that contains wastes returns to your heart in the veins of the systemic circulation system.

Blood Pressure

Physics If you fill a balloon with water and then push on it, the pressure moves through the water in all directions, as illustrated in **Figure 8.** Your circulatory system is like the water balloon. When your heart pumps blood through the circulatory system, the pressure of the push moves through the blood. The force of the blood on the walls of the blood vessels is called blood pressure. This pressure is highest in arteries and lowest in veins. When you take your pulse, you can feel the waves of pressure. This rise and fall of pressure occurs with each heartbeat.

Controlling Blood Pressure Special nerve cells in the walls of some arteries sense changes in blood pressure. When pressure is higher or lower than normal, messages are sent to your brain. Then the brain sends messages that speed up or slow the heart rate. This helps keep blood pressure constant within your arteries. That way, enough blood can reach all organs and tissues in your body and deliver needed nutrients to every cell.

Cardiovascular Disease

Any disease that affects the cardiovascular system—the heart, blood vessels, and blood—can seriously affect the health of your entire body. Heart disease is the leading cause of death in humans.

Atherosclerosis One leading cause of heart disease is called atherosclerosis (ah thur oh skluh ROH sus). In this condition, fatty deposits build up on the walls of arteries. Atherosclerosis can occur in any artery in the body, but fatty deposits in coronary arteries are especially serious. If a coronary artery is blocked, a heart attack can occur. Open-heart surgery then may be needed to correct the problem.

Figure 8 When pressure is exerted on a fluid in a closed container, the pressure is transmitted through the liquid in all directions. Your circulatory system is like a closed container. Blood pressure is measured using a blood pressure cuff and a stethoscope.

Water-filled balloon

Hypertension Another condition of the cardiovascular system is called hypertension (hi pur TEN chun), or high blood pressure. When blood pressure is higher than normal most of the time, the heart must work harder to keep blood flowing. One cause of hypertension is atherosclerosis. A clogged artery can increase pressure within the vessel, causing the walls to become stiff and hard. The artery walls no longer contract and dilate easily because they have lost their elasticity.

Preventing Cardiovascular Disease

Having a healthy lifestyle is important for the health of your cardiovascular system. The choices you make now to maintain good health may reduce your risk of future serious illness. Regular checkups, a healthful diet, and exercise are all part of a heart-healthy lifestyle.

Another way to prevent cardiovascular disease is to not smoke. Smoking causes blood vessels to contract and makes the heart beat faster and harder. Smoking also increases carbon monoxide levels in the blood. Not smoking helps prevent heart disease and a number of respiratory system problems.

Functions of the Lymphatic System

You turn on the water faucet and fill a glass with water. The excess water runs down the drain. In a similar way, your body's tissue fluid is removed by the lymphatic (lihm FA tihk) system, as shown in **Figure 9.** The nutrient, water, and oxygen molecules in blood diffuse through capillary walls to nearby cells. Water and other substances become part of the tissue fluid that is found between cells. This fluid is collected and returned to the blood by the lymphatic system.

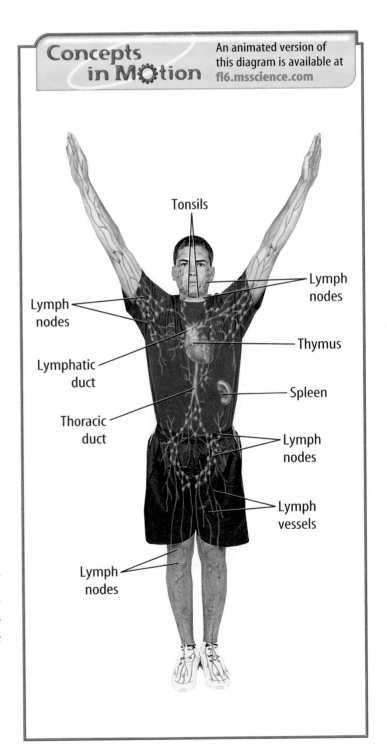

Concepts in Motion

An animated version of this diagram is available at fl6.msscience.com

Tonsils
Lymph nodes
Lymph nodes
Thymus
Lymphatic duct
Spleen
Thoracic duct
Lymph nodes
Lymph vessels
Lymph nodes

Figure 9 The lymphatic system is connected by a network of vessels.
Explain *how muscles help move lymph.*

Lymph After tissue fluid diffuses into the lymphatic capillaries, it is called **lymph** (LIHMF). In addition to water and dissolved substances, lymph contains lymphocytes (LIHM fuh sites), a type of white blood cell. Lymphocytes help your body defend itself against disease-causing organisms. If the lymphatic system is not working properly, severe swelling occurs because the tissue fluid cannot get back to the blood.

✔ **Reading Check** *What is lymph?*

Your lymphatic system carries lymph through a network of lymph capillaries and larger lymph vessels. Then, the lymph passes through lymph nodes, which are bean-shaped organs found throughout the body. Lymph nodes filter out microorganisms and foreign materials that have been taken up by lymphocytes. After it is filtered, lymph enters the bloodstream through large veins near the neck. No heartlike structure pumps the lymph through the lymphatic system. The movement of lymph depends on the contraction of smooth muscles in lymph vessels and skeletal muscles. Lymphatic vessels, like veins, have valves that keep lymph from flowing backward.

section 2 review

Summary

The Body's Delivery System

- Blood vessels carry blood to the body.

The Heart and Types of Circulation

- Your heart controls blood flow through the circulatory system.
- In the lungs, carbon dioxide leaves the blood, and oxygen diffuses into the blood.

Blood Vessels and Blood Pressure

- The three types of blood vessels are arteries, veins, and capillaries.
- The force of the blood on the walls of the blood vessels is called blood pressure.

Cardiovascular Disease

- Heart disease is a leading cause of death.

Functions of the Lymphatic System

- Lymph is tissue fluid from cells that has entered the lymph vessels.
- Lymphocytes help fight disease.

Self Check

1. **Compare and contrast** veins, arteries, and capillaries.
2. **Identify** the vessels in the pulmonary and systemic circulation systems that carry oxygen-rich blood.
3. **Describe** the functions of the lymphatic system. SC.F.1.3.1
4. **Explain** how blood moves through the heart.
5. **Infer** why swollen lymph nodes are usually an indication that an infection is in your body.
6. **Think Critically** What waste product builds up in blood and cells when the heart is unable to pump blood efficiently?

Applying Skills

7. **Use a Database** Research diseases of the circulatory system. Make a database showing what part of the circulatory system is affected by each disease. Categories should include the organs and vessels of the circulatory system.
8. **Concept Map** Make an events-chain concept map to show pulmonary circulation beginning at the right atrium and ending at the aorta.

section 3

Also covers: SC.F.1.3.1 Annually Assessed (pp. 173–175), SC.F.1.3.2 (p. 175), SC.H.1.3.6 (p. 175), SC.H.2.3.1 (p. 175)

Immunity

Lines of Defense

Your body has many ways to defend itself. Its first-line defenses work against harmful substances and all types of disease-causing organisms, called pathogens (PA thuh junz). Your second-line defenses are specific and work against specific pathogens. This complex group of defenses is called your immune system. Tonsils are one of the organs in the immune system that protect your body.

Reading Check *What types of defenses does your body have?*

First-Line Defenses Your skin and respiratory, digestive, and circulatory systems are first-line defenses against pathogens, like those in **Figure 10.** The skin is a barrier that prevents many pathogens from entering your body. However, pathogens can get into your body easily through a cut or through your mouth and the membranes in your nose and eyes. The conditions on the skin can affect pathogens. Perspiration contains substances that can slow the growth of some pathogens. At times, secretions from the skin's oil glands and perspiration are acidic. Some pathogens cannot grow in this acidic environment.

Internal First-Line Defenses Your respiratory system traps pathogens with hairlike structures, called cilia (SIH lee uh), and mucus. Mucus contains an enzyme that weakens the cell walls of some pathogens. When you cough or sneeze, you get rid of some of these trapped pathogens.

Your digestive system has several defenses against pathogens—saliva, enzymes, hydrochloric acid solution, and mucus. Saliva in your mouth contains substances that kill bacteria. Also, enzymes (EN zimez) in your stomach, pancreas, and liver help destroy pathogens. Hydrochloric acid solution in your stomach helps digest your food. It also kills some bacteria and stops the activity of some viruses that enter your body on the food that you eat. The mucus found on the walls of your digestive tract contains a chemical that coats bacteria and prevents them from binding to the inner lining of your digestive organs.

as you read

What You'll Learn
- **Explain** the difference between an antigen and an antibody.
- **Compare and contrast** active and passive immunity.

Why It's Important
Your body's defenses fight the pathogens that you are exposed to every day.

Review Vocabulary
enzyme: a type of protein that speeds up the rate of a chemical reaction in your body

New Vocabulary
- antigen
- antibody
- active immunity
- passive immunity

Stained LM Magnification: 1000✕

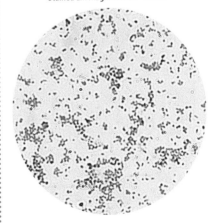

Figure 10 Most pathogens, such as the staphylococci bacteria shown above, cannot get through unbroken skin.

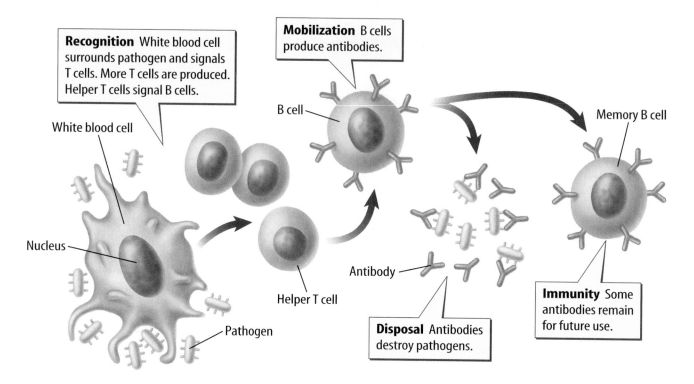

Recognition White blood cell surrounds pathogen and signals T cells. More T cells are produced. Helper T cells signal B cells.

White blood cell

Nucleus

Pathogen

Helper T cell

Mobilization B cells produce antibodies.

B cell

Antibody

Disposal Antibodies destroy pathogens.

Memory B cell

Immunity Some antibodies remain for future use.

Figure 11 The response of your immune system to disease-causing organisms can be divided into four steps—recognition, mobilization, disposal, and immunity.
Describe *the function of B cells.*

White Blood Cells Your circulatory system contains white blood cells that surround and digest foreign organisms and chemicals. These white blood cells constantly patrol your body. They sweep up and digest bacteria that invade your body.

Inflammation When tissue is damaged or infected by pathogens, it can become inflamed—feels warm, becomes red, swells, and hurts. Chemicals released by damaged cells expand capillary walls, allowing more blood to flow into the area. Other chemicals released by damaged tissue attract certain white blood cells that surround and take in pathogens. If pathogens get past these first-line defenses, your body uses another line of defense called specific immunity.

Specific Immunity When your body fights disease, it is battling complex molecules called **antigens** that don't belong there. Antigens can be separate molecules, or they can be found on the surface of a pathogen.

Special lymphocytes called T cells respond when your immune system recognizes foreign molecules, as in **Figure 11.** One type of T cells, called killer T cells, releases enzymes that help destroy invading foreign matter. Another type of T cells, called helper T cells, turns on the immune system. They stimulate other lymphocytes, known as B cells, to form antibodies. An **antibody** is a protein made in response to a specific antigen. The antibody attaches to the antigen and makes it useless.

Memory B Cells Another type of lymphocyte, called memory B cells, also has antibodies for the specific pathogen. Memory B cells remain in the blood, ready to defend against an invasion by that same pathogen at another time.

Active Immunity Antibodies help your body build defenses in two ways—actively and passively. In **active immunity** your body makes its own antibodies in response to an antigen. **Passive immunity** results when antibodies that have been produced in another animal are introduced into your body.

When a pathogen invades your body, the pathogen quickly multiplies, and you get sick. Your body immediately starts to make antibodies to attack the pathogen. After enough antibodies form, you usually get better. Some antibodies stay on duty in your blood, and more are produced rapidly if the pathogen enters your body again. Because of this defense system, you usually don't get certain diseases, such as chicken pox, more than once.

 *How does active immunity differ from passive immunity?*

Vaccination Another way to develop active immunity to a disease is to be inoculated with a vaccine, as shown in **Figure 12.** The process of giving a vaccine by injection or by mouth is called vaccination. A vaccine is a form of the antigen that gives you active immunity against a disease.

A vaccine can prevent a disease, but it is not a cure. As you grow older, you will be exposed to many more types of pathogens and will build a separate immunity to each one.

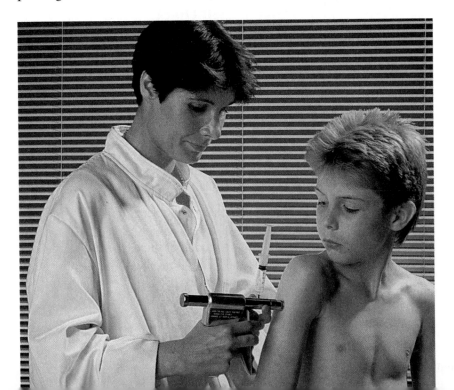

Mini LAB

Determining Reproduction Rates

Procedure

1. Complete a safety worksheet.
2. Place **one penny** on a table. Imagine that the penny is a bacterium that can divide every 10 min.
3. Place **two pennies** below to form a triangle with the first penny. These indicate the two new bacteria present after a bacterium divides.
4. Repeat three more divisions, placing two pennies under each penny in the row above.
5. Calculate how many bacteria you would have after 5 h of reproduction. Graph your data.

Analysis

1. How many bacteria are present after 5 h?
2. Why is it important to take antibiotics promptly if you have an infection?

Try at Home

Figure 12 The Td vaccine protects against tetanus and diphtheria, an infectious disease of the respiratory system. The vaccine usually is injected into the arm.

Table 2 Cases of Disease Before and After Vaccine Availability in the U.S.

Disease	Average Number of Cases per Year Before Vaccine Available	Cases in 1998 After Vaccine Available
Measles	503,282	89
Diphtheria	175,885	1
Tetanus	1,314	34
Mumps	152,209	606
Rubella	47,745	345
Pertussis (whooping cough)	147,271	6,279

Data from the National Immunization Program, CDC

Passive Immunity Passive immunity does not last as long as active immunity does. For example, you were born with all the antibodies that your mother had in her blood. However, these antibodies stayed with you for only a few months. Because newborn babies lose their passive immunity in a few months, they need to be vaccinated to develop their own immunity. Vaccines have helped reduce the number of cases of many childhood diseases, as shown in **Table 2.**

section 3 review

Summary

Lines of Defense

- The purpose of the immune system is to fight disease.

- Your skin and your respiratory, digestive, and circulatory systems are first-line defenses against pathogens.

- Your body's second line of defense is called specific immunity.

- In active immunity, your body makes its own antibodies in response to an antigen.

- Vaccinations can give you active immunity against a disease.

- Passive immunity results when antibodies that have been produced in another animal are introduced into your body.

Self Check

1. **Describe** how harmful bacteria can cause infections in your body.

2. **List** the natural defenses that your body has against harmful substances and disease.

3. **Explain** how an active vaccine works to protect the human body.

4. **Think Critically** Several diseases have symptoms similar to those of measles. Why doesn't the measles vaccine protect you from all of these diseases?

Applying Skills

5. **Make Models** Create models of the different types of T cells, antigens, and B cells from clay, construction paper, or other art materials. Use them to explain how T cells function in the immune system. SC.F.1.3.5

section

4

Diseases

Disease in History

Throughout time, the plague, smallpox, and influenza have killed millions of people worldwide. Today, the causes of these diseases are known, and treatments can prevent or cure them. But even today, some diseases cannot be cured, and outbreaks of new diseases, such as severe acute respiratory syndrome (SARS), occur.

Discovering Disease Organisms With the invention of the microscope in the latter part of the seventeenth century, bacteria, yeast, and mold spores were seen for the first time. However, scientists did not make a connection between microorganisms and disease transmission until the late 1800s and early 1900s.

The French chemist Louis Pasteur learned that microorganisms cause disease in humans. Many scientists of his time did not believe that microorganisms could harm larger organisms, such as humans. However, Pasteur discovered that microorganisms could spoil wine and milk. He then realized that microorganisms could attack the human body in the same way. Pasteur invented **pasteurization** (pas chuh ruh ZAY shun), which is the process of heating a liquid to a temperature that kills most bacteria.

Disease Organisms **Table 3** lists some of the diseases caused by various groups of pathogens. Bacteria and viruses cause many common diseases.

as you read

What **You'll Learn**

- **Describe** the work of Pasteur, Koch, and Lister in the discovery and prevention of disease.
- **Identify** diseases caused by viruses and bacteria.
- **Explain** how HIV affects the immune system.
- **Define** noninfectious diseases and list their causes.
- **Explain** what happens during an allergic reaction.

Why **It's Important**

You can help prevent certain illnesses if you know what causes disease and how disease spreads.

Review Vocabulary

✳ **virus:** tiny piece of genetic material surrounded by a protein coating that infects and multiplies in host cells

New Vocabulary

- pasteurization
- infectious disease
- noninfectious disease
- allergen

✳ FCAT Vocabulary

Table 3 Human Diseases and Their Agents	
Agent	**Diseases**
Bacteria	tetanus, tuberculosis, typhoid fever, strep throat, bacterial pneumonia, plague
Protists	malaria, sleeping sickness
Fungi	athlete's foot, ringworm
Viruses	colds, influenza, AIDS, measles, mumps, polio, smallpox, SARS

INTEGRATE Earth Science

Antibiotics Soil contains many microorganisms—some that are harmful, such as tetanus bacteria, and some that are helpful. Some infections are treated with antibiotics made from bacteria and molds found in the soil. One such antibiotic is streptomycin. In your Science Journal, write a brief report about the drug streptomycin.

Pathogens The conditions in your body, such as temperature and available nutrients, help harmful bacteria that enter your body grow and multiply. Bacteria can slow down the normal growth and metabolic activities of body cells and tissues. Some bacteria even produce toxins that kill cells on contact.

A virus infects and multiplies in host cells. The host cells die when the viruses break out of them. These new viruses infect other cells, leading to the destruction of tissues or the interruption of vital body activities.

Reading Check *What is the relationship between a virus and a host cell?*

Pathogenic protists, such as the organisms that cause malaria, can destroy tissues and blood cells or interfere with normal body functions. In a similar manner, fungus infections can cause athlete's foot, nonhealing wounds, chronic lung disease, or inflammation of the membranes of the brain.

Koch's Rules Many diseases caused by pathogens can be treated with medicines. In many cases, these organisms need to be identified before specific treatment can begin. Today, a method developed in the nineteenth century, as shown in **Figure 14,** still is used to identify organisms.

Infectious Diseases

A disease that is caused by a virus, bacterium, protist, or fungus and is spread from an infected organism or the environment to another organism is called an **infectious disease.** Infectious diseases are spread by direct contact with the infected organism, through water and air, on food, by contact with contaminated objects, and by disease-carrying organisms. These organisms are called biological vectors. Examples of vectors that have been sources of disease are rats, birds, cats, dogs, mosquitoes, fleas, and flies, shown in **Figure 13.**

Figure 13 When flies land on food, they can transport pathogens from one location to another.

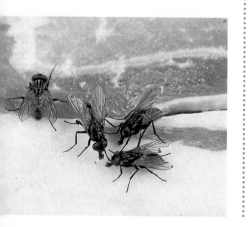

Human Vectors People also can be carriers of disease. Colds and many other diseases are spread through contact. Each time you turn a doorknob or use a telephone, your skin comes in contact with bacteria and viruses. This is why washing your hands frequently should be part of your daily routine.

Joseph Lister, an English surgeon, recognized the relationship between infections and cleanliness. Lister dramatically reduced the number of deaths among his patients by washing their wounds and skin, his hands, and surgical instruments with carbolic (kar BAH lihk) acid—a liquid that kills pathogens.

NATIONAL GEOGRAPHIC

VISUALIZING KOCH'S RULES

Figure 14

In the 1880s, German doctor Robert Koch developed a series of methods for identifying which organism was the cause of a particular disease. Koch's Rules are still in use today. Developed mainly for determining the cause of particular diseases in humans and other animals, these rules have been used for identifying diseases in plants as well.

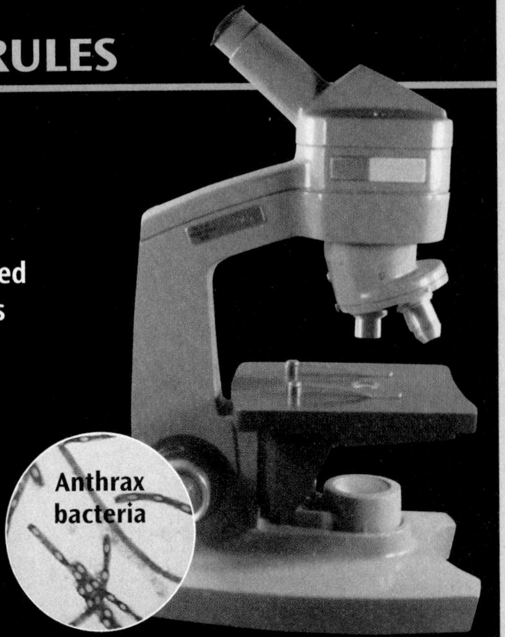
Anthrax
bacteria

A In every case of a particular disease, the organism thought to cause the disease—the pathogen—must be present.

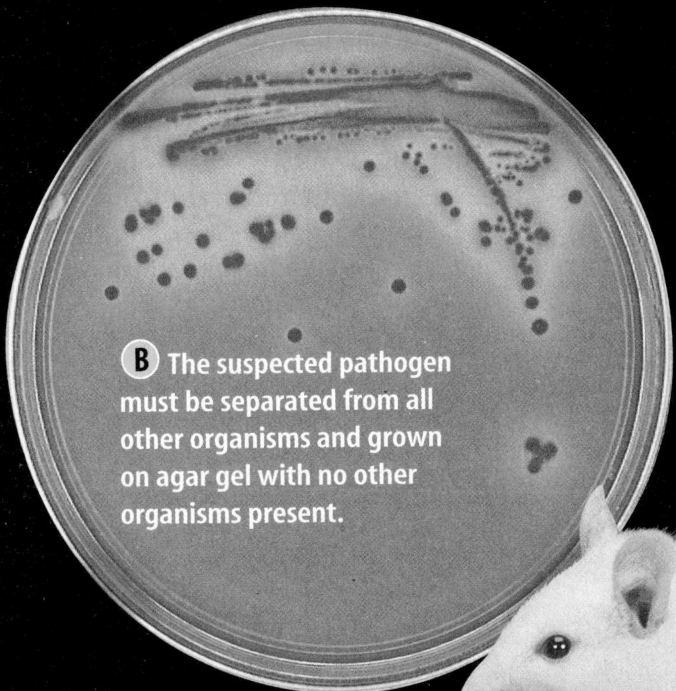

B The suspected pathogen must be separated from all other organisms and grown on agar gel with no other organisms present.

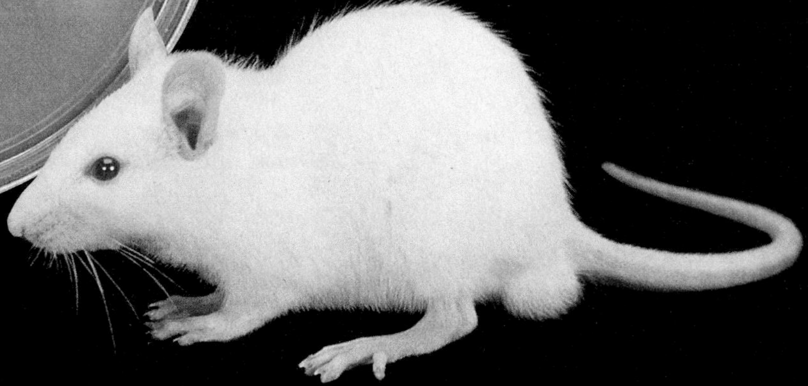

C When inoculated with the suspected pathogen, a healthy host must come down with the original illness.

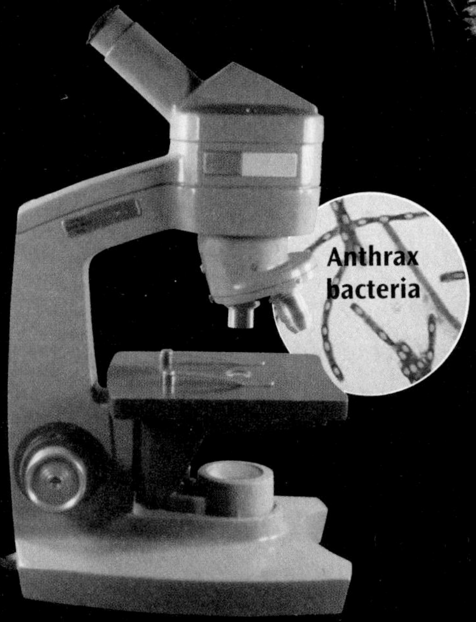
Anthrax
bacteria

D Finally, when the suspected pathogen is removed from the host and grown on agar gel again, it must be compared with the original organism. Only when they match can that organism be identified as the pathogen that causes the disease.

Sexually Transmitted Diseases Infectious diseases that are passed from person to person during sexual contact are called sexually transmitted diseases (STDs). STDs are caused by bacteria or viruses.

Gonorrhea (gah nuh REE uh), chlamydia (kluh MIH dee uh), and syphilis (SIH fuh lus) are STDs caused by bacteria. Antibiotics are used to treat these diseases. If left untreated, gonorrhea and chlamydia can result in a person becoming sterile because reproductive organs can be damaged permanently. Untreated syphilis can infect cardiovascular and nervous systems, resulting in damage to organs that cannot be reversed.

Genital herpes, a lifelong viral disease, causes painful blisters on the sex organs. This type of herpes can be transmitted during sexual contact or from an infected mother to her child during birth. Herpes has no cure, and no vaccine can prevent it. However, the symptoms of herpes can be treated with antiviral medicines.

Reading Check *Why should STDs be treated in the early stages?*

Applying Science

Has the annual percentage of deaths from major diseases changed?

Each year, many people die from diseases. Medical science has found numerous ways to treat and cure disease. Have new medicines, improved surgery techniques, and healthier lifestyles helped decrease the number of deaths from disease? By using your ability to interpret data tables, you can find out.

Percentage of Deaths Due to Major Diseases				
Disease	Year			
	1950	1980	1990	2000
Heart	37.1	38.3	33.5	29.6
Cancer	14.6	20.9	23.5	23.0
Stroke	10.8	8.6	6.7	7.0
Diabetes	1.7	1.8	2.2	2.9
Pneumonia and flu	3.3	2.7	3.7	2.7

Identifying the Problem

The table above shows the percentage of total deaths due to six major diseases for a 50-year time period. Study the data for each disease. Can you see any trends in the percentage of deaths?

Solving the Problem

1. Has the percentage increased for any disease that is listed?

2. What factors could have contributed to this increase?

HIV and Your Immune System

Human immunodeficiency virus (HIV) can exist in blood and body fluids. This virus can hide in body cells, sometimes for years. You can become infected with HIV by having sex with an HIV-infected person or by reusing an HIV-contaminated hypodermic needle for an injection. The risk of getting HIV through blood transfusion is small because all donated blood is tested for the presence of HIV. Also, freshly unwrapped sterile needles cannot transmit infection. A pregnant woman with HIV can infect her child when the virus passes through the placenta. The child also might become infected from contacts with blood during the birth process or when nursing after birth.

HIV cannot multiply outside the body, and it does not survive long in the environment. The virus cannot be transmitted by touching an infected person, by handling objects used by the person unless they are contaminated with body fluids, or from contact with a toilet seat.

AIDS An HIV infection can lead to Acquired Immune Deficiency Syndrome (AIDS), which is a disease that attacks the body's immune system. HIV, shown in **Figure 15,** is different from other viruses. It attacks the helper T cells in the immune system. The virus enters the T cell and multiplies. When the infected T cell bursts open, it is destroyed and more HIV are released that can infect other T cells. Soon, so many T cells are destroyed that not enough B cells are stimulated to produce antibodies. The body no longer has an effective way to fight invading antigens. The immune system is unable to fight HIV or any pathogen.

Through 2002, the estimated diagnosed cases of AIDS in the United States was 886,575, according to the Centers for Disease Control and Prevention. At this time there is no known cure for AIDS but several medications help treat AIDS patients.

Fighting Disease

Washing a small wound with soap and water is the first step in preventing an infection. Cleaning the wound with an antiseptic and covering it with a bandage are other steps. Is it necessary to wash your body to help prevent diseases? Yes! In addition to reducing body odor, washing your body removes and destroys some surface microorganisms.

In your mouth, microorganisms are responsible for mouth odor and tooth decay. Using dental floss and routine tooth brushing keep these organisms under control.

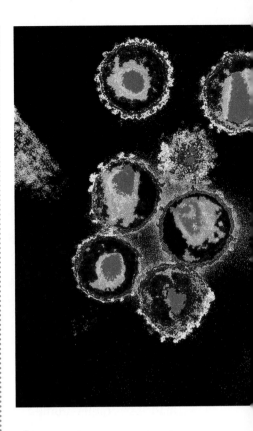

Figure 15 A person can be infected with HIV and not show any symptoms of the infection for several years.
Explain *why this characteristic makes the spread of AIDS more likely.*

FCAT FOCUS **Annually Assessed Benchmark Check**

SC.G.1.3.1 What human body system does HIV depend on for its survival but also damage?

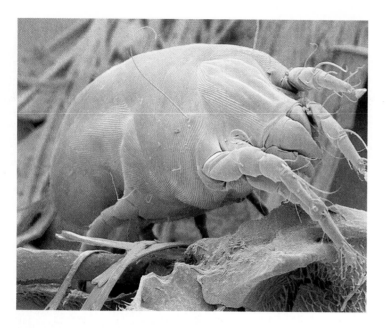

Figure 16 Dust mites are smaller than a period at the end of a sentence. They can live in pillows, mattresses, carpets, furniture, and other places.

Healthy Choices Exercise and good nutrition help the circulatory and respiratory systems work more effectively. Good health habits, including getting enough rest and eating well-balanced meals, can make you less susceptible to the actions of disease organisms such as those that cause colds and flu. Keeping up with recommended immunizations and having annual health checkups also can help you stay healthy.

Chronic Disease

Not all diseases are caused by pathogens. Diseases and disorders such as diabetes, allergies, asthma, cancer, and heart disease are **noninfectious diseases.** They are not spread from one person to another. Many are chronic (KRAH nihk). This means that they can last for a long time. Although some chronic diseases can be cured, others cannot.

Some infectious diseases can be chronic too. For example, deer ticks carry a bacterium that causes Lyme disease. This bacterium can affect the nervous system, heart, and joints for weeks to years. It can become chronic if not treated. Antibiotics will kill the bacteria, but some damage cannot be reversed.

Allergies Many people have allergies. Some people react to cosmetics, shellfish, strawberries, peanuts, or insect stings. An allergy is an overly strong reaction of the immune system to a foreign substance. Most allergic reactions are minor. However, severe allergic reactions can occur, causing shock and even death if they aren't treated promptly.

Substances that cause an allergic response are called **allergens.** Some chemicals, certain foods, pollen, molds, some antibiotics, and dust are allergens for some people. Dust can contain cat and dog dander and dust mites, like the one shown in **Figure 16.**

When you come in contact with an allergen, your immune system usually forms antibodies. Your body reacts by releasing chemicals called histamines (HIHS tuh meenz) that promote red, swollen tissues. Antihistamines are medications that can be used to treat allergic reactions and asthma, a lung disorder associated with reactions to allergens. Some severe allergies are treated with repeated injections of small doses of the allergen. Over time, this allows your body to become less sensitive to the allergen.

Diabetes A chronic disease associated with the levels of insulin produced by the pancreas is diabetes. Insulin is a hormone that enables glucose to pass from the bloodstream into your cells. There are two types of diabetes—Type 1 and Type 2. Type 1 diabetes is the result of too little or no insulin production. In Type 2 diabetes, your body cannot properly process insulin. Symptoms of diabetes include fatigue, excessive thirst, frequent urination, and tingling sensations in the hands and feet.

If glucose levels in the blood remain high for a long time, other health problems can develop. These problems can include blurred vision, kidney failure, heart attack, stroke, loss of feeling in the feet, and the loss of consciousness (diabetic coma).

Cancer

Closely related diseases that result from uncontrolled cell growth are commonly called cancers. They are complicated diseases, and no one fully understands how cancers form. Characteristics of cancer cells are listed in **Table 4.** Tumors can occur anywhere in your body. Cancerous cells can escape from a tumor, spread throughout the body via blood and lymph vessels, and then invade other tissues.

✔ **Reading Check** *How do cancers spread?*

Causes In the latter part of the eighteenth century, a British physician recognized the connection between the exposure to soot and cancer in chimney sweeps. Since that time, scientists have learned more about causes of cancer. Research done in the 1940s and 1950s first related genes to cancer.

Although not all the causes of cancer are known, many causes have been identified. Smoking has been linked to lung cancer—the leading cause of cancer deaths for males in the United States. Exposure to certain chemicals also can increase your chances of developing cancer. These substances, called carcinogens (kar SIH nuh junz), include asbestos, various solvents, heavy metals, alcohol, and home and garden chemicals. Exposure to X rays, nuclear radiation, and ultraviolet radiation of the Sun also increases your risk of cancer.

Table 4 Characteristics of Cancer Cells
Cell growth is uncontrolled.
These cells do not function as part of your body.
The cells take up space and interfere with normal body functions.
The cells travel throughout the body.
The cells produce tumors and abnormal growths anywhere in your body.

Table 5 Early Warning Signs of Cancer

Changes in bowel or bladder habits

A sore that does not heal

Unusual bleeding or discharge

Thickening or lump in the breast or elsewhere

Indigestion or difficulty swallowing

Obvious change in a wart or mole

Nagging cough or hoarseness

from the National Cancer Institute

Prevention Knowing some causes of cancer might help you prevent it. The first step is to know the early warning signs, listed in **Table 5.** Medical attention and treatments such as chemotherapy or surgery in the early stages of some cancers can cure or keep them inactive.

A second step in cancer prevention concerns lifestyle choices. Choosing not to use tobacco and alcohol products can help prevent mouth and lung cancers and the other associated respiratory and circulatory system diseases. Selecting a healthy diet without many foods that are high in fats, salt, and sugar also might reduce your chances of developing cancer. Using sunscreen and limiting the amount of time that you expose your skin to direct sunlight are good preventive measures against skin cancer. Careful handling of harmful home and garden chemicals will help you avoid the dangers connected with these substances.

section 4 review

Summary

Disease in History

- Pasteur, Koch, and Lister made important discoveries about the causes and how to prevent the spread of diseases.

Infectious Diseases and HIV

- Bacteria, fungi, protists, and viruses can cause infectious disease.
- STDs are passed during sexual contact and are caused by bacteria or viruses.
- HIV infection can lead to AIDS, a disease that attacks the immune system.

Fighting Disease

- Good health habits can help prevent the spread of disease.

Chronic Disease and Cancer

- Allergies, diabetes, and cancer are chronic noninfectious diseases.
- Early detection and lifestyle choices can help treat or prevent some cancers.

Self Check

1. **Name** an infectious disease caused by each of the following: a virus, a bacterium, a protist, and a fungus. `SC.G.1.3.1`

2. **Compare and contrast** how HIV and other viruses affect the immune system. `SC.G.1.3.1`

3. **Explain** why diabetes is classified as a noninfectious disease.

4. **Recognize** how poor hygiene is related to the spread of disease.

5. **Describe** how your body might respond to an allergen.

6. **Think Critically** In what ways does Koch's procedure demonstrate the use of scientific methods?

Applying Math

7. **Make and Use Graphs** Make a bar graph using the following data about the number of deaths from AIDS-related diseases for children younger than 13 years old: 1995, 536; 1996, 420; 1997, 209; 1998, 115; and 1999, 76. `MA.E.1.3.1`

Micro Organisms and Disease

Microorganisms are everywhere. Washing your hands and disinfecting items you use helps remove some of these organisms.

Real-World Problem

How do microorganisms cause infection?

Goals

- **Observe** the transmission of microorganisms.
- **Relate** microorganisms to infections.

Materials

fresh apples (6)
rotting apple
rubbing alcohol (5 mL)
self-sealing plastic bags (6)
labels and pencil
gloves

paper towels
sandpaper
cotton ball
soap and water
newspaper

Safety Precautions

Complete a safety worksheet before you begin.

WARNING: *Do not eat the apples. Do not remove goggles until the lab and cleanup are completed. When you complete the experiment, give all bags to your teacher for disposal.*

Procedure

1. **Label** the plastic bags 1 through 6. Put on gloves. Place a fresh apple in bag 1.

2. Rub the rotting apple over the other five apples. This is your source of microorganisms. **WARNING:** *Don't touch your face.*

3. Put one apple in bag 2.

4. Hold one apple 1.5 m above the floor and drop it on a newspaper. Put it in bag 3.

5. Rub one apple with sandpaper. Place this apple in bag 4.

6. Wash one apple with soap and water. Dry it well. Put this apple in bag 5.

7. Use a cotton ball to spread alcohol over the last apple. Let it air-dry. Place it in bag 6.

8. Seal all bags and put them in a dark place.

9. On day 3 and day 7, compare all of the apples without removing them from the bags. Record your observations in a data table.

Apple Observations

Condition	Day 3	Day 7
1. Fresh		
2. Untreated		
3. Dropped		
4. Rubbed with sandpaper	Do not write in this book.	
5. Washed with soap and water		
6. Covered with alcohol		

Conclude and Apply

1. **Infer** How does this experiment relate to infections on your skin?

2. **Explain** why it is important to clean a wound.

Communicating Your Data

Prepare a poster illustrating the advantages of washing hands to avoid the spread of disease. Get permission to put the poster near a school rest room. **For more help, refer to the** Science Skill Handbook.

Benchmark—**SC.H.1.3.4:** The student knows that accurate record keeping, openness, and replication are essential to maintaining an investigator's credibility with other scientists and society; **SC.H.1.3.5:** The student knows that a change in one or more variables may alter the outcome of an investigation.

Design Your Own

Inquiry

Blood Type Reactions

Goals

- **Design** an experiment that simulates the reactions between different blood types.
- **Identify** which blood types can donate to which other blood types.

Possible Materials

simulated blood (10 mL low-fat milk and 10 mL water plus red food coloring)

lemon juice as antigen A (for blood types B and O)

water as antigen A (for blood types A and AB)

droppers

small paper cups

marking pen

10-mL graduated cylinder

Safety Precautions

Complete a safety worksheet before you begin.

WARNING: *Do not taste, eat, or drink any materials used in the lab.*

⊙ *Real-World Problem*

Human blood can be classified into four main blood types— A, B, AB, and O. These types are determined by the presence or absence of antigens on the red blood cells. After blood is collected into a transfusion bag, it is tested to determine the blood type. The type is labeled clearly on the bag. Blood is refrigerated to keep it fresh and available for transfusion. What happens when two different blood types are mixed?

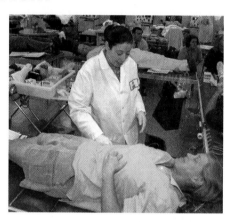

⊙ *Form a Hypothesis*

Based on your reading and observations, form a hypothesis to explain how different blood types will react to each other. Be specific.

⊙ *Test Your Hypothesis*

Make a Plan

1. As a group, agree upon a hypothesis and decide how you will test it. Identify the results that will confirm the hypothesis.

2. **List** the steps you must take and the materials you will need to test your hypothesis. Be specific. Describe exactly what you will do in each step.

3. **Prepare** a data table in your Science Journal to record your observations.

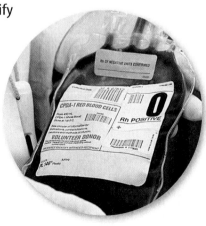

4. Reread the entire experiment to make sure all steps are in logical order.

5. **Identify** constants and variables.

6. **Identify** the control for this experiment.

Follow Your Plan

1. Make sure your teacher approves your plan before you start.

2. Carry out the experiment according to the approved plan.

3. While doing the experiment, record your observations and complete the data table in your Science Journal.

● Analyze Your Data

1. **Compare** the reactions of each blood type (A, B, AB, and O) when antigen A was added to the blood.

2. **Observe** where a change took place.

3. **Compare** your results with those of other groups.

4. What was the control in this experiment? Variables?

● Conclude and Apply

1. Did the results support your hypothesis? Explain.

2. **Predict** what might happen to a person if other antigens are not matched properly.

3. What would happen in an investigation with antigen B added to each blood type?

Communicating Your Data

Write a brief report on how blood is tested to determine blood type. Describe why this is important to know before receiving a blood transfusion. **For more help, refer to the** Science Skill Handbook.

Dr. Daniel Hale Williams was a pioneer in open-heart surgery.

Have a Heart

People didn't always know where blood came from or how it moved through the body.

You prick your finger, and when blood starts to flow out of the cut, you put on a bandage. But if you were a scientist living long ago, you might have also asked yourself some questions: How did your blood get to the tip of your finger? And why and how does it flow through (and sometimes out of!) your body?

As early as the 1500s, a Spanish scientist named Miguel Serveto (mee GEL • ser VEH toh) asked that question. His studies led him to the theory that blood circulated throughout the human body, but he didn't know how or why.

About 100 years later, William Harvey, an English doctor, explored Serveto's idea. Harvey studied animals to develop a theory about how the heart and the circulatory system work. Blood was pumped from the heart throughout the body,

Harvey hypothesized. Then it returned to the heart and recirculated. He published his ideas in 1628 in his famous book, *On the Motion of the Heart and Blood in Animals.* His theories were correct, and Harvey's book became the basis for all modern research on heart and blood vessels.

Medical Pioneer

More than two centuries later, another pioneer, Dr. Daniel Hale Williams, stepped forward and used Harvey's ideas to change the science frontier again. He performed the first open-heart surgery by removing a knife from the heart of a stabbing victim. He stitched the wound in the fluid sac surrounding the heart, and the patient lived for several years afterward.

Report Identify a pioneer in science or medicine who has changed our lives for the better. Find out how this person started in the field, and how they came to make an important discovery. Give a presentation to the class. LA.A.2.3.5 LA.C.3.3.3

TIME

Reviewing Main Ideas

Section 1 Blood

1. Red blood cells carry oxygen and carbon dioxide, platelets form clots, and white blood cells fight infection.

2. A, B, AB, and O blood types are determined by the presence or absence of antigens on red blood cells.

Section 2 Circulation

1. Arteries carry blood away from the heart and veins return blood to the heart. Capillaries connect arteries to veins.

2. The circulatory system can be divided into three sections—coronary, pulmonary, and systemic circulation.

3. Lymph structures filter blood, produce white blood cells, and destroy worn out blood cells.

Section 3 Immunity

1. Your body is protected against most pathogens by the immune system.

2. Active immunity is long lasting, but passive immunity is not.

Section 4 Diseases

1. Pasteur and Koch discovered that microorganisms cause diseases. Lister learned that cleanliness helps control microorganisms.

2. Bacteria, viruses, fungi, and protists can cause infectious diseases.

3. HIV damages your body's immune system, which can cause AIDS.

4. Causes of noninfectious diseases, such as diabetes and cancer, include genetics, a poor diet, chemicals, and uncontrolled cell growth.

Visualizing Main Ideas

Copy and complete this concept map on the functions of the parts of the blood.

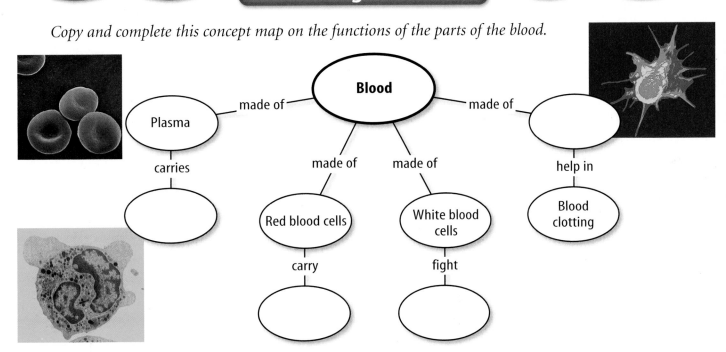

Using Vocabulary

active immunity p. 175	lymph p. 172
allergen p. 182	noninfectious
antibody p. 174	disease p. 182
antigen p. 174	passive immunity p. 175
artery p. 168	pasteurization p. 177
capillary p. 168	plasma p. 162
hemoglobin p. 163	platelet p. 163
infectious disease p. 178	vein p. 168

Match the correct vocabulary word or words with these definitions.

1. the chemical in red blood cells

2. cell fragments that help clot blood

3. occurs when your body makes its own antibodies

4. stimulates histamine release

5. heating a liquid to kill harmful bacteria

6. examples include measles, flu, and the common cold

Checking Concepts

Choose the word or phrase that best answers the question.

7. Where does the exchange of food, oxygen, and wastes occur?
   A) arteries C) veins
   B) capillaries D) lymph vessels

8. How can infectious diseases be caused?
   A) heredity C) chemicals
   B) allergies D) organisms

9. Where is blood under greatest pressure?
   A) arteries C) veins
   B) capillaries D) lymph vessels

10. Which cells fight off infection?
    A) red blood C) white blood
    B) bone D) nerve

11. Of the following, which carries oxygen in blood?
    A) red blood cells C) white blood cells
    B) platelets D) lymph

12. What is required to clot blood?
    A) plasma C) platelets
    B) oxygen D) carbon dioxide

Use the table below to answer question 13.

Table 1 Blood Types		
Blood Type	**Antigen**	**Antibody**
A	A	Anti-B
B	B	Anti-A
AB	A, B	None
0	None	Anti-A, Anti-B

13. Using the table above, what kind of antigen does type O blood have?
    A) A C) A and B
    B) B D) no antigen

14. Where does oxygen-rich blood enter the heart first?
    A) right atrium
    B) left atrium
    C) left ventricle
    D) right ventricle

15. What is formed in the blood to fight invading antigens?
    A) hormones C) pathogens
    B) allergens D) antibodies

16. Which disease is caused by a virus that attacks white blood cells?
    A) AIDS C) flu
    B) measles D) polio

Vocabulary PuzzleMaker fl6.msscience.com

Thinking Critically

17. **Compare and contrast** the life spans of red blood cells, white blood cells, and platelets.

18. **Sequence** blood clotting from the wound to forming a scab.

19. **Compare and contrast** the functions of arteries, veins, and capillaries.

20. **Analyze** how antibodies, antigens, and antibiotics differ.

21. **Recognize Cause and Effect** Use library references to identify the cause—bacteria, virus, fungus, or protist—of each of these diseases: athlete's foot, AIDS, cold, dysentery, flu, pinkeye, acne, and strep throat.

22. **Classify** Using word processing software, make a table to classify the following diseases as infectious or noninfectious: diabetes, gonorrhea, herpes, strep throat, syphilis, cancer, and flu.

Use the graph below to answer question 23.

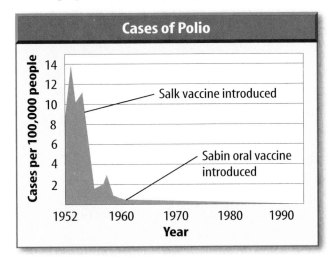

Cases of Polio

Salk vaccine introduced

Sabin oral vaccine introduced

Cases per 100,000 people

1952 1960 1970 1980 1990
Year

23. **Explain** the rate of polio cases between 1952 and 1965. What conclusions can you draw about the effectiveness of the polio vaccine?

Performance Activities

24. **Scientific Drawing** Prepare a drawing of the human heart and label its parts. Use arrows to show the flow of blood through the heart.

25. **Poster** Design and construct a poster to illustrate how a person with the flu could spread the disease to family members, classmates, and others.

26. **Pamphlet** Prepare a pamphlet describing heart transplants. Include an explanation of why the patient is given drugs that suppress the immune system and describe the patient's life after the operation.

Applying Math

27. **Percentages of Blood Cells** A cubic millimeter of blood has about five million red blood cells, 7,500 white blood cells, and 400,000 platelets. Find the total number of red blood cells, white blood cells, and platelets in 1 mm³ of blood. Calculate what percentage of the total each type is. **MA.A.3.3.2**

Use the table below to answer question 28.

Gender and Heart Rate	
Sex	**Pulse/Minute**
Male 1	72
Male 2	64
Male 3	65
Female 1	67
Female 2	84
Female 3	74

28. **Heart Rates** Interpret the data listed in the table above. Find the average heart rate of the three males and the three females, and compare the two averages. **MA.E.1.3.1**

 The assessed Florida Benchmark appears above each question.
Record your answers on the answer sheet provided by your teacher or on a sheet of paper.

Multiple Choice

SC.F.1.3.1

1 Which statement **best** describes the interaction between the circulatory and respiratory systems?

A. Blood carries oxygen from the heart to the lungs.

B. Blood carries oxygen from the body cells to the lungs.

C. Blood carries carbon dioxide from the body cells to the lungs.

D. Blood carries carbon dioxide from the lungs to the body cells.

SC.F.1.3.6

2 Your body creates antibodies in response to an antigen. The diagram below shows a memory B cell with antibodies attached.

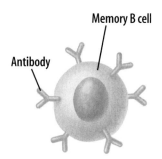

Memory B cell

Antibody

What role will the antibodies play in a future attack by a recognized antigen?

F. They create more T cells.

G. They create more memory B cells.

H. They destroy the antigen.

I. They destroy memory B cells.

SC.F.1.3.1

3 Which correctly describes how the human heart pumps blood?

A. Two muscular atria push blood into the arteries.

B. Two muscular ventricles push blood into the arteries.

C. Two atria and two ventricles push blood into the veins.

D. One atrium and one ventricle push blood into the veins.

SC.F.1.3.6

4 The diagram below shows regular blood cells and misshaped sickle cells within blood vessels.

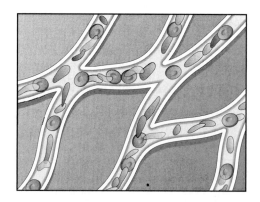

How can sickle-shaped red blood cells affect circulation?

F. They carry less carbon dioxide to body tissues.

G. They fail to fight any infectious agent that enters the body.

H. They block arteries and cause high blood pressure.

I. They stick to capillary walls and tissues receive less oxygen.

SC.F.1.3.1

5 Much of the exchange of materials between body cells and the circulatory system occurs in the capillaries. Which of the following **best** describes the structure and function of capillaries?

  A. They are thick and prevent foreign materials from entering the cells of the body.

  B. They are thin and allow materials to easily move in and out of the bloodstream.

  C. They are thin and wastes can easily move from the bloodstream to the cells.

  D. They are thick and keep the materials from leaving the bloodstream.

Gridded Response

SC.G.1.3.2

6 The table below shows the results of how Ashley's body reacted during certain activities.

Results from Ashley's Activities			
Activity	Pulse Rate (beats/min)	Body Temperature	Degree of Sweating
1	80	98.6°F	None
2	90	98.8°F	Minimal
3	100	98.9°F	Little
4	120	99.1°F	Moderate
5	150	99.5°F	Considerable

In beats per minute, what was the difference of Ashley's heart rate from Activity 4 to Activity 5?

Short Response

SC.G.1.3.2

7 Vaccinations are given to protect the body from serious diseases. Each vaccination contains a form of an antigen carried by a disease-causing agent. How does a vaccination help prevent a disease?

Extended Response

SC.H.1.3.5

8 Nadia wants to see the effect different types of events have on a person's heart rate. She made the table below to record the data for her investigation.

Effect of Events on Heart Rate				
Subject	Event	Heart Rate (beats/minute)		
		At Rest	After Event	Change
A	Tap on the back	80		
B	Sudden loud sound	90		
C	Sudden darkness	70		

PART A Analyze the variables in Nadia's data table. What change should be made in the experimental design?

PART B How might conducting the experiment the way Nadia has planned affect the results of her study?

FCAT Tip

Read Carefully Be sure you understand the question before you read the answer choices. Make special note of words like NOT or EXCEPT. Read and consider all the answer choices before you mark your answer sheet.

Life and the Environment

How Are
Oatmeal & Carpets
Connected?

In the 1850s, the first oatmeal mill began operation in the United States. Over the next few decades, hot, creamy oatmeal became a popular breakfast cereal across the country. By the early 1900s, oatmeal was getting some stiff competition from newly invented cold breakfast cereals such as cornflakes. Hot or cold, cereal had become a breakfast staple. But the processing of oats and corn for cereal leaves behind waste products—oat hulls and corncobs. In 1922, a cereal company discovered it could do something useful with these waste products. The company used oat hulls to make a substance called furfural. Today, furfural also is made from corncobs and other cereal waste products. Manufacturers use furfural in the production of synthetic rubber, plastic, and nylon—including the nylon that goes into carpets.

unit ⚡ projects

Visit unit projects at **fl6.msscience.com** for project ideas and resources. Projects include:

- **Career** You are an environmental scientist as you design your own ecosystem-interaction web to demonstrate relationships from birth to death of your specific organism.
- **Technology** Chart your research results on the manufacturing of different materials. Compare cost, energy use, resources, and environmental concerns.
- **Model** Design your own two-week personal conservation project. Decide how you can make a difference as you reduce, reuse, and recycle.

WebQuest Investigate the *Barrier Islands* ecosystem, then form an opinion as to whether developers should build on these environmentally fragile islands.

Sunshine State Standards—**SC.D.2:** The student understands the need for protection of the natural systems on Earth; **SC.G.1:** The student understands the competitive, interdependent, cyclic nature of living things; **SC.G.2:** The student understands the consequences of using limited natural resources; **SC.H.2.**

Ecology

How do frogs catch insects?

Today is perfect for a field trip to a local stream. Carefully, quietly, you push aside some cattails. You lean in for a closer look when—WHAM! A sticky tongue latches onto a nearby insect and flings it into the waiting mouth of a frog. You jump and the frog leaps into the water. SPLASH! You have just observed a living system in action.

Science Journal   Describe how fallen leaves and insects contribute to the survival of frogs in this system.

Start-Up Activities

 SC.H.2.3.1

What is a living system?

A system is any group of things that interact with one another. Living organisms interact with each other and with the environment to form ecosystems. Ecology is the study of these interactions.

1. Complete a safety worksheet.

2. Choose a small area of grass or weeds near your school. Mark the boundaries of your plot by placing an object at each corner.

3. Carefully observe and record everything in your plot. Be sure to include all parts of your plot, including soil and air.

4. Classify what you observe into two groups—things that are living and things that are not living.

5. **Think Critically** In your Science Journal, describe how you think the parts of the plot you observed form a system.

Science Online
Preview this chapter's content and activities at
fl6.msscience.com

FOLDABLES™ Study Organizer

Ecology Make the following Foldable to help identify what you already know, what you want to know, and what you learned about ecology.

LA.A.1.3.4

STEP 1 Fold a sheet of paper vertically from side to side. Make the front edge about 1.25 cm shorter than the back edge.

STEP 2 Turn lengthwise and **fold** into thirds.

STEP 3 **Unfold and cut** only the top layer along both folds to make three tabs.

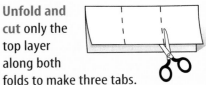

STEP 4 **Label** each tab as shown.

Know? Like to know? Learned?

Identify Questions Before you read the chapter, write what you already know about ecology under the left tab of your Foldable, and write questions about what you'd like to know under the center tab. After you read the chapter, list what you learned under the right tab.

Benchmarks—**SC.D.2.3.1 (p. 205):** The student understands that the quality of life is relevant to personal experience; **SC.G.2.3.2 (pp. 198–205):** The student knows that all biotic and abiotic factors are interrelated and that if one factor is changed or removed, it impacts the availability of other resources within the system; **SC.H.2.3.1 (pp. 197, 198–199):** The student recognizes that patterns exist within and across systems.

Also covers: **SC.D.1.3.4 Annually Assessed (p. 202), SC.G.1.3.4 Annually Assessed (p. 205), SC.H.1.3.5 Annually Assessed (p. 203), SC.H.1.3.7 Annually Assessed (p. 206)**

What is an ecosystem?

as you read

What You'll Learn

- **Describe** the living and nonliving factors in an ecosystem.
- **Explain** how the parts of an ecosystem interact.

Why It's Important

Understanding interactions of an ecosystem will help you understand your role in your ecosystem.

Review Vocabulary

✹ **organism:** any living thing; uses energy, is made of cells, reproduces, responds, and grows

New Vocabulary

- ✹ **ecosystem**
- ✹ **environment**
- ● **ecology**
- ● **biosphere**
- ✹ **biotic factor**
- ✹ **abiotic factor**

✹ FCAT Vocabulary

Ecosystems

Take a walk outside and look around. If you observe an area closely, you might see many different organisms (OR guh nih zumz) living there. In your backyard, you might see squirrels, birds, insects, grass, and shrubs. These organisms, along with the nonliving things in the yard, such as soil, air, and light, make an ecosystem (EE koh sihs tum). An **ecosystem** is made up of organisms interacting with one another and with nonliving factors to form a working unit. **Figure 1** shows an example of a stream ecosystem.

What does it mean to say that one organism interacts with another organism? Think back to the field trip at the beginning of the chapter. When the frog ate the insect, an interaction occurred between two organisms living in the same ecosystem.

What does it mean to say that an organism interacts with the nonliving parts of an ecosystem? Think about the field trip again. What did the frog do when it spotted your movement? It dove into the stream, probably for safety. The frog uses the stream for shelter. This is an example of an interaction between a living organism and a nonliving part of an ecosystem. All conditions, both living and nonliving, that surround and affect an organism are called its **environment.**

Patterns that exist in one environment can affect other environments. For example, a hurricane over an ocean environment has a great effect when it travels over land environments.

Figure 1 Let's identify the living and nonliving parts of this stream ecosystem. Rocks and water are nonliving things. Water striders are alive— these insects skim the surface of the water. Algae, fish, crayfish, and mosses covering rocks are other living parts of this ecosystem.
Describe *how these living organisms interact with nonliving parts of the ecosystem.*

The Study of Ecosystems When you study the interactions in an ecosystem, you are studying the science of ecology (ih KAH luh jee). **Ecology** is the study of the interactions that take place among the living organisms and nonliving parts of an ecosystem. Ecologists spend most of their time outdoors, observing the subject matter in the field. Just as you knelt quietly in the cattails on your field trip, an ecologist might spend hours by a stream, watching, recording, and analyzing what goes on there. In addition, like other scientists, ecologists also conduct experiments in laboratories. For instance, they might need to analyze samples of stream water. The observations in the field and laboratory work help give a complete picture of an ecosystem.

The Largest Ecosystem Ecosystems come in all sizes. Some are small, like a pile of leaves. Others are big, like a forest. **Figure 2** shows the biosphere (BI uh sfihr), the largest ecosystem on Earth. The **biosphere** is the part of Earth where organisms can live. It includes the topmost layer of Earth's crust; all the oceans, rivers, and lakes; and the surrounding atmosphere. The biosphere is made up of all the ecosystems on Earth combined.

How many different ecosystems are part of the biosphere? Let's list a few. There are deserts, mountains, rivers, prairies, wetlands, forests, plains, oceans—the list can go on and on, and we haven't even gotten to smaller ecosystems yet, such as a vacant lot or a rotting tree trunk. The number of ecosystems that make up the biosphere is almost too many to count. How would you describe your ecosystem?

Figure 2 The biosphere is the part of Earth that contains all the living things on the planet. Each ecosystem that you study is part of the biosphere.

Living Parts of Ecosystems

Each ecosystem in the biosphere contains many different living organisms. Think about a rotting tree trunk. It's a small ecosystem compared to a forest, but the tree trunk may be home to bacteria, bees, beetles, mosses, mushrooms, slugs, snails, snakes, wildflowers, woodpeckers, and worms. The organisms that make up the living part of an ecosystem are called **biotic factors.** An organism depends on other biotic (bi AH tihk) factors for food, shelter, protection, and reproduction. For example, a snake might use a rotting log for shelter. Termites are insects that depend on the same log for food. **Figure 3** shows some of the biotic factors in an estuary ecosystem.

Figure 3

Water birds, oysters, jellies, and fish are just some of the organisms that make up an estuary's living, or biotic, factors. An estuary is an ecosystem formed where freshwater from rivers and streams mixes with the salty water from the ocean, like the Apalachee Bay near Tallahassee, Florida. Water in an estuary is saltier than freshwater but less salty than water from the ocean. An estuary is protected from tides by reefs, islands, mud, or sand. These conditions make a unique habitat.

Life in an estuary is specially adapted to living there. An estuary provides a rest stop for migrating birds, a protected nursery for fish and shellfish, as well as a home for many plants and other animals. Organisms such as horseshoe crabs, ospreys, manatees, mangroves, and seagrasses thrive in this habitat. They interact with each other and with the nonliving parts of the ecosystem, such as the sunlight, air, water, and soil.

The osprey, a member of the eagle family, has a diet consisting mostly of fish. The shallow waters of the estuary make hunting easier.

Osprey nest

Cypress tree

Brown pelican

Red mangrove

Redhead duck

Plankton

Bay scallop

Striped mullet

The manatee is protected from predators in the slow-moving water of the estuary. The manatee's primary food source, seagrass, is abundant in the shallow waters of the estuary.

Seagrasses provide habitat and food for many species.

The low salt content of the water of the estuary keeps the predators of the American oyster away.

The horseshoe crab comes on land once a year to mate and lay eggs.

Figure 4 Different types of soil support different kinds of plant life. Cactus and other desert plants can thrive in dry, sandy, or rocky soils. Forest soils are deep, moist, and full of nutrients from decaying leaves.

Nonliving Parts of Ecosystems

Earlier, you listed the parts that make up an ecosystem near your school. Was your list limited to the living organisms—the biotic factors—only? No. You included nonliving factors, too, such as air and soil. The nonliving things found in an ecosystem are called **abiotic** (ay bi AH tihk) **factors.** Look for some abiotic factors in the estuary shown in **Figure 3.** Abiotic factors affect the type and number of organisms living in ecosystems. Let's take a closer look at some abiotic factors.

Soil One abiotic factor that can affect which plants and other organisms are found in an ecosystem is soil. It is made up of several ingredients, much like a recipe. Soil is made up of a combination of minerals, water, air, and organic matter—the decaying parts of plants and animals. You know that salt, flour, and sugar are found in many recipes. But not all foods made from these same ingredients taste or look the same. Cakes and cookies look and taste different because different amounts of salt, flour, and sugar are used to make them. It's the same with soil. Different amounts of minerals, organic matter, water, and air make different types of soil, as shown in **Figure 4.**

Reading Check *What ingredients make up soil?*

Different soils offer different materials and conditions for organisms. If you've ever visited a gardening store, you've seen all kinds of products gardeners add to their soil to make it just right for the types of plants they want to grow. The next time you dig a hole, take a close look at the soil. Is it dry? Does it have a lot of dead leaves and twigs in it? Is it tightly packed or loose and airy?

Temperature Soil is only one of the factors that affect the organisms that live in an ecosystem. Temperature also determines which organisms live in a particular place. How do the tropical plants shown in **Figure 5** compare with the mountainside plants? Predict what would happen if the organisms on the mountainside were moved to a hot climate such as a tropical rain forest.

Figure 5 Plants have adaptations for their environments. The mountainside wildflowers grow in clusters close to the ground, which protects them from strong winds. The tropical plants have large leaves to absorb as much light as possible in the dim light of the rain forest floor.

SC.H.1.3.5

Mini LAB

Observing Soil Characteristics

Procedure
1. Complete a safety worksheet.
2. Using different amounts of the materials available to create two different "soil recipes," fill **two cups** with **soil**. Pack the soil equally into each cup.
3. Pour equal amounts of **water** into each cup.
4. After a minute or so, tip the cups over to see if any water pours out.
5. Observe the characteristics of the soils you made. Record your observations in your Science Journal.

Analysis
1. What was the difference between the soil in the two cups to start with?
2. Was there a difference in how the soil in each cup held water? What environments might have soils like these?

Water Another important abiotic factor is water. In the field trip to the stream at the beginning of the chapter, maybe you saw a sleek trout dart through the water. Some organisms, such as fish, whales, and algae (AL jee), are adapted for life in water, not on land. But these organisms depend upon water for more than just a home. Water helps all living things carry out important life processes such as digestion and waste removal. In fact, most cells are made up largely of water. Iceberg lettuce is about 95 percent water! Scientists estimate that two-thirds of the weight of the human body is water, as shown in **Figure 6.** Do you know how much you weigh? Calculate about how much of your weight is made up of water.

Because water is so important to living things, it is also important to an ecosystem. The amount of water available in an ecosystem can determine how many organisms can live in a particular area. It can also serve as shelter and as a way to move from place to place.

Sunlight The Sun is the main source of energy for most organisms on Earth. Energy from the Sun is used by green plants to produce food. Humans and other animals then obtain their energy by eating these plants and other organisms that have fed on the plants. When you eat food produced by a plant, you are consuming energy that started out as sunlight. You'll learn more about the transfer of energy in an ecosystem later in this chapter.

✔ Reading Check *Why are water and sunlight important to ecosystems?*

Figure 6 Sunlight and water are two abiotic factors essential to ecosystems. Water is important to humans because about 66 percent of our bodies is composed of water.
Explain *why most ecosystems could not exist without sunlight.*

A Balanced System

Every ecosystem is made up of many different biotic and abiotic factors working together. When these factors are in balance, the system is in balance, too.

Ecosystems are constantly changing. These changes affect the quality of life in different ways for different organisms. For example, hurricanes can change an ecosystem greatly, as shown in **Figure 7.** They are extremely destructive, causing erosion, fish kills, and loss of beach vegetation. The beach vegetation clogs the waterways causing oxygen depletion. However, the flooding caused by hurricanes adds soil and nutrients to marshes. This can make the marshes healthier by allowing new growth and habitat. Nutrients tied up in the bottom water can be stirred up and mixed back into the aquatic system, having beneficial, long-term effects. Studies also have shown that some aquatic animals thrive after a hurricane, due to less competition and nutrient-rich waters. Now the ecosystem must reach a new balance.

Figure 7 Hurricane-force winds destroyed the trees and fruit in this orange grove. This environment might recover over time but habitats have been lost temporarily.

section 1 review

Summary

Ecosystems

- Ecosystems are made up of organisms that interact with each other and with the nonliving parts of the environment.
- Ecology is the study of interactions that occur in ecosystems.
- The biosphere is the part of Earth that supports life.

Living Parts of Ecosystems

- Biotic factors are the organisms in an ecosystem.

Nonliving Parts of Ecosystems

- Abiotic factors include soil, temperature, water, and sunlight.

A Balanced System

- Ecosystems change over time.

Self Check

1. **Describe** two ways in which an organism can interact with the other biotic factors of the ecosystem in which it lives. `SC.G.2.3.1`

2. **Explain** four ways in which abiotic factors are important to an ecosystem. `SC.G.2.3.1`

3. **Compare and contrast** the meanings of the terms *ecosystem* and *biosphere.*

4. **Think Critically** You have been asked to design a space station on the Moon. Use your knowledge of ecosystems to describe how you would develop your design.

Applying Skills

5. **Describe** the ecosystem that you are a part of. What are the biotic factors? The abiotic factors? What kinds of interactions take place in your ecosystem? `SC.G.2.3.1`

Benchmark—**SC.F.2.3.3:** The student knows that generally organisms in a population live long enough to reproduce because they have survival characteristics; **SC.G.2.3.3:** The student knows that a brief change in the limited resources of an ecosystem may alter the size of a population or the average size of individual organisms and that long-term change may result in the elimination of animal and plant populations inhabiting the Earth; **SC.H.1.3.5:** The student knows that a change in one or more variables may alter the outcome of an investigation; **SC.H.1.3.7:** The student knows that when similar investigations give different results, the scientific challenge is to verify whether the differences are significant by further study.

Toothpick Fish

The environment not only affects how each species interacts with biotic and abiotic factors, it also can affect the genes that are passed to another generation.

Number of Fish Offspring					
Environment	Generation	Green	Red	Orange	Yellow
Green seaweed grows everywhere.	First				
	Second		Do not write in this book.		
	Third				
	Fourth				
The seaweed dies.	Fifth	0			

▶ Real-World Problem

How does the environment affect a species' genetics?

Goals

- **Identify** how the environment can affect the genes of a species.
- **Demonstrate** that environmental factors can result in the extinction of a species on Earth.

Materials

cup
toothpicks (24 total: 8 green, 8 red, 8 yellow)

Safety Precautions

Complete a safety worksheet before you begin.

▶ Procedure

1. Place the toothpicks in the cup. The cup represents all of the genes of a fish species in an ecosystem. The colored toothpicks represent genes, and a pair of toothpicks represents a fish. One or two green toothpicks is a fish with green skin, two red toothpicks is a fish with red skin, and two yellow toothpicks is a fish with yellow skin. A red and a yellow toothpick is a fish with orange skin.

2. Without looking, remove two toothpicks from the cup. Record the color of this fish in your Science Journal.

3. Repeat step 2 until the cup is empty.

4. A pollutant kills the plants along the shore. The green fish have no place to hide to escape predators. Put all but your green fish back into the cup.

5. Repeat steps 2, 3, and 4 two more times to model the passing of genes over time.

▶ Conclude and Apply

1. **Explain** why the green toothpicks did not go back into the gene pool.

2. **Describe** how the long-term environmental change affected the fish population.

3. **Infer** how environmental changes could lead to the extinction of a species.

Communicating Your Data

Combine the data from all students in your class. Calculate the average number of each fish color for each trail. How does your data compare to the class averages? Were any students' results significantly different from the average? If so, determine why.

Also covers: SC.D.1.3.2 Annually Assessed (p. 207), SC.G.2.3.3 (p. 209)

Relationships Among Living Things

Organizing Ecosystems

Imagine trying to study all of the living things on Earth at once! When ecologists study living things, they usually don't start by studying the entire biosphere. Remember, the biosphere consists of all the parts of Earth where organisms can live. It's much easier to begin by studying smaller parts of the biosphere.

To separate the biosphere into smaller systems that are easier to study, ecologists find it helpful to organize living things into groups. They then study how members of a group interact with each other and their environments.

Groups of Organisms Look at the fish in **Figure 8.** This particular kind of fish lives in a coral reef in the warm, shallow waters near Florida. The fish uses energy, grows, reproduces, and eventually dies. The coral reef is the ecosystem the fish lives in. All of the fish that live in this particular coral reef make up a population. A **population** is a group of the same type of organisms living in the same place at the same time. Some other populations that you might find in a coral reef ecosystem are sponges, algae, sharks, and coral. What are some populations of organisms that live around your school?

as you read

What **You'll Learn**

- **Explain** how ecologists organize living systems.
- **Describe** relationships among living things.

Why **It's Important**

Learning how living things relate to one another will help you understand how you depend on other organisms for survival.

Review Vocabulary

✳ **adaptation:** any variation that makes an organism better suited to its environment

New Vocabulary

✳ **population**
✳ **community**
● limiting factor
● niche
✳ **habitat**

✳ FCAT Vocabulary

Figure 8 This school of blue-striped grunt fish belongs to the population of fish living in a coral reef ecosystem.

Calculating Population Density

Procedure

1. Using a **measuring tape,** calculate the total area of your home by multiplying the length times the width of each room and adding all the products together.
2. Count the number of people who live in your home.
3. Divide the number of people living in your home by the total area to determine the population density.

Analysis

1. Calculate what would happen to the population density if the number of people living in your home doubled. If it doubled again?
2. Explain how increasing population density in your home could affect availability of resources in your home.

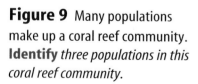

Groups of Populations Many populations live in an ecosystem like the coral reef in **Figure 9.** All of the populations that live in an area make up a **community** (kuh MYEW nuh tee). The members of a community depend on each other for food, shelter, and other needs. For example, a shark depends on the fish populations for food. The fish populations, on the other hand, depend on coral animals to build the reef that they use to hide from the sharks.

No matter where you live, you are part of a community. Make a list of as many of the populations that make up your community as you can. Compare your list with the lists of your classmates. How many populations did the class come up with?

Reading Check *In what ways do the members of a community depend on each other?*

Characteristics of Populations Look around your classroom. Is the room big or small? How many students are in your class? Are there enough books and supplies for everyone? Ecologists ask questions like these to describe populations. They want to know the size of the population, where its members live, and how it is able to stay alive. These characteristics exist for any population, from bacteria to people.

Population Density Think about your classroom. A population of 25 students in a large room has plenty of space. How would the same 25 students fit into a smaller room? Ecologists determine population density (DEN suh tee) by comparing the size of a population with its area. For instance, if 100 dandelions are growing in a field that is one square kilometer in size, then the population density is 100 dandelions per square kilometer.

Figure 9 Many populations make up a coral reef community. **Identify** *three populations in this coral reef community.*

Studying Populations One method an ecologist uses to study populations is mark and recapture. An organism is caught, tagged, and released, then evaluated when it is caught again. This evaluation can include general health, number of times caught, or where the organism is caught. Mark and recapture often is used to track migrations, or seasonal movements, of an organism. The monarch butterfly, shown in **Figure 10,** is tracked using this method. Populations also can be studied by observation, population count, population sampling, and life history.

Limits to Populations

Populations cannot grow larger and larger forever. There wouldn't be enough food, water, living space, and other resources. The resources that limit the size of a population, such as the amount of rainfall or food, are called **limiting factors.** Over time, these factors can alter the size of a population. For example, frogs eat mosquitoes. If a lack of rain caused the mosquito population to decrease, then the frog population might not have enough food and its population size also might decline. These factors also can affect the average size of a population. The Key deer is found only in the Florida Keys. Due to the limited resources found on the islands, only the smaller deer survived and produced offspring.

Competition Are frogs the only organisms in the stream community that eat mosquitoes? No, there are many animals that eat them, including some birds and spiders. That means that frogs must compete with birds and spiders for the same food.

Imagine a bowl of popcorn in your classroom. If it were small, you would have to compete with your classmates to get popcorn. The larger the population of an area, the greater the competition for resources such as food. Organisms also can compete for space, water, light, shelter, and any other resources that may be limited in a particular ecosystem.

Figure 10 Monarch butterflies often are tagged to study their migrations.

LA.B.2.3.4

Sciencenline

Topic: Animal Migration
Visit fl6.msscience.com for Web links to information about tracking animal migrations.

Activity In your Science Journal, draw a map showing the migration route of an animal species.

LA.A.2.3.5
LA.B.2.3.2

INTEGRATE
History

Compasses Monarchs may be able to use Earth's magnetic field as a kind of compass as they fly. Humans have used compasses for centuries. Research the history of compasses and create a time line.

Where and How Organisms Live

How can a small ecosystem such as a classroom aquarium support a variety of different organisms? It's possible because each type of organism has a different role to play in the ecosystem. A typical classroom aquarium may contain snails, fish, algae, and bacteria. The role of snails is to feed on algae. The glass of an aquarium can become clouded by the growth of too much algae. Snails eat the algae, helping keep the glass clear so light can get in. The role of the algae is to provide food for snails and fish, and to provide oxygen for the system through photosynthesis. The role of an organism in an ecosystem is called the organism's **niche** (NICH).

What do you think the role of the fish might be in an aquarium ecosystem? The niche of the fish includes adding nutrients to the ecosystem through its waste products that encourage the growth of algae. All the interactions in which an organism takes part make up its niche.

How would you describe your niche? Perhaps you help dispose of wastes by recycling, or obtain food by grocery shopping. What other activities does your niche include?

Applying Science

Graph Populations

One way to understand more about relationships among organisms in an ecosystem is to keep track of, or monitor, and graph populations. Use the information in **Table 1** to make a graph of population size over time for barn owls and field mice. Then, answer the questions that follow.

Table 1 Monthly Population Size per Hectare (in 100s)									
Month	J	F	M	A	M	J	J	A	S
Field mice	6	5	4	3	3	4	5	4	6
Barn owls	2	3	4	4	2	1	4	3	4

Identifying the Problem

Set up your graph with months on the *x*-axis and numbers of organisms on the *y*-axis. Use two colors to plot your data. For more help, refer to the Math Skill Handbook. Use your graph to infer how the population of field mice affects the population of barn owls.

Solving the Problem

1. Predict how the next two months of the graph will look.
2. Field mice eat green plants and grains. What do you think would happen to the population of barn owls if there were no rain in the area for a long time?

The place where an organism lives is called its **habitat** (HA buh tat). The habitat of a catfish is the muddy bottom of a lake or pond. The habitat of a penguin is the icy waters of the Antarctic. How would you describe the habitat of the pet reptile shown in **Figure 11?**

Different species of organisms often live in the same habitat. Resources, such as food, living space, and shelter, are shared among all the species living in a habitat. For example, the branches of an apple tree provide a habitat for spiders, fruit flies, beetles, caterpillars, and birds. How can all these organisms share the same home? They have different ways of feeding, seeking shelter, and using other resources. In other words, they have different niches. For example, spiders feed on beetles and other insects. Caterpillars eat leaves. Fruit flies feed on apples. Birds eat spiders, caterpillars, or flies. Each species has a different niche within the same habitat.

Figure 11 Each organism in an ecosystem has its own job, or niche. **Explain** *how the reptile and the plant can share the same habitat.*

section 2 review

Summary

Organizing Ecosystems

- A population is a group of the same type of organisms living together in the same place.
- A community is made up of all the populations in an ecosystem.

Limits to Populations

- Limiting factors prevent a population from growing larger.

Where and How Organisms Live

- An organism's role in an ecosystem is its niche.
- An organism's home is its habitat.

Self Check

1. **Identify** a population that lives in your community.
2. **Explain** how the number of trees in a forest could affect the size of a bird population. `SC.G.2.3.2` `SC.G.2.3.3`
3. **Design an experiment** to identify a limiting factor that prevents the snail population in a home aquarium from growing larger.
4. **Think Critically** Ladybug beetles help gardeners control insect pests called aphids. What kind of interaction might take place between ladybug beetles and aphids? `SC.G.2.3.2` `SC.G.2.3.3`

Applying Math

5. **Calculate** the population density of buttercups in a meadow. There are 550 buttercups in a meadow that measures 100 m by 66 m.

section

3

Benchmarks—SC.G.1.3.4 Annually Assessed (pp. 212–214): The student knows that the interactions of organisms with each other and with the non-living parts of their environments result in the flow of energy and the cycling of matter throughout the system.

Also covers: SC.B.1.3.4 (p. 212), SC.B.2.3.1 Annually Assessed (p. 212), SC.D.1.3.4 Annually Assessed (p. 213), SC.G.1.3.5 Annually Assessed (pp. 212–215), SC.G.2.3.2 (p. 213), SC.H.1.3.5 Annually Assessed (pp. 216–217), SC.H.1.3.7 Annually Assessed (p. 217), SC.H.2.3.1 (p. 214)

Energy Through the Ecosystem

as you read

What **You'll Learn**

- **Explain** how organisms get the energy they need.
- **Describe** how energy flows through an ecosystem.

Why **It's Important**

The energy most living things require comes directly or indirectly from the Sun.

Review Vocabulary

recycling: reuse of an item or natural resource that requires changing or reprocessing it

New Vocabulary

✹ **producer**   ✹ **prey**
✹ **consumer**   ✹ **decomposer**
✹ **predator**

✹ FCAT Vocabulary

The Flow of Energy

Energy for most organisms comes from the Sun. This continuous input of energy is moved through the ecosystem in the form of food. Energy transfers never are one hundred percent efficient. At each feeding level the amount of useable energy is reduced because some energy is transformed to heat. For instance, in **Figure 12,** the Sun is the energy source for a plant. When it is eaten by the grasshopper, only some of this energy is transferred. Some of the energy is used by the plant for its life processes, and some is given off as heat. When the bird eats the grasshopper, it receives even less energy. This decrease occurs at every step in the food web. The interactions of organisms with each other and with the nonliving parts of their environments, such as the Sun, result in the flow of energy throughout the system. All energy in an ecosystem is eventually cycled through the ecosystem and used again and again.

Figure 12 In any community, energy flows through the living organisms.

Interactions in Communities

Many different populations can interact in a backyard ecosystem, including plants, birds, insects, squirrels, and fungi, as shown in **Figure 12.** The plants in the ecosystem produce food through photosynthesis. An organism that makes its own food, like a plant, is called a **producer.** The grasshopper that nibbles on the plants is a **consumer.** A consumer eats other organisms.

Consumers There are different types of consumers in an ecosystem. The bird in **Figure 13** is a **predator,** which means it captures and eats other animals. The ladybug is its **prey,** an organism that is hunted and caught for food by another animal. This relationship can be seen in a food chain, like the one shown in **Figure 13.** A food chain shows a sequence of organisms, each of which obtains energy from the next lower member of the sequence as food.

Decomposers Some of the consumers in an ecosystem are so small that you might not notice them, but they have an important role to play. They are the decomposers, such as bacteria and fungi. **Decomposers** use dead organisms and the waste material of other organisms for food.

✔ Reading Check *Identify four ways organisms interact in an ecosystem.*

Organisms That Live Together There are other types of relationships among organisms. In one type of interaction, both organisms in the relationship benefit. The African tick-bird, for instance, gets its food by eating insects off the skin of zebras. The tickbird gets food, while the zebra gets rid of harmful insects. In another type of relationship, only one organism benefits. The other organism doesn't benefit, but is not harmed. A bird building a nest in a tree gets protection from the tree, but the tree isn't harmed. In still another relationship, one organism is helped while the other is harmed. Have you ever been bitten by a mosquito? That's a first-hand experience of this type of relationship. The mosquito benefits because your blood provides nutrients for the female mosquito's eggs. You are harmed and your body will have an immune reaction—an itchy, red bump. You also could get a disease like malaria if you are bitten by an infected mosquito.

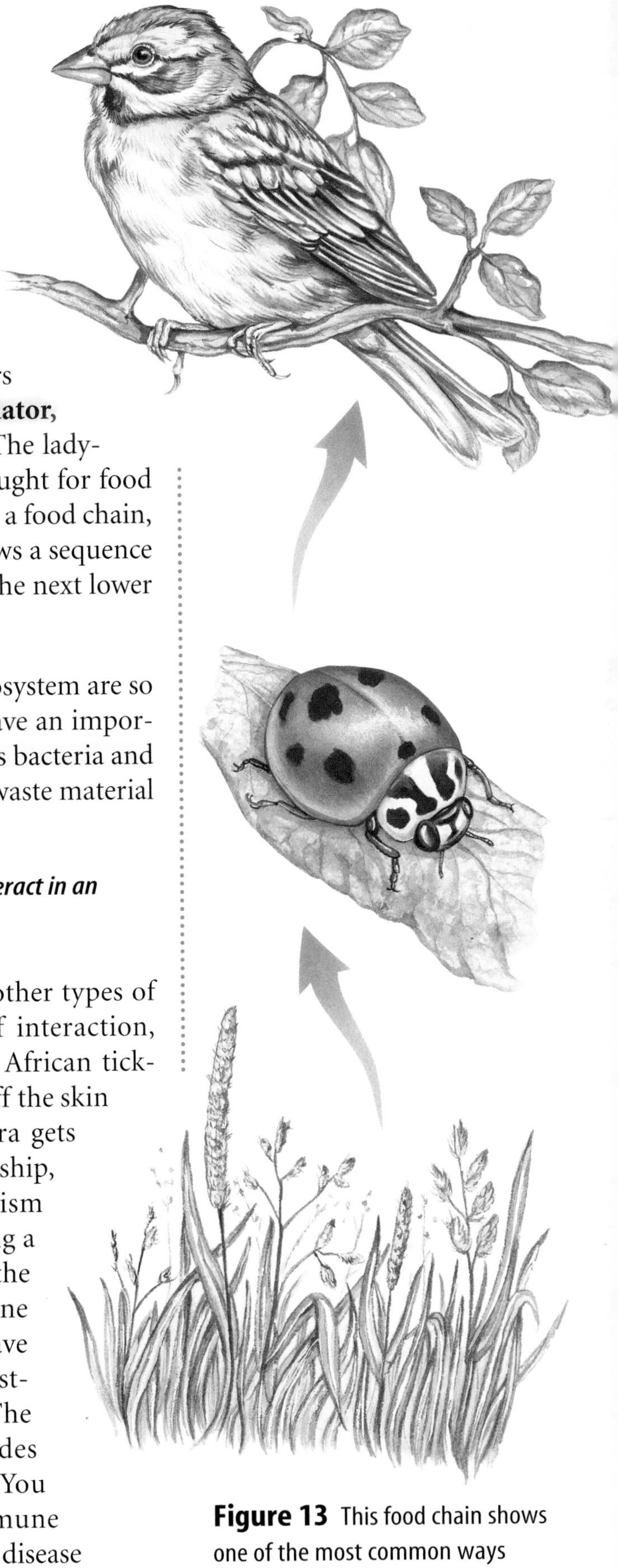

Figure 13 This food chain shows one of the most common ways organisms interact in a community.

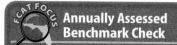

FCAT FOCUS

Annually Assessed Benchmark Check

SC.G.1.3.4 Arrange the following to show the flow of energy: algae, bacteria, fish, osprey, and Sun. How is this matter recycled?

Figure 14 The Sun provides the energy for this food web.

Modeling the Flow of Energy

The food chain in **Figure 13** is a simple model that shows how energy from food passes from one organism to another. Each organism is linked by an arrow. The arrows show that energy moves from one organism to another. However, a food chain does not show every species in the community. For instance, a bird may eat seeds and in turn be eaten by a hawk. The hawk also might eat a snake or a mouse. One food chain cannot model all these overlapping relationships. We need a more complex model to show all the feeding interactions in an ecosystem.

Scientists use a more complicated model, called a food web, to show the transfer of energy in an ecosystem. A food web, shown in **Figure 14,** is a series of overlapping food chains that shows possible feeding relationships in an ecosystem.

☑ **Reading Check** *What does a food web model?*

Feeding patterns and relationships occur throughout all ecosystems. Every organism is part of a food web. In an ocean food web, plankton use the Sun's energy. Some of this energy eventually is transferred to the orca. From the orca, some energy is transferred to decomposers, such as bacteria that feed on the orca's remains. All food webs include an energy source, producers, consumers, and decomposers.

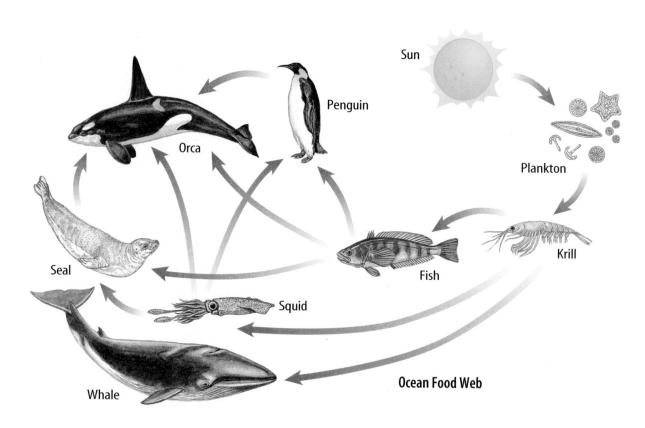

Sun

Penguin

Orca

Plankton

Krill

Seal

Fish

Squid

Whale

Ocean Food Web

Cycling of Materials

What happens when you recycle a soda can? The can is taken to a processing plant and melted so that the aluminum can be used again. This is an example of a simple cycle. The same aluminum can be used over and over again. Cycles are important to ecosystems. Instead of aluminum cans, however, it's the materials that make up organisms that get recycled in an ecosystem.

The bodies of living things are made up of matter, including water and chemicals like nitrogen and carbon. To get the matter needed to build bones, muscles, and skin, you need to eat food made of the right kinds of matter, as the horse in **Figure 15** is doing. In an ecosystem, matter cycles through food chains. The amount of matter on Earth never changes. So matter in ecosystems is recycled, or used again and again.

Living organisms depend on these cycles for survival. Organisms also depend on one another for food, shelter, and other needs. All the different things that make up the biosphere—from a tiny insect to a raging river—have a unique role to play.

FCAT FOCUS — **Annually Assessed Benchmark Check**

SC.G.1.3.5 Imagine a horse eating an apple. Where did the energy come from to grow the apple? How are the atoms of the apples recycled?

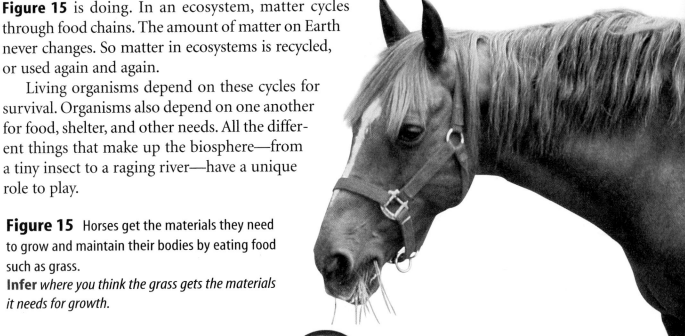

Figure 15 Horses get the materials they need to grow and maintain their bodies by eating food such as grass.
Infer *where you think the grass gets the materials it needs for growth.*

section 3 review

Summary

It's All About Food

- Energy moves through ecosystems in the form of food.
- Producers make their own food.
- Consumers obtain food by eating other organisms.
- Decomposers break down dead organisms.

Modeling the Flow of Energy

- Food chains and food webs show how food energy passes from one organism to another.

Cycling of Materials

- All matter on Earth is recycled through food chains.

Self Check

1. **List** some organisms that are consumers. Give an example of the type of food each eats.
2. **Explain** how the Sun's energy reaches a cat that eats a bird. SC.G.1.3.3
3. **Compare and contrast** food chains and food webs. SC.G.1.3.4
4. **Think Critically** Explain why more energy is available in the first link of a food chain than in the fourth link of the same food chain. SC.B.1.3.4

Applying Skills

5. **Sequence** Use an events-chain concept map to trace the path of energy that flows from the Sun to your body when you eat a piece of chicken. SC.G.1.3.4

Benchmark—**SC.G.2.3.1:** The student knows that some resources are renewable and others are nonrenewable; **SC.H.1.3.5:** The student knows that a change in one or more variables may alter the outcome of an investigation.

Design Your Own

What's the limit? Inquiry

Goals

- **Observe** how space, light, water, or temperature affect how many bean plants are able to grow in a pot.
- **Design an experiment** that shows whether a certain abiotic factor limits a plant population using the materials listed.

Possible Materials

bean seeds
small planting containers
soil
water
labels
spoons
aluminum foil
sunny window or other light source
refrigerator or heater

Safety Precautions

Complete a safety worksheet before you begin.
WARNING: *Wash your hands after you handle soil and seeds.*

⦿ Real-World Problem

How many blades of grass are in a park? It may seem to you like there's no limit to the number of blades of grass that can grow there. However, as you've discovered, there are many factors that organisms like the plants in the park need to live and grow. By experimenting with these factors, you can see how they limit the size of the population. How do space, light, water, and temperature limit plant populations?

⦿ Form a Hypothesis

Think about what you already know about the needs of plants. As a group, form a hypothesis to explain how one abiotic factor may limit the number of bean plants that can grow in a single pot.

⦿ Test Your Hypothesis

Make a Plan

1. **Decide** on a way to test your group's hypothesis. Make a complete materials list as you plan the steps of your experiment.

2. What is the one abiotic factor you will be testing? How will you test it? What factors will you need to control? Be specific in describing how you will handle the other abiotic factors.

3. How long will you run your experiment? How many trials of your experiment will you run?

4. **Decide** what data you will need to collect. Prepare a data table in your Science Journal.

5. **Identify** the variables in your experiment.

6. **Identify** the controls in your experiment.

7. Read over your entire experiment and imagine yourself doing it. Make sure the steps are in logical order.

Follow Your Plan

1. Make sure your teacher has approved your plan and your data table before you proceed.

2. Carry out your plan.

3. **Record** your observations during the experiment.

4. **Complete** your data table in your Science Journal.

▶ *Analyze Your Data*

1. **Make a graph** to show your results.

2. Use a bar graph to compare the number of seedlings that grew in the experimental containers with the number of seedlings that grew in the control containers.

▶ *Conclude and Apply*

1. **Explain** how the abiotic factor you tested affected the bean plant population.

2. **Predict** what would happen to your plant population if you added another kind of plant or animal to the containers.

▶ *Extending Inquiry*

Choose a plant species to study in a local park or green space. Observe different abiotic factors and document where the plant thrives and where it does not.

*C*ommunicating
Your Data

Compare your results with other groups. Explain how different factors affected the plants grown by each group. Investigate further any differences in results to determine if the differences are significant.

Gators at the Gate!

When you think about Florida, you probably picture sandy beaches and palm trees. But do you think about alligators? Alligators are among the best-known animals that live in Florida. They can grow to be 13 feet long and weigh more than 600 pounds.

Endangered Alligators

By the 1960s, the number of alligators was greatly reduced in Florida due to hunting and habitat loss. The numbers became so low that alligators were placed on the endangered species list. A species is listed as endangered

when so few of its members are living that the entire species is in danger of becoming extinct. In the United States, it became illegal to hunt alligators. Gradually the number of alligators went up. By 1977, they were renamed as a threatened species. A threatened species still needs to be protected but is not in immediate danger of becoming extinct. Now, more than a million alligators live on farms and in the wild. Good news, right? Think again. There are problems—big problems from big alligators.

Alligator Problems

Today more people live, work, and play in areas where alligators live. Alligators have been found in swimming pools and on golf courses. Many people believe that the size of Florida's alligator population should be tightly controlled. They fear that more alligators will lead to more encounters with humans and increase the possibility of alligator attacks.

Other people point out that, as the number of houses, roads, and shopping centers in Florida increases, alligators are left with fewer and fewer places to live and hunt. These people suggest that more wilderness areas must be set aside for alligators and other predators.

Write Alligators are not the only predators people fear. Some parts of the country also have problems with bears, wolves, cougars, or other animals. Write a short paper about encounters between people and predators in your area.

TIME

For more information, visit
fl6.msscience.com

Reviewing Main Ideas

Section 1 **What is an ecosystem?**

1. An ecosystem is made up of organisms interacting with each other and with the nonliving factors in the system.

2. The biosphere is made up of all the ecosystems on Earth.

Section 2 **Relationships Among Living Things**

1. A population is made up of the same type of organisms living together in the same place at the same time.

2. A community is made up of all the populations in an ecosystem.

3. Limiting factors, which may be living or nonliving, influence the size of a population.

Section 3 **Energy Through the Ecosystem**

1. Energy is transferred through an ecosystem in the form of food.

2. The feeding relationships in an ecosystem can be illustrated by food chains and food webs.

Visualizing Main Ideas

Copy and complete this concept map about ecosystems.

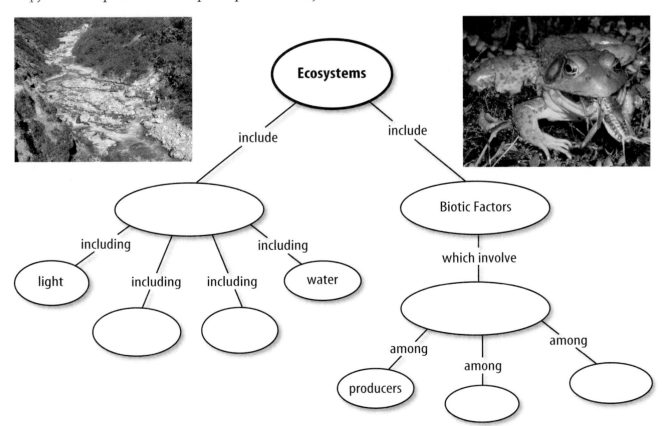

Using Vocabulary

✳ abiotic factor p. 202   ✳ environment p. 199
  biosphere p. 200   ✳ habitat p. 211
✳ biotic factor p. 200   limiting factor p. 209
✳ community p. 208   niche p. 210
✳ consumer p. 213   ✳ population p. 207
✳ decomposer p. 213   ✳ predator p. 213
  ecology p. 200   ✳ prey p. 213
✳ ecosystem p. 198   ✳ producer p. 213
✳ FCAT Vocabulary

Explain the difference between the vocabulary words in each of the following sets.

1. abiotic factor—biotic factor   **SC.G.2.3.2**

2. biosphere—ecology

3. community—population

4. ecosystem—limiting factor

5. niche—habitat

6. producer—consumer

7. consumer—decomposer

Checking Concepts

Choose the word or phrase that completes the sentence.

8. Which of the following is **NOT** a biotic factor?   **SC.G.2.3.2**
   A) raccoons   C) pine trees
   B) sunlight   D) mushrooms

9. Ponds, streams, and prairies are examples of what parts of the environment?
   A) niches   C) populations
   B) producers   D) ecosystems

10. What is a group of the same type of organism living in the same place at the same time?
    A) habitat   C) community
    B) population   D) ecosystem

11. Which of the following is an example of a producer?
    A) grass   C) fungus
    B) horse   D) fish

Use the illustration below to answer question 12.

12. What is the diagram shown above an example of?
    A) food chain   C) ecosystem
    B) food web   D) population

13. All of the following are abiotic factors except   **SC.G.2.3.2**
    A) sunlight.   C) bacteria.
    B) water.   D) temperature.

14. All ecosystems on Earth make up the
    A) atmosphere.   C) lithosphere.
    B) biosphere.   D) hydrosphere.

15. All the populations in an ecosystem make up a
    A) community.   C) habitat.
    B) niche.   D) limiting factor.

16. In an estuary ecosystem, lightning whelks feed on American oysters. When the oyster population is small, there is less food for the whelks. What is the oyster population in relation to the whelk population in this ecosystem?   **SC.G.2.3.2**
    A) niche   C) producer
    B) habitat   D) limiting factor

17. A food web is a model that shows how
    A) energy moves through an ecosystem.
    B) ecosystems change over time.   **SC.G.1.3.4**
    C) producers use sunlight.
    D) abiotic factors affect populations.

Thinking Critically

18. **Infer** why it is correct to say that decomposers are also consumers.

19. **List** examples of foods you would eat if you were eating low on the food chain.

20. **Draw and label** a diagram of an ecosystem. Label biotic and abiotic factors. Describe three interactions among organisms in the ecosystem. SC.G.2.3.2

21. **Identify** three possible limiting factors for an aquarium ecosystem. Describe how each factor can limit population growth.

22. **Describe** your own habitat and niche. SC.G.2.3.2

23. **Classify** each of your ten favorite foods as coming from a producer, consumer, or decomposer. Write a short explanation of your classification of each item.

Use the graph below to answer question 24.

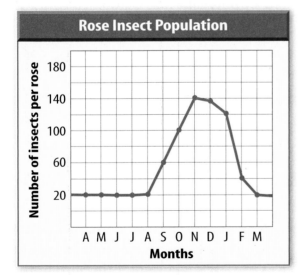

Rose Insect Population

24. **Make and Use Graphs** The graph above shows the changes in the size of a population of insects living on roses over the course of a year. During what month is the insect population the smallest? During what month is the population the largest?

25. **Predict** what would happen to an ecosystem if its decomposers were removed. SC.G.2.3.2

Performance Activities

26. **Develop Multimedia Presentations** Find slides or photographs that show different ecosystems. Arrange a slide presentation or photo display of these images. Use titles or captions to identify each one.

27. **Research Information** Choose an ecosystem to research. Find out what organisms are found there and how they interact. Make a poster or a computer slideshow illustrating a food web in this ecosystem.

Applying Math

28. **Population Density** The population density of rabbits living along the banks of a stream is about one rabbit per 100 m². How many rabbits are likely to be found in a 900-m by 25-m section of the stream bank?

Use the table below to answer question 29.

Changes in Population Size (in 100s)		
Year	Rabbit Population	Bobcat Population
1970	100	39
1975	133	80
1980	94	61
1985	65	63
1990	80	45

29. **Changes in Population Size** Use the data from the table above to make a graph of population size over time for rabbits and bobcats. Based on your graph, infer how the size of the rabbit population affects the size of the bobcat population.

 The assessed Florida Benchmark appears above each question.
Record your answers on the answer sheet provided by your teacher or on a sheet of paper.

Multiple Choice

SC.G.2.3.2

1 Beavers in a forest ecosystem gnaw down trees to build a dam across a stream. In which way could this behavior affect the biotic factors within the ecosystem?

A. It increases the amount of water within the ecosystem.

B. It destroys the habitats of animals that used the trees as homes.

C. It may cause soil to be washed away in the areas that were cleared of trees.

D. It may raise the average temperature of the ecosystem because there is less shade.

SC.G.1.3.4

2 Which conclusion is **best** supported by the diagram below?

F. A food chain shows that producers rely on sunlight.

G. A food chain shows how ecosystems change over time.

H. A food chain shows that abiotic factors affect populations.

I. A food chain shows how energy moves through an ecosystem.

SC.G.2.3.3

3 The graph below shows the changes in a prey population over time.

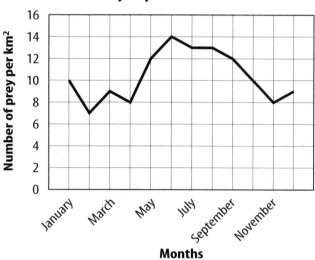

What was the approximate density of the prey population in October?

A. 13 prey per square kilometer

B. 10 prey per square kilometer

C. 9 prey per square kilometer

D. 7 prey per square kilometer

SC.G.1.3.4

4 Which represents a likely food chain in an ecosystem?

F. A producer eats a consumer. Then the producer is eaten by another producer.

G. A producer eats a consumer. Then the producer is eaten by another consumer.

H. A consumer eats another consumer. Then the consumer is eaten by a producer.

I. A consumer eats a producer. Then the consumer is eaten by another consumer.

Gridded Response

SC.G.2.3.3

5 There are 48 dogs that live within a town with an area of 16 square kilometers. What is the population density of dogs per square kilometer?

Short Response

SC.H.2.3.1

6 Marika wanted to know if temperature affects the flying-insect population at her school's pond. Marika recorded the average high temperature and the average number of flying insects at the pond each month for one year. Her results are shown in the graph below.

Flying Insect Population at the School Pond

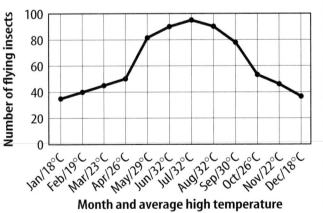

When was the flying-insect population the greatest? Based on the graph, describe the relationship between average temperature and the flying-insect population at the pond.

Extended Response

SC.G.1.3.4

7 The diagram below shows one type of ocean food web. In this food web, plankton is the producer.

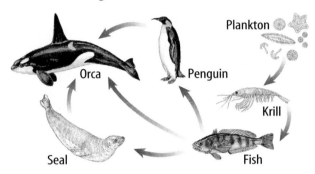

PART A Describe how the energy used by the penguin originally comes from the Sun.

PART B What might happen to this food web if there were as many orcas as there were krill?

FCAT Tip

When In Doubt If you don't know the answer to a multiple-choice question, try to eliminate as many incorrect answers as possible. Mark your best guess from the remaining answers before moving on to the next question.

---

chapter

8

Sunshine State Standards—**SC.D.1:** The student recognizes that processes in the lithosphere, atmosphere, hydrosphere, and biosphere interact to shape the Earth; **SC.D.2:** understands the need for protection of the natural systems on Earth; **SC.G.2:** understands the consequences of using limited natural resources; **SC.H.2.**

Ecosystems

chapter preview

The Benefits of Wildfires

Ecosystems are places where organisms, including humans, interact with each other and with their physical environment. In some ecosystems, wildfires are an essential part of the physical environment. Organisms in these ecosystems are well adapted to the changes that fire brings, and can benefit from wildfires.

Science Journal What traits might plants on this burning hillside have that enable them to survive?

Start-Up Activities

What environment do houseplants need?

The plants growing in your classroom or home may not look like the same types of plants that you find growing outside. Many indoor plants don't grow well outside in most North American climates. Do the lab below to determine what type of environment most houseplants thrive in.

1. Complete a safety worksheet.

2. Examine a healthy houseplant in your classroom or home.

3. Describe the environmental conditions found in your classroom or home. For example, is the air humid or dry? Is the room warm or cool? Does the temperature stay about the same, or change during the day?

4. Using observations from step 1 and descriptions from step 2, hypothesize about the natural environment of the plants in your classroom or home.

5. **Think Critically** In your Science Journal, record the observations that led to your hypothesis. How would you design an experiment to test your hypothesis?

Primary and Secondary Succession Make the following Foldable to help you illustrate the main ideas about succession.

LA.A.1.3.4

STEP 1 Fold a vertical sheet of paper in half from top to bottom.

STEP 2 Fold in half from side to side with the fold at the top.

STEP 3 Unfold the paper once. Cut only the fold of the top flap to make two tabs.

STEP 4 Turn the paper vertically and label on the front tabs as shown.

Illustrate and Label As you read the chapter, define terms and collect information under the appropriate tabs.

Science Online Preview this chapter's content and activities at fl6.msscience.com

section 1

Also covers: SC.G.1.3.2 (p. 228)

How Ecosystems Change

as you read

What You'll Learn

- **Explain** how ecosystems change over time.
- **Describe** how new communities begin in areas without life.
- **Compare** pioneer species and climax communities.

Why It's Important

Understanding ecosystems and your role in them can help you manage your impact on them and predict the changes that may happen in the future.

Review Vocabulary

✳ **ecosystem:** community of living organisms interacting with each other and their physical environment

New Vocabulary

- succession
- pioneer species
- climax community

✳ FCAT Vocabulary

Ecological Succession

What would happen if the lawn at your home were never cut? The grass would get longer, as in **Figure 1,** and soon it would look like a meadow. Later, larger plants would grow from seeds brought to the area by animals or wind. Then, trees might sprout. In fact, in 20 years or less you wouldn't be able to tell that the land was once a mowed lawn. An ecologist can tell you what type of ecosystem your lawn would become. If it would become a forest, they can tell you how long it would take and predict the type of trees that would grow there. **Succession** refers to the pattern of gradual changes that occur in the types of species that live in an area. Succession occurs differently in different places around the world.

Primary Succession As lava flows from the mouth of a volcano, it is so hot that it destroys everything in its path. When it cools, lava forms new land composed of rock. It is hard to imagine that this land eventually could become a forest or grassland someday.

The process of succession that begins in a place previously without plants is called primary succession. It starts with the arrival of living things such as lichens (LI kunz). These living things, called **pioneer species,** are the first to inhabit an area. They survive drought, extreme heat and cold, and other harsh conditions and often start the soil-building process.

Figure 1 This once-mowed cemetery is now full of long grasses and wildflowers due to secondary succession.

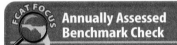

Annually Assessed Benchmark Check

SC.D.1.3.4 How do plants, lichens, and other organic matter change the landscape?

New Soil During primary succession, soil begins to form as lichens and the forces of weather and erosion help break down rocks into smaller pieces. When lichens die, they decay, adding small amounts of organic matter to the rock. Plants such as mosses and ferns can grow in this new soil. Eventually, these plants die, adding more organic material. The soil layer thickens, and grasses, wildflowers, and other plants begin to take over. When these plants die, they add more nutrients to the soil. This buildup is enough to support the growth of shrubs and trees. All the while, insects, small birds, and mammals have begun to move in. What was once bare rock now supports a variety of life, as shown in **Figure 2.**

Secondary Succession What happens when a fire, such as the one in **Figure 3,** disturbs a forest or when a building is torn down in a city? After a forest fire, not much seems to be left except dead trees and ash-covered soil. After the rubble of a building is removed, all that remains is bare soil. However, these places do not remain lifeless for long. The soil already contains the seeds of weeds, grasses, and trees. More seeds are carried to the area by wind and birds. Other wildlife may move in. Succession that begins in a place that already has soil and was once the home of living organisms is called secondary succession. Because soil already is present, secondary succession occurs faster and has different pioneer species than primary succession does.

LA.A.1.3.4
LA.B.2.3.4

Topic: Eutrophication
Visit fl6.msscience.com for Web links to information about eutrophication (yoo truh fih KAY shun)—secondary succession in an aquatic ecosystem.

Activity Using the information that you find, illustrate or describe in your Science Journal this process for a small freshwater lake.

 *Which type of succession usually starts without soil?*

Figure 3

In the summer of 1988, wind-driven flames like those shown in the background photo swept through Yellowstone National Park, scorching nearly a million acres. The Yellowstone fire was one of the largest forest fires in United States history. The images on this page show secondary succession—the process of ecological regeneration—triggered by the fire.

▶ After the fire, burned timber and blackened soil seemed to be all that remained. However, the fire didn't destroy the seeds that were protected under the soil.

◀ Within weeks, grasses and other plants were beginning to grow in the burned areas. Ecological succession was underway.

▶ Many burned areas in the park opened new plots for stands of trees. This picture shows young lodgepole pines in August 1999. The forest habitat of America's oldest national park is being restored gradually through secondary succession.

Figure 4 This beech-maple forest is an example of a climax community.

Climax Communities A community of plants that is relatively stable and undisturbed and has reached an end stage of succession is called a **climax community.** The beech-maple forest shown in **Figure 4** is an example of a community that has reached the end of succession. New trees grow when larger, older trees die. The individual trees change, but the species remain stable. There are fewer changes of species in a climax community over time, as long as the community isn't disturbed by wildfire, avalanche, or human activities.

Primary succession begins in areas with no previous vegetation. It can take hundreds or even thousands of years to develop into a climax community. Secondary succession is usually a shorter process, but it still can take a century or more.

section 1 review

Summary

Ecological Succession

- Succession is the natural, gradual changes over time of species in a community.

- Primary succession occurs in areas that previously were without soil or plants.

- Secondary succession occurs in areas where soil has been disturbed.

- Climax communities have reached an end stage of succession and are stable.

- Climax communities have less diversity than communities in mid-succession.

Self Check

1. **Compare** primary and secondary succession.
2. **Describe** adaptations of pioneer species. `SC.G.1.3.2`
3. **Infer** the kind of succession that will take place on an abandoned, unpaved country road.
4. **Think Critically** Show the sequence of events in primary succession. Include the term *climax community*.

Applying Math

5. **Solve One-Step Equations** A tombstone etched with 1802 as the date of death has a lichen on it that is 6 cm in diameter. If the lichen began growing in 1802, calculate its average yearly rate of growth. `MA.D.2.3.1`

section 2

Biomes

as you read

What You'll Learn

- **Explain** how climate influences land environments.
- **Identify** seven biomes of Earth.
- **Describe** the adaptations of organisms found in each biome.

Why It's Important

Resources that you need to survive are found in a variety of biomes.

Review Vocabulary

climate: the average weather conditions of an area over many years

New Vocabulary

- biome
- tundra
- taiga
- temperate deciduous forest
- temperate rain forest
- tropical rain forest
- desert
- grassland

Factors That Affect Biomes

Does a desert in Arizona have anything in common with a desert in Africa? Both have heat, little rain, poor soil, water-conserving plants with thorns, and lizards. Even widely separated regions of the world can have similar biomes because they have similar climates. Climate is the average weather pattern in an area over a long period of time. The two most important climatic factors that affect life in an area are temperature and precipitation.

Major Biomes

Large geographic areas that have similar climates and ecosystems are called **biomes** (BI ohmz). Seven common types of land biomes are mapped in **Figure 5.** Areas with similar climates produce similar climax communities. Tropical rain forests are climax communities found near the equator, where temperatures are warm and rainfall is plentiful. Coniferous forests grow where winter temperatures are cold and rainfall is moderate.

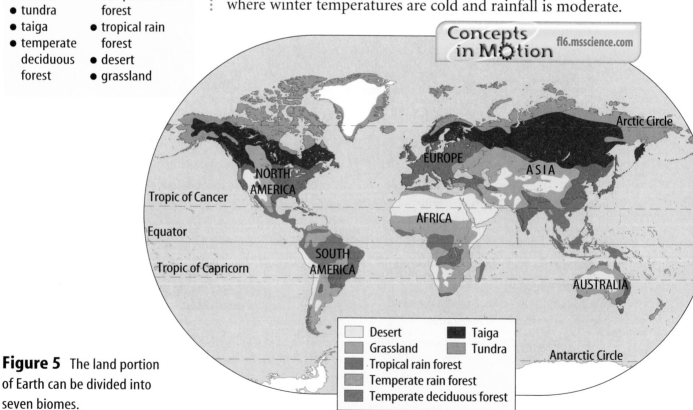

Concepts in Motion
fl6.msscience.com

Legend	
Desert	Taiga
Grassland	Tundra
Tropical rain forest	
Temperate rain forest	
Temperate deciduous forest	

Figure 5 The land portion of Earth can be divided into seven biomes.

Tundra At latitudes just south of the north pole or at high elevations, a biome can be found that receives little precipitation but is covered with ice most of the year. The **tundra** is a cold, dry, treeless region, sometimes called a cold desert. Precipitation averages less than 25 cm per year. Winters in the Arctic can be six to nine months long. For some of these months, the Sun never appears above the horizon and it is dark 24 hours a day. The average daily temperature is about −12°C. For a few days during the short, cold summer, the Sun is always visible. Only the top portion of soil thaws in the summer. Below the thawed surface is a layer of permanently frozen soil called permafrost, shown in **Figure 6.** Alpine tundra, found above the treeline on high mountains, have similar climates. Tundra soil has few nutrients because the cold temperatures slow the process of decomposition.

Figure 6 This permafrost in Alaska is covered by soil that freezes in the winter and thaws in the summer.
Infer *what types of problems this might cause for people living in this area.*

Tundra Life Tundra plants are adapted to drought and cold. They include mosses, grasses, and small shrubs, as seen in **Figure 7.** Many lichens grow on the tundra. During the summer, mosquitoes, blackflies, and other biting insects fill the air. Migratory birds such as ducks, geese, shorebirds, and songbirds nest on the Arctic tundra during the summer. Other inhabitants include hawks, snowy owls, and willow grouse. Mice, voles, lemmings, arctic hares, caribou, reindeer, and musk oxen also are found there.

People are concerned about overgrazing by animals on the tundra. Fences, roads, and pipelines have disrupted the migratory routes of some animals and forced them to stay in a limited area. Because the growing season is so short, plants and other vegetation can take decades to recover from damage.

Figure 7 Lichens, mosses, grasses, and small shrubs thrive on the tundra. Ptarmigan also live on the tundra. In winter, their feathers turn white. Extra feathers on their feet keep them warm and prevent them from sinking into the snow.

Tundra

Ptarmigan

Taiga South of the tundra—between latitudes 50°N and 60°N and stretching across North America, northern Europe, and Asia—is the world's largest biome. The **taiga** (TI guh), shown in **Figure 8,** is a cold, forest region dominated by cone-bearing evergreen trees. Although the winter is long and cold, the taiga is warmer and wetter than the tundra. Precipitation is mostly snow and averages 35 cm to 100 cm each year.

Most soils of the taiga thaw completely during the summer, making it possible for trees to grow. However, permafrost is present in the extreme northern regions of the taiga. The forests of the taiga might be so dense that little sunlight penetrates the trees to reach the forest floor. However, some lichens and mosses do grow on the forest floor. Moose, lynx, shrews, bears, and foxes are some of the animals that live in the taiga.

Figure 8 The taiga is dominated by cone-bearing trees. The lynx, a mammal adapted to life in the taiga, has broad, heavily furred feet that act like snowshoes to prevent it from sinking in the snow.
Infer *why "snowshoe feet" are important for a lynx.*

Temperate Deciduous Forest Temperate regions usually have four distinct seasons each year. Annual precipitation ranges from about 75 cm to 150 cm and is distributed throughout the year. Temperatures range from below freezing during the winter to 30°C or more during the warmest days of summer. Most of Florida is in the temperate deciduous biome, with an average rainfall between 120 cm to 150 cm. The average temperature range is 15°C to 29°C.

Figure 9 White-tailed deer are one of many species that you can find in a deciduous forest. In autumn, the leaves on deciduous trees change color and fall to the ground.

Temperate Forest Life Many evergreen trees grow in the temperate regions of the world. However, most of the temperate forests in Europe and North America are dominated by climax communities of deciduous trees, which lose their leaves every autumn. These forests, like the one in **Figure 9,** are called **temperate deciduous forests.** In the United States, most of them are located east of the Mississippi River.

A unique aspect of organisms in a temperate deciduous biome is that they have adaptations that allow them to withstand environmental seasonal changes. Each season has a different range of temperatures and amounts of precipitation. The loss of leaves by trees is one adaptation. In winter there is not enough sunlight and water for deciduous trees to make their own food. The leaves drop and trees use stored energy. Some plants go dormant in cold weather. Extra fur grows on some mammals, which insulates them in cold weather. This fur is shed in hot weather. Some animals become inactive during cold weather, and some become inactive in hot weather.

Temperate Rain Forest New Zealand, southern Chile, and the Pacific Northwest of the United States are some of the places where **temperate rain forests,** shown in **Figure 10,** are found. The average temperature of a temperate rain forest ranges from 9°C to 12°C. Precipitation ranges from 200 cm to 400 cm per year.

Trees with needlelike leaves dominate these forests, including the Douglas fir, western red cedar, and spruce. Many grow to great heights. Animals of the temperate rain forest include the black bear, cougar, bobcat, northern spotted owl, and marbled murrelet. Many species of amphibians also inhabit the temperate rain forest, including salamanders.

The logging industry in the Northwest provides jobs for many people. However, it also removes large parts of the temperate rain forest and destroys the habitat of many organisms. Many logging companies now are required to replant trees to replace the ones they cut down. Also, some rain forest areas are protected as national parks and forests.

Figure 10 In the Olympic rain forest in Washington State, mosses and lichens blanket the ground and hang from the trees. Wet areas are perfect habitats for amphibians like the Pacific giant salamander above.

Figure 11 Tropical rain forests are lush environments that contain such a large variety of species that many have not been discovered.

Mini LAB

Modeling Rain Forest Leaves

Procedure

1. Draw an oval leaf about 10 cm long on a piece of **poster board.** Cut it out.
2. Draw a second leaf the same size but make one end pointed. This is called a drip tip. Cut this leaf out.
3. Hold your hands palm-side up over a **sink** and have someone lay a leaf on each one. Point the drip tip away from you. Tilt your hands down but do not allow the leaves to fall off.
4. Have someone gently spray **water** on the leaves and observe what happens.

Analysis

1. From which leaf does water drain faster?
2. Infer why it is an advantage for a leaf to get rid of water quickly in a rain forest.

Try at Home

Tropical Rain Forest Warm temperatures, wet weather, and lush plant growth are found in **tropical rain forests.** These forests are warm because they are near the equator. The average temperature, about 25°C, doesn't vary much between night and day. Most tropical rain forests receive at least 200 cm of rain annually. Some receive as much as 600 cm of rain each year.

Tropical rain forests, like the one in **Figure 11,** are home to an astonishing variety of organisms. They are one of the most biologically diverse places in the world. For example, one tree in a South American rain forest might contain more species of ants than exist in all of the British Isles.

Tropical Rain Forest Life Different animals and plants live in different parts of the rain forest. Scientists divide the rain forest into zones based on the types of plants and animals that live there, just as a library separates books about different topics onto separate shelves. The zones include: forest floor, understory, canopy, and emergents, as shown in **Figure 12.** These zones often blend together, but their existence provide different habitats for many diverse organisms to live in the tropical rain forest.

✓ **Reading Check** *What are the four zones of a tropical rain forest?*

Although tropical rain forests support a huge variety of organisms, the soil of the rain forest contains few nutrients. Over the years, nutrients have been washed out of the soil by rain. On the forest floor, decomposers immediately break down organic matter, making nutrients available to the plants again.

Human Impact Farmers that live in tropical areas clear the land to farm and to sell the valuable wood. After a few years, the crops use up the nutrients in the soil, and the farmers must clear more land. As a result, tropical rain forest habitats are being destroyed. Through education, people are realizing the value and potential value of preserving the species of the rain forest. In some areas, logging is prohibited. In other areas, farmers are taught new methods of farming so they do not have to clear rain forest lands continually.

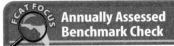

FCAT FOCUS **Annually Assessed Benchmark Check**

SC.D.2.3.2 Name a positive and a negative impact of human action in a tropical rainforest.

Figure 12 Tropical rain forests contain abundant and diverse organisms.

Desertification When vegetation is removed from soil in areas that receive little rain, the dry, unprotected surface can be blown away. If the soil remains bare, a desert might form. This process is called desertification. Look on a biome map and hypothesize about which areas of the United States are most likely to become deserts.

Figure 13 Desert plants, like these in the Sonoran Desert, are adapted for survival in the extreme conditions of the desert biome. The giant hairy scorpion found in some deserts has a venomous sting.

Desert The driest biome on Earth is the **desert.** Deserts receive less than 25 cm of rain each year and support little plant life. Some desert areas receive no rain for years. When rain does come, it quickly drains away. Any water that remains on the ground evaporates rapidly.

Most deserts, like the one in **Figure 13,** are covered with a thin, sandy, or gravelly soil that contains little organic matter. Due to the lack of water, desert plants are spaced far apart and much of the ground is bare. Barren, windblown sand dunes are characteristics of the driest deserts.

✓ Reading Check *Why is much of a desert bare ground?*

Desert Life Desert plants are adapted for survival in the extreme dryness and hot and cold temperatures of this biome. Most desert plants are able to store water. Cactus plants are probably the most familiar desert plants of the western hemisphere. Desert animals also have adaptations that help them survive the extreme conditions. Some, like the kangaroo rat, never need to drink water. They get all the moisture they need from the breakdown of food during digestion. Most animals are active only during the night, late afternoon, or early morning when temperatures are less extreme. Few large animals are found in the desert.

In order to provide water for desert cities, rivers and streams have been diverted. When this happens, wildlife tends to move closer to cities in their search for food and water. Education about desert environments has led to an awareness of the impact of human activities. As a result, large areas of desert have been set aside as national parks and wilderness areas to protect desert habitats.

Grasslands Temperate and tropical regions that receive between 25 cm and 75 cm of precipitation each year and are dominated by climax communities of grasses are called **grasslands.** Most grasslands have a dry season, when little or no rain falls. This lack of moisture prevents the development of forests. Grasslands are found in many places around the world, and they have a variety of names. The prairies and plains of North America, the steppes of Asia, the savannas of Africa shown in **Figure 14,** and the pampas of South America are types of grasslands.

Grasslands Life The most noticeable animals in grassland biomes are usually mammals that graze on the stems, leaves, and seeds of grass plants. Kangaroos graze in the grasslands of Australia. In Africa, communities of animals such as wildebeests, impalas, and zebras thrive in the savannas.

Grasslands are perfect for growing many crops such as wheat, rye, oats, barley, and corn. Grasslands also are used to raise cattle and sheep. However, overgrazing can result in the death of grasses and the loss of valuable topsoil from erosion. Most farmers and ranchers take precautions to prevent the loss of valuable habitats and soil.

Figure 14 Animals such as zebras and wildebeests are adapted to life on the savannas in Africa.

section 2 review

Summary

Major Biomes

- Tundra, sometimes called a cold desert, can be divided into two types: arctic and alpine.

- Taiga is the world's largest biome. It is a cold forest region with long winters.

- Temperate regions have either a deciduous forest biome or a rain forest biome.

- Tropical rain forests are one of the most biologically diverse biomes.

- Humans have a huge impact on tropical rain forests.

- The driest biome is the desert. Desert organisms are adapted for extreme dryness and temperatures.

- Grasslands provide food for wildlife, livestock, and humans.

Self Check

1. **Determine** which two biomes are the driest. `SC.G.2.3.2`

2. **Compare and contrast** tundra organisms and desert organisms.

3. **Identify** the biggest climatic difference between a temperate rain forest and a tropical rain forest. `SC.G.2.3.2`

4. **Explain** why the soil of tropical rain forests makes poor farmland. `SC.G.2.3.2`

5. **Think Critically** If you climb a mountain in Arizona, you might reach an area where the trees resemble the taiga trees in northern Canada. Why would a taiga forest exist in Arizona? `SC.G.2.3.2`

Applying Skills

6. **Record Observations** Animals have adaptations that help them survive in their environments. Make a list of animals that live in your area, and record the physical or behavioral adaptations that help them survive.

Benchmark—SC.G.2.3.2: The student knows that all biotic and abiotic factors are interrelated and that if one factor is changed or removed, it impacts the availability of other resources within the system; **SC.H.1.3.1; SC.H.1.3.4; SC.H.1.3.7; SC.H.2.3.1**

Studying a Land Ecosystem *Inquiry*

An ecological study includes observation and analysis of organisms and the physical features of the environment.

▶ *Real-World Problem*

How do you study an ecosystem?

Goals
- **Observe** biotic factors and abiotic factors of an ecosystem.
- **Analyze** the relationships among organisms and their environments.

Materials

graph paper	field guides
binoculars	notebook
thermometer	compass
pencil	tape measure
magnifying lens	

Safety Precautions

Complete a safety worksheet before you begin.

▶ *Procedure*

1. Choose a portion of an ecosystem and determine the boundaries of your study area.

2. Using a tape measure and graph paper, make a map of your area. Determine the scale; for example, one square of graph paper equals one square centimeter or one square meter of land. Determine north.

3. **Observe** the organisms in your study area. Use field guides to identify them. Use a magnifying lens to study small organisms and binoculars to study animals you can't get near. Look for evidence (such as tracks or feathers) of organisms you do not see.

4. **Record** your observations in a table.

5. Measure and record the air temperature.

6. Visit your study area many times and at different times of day for one week. At each visit, make the same measurements and record all observations. Note how the living and nonliving parts of the ecosystem interact.

Environmental Observations		
Date		
Time of day		
Temperature	Do not write in this book.	
Organisms observed		
Comments		

▶ *Conclude and Apply*

1. **Predict** what might happen if one or more abiotic factors were changed suddenly.

2. **Infer** what might happen if one or more populations of plants or animals were removed from the area.

3. **Infer** how a new population of organisms might affect your ecosystem.

4. **Identify** possible sources of error in your data.

Communicating Your Data

Make a classroom display of all data recorded. **Compare and contrast** your results with those of your classmates and investigate differences further. **For more help, refer to the** Science Skill Handbook.

Benchmarks—SC.D.2.3.1 (pp. 240, 241): The student understands that the quality of life is relevant to personal experience; SC.D.2.3.2 Annually Assessed (pp. 240, 241): knows the positive and negative consequences of human action on the Earth's systems; SC.G.2.3.3 (pp. 240, 241)

Also covers: SC.G.2.3.2 (pp. 240, 241), SC.G.2.3.4 Annually Assessed (pp. 240, 241), SC.H.1.3.4 Annually Assessed (pp. 246–247), SC.H.1.3.5 Annually Assessed (pp. 240, 246–247), SC.H.1.3.6 (p. 244), SC.H.3.3.4 (p. 248)

Aquatic Ecosystems

Freshwater Ecosystems

In a land environment, temperature and precipitation are the most important factors that determine which species can survive. In aquatic environments, water temperature, the amount of sunlight present, and the amounts of dissolved oxygen and salt in the water are important. Earth's freshwater ecosystems include flowing water such as rivers and streams and standing water such as lakes, ponds, and wetlands.

Rivers and Streams Flowing freshwater environments vary from small, gurgling brooks to large, slow-moving rivers. Currents can quickly wash loose particles downstream, leaving a rocky or gravelly bottom. As the water tumbles and splashes, as shown in **Figure 15,** air from the atmosphere mixes in. Naturally fast-flowing streams usually have clearer water and higher oxygen content than slow-flowing streams.

Most nutrients that support life in flowing-water ecosystems are washed into the water from land. In areas where the water movement slows, such as in the pools of streams or in large rivers, debris settles to the bottom. These environments tend to have higher nutrient levels and more plant growth. They contain organisms that are not as well adapted to swiftly flowing water, such as freshwater mussels, minnows, and leeches.

as you read

What You'll Learn

- **Compare** flowing freshwater and standing freshwater ecosystems.
- **Identify** and describe important saltwater ecosystems.
- **Identify** problems that affect aquatic ecosystems.

Why It's Important

All of the life processes in your body depend on water.

Review Vocabulary
aquatic: growing or living in water

New Vocabulary
- wetland
- intertidal zone
- coral reef
- estuary

Figure 15 Streams like this one are high in oxygen because of the swift, tumbling water.
Determine *where most nutrients in streams come from.*

Mini LAB

Modeling River Pollution

Procedure 🥽 🧤 ⚗️

1. Complete a safety worksheet.
2. Fill several **small aquariums** (or **other clear containers**) with **water**. Place **aquarium plants** in the containers.
3. Have students put "pollutants" (such as **salt, cooking oil, soap, etc.**) in the containers and observe what takes place over the next few weeks. One container should have no pollutants.

Analysis

1. What might be the result if you used stronger pollutants?
2. Identify the types of pollution in streams and rivers. What is the source of this pollution?
3. List some steps that you can take to limit the pollution getting to waterways.

Human Impact People use rivers and streams for many activities. Once regarded as a free place to dump sewage and other pollutants, many people now recognize the damage this causes. Treating sewage and restricting pollutants have led to an improvement in the water quality in some rivers.

Lakes and Ponds When a low place in the land fills with rainwater, snowmelt, or water from an overflowing stream, a lake or pond might form. Pond or lake water hardly moves. It contains more plants than flowing-water environments contain.

Lakes are larger and deeper than ponds. Plants and microscopic organisms called plankton grow in the shallow, sunlit areas of a lake. Life at the shorelines and near the surface is very similar to that found in ponds. Colder temperatures and lower light levels in deep lake waters limit the types of organisms that live there. **Figure 16** shows Lake Okeechobee, located in south central Florida. It is home to many organisms, including herons, egrets, bass, bluegill, white mussel, and red maple and bald cypress trees. A relatively shallow lake, its average depth is nine feet, but reaches 17 feet deep. At its deepest areas there are few plants or algae growing.

A pond is a small, shallow body of water. Because ponds are shallow, they are filled with animal and plant life. Sunlight usually penetrates to the bottom. The warm, sunlit water promotes the growth of plants and algae. In fact, many ponds are filled almost completely with plant material, so the only clear, open water is at the center. Because of the lush growth in pond environments, they tend to be high in nutrients.

Figure 16 Lake Okeechobee is the second largest natural lake in the continental United States. It is 730 square miles and holds more than a trillion gallons of water.

Water Pollution Human activities can harm freshwater environments. Fertilizer-filled runoff from farms and lawns, as well as sewage dumped into the water, can lead to excessive growth of algae and plants in lakes and ponds. The growth and decay of these organisms reduces the oxygen level in the water, which makes it difficult for some organisms to survive. To prevent problems, sewage is treated before it is released. People also are being educated about problems associated with polluting lakes and ponds. Fines and penalties are issued to people caught polluting waterways. These controls have led to the recovery of many freshwater ecosystems.

Wetlands As the name suggests, **wetlands,** shown in **Figure 17,** are regions that are wet for all or most of a year. They are found in regions that lie between landmasses and water. Other names for wetlands include swamps, bogs, and fens. Some people refer to wetlands as biological supermarkets. They are fertile ecosystems, but only plants that are adapted to waterlogged soil survive there. Wetland animals include beavers, muskrats, alligators, and the threatened bog turtle. Many migratory bird populations use wetlands as breeding grounds.

✔ **Reading Check** *Where are wetlands found?*

Wetlands once were considered to be useless, disease-ridden places. Many were drained and destroyed to make roads, farmland, shopping centers, and housing developments. Only recently have people begun to understand the importance of wetlands. Products that come from wetlands, including fish, shellfish, cranberries, and plants, are valuable resources. Now many developers are restoring wetlands, and in most states access to land through wetlands is prohibited.

Figure 17 Life in the Florida Everglades was threatened due to pollution, drought, and draining of the water. Conservation efforts are being made in an attempt to preserve this ecosystem.

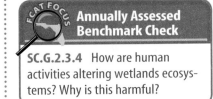

FCAT FOCUS **Annually Assessed Benchmark Check**

SC.G.2.3.4 How are human activities altering wetlands ecosystems? Why is this harmful?

Saltwater Ecosystems

About 95 percent of the water on the surface of Earth contains high concentrations of various salts. The amount of dissolved salts in water is called salinity. The average ocean salinity is about 35 g of salts per 1,000 g of water. Saltwater ecosystems include oceans, seas, a few inland lakes such as the Great Salt Lake in Utah, coastal inlets, and estuaries.

Applying Math   Convert Units

TEMPERATURE Organisms that live around hydrothermal vents in the ocean deal with temperatures that range from 1.7°C to 371°C. You have probably seen temperatures measured in degrees Celsius (°C) and degrees Fahrenheit (°F). Which one are you familiar with? If you know the temperature in one system, you can convert it to the other.

You have a Fahrenheit thermometer and measure the water temperature of a pond at 59°F. What is that temperature in degrees Celsius?

Solution

1 *This is what you know:*   water temperature in degrees Fahrenheit = 59°F

2 *This is what you need to find out:*   The water temperature in degrees Celsius.

3 *This is the procedure you need to use:*
- Solve the equation for degrees Celsius:
  (°C × 1.8) + 32 = °F
  °C = (°F − 32)/1.8
- Substitute the known value:
  °C = (59°F − 32)/1.8 = 15°C
- Water temperature that is 59°F is 15°C.

4 *Check your answer:*   Substitute the Celsius temperature back into the original equation. You should get 59.

Practice Problems

1. The thermometer outside your classroom reads 78°F. What is the temperature in degrees Celsius? MA.B.2.3.2

2. If lake water was 12°C in October and 23°C in May, what is the difference in degrees Fahrenheit? MA.B.2.3.2

Math Practice | For more practice, visit fl6.msscience.com

Open Oceans Life abounds in the open ocean. Scientists divide the ocean into different life zones, based on the depth to which sunlight penetrates the water. The lighted zone of the ocean is the upper 200 m or so. It is the home of the plankton that make up the foundation of the food chain in the open ocean. Below about 200 m is the dark zone of the ocean. Animals living in this region feed on material that floats down from the lighted zone, or they feed on each other. A few organisms are able to produce their own food.

Coral Reefs One of the most diverse ecosystems in the world is the coral reef. **Coral reefs** are formed over long periods of time from the calcium carbonate exoskeletons secreted by animals called corals. When corals die, their exoskeletons remain. Over time, the exoskeleton deposits form reefs such as Molasses Reef off the coast of the Florida Keys, shown in **Figure 18.**

Reefs do not adapt well to long-term stress. Runoff from fields, sewage, and increased sedimentation from cleared land harm reef ecosystems. Organizations like the Environmental Protection Agency have developed management plans to protect the diversity of coral reefs. These plans treat a coral reef as a system that includes all the areas that surround the reef. Keeping the areas around reefs healthy will result in a healthy environment for the coral reef ecosystem.

Science nline

Topic: Coral Reefs
Visit **fl6.msscience.com** for Web links to information about coral reef ecosystems.

Activity Construct a diorama of a coral reef. Include as many different kinds of organisms as you can for a coral reef ecosystem.

Inquiry

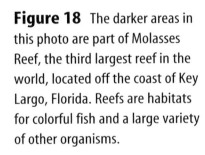

Figure 18 The darker areas in this photo are part of Molasses Reef, the third largest reef in the world, located off the coast of Key Largo, Florida. Reefs are habitats for colorful fish and a large variety of other organisms.

Figure 19 As the tide recedes, small pools of seawater are left behind. These pools contain a variety of organisms such as sea stars and periwinkles.

Sea star

Periwinkles

INTEGRATE
Career

Environmental Author
Rachel Carson (1907–1964) was a scientist that turned her knowledge and love of the environment into articles and books. After 15 years as an editor for the U.S. Fish and Wildlife Service, she resigned and devoted her time to writing. She probably is known best for her book *Silent Spring,* in which she warned about the long-term effects of the misuse of pesticides. In your Science Journal, compile a list of other authors who write about environmental issues.

INTEGRATE Earth Science

Seashores All of Earth's landmasses are bordered by ocean water. The shallow waters along the world's coastlines contain a variety of saltwater ecosystems, all of which are influenced by the tides and by the action of waves. The gravitational pull of the Moon, and to a lesser extent, the Sun, on Earth causes the tides to rise and fall each day. The height of the tides varies according to the phases of the Moon, the season, and the slope of the shoreline. The **intertidal zone** is the portion of the shoreline that is covered with water at high tide and exposed to the air during low tide. Organisms that live in the intertidal zone, such as those in **Figure 19,** must be adapted to dramatic changes in temperature, moisture, and salinity and must be able to withstand the force of wave action.

Estuaries Almost every river on Earth eventually flows into an ocean. The area where a river meets an ocean and contains a mixture of freshwater and salt water is called an **estuary** (ES chuh wer ee). Other names for estuaries include bays, lagoons, harbors, inlets, and sounds. They are located near coastlines and border the land. Salinity in estuaries changes with the amount of freshwater brought in by rivers and streams, and with the amount of salt water pushed inland by the ocean tides.

Estuaries, shown in **Figure 20,** are extremely fertile, productive environments because freshwater streams bring in tons of nutrients washed from inland soils. Therefore, nutrient levels in estuaries are higher than in freshwater ecosystems or other saltwater ecosystems.

Figure 20 The Crystal River estuary is rich in resources. Fish and shrimp are harvested by commercial fishing boats.
Describe *what other resources can be found in estuaries.*

Estuary Life Organisms found in estuaries include many species of algae, salt-tolerant grasses, shrimp, crabs, clams, oysters, snails, worms, and fish. Estuaries also serve as important nurseries for many species of ocean fish. Estuaries provide much of the seafood consumed by humans.

 **Reading Check** *Why are estuaries more fertile than other aquatic ecosystems?*

section 3 review

Summary

Freshwater Ecosystems

● Temperature, light, salt, and dissolved oxygen are important factors.

● Rivers, streams, lakes, ponds, and wetlands are freshwater ecosystems.

● Human activities, such as too much lawn fertilizer, can pollute aquatic ecosystems.

Saltwater Ecosystems

● About 95 percent of Earth's water contains dissolved salts.

● Saltwater ecosystems include open oceans, coral reefs, seashores, and estuaries.

● Organisms that live on seashores have adaptations that enable them to survive dramatic changes in temperature, moisture, and salinity.

● Estuaries serve as nursery areas for many species of ocean fish.

Self Check

1. **Identify** the similarities and differences between a lake and a stream.

2. **Compare and contrast** the dark zone of the ocean with the forest floor of a tropical rain forest. What living or nonliving factors affect these areas? `SC.G.2.3.2` `SC.G.2.3.2`

3. **Explain** why fewer plants are at the bottom of deep lakes.

4. **Infer** what adaptations are necessary for organisms that live in the intertidal zone. `SC.G.1.3.2`

5. **Think Critically** Would you expect a fast moving mountain stream or the Mississippi River to have more dissolved oxygen? Explain.

Applying Skills

6. **Communicate** Wetlands trap and slowly release rain, snow, and groundwater. Describe in your Science Journal what might happen to a town located on a floodplain if nearby wetlands are destroyed.

Benchmark—SC.D.2.3.2: The student knows the positive and negative consequences of human action on the Earth's systems; **SC.H.1.3.4:** The student knows that accurate record keeping, openness, and replication are essential to maintaining an investigator's credibility with other scientists and society; **SC.H.1.3.5:** The student knows that a change in one or more variables may alter the outcome of an investigation.

Use the Internet

Explori🚶‍♀️g Wetlands

Goals

- **Identify** wetland regions in the United States.
- **Describe** the significance of the wetland ecosystem.
- **Identify** plant and animal species native to a wetland region.
- **Identify** strategies for supporting the preservation of wetlands.

Data Source

Internet Lab

Visit **fl6.msscience.com** for more information about wetland environments and for data collected by other students.

Real-World Problem

Wetlands, such as the one shown below, are an important part of the environment. These fertile ecosystems support unique plants and animals that can survive only in wetland conditions. The more you understand the importance of wetlands, the more you can do to preserve and protect them. Why are wetlands an important part of the ecosystem?

⦿ Make a Plan

1. **Determine** where some major wetlands are located in the United States.

2. **Identify** one wetland area to study in depth. Where is it located? Is it classified as a marsh, bog, or something else?

3. **Explain** the role this ecosystem plays in the overall ecology of the area.

4. **Research information** about the plants and animals that live in the wetland environment you are researching.

5. **Investigate** what laws protect the wetland you are studying.

⦿ Follow Your Plan

1. Make sure your teacher approves your plan before you start.

2. Perform the investigation.

3. Post your data at the link shown below.

⦿ Analyze Your Data

1. **Describe** the wetland area you have researched. What region of the United States is it located in? What other ecological factors are found in that region?

2. **Outline** the laws protecting the wetland you are investigating. How long have the laws been in place?

3. **List** the plants and animals native to the wetland area you are researching. Are those plants and animals found in other parts of the region or the United States? What adaptations do the plants and animals have that help them survive in a wetland environment?

⦿ Conclude and Apply

1. **Infer** Are all wetlands the same?

2. **Determine** what the ecological significance of the wetland area that you studied for that region of the country is.

3. **Draw Conclusions** Why should wetland environments be protected?

4. **Summarize** what people can do to support the continued preservation of wetland environments in the United States.

Communicating Your Data

Find this lab using the link below. **Post** your data in the table provided. **Review** other students' data to learn about other wetland environments in the United States.

Internet Lab
fl6.msscience.com

Creating Wetlands to Purify Wastewater

Pebbles were added to the Corrales wetlands to help with drainage.

2

Water irises thrived in the wetlands, less than a year after planting.

Students enjoy pure water from the Corrales wetlands after it is filtered.

When you wash your hands or flush the toilet, do you think about where the wastewater goes? In most places, it eventually ends up being processed in a traditional sewage-treatment facility. But some places are experimenting with a new method that processes wastewater by creating wetlands. Wetlands are home to filtering plants, such as cattails, and sewage-eating bacteria.

In 1996, school officials at the Corrales Elementary School in Albuquerque, New Mexico, faced a big problem. The old wastewater-treatment system had failed. Replacing it was going to cost a lot of money. Instead of constructing a new sewage-treatment plant, school officials decided to create a natural wetlands system. The wetlands system could do the job less expensively, while protecting the environment.

Today, this wetlands efficiently converts polluted water into cleaner water that's good for the environment. U.S. government officials are monitoring this alternative sewage-treatment system to see if it is successful. So far, so good!

Wetlands filter water through the actions of the plants and microorganisms that live there. When plants absorb water into their roots, some also take up pollutants. The plants convert the pollutants to forms that are not dangerous. At the same time, bacteria and other microorganisms are filtering water as they feed. Water moves slowly through wetlands, so the organisms have plenty of time to do their work. Wetlands built by people to filter small amounts of pollutants are called "constructed wetlands". In many places, constructed wetlands are better at cleaning wastewater than sewers or septic systems.

Visit and Observe Visit a wetlands and create a field journal of your observations. Draw the plants and animals you see. Use a field guide to help identify the wildlife. If you don't live near a wetlands, use resources to research wetlands environments.

Reviewing Main Ideas

Section 1 How Ecosystems Change

1. Ecological succession is the gradual change from one plant community to another.

2. Primary succession begins in a place where no plants were before.

3. Secondary succession begins in a place that has soil and was once the home of living organisms.

4. A climax community has reached a stable stage of ecological succession.

Section 2 Biomes

1. Temperature and precipitation help determine the climate of a region.

2. Large geographic areas with similar climax communities are called biomes.

3. Earth's land biomes include tundra, taiga, temperate deciduous forest, temperate rain forest, tropical rain forest, grassland, and desert.

Section 3 Aquatic Ecosystems

1. Freshwater ecosystems include streams, rivers, lakes, ponds, and wetlands.

2. Wetlands are areas that are covered with water most of the year. They are found in regions that lie between land-masses and water.

3. Saltwater ecosystems include estuaries, sea-shores, coral reefs, a few inland lakes, and the deep ocean.

4. Estuaries are fertile transitional zones between freshwater and saltwater environments.

Visualizing Main Ideas

Copy and complete this concept map about land biomes.

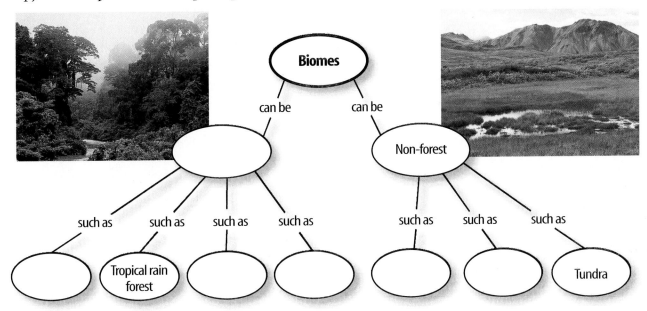

Biomes

can be   can be

Non-forest

such as   such as   such as   such as   such as   such as   such as

Tropical rain forest

Tundra

Using Vocabulary

biome p. 230	succession p. 226
climax community p. 229	taiga p. 232
coral reef p. 243	temperate deciduous
desert p. 236	forest p. 233
estuary p. 244	temperate rain forest p. 233
grassland p. 237	tropical rain forest p. 234
intertidal zone p. 244	tundra p. 231
pioneer species p. 226	wetland p. 241

Answer with the correct vocabulary word or words.

1. the normal changes in the types of species that live in communities

2. a group of organisms found in a stable stage of succession

3. place where deciduous trees are dominant

4. the average temperature is between 9°C and 12°C

5. the most biologically diverse biomes in the world

6. an area where freshwater meets the ocean

Checking Concepts

Choose the word or phrase that best answers the question.

7. What are tundra and desert examples of?
   A) ecosystems
   C) habitats
   B) biomes
   D) communities

8. What is a biome that receives less than 25 cm of rain called?   SC.G.2.3.2
   A) desert
   C) coral reef
   B) tundra
   D) grassland

9. Where would organisms that are adapted to live in slightly salty water be found?
   A) lake
   C) open ocean
   B) estuary
   D) intertidal zone

10. Which biome contains mostly frozen soil called permafrost?
    A) taiga
    B) temperate rain forest
    C) tundra
    D) temperate deciduous forest

11. A new island is formed from a volcanic eruption. Which species probably would be the first to grow and survive?
    A) palm trees
    C) grasses
    B) lichens
    D) ferns

12. What would the changes in communities that take place on a recently formed volcanic island best be described as?
    A) primary succession
    B) secondary succession
    C) tertiary succession
    D) magma

13. What is the stable end stage of succession?
    A) pioneer species
    B) climax community
    C) limiting factor
    D) permafrost

Use the illustration below to answer question 14.

Observed Fire Danger Class—June, 2003

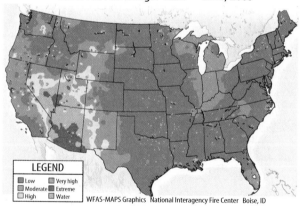

LEGEND
☐ Low   ☐ Very high
☐ Moderate ■ Extreme
☐ High   ☐ Water

WFAS-MAPS Graphics National Interagency Fire Center Boise, ID

14. Which area of the U.S. had the highest observed fire danger on June 20, 2003?
    A) northeast
    C) northwest
    B) southeast
    D) southwest

Vocabulary PuzzleMaker fl6.msscience.com

Thinking Critically

15. Explain In most cases, would a soil sample from a temperate deciduous forest be more or less nutrient-rich than a soil sample from a tropical rain forest? `SC.G.2.3.2`

16. Explain why some plant seeds need fire in order to germinate. How does this give these plants an advantage in secondary succession?

17. Determine A grassy meadow borders a beech-maple forest. Is one of these ecosystems undergoing succession? Why?

18. Infer why tundra plants are usually small.

19. Make and Use a Table Copy and complete the following table about aquatic ecosystems. Include the terms: *intertidal zone, lake, pond, coral reef, open ocean, river, estuary,* and *stream.*

Aquatic Ecosystems

Saltwater	Freshwater
Do not write in this book.	

20. Recognize Cause and Effect Wildfires like the one in Yellowstone National Park in 1988, cause many changes to the land. Determine the effect of a fire on an area that has reached its climax community.

Performance Activities

21. Oral Presentation Research a biome not in this chapter. Find out about its climate and location, and which organisms live there. Present this information to your class. `SC.G.2.3.2`

Applying Math

Use the table below to answer question 22.

Rainfall Amounts

Biome	Average Precipitation/Year (cm)
Taiga	50
Temperate rain forest	200
Tropical rain forest	400
Desert	25
Temperate deciduous forest	150
Tundra	25

22. Biome Precipitation How many times more precipitation does the tropical rain forest biome receive than the taiga or desert? `SC.G.2.3.2`

Use the graph below to answer question 23.

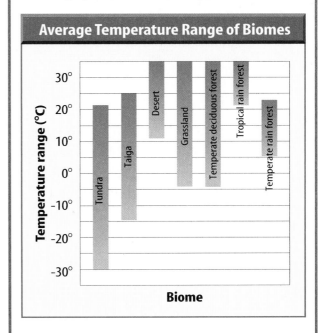

Average Temperature Range of Biomes

23. Biome Temperatures According to the graph, which biome has the greatest and which biome has the least variation in temperature throughout the year? Estimate the difference between the two. `SC.G.2.3.2` `MA.E.1.3.1`

The assessed Florida Benchmark appears above each question.
Record your answers on the answer sheet provided by your teacher or on a sheet of paper.

Multiple Choice

SC.H.2.3.1

1 What biome is found primarily near the Arctic Circle?

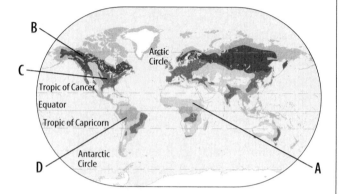

A. grassland

B. taiga

C. temperate deciduous forest

D. tropical rain forest

SC.G.2.3.3

2 Over time the number and size of trees surrounding a small pond have increased, reducing the amount of sunlight the pond receives. What effect will the increased amount of shade **most** likely have on the pond?

F. The volume of water in the pond will decrease.

G. The population of plants in the pond will decrease.

H. The amount of algae growing in the pond will increase.

I. The average temperature of the water in the pond will increase.

SC.G.1.3.2

3 A plant called saxifrage grows near the ground and can absorb heat from the ground during summer. It is protected from harsh winter weather by a layer of snow. Based on this information, which **best** explains why saxifrage is well-adapted to the tundra?

A. The saxifrage has adapted to survive the extreme cold in the tundra.

B. The saxifrage has adapted to use the nutrient-rich soil in the tundra.

C. The saxifrage has adapted to be pollinated by the many types of birds in tundra.

D. The saxifrage has adapted to use the moderate amount of precipitation in the tundra.

SC.G.2.3.3

4 Look at the diagram below. What is most likely to happen next in this community?

F. The bare soil will remain lifeless for many years.

G. Lichens and erosion will slowly break down rocks to form new soil.

H. A variety of plants will begin to grow from seeds already in the soil.

I. Only small plants such as mosses and ferns will have enough nutrients to grow.

SC.G.2.3.4

5 How might grassland **most** likely be affected if livestock overgraze it?

A. Erosion of topsoil will increase as the grasses die.

B. The grasses will be replaced by a temperate forest.

C. The length of the dry season in the grassland will decrease.

D. Ranchers will be able to raise more animals on the grassland.

 Gridded Response

SC.G.2.3.2

6 The table below shows the average yearly rainfall in four desert cities.

City	Average Yearly Rainfall (mm)
Agadez, Niger	143
Aleppo, Syria	329
Carson City, United States	285
Iquique, Chile	2

Based on the information in the table, how many years would it take for Iquique to receive the amount of rainfall that Agadez receives in a single year?

 Short Response

SC.G.2.3.2

7 Explain why primary succession takes longer than secondary succession.

 Extended Response

SC.D.2.3.2   SC.G.2.3.4

8 The diagram below shows a farm and a sewage plant located near a lake.

PART A Based on the diagram, describe the effects that pollutants released from the farm and the sewage plant might be having on the organisms that live in the lake.

PART B Explain how these effects could be prevented.

FCAT Tip

Show All Your Work For "Read, Inquire, Explain" questions, show all of your work and any calculations on your answer sheet.

Sunshine State Standards—**SC.A.2:** The student understands the basic principles of atomic theory; **SC.D.2:** The student understands the need for protection of the natural systems on Earth; **SC.G.2:** understands the consequences of using limited natural resources.

Earth's Energy and Mineral Resources

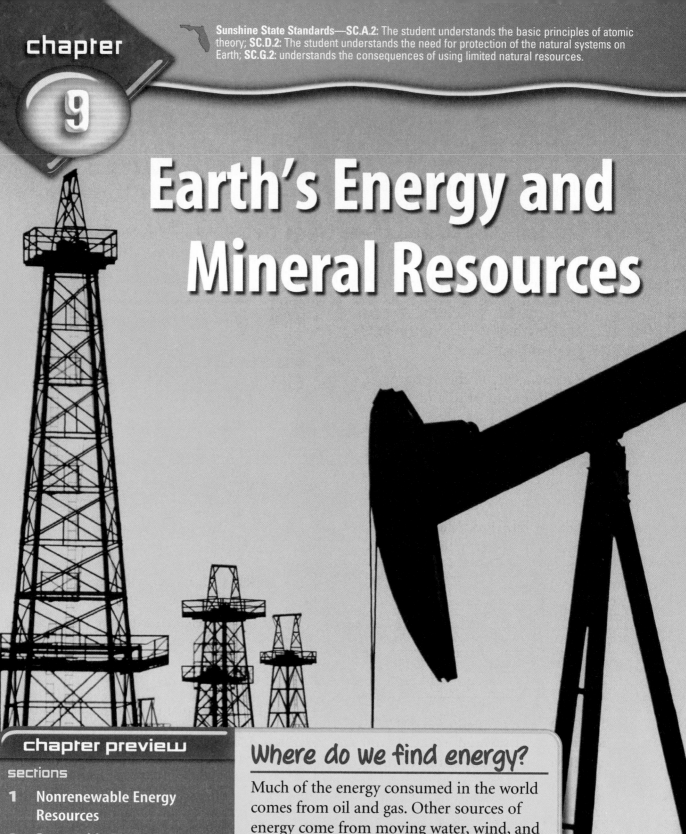

chapter preview

sections

1 Nonrenewable Energy Resources

2 Renewable Energy Resources
  Lab Soaking Up Solar Energy

3 Mineral Resources
  Lab Home Sweet Home

  Virtual Lab What are the advantages of alternative energy sources?

Where do we find energy?

Much of the energy consumed in the world comes from oil and gas. Other sources of energy come from moving water, wind, and the Sun's rays. In this chapter you'll learn about many types of energy resources and the importance of conserving these resources.

Science Journal Write three ways electricity is generated at a power plant.

Start-Up Activities

Finding Energy Reserves

The physical properties of Earth materials determine how easily liquids and gases move through them. Geologists use these properties, in part, to predict where reserves of energy resources like petroleum or natural gas can be found.

1. Complete a safety worksheet.
2. Obtain a sample of sandstone and a sample of shale from your teacher.
3. Make sure that your samples can be placed on a tabletop so that the sides facing up are reasonably flat and horizontal.
4. Place the two samples side by side in a shallow baking pan.
5. Using a dropper, place three drops of cooking oil on each sample.
6. For ten minutes, observe what happens to the oil on the samples.
7. **Think Critically** Write your observations in your Science Journal. Infer which rock type might be a good reservoir for petroleum.

Science Online | **Preview this chapter's content and activities at** fl6.msscience.com

Energy Resources Make the following Foldable to help you identify energy resources.

LA.A.1.3.4
LA.A.2.3.1

STEP 1 Fold a sheet of paper in half lengthwise. Make the back edge about 1.25 cm longer than the front edge.

STEP 2 Turn lengthwise and fold into thirds.

STEP 3 Unfold and cut only the top layer along both folds to make three tabs.

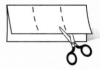

STEP 4 Label each tab as shown.

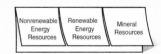

Find Main Ideas As you read the chapter, list examples on the front of the tabs and write about each type of resource under the tabs.

Benchmarks—SC.A.2.3.3 Annually Assessed (pp. 256, 263, 265): The student knows that radiation, light, and heat are forms of energy . . . ; SC.D.2.3.2 Annually Assessed (pp. 263–264): knows the positive and negative consequences of human action on the Earth's systems; SC.G.2.3.4 Annually Assessed (pp. 263–264): understands that humans are a part of an ecosystem . . . .

Also covers: SC.B.1.3.1 (pp. 256–272), SC.B.2.3.2 (pp. 256–259), SC.D.2.3.1 (pp. 263–264), SC.G.2.3.1 (pp. 256–265), SC.H.3.3.4 (pp. 264–265)

section 1

Nonrenewable Energy Resources

as you read

What You'll Learn

- **Identify** examples of nonrenewable energy resources.
- **Describe** the advantages and disadvantages of using fossil fuels.
- **Explain** the advantages and disadvantages of using nuclear energy.

Why It's Important

Nonrenewable resources should be conserved to ensure their presence for future generations.

Review Vocabulary

fuel: a material that provides useful energy

New Vocabulary

☀ resource
☀ nonrenewable resource
☀ fossil fuel
● coal
● oil
● natural gas
● reserve
☀ conservation
● nuclear energy

☀ FCAT Vocabulary

Energy

A **resource** is any material that can be used to satisfy a need. Some resources are used to provide energy. The world's population relies on energy of all kinds. Most of the energy resources used to generate electricity are nonrenewable. **Nonrenewable resources** are being used faster than natural Earth processes can replace them.

Fossil Fuels

Nonrenewable energy resources include fossil fuels. **Fossil fuels** are fuels such as coal, oil, and natural gas that form from the remains of plants and other organisms that were buried and altered over millions of years. Coal is a sedimentary rock formed from the compacted and transformed remains of ancient plant matter. Oil is a liquid hydrocarbon that often is referred to as petroleum. Hydrocarbons are compounds that contain hydrogen and carbon atoms. Other naturally occurring hydrocarbons occur in the gas or semisolid states. Fossil fuels are processed to make gasoline for cars, to heat homes, and for many other uses, as shown in **Table 1.**

Table 1 Uses of Fossil Fuels	
🛒 Coal	▪ To generate electricity
🛢 Oil	▪ To produce gasoline and other fuels ▪ As lubricants ▪ To make plastics, home shingles, and other products
🔥 Natural Gas	▪ To heat buildings ▪ As a source of sulfur

Figure 1 This coal layer is located in Castle Gate, Utah. **Analyze and Conclude** *Using the map and legend below, can you determine what type of coal it is?*

Coal

Legend:
- Anthracite
- Bituminous
- Lignite

C A N A D A

U N I T E D   S T A T E S

M E X I C O

Coal

The most abundant fossil fuel in the world is coal, shown in **Figure 1.** If the consumption of coal continues at the current rate, it is estimated that the coal supply will last for about another 250 years.

Coal is a rock that contains at least 50 percent plant remains. Coal begins to form when plants die in a swampy area. The dead plants are covered by more plants, water, and sediment, preventing atmospheric oxygen from coming into contact with the plant matter. The lack of atmospheric oxygen prevents the plant matter from decaying rapidly. Bacterial growth within the plant material causes a gradual breakdown of molecules in the plant tissue, leaving carbon and some impurities behind. This is the material that eventually will become coal after millions of years. Bacteria also cause the release of methane gas, carbon dioxide, ammonia, and water as the original plant matter breaks down.

Reading Check *What happens to begin the formation of coal in a swampy area?*

Synthetic Fuels

Unlike gasoline, which is refined from petroleum, other fuels called synthetic fuels are extracted from solid organic material. Synthetic fuels can be created from coal—a sedimentary rock containing hydrocarbons. The hydrocarbons are extracted from coal to form liquid and gaseous synthetic fuels. Liquid synthetic fuels can be processed to produce gasoline for automobiles and fuel oil for home heating. Gaseous synthetic fuels are used to generate electricity and heat buildings.

LA.A.2.3.5
LA.B.2.3.1

INTEGRATE Life Science

Coal Formation The coal found in the eastern and midwestern United States formed from plants that lived in great swamps about 300 million years ago during the Pennsylvanian Period of geologic time. Research the Pennsylvanian Period to find out what types of plants lived in these swamps. Describe the plants in your Science Journal.

Stages of Coal Formation As decaying plant material loses gas and moisture, the concentration of carbon increases. The first step in this process, shown in the "A" portion of **Figure 2,** results in the formation of peat. Peat is a layer of organic sediment. When peat burns, it releases large amounts of smoke because it has a high concentration of water and impurities.

As peat is buried under more sediment, it changes into lignite, which is a soft, brown coal with much less moisture. Heat and pressure, produced by burial, force water out of peat and concentrate carbon in the lignite. Lignite releases more energy and less smoke than peat when it is burned.

As the layers are buried deeper, bituminous coal, or soft coal, forms. Bituminous coal is compact, black, and brittle. It provides lots of heat energy when burned. Bituminous coal contains various levels of sulfur, which can pollute the environment.

If enough heat and pressure are applied to buried layers of bituminous coal, anthracite coal forms. Anthracite coal contains the highest amount of carbon of all forms of coal. Therefore, anthracite coal is the cleanest burning of all coals.

Figure 2 Coal is formed in four basic stages.

A Dead plant material accumulates in swamps and eventually forms a layer of peat.

B Over time, heat and pressure cause the peat to change into lignite coal.

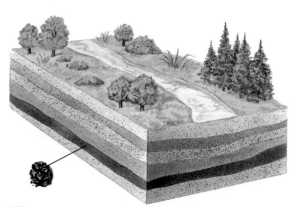

C As the lignite coal becomes buried by more sediments, heat and pressure change it into bituminous coal.

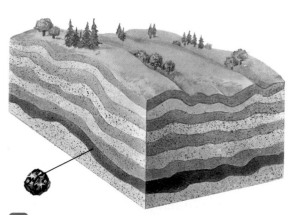

D When bituminous coal is heated and squeezed during metamorphism, anthracite coal forms.

Oil and Natural Gas Coal isn't the only fossil fuel used to obtain energy. Two other fossil fuels that provide large quantities of the energy used today are oil and natural gas. **Oil** is a thick, black liquid formed from the buried remains of microscopic marine organisms. **Natural gas** forms under similar conditions and often with oil, but it forms in a gaseous state. Oil and natural gas are hydrocarbons. However, natural gas is composed of hydrocarbon molecules that are lighter than those in oil.

Residents of the United States burn vast quantities of oil and natural gas for daily energy requirements. As shown in **Figure 3,** people in Florida obtain most of their energy from these sources. Natural gas is used mostly for heating and cooking. Oil is used in many ways, including heating oil, gasoline, lubricants, and in the manufacture of plastics and other important compounds.

Formation of Oil and Natural Gas Most geologists agree that petroleum forms over millions of years from the remains of tiny marine organisms in ocean sediment. The process begins when marine organisms called plankton die and fall to the seafloor. Similar to the way that coal is buried, sediment is deposited over them. The temperature rises with depth in Earth, and increased heat eventually causes the dead plankton to change to oil and gas after they have been buried deeply by sediment.

Oil and natural gas often are found in layers of rock that have become tilted or folded. Because they are less dense than water, oil and natural gas are forced upward. Rock layers that are impermeable, such as shale, stop this upward movement. When this happens, a folded shale layer can trap the oil and natural gas below it. Such a trap for oil and gas is shown in **Figure 4.** The rock layer beneath the shale in which the petroleum and natural gas accumulate is called a reservoir rock.

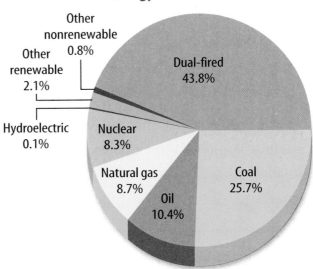

Energy Use in Florida, 2002

- Other nonrenewable 0.8%
- Other renewable 2.1%
- Hydroelectric 0.1%
- Dual-fired 43.8%
- Nuclear 8.3%
- Natural gas 8.7%
- Coal 25.7%
- Oil 10.4%

Figure 3 This circle graph shows the percentages of energy that Florida derives from various energy resources. Dual-fired indicates that two types of fossil fuels are used: coal and natural gas, coal and oil, or oil and natural gas.

Figure 4 Oil and natural gas are fossil fuels formed when marine organisms are buried. These fuels can be trapped and accumulate beneath Earth's surface.

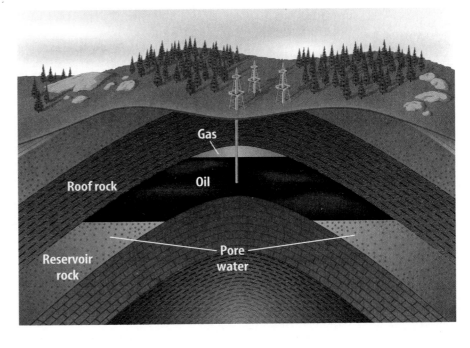

Gas

Oil

Roof rock

Reservoir rock

Pore water

Removing Fossil Fuels from the Ground

Coal is removed from the ground using one of several methods of excavation. The two most common methods, shown in **Figure 5,** are strip mining, also called open-pit mining, and underground mining. Oil and natural gas are removed by pumping them out of the ground.

Coal Mining During strip mining, layers of soil and rock above coal are removed and piled to one side. The exposed coal then is removed and loaded into trucks or trains and transported elsewhere. After the coal has been removed, mining companies often return the soil and rock to the open pit and cover it with topsoil. Trees and grass are planted in a process called land reclamation. If possible, animals native to the area are reintroduced. Strip mining is used only when the coal deposits are close to the surface.

In one method of underground coal mining, tunnels are dug and pillars of rock are left to support the rocks surrounding the tunnels. Two types of underground coal mines are drift mines and slope mines. Drift mining is the removal of coal that is not close to Earth's surface through a horizontal opening in the side of a hill or mountain. In slope mining, an angled opening and air shaft are made in the side of a mountain to remove coal.

Figure 5 Coal is a fossil fuel that can be removed from Earth in many different ways.

During strip mining, coal is accessed by removing the soil and rock above it.

During drift mining, tunnels are made into Earth.
Explain *how you think the coal is removed from these tunnels.*

Drilling for Oil and Gas Oil and natural gas are fossil fuels that can be pumped from underground deposits. Geologists and engineers drill wells through rocks where these resources might be trapped, as shown in **Figure 6.** As the well is being drilled, it is lined with pipe to prevent it from caving in. When the drill bit reaches the rock layer containing oil, drilling is stopped. Equipment is installed to control the flow of oil. The surrounding rock then is fractured to allow oil and gas to flow into the well. The oil and gas are pumped to the surface.

 *How are oil and natural gas brought to Earth's surface?*

Fossil Fuel Reserves

The amount of a fossil fuel that can be extracted at a profit using current technology is known as a **reserve.** This is not the same as a fossil fuel resource. A fossil fuel resource has fossil fuels that are concentrated enough that they can be extracted from Earth in useful amounts. However, a resource is not classified as a reserve unless the fuel can be extracted economically. What might cause a known fossil fuel resource to become classified as a reserve?

Methane Hydrates You have learned that current reserves of coal will last about 250 years. Enough natural gas is located in the United States to last about 60 more years. However, recent studies indicate that a new source of methane, which is the main component of natural gas, might be located beneath the seafloor. Icelike substances known as methane hydrates could provide tremendous reserves of methane.

Methane hydrates are stable molecules found hundreds of meters below sea level in ocean floor sediment. They form under conditions of relatively low temperatures and high pressures. The hydrocarbons are trapped within the cagelike structure of ice, as described in **Figure 7.** Scientists estimate that more carbon is contained in methane hydrates than in all current fossil fuel deposits combined. Large accumulations of methane hydrates are estimated to exist off the eastern coast of the United States. Can you imagine what it would mean to the world's energy supply if relatively clean-burning methane could be extracted economically from methane hydrates?

Figure 6 Oil and natural gas are recovered from Earth by drilling deep wells.

LA.B.2.3.4

Science Online

Topic: Methane Hydrates
Visit fl6.msscience.com for Web links to information about methane hydrates.

Activity Identify which oceans might contain significant amounts of methane hydrates.

Figure 7

Reserves of fossil fuels—such as oil, coal, and natural gas—are limited and will one day be used up. Methane hydrates could be an alternative energy source. This icelike substance has been discovered in ocean floor sediments and in permafrost regions worldwide. If scientists can harness this energy, the world's gas supply could be met for years to come.

Methane hydrates are highly flammable compounds made up of methane—the main component of natural gas—trapped in a cage of frozen water. Methane hydrates represent an enormous source of potential energy. However, they contain a greenhouse gas that might intensify global warming. More research is needed to determine how to safely extract them from the seafloor.

In the photo above, a Russian submersible explores a site in the North Atlantic that contains methane hydrate deposits.

Conserving Fossil Fuels Do you sometimes forget to turn off the lights when you walk out of a room? Wasteful habits might mean that electricity to run homes and industries will not always be as plentiful and cheap as it is today. Fossil fuels take millions of years to form and are used much faster than Earth processes can replenish them.

Today, coal provides about 25 percent of the energy that is used worldwide and 22 percent of the energy used in the United States. Oil and natural gas provide almost 61 percent of the world's energy and about 65 percent of the U.S. energy supply. At the rate these fuels are being used, they could run out someday. How can this be avoided?

Conservation is the controlled use and maintenance of natural resources—the efforts to preserve or protect natural resources. By remembering to turn off lights and appliances, you can avoid wasting fossil fuels. Another way to conserve fossil fuels is to make sure doors and windows are shut tightly during cold weather so heat doesn't leak out of your home. If you have air-conditioning, run it as little as possible. Ask the adults you live with if more insulation could be added to your home or if an insulated jacket could be put on the water heater.

Energy from Atoms

Most electricity in the United States is produced by burning coal. However, alternate sources of energy exist. **Nuclear energy** is an alternate energy source produced from atomic reactions. When the nucleus of a heavy element is split, lighter elements form and energy is released. This energy can be used to light a home or power the submarines shown in **Figure 8.**

The splitting of heavy elements to produce energy is called nuclear fission. Nuclear fission is carried out in nuclear power plants using a type of uranium as fuel.

Mini LAB

Practicing Energy Conservation

Procedure
1. Complete a safety worksheet.
2. Have an adult help you find the **electric meter** for your home and record the reading in your **Science Journal.**
3. Do this for several days, taking your meter readings at about the same time each day.
4. List things you and your family can do to reduce your electricity use.
5. Encourage your family to try some of the listed ideas for several days.

Analysis
1. Keep taking meter readings and infer whether the changes make any difference.
2. Have you and your family helped conserve energy?

Try at Home

Figure 8 Atoms can be a source of energy.

These submarines are powered by nuclear fission.

During nuclear fission, energy is given off when a heavy atom, like uranium, splits into lighter atoms.

Heavy atom

Lighter atoms

+ **Energy**

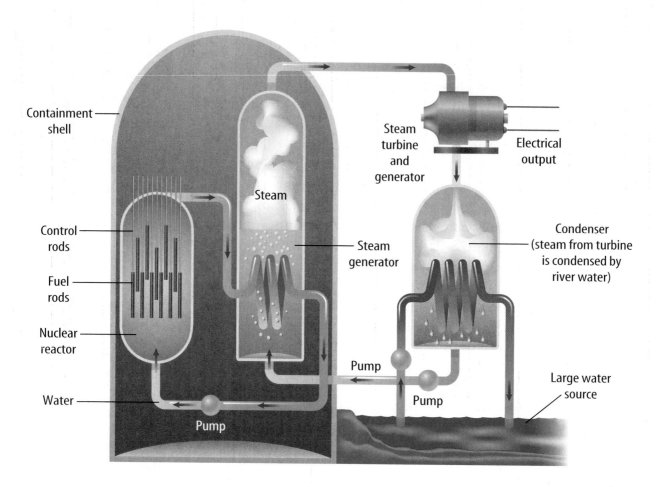

Containment shell

Control rods

Fuel rods

Nuclear reactor

Water

Pump

Steam

Steam generator

Steam turbine and generator

Electrical output

Condenser (steam from turbine is condensed by river water)

Pump

Pump

Large water source

Figure 9 Heat released in nuclear reactors produces steam, which in turn is used to produce electricity. This is an example of transforming nuclear energy into electrical energy.
Infer *Why do you think nuclear power plants are located near rivers and lakes?*

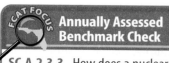

Annually Assessed Benchmark Check

SC.A.2.3.3 How does a nuclear power plant provide energy? What type of energy is this?

Electricity from Nuclear Energy A nuclear power plant, shown in **Figure 9,** has a large chamber called a nuclear reactor. Within the nuclear reactor, uranium fuel rods sit in a pool of cooling water. Neutrons are fired into the fuel rods. When the uranium-235 atoms are hit, they break apart and fire out neutrons that hit other atoms, beginning a chain reaction. As each atom splits, it not only fires neutrons but also releases heat that is used to boil water to make steam. The steam drives a turbine, which turns a generator that produces electricity.

Reading Check *How is nuclear energy used to produce electricity?*

Nuclear energy from fission is considered to be a nonrenewable energy resource because it uses uranium-235 as fuel. A limited amount of uranium-235 is available for use. Another problem with nuclear energy is the waste material that it produces. Nuclear waste from power plants consists of highly radioactive elements formed by the fission process. Some of this waste will remain radioactive for thousands of years. The Environmental Protection Agency (EPA) has determined that nuclear waste must be stored safely and contained for at least 10,000 years before reentering the environment.

Fusion Environmental problems related to nuclear power could be eliminated if usable energy could be obtained from fusion. The Sun is a natural fusion power plant that provides energy for Earth and the solar system. Someday fusion also might provide energy for your home.

During fusion, materials of low mass are fused together to form a substance of higher mass. No fuel problem exists if the low-mass material is a commonly occurring substance. Also, if the end product is not radioactive, storing nuclear waste is not a problem. In fact, fusion of hydrogen into helium would satisfy both of these conditions. However, technologies do not currently exist to enable humans to fuse hydrogen into helium at reasonably low temperatures in a controlled manner. But research is being conducted, as shown in **Figure 10.** If this is accomplished, nuclear energy could be considered a renewable fuel resource. You will learn the importance of renewable energy resources in the next section.

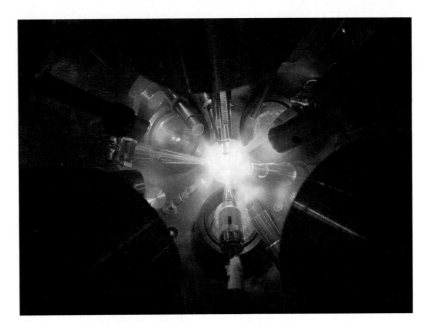

Figure 10 Lasers are used in research facilities to help people understand and control fusion.

---

section 1 review

Summary

Fossil Fuels

- Coal, natural gas, and oil are all nonrenewable energy sources.
- Synthetic fuels are human-made fuels that can be derived from coal.
- The four stages of coal formation are peat, lignite, bituminous coal, and anthracite coal.
- Oil and gas are made from the decay of ancient marine organisms.
- Strip mining and underground mining are two common methods that are used to extract coal reserves.

Energy from Atoms

- Energy is released during a fission reaction when a heavy atom is split into lighter atoms.
- Fusion occurs when two atoms come together to form a single atom.

Self Check

1. **Explain** why fossil fuels are considered to be non-renewable energy resources. SC.B.2.3.2
2. **List** ways that you can practice energy conservation. SC.G.2.3.4
3. **Describe** two disadvantages of nuclear energy.
4. **Think Critically** Why are you likely to find natural gas and oil deposits in the same location, but less likely to find coal and petroleum deposits in the same location?

Applying Math

5. **Design a Graph** Current energy consumption by source in the U.S. is as follows: oil, 39%; natural gas, 24%; coal, 23%; nuclear energy, 8%; renewable resources, 6%. Design a bar graph to show the energy consumption by source in the U.S. Display the sources from greatest to least. MA.E.1.3.1

---

section

2

Benchmarks—SC.A.2.3.3 Annually Assessed (pp. 266–271): The student knows that radiation, light, and heat are forms of energy . . . ; SC.D.2.3.2 Annually Assessed (pp. 266–271): knows the positive and negative consequences of human action on the Earth's systems; SC.G.2.3.4 Annually Assessed (pp. 266–271): understands that humans are a part of an ecosystem . . . .

Also covers: SC.B.1.3.1 (pp. 266–271), SC.D.2.3.1 (pp. 266–271), SC.G.2.3.1 (pp. 266–271), SC.H.1.3.5 Annually Assessed (p. 272), SC.H.1.3.6 (p. 267), SC.H.3.3.4 (pp. 267–271)

Renewable Energy Resources

as you read

What You'll Learn

- **Compare and contrast** inexhaustible and renewable energy resources.
- **Explain** why inexhaustible and renewable resources are used less than nonrenewable resources.

Why It's Important

As fossil fuel reserves continue to diminish, alternate energy resources will be needed.

Review Vocabulary

❋ **energy:** the ability to cause change

New Vocabulary

❋ **renewable resource**
- solar energy
- wind farm
- hydroelectric energy
- geothermal energy
- biomass energy

❋ FCAT Vocabulary

Renewable Energy Resources

How soon the world runs out of fossil fuels depends on how they are used and conserved. A **renewable resource** can be replaced or restored as it is used or within a reasonable amount of time. Sources of renewable energy include the Sun, wind, water, and geothermal energy.

Energy from the Sun When you sit in the Sun, walk into the wind, or sail against an ocean current, you are experiencing the power of solar energy. **Solar energy** is energy from the Sun. You already know that the Sun's energy heats Earth, and it causes circulation in Earth's atmosphere and oceans. Global winds and ocean currents are examples of nature's use of solar energy. Thus, solar energy is used indirectly when the wind and some types of moving water are used to do work.

People can use solar energy in a passive way or in an active way. Windows facing the Sun act as passive solar collectors, warming exposed rooms. Solar cells actively collect energy from the Sun and transform it into electricity. Solar cells were invented to generate electricity for satellites. Now they also are used to power calculators, streetlights, and experimental cars. Some people have installed solar energy cells on their roofs, as shown in **Figure 11.**

Figure 11 Solar panels, such as on this zero-energy home in New Smyrna, Florida, can be used to collect inexhaustible solar energy to power appliances and heat water. The white roof reflects sunlight, which helps to keep the house cool.

Figure 12 Wind farms are used to produce electricity.
Evaluate *Some people might argue that windmills produce visual pollution. Why do you think this is?*

Disadvantages of Solar Energy Solar energy is clean and inexhaustible, but it does have some disadvantages. Solar cells work less efficiently on cloudy days and cannot work at all at night. Some systems use batteries to store solar energy for use at night or on cloudy days, but it is difficult to store large amounts of energy in batteries. Worn out batteries also must be discarded. This can pollute the environment if not done properly.

Energy from Wind What is better to do on a warm, windy day than fly a kite? A strong wind can lift a kite high in the sky and whip it around. The pull of the wind is so great that you wonder if it will whip the kite right out of your hands. Wind is a source of energy. It was and still is used to power sailing ships. Windmills have used wind energy to grind corn and pump water. Today, windmills can be used to generate electricity. When a large number of windmills are placed in one area for the purpose of generating electricity, the area is called a **wind farm,** as shown in **Figure 12.**

Wind is nonpolluting and free. However, only a few regions of the world have winds strong enough to generate electricity. Sometimes wind blows too hard and at other times it is too weak or stops entirely. For an area to use wind energy consistently, the area must have a persistent wind that blows at an appropriate speed. Windmills also can be a problem for birds, who cannot see the blades turning. Also, habitats need to be destroyed to place the windmills.

 *Why are some regions better suited for wind farms than others?*

LA.A.2.3.5
LA.B.2.3.1

INTEGRATE
Career

Physicists The optimal speed of wind needed to rotate blades on a windmill is something a physicist would study. They can calculate the energy produced based on the speed at which the blades turn. Some areas in the country are better suited for wind farms than others. Find out which areas utilize wind farms and report in your Science Journal how much electricity is produced and what it is used for. What kinds of organizations would a physicist work for in these locations?

Energy from Water For a long time, waterwheels steadily spun next to streams and rivers. The energy in the flowing water powered the wheels that ground grain or cut lumber. Running water also can be used to generate electricity. Electricity produced by waterpower is called **hydroelectric energy.** To generate electricity from water running in a river, a large concrete dam is built to retain water, as illustrated in **Figure 13.** A lake forms behind the dam. As water is released, its force turns turbines at the base of the dam. The turbines then turn generators that make electricity. In Florida, Lake Seminole was formed when the Apalachicola River was dammed to provide hydroelectric power. The plant produces enough power for about 50,000 homes.

At first, it might appear that hydroelectric energy doesn't create any environmental problems and that the water is used with little additional cost. However, when dams are built, upstream lakes fill with sediment and downstream erosion increases. Land above the dam is flooded, and wildlife habitats are damaged.

Energy from Earth Erupting volcanoes and geysers like Old Faithful are examples of geothermal energy in action. The energy that causes volcanoes to erupt or water to shoot up as a geyser also can be used to generate electricity. Energy obtained by using hot magma or hot, dry rocks inside Earth is called **geothermal energy.**

Bodies of magma can heat large reservoirs of groundwater. Geothermal power plants use steam from the reservoirs to produce electricity, as shown in **Figure 14.** Water becomes steam when it is pumped through broken, hot, dry rocks. The steam then is used to turn turbines that run generators to make electricity. The advantage of using hot, dry rocks is that they are found just about everywhere. Geothermal energy presently is being used in Hawaii and in parts of the western United States.

Figure 13 Hydroelectric power is important in many regions of the United States. Hoover Dam was built on the Colorado River to supply electricity for a large area.

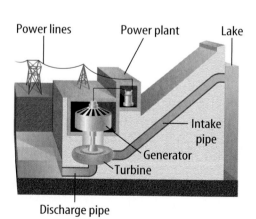

The power of running water is converted to usable energy in a hydroelectric power plant.

Figure 14 Geothermal energy is used to supply electricity to industries and homes.

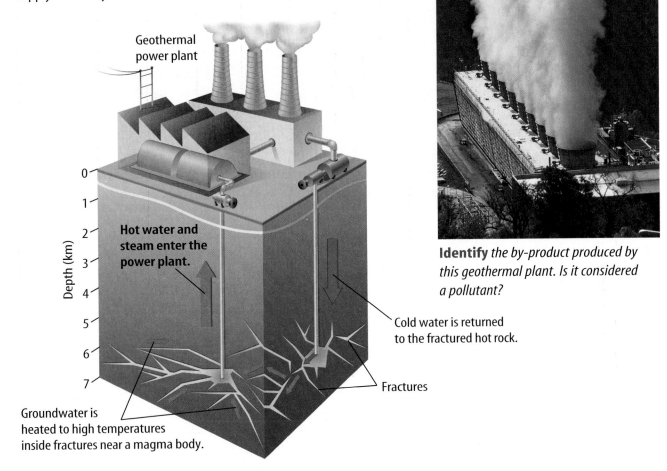

Geothermal power plant

Depth (km)

Hot water and steam enter the power plant.

Cold water is returned to the fractured hot rock.

Fractures

Groundwater is heated to high temperatures inside fractures near a magma body.

Identify *the by-product produced by this geothermal plant. Is it considered a pollutant?*

Disadvantages of Geothermal Energy Geothermal energy sounds like the perfect solution—harness the heat energy already in Earth. However, often the hot, dry rocks or magma are located deep within Earth. More energy would be used to get to the rocks or magma than would be taken from it. Also, digging for the energy destroys habitat in much the same way that drilling for fossil fuels does.

Other Renewable Energy Resources

Some other energy resources are not inexhaustible but, if used responsibly, can be replaced within a human lifetime. These are replaced either by nature or humans. For example, trees can be cut down and others can be planted in their place.

Biomass Energy A major renewable energy resource is biomass materials. **Biomass energy** is energy derived from burning organic material such as wood, alcohol, and garbage. The term *biomass* is derived from the words *biological* and *mass*.

LA.A.1.3.4

LA.B.2.3.4

Science nline

Topic: Biomass Energy
Visit fl6.msscience.com for Web links to information about biomass energy.

Activity List three new technologies that turn biomass into useable energy. Give two examples of each type of biomass and its energy technology.

Figure 15 These campers are using wood, a renewable energy resource, to produce heat and light.

Discuss *Why do you think wood is the most commonly used biomass fuel?*

Energy from Wood If you've ever sat around a campfire, like the campers shown in **Figure 15,** or close to a wood-burning fireplace to keep warm, you have used energy from wood. The burning wood is releasing stored solar energy as heat energy. Humans have long used wood as an energy resource. Much of the world still cooks with wood. In fact, firewood is used more widely today than any other type of biomass fuel.

Using wood as a biomass fuel has its problems. Gases and small particles are released when wood is burned. These materials can pollute the air. When trees are cut down for firewood, natural habitats are destroyed. However, if proper conservation methods are employed or if tree farms are maintained specifically for use as fuel, energy from wood can be a part of future energy resources.

Energy from Alcohol Biomass fuel can be burned directly, such as when wood or peat is used for heating and cooking. However, it also can be transformed into other materials that might provide cleaner, more efficient fuels.

For example, during distillation, biomass fuel, such as corn, is changed to an alcohol such as ethanol. Ethanol then can be mixed with another fuel. When the other fuel is gasoline, the mixture is called gasohol. Gasohol can be used in the same way as gasoline, as shown in **Figure 16,** but it cuts down on the amount of fossil fuel needed to produce gasoline. Fluid biomass fuels are more efficient and have more uses than solid biomass fuels do.

The problem with this technology is that presently growing the corn and distilling the ethanol often uses more energy from burning fossil fuels than the amount of energy that is derived from burning ethanol. At present, biomass fuel is best used locally.

Figure 16 Gasohol sometimes is used to reduce dependence on fossil fuels.

✓ **Reading Check** *What are the drawbacks of biomass fuels?*

Energy from Garbage Every day humans throw away a tremendous amount of burnable garbage. As much as two thirds of what is thrown away could be burned. If more garbage were used for fuel, as shown in **Figure 17,** human dependence on fossil fuels would decrease. Burning garbage is a cheap source of energy and also helps reduce the amount of material that must be dumped into landfills.

Compared to other nations, the United States lags in the use of municipal waste as a renewable energy resource. For example, in some countries in Western Europe, as much as half of the waste generated is used for biomass fuel. When the garbage is burned, heat is produced, which turns water to steam. The steam turns turbines that run generators to produce electricity.

Unfortunately, some environmental constraints can be associated with using energy from garbage. Burning municipal waste can produce toxic ash residue and air pollution. Substances such as heavy metals could find their way into the smoke from garbage and thus into the atmosphere.

Figure 17 Garbage can be burned to produce electricity at trash-burning power plants.

section 2 review

Summary

Renewable Energy Resources

- Solar cells are used to collect the Sun's energy.
- Wind energy produces no waste or pollution, however only a few areas are conducive for creating significant energy supplies.
- Dams are used to help provide running water, which is used to produce electricity.
- Energy obtained by using heat from inside Earth is called geothermal energy.

Other Renewable Energy Resources

- Biomass energy is produced when organic material such as wood, alcohol, or garbage is burned.
- Trash-burning power plants convert waste into electricty by burning garbage.

Self Check

1. **List** three advantages and disadvantages of using solar energy, wind energy, and hydroelectric energy.
2. **Explain** the difference between nonrenewable and renewable energy resources. Give two examples of each. SC.G.2.3.1
3. **Describe** how geothermal energy is used to create electricity.
4. **Infer** why nonrenewable resources are used more than renewable resources. SC.G.2.3.1
5. **Think Critically** How could forests be classified as a renewable and nonrenewable resource?

Applying Skills

6. **Use a Spreadsheet** Make a table of energy resources. Include an example of how each resource is used. Then describe how you could reduce the use of energy resources at home. SC.G.2.3.4

Soaking Up Solar Energy

Winter clothing tends to be darker in color than summer clothing. The color of the material used in the clothing affects its ability to absorb energy. In this lab, you will use different colors of soil to study this effect.

▶ Real-World Problem

How does color affect the absorption of energy?

Goals

- **Determine** whether color has an effect on the absorption of solar energy.
- **Relate** the concept of whether color affects absorption to other applications.

Materials

dry, black soil	clear, glass or plastic
dry, brown soil	dishes (3)
dry, sandy,	200-watt gooseneck
white soil	lamps (3)
thermometers (3)	*200-watt lamp with
graph paper	reflector and clamp (3)
colored pencils (3)	*ring stand (3)
metric ruler	watch or clock
*stopwatch	with second hand
*Alternate materials	

Safety Precautions

Complete a safety worksheet before you begin.

WARNING: *Handle glass with care so as not to break it. Wear thermal mitts when handling the light source.*

▶ Procedure

1. Fill each dish with a different color of soil to a depth of 2.5 cm and distribute one dish per lab group.

Time and Temperature

Time (min)	Temperature Dish A (°C)	Temperature Dish B (°C)	Temperature Dish C (°C)
0.0			
0.5	Do not write in this book.		
1.0			
1.5			

2. Place a thermometer in each dish. Be sure to cover the thermometer bulb in each dish completely with the soil.

3. Position the lamp over all three dishes at the same distance from each dish.

4. Read the temperature of each dish every 30 s for 10 min after the light is turned on. Record your results in a table.

5. Turn on the light and begin your experiment. One student in the lab group should read the stopwatch, one should read the temperature, and one should record the temperature.

6. Use the data to construct a graph. Time should be plotted on the horizontal axis and temperature on the vertical axis. Use a different colored pencil to plot the data for each type of soil, or use a computer to design a graph that illustrates your data.

▶ Conclude and Apply

1. **Observe** which soil had the greatest temperature change. The least?

2. **Determine** why the curves on the graph flatten.

3. **Predict** what would be the best location for using solar energy. What color would the collector be? Why?

Benchmarks—SC.D.2.3.2 Annually Assessed (pp. 276–277): The student knows the positive and negative consequences of human action on the Earth's systems; SC.G.2.3.4 Annually Assessed (pp. 276–277):
The student understands that humans are a part of an ecosystem and their activities may deliberately
or inadvertently alter the equilibrium in ecosystems.

section 3

Mineral Resources

Metallic Mineral Resources

If your room at home is anything like the one shown in
Figure 18, you will find many metal items. Metals are obtained
from Earth materials called metallic mineral resources. A
mineral resource is a deposit of useful minerals. See how many
metals you can find. Is there anything in your room that contains iron? What about the metal in the frame of your bed? Is it
made of iron? If so, the iron might have come from the mineral
hematite. What about the framing around the windows in your
room? Is it aluminum? Aluminum, like that in a soft-drink can,
comes from a mixture of minerals known as bauxite. Many minerals contain these and other useful elements. Hematite (iron)
and bauxite (aluminum) are among minerals that are mined as
sources for the materials you use every day.

Ores Deposits in which a mineral or minerals exist in large
enough amounts to be mined at a profit are called **ores.**
Generally, the term ore is used for metallic deposits, but this is
not always the case. The hematite that was mentioned earlier as
an iron ore and the bauxite that was mentioned earlier as an aluminum ore are metallic ores.

as you read

What You'll Learn

- **Explain** the conditions needed
  for a mineral to be classified as
  an ore.
- **Describe** how market conditions
  can cause a mineral to lose its
  value as an ore.
- **Compare and contrast** metallic
  and nonmetallic mineral
  resources.

Why It's Important

Many products you use are made
from mineral resources.

Review Vocabulary
metal: a solid material that is
generally hard, shiny, pliable and
a good electrical conductor

New Vocabulary
- mineral resource
- ore
- recycling

Copper in wires
found in electrical
equipment comes
from the mineral
chalcopyrite.

Many bed frames contain iron,
which is extracted from minerals
such as hematite.

Aluminum comes from
a mixture of minerals
called bauxite.

Stainless steel contains
chromium, which comes
from the mineral chromite.

Figure 18 Many items in your
home are made from metals
obtained from metallic mineral
resources.

Figure 19 Iron ores are smelted to produce nearly pure iron.
List *three examples of what this iron could be used for.*

Economic Constraints When is a mineral deposit considered an ore? The mineral in question must be in demand. Enough of it must be present in the deposit to make it worth removing. Some mining operations are profitable only if a large amount of the mineral is needed. It also must be fairly easy to separate the mineral from the material in which it is found. If any one of these conditions isn't met, the deposit might not be considered an ore.

Supply and demand is an important part of life. You might have noticed that when the supply of fresh fruit is down, the price you pay for it at the store goes up. Economic factors largely determine what an ore is.

Refining Ore The process of extracting a useful substance from an ore involves two operations—concentrating and refining. After a metallic ore is mined from Earth's crust, it is crushed and the waste rock is removed. The waste rock that must be removed before a mineral can be used is called gangue (GANG).

 Refining produces a pure or nearly pure substance from ore. For example, iron can be concentrated from the ore hematite, which is composed of iron oxide. The concentrated ore then is refined to be as close to pure iron as possible. One method of refining is smelting, illustrated in **Figure 19.** Smelting is a chemical process that removes unwanted elements from the metal that is being processed. During one smelting process, a concentrated ore of iron is heated with a specific chemical. The chemical combines with oxygen in the iron oxide, resulting in pure iron. Note that one resource, fossil fuel, is burned to produce the heat that is needed to obtain the finished product of another resource, in this case iron.

Nonmetallic Mineral Resources

Any mineral resources not used as fuels or as sources of metals are nonmetallic mineral resources. These resources are mined for the nonmetallic elements contained in them and for the specific physical and chemical properties they have. Generally, nonmetallic mineral resources can be divided into two different groups—industrial minerals and building materials. Some materials, such as limestone, belong to both groups of nonmetallic mineral resources, and others are specific to one group or the other.

Industrial Minerals Many useful chemicals are obtained from industrial minerals. Sandstone is a source of silica (SiO_2), which is a compound that is used to make glass. Some industrial minerals are processed to make fertilizers for farms and gardens. For example, sylvite, a mineral that forms when seawater evaporates, is used to make potassium fertilizer.

Many people enjoy a little sprinkle of salt on french fries and pretzels. Table salt is a product derived from halite, a nonmetallic mineral resource. Halite also is used to help melt ice on roads and sidewalks during winter and to help soften water.

Other industrial minerals are useful because of their characteristic physical properties. For example, abrasives are made from deposits of corundum and garnet. Both of these minerals are hard and able to scratch most other materials they come into contact with. Small particles of garnet can be glued onto a sheet of heavy paper to make abrasive sandpaper. **Figure 20** illustrates just a few ways in which nonmetallic mineral resources help make your life more convenient.

Figure 20 You benefit from the use of industrial minerals every day.

Road salt melts ice on streets.

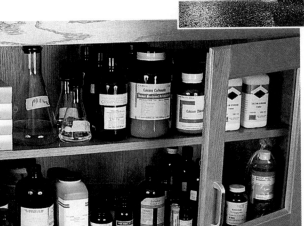

Many important chemicals are made from industrial minerals.

An industrial mineral called trona is important for making glass.

SC.G.2.3.4

Mini LAB

Observing Mineral Mining

Procedure

1. Complete a safety worksheet.
2. Divide into lab groups of four to six students. Pour **0.68 kg of birdseed** into a **shallow pan**. Add **15 colored beads** to each pan.
3. Have students "mine" for the beads using **tweezers** and **probes** for five minutes. Any birdseed on the table is considered a mining violation for going out of permit bounds. Two violations will disqualify the group. The group with the most beads wins.

Analysis

1. Identify what problems might arise when mining for "minerals" or "gems."
2. Infer what might be some responsibilities of the mining company.

Building Materials One of the most important nonmetallic mineral resources is aggregate. Aggregate is composed of crushed stone or a mixture of gravel and sand and has many uses in the building industry. For example, aggregates can be mixed with cement and water to form concrete. Quality concrete is vital to the building industry. Limestone also has industrial uses. It is used as paving stone and as part of concrete mixtures. Have you ever seen the crushed rock in a walking path or driveway? The individual pieces might be crushed limestone. Gypsum, a mineral that forms when seawater evaporates, is soft and lightweight and is used in the production of plaster and wallboard. If you handle a piece of broken plaster or wallboard, note its appearance, which is similar to the mineral gypsum.

Rock also is used as building stone. You might know of buildings in your region that are made from granite, limestone, or sandstone. These rocks and others are quarried and cut into blocks and sheets. The pieces then can be used to construct buildings. Some rock also is used to sculpt statues and other pieces of art.

Annually Assessed Benchmark Check

SC.D.2.3.2 Explain the negative impacts of mineral mining. What positive steps are some people taking to offset these impacts?

Reading Check *What are some important nonmetallic mineral resources?*

Applying Science

Why should you recycle?

Recycling in the United States has become a way of life. In 2000, 88 percent of Americans participated in recycling. Recycling is important because it saves precious raw materials and energy. Recycling aluminum saves 95 percent of the energy required to obtain it from its ore. Recycling steel saves up to 74 percent in energy costs, and recycling glass saves up to 22 percent.

Identifying the Problem

The following table includes materials that currently are being recycled and rates of recycling for the years 1995, 1997, and 2001. Examine the table to determine materials for which recycling increased or decreased between 1995 and 2001.

Recycling Rates in the United States

Material	1995 (%)	1997 (%)	2001 (%)
Glass	24.5	24.3	27.2
Steel	36.5	38.4	43.5 (est.)
Aluminum	34.6	31.2	33.0
Plastics	5.3	5.2	7.0

Solving the Problem

1. Has the recycling of materials increased or decreased over time? Which materials are recycled most? Which materials are recycled least? Discuss why some materials might be recycled more than others.
2. How can recycling benefit society? Explain your answer.

Recycling Mineral Resources

Mineral resources are nonrenewable, and most mineral resources take millions of years to form. Have you ever thrown away an empty soft-drink can? Many people do, and then new materials must be mined. Wouldn't it be better if these cans and other items made from mineral resources were recycled?

Recycling is using old materials to make new ones through manufacturing processes. Recycling has many advantages. It reduces the demand for new mineral resources. When fewer resources need to be mined, fewer habitats are destroyed to get to those resources. The recycling process often uses less energy than it takes to obtain new material. Because supplies of some minerals might become limited in the future, recycling could be required to meet needs for certain materials, as shown in **Figure 21.**

Other ways to conserve mineral resources are reducing and reusing. Reducing means using only what is necessary. Perhaps instead of choosing soft drinks in cans, choose a two-liter bottle. This reduces the amount of aluminum cans being used. An example of reuse is a house made entirely of aluminum cans.

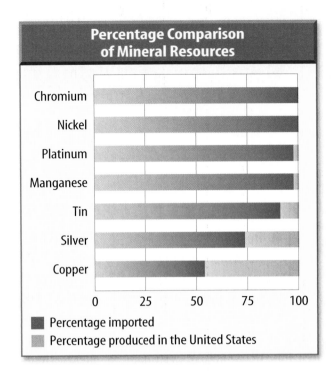

Percentage Comparison of Mineral Resources

- ■ Percentage imported
- ■ Percentage produced in the United States

Figure 21 The United States produces only a small percentage of the metallic resources it consumes.

---

section 3 review

Summary

Metallic Mineral Resources

- Minerals found in rocks that can be mined for an economic profit are called ores.

Nonmetallic Mineral Resources

- Nonmetallic mineral resources can be classified into groups: industrial minerals and building materials.
- Sedimentary rocks such as limestone and sandstone can be used as building materials to make things like buildings and statues.

Recycling Mineral Resources

- Recycling materials helps to preserve Earth's resources by reusing old or used materials without extracting new resources from Earth.
- The recycling process may use fewer resources than it takes to obtain new material.

Self Check

1. **Explain** how metals obtained from metallic mineral resources are used in your home and school. Which of these products could be recycled easily?
2. **List** two industrial uses for nonmetallic mineral resources.
3. **Explain** how supply and demand of a material can cause a mineral to become an ore.
4. **Think Critically** Gangue is waste rock remaining after a mineral ore is removed. Why is gangue sometimes reprocessed?

Applying Skills

5. **Classify** the following mineral resources as metallic or nonmetallic: *hematite, limestone, bauxite, sandstone, garnet,* and *chalcopyrite*. Explain why you classified each one as you did.

Model and Invent

Inquiry

Home Sweet Home

▶ Real-World Problem

As fossil fuel supplies continue to be depleted, an increasing U.S. population has recognized the need for alternative energy sources. United States residents might be forced to consider using renewable energy resources to meet some of their energy needs. The need for energy-efficient housing is more relevant now than ever before. A designer of energy-efficient homes considers proper design and structure, a well

chosen building site with wise material selection, and selection of efficient energy generation systems to power the home. Energy-efficient housing uses less energy and produces fewer pollutants. What does the floor plan, building plan, or a model of an energy efficient home look like? How and where should your house be designed and built to efficiently use the alternative energy resources you've chosen?

Goals

- **Research** various renewable energy resources available to use in the home.
- **Design** blueprints for an energy-efficient home and/or design and build a model of an energy-efficient home.

Possible Materials

paper	glue
ruler	aluminum foil
pencils	plastic wrap
cardboard	

Safety Precautions

Complete a safety worksheet before you begin.

⊙ Make a Model

Plan

1. **Research** current information about energy-efficient homes.
2. **Research** renewable energy resources such as wind, geothermal power, hydroelectric power, or solar power, as well as energy conservation. Decide which energy resources are most efficient for your home design.
3. Decide where your house should be built to use energy efficiently.
4. Decide how your house will be laid out and draw mock blueprints for your home. Highlight energy issues such as where solar panels can be placed.
5. Build a model of your energy-efficient home.

Do

1. Ask your peers for input on your home. As you research, become an expert in one area of alternative energy generation and share your information with your classmates.
2. **Compare** your home's design to energy-efficient homes you learn about through your research.

⊙ Test Your Model

1. Think about how most of the energy in a home is used. Remember as you plan your home that energy-efficient homes not only generate energy—they also use it more efficiently.
2. Carefully consider where your home should be built. For instance, if you plan to use wind power, will your house be built in an area that receives adequate wind?
3. Be sure to plan for backup energy generation. For instance, if you plan to use mostly solar energy, what will you do if it's a cloudy day?

⊙ Analyze Your Data

Devise a budget for building your home. Could your energy-efficient home be built at a reasonable price?

⊙ Conclude and Apply

Create a list of pro and con statements about the use of energy-efficient homes. Why aren't renewable energy sources widely used in homes today?

Communicating Your Data

Present your model to the class. Explain which energy resources you chose to use in your home and why. Have an open house. Take prospective home owners/classmates on a tour of your home and sell it.

BLACK GOLD!

What if you went out to your backyard, started digging a hole, and all of the sudden oil spurted out of the ground? Dollar signs might flash before your eyes.

It wasn't quite that exciting for Charles Tripp. Tripp, a Canadian, is credited with being the first person to strike oil. And he wasn't even looking for what has become known as "black gold."

In 1851, Tripp built a factory in Ontario, Canada, not far from Lake Erie. He used a natural, black, thick, sticky substance that could be found nearby to make asphalt for paving roads and to construct buildings.

In 1855, Tripp dug a well looking for fresh-water for his factory. After digging just 2 m or so, he unexpectedly came upon liquid. It wasn't clear, clean, and delicious; it was smelly, thick, and black. You guessed it—oil! Tripp didn't understand the importance of his find. Two years after his accidental discovery, Tripp sold his company to James Williams.

Some people used TNT to search for oil. This photo was taken in 1943.

In 1858, Williams continued to search for water for the factory, but, as luck would have it, diggers kept finding oil.

Some people argue that the first oil well in North America was in Titusville, Pennsylvania, when Edwin Drake hit oil in 1859. However, most historians agree that Williams was first in 1858. But they also agree that it was Edwin Drake's discovery that led to the growth of the oil industry. So, Drake and Williams can share the credit!

The Titusville, Pennsylvania oil well drilled by Edwin Drake. This photo was taken in 1864.

Today, many oil companies are drilling beneath the sea for oil.

LA.B.2.3.4

Make a Graph Research the leading oil-producing nations and make a bar graph of the top five producers. Research how prices of crude oil affect the U.S. and world economies. Share your findings with your class.

Oops!

For more information, visit fl6.msscience.com

Reviewing Main Ideas

Section 1 **Nonrenewable Energy Resources**

1. Fossil fuels are considered to be non-renewable energy resources.

2. The higher the concentration of carbon in coal is, the cleaner it burns.

3. Oil and natural gas form from altered and buried marine organisms and often are found near one another.

4. Nuclear energy is obtained from the fission of heavy isotopes.

Section 2 **Renewable Energy Resources**

1. Some energy resources—solar energy, wind energy, hydroelectric energy, and geother-mal energy—are constant and will not run out.

2. Renewable energy resources are replaced within a relatively short period of time.

3. Biomass energy is derived from organic material such as wood and corn.

Section 3 **Mineral Resources**

1. Metallic mineral resources provide metals.

2. Ores are mineral resources that can be mined at a profit.

3. Smelting is a chemical process that removes unwanted elements from a metal that is being processed.

4. Nonmetallic mineral resources are classified as industrial minerals or building materials.

Visualizing Main Ideas

LA.B.2.3.1

Copy and complete the following table that lists advantages and disadvantages of energy resources.

Energy Resources		
Resource	Advantages	Disadvantages
Fossil fuels		
Nuclear energy		
Solar energy	Do not write in this book.	
Wind energy		
Geothermal energy		
Biomass fuel		

Using Vocabulary

biomass energy p. 269
coal p. 257
❋ conservation p. 263
❋ fossil fuel p. 256
geothermal energy p. 268
hydroelectric energy p. 268
mineral resource p. 273
natural gas p. 259
❋ nonrenewable
    resource p. 256

nuclear energy p. 263
oil p. 259
ore p. 273
recycling p. 277
❋ renewable resource p. 266
reserve p. 261
❋ resource p. 256
solar energy p. 266
wind farm p. 267

❋ FCAT Vocabulary

Each phrase below describes a vocabulary word from the list. Write the word that matches the phrase describing it.

1. mineral resource mined at a profit

2. fuel that is composed mainly of the remains of dead plants

3. method of conservation in which items are processed to be used again

4. renewable energy resource that is used to power the *Hubble Space Telescope*

5. energy resource that is based on fission

6. liquid from remains of marine organisms

Checking Concepts

Choose the word or phrase that best answers the question.

7. Which has the highest content of carbon?
   A) peat
   B) lignite
   C) bituminous coal
   D) anthracite coal

8. Which is the first step in coal formation?
   A) peat
   B) lignite
   C) bituminous coal
   D) anthracite

9. Which of the following is an example of a fossil fuel?
   A) wind
   B) water
   C) natural gas
   D) uranium-235

10. What is the waste material that must be separated from an ore?
    A) smelter
    B) gangue
    C) mineral resource
    D) petroleum

11. What common rock structure can trap oil and natural gas under it?
    A) folded rock
    B) sandstone rock
    C) porous rock
    D) permeable rock

Use the figure below to answer question 12.

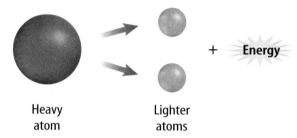

Heavy atom   Lighter atoms   + Energy

12. What other particles are released in the reaction above?
    A) protons
    B) neutrons
    C) uranium atoms
    D) heavy atoms

13. What is a region where many windmills are located in order to generate electricity from wind called?
    A) wind farm
    B) hydroelectric dam
    C) oil well
    D) steam-driven turbine

14. Which of the following is a deposit of hematite that can be mined at a profit?
    A) ore
    B) anthracite
    C) gangue
    D) energy resource

15. What is an important use of petroleum?
    A) making plaster
    B) making glass
    C) as abrasives
    D) making gasoline

16. Which of the following is a nonrenewable energy resource?   SC.G.2.3.1
    A) water
    B) wind
    C) geothermal
    D) petroleum

Vocabulary PuzzleMaker fl6.msscience.com

Thinking Critically

17. Describe the major problems associated with generating electricity using nuclear power plants. `SC.H.3.3.4`

18. Explain why wind is considered to be an renewable energy resource. `SC.G.2.3.1`

19. Determine which type of energy resources are considered to be biomass fuels. List three biomass fuels.

20. Discuss two conditions which could occur to cause gangue to be reclassified as an ore.

21. Predict If a well were drilled into a rock layer containing petroleum, natural gas, and water, which substance would be encountered first? Illustrate your answer with a labeled diagram.

22. Compare and contrast solar energy and wind energy by creating a table.

23. Concept Map Copy and complete the following concept map about mineral resources.

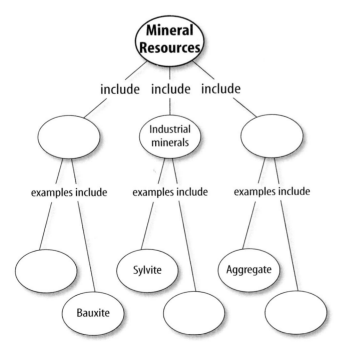

Performance Activities

24. Make Models Make a blueprint of a house that has been built to use passive solar energy. Which side of the house will face the Sun?

25. Letter Write a letter to the Department of Energy asking how usable energy might be obtained from methane hydrates in the future. Also inquire about methods to extract methane hydrates.

Applying Math

Use the table below to answer questions 26–28.

Big Canyon Mine			
Ore Mineral	Metal	Percent Composition	Value (dollars/kg)
Bauxite	Aluminum	5	1.00
Hematite	Iron	2	4.00
Chalcopyrite	Copper	1	6.00
Galena	Lead	7	1.00

26. Ore Composition If 100 kg of rock are extracted from this mine, what percentage of the rock is gangue? `MA.E.1.3.1`

   A. 15%   **C.** 74%

   B. 26%   **D.** 85%

27. Total Composition Graph the total composition of the extracted rock using a circle graph. Label each component clearly. Provide a title for your graph. `MA.E.1.3.1`

28. Economic Geology Of that 100 kg of extracted rock, determine how many kilograms of each ore mineral is extracted. List the total dollar value for each metal after the gangue has been eliminated and the ore mineral extracted. `MA.D.2.3.1`

 The assessed Florida Benchmark appears above each question.
Record your answers on the answer sheet provided by your teacher or on a sheet of paper.

Multiple Choice

SC.A.2.3.3

1 The diagram below shows a process that is used to obtain energy.

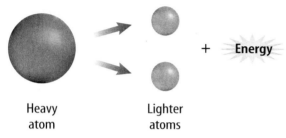

Heavy atom   Lighter atoms   + **Energy**

Which of the following **best** describes how energy is obtained from this process?

A. Nuclear energy is released when an atom splits apart.

B. Nuclear energy is released when atoms join together.

C. Nuclear energy is released when atoms move through wires.

D. Nuclear energy is released when atoms are burned to heat magma.

SC.A.2.3.3

2 Which of the following is a renewable resource for energy?

F. coal

G. nuclear

H. oil

I. solar

SC.G.2.3.1

3 Which of the following is an **advantage** of using wood as an energy source?

A. It is a free energy source.

B. It does not produce waste.

C. It is a renewable source of energy.

D. Its use does not affect ecosystems.

SC.A.2.3.3

4 The illustration shows how electricity is produced in one type of power plant.

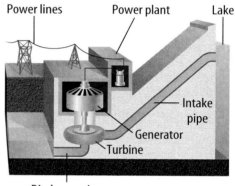

Power lines   Power plant   Lake
Intake pipe
Generator
Turbine
Discharge pipe

In this power plant, when the turbines turn, they cause generators to turn. The turning generators then produce electricity. Which of the following causes the turbines to turn?

F. steam produced by burning fossil fuels

G. hot water from beneath Earth's surface

H. wind blowing through tunnels

I. the energy of moving water

SC.G.2.3.4

5 How does recycling protect resources in the environment?

   A. It converts energy into useful products.

   B. It increases the demand for used materials.

   C. It uses old materials instead of disturbing new resources.

   D. It increases the rate at which nonrenewable resources are formed.

Gridded Response

SC.B.1.3.1

6 The energy stored in many of Earth's resources is transformed into electrical energy. The circle graph below shows how energy resources were used in the United States during 2002.

Energy Use in the United States, 2002

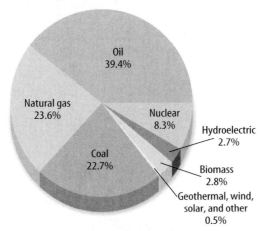

Oil 39.4%

Natural gas 23.6%

Nuclear 8.3%

Hydroelectric 2.7%

Coal 22.7%

Biomass 2.8%

Geothermal, wind, solar, and other 0.5%

According to the graph, what percentage of energy used in the United States in 2002 came from fossil fuels?

Short Response

SC.G.2.3.4

7 Moving wind and water are two types of energy resources that are renewable. Every energy resource has advantages and disadvantages. Describe one advantage and one disadvantage of the use of water and wind as an energy resource.

Extended Response

SC.A.2.3.3

8 The diagram below shows how one type of energy resource is formed.

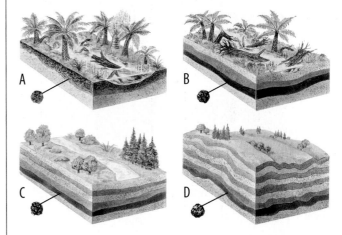

A

B

C

D

   PART A What energy resource formation is shown in the diagram?

   PART B Trace the flow of energy from its source to its use by humans.

FCAT Tip

List and Organize First For extended-response "Read, Inquire, Explain" questions, spend a few minutes listing and organizing the main points that you plan to discuss.

Shaping Earth

How Are
Bats & Tornadoes
Connected?

286

NATIONAL
GEOGRAPHIC

Bats are able to find food and avoid obstacles without using their vision. They do this by producing high-frequency sound waves which bounce off objects and return to the bat. From these echoes, the bat is able to locate obstacles and prey. This process is called echolocation. If the reflected waves have a higher frequency than the emitted waves, the bat senses the object is getting closer. If the reflected waves have a lower frequency, the object is moving away. This change in frequency is called the Doppler effect. Like echolocation, sonar technology uses sound waves and the Doppler effect to determine the position and motion of objects. Doppler radar also uses the Doppler effect, but with radar waves instead of sound waves. Higher frequency waves indicate if an object, such as a storm, is coming closer, while lower frequencies indicate if it is moving away. Meteorologists use frequency shifts indicated by Doppler radar to detect the formation of tornadoes and to predict where they will strike.

unit projects

Visit unit projects at **fl6.msscience.com** for project ideas and resources.
Projects include:
- **Technology** Predict and track the weather of a city in a different part of the world, and compare it to your local weather pattern.
- **Career** Explore weather-related careers while investigating different types of storms. Compare and contrast career characteristics and history.
- **Model** Research animal behavior to discover if animals are able to predict the weather. Present your samples of weather-predicting proverbs as a collection, or use them in a folklore tale.

WebQuest *Hurricanes!* investigates a variety of tropical storms, their source of energy, classifications, and destructive forces.

chapter

10

Sunshine State Standards—SC.B.1: The student recognizes that energy may be changed in form with varying efficiency; SC.D.1: recognizes that processes in the lithosphere, atmosphere, hydrosphere, and biosphere interact to shape the Earth.

The Atmosphere in Motion

chapter preview

sections

Record Tying Hurricanes

Ivan (above) and Jeanne (at right) were the last two of the four hurricanes that struck the Florida coast in 2004. This tied Florida with Texas for the most hurricanes to strike the same state in one season. Some scientists have predicted that this is the start of a 40-year hurricane cycle.

Science Journal Write a short newspaper article to warn people about the dangers of an approaching hurricane.

Start-Up Activities

SC.D.1.3.3
SC.H.1.3.5

How does temperature affect gas molecules?

The temperature of air affects the movement of gas molecules. In the lab below, you will increase and then decrease the temperature of air and observe the changes that occur as a result of the movement of air molecules.

1. Complete a safety worksheet.

2. With your finger, rub a mixture of water and dish-washing liquid across the top of a narrow-necked plastic bottle until a thin film forms over the opening.

3. Hold the bottle in a beaker that is half-filled with hot water and observe what happens to the soap film.

4. Without breaking the film, remove the bottle from the hot water and place it in a beaker that is half-filled with ice water. Observe what happens to the film.

5. **Think Critically** In your Science Journal, describe what you observed. Infer what happened to change the shape of the film on top of the bottle.

FOLDABLES™
Study Organizer

Earth's Atmosphere Make the following Foldable to identify what you already know, what you want to know, and what you learned about the atmosphere.

LA.A.1.3.4

STEP 1 **Fold** a vertical sheet of paper from side to side. Make the front edge about 1.25 cm shorter than the back edge.

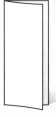

STEP 2 **Turn** lengthwise and **fold** into thirds.

STEP 3 **Unfold and cut** only the top layer along both folds to make three tabs. **Label** each tab as shown.

Know? | Want to know? | Learned?

Read and Write Before you read the chapter, write what you already know and what you want to know about the atmosphere under the tabs. As you read the chapter, write what you learned.

Preview this chapter's content and activities at
fl6.msscience.com

Benchmarks—**SC.D.1.3.3 (p. 291):** The student knows how conditions that exist in one system influence the conditions that exist in other systems; **SC.D.1.3.5 (pp. 291–295):** The student understands concepts of time and size relating to the interaction of Earth's processes.

Also covers: **SC.A.1.3.5 (p. 289), SC.A.1.3.6 Annually Assessed (p. 290), SC.B.1.3.3 Annually Assessed (pp. 292–293), SC.H.1.3.5 Annually Assessed (pp. 289, 295), SC.H.2.3.1 (p. 294), SC.H.3.3.5 (p. 290)**

The Atmosphere

as you read

What **You'll Learn**

- **Explain** why air has pressure.
- **Describe** the composition of the atmosphere.
- **Describe** how energy causes water on Earth to cycle.

Why **It's Important**

Movements within the atmosphere create weather changes.

Review Vocabulary

✷ **evaporation:** the process by which a liquid is converted to a gas

New Vocabulary

✷ **atmosphere**
● **aerosol**
● **troposphere**
✷ **water cycle**

✷ FCAT Vocabulary

Figure 1 The flask with air injected weighs more than the flask with no air injected.

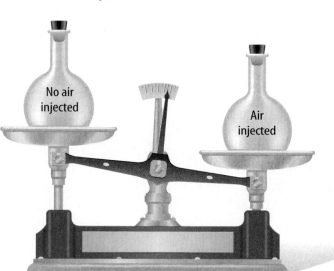

Investigating Air

Air, air . . . everywhere. It's always there. You might take it for granted, but without it, Earth would be unfit for life. The **atmosphere**—the layer of gases surrounding Earth—provides Earth with all the gases necessary to support life. It protects living things against harmful doses of ultraviolet and X-ray radiation. At the same time, it absorbs and distributes warmth.

Galileo Galilei (1564–1642), an Italian astronomer and physicist, suspected that air was more than just empty space. He weighed a flask, then injected air into it and weighed it again. As shown in **Figure 1,** Galileo observed that the flask weighed more after injecting the air. He concluded that air must have weight and therefore must contain matter. Today scientists know that the atmosphere has other properties, as well. Air stores and releases heat and holds moisture. Because it has weight, air can exert pressure. All of these properties, when combined with energy from the Sun, create Earth's daily weather.

Composition of the Atmosphere

What else do scientists know about the atmosphere? Because it is composed of matter and has mass, it is subject to the pull of gravity. This is what keeps the atmosphere around Earth and prevents it from moving into space. Because it exerts pressure in all directions, you barely notice the atmosphere. Yet its weight is equal to a layer of water more than 10 m deep covering Earth. Scientists also know that the atmosphere is composed of a mixture of gases, liquid water, and microscopic particles of solids and other liquids.

 **Reading Check** *What is Earth's atmosphere composed of?*

Gases Although the atmosphere contains many gases, two of them make up approximately 99 percent of the total. **Figure 2** shows a graph of the gases found in the atmosphere. Nitrogen (N_2) is the most abundant gas—it makes up about 78 percent of the atmosphere. Oxygen (O_2), the gas necessary for human life, makes up about 21 percent. A variety of trace gases makes up the rest.

Of the trace gases, two have important roles within the atmosphere. Water vapor (H_2O) makes up from 0.0 to 4.0 percent of the atmosphere and is critical to weather. Water in the atmosphere is responsible for clouds and precipitation. Much of the life on Earth depends on water from precipitation. The other important trace gas, carbon dioxide (CO_2), is present in small amounts. Carbon dioxide is needed for plants to make food. Also, carbon dioxide in the atmosphere absorbs heat and emits it back toward Earth's surface, helping keep Earth warm.

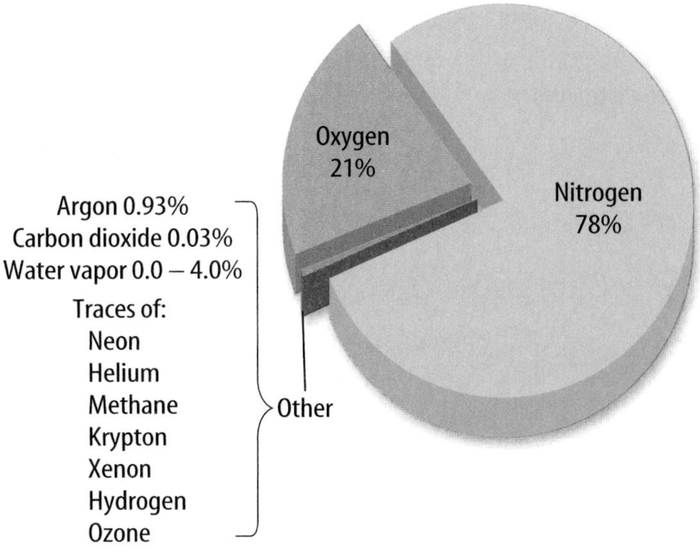

Aerosols Solids such as dust, salt, and pollen and tiny liquid droplets such as acids in the atmosphere are called **aerosols** (AR uh sahlz). Dust enters the atmosphere when wind picks tiny soil particles off the ground or when ash is emitted from volcanoes. Salt enters the atmosphere when wind blows across the oceans. Pollen enters the atmosphere when it is released by plants. Such human activities as burning coal in power plants also release aerosols into the air. Some aerosols, such as those given off by the volcano in **Figure 3,** reflect incoming solar energy, which can affect weather and climate.

Argon 0.93%
Carbon dioxide 0.03%
Water vapor 0.0 – 4.0%

Traces of:
Neon
Helium
Methane
Krypton
Xenon
Hydrogen
Ozone

Oxygen 21%

Nitrogen 78%

Other

Figure 2 The percentages of gases in the atmosphere vary slightly. For example, water vapor makes up from 0.0 to 4.0 percent of the atmosphere.
Predict *what happens to the percentages of other gases when the percentage of water vapor is higher.*

Figure 3 Volcanoes add many aerosols to the atmosphere. Some volcanic aerosols can remain suspended in the atmosphere for months or even years.
Infer *what happens if many aerosols are in the atmosphere.*

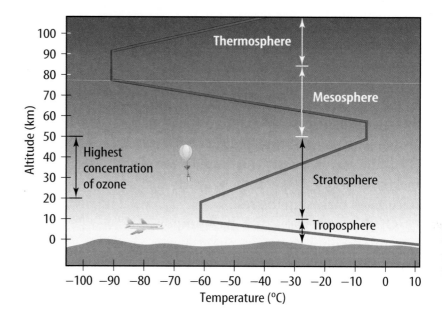

Figure 4 Temperature variations separate Earth's atmosphere into distinct layers.

The Ozone Layer Ozone in the stratosphere shields Earth's surface from the Sun's ultraviolet (UV) radiation. However, scientists have discovered that the ozone layer has been damaged, allowing more UV radiation to reach Earth. This radiation can cause skin cancers and cataracts, which damage vision. What should you do to protect your skin and eyes when you are outdoors?

Layers of the Atmosphere

The atmosphere is divided into the layers that you see in **Figure 4.** These layers are based on temperature changes that occur with altitude. Each atmospheric layer has unique properties. Find each layer as you read about it. The lower layers are the troposphere and stratosphere. The upper layers are the mesosphere and the thermosphere. The exosphere is located beyond the thermosphere.

Troposphere The **troposphere** (TROH puh sfihr) is the atmospheric layer closest to Earth's surface. Notice that it extends upward to about 10 km. The troposphere contains about three fourths of the matter in Earth's entire atmosphere and nearly all of its clouds and weather. Part of the Sun's energy is reflected into space and some is absorbed in the layers of the atmosphere. However, nearly 50 percent of the energy passes through the troposphere and reaches Earth's surface. This energy heats Earth. The atmosphere near Earth's surface is heated by the process of conduction. This means that the source of most of the troposphere's heat is Earth's surface. Therefore, temperatures in the troposphere are usually warmest near the surface and tend to cool as altitude increases. Temperatures cool at a rate of about 6.5 Celsius degrees per kilometer of altitude. If you ever climb a mountain, you will notice that it gets colder as you go higher.

 *What is the troposphere?*

Stratosphere Above the troposphere is the stratosphere (STRAH tuh sfihr). The stratosphere extends from about 10 km to about 50 km above Earth's surface. As shown in **Figure 4,** most atmospheric ozone is contained in the stratosphere. This ozone absorbs much of the Sun's ultraviolet radiation. As a result, the stratosphere warms as you go upward through it, which is just the opposite of the troposphere. Without the ozone in this layer, too much radiation would reach Earth's surface, causing health problems for plants and animals.

Upper Layers Above the stratosphere is the mesosphere (ME zuh sfihr). This layer extends from approximately 50 km to 85 km above Earth's surface. This layer contains little ozone, so much less heat is absorbed. Notice in **Figure 4** how the temperature in this layer drops to the lowest temperatures in the atmosphere.

The thermosphere (THUR muh sfihr) is above the mesosphere. The thermosphere extends from about 85 km to approximately 500 km above Earth's surface. Temperatures increase rapidly in this layer to more than 1,700°C. The thermosphere layer filters out harmful X rays and gamma rays from the Sun.

Because of intense interaction with the Sun's radiation, atoms can become electrically charged particles called ions. For this reason a part of the thermosphere and mesosphere is called the ionosphere (i AH nuh sfihr). This layer of ions is useful because it can reflect AM radio waves, as shown in **Figure 5,** making long-distance communication possible. If the interaction between the Sun's radiation and this layer is too active, however, the quality of radio reception is reduced. Radio signals break up and a lot of static can be heard.

The outermost layer of the atmosphere is the exosphere. It extends outward to where space begins and contains few atoms. No clear boundary separates the exosphere from space.

Earth's Water

Earth often is referred to as the water planet. This is because Earth's surface is about 70 percent water. Because water can exist in three separate states it can be stored throughout the entire land-ocean-atmosphere system. As **Table 1** shows, water exists as solid snow or ice in glaciers. In oceans, lakes, and rivers water exists as a liquid and in the atmosphere it exists as gaseous water vapor.

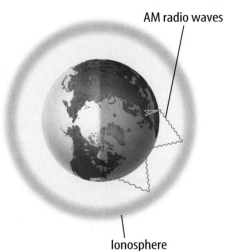

Figure 5 Radio waves are reflected by the ionosphere.

Table 1 Distribution of Earth's Water	
Location	**Amount of Water (%)**
Oceans	97.2
Ice caps and glaciers	2.05
Groundwater	0.62
Rivers and lakes	0.009
Atmosphere	0.001
Total (rounded)	100.00

Figure 6

As the diagram below shows, energy for the water cycle is provided by the Sun. Water continuously cycles between oceans, land, and the atmosphere through the processes of evaporation, transpiration, condensation, and precipitation.

▲ Droplets inside clouds join to form bigger drops. When they become heavy enough, they fall as rain, snow, or some other form of precipitation.

▲ As it rises into the air, water vapor cools and condenses into water again. Millions of tiny water droplets form a cloud.

▶ Rain runs off the land into streams and rivers. Water flows into lakes and oceans. Some water is taken up by plants.

▲ Water evaporates from oceans, lakes, and rivers. Plants release water vapor through transpiration.

The Water Cycle Earth's water is in constant motion in a never-ending pattern called the **water cycle,** shown in **Figure 6.** The Sun's radiant energy powers the cycle. Water on Earth's surface—in oceans, lakes, rivers, and streams—absorbs energy and stores it as heat. When water has enough heat energy, it changes from liquid water into water vapor in a process called evaporation. Water vapor then enters the atmosphere.

Evaporation occurs from all bodies of water, no matter how large or small. Have you ever noticed that a puddle of water left on the sidewalk from a rainstorm disappears after a while? The water evaporates into the atmosphere. Water also is transferred into the atmosphere from plant leaves in a process called transpiration. As water vapor moves up through the atmosphere, it becomes cooler. The molecules begin to slow down. Eventually, the water molecules change back into droplets of liquid water. This process is called condensation.

✔ Reading Check *How do evaporation and condensation differ?*

Water droplets grow in size when two or more droplets run into each other and combine to form a larger droplet. Eventually, these droplets become large enough to be visible, forming a cloud. If the water droplets continue to grow, they become too large to remain suspended in the atmosphere and fall to Earth as precipitation. You will learn about the different forms of precipitation in the next section. After it is on the ground, some water evaporates. Most water enters streams or soaks into the soil to become groundwater. Much of this water eventually makes its way back to lakes or to the oceans, where more evaporation occurs and the water cycle continues.

SC.H.1.3.5

Mini LAB

Observing Evaporation and Condensation

Procedure 🔧 👓 ✋
1. Mark one of **two clear-plastic cups** with a thin line at the half-full point.
2. Carefully fill the cup to the line with **hot water.**
3. Immediately place the second cup upside down on the first.
4. Seal the cups together with **tape.**
5. Place a small **ice cube** on top and wait.
6. After 30 min, observe the water level in the bottom cup and also what happened inside the top cup.
7. Record the changes in your **Science Journal.**

Analysis
1. What happened to the water level you marked?
2. Explain how moisture appeared in the top cup.

Try at Home

---

section 1 review

Summary

Investigating Air
● Air exerts pressure in all directions.

Composition of the Atmosphere
● The atmosphere consists of nitrogen, oxygen, and trace gases, such as water vapor and carbon dioxide.

Layers of the Atmosphere
● The atmosphere is divided into layers based on temperature changes.

Earth's Water
● A model that shows how water cycles is called the water cycle.

Self Check

1. **Explain** why air has pressure. SC.B.2.3.1
2. **Identify** three solid particles that occur in the atmosphere.
3. **List** the five layers of Earth's atmosphere starting at Earth's surface.
4. **Describe** four important processes that are part of the water cycle. SC.D.1.3.3
5. **Think Critically** Why is it possible for a high mountain at the equator to be covered by snow?

Applying Skills SC.D.1.3.3

6. **Recognize Cause and Effect** A closed, metal can collapses when the air is pumped out of it. Explain why.

Benchmarks—**SC.B.1.3.5 (pp. 296–299, 302–303):** The student knows the processes by which thermal energy tends to flow from a system of higher temperature to a system of lower temperature; **SC.D.1.3.3 (pp. 296–303):** knows how conditions that exist in one system influence the conditions that exist in other systems.

Also covers: **SC.A.1.3.3 (p. 296), SC.B.2.3.1 Annually Assessed (p. 297), SC.D.1.3.5 (pp. 296–303), SC.H.2.3.1 (pp. 296–303)**

section 2

Earth's Weather

as you read

What You'll Learn

- **Compare** ways that heat is transferred on Earth.
- **Describe** the formation of different kinds of clouds and precipitation.
- **Explain** what causes wind.

Why It's Important

Weather affects your life every day.

Review Vocabulary

☀ **condensation:** the process of changing from a gas to a liquid

New Vocabulary

- weather
- humidity
- dew point
- relative humidity
- precipitation

☀ FCAT Vocabulary

Weather

Your favorite television show is interrupted by a special weather bulletin. Severe weather is headed your way. Will there be strong winds? Flooding? If there are downed trees and power lines, will you be able to get to school? How might this weather affect your family? **Weather** describes the current condition of the atmosphere. Factors of weather include temperature, cloud cover, wind speed, wind direction, humidity, and air pressure. It is the task of meteorologists (mee tee uh RAH luh jists) to monitor all weather data continuously in an attempt to forecast weather.

Temperature   You learned earlier that the Sun's radiant energy powers the water cycle. In fact, the Sun is the source of almost all of the energy on Earth. When the Sun's rays reach Earth, energy is absorbed. Gas molecules are constantly in motion, but when they absorb more energy, they move faster and farther apart, as shown in **Figure 7.** Temperature is a measure of how fast air molecules are moving. When air molecules are moving rapidly, temperature is high. Temperature is measured with a thermometer that has a particular scale. The Celsius and Fahrenheit scales commonly are used to measure air temperature.

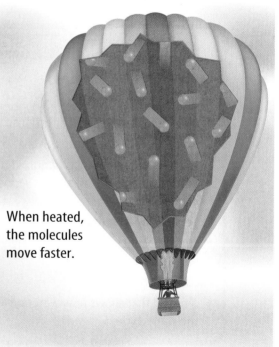
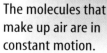

Figure 7 Temperature is a measure of the average movement of molecules. The faster they're moving, the higher the temperature is.

The molecules that make up air are in constant motion.

When heated, the molecules move faster.

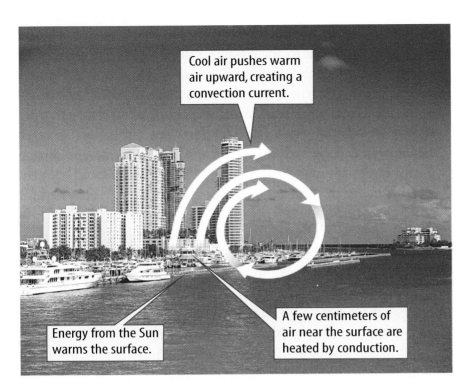

Cool air pushes warm air upward, creating a convection current.

Energy from the Sun warms the surface.

A few centimeters of air near the surface are heated by conduction.

Figure 8 Energy from the Sun warms Earth's surface. Conduction and convection transfer heat on Earth.

Energy Transfer Fast-moving molecules transfer energy to slower-moving molecules when they bump into each other. The transfer of energy that results when molecules collide is called conduction. It is conduction that transfers heat from Earth's surface to those molecules in the air that are in contact with it. After it is in the atmosphere, heated air will move upward as long as it is warmer than the surrounding air. The rising air cools as it gets higher. If it becomes cooler than the surrounding air, it will sink. The process of warm air rising and cool air sinking is called convection. It is the main way heat is transferred throughout the atmosphere. Both processes are shown in **Figure 8.**

Atmospheric Pressure As you have learned, air has particles, and the pull of gravity on them gives air weight. Therefore, the weight of air exerts pressure. Air pressure decreases with altitude in the atmosphere. This is because as you go higher, the weight of the atmosphere above you is less.

Temperature and pressure are related. When air is heated, its molecules move faster, and the air expands. This makes the air less dense, which is why heated air gets moved upward. Less dense air also exerts less pressure on anything below it, creating lower pressure. Cooled air becomes more dense and sinks as the molecules slow down and move closer together, creating more pressure. Therefore, rising air generally means lower pressure and sinking air means higher pressure. Air pressure varies over Earth's surface.

Natural Thermometers
Crickets chirp more often and rattlesnakes rattle faster when they're warm. How could these animals be used as natural thermometers?

Humidity As air warms up, it can cause water that is in contact with it to evaporate to form water vapor. The amount of water vapor in the atmosphere is called **humidity.** The graph in **Figure 9** shows how temperature affects how much moisture can be present in the air. When air is warmer, evaporation occurs more quickly, and more water vapor can be added to the air. More water vapor can be present in warm air than in cool air. When air is holding as much water vapor as it can, it is said to be saturated and condensation can occur. The temperature at which this takes place is called the **dew point.**

Relative Humidity Suppose a mass of air is chilled. The air particles lose energy and move closer together. Unless condensation occurs, the water vapor in the air remains the same, but less moisture can be absorbed. **Relative humidity** is a measure (in percent) of the amount of water vapor that is present compared to the amount that could be held at a specific temperature. As air cools, relative humidity increases if the amount of water vapor stays the same. When air is saturated it has 100 percent relative humidity. As shown in **Figure 9,** air at 40°C can hold 50 g/m^3 when saturated. If it only has 25 g/m^3, the relative humidity is 50 percent.

✔ **Reading Check** *What is relative humidity?*

Sometimes local TV weather reports give the dew point on summer days. If the dew point is close to the air temperature, the relative humidity is high. If the dew point is much lower than the air temperature, relative humidity is low.

Figure 9 This graph shows how temperature affects the amount of water vapor that air can hold. **Determine** *how much water vapor the air can hold if its temperature is 30°C. How much can it hold if the temperature drops to 10°C?*

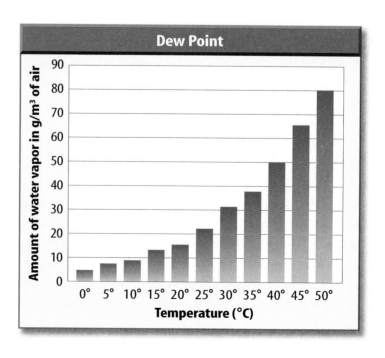

Clouds

One of the best indications that Earth has an atmosphere in motion is the presence of clouds. Clouds form when air rises, cools to its dew point, and becomes saturated. Water vapor in the air then condenses onto small particles in the atmosphere. If the temperature is not too cold, the clouds will be made of small drops of water. If the temperature is cold enough, clouds can consist of small ice crystals.

Clouds commonly are classified according to the altitude at which they begin to form. The most common classification method is one that separates clouds into low, middle, or high groups. Some cloud types are shown in **Figure 10.**

Low Clouds The low-cloud group consists of clouds that form at about 2,000 m or less in altitude. These clouds include the cumulus (KYEW myuh lus) type, which are puffy clouds that form when air currents rise, carrying moisture with them. Sometimes cumulus clouds are fair weather clouds. However, when they have high vertical development, they can produce thunder, lightning, and heavy rain. Another type of low cloud includes layered stratus (STRA tus) clouds. Stratus clouds form dull, gray sheets that can cover the entire sky. Nimbostratus (nihm boh STRA tus) clouds form low, dark, thick layers that blot out the Sun. If you see either of these types of clouds, you can expect some kind of precipitation. Fog is a type of stratus cloud that is in contact with the ground.

Middle Clouds Clouds that form between about 2,000 m and 8,000 m are known as the middle-cloud group. Most of these clouds are of the layered variety. Their names often have the prefix *alto-* in front of them, such as altocumulus and altostratus. Sometimes they contain enough moisture to produce light precipitation. Middle clouds can be made up of a mixture of liquid water and ice crystals.

Figure 10 Clouds are grouped according to how high they are above the ground. The types of clouds can be used to predict weather.

High and Vertical Clouds Some clouds occur in air that is so cold they are made up entirely of ice crystals. Because this usually happens high in the atmosphere, these are known as the high-cloud group. They include cirrus (SIHR us) clouds, which are wispy, high-level clouds. Another type is cirrostratus clouds, which are high, layered clouds that sometimes cover the entire sky.

Some clouds can extend vertically throughout all the levels of the atmosphere. These are clouds of vertical development, and the most common type is cumulonimbus (kyew myuh loh NIHM bus). When you see the term *nimbus* attached to a cloud name, it usually means the cloud is creating precipitation. Cumulonimbus clouds create the heaviest precipitation of all. Known as thunderstorm clouds, they start to form at heights of less than 1,000 m but can build to more than 16,000 m high.

Precipitation

When drops of water or crystals of ice become too large to be suspended in a cloud, they fall as **precipitation.** Precipitation can be in the form of rain, freezing rain, sleet, snow, or hail. The type of precipitation that falls depends on the temperature of the atmosphere. For example, rain falls when the temperature of the atmosphere is above freezing. However, if air aloft is above freezing while air near Earth's surface is below freezing, freezing rain might occur. Hail consists of balls of ice that form within cumulonimbus clouds. Within the storm cloud, strong winds toss ice crystals up and down, as shown in **Figure 11.** As the ice crystals move, droplets of water freeze around them. Hailstones keep growing until they are too heavy for the winds to keep up. Then they fall to the ground.

Figure 11 Hailstones develop in cumulonimbus clouds. Most hailstones are the size of peas, but some can reach the size of softballs. **Explain** *what this tells you about the strength of the winds in the cloud.*

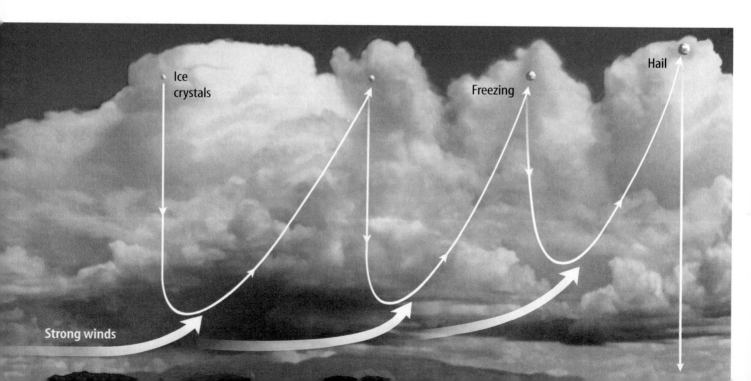

Ice crystals

Freezing

Hail

Strong winds

Wind

As you learned earlier, air pressure is related to temperature. When molecules in the atmosphere are heated, they move more rapidly and spread apart. The air becomes less dense and is moved upward. This causes regions of low air pressure. When cooled, those molecules move more slowly and move closer together. The air becomes more dense and sinks, forming regions of high pressure. Typically, air moves from high-pressure areas toward low-pressure areas. Because pressure and temperature are directly related, wind can be thought of simply as air moving from one temperature or pressure area to another. The greater the difference in temperature or pressure between two areas, the stronger the winds that blow between them will be. Wind speed is measured by an instrument called an anemometer (an uh MAH muh tur), which indicates wind speed by how fast an array of cups that catch the wind rotate. The fastest wind speed ever measured was 371 km/h measured on Mount Washington, New Hampshire, in 1934.

Indian Monsoon A monsoon is a shift in wind direction that occurs during particular seasons. India is a country that is strongly affected by monsoons. During June and July, low pressure forms over the Indian continent. This causes moist winds to blow from the ocean. These winds produce the heavy rains needed for Indian agriculture. During winter, high pressure forms over India, and dry winds blow from the land to the sea.

Applying Math Solve a One-Step Equation

WIND SPEED Air moves from an area of high air pressure to an area of low air pressure. The wind that is created travels a distance of 14 km in 2 h. What is the wind speed?

Solution

1 *This is what you know:*

- distance: $d = 14$ km
- time: $t = 2$ h

2 *This is what you need to find:*

speed (rate): r

3 *This is the procedure you need to use:*

- substitute into the equation, $r = d/t$
- $r = 14$ km/2 h $= 7$ km/h

4 *Check your answer:*

Multiply your answer by the time. Do you calculate the same distance that was given?

Practice Problems

1. Air moves from a cool area to a warmer area. The wind that is created moves 20 km in 2 h. What is the wind speed? **MA.D.2.3.1**

2. Air moves from an area of high air pressure to an area of low air pressure. The wind that is created travels a distance of 69 km in 3 h. What is the wind speed? **MA.D.2.3.1**

Math Practice | For more practice, visit fl6.msscience.com

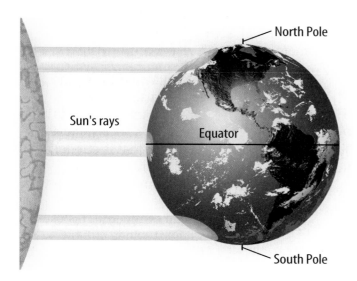

Figure 12 The angle of the Sun's rays is higher near the equator than near the poles.

Global Air Circulation Look at **Figure 12.**

In any given year, the Sun's rays strike Earth at a higher angle near the equator than near the poles. As a result, Earth's tropical areas heat up more than the polar regions do. Because of this imbalance of heat, warm air flows toward the poles from the tropics and cold air flows toward the equator from the poles. Because Earth rotates, this moving air is deflected to the right in the northern hemisphere and to the left south of the equator. This is known as the Coriolis (kor ee OH lus) effect.

 **Reading Check** *What is the Coriolis effect?*

Surface Winds **Figure 13** shows Earth's major surface winds. Air at the equator is heated by the rays of the Sun. This air expands, becomes less dense, and gets pushed upward. Farther from the equator, at about 30° latitude, the air is somewhat cooler. This air sinks and flows toward the equator. As this air flows, it is turned by the Coriolis effect, creating steady winds called the trade winds. Trade winds also are called tropical easterlies because they blow in a general east-to-west direction. Find the trade winds in **Figure 13.**

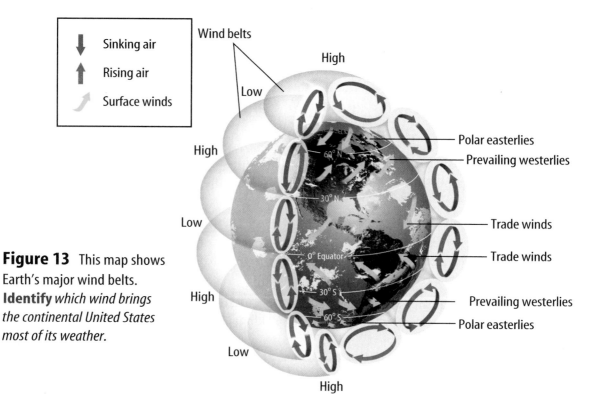

Figure 13 This map shows Earth's major wind belts. **Identify** *which wind brings the continental United States most of its weather.*

Westerlies and Easterlies Major wind cells also are located between 30° and 60° latitude north and south of the equator. They blow from the west and are called the prevailing westerlies. These winds form the boundary between cold air from the poles and milder air closer to the equator. Many of Earth's major weather systems form along these boundaries, so these regions are known for frequent storms.

Near the poles, cold, dense air sinks and flows away from the poles. It is replaced by warmer air flowing in from above. As the cold air flows away from the poles, it is turned by the Coriolis effect. These winds, the polar easterlies, blow from the east.

Jet Streams Within the zone of prevailing westerlies are bands of strong winds that develop at higher altitudes. Called jet streams, they are like giant rivers of air, as shown in **Figure 14.** They blow near the top of the troposphere from west to east at the northern and southern boundaries of the prevailing westerlies. Their positions in latitude and altitude change from day to day and from season to season. Jet streams are important because weather systems move along their paths.

Other Winds Besides the major winds, other winds constantly are forming. Slight differences in pressure create gentle breezes. Great differences create strong winds. The strongest winds occur when air rushes into the center of low pressure. This can cause severe weather like tornadoes and hurricanes.

Figure 14 Weather forecasters often show the position of a jet stream to help explain the movements of weather systems.

---

section 2 review

Summary

Weather
- Weather describes the current condition of the atmosphere.

Clouds
- Clouds are classified according to the altitude at which they form.

Precipitation
- Types of precipitation include rain, freezing rain, sleet, snow, and hail.

Wind
- Air moves as wind because of pressure differences on Earth.

Self Check

1. **Explain** the processes that heat the troposphere. **SC.D.1.3.3**
2. **Describe** what happens when water vapor rises and cools to the dew point.
3. **Explain** how air pressure is related to temperature.
4. **Define** a jet stream. **SC.D.1.3.3**
5. **Think Critically** Why doesn't precipitation fall from every cloud?

Applying Math

6. **Solve** The air temperature is 40°C and the relative humidity is 20 percent. How many g/m³ of moisture does the air hold? **MA.D.2.3.1**

---

section 3

Air Masses and Fronts

Air Masses

Weather can change quickly. It can be sunny with calm winds in the morning and turn stormy by noon. Weather changes quickly when a different air mass enters an area. An **air mass** is a large body of air that develops over a particular region of Earth's surface.

Types of Air Masses A mass of air that remains over a region for a few days acquires the characteristics of the area over which it occurs. For example, an air mass over tropical oceans becomes warm and moist. **Figure 15** shows the location of the major air masses that affect weather in North America.

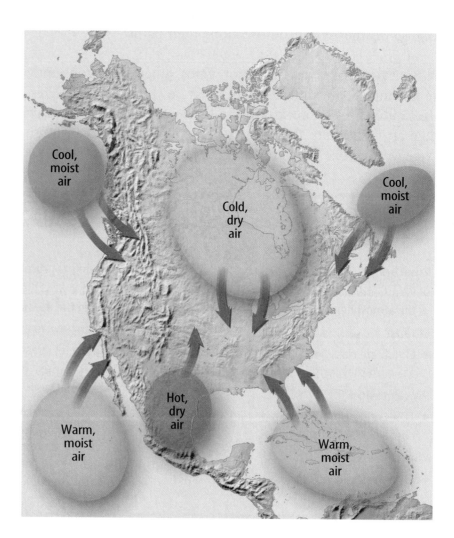

Figure 15 Six major air masses affect North America.
Infer *the characteristics of an air mass that originates over the North Pacific Ocean.*

Fronts

Where air masses of different temperatures meet, a boundary between them, called a **front,** is created. Along a front, the air doesn't mix. Because cold air is more dense, it sinks beneath warm air. The warm air is forced upward and winds develop. Fronts usually bring a change in temperature as they pass, and they always bring a change in wind direction. The four kinds of fronts are shown in **Figures 16, 17,** and **18.**

Reading Check *What is a front?*

Cold Fronts When a cold, dense air mass advances and pushes under a warm air mass, the warm air is forced to rise. The boundary is known as a cold front, shown in **Figure 16.** As water condenses, clouds and precipitation develop. If the air is pushed upward quickly enough, a narrow band of violent storms can result. Cumulus and cumulonimbus clouds can develop. As the name implies, a drop in temperature occurs with a cold front.

Warm Fronts If warm air is advancing into a region of colder air, a warm front is formed. Notice in **Figure 16** that warm, less dense air slides up and over the colder, denser air mass. As the warm air mass moves upward, it cools. Water vapor condenses and precipitation occurs over a wide area. As a warm front approaches, high cirrus clouds are seen where condensation begins. The clouds become progressively lower as you get nearer the front.

LA.B.2.3.4

Science Online

Topic: Air Masses and Fronts
Visit fl6.msscience.com for Web links to information about air masses and fronts.

Activity Examine a current weather map. Use the Weather Map Symbols in the Reference Handbook in the back of this book to identify any approaching fronts. Track the changes in temperature, pressure, precipitation, wind direction, and cloud cover as the front passes.

Figure 16 Cold and warm fronts always bring changes in the weather.
Describe *how precipitation differs between cold and warm fronts.*

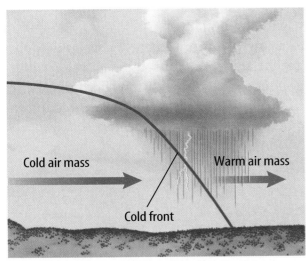

A cold front often produces short periods of storms with heavy precipitation. After the front passes, wind changes direction, skies begin to clear, and the temperature usually drops.

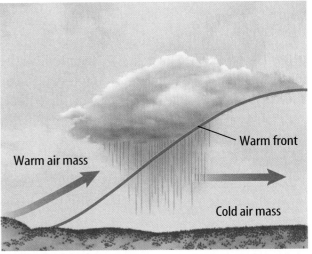

A warm front usually produces a long period of steady precipitation over a wide area. After the front passes, the sky clears, wind direction changes, and the temperature rises.

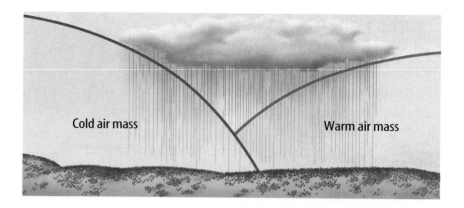

Figure 17 A stationary front can result in days of steady precipitation over the same area.

Cold air mass

Warm air mass

Stationary Fronts A stationary front, shown in **Figure 17,** is a front where a warm air mass and a cold air mass meet but neither advances. This kind of front can remain in the same location for several days. Cloudiness and precipitation occur along the front. Some precipitation can be heavy because the front moves so little.

Occluded Fronts **Figure 18** illustrates how an occluded front forms when a fast-moving cold front overtakes a slower warm front. Occluded fronts also form in other ways, but all types of occluded fronts can produce cloudy weather with precipitation.

High- and Low-Pressure Centers

In areas where pressure is high, air sinks. As it reaches the ground, it spreads outward away from the high-pressure center. As it spreads, the Coriolis effect turns the air in a clockwise direction in the northern hemisphere. Because the air is sinking, moisture cannot rise and condense, so air near a high-pressure center is usually dry with few clouds.

As air flows into a low-pressure center, it rises and cools. Eventually, the air reaches its dew point and the water vapor condenses, forming clouds and precipitation. Because of the Coriolis effect, air circulates in a counterclockwise direction in the northern hemisphere in a low-pressure center.

Figure 18 An occluded front produces weather similar to, but less severe than, the weather along a cold front.

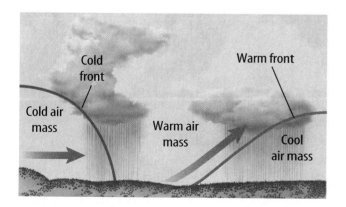

Cold front

Cold air mass

Warm air mass

Warm front

Cool air mass

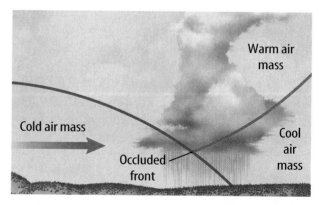

Cold air mass

Warm air mass

Occluded front

Cool air mass

Severe Weather

Severe weather causes strong winds and heavy precipitation. People can be injured and property can be damaged. How can you prepare for severe weather? To prepare, you must first understand it.

Thunderstorms Thunderstorms develop from cumulonimbus clouds. Recall that cumulonimbus clouds often form along cold fronts where air is forced rapidly upward, causing water droplets to form. Falling droplets collide with other droplets and grow bigger. As these large droplets fall, they cool the surrounding air, creating downdrafts that spread out at the surface. These are the strong winds associated with thunderstorms. Dangerous hail can develop in these storms.

Lightning and thunder also are created in cumulonimbus clouds. Where air uplifts rapidly, electric charges form, as shown in **Figure 19.** Lightning is the almost instantaneous energy flow that occurs between areas of opposite electrical charge. A bolt of lightning can be five times hotter than the Sun's surface. Its extreme temperature heats the air nearby. The heated air expands faster than the speed of sound, which produces a sonic boom. This is the thunder that is heard after a lightning flash. Close to the lightning, the thunder sounds like a sharp bang. Farther away, the thunder is a dull rumble.

Reading Check *What causes thunder?*

Figure 19 During a thunderstorm, the bottom of the storm cloud has a negative charge. The ground has a positive charge. The negative charge rushes toward the ground. At the same time, the positive charge rushes toward the cloud.

Mini LAB

SC.D.1.3.3

Creating a Low-Pressure Center

Procedure
1. Complete a safety worksheet.
2. Fasten a **birthday candle** firmly to the bottom of a **pie pan or plate** with **clay.**
3. Fill a **tall, narrow jar** halfway with **water,** and pour the water into the pan or plate.
4. Light the candle. Invert the jar over the candle. Set the jar mouth down into the water and rest its edge on a **penny.**
5. In your **Science Journal,** write a brief description of what happens to the water level inside the jar when the candle goes out.

Analysis
1. Infer what happens to the air inside the jar when the candle is lit.
2. Infer what happens to the air and water in the jar when the candle goes out.

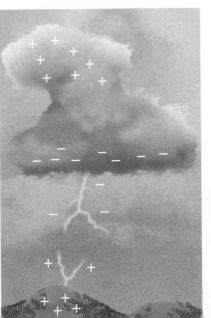

Tornadoes Along some frontal boundaries, cumulonimbus clouds create severe weather. If conditions are just right, updrafts of rising air can start to spin into a rotating vortex. This creates a funnel cloud. **Figure 20** shows the steps in the formation of a funnel cloud. If the funnel cloud reaches Earth's surface, it becomes a tornado like the one shown. A **tornado** is a violent, whirling wind that moves in a narrow path over land. Although tornadoes are usually less than 200 m in diameter, seldom travel on the ground for more than 10 km, and generally last less than 15 min, they are extremely destructive. The powerful updrafts into the low pressure in the center of a tornado act like a giant vacuum cleaner, sucking up anything in its path.

Concepts in Motion

An animated version of this diagram is available at fl6.msscience.com

Strong updrafts and downdrafts develop within cumulonimbus clouds when warm, moist air meets cool, dry air.

Winds within the clouds cause air to spin faster and faster.

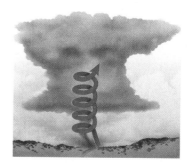

A funnel of spinning air drops downward through the base of the cloud toward the ground.

Figure 20 A tornado's winds can reach nearly 500 km/h, and it can move across the ground at speeds of up to 100 km/h.

Figure 21 Hurricanes begin as low-pressure areas over warm oceans.

Air circulation in a hurricane produces updrafts and downdrafts. The downdrafts prevent cloud formation, creating the calm eye of the storm.

As seen from a satellite, the swirling storm clouds of a hurricane are easy to spot. In 1996, Hurricane Fran turned north and came ashore in North Carolina.

Hurricanes

Unlike tornadoes, hurricanes can last for weeks and travel thousands of kilometers. The diameter of a hurricane can be up to 1,000 km. A **hurricane** is a large storm that begins as an area of low pressure over tropical oceans. The hurricanes that affect the East Coast and Gulf Coast of the United States often begin over the Atlantic Ocean west of Africa. Look at **Figure 21** as you read how a hurricane forms. The Coriolis effect causes winds to rotate counterclockwise around the center of the storm. As the storm moves, carried along by upper wind currents, it pulls in moisture. The heat energy from the moist air is converted to wind. When the winds reach 120 km/h, the low-pressure area is called a hurricane. The sustained winds in a hurricane can reach 250 km/h with gusts up to 300 km/h. **Figure 21** also shows a satellite photo of a hurricane over the ocean.

Sometimes a hurricane spends its entire existence at sea and is a danger only to ships. However, when a hurricane passes over land, high winds, tornadoes, heavy rains, and storm surge pound the affected region. Crops can be destroyed, land flooded, and people and animals killed or injured. After the storm begins traveling over land, however, it no longer has the warm, moist air to provide it with energy, and it begins losing power. Gradually, its winds decrease and the storm disappears.

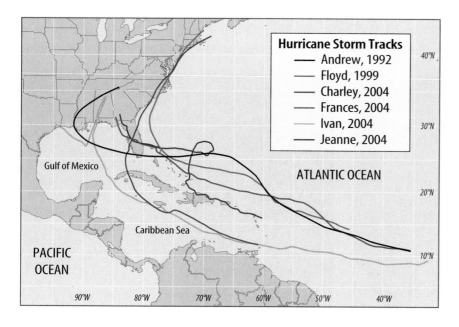

Figure 22 The map shows the paths of the history-making storms from 1992 to 2004.

Winds During the 2004 hurricane season, the state of Florida was struck by the four major hurricanes shown in **Figure 22.** Whether a hurricane is fast-moving or slow-moving, the speed of winds produced and the storm surge they cause determine the damage done as it comes ashore.

Mobile Doppler radar, mobile weather towers, and houses built with special sensors are providing new evidence about hurricane winds. **Figure 23** shows how wind speed is used to predict the category of a hurricane.

Wind Gusts Although sustained winds are dangerous, most damage to buildings is caused by high-speed wind gusts. In the top layer of a storm the wind speeds can exceed 250 kph. These high speed winds are pulled down and strike land as gusts. Poorly built and mobile structures sustain the most damage. Flying debris can become deadly projectiles when picked up by hurricane-force winds. Broken power lines can prove to be an additional danger.

Figure 23 The Saffir-Simpson Hurricane Scale is used to measure the severity of a hurricane and predict the damage it may cause.

Storm Surge Though the winds of a hurricane can be deadly, most deaths are caused by drowning. As a hurricane develops, the pressure in its center drops. This low pressure creates a suction that draws the ocean water into a dome. The counterclockwise motion of the storm drives the dome onto the land. This is the storm surge. The surge of ocean water, which weighs 770 kg per cubic meter, produces a tremendously destructive force to both land and property. When the land is near sea level and the coastlines are shallow, the combination is costly. As shown in **Table 2,** 1,723 lives were lost due to hurricanes in 2004. Damage to homes, agriculture, and business totaled over $35 billion.

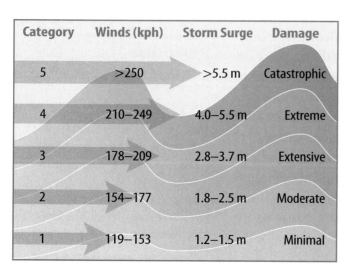

Category	Winds (kph)	Storm Surge	Damage
5	>250	>5.5 m	Catastrophic
4	210–249	4.0–5.5 m	Extreme
3	178–209	2.8–3.7 m	Extensive
2	154–177	1.8–2.5 m	Moderate
1	119–153	1.2–1.5 m	Minimal

Table 2 Data Comparisons of Recent Hurricanes

Name of Hurricane	Andrew	Floyd	Charley	Frances	Ivan	Jeanne
Year	1992	1999	2004	2004	2004	2004
Category	5	2	4	4	5	3
*Damage (billion)	$20	$3–6	$13–15	$4.4	$6	$8
Deaths (total)	26	50	36	35	115	1,537

*Data available as of Winter, 2004

Beach Erosion The action of water and wind combine to create a tremendous erosional force. Normally the action of the ocean waves causes some beach erosion. A hurricane can increase the size and effect of the waves as much as six times. The increased height of waves, the storm surge, and the accompanying rain cause most coastal land areas to flood. Beaches can be washed away or transported inland. Houses built on dunes can be destroyed as the dunes are carried away. Sand bar islands, common along the coasts, can be either created or breached. **Figure 24** shows the storm surge action and the results of that surge.

☑ **Reading Check** *What causes beach erosion?*

Evacuation A hurricane can deposit ten to twenty inches of rain in less than an hour. Most of the deaths attributed to hurricanes come from flooding. As storms approach land, millions of people may be directed to evacuate hundreds of miles of coastline. They must move inland to higher ground. Shelters are set up in schools and other large buildings. According to the Federal Emergency Management Administration (FEMA), the 2004 hurricane effort was the largest since the 1994 Los Angeles Northridge earthquake.

Figure 24 The storm surge, at the left below, pounds the shore as the hurricane makes landfall. The resulting property damage from the waves and flooding is seen at right.

Figure 25 These scientists are placing weather instruments in the path of a tornado. Their research helps forecasters better understand and predict tornadoes.

Weather Safety In the United States, the National Weather Service carefully monitors weather. Using technology such as Doppler radar as well as weather balloons, satellites, and computers, the position and strength of storms are watched constantly. Predicting the movement of storms is sometimes difficult because the conditions that affect them are always changing. If the National Weather Service believes conditions are right for severe weather to develop in a particular area, it issues a severe weather watch. If the severe weather already is occurring or has been indicated by radar, a warning is issued. **Figure 22** shows the different levels of damage potential caused by the five categories of hurricanes.

Watches and Warnings Watches and warnings are issued for severe thunderstorms, tornadoes, tropical storms, hurricanes, blizzards, and floods. Local radio and television stations announce watches and warnings, along with the National Weather Service's own radio network, called NOAA (NOH ah) Weather Radio.

The best preparation for severe weather is to understand how storms develop and to know what to do during watches and warnings. During a watch, stay tuned to a radio or television station and have a plan of action in case a warning is issued. If the National Weather Service does issue a warning, take immediate action to protect yourself.

section 3 review

Summary

Air Masses

- Air masses have the characteristics of the region where they developed.

Fronts

- Front types include cold, warm, stationary, and occluded.
- Precipitation often occurs along fronts.

High and Low Pressure Centers

- In the northern hemisphere, wind spirals clockwise around high pressure. It spirals counterclockwise around low-pressure regions.

Severe Weather and Hurricanes

- If a severe weather warning is issued, take action to protect yourself.

Self Check

1. **Summarize** the characteristics of the four types of fronts. `SC.D.1.3.3`
2. **Explain** why thunderstorms often occur along cold fronts. `SC.D.1.3.3`
3. **Define** a severe weather watch and a severe weather warning.
4. **Explain** why technology is important for forecasting the weather.
5. **Think Critically** Why do southerly winds occur on the trailing side of a high pressure region? `SC.D.1.3.3`

Applying Math

6. **Solve One-Step Equations** Calculate the average speed of a hurricane if it travels 3,500 km in nine days. What is the average speed of a tornado that travels 8 km in 10 min? `SC.D.1.3.5` `MA.D.2.3.1`

Benchmark—SC.D.1.3.3: The student knows how conditions that exist in one system influence the conditions that exist in other systems; **SC.H.2.3.1:** The student recognizes that patterns exist within and across systems.

Interpreting Satellite Images

Satellite images show the pattern of clouds and weather systems across a large region. In this lab, you'll learn to interpret weather from a satellite image.

▶ Real-World Problem

What can you learn about the weather from satellite images?

Goals
- **Interpret** a satellite image.
- **Predict** future weather from the image.
- **Explain** the advantages of satellite technology for weather forecasting.

Materials
satellite image on this page

▶ Procedure

1. Examine the satellite image shown on this page. Identify the color that represents clouds. What color is ocean water? Where is the United States in this image? Where is your state?

2. Describe which regions in the United States have clear skies. Which regions have cloud cover? How do you know?

3. Locate your town or city on the satellite image. What can you infer about the weather conditions at your location when this satellite image was made?

▶ Conclude and Apply

1. **Identify** A tropical storm, named Bill, can be seen in this satellite image. Where is tropical storm Bill located? Which regions of the United States might be affected by this storm if it is moving toward the north? Will tropical storm watches and warnings be issued?

2. **Locate** A stationary front is causing some precipitation in the Midwest. Locate the stationary front on this map. How do you know its position? List some states that are receiving rainfall from this front. Which regions might receive rainfall tomorrow if the front is moving slowly toward the south?

3. **Observe** Find a region of low pressure in Canada. What shape can you see in the pattern of clouds?

4. **Explain** why satellite images are helpful for weather forecasters. What could you learn from the satellite image in today's newspaper?

Benchmark—SC.H.1.3.4: The student knows that accurate record keeping, openness, and replication are essential to maintaining an investigator's credibility with other scientists and society; **SC.H.2.3.1:** The student recognizes that patterns exist within and across systems.

Design Your Own

CREATING YOUR OWN WEATHER STATION

Goals

■ Use weather instruments for measuring air pressure, wind data, temperature, and precipitation.

■ **Design** a weather station using your weather instruments.

■ **Evaluate** current weather conditions and predict future conditions using your weather station.

Possible Materials

peanut butter jar
olive jar
permanent marker
metric ruler
meterstick
confetti
*shredded tissue paper
wind vane
anemometer
compass
coffee can
barometer
thermometer
*grease pencil
*Alternate materials

Safety Precautions

Complete a safety worksheet before you begin.

▶ Real-World Problem

The weather can be very unpredictable. Being able to forecast severe weather such as thunderstorms, tornadoes, and flash floods can save property or lives. Weather stations use instruments to help predict weather patterns. Simple instruments that can be found in a weather station include thermometers for measuring temperature, barometers for observing changes in air pressure, anemometers for measuring wind speed, and rain gauges for measuring precipitation. How can you use weather instruments and design your own weather station to monitor and predict weather conditions?

▶ Form a Hypothesis

Based on your reading in the text and your own experiences with the weather, form a hypothesis about how you could study weather patterns using the instruments in your weather station. Be specific. Describe each instrument and determine how it will help you measure and predict weather conditions.

▶ Test Your Hypothesis

Make a Plan

1. Decide which materials you will need to construct a rain gauge. Decide how you will mark your rain gauge to accurately measure centimeters of rainfall.

2. Decide which materials you will use to measure wind speed.

3. Decide which material you will use to measure wind direction.

4. Decide where you will place your thermometer.

5. Decide where you will place your barometer.

6. Prepare a data table in your Science Journal or on a computer to record your measurements.

7. **Describe** how you will use your weather instruments to evaluate current weather conditions and predict future conditions.

Follow Your Plan

1. Ask your teacher to examine your plans and your data table before you start.

2. **Assemble** your weather instruments.

3. Use the weather instruments to monitor weather conditions for several days.

4. **Record** your weather data.

ⓞ *Analyze Your Data*

1. **Compare** your weather data with those given on the nightly news or in the newspaper.

2. How well did your weather equipment measure current weather conditions?

3. Describe any patterns you see in your data. What relationships do you see between your measurements from day to day?

4. **Compare** your barometer readings with the dates it rained in your area. What can you conclude?

ⓞ *Conclude and Apply*

1. **Determine** Did the results of your experiment support your hypothesis?

2. **Identify** ways your weather instruments could be improved for greater accuracy.

3. **Determine** what kinds of weather patterns you could study if you used your instruments for a year.

4. **Infer** how you could use weather data to make weather predictions.

𝒞ommunicating
Your Data

Post your weather measurements each day. How do your measurements compare to those of other students? Discuss any differences.

How ZOOS Prepare for Hurricanes

Humans aren't the only ones to take cover when hurricanes strike

Flamingos are herded into the zoo's rest room for safety.

A s you step into the rest room, you notice a crunch under your feet. When you look up expecting to see sinks and stalls, you see a flock of pink flamingos standing on a bed of straw. What's going on here?

The Miami Metrozoo is preparing for a hurricane, which means herding all of the flamingos into the shelter of the rest room. Why so much fuss?

In 1992, the Metrozoo was devastated by Hurricane Andrew, which killed five mammals and 50 to 75 birds. The zoo, along with many other Florida zoos, has since been forced to rethink how it gets ready for a hurricane and how to deal with its residents after the storm blows over.

Before the Storm

Where do the animals go before a storm at Metrozoo? The lions, tigers, bears, and monkeys are kept in their solid, strong, concrete overnight pens. Poisonous snakes must be bagged because it could be disastrous if they escaped. Other small animals are put into whatever containers can be found, including dog carriers and shipping crates. Some animals are shipped to warehouses or to other zoos that can care for them and are out of the hurricane's path.

Some animals can trust their instincts to tell them what to do. Larger animals may be given the option of coming under shelter or staying out and braving the storm. According to a spokesperson from Seaworld, "The killer whales stay under water longer," which is what they would do in the wild.

Even after the animals are locked up tight, zookeepers worry that the animals could be hurt psychologically by the storm. After Hurricane Andrew, some frightened animals were running around after the storm or just sitting alone. For many zookeepers, the most frustrating thing is being unable to go to an animal and hold it and say, "It's going to be okay."

Make a List List animal safety tips in case of severe weather in your area. What should you have on hand to keep your pets safe? What should you do with your pets during a weather disaster? If you live on a farm, how can you keep the livestock safe?

TIME

For more information, visit fl6.msscience.com

Section 1 **The Atmosphere**

1. The atmosphere is made of gases, liquids, and solids.

2. The troposphere is warmest near the surface and grows cooler with height. Above the troposphere are four additional layers of the atmosphere, each with different characteristics.

3. Water circulates between Earth's surface and the atmosphere in the water cycle.

Section 2 **Earth's Weather**

1. Conduction and convection are two ways that heat is distributed on Earth.

2. Precipitation occurs when droplets or ice crystals become too heavy to be supported by the air.

3. Wind is air molecules moving from high-pressure centers to low-pressure centers.

Section 3 **Air Masses and Fronts**

1. Air masses are dry or moist and warm or cool, depending on where they originate.

2. Fronts develop where air masses of different temperatures collide, forming a boundary. The four kinds of fronts are cold, warm, stationary, and occluded.

3. Severe weather develops from low-pressure centers. Thunderstorms and tornadoes often form near fronts. Hurricanes develop from lows over tropical waters.

4. Knowing what to do when weather watch and warning advisories are made can save your life.

Visualizing Main Ideas

Copy and complete the following concept map about air masses and fronts.

Air Masses Meet

Cold air mass and warm air mass meet but don't move very much.

Warm air mass slides over cold air mass.

forming a

forming a — Cold front

forming a

forming a

Using Vocabulary

aerosol p. 291
air mass p. 304
✳ atmosphere p. 290
dew point p. 298
front p. 305
humidity p. 298
hurricane p. 309

precipitation p. 300
relative humidity p. 298
tornado p. 308
troposphere p. 292
✳ water cycle p. 295
weather p. 296

✳ FCAT Vocabulary

Fill in the blanks with the correct word or words.

1. The _____ describes the current condition of the atmosphere.

2. The boundary between different air masses is called a(n) _____.

3. A(n) _____ is a violent, whirling wind that forms over land.

4. Dust, salt, pollen, and acid droplets in the atmosphere are called _____.

5. A large body of air that develops over a particular region of Earth's surface is called a(n) _____.

Checking Concepts

6. Which layer of Earth's atmosphere contains the ozone that protects living things from too much ultraviolet radiation?
   A) thermosphere   C) stratosphere
   B) ionosphere   D) troposphere

7. Air at 30°C can hold 32 g of water vapor per cubic meter of air. If the air is holding 16 g of water vapor, what is the relative humidity?
   A) 15 percent   C) 50 percent
   B) 30 percent   D) 100 percent

8. Which atmospheric layer is farthest from Earth's surface?
   A) troposphere   C) stratosphere
   B) exosphere   D) ionosphere

Use the illustration below to answer question 9.

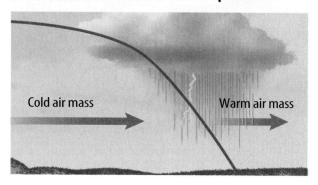

Cold air mass   Warm air mass

9. Which type of front is shown above?
   A) warm   C) cold
   B) stationary   D) occluded

10. What causes low-pressure centers to rotate counterclockwise in the northern hemisphere?   SC.D.1.3.3
    A) trade winds
    B) prevailing westerlies
    C) Coriolis effect
    D) jet stream

11. Who first proved that air has weight?
    A) Robert Hooke
    B) Evangelista Torricelli
    C) Robert Boyle
    D) Galileo Galilei

12. Which step in the water cycle occurs when water vapor changes to liquid water?
    A) condensation   C) precipitation
    B) evaporation   D) transpiration

13. What kind of cloud touches the ground?
    A) altostratus   C) stratocumulus
    B) stratocirrus   D) fog

14. Which occurs when colliding molecules transfer energy?
    A) precipitation   C) radiation
    B) conduction   D) convection

15. What occurs when strong winds toss ice crystals up and down within a cloud?
    A) rain   C) snow
    B) freezing rain   D) hail

Vocabulary PuzzleMaker fl6.msscience.com

Thinking Critically

16. **Explain** how hurricanes are formed. `SC.D.1.3.3`

17. **Infer** why air pressure is higher at sea level than on top of a mountain.

18. **Compare and contrast** condensation and precipitation.

19. **Describe** what happens to gas molecules when air is heated.

20. **Recognize Cause and Effect** How can a cloud produce both rain and hail? `SC.D.1.3.3`

21. **Concept Map** Copy and complete the concept map of the water cycle below.

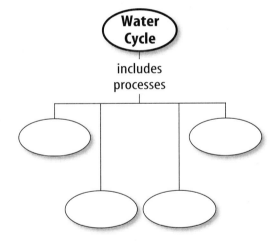

22. **Classify** You observe a tall, dark, puffy cloud. Rain is falling from its lower surface. How would you classify this cloud?

23. **Use Scientific Explanations** Explain why thunder is heard after a flash of lightning. `SC.D.1.3.5`

24. **Venn Diagram** Make a Venn diagram to compare and contrast tornadoes and hurricanes.

25. **Research Information** Do research to learn how sleet forms. Write a paragraph about sleet in your Science Journal.

Performance Activities

26. **Pamphlet** Research three destructive hurricanes and make a pamphlet using the information you collect. Discuss the paths the hurricanes took, how fast they moved, and the damage they caused.

27. **Oral Presentation** Imagine that you work for a television network. Prepare a weather advisory message and announce your watch or warning to the class. Discuss what actions people should take to stay safe.

28. **Poem** Write a poem about the water cycle. Display your poem with those of your classmates on a decorated bulletin board.

Applying Math

Use the equations below to answer questions 29–33.

$$°F = 9/5°C + 32$$
$$°C = 5/9(°F - 32)$$

29. **A Hot Summer Day** The Sun is shining and the temperature is a sweltering 95°F. What is the temperature in degrees Celsius? `MA.B.2.3.2`

30. **A Frigid Winter Morning** The thermometer shows a temperature of −10°C. What's the temperature in degrees Fahrenheit? `MA.B.2.3.2`

31. **A Pleasant Day** A gentle breeze is blowing and the temperature is a comfortable 78°F. What's the temperature in degrees Celsius? `MA.B.2.3.2`

32. **Record Cold** The coldest temperature recorded on Earth occurred at Vostok, Antarctica on July 21, 1983. It was −89.4°C. What was the temperature in degrees Fahrenheit? `MA.B.2.3.2`

33. **Record Heat** The hottest temperature occurred in El Azizia, Libya on September 13, 1922. A scorching 136°F was recorded. What was the temperature in degrees Celsius? `MA.B.2.3.2`

 The assessed Florida Benchmark appears above each question.
Record your answers on the answer sheet provided by your teacher or on a sheet of paper.

Multiple Choice

SC.B.1.3.3

1 Solar radiation causes ions to continually form in Earth's ionosphere. One valuable characteristic of the ionosphere is that it reflects radio waves. Which of the following human activities is made possible by this property of the ionosphere?

A. long-distance communication

B. cooking with microwaves

C. locating distant objects

D. safer medical tests

SC.D.1.3.3

2 Over a period of time, weather conditions were observed and recorded in a student's science journal. Some of the data from the journal is shown below.

Weather Conditions on Monday			
Condition	**Morning**	**Afternoon**	**Evening**
Temperature	35	40	50
Humidity	low	high	high
Cloud cover	some	a lot	little
Rainfall	none	light rain	no rain

Which of the following may have passed through the area while the student was recording data?

F. a cold front

G. a warm front

H. a stationary front

I. an occluded front

SC.B.2.3.1

3 Which of the following **best** describes energy transfer in a hurricane?

A. Thermal energy in the water is converted to the energy in waves.

B. Energy from the Sun is converted to the energy in the waves.

C. Energy in the ocean waves is converted to wind energy.

D. Thermal energy in the air is converted to wind energy.

SC.B.1.3.5

4 What conclusion about temperature and water vapor can be made based on data presented in the graph below?

Dew Point

Amount of water vapor in grams per cubic meter of air

(y-axis: 0, 10, 20, 30, 40, 50, 60, 70, 80, 90)

Temperature (°C): 0° 5° 10° 15° 20° 25° 30° 35° 40° 45° 50°

F. As the temperature decreases, the greater the amount of water vapor in the air.

G. As the temperature increases, the lesser the amount of water vapor in the air.

H. As the temperature increases, the greater the amount of water vapor in the air.

I. Temperature has no affect on the amount of water vapor that the air can hold.

SC.D.1.3.5

5 Tornadoes and hurricanes are two types of severe storms in which air spins around a low-pressure center. Which of the following is the main difference between tornadoes and hurricanes that affect the United States?

   A. presence of destructive winds

   B. size and duration of the storms

   C. direction in which the air spins

   D. association with rain and lightning

Short Response

SC.D.1.3.3

6 The figure below shows an important interaction between the Sun and Earth.

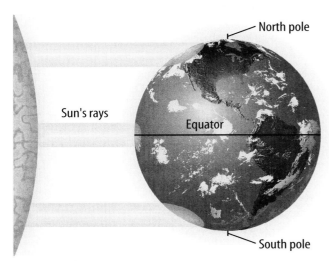

Identify this interaction and explain how this interaction helps in the creation of winds.

Gridded Response

SC.D.1.3.3

7 In a hurricane, winds circulate around a low-pressure center usually located over an ocean. At what speed, in kilometers per hour (km/h), must these winds move for a storm over the ocean to be called a hurricane?

READ INQUIRE EXPLAIN
Extended Response

SC.B.1.3.3

8 The diagram below shows the layers of Earth's atmosphere. If you were using a weather balloon to measure Earth's atmospheric temperature, what would happen to the temperature as it passed through each layer?

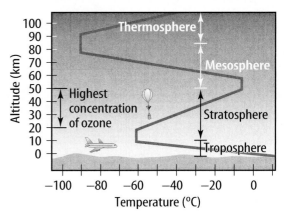

FCAT Tip

Keep Track of Time Allow about five minutes to answer short-response questions and about 10 to 15 minutes to answer extended-response questions.

Sunshine State Standards—SC.D.1: The student recognizes that processes in the lithosphere, atmosphere, hydrosphere, and biosphere interact to shape the Earth.

Weathering and Soil

What's a tor?

A tor, shown in the photo, is a pile of boulders left on the land. Tors form because of weathering, which is a natural process that breaks down rock. Weathering weakened the rock that used to be around the boulders. This weakened rock then was eroded away, and the boulders are all that remain.

Science Journal Write a poem about a tor. Use words in your poem that rhyme with the word *tor.*

Start-Up Activities

 SC.D.1.3.1

Stalactites and Stalagmites

During weathering, minerals can be dissolved by acidic water. If this water seeps into a cave, minerals might precipitate. In this lab, you will model the formation of stalactites and stalagmites.

1. Complete a safety worksheet.

2. Pour 700 mL of water into two 1,000-mL beakers and place the beakers on a large piece of cardboard. Stir Epsom salt into each beaker until no more will dissolve.

3. Add two drops of yellow food coloring to each beaker and stir.

4. Measure and cut three 75-cm lengths of cotton string. Hold the three pieces of string in one hand and twist the ends of all three pieces to form a loose braid of string.

5. Tie each end of the braid to a large steel nut.

6. Soak the braid of string in one of the beakers until it is wet with the solution. Drop one nut into one beaker and the other nut into the second beaker. Allow the string to sag between the beakers. Observe for several days.

7. **Think Critically** Record your observations in your Science Journal. How does this activity model the formation of stalactites and stalagmites?

FOLDABLES™
Study Organizer

Weathering and Soil Make the following Foldable to help you understand the vocabulary terms in this chapter.

LA.A.1.3.4

STEP 1 **Fold** a vertical sheet of notebook paper from side to side.

STEP 2 **Cut** along every third line of only the top layer to form tabs.

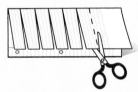

STEP 3 **Label** each tab.

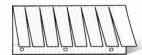

Build Vocabulary As you read the chapter, list the vocabulary words about weathering and soil on the tabs. As you learn the definitions, write them under the tab for each vocabulary word.

Preview this chapter's content and activities at fl6.msscience.com

Benchmarks—SC.D.1.3.1 (pp. 324–329): The student knows that mechanical and chemical activities shape and reshape the Earth's land surface by eroding rock and soil in some areas and depositing them in other areas, sometimes in seasonal layers; SC.D.1.3.4 Annually Assessed (pp. 324–329): The student knows the ways in which plants and animals reshape the landscape.

Also covers: SC.D.1.3.5 (pp. 324, 326, 328)

section

1

Weathering

Weathering and Its Effects

Can you believe that tiny moss plants, earthworms, and even oxygen in the air can affect solid rock? These things weaken and break apart rock at Earth's surface. Surface processes that work to break down rock are called **weathering.**

Weathering breaks rock into smaller and smaller particles, such as sand, silt, and clay. These particles are called sediment. The terms *sand, silt,* and *clay* are used to describe specific particle sizes which contribute to soil texture. Sand grains are larger than silt, and silt is larger than clay. Soil texture influences virtually all mechanical and chemical processes in the soil, including the ability to hold moisture and nutrients.

Over millions of years, weathering has changed Earth's surface. The process continues today. Weathering wears mountains down to hills, as shown in **Figure 1.** Rocks at the top of mountains are broken down by weathering, and the sediment is moved downhill by gravity, water, and ice. Weathering also produces strange rock formations like those shown at the beginning of this chapter. Two different types of weathering— mechanical weathering and chemical weathering—work together to shape Earth's surface.

Figure 1 Over long periods of time, weathering wears mountains down to rolling hills.
Explain *how this occurs.*

Figure 2 Growing tree roots can be agents of mechanical weathering.

Tree roots can crack a sidewalk.

Tree roots also can grow into cracks and break rock apart.

Mechanical Weathering

Mechanical weathering occurs when rocks are broken apart by physical processes. This means that the overall chemical makeup of the rock stays the same. Each fragment has characteristics similar to the original rock. Growing plants, burrowing animals, and expanding ice are some of the things that can mechanically weather rock. These physical processes produce enough force to break rocks into smaller pieces.

Reading Check *What can cause mechanical weathering?*

Figure 3 Small animals mechanically weather rock when they burrow by breaking apart sediment.

Plants and Animals Water and nutrients that collect in the cracks of rocks result in conditions in which plants can grow. As the roots grow, they enlarge the cracks. You've seen this kind of mechanical weathering if you've ever tripped on a crack in a sidewalk near a tree, as shown in **Figure 2.** Sometimes tree roots wedge rock apart, also shown in **Figure 2.**

Burrowing animals also cause mechanical weathering, as shown in **Figure 3.** As these animals burrow, they loosen sediment and push it to the surface. Once the sediment is brought to the surface, other weathering processes act on it.

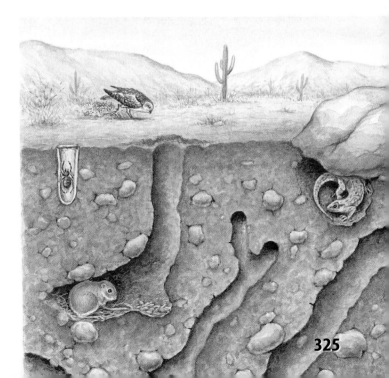

Figure 4 When water enters cracks in rock and freezes, it expands, causing the cracks to enlarge and the rock to break apart.

Figure 5 As rock is broken apart by mechanical weathering, the amount of rock surface exposed to air and water increases. The background squares show the total number of surfaces exposed.

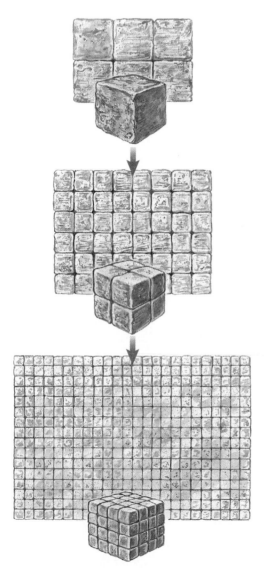

Ice Wedging A mechanical weathering process called ice wedging is shown in **Figure 4. Ice wedging** occurs in temperate and cold climates where water enters cracks in rocks and freezes. Because water expands when it turns to ice, pressure builds up in the cracks. This pressure can extend the cracks and break apart rock. The ice then melts, allowing more water to enter the crack, where it freezes and breaks the rock even more. Ice wedging is most noticeable in the mountains, where warm days and cold nights are common. It is one process that wears down mountain peaks. This cycle of freezing and thawing not only breaks up rocks, but also can break up roads and highways. When water enters cracks in road pavement and freezes, it forces the pavement apart. This causes potholes to form in roads.

Surface Area Mechanical weathering by plants, animals, and ice wedging reduces rocks to smaller and smaller pieces. These small pieces have more surface area than the original rock body, as shown in **Figure 5.** As the amount of surface area increases, more rock is exposed to water and oxygen. This speeds up a different type of weathering, called chemical weathering, which continues to reduce the particle size of sediments from a coarse to a finer texture.

Chemical Weathering

The second type of weathering, **chemical weathering,** occurs when chemical processes dissolve or alter the minerals in rocks or change them into different minerals. This type of weathering occurs at or near Earth's surface and changes the chemical composition of the rock, which can weaken the rock.

Natural Acids Naturally formed acids can weather rocks. When water reacts with carbon dioxide in the air or soil, a weak acid, called carbonic acid, forms. Carbonic acid reacts with minerals such as calcite, which is the main mineral that makes up limestone. This reaction causes the calcite to dissolve. Over many thousands of years, carbonic acid has weathered so much limestone that caves have formed, as shown in **Figure 6.**

Chemical weathering also occurs when naturally formed acids come in contact with other types of rocks. Over a long time, the mineral feldspar, which is found in granite, some types of sandstone, and other rocks, is broken down into a clay mineral called kaolinite (KAY oh luh nite). Kaolinite clay is common in some soils. Clay is an end product of weathering.

Reading Check *How does kaolinite clay form?*

Plant Acids Some roots and decaying plants give off acids that dissolve minerals in rock. When the minerals dissolve, the rock is weakened. Eventually, the rock breaks into smaller pieces. As the rock weathers, nutrients become available to plants.

Science Online

LA.B.2.3.4

Topic: Chemical Weathering
Visit fl6.msscience.com for Web links to information about chemical weathering.

Activity List different types of chemical weathering. Next to each type, write an effect that you have observed.

Figure 6 Caves form when slightly acidic groundwater dissolves limestone.
Explain *why the groundwater is acidic.*

Carbon dioxide + Water = Carbonic acid
Carbonic acid dissolves limestone.

Mini LAB

Observing Chemical and Mechanical Weathering

Procedure 🥽 🧤 🚫

1. Collect and rinse two handfuls of **common rock or shells**.
2. Place equal amounts of rock into two **plastic bottles.**
3. Fill one bottle with **water** to cover the rock and seal with a **lid.**
4. Cover the rock in the second bottle with **lemon juice** and seal.
5. Shake both bottles for ten minutes.
6. Tilt the bottles so you can observe the liquids in each.

Analysis

1. Describe the appearance of each liquid.
2. Explain any differences.

Figure 7 Iron-containing minerals like the magnetite shown here can weather to form a rustlike material called limonite.

INTEGRATE Chemistry

pH Scale The strength of acids and bases is measured on the pH scale with a range of 0 to 14. On this scale, 0 is extremely acidic, 14 is extremely basic or alkaline, and 7 is neutral. Most minerals are more soluble in acidic soils than in neutral or slightly alkaline soils. Different plants grow best at different pH values. For example, peanuts grow best in soils that have a pH of 5.3 to 6.6, while alfalfa grows best in soils having a pH of 6.2 to 7.8.

Oxygen Oxygen also causes chemical weathering. **Oxidation** (ahk sih DAY shun) occurs when some materials are exposed to oxygen and water. For example, when minerals containing iron are exposed to water and the oxygen in the air, the iron in the mineral reacts to form a new material that resembles rust. One common example of this type of weathering is the alteration of the iron-bearing mineral magnetite to a rustlike material called limonite, as shown in **Figure 7.** Oxidation of minerals gives some rock layers a red color.

✓ **Reading Check** *How does oxygen cause weathering?*

Effects of Climate

Climate affects soil temperature and moisture and also affects the rate of mechanical and chemical weathering. **Climate** is the pattern of weather that occurs in a particular area over many years. In cold climates, where freezing and thawing are frequent, mechanical weathering rapidly breaks down rock through a process of ice wedging. Chemical weathering is more rapid in warm, wet climates. High temperatures tend to increase the rate of chemical reactions. Thus, chemical weathering tends to occur quickly in tropical areas. Lack of moisture in deserts and low temperatures in polar regions slow down chemical weathering.

Magnetite

Limonite

Marble statue

Granite statue

Figure 8 Different types of rock weather at different rates. In humid climates, marble statues weather rapidly and become discolored. Granite statues weather more slowly.

Effects of Rock Type Rock type also can affect the rate of weathering in a particular climate. In wet climates, for example, marble weathers more rapidly than granite, as shown in **Figure 8.** The weathering of rocks and the processes of soil formation alter rock minerals so that soil minerals are mostly inherited from the parent rock type. Weathering begins the process of forming soil from rock and sediment and also affects particle size and soil texture. Sand, silt, and clay simply refer to different particle sizes of the soil's mineral content.

section 1 review

Summary

Weathering and Its Effects
- Weathering includes processes that break down rock.
- Weathering affects Earth's landforms.

Mechanical Weathering
- During mechanical weathering, rock is broken apart, but it is not changed chemically.
- Plant roots, burrowing animals, and expanding ice all weather rock.

Chemical Weathering
- During chemical weathering, minerals in rock dissolve or change to other minerals.
- Agents of chemical weathering include natural acids and oxygen.

Self Check

1. **Describe** how weathering reduces the height of mountains through millions of years. `SC.D.1.3.5`
2. **Explain** how both tree roots and prairie dogs mechanically weather rock. `SC.D.1.3.4`
3. **Summarize** the effects of carbonic acid on limestone.
4. **Describe** how climate affects weathering. `SC.D.1.3.1`
5. **Think Critically** Why does limestone often form cliffs in dry climates but rarely form cliffs in wet climates?

Applying Skills

6. **Venn Diagram** Make a Venn diagram to compare and contrast mechanical weathering and chemical weathering. Include the causes of mechanical and chemical weathering in your diagram.

Benchmarks—SC.D.1.3.4 Annually Assessed (pp. 330–336): The student knows the ways in which plants and animals reshape the landscape (e.g., bacteria, fungi, worms, rodents, and other organisms add organic matter to the soil, increasing soil fertility, encouraging plant growth, and strengthening resistance to erosion).

Also covers: SC.D.1.3.5 (pp. 330, 334)

section 2

The Nature of Soil

as you read

What You'll Learn

- **Explain** how soil forms.
- **Describe** soil characteristics.
- **Describe** factors that affect the development of soil.

Why It's Important

Much of the food that you eat is grown in soil.

Review Vocabulary

profile: a vertical slice through rock, sediment, or soil

New Vocabulary

- soil
- soil profile
- humus
- litter
- horizon
- leaching

Formation of Soil

The word *ped* is from a Greek word that means "ground" and from a Latin word that means "foot." The pedal under your foot, when you're bicycling, comes from the word *ped*. The part of Earth under your feet, when you're walking on the ground, is the pedosphere, or soil. Soil science is called pedology.

What is soil and where does it come from? A layer of rock and mineral fragments produced by weathering covers the surface of Earth. As you learned in Section 1, weathering gradually breaks rocks into smaller and smaller fragments. However, these fragments do not become high-quality soil until plants and animals live in them. Plants and animals add organic matter, the remains of once-living organisms, to the rock fragments. Organic matter can include leaves, twigs, roots, and dead worms and insects. **Soil** is a mixture of weathered rock, decayed organic matter, mineral fragments, water, and air.

Soil can take thousands of years to form and ranges from 60 m thick in some areas to just a few centimeters thick in others. Climate, slope, types of rock, types of vegetation, and length of time that rock has been weathering all affect the formation of soil, as shown in **Figure 9.** For example, different kinds of soils develop in tropical regions than in polar regions. Soils that develop on steep slopes are different from soils that develop on flat land. **Figure 10** illustrates how soil develops from rock.

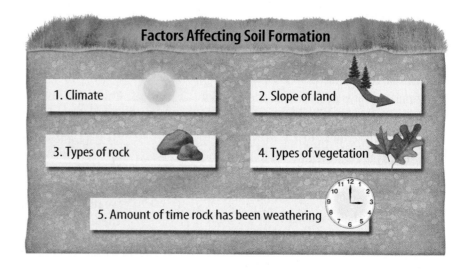

Factors Affecting Soil Formation

1. Climate
2. Slope of land
3. Types of rock
4. Types of vegetation
5. Amount of time rock has been weathering

Figure 9 Five different factors affect soil formation.
Explain *how time influences the development of soils.*

Figure 10

It may take thousands of years to form, but soil is constantly evolving from solid rock, as this series of illustrations shows. Soil is a mixture of weathered rock, mineral fragments, and organic material—the remains of dead plants and animals—along with water and air.

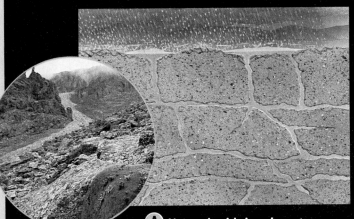

A Natural acids in rainwater weather the surface of exposed bedrock. Water can also freeze in cracks, causing rocks to fracture and break apart. The inset photo shows weathered rock in the Tien Shan Mountains of Central Asia.

B Plants take root in the cracks and among bits of weathered rock—shown in the inset photo above. As they grow, plants, along with other natural forces, continue the process of breaking down rocks, and a thin layer of soil begins to form.

C Like the grub in the inset photo, insects, worms, and other living things live among plant roots. Their wastes, along with dead plant material, add organic matter to the soil.

D As organic matter increases and underlying bedrock continues to break down, the soil layer thickens. Rich topsoil supports trees and other plants with large root systems.

Mini LAB

Comparing Components of Soil

Procedure

1. Complete a safety worksheet.
2. Collect a sample of **soil**.
3. Observe it closely with a **magnifying lens.**
4. Record evidence of plant and animal components or their activities.

Analysis

1. Describe the different particles found in your sample. Did you find any remains of organisms?
2. Explain how living organisms might affect the soil.
3. Compare and contrast your sample with those other students have collected.

Composition of Soil

Soil is made up of rock and mineral fragments, organic matter, air, and water. The rock and mineral fragments come from rocks that have been weathered. Most of these fragments are small particles of sediment such as clay, silt, and sand.

Most organic matter in soil comes from plants. Plant leaves, stems, and roots all contribute organic matter to soil. Animals and microorganisms provide additional organic matter when they die. After plant and animal material gets into soil, fungi and bacteria cause it to decay. The decayed organic matter turns into a dark-colored material called **humus** (HYEW mus). Humus serves as a source of nutrients for plants. As worms, insects, and rodents burrow throughout soil, they mix the humus with the fragments of rock. Good-quality surface soil has approximately equal amounts of humus and weathered rock material.

Water Infiltration Soil has many small spaces between individual soil particles that are filled with water and air. When soil is moist, the spaces hold the water that plants need to grow. During a drought, the spaces, or pores, are almost entirely filled with air. When water soaks into the ground, it infiltrates the pores. Infiltration rate is determined by calculating the time it takes for water sitting on soil to drop a fixed distance. This rate changes as the soil pore spaces fill with water.

Figure 11 This soil, which developed beneath a grassy prairie, has three main horizons.
Describe *how the A horizon is different from the other two horizons.*

Soil Profile

You have seen layers of soil if you've ever dug a deep hole or driven along a road that has been cut into a hillside. You probably observed that most plant roots grow in the top layer of soil. The top layer typically is darker than the soil layers below it. These different layers of soil are called **horizons.** All the horizons of a soil form a **soil profile.** Most soils have three horizons—labeled A, B, and C, as shown in **Figure 11.**

A horizon

B horizon

C horizon

A Horizon The A horizon is the top layer of soil. In a forest, the A horizon might be covered with litter. **Litter** consists of leaves, twigs, and other organic material that eventually can be changed to humus by decomposing organisms. Litter helps prevent erosion and evaporation of water from the soil. The A horizon also is known as topsoil. Topsoil has more humus and fewer rock and mineral particles than the other layers in a soil profile. The A horizon generally is dark and fertile. The dark color of the soil is caused by the humus, which provides nutrients for plant growth.

Since dark color absorbs solar energy more readily, soil color can greatly affect soil temperature. Darker color also may indicate higher soil moisture. Soil moisture and soil temperature are important in determining seed germination for plants and the vitality of decomposing organisms.

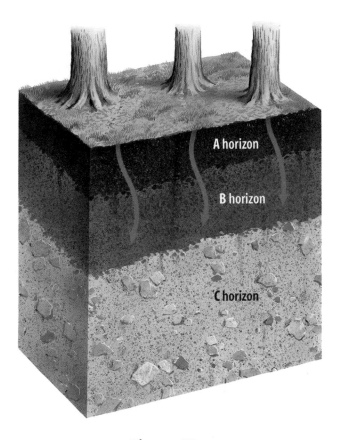

B Horizon The layer below the A horizon is the B horizon. Because less organic matter is added to this horizon, it is lighter in color than the A horizon and contains less humus. As a result, the B horizon is less fertile. The B horizon contains material moved down from the A horizon by the process of leaching.

Leaching is the removal of minerals that have been dissolved in water. In soil, water seeps through the A horizon and reacts with humus and carbon dioxide to form acid. The acid dissolves some of the minerals in the A horizon and carries the material down into the B horizon, as shown in **Figure 12.**

Figure 12 Leaching removes material from the upper layer of soil. Much of this material then is deposited in the B horizon.

Reading Check *How does leaching transport material from the A horizon to the B horizon?*

C Horizon The C horizon consists of partially weathered rock and is the bottom horizon in a soil profile. It is often the thickest soil horizon. This horizon does not contain much organic matter and is not strongly affected by leaching. It usually is composed of coarser sediment than the soil horizons above it. What would you find if you dug to the bottom of the C horizon? As you might have guessed, you would find rock—the rock that gave rise to the soil horizons above it. This rock is called the parent material of the soil. The C horizon is the soil layer that is most like the parent material.

Soil Fertility Plants need a variety of nutrients for growth. They need things like nitrogen, phosphorous, potassium, sulfur, calcium, and magnesium called macronutrients. They get these nutrients from the minerals and organic material in soil. Soil fertility usually is determined in a laboratory by a soil chemist. However, fertility sometimes can be inferred by looking at plants. Do research to discover more important plant nutrients.

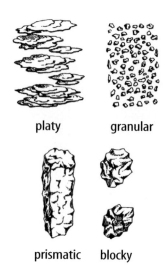

platy   granular

prismatic   blocky

Figure 13 Four major classes characterize soil structure.

Soil Structure Individual soil particles clump or bind together. Examine soil closely and you will see natural clumps called *peds*. Soil structure affects pore space and will affect a plant's ability to penetrate roots. **Figure 13** shows four classes of soil structure. Granular structures are common in surface soils with high organic content that glues minerals together. Earthworms, frost, and rodents mix the soil, keeping the peds small, which provides good porosity and movement of air and water. Platy structures are often found in subsurface soils that have been leached or compacted by animals or machinery. Blocky structures are common in subsoils or surface soils with high clay content, which shrinks and swells, producing cracks. Prismatic structures, found in B horizons, are very dense and difficult for plant roots to penetrate. Vertical cracks result from freezing and thawing, wetting and drying, and downward movement of water and roots. Soil consistency refers to the ability of peds and soil particles to stick together and hold their shapes.

Applying Math   Calculate Percentages

SOIL TEXTURE Some soil is coarse, some is fine. This property of soil is called soil texture. The texture of soil often is determined by finding the percentages of sand, silt, and clay. Calculate the percentage of clay shown by the circle graph.

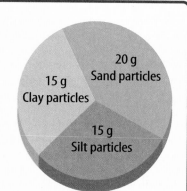

Solution

1 *This is what you know:*

- sand weight: 20 g
- clay weight: 15 g
- silt weight: 15 g

2 *This is what you need to find:*

- total weight of the sample
- percentage of clay particles

3 *This is the procedure you need to use:*

- Add all the masses to determine the total sample mass:
  20 g sand + 15 g silt + 15 g clay = 50 g sample
- Divide the clay mass by the sample mass; multiply by 100:
  15 g clay/50 g sample × 100 = 30% clay in the sample

Practice Problems

1. Calculate the percentage of sand in the sample. **MA.E.3.3.1**
2. Calculate the percentage of silt in the sample. **MA.E.3.3.1**

Math Practice | For more practice, visit fl6.msscience.com

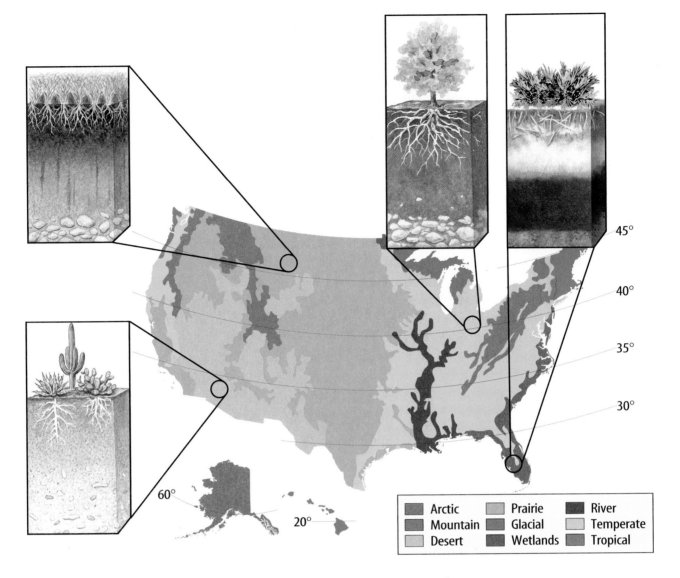

Figure 14 The United States has many different soil types. They vary in color, depth, texture, and fertility.
Identify *the soil type in your region.*

Soil Types

If you travel across the country, you will notice that not all soils are the same. Some are thick and red. Some are brown with hard rock nodules, and some have thick, black A horizons. They vary in color, depth, texture, fertility, pH, temperature, and moisture content. Many soils exist, as shown in **Figure 14.**

Soil Types Reflect Climate Different regions on Earth have different climates. Deserts are dry, prairies are semidry, and temperate forests are mild and moist. These places also have different types of soils. Soil temperature and moisture content affect the quality of soils. Soils in deserts contain little organic material and are thinner than soils in wetter climates. Prairie soils have thick, dark A horizons because the grasses that grow there contribute lots of organic matter. Temperate forest soils have less organic matter and thinner A horizons than prairie soils. Other regions also have distinct soils such as the permafrost soils of the tundra and laterite soils of tropical areas.

Other Factors Parent rock material affects soils that develop from it. Clay soils develop on rocks like basalt, because minerals in the rock weather to form clay. Rock type also affects vegetation, because different rocks provide different amounts of nutrients.

Soil pH controls many chemical and biological activities that take place in soil. Activities of organisms, acid rain, or land management practices could affect soil quality.

Time also affects soil development. If weathering has been occurring for only a short time, the parent rock determines the soil characteristics. As weathering continues, the soil resembles the parent rock less and less.

Slope also is a factor affecting soil profiles, as shown in **Figure 15.** On steep slopes, soils often are poorly developed, because material moves downhill before it can be weathered much. In bottomlands, sediment and water are plentiful. Bottomland soils are often thick, dark, and full of organic material.

Figure 15 The slope of the land affects soil development. Thin, poorly developed soils form on steep slopes, but valleys often have thick, well-developed soils. **Infer** *why this is so.*

section 2 review

Summary

Formation of Soil

- Soil is a mixture of rock and mineral fragments, decayed organic matter, water, and air.

Composition of Soil

- Organic matter gradually changes to humus.
- Soil moisture is important for plant growth.

Soil Profile

- The layers in a soil profile are called horizons.
- Most soils have an A, B, and C horizon.

Soil Types

- Many different types of soils occur in the United States.
- Climate and other factors determine the type of soil that develops.

Self Check

1. **List** the five factors that affect soil development. `SC.D.1.3.5`
2. **Explain** how soil forms.
3. **Explain** why A horizons often are darker than B horizons or C horizons.
4. **Describe** how leaching affects soil.
5. **Think Critically** Why is a soil profile in a tropical rain forest different from one in a desert? A prairie? `SC.D.1.3.4`

Applying Math

6. **Use Statistics** A farmer collected five soil samples from a field and tested their acidity, or pH. His data were the following: 7.5, 8.2, 7.7, 8.1, and 8.0. Calculate the mean of these data. Also, determine the range and median. `MA.E.1.3.2`

Benchmark—SC.D.1.3.5: The student understands concepts of time and size relating to the interaction of Earth's processes (e.g., lightning striking in a split second as opposed to the shifting of the Earth's plates altering the landscape, distance between atoms measured in Angstrom units as opposed to distance between stars measured in light-years).

Soil Texture

Soils have different amounts of different sizes of particles. When you determine how much sand, silt, and clay a soil contains, you describe the soil's texture.

▶ Real-World Problem

What is the texture of your soil?

Goals

■ **Determine** soil texture by making a ribbon.

Materials

soil sample (100 g)   water bottle

Safety Precautions

Complete a safety worksheet before you begin.

▶ Procedure

1. Take some soil and make it into a ball. Work the soil with your fingers. Slowly add water to the soil until it is moist.

2. After your ball of soil is moist, try to form a thin ribbon of soil. Use the following descriptions to categorize your soil:
   a. If you can form a long, thin ribbon, you have a clay soil.
   b. If you formed a long ribbon but it breaks easily, you have a clay loam soil.
   c. If you had difficulty forming a long ribbon, you have loam soil.

3. Now make your soil classification more detailed by selecting one of these descriptions:
   a. If the soil feels smooth, add the word *silty* to your soil name.
   b. If the soil feels slightly gritty, don't add any word to your soil name.
   c. If the soil feels very gritty, add the word *sandy* before your soil name.

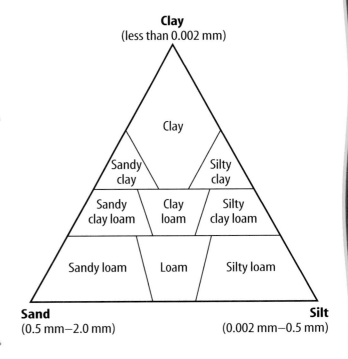

Clay
(less than 0.002 mm)

Clay

Sandy clay

Silty clay

Sandy clay loam

Clay loam

Silty clay loam

Sandy loam

Loam

Silty loam

Sand
(0.5 mm–2.0 mm)

Silt
(0.002 mm–0.5 mm)

▶ Conclude and Apply

1. **Classify** Which texture class name did you assign to your soil?

2. **Observe** Find your soil texture class name on the triangle above. Notice that the corners of the triangle are labeled *sand, silt,* and *clay.*

3. **Determine** Is your soil texture class close to one of the three corners or near the middle of the diagram? If your soil texture class is close to a corner, which one?

4. **Describe** Does your soil contain mostly sand, silt, or clay, or does it have nearly equal amounts of each? *Hint: If your soil name is close to a corner, it has mostly that size of sediment. If your soil name is in the middle of the triangle, it has nearly equal amounts of each sediment size.*

Benchmarks—SC.D.1.3.1 (pp. 338, 340): The student knows that mechanical and chemical activities shape and reshape the Earth's land surface by eroding rock and soil in some areas and depositing them in other areas, sometimes in seasonal layers; SC.D.1.3.4 Annually Assessed (pp. 338–341): The student knows the ways in which plants and animals reshape the landscape.

Also covers: SC.D.1.3.5 (pp. 338–340), SC.H.1.3.3 (p. 339), SC.H.1.3.4 Annually Assessed (pp. 342–343), SC.H.1.3.5 Annually Assessed (pp. 342–343), SC.H.1.3.6 (pp. 339, 344)

section 3

Soil Erosion

as you read

What You'll Learn

- **Explain** why soil is important.
- **Evaluate** ways that human activity has affected Earth's soil.
- **Describe** ways to reduce soil erosion.

Why It's Important

If topsoil is eroded, soil becomes less fertile.

Review Vocabulary

☀ **erosion:** the picking up and moving of sediment or soil

New Vocabulary

- no-till farming
- contour farming
- terracing

☀ FCAT Vocabulary

Figure 16 Removing vegetation can increase soil erosion.

Soil—An Important Resource

While picnicking at a local park, a flash of lightning and a clap of thunder tell you that a storm is upon you. Watching the pounding rain from the park shelter, you notice that the water flowing off of the ball diamond is muddy, not clear. The flowing water is carrying away some of the sediment that used to be on the field. This process is called soil erosion. Soil erosion is harmful because plants do not grow as well when topsoil has been removed.

Causes and Effects of Soil Erosion

Soil erodes when it is moved from the place where it formed. Erosion occurs as water flows over Earth's surface or when wind picks up and transports sediment. Generally, erosion is more severe on steep slopes than on gentle slopes. It's also more severe in areas where there is little vegetation. Under normal conditions, a balance between soil production and soil erosion often is maintained. This means that soil forms at about the same rate as it erodes. However, humans sometimes cause erosion to occur faster than new soil can form. One example is when people remove ground cover. Ground cover is vegetation that covers the soil and protects it from erosion. When vegetation is cleared, as shown in **Figure 16,** soil erosion often increases.

Trees protect the soil from erosion in forested regions.

When forest is removed, soil erodes rapidly.

Figure 17 Tropical rain forests often are cleared by burning. **Explain** *how this can increase soil erosion.*

Agricultural Cultivation Soil erosion is a serious problem for agriculture. Topsoil contains many nutrients, holds water well, and has a porous structure that is good for plant growth. If topsoil is eroded, the quality of the soil is reduced. For example, plants need nutrients to grow. Each year, nutrients are both added to the soil and removed from the soil. The difference between the amount of nutrients added and the amount of nutrients removed is called the nutrient balance. If topsoil erodes rapidly, the nutrient balance might be negative. Farmers might have to use more fertilizer to compensate for the nutrient loss. In addition, the remaining soil might not have the same open structure and water-holding ability that topsoil does.

Forest Harvesting When forests are removed, soil is exposed and erosion increases. This creates severe problems in many parts of the world, but tropical regions are especially at risk. Each year, thousands of square kilometers of tropical rain forest are cleared for lumber, farming, and grazing, as shown in **Figure 17.** Soils in tropical rain forests appear rich in nutrients but are almost infertile below the first few centimeters. The soil is useful to farmers for only a few years before the topsoil is gone. Farmers then clear new land, repeating the process and increasing the damage to the soil.

Overgrazing In most places, land can be grazed with little damage to soil. However, overgrazing can increase soil erosion. In some arid regions of the world, sheep and cattle raised for food are grazed on grasses until almost no ground cover remains to protect the soil. When natural vegetation is removed from land that receives little rain, plants are slow to grow back. Without protection, soil is carried away by wind, and the moisture in the soil evaporates.

INTEGRATE
Career

Soil Scientist Elvia Niebla is a soil scientist at the U.S. Environmental Protection Agency (EPA). Soil scientists at the EPA work to reduce soil erosion and pollution. Niebla's research even helped keep hamburgers safe to eat. How? In a report for the EPA, she explained how meat can be contaminated when cattle graze on polluted soil.

LA.B.2.3.4

LA.C.3.3.3

Topic: Land Use
Visit fl6.msscience.com for Web links to information about how land use affects Earth's soil and about measures taken to reduce the impact.

Activity Debate with classmates about the best ways to protect rich farmland. Consider advantages and disadvantages of each method.

Excess Sediment If soil erosion is severe, sediment can damage the environment. Severe erosion sometimes occurs where land is exposed. Examples might include strip-mined areas or large construction sites. Eroded soil is moved to a new location where it is deposited. If the sediment is deposited in a stream, as shown in **Figure 18,** the stream channel might fill.

Figure 18 Erosion from exposed land can cause streams to fill with excessive amounts of sediment.

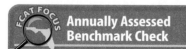
Annually Assessed Benchmark Check

SC.D.1.3.4 Why is it important to leave vegetation on crop fields after harvesting the crop?

Figure 19 No-till farming decreases soil erosion because fields are not plowed.

Preventing Soil Erosion

Each year more than 1.5 billion metric tons of soil are eroded in the United States. Soil is a natural resource that must be monitored, managed, and protected. People can do several things to conserve soil.

Manage Crops All over the world, farmers work to slow soil erosion. They plant shelter belts of trees to break the force of the wind and plant crops to cover the ground after the main harvest. In dry areas, instead of plowing under crops, many farmers graze animals on the vegetation. Proper grazing management can maintain vegetation and reduce soil erosion.

In recent years, many farmers have begun to practice no-till farming. Normally, farmers till or plow their fields one or more times each year. Using **no-till farming,** seen in **Figure 19,** farmers leave plant stalks in the field over the winter months. At the next planting, they seed crops without destroying these stalks and without plowing the soil. Farm machinery makes a narrow slot in the soil, and the seed is planted in this slot. No-till farming provides cover for the soil year-round, which reduces water runoff and soil erosion. One study showed that no-till farming can leave as much as 80% of the soil covered by plant residue. The leftover stalks also keep weeds from growing in the fields.

Reading Check *How can farmers reduce soil erosion?*

Reduce Erosion on Slopes On gentle slopes, planting along the natural contours of the land, called **contour farming,** reduces soil erosion. This practice, shown in **Figure 20,** slows the flow of water down the slope and helps prevent the formation of gullies.

Where slopes are steep, terracing often is used. **Terracing** (TER uh sing) is a method in which steep-sided, level topped areas are built onto the sides of steep hills and mountains so that crops can be grown. These terraces reduce runoff by creating flat areas and shorter sections of slope. In the Philippines, Japan, China, and Peru, terraces have been used for centuries.

Reduce Erosion of Exposed Soil A variety of methods are used to control erosion where soil is exposed. During the construction process water is sometimes sprayed onto bare soil to prevent erosion by wind. When construction is complete, topsoil is added in areas where it was removed and trees are planted. At strip mines, water flow can be controlled so that most of the eroded soil is kept from leaving the mine. After mining is complete, the land is reclaimed. This means that steep slopes are flattened and vegetation is planted.

Figure 20 This orchard was planted along the natural contours of the land.
Summarize *the benefits of using contour farming on slopes.*

section 3 review

Summary

Soil—An Important Resource

- Soil erosion is a serious problem because topsoil is removed from the land.

Causes and Effects of Soil Erosion

- Soil erosion occurs rapidly on steep slopes and areas that are not covered by vegetation.
- The quality of farmland is reduced when soil erosion occurs.

Preventing Soil Erosion

- Farmers reduce erosion by planting shelter belts, using no-till farming, and planting cover crops after harvesting.
- Contour farming and terracing are used to control erosion on slopes.

Self Check

1. **Explain** why soil is important.
2. **Explain** how soil erosion damages soil.
3. **Describe** no-till farming. `SC.D.1.3.4`
4. **Explain** how overgrazing increases soil erosion. `SC.D.1.3.4`
5. **Think Critically** How does contour farming help water soak into the ground?

Applying Skills

6. **Communicate** Do research to learn about the different methods that builders use to reduce soil erosion during construction. Write a newspaper article describing how soil erosion at large construction sites is being controlled in your area.

Benchmark—SC.D.1.3.1: The student knows that mechanical and chemical activities shape and reshape the Earth's land surface . . . ; **SC.D.1.3.5; SC.H.1.3.4; SC.H.1.3.5; SC.H.1.3.7**

LAB

Design Your Own

WEATHERING CHALK

Goals

- **Design** experiments to evaluate the effects of acidity, surface area, and temperature on the rate of chemical weathering of chalk.
- **Describe** factors that affect chemical weathering.
- **Explain** how the chemical weathering of chalk is similar to the chemical weathering of rocks.

Possible Materials

pieces of chalk (6)
250-mL beakers (2)
metric ruler
water
white vinegar (100 mL)
hot plate
250-mL graduated cylinder
computer probe for
    temperature

Safety Precautions

Complete a safety worksheet before you begin.

WARNING: *When mixing acid and water, always add acid to water.*

▶ Real-World Problem

Chalk is a type of limestone made of the shells of microscopic organisms. The famous White Cliffs of Dover, England, are made up of chalk. This lab will help you understand how chalk can be chemically weathered. How can you simulate chemical weathering of chalk?

▶ Form a Hypothesis

How do you think acidity, surface area, and temperature affect the rate of chemical weathering of chalk? What happens to chalk in water? What happens to chalk in acid (vinegar)? How will the size of the chalk pieces affect the rate of weathering? What will happen if you heat the acid? Make hypotheses that explain your predictions.

Test Your Hypothesis

Make a Plan

1. **Develop** hypotheses about the effects of acidity, surface area, and temperature on the rate of chemical weathering.

2. Decide how to test your first hypothesis. List the steps needed to test the hypothesis.

3. Repeat step 2 for your other two hypotheses.

4. **Design** data tables in your Science Journal. Make one for acidity, one for surface area, and one for temperature.

5. **Identify** what remains constant in your experiment and what varies. Change only one variable in each procedure.

6. **Summarize** your data in a graph. Decide from reading the Science Skill Handbook which type of graph to use.

Follow Your Plan

1. Make sure your teacher approves your plan before you start.

2. Carry out the three experiments as planned.

3. While you are conducting the experiments, record your observations and complete the data tables in your Science Journal.

4. Graph your data to show how each variable affected the rate of weathering.

Analyze Your Data

1. **Analyze** your graph to find out which substance—water or acid—weathered the chalk more quickly. Was your hypothesis supported by your data?

2. **Infer** from your data whether the amount of surface area makes a difference in the rate of chemical weathering. Explain.

Conclude and Apply

1. **Explain** how the chalk was chemically weathered.

2. How does heat affect the rate of chemical weathering?

3. What does this imply about weathering in the tropics and in polar regions?

*C*ommunicating Your Data

Compare your results with those of your classmates. How were your data similar? How were they different? **For more help, refer to the** Science Skill Handbook.

Science and Language Arts

Landscape, History, and the Pueblo Imagination

by Leslie Marmon Silko

Leslie Marmon Silko, a woman of Pueblo, Hispanic, and American heritage, explains what ancient Pueblo people believed about the circle of life on Earth.

You see that after a thing is dead, it dries up. It might take weeks or years, but eventually if you touch the thing, it crumbles under your fingers. It goes back to dust. The soul of the thing has long since departed. With the plants and wild game the soul may have already been borne back into bones and blood or thick green stalk and leaves. Nothing is wasted. What cannot be eaten by people or in some way used must then be left where other living creatures may benefit. What domestic animals or wild scavengers can't eat will be fed to the plants. The plants feed on the dust of these few remains.

. . . Corn cobs and husks, the rinds and stalks and animal bones were not regarded by the ancient people as filth or garbage. The remains were merely resting at a mid-point in their journey back to dust. . . .

The dead become dust . . . . The ancient Pueblo people called the earth the Mother Creator of all things in this world. Her sister, the Corn mother, occasionally merges with her because all . . . green life rises out of the depths of the earth.

Rocks and clay . . . become what they once were. Dust.

A rock shares this fate with us and with animals and plants as well.

Understanding Literature

Repetition The recurrence of sounds, words, or phrases is called repetition. What is Silko's purpose of the repeated use of the word *dust*? `LA.E.1.3.3`

Respond to the Reading

1. What one word is repeated throughout this passage?
2. What effect does the repetition of this word have on the reader?
3. **Linking Science and Writing** Using repetition, write a one-page paper on how to practice a type of soil conservation. `LA.B.2.3.1`

INTEGRATE Earth Science This chapter discusses how weathered rocks and mineral fragments combine with organic matter to make soil. Silko's writing explains how the ancient Pueblo people understood that all living matter returns to the earth, or becomes dust. Lines such as "green life rises out of the depths of the earth," show that the Pueblo people understood that the earth, or rocks and mineral fragments, must combine with living matter in order to make soil and support plant life.

Reviewing Main Ideas

Section 1 Weathering

1. Weathering helps to shape Earth's surface.

2. Mechanical weathering breaks apart rock without changing its chemical composition. Plant roots, animals, and ice wedging are agents of mechanical weathering.

3. Chemical weathering changes the chemical composition of rocks. Natural acids and oxygen in the air can cause chemical weathering.

Section 2 The Nature of Soil

1. Soil is a mixture of rock and mineral fragments, organic matter, air, and water.

2. A soil profile contains different layers that are called horizons.

3. Climate, parent rock, slope of the land, type of vegetation, and the time that rock has been weathering are factors that affect the development of soil.

Section 3 Soil Erosion

1. Soil is eroded when it is moved to a new location by wind or water.

2. Human activities can increase the rate of soil erosion.

3. Windbreaks, no-till farming, contour farming, and terracing reduce soil erosion on farm fields.

Visualizing Main Ideas

Copy and complete the following concept map about weathering.

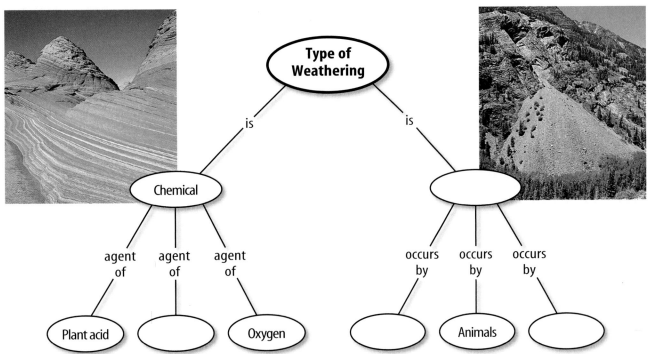

Using Vocabulary

※ chemical weathering
p. 327

climate p. 328

contour farming p. 341

horizon p. 332

humus p. 332

ice wedging p. 326

leaching p. 333

litter p. 333

mechanical weathering
p. 325

no-till farming p. 340

oxidation p. 328

soil p. 330

soil profile p. 332

terracing p. 341

※ weathering p. 324

※ FCAT Vocabulary

Fill in the blanks with the correct vocabulary word or words.

1. _____ changes the composition of rock.

2. _____ forms from organic matter such as leaves and roots.

3. The horizons of a soil make up the _____.

4. _____ transports material to the B horizon.

5. _____ occurs when many materials containing iron are exposed to oxygen and water.

6. _____ means that crops are planted along the natural contours of the land.

7. _____ is the pattern of weather that occurs in a particular area for many years.

Checking Concepts

Choose the word or phrase that best answers the question.

8. Which of the following can be caused by acids produced by plant roots? SC.D.1.3.4
   A) soil erosion
   B) oxidation
   C) mechanical weathering
   D) chemical weathering

Use the graph below to answer question 9.

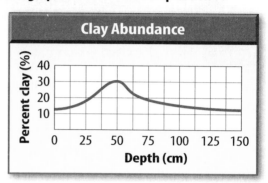

9. The above graph shows the percentage of clay in a soil profile at varying depths. Which depth has the highest amount of clay?
   A) 25 cm   C) 50 cm
   B) 150 cm   D) 100 cm

10. Which of the following is an agent of mechanical weathering? SC.D.1.3.4
    A) animal burrowing
    B) carbonic acid
    C) leaching
    D) oxidation

11. In which region is chemical weathering most rapid? SC.D.1.3.1
    A) cold, dry   C) warm, moist
    B) cold, moist   D) warm, dry

12. What is a mixture of rock and mineral fragments, organic matter, air, and water called?
    A) soil   C) horizon
    B) limestone   D) clay

13. What is organic matter in soil?
    A) leaching   C) horizon
    B) humus   D) profile

14. What is done to reduce soil erosion on steep slopes?
    A) no-till farming
    B) contour farming
    C) terracing
    D) grazing

Thinking Critically

15. Predict which type of weathering—mechanical or chemical—you would expect to have a greater effect in a polar region. Explain.
SC.D.1.3.5

16. Recognize Cause and Effect How does soil erosion reduce the quality of soil?

17. Concept Map Copy and complete the concept map about layers in soil.

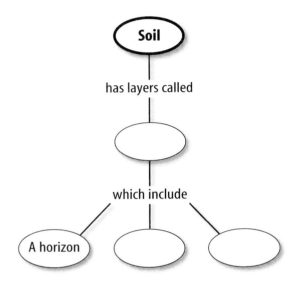

18. Recognize Cause and Effect Why do rows of trees along the edges of farm fields reduce wind erosion of soil?
SC.D.1.3.4

19. Form a Hypothesis A pile of boulders lies at the base of a high-mountain cliff. Form a hypothesis explaining how the pile of rock might have formed.
SC.D.1.3.1

20. Test a Hypothesis How would you test your hypothesis from question 19?

21. Identify a Question Many scientists are conducting research to learn more about how soil erosion occurs and how it can be reduced. Write a question about soil erosion that you would like to research. With your teacher's help, carry out an investigation to answer your question.

Performance Activities

22. Design a Landscape Find a slope in your area that might benefit from erosion maintenance. Develop a plan for reducing erosion on this slope. Make a map showing your plan.

23. Describing Peds Natural clumps of soil are called peds. Collect a large sample of topsoil. Describe the shape of the peds. Sketch the peds in your Science Journal.

Applying Math

Use the illustration below to answer questions 24–26.

24. Fertilizer Nutrients A bag of fertilizer is labeled to list the nutrients as three numbers. The numbers represent the percentages of nitrogen, phosphate, and potash in that order. What are the percentages of these nutrients for a fertilizer with the following information on the label: 5-10-10?
MA.A.3.3.2

25. Fertilizer Ratio The fertilizer ratio tells you the proportions of the different nutrients in a fertilizer. To find the fertilizer ratio, divide each nutrient value by the lowest value. Calculate the fertilizer ratio for the fertilizer in question 24.
MA.A.3.3.2

26. Relative Amounts of Nutrients Which nutrient is least abundant in the fertilizer? Which nutrients are most abundant? How many times more potash does the fertilizer contain than nitrogen?
MA.A.3.3.2

 The assessed Florida Benchmark appears above each question.
Record your answers on the answer sheet provided by your teacher or on a sheet of paper.

Multiple Choice

SC.D.1.3.1

1 How does the soil profile shown below differ from the soil profile in most deserts?

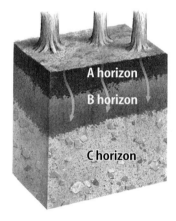

A horizon
B horizon
C horizon

A. In a desert, the A horizon is likely to be much thinner.

B. In a desert, the B horizon is likely to contain more humus.

C. In a desert, the A horizon is likely to be thicker than the C horizon.

D. In a desert, the B horizon is likely to be thinner than the A horizon.

SC.D.1.3.1

2 If an iron-containing mineral is exposed to rain, a rust-like material forms on its surface. Which **best** explains this?

F. chemical weathering involving carbon dioxide and water

G. chemical weathering involving oxygen and water

H. mechanical weathering caused by strong winds

I. mechanical weathering caused by rain

SC.D.1.3.1

3 Which area is likely to be **most** affected by soil erosion?

A. a steep slope after a fire burned all the vegetation

B. a section of low-elevation tropical rainforest

C. a meadow with several kinds of grass

D. a hillside that has been terrace-farmed

SC.D.1.3.1

4 Which statue is likely to be affected the **most** by chemical weathering?

F. a marble statue in a cool, dry climate

G. a granite statue in a cool, dry climate

H. a marble statue in a warm, wet climate

I. a granite statue in a warm, wet climate

SC.D.1.3.4

5 Which method of reducing soil erosion on hillsides is shown in the diagram below?

A. terracing

B. shelter belts

C. no-till farming

D. contour farming

SC.D.1.3.4

6 What is the main reason that plants benefit from the presence of decaying organic material in the soil?

F. It adds nutrients to the soil.

G. It encourages mechanical weathering.

H. It speeds the rate of evaporation from soil.

I. It protects the plants from harmful insects.

Gridded Response

SC.A.1.3.1

7 The table below shows the percentages of sand, silt, and clay in each horizon of a soil profile.

Texture Data for a Soil Profile			
Horizon	**Percent**		
	Sand	**Silt**	**Clay**
A	16.2	54.4	29.4
B	10.5	50.2	39.3
C	31.4	48.4	20.2

Particles of clay have a diameter of less than 0.002 mm, particles of silt have a diameter between 0.002 mm and 0.05 mm, and particles of sand have a diameter between 0.05 mm and 2 mm. What percentage of the soil in Horizon C is composed of particles with a diameter of less than 0.05 mm?

Short Response

SC.D.1.3.4

8 Describe how plants and animals can contribute to the mechanical weathering of rock.

Extended Response

SC.D.1.3.4

9 A farmer tried a new method of farming in a cornfield. The table shows how the farmer treated the field each season.

Work Done Each Season		
Fall/Winter	**Spring**	**Summer**
Harvested crops; left stalks in field	Planted seeds without plowing soil	Watered and fertilized plants when necessary

PART A Explain how this method of farming helps decrease erosion.

PART B Describe two ways this practice can help farmers in the long term.

FCAT Tip

Write Clearly Write your explanations neatly in clear, concise language. Use only the space provided in the Sample Answer Book.

chapter

12

Sunshine State Standards—SC.D.1: The student recognizes that processes in the lithosphere, atmosphere, hydrosphere, and biosphere interact to shape the Earth.

Water Erosion and Deposition

Nature's Sculptor

Bryce Canyon National Park in Utah is home to the Hoodoos—tall, column-like formations. They were made by one of the most powerful forces on Earth—moving water. In this chapter you will learn how moving water shapes Earth's surface.

Science Journal What might have formed the narrowing of each Hoodoo? What will happen if this narrowing continues?

Start-Up Activities

 **SC.D.1.3.1**
SC.H.1.3.5

Model How Erosion Works

Moving water has great energy. Sometimes rainwater falls softly and soaks slowly into soil. Other times it rushes down a slope with tremendous force and carries away valuable topsoil. What determines whether rain soaks into the ground or runs off and wears away the surface?

1. Complete a safety worksheet.

2. Place an aluminum pie pan on your desktop.

3. Put a pile of dry soil about 7 cm high into the pan.

4. Slowly drip water from a dropper onto the pile and observe what happens next.

5. Drip the water faster and continue to observe what happens.

6. Repeat steps 1 through 4, but this time change the slope of the hill by increasing the central pile. Start again with dry soil.

7. **Think Critically** In your Science Journal, write about the effect the water had on the different slopes.

FOLDABLES™
Study Organizer

Characteristics of Surface Water, Groundwater, and Shoreline Water Make the following Foldable to help you identify the main concepts relating to surface water, groundwater, and shoreline water.

LA.A.1.3.4

STEP 1 **Fold** the top of a vertical piece of paper down and the bottom up to divide the paper into thirds.

STEP 2 **Turn** the paper horizontally; **unfold and label** the three columns as shown.

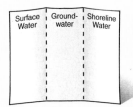

Read for Main Ideas As you read the chapter, list the concepts relating to surface water, groundwater, and shoreline water.

 **Preview this chapter's content and activities at** fl6.msscience.com

Benchmarks—**SC.D.1.3.1 (pp. 352–362):** The student knows that mechanical and chemical activities shape and reshape the Earth's land surface by eroding rock and soil in some areas and depositing them in other areas, sometimes in seasonal layers; **SC.D.1.3.5 (pp. 352–362):** The student understands concepts of time and size relating to the interaction of Earth's processes ....

Also covers: **SC.D.1.3.3 (pp. 352–362), SC.D.1.3.4 Annually Assessed (p. 353), SC.H.1.3.5 Annually Assessed (p. 361), SC.H.1.3.6 (p. 353), SC.H.2.3.1 (pp. 352–362)**

section 1

Surface Water

as you read

What **You'll Learn**

- **Identify** the causes of runoff.
- **Compare** rill, gully, sheet, and stream erosion.
- **Identify** three different stages of stream development.
- **Explain** how alluvial fans and deltas form.

Why **It's Important**

Runoff and streams shape Earth's surface.

Review Vocabulary

✹ **erosion:** transport of surface materials by agents such as gravity, wind, water, or glaciers

New Vocabulary

- runoff
- ✹ erosion
- channel
- drainage basin
- meander
- ✹ deposition

✹ FCAT Vocabulary

Runoff

Picture this. You pour a glass of milk and it overflows, spilling onto the table. You grab a towel to clean up the mess, but the milk is already running through a crack in the table, over the edge, and onto the floor. This is similar to what happens to rainwater when it falls to Earth. Some rainwater soaks into the ground and some evaporates, turning into a gas. The rainwater that doesn't soak into the ground or evaporate runs over the ground. Eventually, it enters streams, lakes, or the ocean. Water that doesn't soak into the ground or evaporate but instead flows across Earth's surface is called **runoff.** If you've ever spilled milk while pouring it, you've experienced something similar to runoff.

Factors Affecting Runoff What determines whether rain soaks into the ground or runs off? The amount of rain and the length of time it falls are two factors that affect runoff. Light rain falling over several hours probably will have time to soak into the ground. Heavy rain falling in less than an hour or so will run off because it cannot soak in fast enough, or it can't soak in because the ground cannot hold any more water.

Figure 1 In areas with gentle slopes and vegetation, little runoff and erosion take place. Lack of vegetation has led to severe soil erosion in some areas.

Other Factors Another factor that affects the amount of runoff is the steepness, or slope, of the land. Gravity causes water to move down slopes. Water moves rapidly down steep slopes so it has little chance to soak into the ground. Water moves more slowly down gentle slopes and across flat areas. Slower movement allows water more time to soak into the ground.

Vegetation, such as grass and trees, also affects the amount of runoff. Just like milk running off the table, water will run off smooth surfaces that have little or no vegetation. Imagine a tablecloth on the table. What would happen to the milk then? Runoff slows down when it flows around plants. Slower-moving water has a greater chance to sink into the ground. By slowing down runoff, plants and their roots help prevent soil from being carried away. Large amounts of soil may be carried away in areas that lack vegetation, as shown in **Figure 1.**

INTEGRATE Physics

Effects of Gravity When you lie on the ground and feel as if you are being held in place, you are experiencing the effects of gravity. Gravity is an attracting force that all objects have for one another. The greater the mass of an object is, the greater its force of gravity is. Because Earth has a much greater mass than any of the objects on it, Earth's gravitational force pulls objects toward its center. Water runs downhill because of Earth's gravitational pull. When water begins to run down a slope, it picks up speed. As its speed increases, so does its energy. Fast-moving water, shown in **Figure 2,** carries more soil than slow-moving water does.

INTEGRATE Career

Conservation Farmers sometimes have to farm on some kind of slope. The steeper the slope, the more erosion will occur. Not only is slope an important factor, but other factors have to be considered as well. The Natural Resources Conservation Service, a government agency, studies these factors to determine soil loss from a given area. Find out what other factors this agency uses to determine soil loss.

Figure 2 During floods, the high volume of fast-moving water erodes large amounts of soil.

Figure 3 Heavy rains can remove large amounts of sediment, forming deep gullies in the side of a slope.

Water Erosion

Suppose you and several friends walk the same way to school each day through a field or an empty lot. You always walk in the same footsteps as you did the day before. After a few weeks, you've worn a path through the field. When water travels down the same slope time after time, it also wears a path. **Erosion** is a combination of natural processes that wears away surface materials and moves them from one place to another.

Rill and Gully Erosion You may have noticed a groove or small ditch on the side of a slope that was left behind by running water. This is evidence of rill erosion. Rill erosion begins when a small stream forms during a heavy rain. As this stream flows along, it has enough energy to erode and carry away soil. Water moving down the same path creates a groove, called a **channel,** on the slope where the water eroded the soil. If water frequently flows in the same channel, rill erosion may change over time into another type of erosion called gully erosion.

During gully erosion, a rill channel becomes broader and deeper. **Figure 3** shows gullies that were formed when water carried away large amounts of soil.

Sheet Erosion Water often erodes without being in a channel. Rainwater that begins to run off during a rainstorm often flows as thin, broad sheets before forming rills and streams. For example, when it rains over an area, the rainwater accumulates until it eventually begins moving down a slope as a sheet, like the water flowing off the hood of the car in **Figure 4.** Water also can flow as sheets if it breaks out of its channel.

Figure 4 When water accumulates, it can flow in sheets like the water seen flowing over the hood of this car.

Floodwaters spilling out of a river can flow as sheets over the surrounding flatlands. Streams flowing out of mountains fan out and may flow as sheets away from the foot of the mountain. Sheet erosion occurs when water that is flowing as sheets picks up and carries away sediments.

Stream Erosion Sometimes water continues to flow along a low place it has formed. As the water in a stream moves along, it picks up sediments from the bottom and sides of its channel. By this process, a stream channel becomes deeper and wider.

The sediment that a stream carries is called its load. Water picks up and carries some of the lightweight sediments, called the suspended load. Larger, heavy particles called the bed load just roll along the bottom of the stream channel, as shown in **Figure 5.** Over time, water can even dissolve some rocks and carry them away in solution. The different-sized sediments scrape against the bottom and sides of the channel like a piece of sandpaper. Gradually, these sediments can wear away the rock by a process called abrasion.

Figure 5 This cross section of a stream channel shows the location of the suspended load and the bed load.
Describe *how the stream carries dissolved material.*

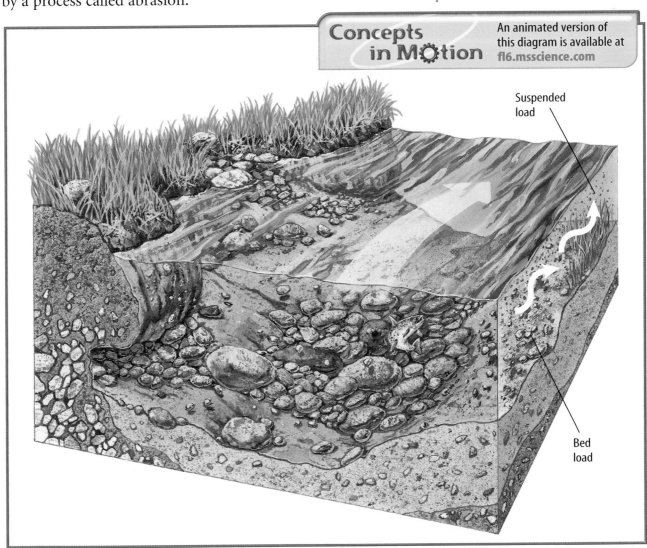

Concepts in M⊙tion

An animated version of this diagram is available at fl6.msscience.com

Suspended load

Bed load

River System Development

Have you spent time near a river or stream in your community? Each day, millions of liters of water probably flow through that stream. Where does all the water come from? Where is it flowing to?

River Systems Streams are parts of river systems. The water comes from rills, gullies, and smaller streams located upstream. Just as the tree in **Figure 6** is a system containing twigs, branches, and a trunk, a river system also has many parts. Runoff enters small streams, which join together to form larger streams. Larger streams come together to form rivers. Rivers grow and carry more water as more streams join.

Drainage Basins A **drainage basin** is the area of land from which a stream or river collects runoff. Compare a drainage basin to a bathtub. Water that collects in a bathtub flows toward one location—the drain. Likewise, all of the water in a river system eventually flows to one location—the main river, or trunk. The largest drainage basin in the United States is the Mississippi River drainage basin, shown in **Figure 6.**

Reading Check *What is a drainage basin?*

Figure 6 River systems can be compared with the structure of a tree.

The system of twigs, branches, and trunk that make up a tree is similar to the system of streams and rivers that make up a river system.

A large number of the streams and rivers in the United States are part of the Mississippi River drainage basin, or watershed.

Identify *What river represents the trunk of this system?*

Stages of Stream Development

Streams come in a variety of forms. Some are narrow and swift-moving, and others are wide and slow-moving. Streams differ because they are in different stages of development. These stages depend on the slope of the ground over which the stream flows. Streams are classified as young, mature, or old. **Figure 8** shows how the stages come together to form a river system.

The names of the stages of development aren't always related to the actual age of a river. The New River in West Virginia is one of the oldest rivers in North America. However, it has a steep valley and flows swiftly. As a result, it is classified as a young stream.

Young Streams A stream that flows swiftly through a steep valley is a young stream. A young stream may have white-water rapids and waterfalls. Water flowing through a steep channel with a rough bottom has a high level of energy and erodes the stream bottom faster than its sides.

Mature Streams The next stage in the development of a stream is the mature stage. A mature stream flows more smoothly through its valley. Over time, most of the rocks in the streambed that cause waterfalls and rapids are eroded by running water and the sediments it carries.

Erosion is no longer concentrated on the bottom in a mature stream. A mature stream starts to erode more along its sides, and curves develop. These curves form because the speed of the water changes throughout the width of the channel.

Water in a shallow area of a stream moves slower because it drags along the bottom. In the deeper part of the channel, the water flows faster. If the deep part of the channel is next to one side of the river, water will erode that side and form a slight curve. Over time, the curve grows to become a broad arc called a **meander** (mee AN dur), as shown in **Figure 7.**

The broad, flat valley floor formed by a meandering stream is called a floodplain. When a stream floods, it often will cover part or all of the floodplain.

Figure 7 A meander is a broad bend in a river or stream. As time passes, erosion of the outer bank increases the bend.

Figure 8

Although no two streams are exactly alike, all go through three main stages—young, mature, and old—as they flow from higher to lower ground. A young stream, below, surging over steep terrain, moves rapidly. In a less steep landscape, right, a mature stream flows more smoothly. On nearly level ground, the stream—considered old—winds leisurely through its valley. The various stages of a stream's development are illustrated here.

Waterfall

Rapids

A A young stream begins at a source—here, a melting mountain glacier. From its source, the stream flows swiftly downhill, cutting a narrow valley.

B A mature stream flows smoothly through its valley. Mature streams often develop broad curves called meanders.

C Old streams flow through broad, flat floodplains. Near its mouth, the stream gradually drops its load of silt. This sediment forms a delta, an area of flat, fertile land extending into the ocean.

Oxbow lake

Old Streams   The last stage in the development of a stream is the old stage. An old stream flows smoothly through a broad, flat floodplain that it has deposited. South of St. Louis, Missouri, the lower Mississippi River is in the old stage.

Major river systems, such as the Mississippi River, usually contain streams in all stages of development. In the upstream portion of a river system, you find whitewater streams moving swiftly down mountains and hills. At the bottom of mountains and hills, you find streams that start to meander and are in the mature stage of development. These streams meet at the trunk of the drainage basin and form a major river.

 **Reading Check**   *How do old streams differ from young streams?*

Too Much Water

Sometimes heavy rains or a sudden melting of snow can cause large amounts of water to enter a river system. What happens when a river system has too much water in it? The water needs to go somewhere, and out and over the banks is the only choice. A river that overflows its banks can bring disaster by flooding homes or washing away bridges or crops.

Dams and levees are built in an attempt to prevent this type of flooding. A dam is built to control the water flow downstream. It may be built of soil, sand, or steel and concrete. Levees are mounds of earth that are built along the sides of a river. Dams and levees are built to prevent rivers from overflowing their banks. Unfortunately, they do not stop the water when flooding is great. This was the case in 1993 when heavy rains caused the Mississippi River to flood parts of nine midwestern states. Flooding resulted in billions of dollars in property damage. **Figure 9** shows some of the damage caused by this flood.

As you have seen, floods can cause great amounts of damage. But at certain times in Earth's past, great floods have completely changed the surface of Earth in a large region. Such floods are called catastrophic floods.

Figure 9   Flooding causes problems for people who live along major rivers. Floodwater broke through a levee during the Mississippi River flooding in 1993.

Figure 10 The Channeled Scablands formed when Lake Missoula drained catastrophically.

These channels were formed by the floodwaters.

Catastrophic Floods During Earth's long history, many catastrophic floods have dramatically changed the face of the surrounding area. One catastrophic flood formed the Channeled Scablands in eastern Washington State, shown above in **Figure 10.** A vast lake named Lake Missoula covered much of western Montana. A natural dam of ice formed this lake. As the dam melted or was eroded away, tremendous amounts of water suddenly escaped through what is now the state of Idaho into Washington. In a short period of time, the floodwater removed overlying soil and carved channels into the underlying rock, some as deep as 50 m. Flooding occurred several more times as the lake refilled with water and the dam broke loose again. Scientists say the last such flood occurred about 13,000 years ago.

Deposition by Surface Water

As water moves throughout a river system, it loses some of its energy of motion and slows down. The water can no longer carry some of its sediment. As a result, it drops the sediment to the bottom of the stream. The dropping of sediment when water or another agent of erosion loses energy is called **deposition.**

Some stream sediment is carried only a short distance. In fact, sediment often is deposited within the stream channel. Other stream sediment is carried great distances before being deposited. Sediment picked up when rill and gully erosion occur is an example of this. Water usually has a lot of energy as it moves down a steep slope. When water begins flowing on a level surface, it slows, loses energy, and deposits its sediment. Water also loses energy and deposits sediment when it empties into an ocean or lake.

SC.D.1.3.5

Mini LAB

Observing Runoff Collection

Procedure
1. Complete a safety worksheet.
2. Put a plastic **graduated cylinder** into a **heavy drinking glass** and place the glass in the **sink.**
3. Fill a plastic **sprinkling can** with **water.**
4. Hold the sprinkling can one-half meter above the sink and sprinkle water onto the cylinder for 30 s.
5. Record the amount of water in the cylinder.
6. After emptying the cylinder, place a **plastic funnel** into the cylinder and sprinkle again for 30 s.
7. Record the amount of water in the cylinder.

Analysis
Explain how a small amount of rain falling on a drainage basin can have a big effect on a river or stream.

Figure 11 This satellite image of the Nile River Delta in Egypt shows the typical triangular shape. The green color shows areas of vegetation.

Agriculture is important on the Nile Delta.

Deltas and Fans Sediment that is deposited as water empties into an ocean or lake forms a triangular, or fan-shaped, deposit called a delta, shown in **Figure 11.** When the river waters empty from a mountain valley onto an open plain, the deposit is called an alluvial (uh LEW vee ul) fan. The Mississippi River exemplifies the topics presented in this section. Runoff causes rill and gully erosion. Sediment is picked up and carried into the larger streams that flow into the Mississippi River. As the Mississippi River flows, it cuts into its banks and picks up more sediment. Where the land is flat, the river deposits some of its sediment in its own channel. As the Mississippi enters the Gulf of Mexico, it slows, dropping much of its sediment and forming the Mississippi River delta. In this way, seasonal layers of silt can provide fresh nutrients for vegetation.

section 1 review

Summary

Runoff

- Rainwater that doesn't soak into the ground or evaporate becomes runoff.
- Slope of land and vegetation affect runoff.

Water Erosion

- Water flowing over the same slope causes rills and gullies to form.

River System Development

- A drainage basin is an area of land from which a stream or river collects runoff.

Self Check

1. **Explain** how the slope of an area affects runoff. SC.D.1.3.1
2. **Compare and contrast** rill and gully erosion.
3. **Describe** the three stages of stream development. SC.D.1.3.1
4. **Think Critically** How is a stream's rate of flow related to the amount of erosion it causes? How is it related to the size of the sediments it deposits? SC.D.1.3.5

Applying Skills

5. **Compare and contrast** the formation of deltas and alluvial fans. SC.D.1.3.1

Benchmarks—SC.D.1.3.1 (pp. 363–368): The student knows that mechanical and chemical activities shape and reshape the Earth's land surface by eroding rock and soil in some areas and depositing them in other areas, sometimes in seasonal layers; SC.D.1.3.5 (pp. 364–367): The student understands concepts of time and size relating to the interaction of Earth's processes ....

Also covers: SC.D.1.3.3 (pp. 363–368), SC.H.1.3.5 Annually Assessed (p. 364)

section 2

Groundwater

Groundwater Systems

What would have happened if the spilled milk in Section 1 ran off the table onto a carpeted floor? It probably would have quickly soaked into the carpet. Water that falls on Earth can soak into the ground just like the milk into the carpet.

Water that soaks into the ground becomes part of a system, just as water that stays above ground becomes part of a river system. Soil is made up of many small rock and mineral fragments. These fragments are all touching one another, as shown in **Figure 12,** but some empty space remains between them. Holes, cracks, and crevices exist in the rock underlying the soil. Water that soaks into the ground collects in these pores and empty spaces and becomes part of what is called **groundwater.**

How much of Earth's water do you think is held in the small openings in rock? Scientists estimate that 14 percent of all freshwater on Earth exists as groundwater. This is almost 30 times more water than is contained in all of Earth's lakes and rivers.

Figure 12 Soil has many small, connected pores that are filled with water when soil is wet.

Soil or rock fragment

Pore space

Water

as you read

What You'll Learn

- **Recognize** the importance of groundwater.
- **Describe** the effect that soil and rock permeability have on groundwater movement.
- **Explain** how groundwater dissolves and deposits minerals.

Why It's Important

The groundwater system is an important source of your drinking water.

Review Vocabulary

pore: a small, or minute, opening in rock or soil

New Vocabulary

- groundwater
- permeable
- impermeable
- aquifer
- water table
- spring
- geyser
- cave

Mini LAB

Measuring Pore Space

Procedure 🚫 🌊 📋

1. Use two identical, **clear-plastic containers.**
2. Put 3 cm of **sand** in one container and 3 cm of **gravel** in the other.
3. Pour **water** slowly into the containers and stop when the water just covers the top of the sediment.
4. Record the volume of water used in each.

Analysis
Which substance has more pore space—sand or gravel?

Try at Home

Permeability A groundwater system is similar to a river system. However, instead of having channels that connect different parts of the drainage basin, the groundwater system has connecting pores. Soil and rock are **permeable** (PUR mee uh bul) if the pore spaces are connected and water can pass through them. Sandstone is an example of a permeable rock.

Soil or rock that has many large, connected pores is permeable. Water can pass through it easily. However, if a rock or sediment has few pore spaces or they are not well-connected, then the flow of groundwater is blocked. These materials are **impermeable,** which means that water cannot pass through them. Granite has few or no pore spaces at all. Clay has many small pore spaces, but the spaces are not well-connected.

✓ **Reading Check** *How does water move through permeable rock?*

Groundwater Movement How deep into Earth's crust does groundwater go? **Figure 13** shows a model of a groundwater system. Groundwater keeps going deeper until it reaches a layer of impermeable rock. When this happens, the water stops moving down. As a result, water begins filling up the pores in the rocks above. A layer of permeable rock that lets water move freely is an **aquifer** (AK wuh fur). The area where all of the pores in the rock are filled with water is the zone of saturation. The upper surface of this zone is the **water table.**

Figure 13 A stream's surface level is the water table. Below that is the zone of saturation.

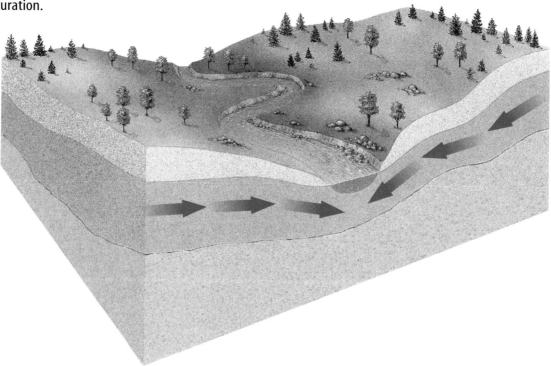

Water Table

Why are the zone of saturation and the water table so important? An average United States resident uses about 626 L of water per day. That's enough to fill nearly two thousand soft-drink cans. Many people get their water from groundwater through wells that have been drilled into the zone of saturation. However, the supply of groundwater is limited. During a drought, the water table drops. This is why you should conserve water.

Applying Math   Calculate Rate of Flow

GROUNDWATER FLOW You and your family are hiking and the temperature is hot. You feel as if you can't walk one step farther. Luckily, relief is in sight. On the side of a nearby hill you see a stream, and you rush to splash some water on your face. Although you probably feel that it's taking you forever to reach the stream, your pace is quick when compared to how long it takes groundwater to flow through the aquifer that feeds the stream. The following problem will give you some idea of just how slowly groundwater flows through an aquifer.

The groundwater flows at a rate of 0.6 m/day. You've run 200 m to get some water from a stream. How long does it take the groundwater in the aquifer to travel the same distance?

Solution

1 *This is what you know:*

- the distance that the groundwater has to travel: $d = 200$ m

- the rate that groundwater flows through the aquifer: $r = 0.6$ m/day

2 *This is what you want to find:*   time $= t$

3 *This is the equation you use:* $r \times t = d$ (rate $\times$ time $=$ distance)

4 *Solve the equation for* t *and then substitute known values:* $t = \dfrac{d}{r} = \dfrac{(200\ \text{m})}{(0.6\ \text{m/day})} = 333.33$ days

Practice Problems

1. The groundwater in an aquifer flows at a rate of 0.5 m/day. How far does the groundwater move in a year? `MA.D.2.3.1`

2. How long does it take groundwater in the above aquifer to move 100 m? `MA.D.2.3.1`

Math Practice | For more practice, visit fl6.msscience.com

Figure 14 The years on the pole show how much the ground level dropped in the San Joaquin Valley, California, between 1925 and 1977.

Figure 15 The pressure of water in a sloping aquifer keeps an artesian well flowing.
Describe *what limits how high water can flow in an artesian well.*

Wells A good well extends deep into the zone of saturation, past the top of the water table. Groundwater flows into the well, and a pump brings it to the surface. Because the water table sometimes drops during very dry seasons, even a good well can go dry. Then time is needed for the water table to rise, either from rainfall or through groundwater flowing from other areas of the aquifer.

Where groundwater is the main source of drinking water, the number of wells and how much water is pumped out are important. If a large factory were built in such a town, the demand on the groundwater supply would be even greater. Even in times of normal rainfall, the wells could go dry if water were taken out at a rate greater than the rate at which it can be replaced.

In areas where too much water is pumped out, the land level can sink from the weight of the sediments above the now-empty pore spaces. **Figure 14** shows what occurred when too much groundwater was removed in a region of California.

One type of well doesn't need a pump to bring water to the surface. An artesian well is a well in which water rises to the surface under pressure. Artesian wells are less common than other types of wells because of the special conditions they require.

As shown in **Figure 15,** the aquifer for an artesian well needs to be located between two impermeable layers that are sloping. Water enters at the high part of the sloping aquifer. The weight of the water in the higher part of the aquifer puts pressure on the water in the lower part. If a well is drilled into the lower part of the aquifer, the pressurized water will flow to the surface. Sometimes, the pressure is great enough to force the water into the air, forming a fountain.

✓ **Reading Check** *How does water move through permeable rock?*

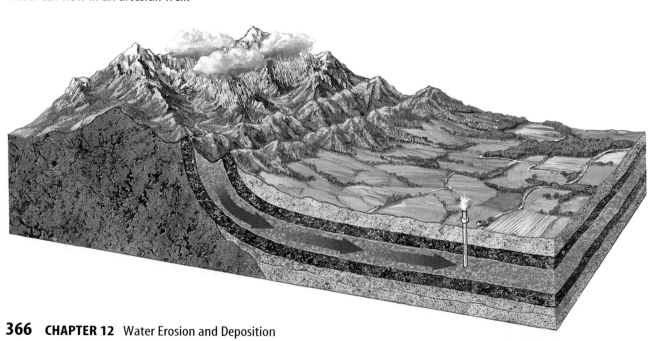

Springs In some places, the water table is so close to Earth's surface that water flows out and forms a **spring.** Springs are found on hillsides or other places where the water table meets a sloping surface. Springs often are used as a source of freshwater.

The water from most springs is a constant, cool temperature because soil and rock are good insulators and protect the groundwater from changes in temperature on Earth's surface. However, in some places, magma rises to within a few kilometers of Earth's surface and heats the surrounding rock. Groundwater that comes in contact with these hot rocks is heated and can come to the surface as a hot spring.

Geysers When water is put into a teakettle to boil, it heats slowly at first. Then some steam starts to come out of the cap on the spout, and suddenly the water starts boiling. The teakettle starts whistling as steam is forced through the cap. A similar process can occur with groundwater. One of the places where groundwater is heated is in Yellowstone National Park in Wyoming. Yellowstone has hot springs and geysers. A **geyser** is a hot spring that erupts periodically, shooting water and steam into the air. Groundwater is heated to high temperatures, causing it to expand underground. This expansion forces some of the water out of the ground, taking the pressure off the remaining water. The remaining water boils quickly, with much of it turning to steam. The steam shoots out of the opening like steam out of a teakettle, forcing the remaining water out with it. Yellowstone's famous geyser, Old Faithful, pictured in **Figure 16,** shoots between 14,000 and 32,000 L of water and steam into the air about once every 80 min.

The Work of Groundwater

Although water is the most powerful agent of erosion on Earth's surface, it also can have a great effect underground. Water mixes with carbon dioxide gas to form a weak acid called carbonic acid. Some of this carbon dioxide is absorbed from the air by rainwater or surface water. Most carbon dioxide is absorbed by groundwater moving through soil. One type of rock that is dissolved easily by this acid is limestone. Acidic groundwater moves through natural cracks and pores in limestone, dissolving the rock. Gradually, the cracks in the limestone enlarge until an underground opening called a **cave** is formed.

LA.B.2.3.1

INTEGRATE Chemistry

Acid Rain Effects Acid rain occurs when gases released by burning oil and coal mix with water in the air. Infer what effect acid rain can have on a statue made of limestone.

Figure 16 Yellowstone's famous geyser, Old Faithful, used to erupt once about every 76 min. An earthquake on January 9, 1998, slowed Old Faithful's "clock" by 4 min to an average of one eruption about every 80 min. The average height of the geyser's water is 40.5 m.

Figure 17 Water dissolves rock to form caves and also deposits material to form spectacular formations, such as these in Carlsbad Caverns in New Mexico.

Cave Formation You've probably seen a picture of the inside of a cave, like the one shown in **Figure 17,** or perhaps you've visited one. Groundwater not only dissolves limestone to make caves, but it also can make deposits on the insides of caves.

Water often drips slowly from cracks in the cave walls and ceilings. This water contains calcium ions dissolved from the limestone. If the water evaporates while hanging from the ceiling of a cave, a deposit of calcium carbonate is left behind. Stalactites form when this happens over and over. Where drops of water fall to the floor of the cave, a stalagmite forms. The words *stalactite* and *stalagmite* come from Greek words that mean "to drip."

Sinkholes If underground rock is dissolved near the surface, a sinkhole may form. A sinkhole is a depression on the surface of the ground that forms when the roof of a cave collapses or when material near the surface dissolves. Sinkholes are common features in places like Florida and Kentucky that have lots of limestone and enough rainfall to keep the groundwater system supplied with water. Sinkholes can cause property damage if they form in a populated area.

In summary, when rain falls and becomes groundwater, it might dissolve limestone and form a cave, erupt from a geyser, or be pumped from a well to be used at your home.

section 2 review

Summary

Groundwater Systems

- Water that soaks into the ground and collects in pore spaces is called groundwater.
- 14 percent of all freshwater on Earth exists as groundwater.
- Groundwater systems have connecting pores.
- The zone of saturation is the area where all pores in the rock are filled with water.

Water Table

- The supply of groundwater is limited.

Self Check

1. **Describe** how the permeability of soil and rocks affects the flow of groundwater.
2. **Describe** why a well might go dry. `SC.D.1.3.3`
3. **Explain** how caves form. `SC.D.1.3.3`
4. **Think Critically** Why would water in wells, geysers, and hot springs contain dissolved materials? `SC.D.1.3.1`

Applying Skills

5. **Compare and contrast** wells, geysers, and hot springs.

Benchmarks—**SC.D.1.3.1 (pp. 369–372):** The student knows that mechanical and chemical activities shape and reshape the Earth's land surface by eroding rock and soil in some areas and depositing them in other areas, sometimes in seasonal layers; **SC.D.1.3.5 (pp. 369–372):** The student understands concepts of time and size relating to the interaction of Earth's processes ....

Also covers: **SC.D.1.3.3 (pp. 369–372), SC.H.1.3.4 Annually Assessed (p. 373), SC.H.1.3.5 Annually Assessed (pp. 374–375)**

section

3

Ocean Shoreline

The Shore

Picture yourself sitting on a beautiful, sandy beach like the one shown in **Figure 18.** Nearby, palm trees sway in the breeze. Children play in the quiet waves lapping at the water's edge. It's hard to imagine a place more peaceful. Now, picture yourself sitting along another shore. You're on a high cliff watching waves crash onto boulders far below. Both of these places are shorelines. An ocean shoreline is where land meets the ocean.

The two shorelines just described are different, even though both experience surface waves, tides, and currents. These actions cause shorelines to change constantly. Sometimes you can see these changes from hour to hour. Why are shorelines so different? You'll understand why they look different when you learn about the forces that shape shorelines.

Figure 18 Waves, tides, and currents cause shorelines to change constantly. Waves approaching the shoreline at an angle create a longshore current.

as you read

What **You'll Learn**

- **Identify** the different causes of shoreline erosion.
- **Compare and contrast** different types of shorelines.
- **Describe** some origins of sand.

Why **It's Important**

Constantly changing shorelines impact the people who live and work by them.

Review Vocabulary

✳ **spring tide:** the tide of increased range that occurs twice monthly at the new and full phases of the Moon

New Vocabulary

- longshore current
- beach

✳ FCAT Vocabulary

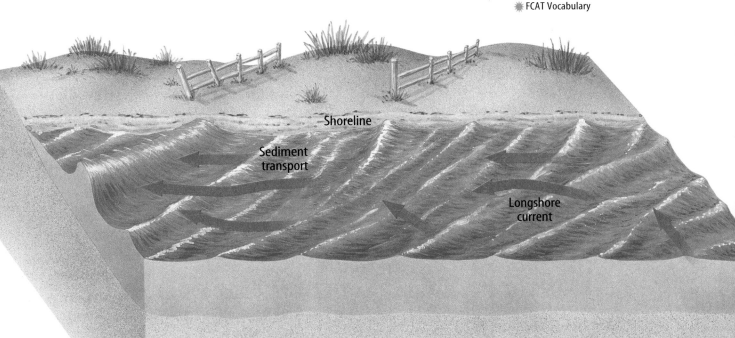

Shoreline

Sediment transport

Longshore current

369

Shoreline Forces When waves constantly pound against the shore, they break rocks into smaller and smaller pieces. Currents move many metric tons of sediment along the shoreline. The sediment grains grind against each other like sandpaper. The tide goes out carrying sediment to deeper water. When the tide returns, it brings new sediment with it. These forces are always at work, slowly changing the shape of the shoreline. Water is always in motion along the shore.

The three major forces at work on the shoreline are waves, currents, and tides. Winds blowing across the water make waves. Waves, crashing against a shoreline, are a powerful force. They can erode and move large amounts of material in a short time. Waves usually collide with a shore at slight angles. This creates a **longshore current** of water that runs parallel to the shoreline. Longshore currents, shown in **Figure 18,** carry many metric tons of loose sediments and act like rivers of sand in the ocean.

Reading Check *How does a longshore current form?*

Tides create currents that move at right angles to the shore. These are called tidal currents. Outgoing tides carry sediments away from the shore, and incoming tides bring new sediments toward the shore. Tides work with waves to shape shorelines. You've seen the forces that affect all shorelines. Now you will see the differences that make one shore a flat, sandy beach and another shore a steep, rocky cliff.

Figure 19 Along a rocky shore-line, the force of pounding waves breaks rock fragments loose, then grinds them into smaller and smaller pieces.

Rocky Shorelines

Rocks and cliffs are the most common features along rocky shorelines like the one in **Figure 19.** Waves crash against the rocks and cliffs. Sediments in the water grind against the cliffs, slowly wearing the rock away. Then rock fragments broken from the cliffs are ground up by the endless motion of waves. They are transported as sediment by longshore currents.

Softer rocks become eroded before harder rocks do, leaving islands of harder rocks. This takes thousands of years, but remember that the ocean never stops. In a single day, about 14,000 waves crash onto shore.

This Florida beach consists primarily of seashell fragments.

Some Hawaiian beaches are composed of black basalt sand.

Sandy Beaches

Smooth, gently sloping shorelines are different from steep, rocky shorelines. **Beaches,** the main feature of these shorelines, are deposits of sediment that are parallel to the shore.

Beaches can be made from different materials. Some are made of rock fragments from the shoreline. Many beaches consist of grains of quartz, and others consist of seashell fragments. These fragments range in size from stones larger than your hand to fine sand. Sand grains range from 0.06 mm to 2 mm in diameter. Why do many beaches have particles of this size? Waves break rocks and seashells down to sand-sized particles like those shown in **Figure 20.** The constant wave motion bumps sand grains together. This bumping not only breaks particles into smaller pieces but also smooths off their jagged corners, making them more rounded.

✔ **Reading Check** *How do waves affect beach particles?*

Sand in some places is made of other things. For example, Hawaii's black sands are made of basalt, and its green sands are made of the mineral olivine. Jamaica's white sands are made of coral and shell fragments.

Figure 20 Many people are familiar with quartz sand. However, beach sand can vary in size, color, and composition. Sometimes beach sand can be black, white, tan, red, and even green.
Explain *why beaches are different colors.*

Figure 21 Shorelines change constantly. Human development is often at risk from shoreline erosion.

Sand Erosion and Deposition

Longshore currents carry sand along beaches to form features such as barrier islands, spits, and sandbars. Storms and wind also move sand. Thus, beaches are fragile, short-term land features that are damaged easily by storms and human activities such as some types of construction. Communities in widely separated places such as Long Island, New York; Malibu, California; and Padre Island, Texas, have problems because of beach erosion.

Barrier Islands Barrier islands are sand deposits that lie parallel to the shore but are separated from the mainland. These islands start as underwater sand ridges formed by breaking waves. Hurricanes and storms add sediment to them, raising some to sea level. When a barrier island becomes large enough, the wind blows the loose sand into dunes, keeping the new island above sea level. As with all seashore features, barrier islands are short term, lasting from a few years to a few centuries.

The forces that build barrier islands also can erode them. Storms and waves carry sediments away. Beachfront development, as in **Figure 21,** can be affected by shoreline erosion.

section 3 review

Summary

The Shore

● An ocean shoreline is where land meets the ocean.

● The forces that shape shorelines are waves, currents, and tides.

Rocky Shorelines

● Rocks and cliffs are the most common features along rocky shorelines.

Sandy Beaches

● Beaches are made up of different materials. Some are made of rock fragments and others are made of seashell fragments.

Sand Erosion and Deposition

● Longshore currents, storms, and wind move sand.

● Beaches are fragile, short-term land features.

Self Check

SC.D.1.3.1

1. **Identify** major forces that cause shoreline erosion.

2. **Compare and contrast** the features you would find along a steep, rocky shoreline with the features you would find along a gently sloping, sandy shoreline.

3. **Explain** how the type of shoreline could affect the types of sediments you might find there. SC.D.1.3.3

4. **List** several materials that beach sand might be composed of. Where do these materials come from?

5. **Think Critically** How would erosion and deposition of sediment along a shoreline be affected if the longshore current was blocked by a wall built out into the water?

Applying Math

6. **Solve One-Step Equations** If 14,000 waves crash onto a shore daily, how many waves crash onto it in a year? How many crashed onto it since you were born? MA.D.2.3.1

Benchmark—**SC.D.1.3.5:** The student understands concepts of time and size relating to the interaction of Earth's processes; **SC.H.1.3.4:** The student knows that accurate record keeping, openness, and replication are essential to maintaining an investigator's credibility with other scientists and society.

Classifying Types of Sand

Sand is made of different kinds of grains, but did you realize that the slope of a beach is related to the size of its grains? The coarser the grain size is, the steeper the beach is. The composition of sand also is important.

🔘 *Real-World Problem*

What characteristics can be used to classify different types of beach sand?

Goals
- **Observe** differences in sand.
- **Identify** characteristics of beach sand.
- **Infer** sediment sources.

Materials
samples of different sands (3)
magnifying lens
*stereomicroscope
magnet
*Alternate materials

Safety Precautions

Complete a safety worksheet before you begin.

🔘 *Procedure*

1. **Design** a five-column data table to compare the three sand samples. Use column one for the samples and the others for the characteristics you will be examining.

Angular   Sub-angular   Sub-rounded   Rounded

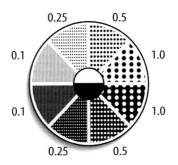

Sand gauge
(measurements in mm)

2. **Use the diagram** in the previous column to determine the average roundness of each sample.

3. **Identify** the grain size of your samples by using the sand gauge above. To determine the grain size, place sand grains in the middle of the circle of the sand gauge. Use the upper half of the circle for dark-colored particles and the bottom half for light-colored particles.

4. **Decide** on two other characteristics to examine that will help you classify your samples.

🔘 *Conclude and Apply*

1. **Compare and contrast** some characteristics of beach sand.

2. **Describe** why there are variations in the characteristics of different sand samples.

3. **Explain** what your observations tell you about the sources of the three samples.

*C*ommunicating Your Data

Compare your results with those of other students.

Benchmark—SC.D.1.3.1: The student knows that mechanical and chemical activities shape and reshape the Earth's land surface by eroding rock and soil in some areas and depositing them in other areas, sometimes in seasonal layers; SC.D.1.3.3: knows how conditions that exist in one system influence the conditions that exist in other systems; SC.D.1.3.5: understands concepts of time and size relating to the interaction of Earth's processes; SC.H.1.3.5

Water Speed and Erosion

Goals

- **Assemble** an apparatus for measuring the effect of water speed on erosion.
- **Observe and measure** the ability of water traveling at different speeds to erode sand.

Materials

paint roller pan
disposable wallpaper trays
sand
1-L beaker
rubber tubing (20 cm)
metric ruler
water
stopwatch
fine-mesh screen
wood block
Alternate materials

Safety Precautions

Complete a safety worksheet before you begin. Wash your hands after you handle the sand. Immediately clean up any water that spills on the floor.

▶ Real-World Problem

What would it be like to make a raft and use it to float on a river? Would it be easy? Would you feel like Tom Sawyer? Probably not. You'd be at the mercy of the current. Strong currents create fast rivers. But does fast moving water affect more than just floating rafts and other objects? How does the speed of a stream or river affect its ability to erode?

▶ Procedure

1. Copy the data table on the following page.
2. Place the screen in the sink. Pour moist sand into your pan and smooth out the sand. Set one end of the pan on the wood block and hang the other end over the screen in the sink. Excess water will flow onto the screen in the sink.
3. Attach one end of the hose to the faucet and place the other end in the beaker. Turn on the water so that it trickles into the beaker. Time how long it takes for the trickle of water to fill the beaker to the 1-L mark. Divide 1 L by your time in seconds to calculate the water speed. Record the speed in your data table.
4. Without altering the water speed, hold the hose over the end of the pan that is resting on the wood block. Allow the water to flow into the sand for 2 min. At the end of 2 min, turn off the water.
5. **Measure** the depth and length of the eroded channel formed by the water. Count the number of branches formed on the channel. Record your measurements and observations in your data table.

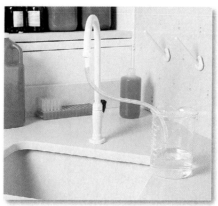

Water Speed and Erosion			
Water Speed (Liters per Second)	Depth of Channel	Length of Channel	Number of Channel Branches
	Do not write in this book.		

6. Empty the excess water from the tray and smooth out the sand. Repeat steps 3 through 5 two more times, increasing your water speed each time.

Conclude and Apply

1. **Identify** the constants and variables in your experiment.

2. **Observe** Which water speed created the deepest and longest channel?

3. **Observe** Which water speed created the greatest number of branches?

4. **Infer** the effect that water speed has on erosion.

5. **Predict** how your results would have differed if one end of the pan had been raised higher.

6. **Infer** how streams and rivers can shape Earth's surface.

7. **Predict** how changing seasons might affect erosion and deposition.

Communicating Your Data

Write a pamphlet for people buying homes near rivers or streams that outlines the different effects that water erosion could have on their property.

Is there hope for America's coastlines or is beach erosion a "shore" thing?

Sands in Time

Water levels are rising along the coastline of the United States. Serious storms and the building of homes and businesses along the shore are leading to the erosion of anywhere from 70 percent to 90 percent of the U.S. coastline. A report from the Federal Emergency Management Agency (FEMA) confirms this. The report says that one meter of United States beaches will be eaten away each year for the next 60 years. Since 1965, the federal government has spent millions of dollars replenishing more than 1,300 eroding sandy shores around the country. And still beaches continue to disappear.

The slowly eroding beaches are upsetting to residents and officials of many communities, who depend on their shore to earn money from visitors. Some city and state governments are turning to beach nourishment— a process in which sand is taken from the seafloor and dumped on beaches. The process is expensive, however. The state of Delaware, for example, is spending 7,000,000 dollars to bring in sand for its beaches.

This beach house will collapse as its underpinnings are eroded.

Other methods of saving eroding beaches are being tried. In places along the Great Lakes shores and coastal shores, one company has installed fabrics underwater to slow currents. By slowing currents, sand is naturally deposited and kept in place.

Another shore-saving device is a synthetic barrier that is shaped like a plastic snowflake. A string of these barriers is secured just offshore. They absorb the energy of incoming waves. Reducing wave energy can prevent sand from being eroded from the beach. New sand also might accumulate because the barriers slow down the currents that flow along the shore.

Many people believe that communities along the shore must restrict the beachfront building of homes, hotels, and stores. Since some estimates claim that by the year 2025, nearly 75 percent of the U.S. population will live in coastal areas, it's a tough solution. Says one geologist, "We can retreat now and save our beaches or we can retreat later and probably ruin the beaches in the process."

(LA.A.2.3.5)   (LA.B.2.3.1)   (LA.C.2.3.3)

Debate Using the facts in this article and other research you have done in your school media center or through Web links at fl6.msscience.com, make a list of methods that could be used to save beaches. Debate the issue with your classmates.

Reviewing Main Ideas

Section 1 Surface Water

1. Rainwater that does not soak into the ground is pulled down the slope by gravity. This water is called runoff.

2. Runoff can erode sediment. Factors such as steepness of slope and number and type of plants affect the amount of erosion. Rill, gully, and sheet erosion are types of surface water erosion caused by runoff.

3. Runoff generally flows into streams that merge with larger rivers until emptying into a lake or ocean. Major river systems usually contain several different types of streams.

4. Young streams flow through steep valleys and have rapids and waterfalls. Mature streams flow through gentler terrain and have less energy. Old streams often are wide and meander across their floodplains.

Section 2 Groundwater

1. When water soaks into the ground, it becomes part of a vast groundwater system.

2. Although rock may seem solid, many types are filled with connected spaces called pores. Such rocks are permeable and can contain large amounts of groundwater.

Section 3 Ocean Shoreline

1. Ocean shorelines are always changing.

2. Waves and currents have tremendous amounts of energy which break up rocks into tiny fragments called sediment. Over time, the deposition and relocation of sediment can change beaches, sandbars, and barrier islands.

Visualizing Main Ideas

Copy and complete the following concept map on caves.

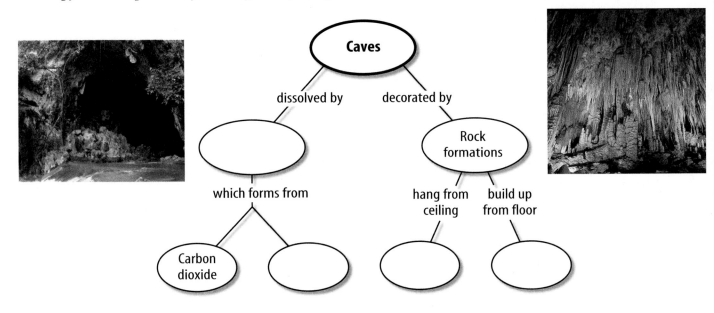

Using Vocabulary

aquifer p. 364
beach p. 371
cave p. 367
channel p. 354
✸ deposition p. 361
drainage basin p. 356
✸ erosion p. 354
geyser p. 367

groundwater p. 363
impermeable p. 364
longshore current p. 370
meander p. 357
permeable p. 364
runoff p. 352
spring p. 367
water table p. 364

✸ FCAT Vocabulary

Explain the difference between the vocabulary words in each of the following sets.

1. runoff—erosion

2. channel—drainage basin

3. aquifer—cave

4. spring—geyser

5. permeable—impermeable

6. erosion—deposition

7. groundwater—water table

8. permeable—aquifer

9. longshore current—channel

10. meander—channel

Checking Concepts

Choose the word or phrase that best answers the question.

11. Where are beaches most common?
    A) rocky shorelines   SC.D.1.3.1
    B) flat shorelines
    C) aquifers
    D) young streams

12. What is the network formed by a river and all the smaller streams that contribute to it?
    A) groundwater system
    B) zone of saturation
    C) river system
    D) water table

13. Why does water rise in an artesian well?
    A) a pump   **C)** heat
    B) erosion   **D)** pressure

14. Which term describes rock through which fluids can flow easily?
    A) impermeable   **C)** saturated
    B) meanders   **D)** permeable

15. Identify an example of a structure created by deposition.   SC.D.1.3.1
    A) beach   **C)** cave
    B) rill   **D)** geyser

16. Which stage of development are mountain streams in?
    A) young   **C)** old
    B) mature   **D)** meandering

17. What forms as a result of the water table meeting Earth's surface?
    A) meander   **C)** aquifer
    B) spring   **D)** stalactite

18. What contains heated groundwater that reaches Earth's surface?
    A) water table   **C)** aquifer
    B) cave   **D)** hot spring

19. What is a layer of permeable rock that water flows through?   SC.D.1.3.3
    A) an aquifer   **C)** a water table
    B) a pore   **D)** impermeable

20. Name the deposit that forms when a mountain river runs onto a plain.   SC.D.1.3.1
    A) subsidence   **C)** infiltration
    B) an alluvial fan   **D)** water diversion

Thinking Critically

21. Concept Map Copy and complete the concept map below using the following terms: *developed meanders, gentle curves, gentle gradient, old, rapids, steep gradient, wide floodplain,* and *young.*

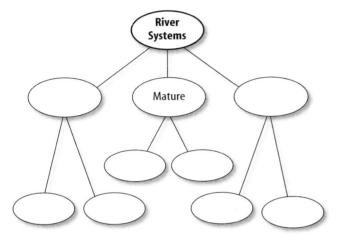

22. Describe what determines whether a stream erodes its bottom or its sides. SC.D.1.3.1

23. Interpret Data The rate of water flowing out of the Brahmaputra River in India, the La Plata River in South America, and the Mississippi River in North America are given in the table below. Infer which river carries the most sediment. SC.D.1.3.5

River Flow Rates	
River	**Flow (m³/s)**
Brahmaputra River, India	19,800
La Plata River, South America	79,300
Mississippi River, North America	175,000

24. Explain why the Mississippi River has meanders along its course.

25. Outline Make an outline that explains the three stages of stream development. SC.D.1.3.1

26. Form Hypotheses Hypothesize why most of the silt in the Mississippi delta is found farther out to sea than the sand-sized particles are. SC.D.1.3.5

27. Infer Along what kind of shoreline would you find barrier islands? SC.D.1.3.1

28. Explain why you might be concerned if developers of a new housing project started drilling wells near your well.

29. Use Variables, Constants, and Controls Explain how you could test the effect of slope on the amount of runoff produced. SC.D.1.3.3

Performance Activities

30. Poster Research a beach that interests you. Make a poster that shows different features you would find at a beach.

Applying Math

Use the illustration below to answer questions 31 and 32.

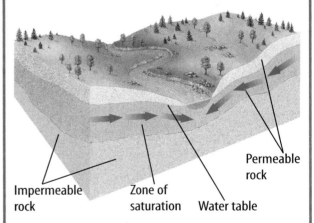

Impermeable rock Zone of saturation Water table Permeable rock

31. Flow Distance The groundwater in an aquifer flows at a rate of 0.2 m/day. How far does the groundwater move in one week? MA.D.2.3.1

32. Flow Time If groundwater in an aquifer flows at a rate of 0.4 m/day, how long does it take groundwater to move 24 m? MA.D.2.3.1

 The assessed Florida Benchmark appears above each question.
Record your answers on the answer sheet provided by your teacher or on a sheet of paper.

Multiple Choice

SC.D.1.3.1

1 The Channeled Scablands in Washington State is an area covered by many deep channels. The channels formed when a large lake drained quickly. Which of the following processes could cause a similar area to develop in Florida?

  A. catastrophic flooding

  B. chemical weathering

  C. sediment deposition

  D. sheet erosion

SC.D.1.3.1

2 The diagram below shows a formation that often develops on slopes covered by loose soil and very little vegetation.

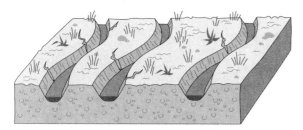

Which of the following **best** describes this type of erosion?

  F. sheet deposition

  G. rill erosion

  H. gully deposition

  I. groundwater erosion

SC.D.1.3.4

3 Which **best** describes the effect of clear cutting the vegetation in a forest?

  A. It results in less flooding in these areas.

  B. It results in greater erosion in these areas.

  C. It results in less runoff into rivers in these areas.

  D. It results in greater amounts of rainfall in these areas.

SC.D.1.3.4

4 A highway department is studying ways to improve state highways. The diagram below shows a cross section of one highway studied. Side A has little vegetation and side B is planted with grass and other plants.

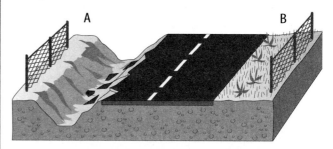

Which can be inferred from the diagram?

  F. Removing plants from roadsides will protect the edges of the roads.

  G. Highways with plants growing next to them tend to have more traffic.

  H. Planting seeds along a highway may reduce erosion and repair costs.

  I. Highways are more likely to be affected by flooding if plants grow nearby.

SC.A.1.3.5

5 Water moves at different rates in different kinds of aquifers. Through which type of rock is water likely to move the fastest?

A. marble, which has few or no pore spaces

B. limestone, which has many, well connected pore spaces

C. shale, which has small, poorly connected pore spaces

D. pumice, which has large, poorly connected pore spaces

SC.D.1.3.5

6 Which of the following would **most** likely take the longest period of time to occur?

F. the development of a river

G. the runoff from a thunderstorm

H. the formation of a hurricane

I. the change from high and low tide

Gridded Response

SC.D.1.3.5

7 Scientists sometimes use dye to study the rate at which water flows in an aquifer. In one test, a dye was found to travel 28.2 kilometers in 3 days. At what rate, in kilometers per day, did the water in the aquifer flow?

FCAT Tip

Double-Check Your Answer When you have finished each question, reread your answer to make sure it is reasonable and that it is the *best* answer to the question.

 Short Response

READ
INQUIRE
EXPLAIN

SC.D.1.3.1

8 The diagram below shows a stream formation seen in many rivers in Florida.

What stream formation does the diagram show? Explain how differing speeds of water in a stream can cause this type of stream formation.

READ
INQUIRE
EXPLAIN

Extended Response

SC.D.1.3.4

9 Carlos observed two different vacant lots near his school. He recorded what he saw in the table below.

Characteristics of Two Vacant Lots		
Lot	Slope of lot	Vegetation present
A	Slight incline	Grasses, shrubs, trees
B	Steep incline	Few trees

PART A Compare and contrast the two lots.

PART B Describe the amount of runoff that will occur on each lot. Explain your answer.

Sunshine State Standards——**SC.D.1:** The student recognizes that processes in the lithosphere, atmosphere, hydrosphere, and biosphere interact to shape the Earth; **SC.H.1:** The student uses the scientific processes and habits of mind to solve problems.

Plate Tectonics

Will this continent split?

Ol Doinyo Lengai is an active volcano in the East African Rift Valley, a place where Earth's crust is being pulled apart. If the pulling continues over millions of years, Africa will separate into two landmasses. In this chapter, you'll learn about rift valleys and other clues that the continents move over time.

Science Journal Pretend you're a journalist with an audience that assumes the continents have never moved. Write about the kinds of evidence you'll need to convince people otherwise.

Start-Up Activities

Reassemble an Image

Can you imagine a giant landmass that broke into many separate continents and Earth scientists working to reconstruct Earth's past? Do this lab to learn about clues that can be used to reassemble a supercontinent.

1. Complete a safety worksheet.

2. Collect interesting photographs from an old magazine.

3. You and a partner each select one photo, but don't show them to each other. Then each of you cut your photos into pieces no smaller than about 5 cm or 6 cm.

4. Trade your cut-up photo for your partner's.

5. Observe the pieces, and reassemble the photograph your partner has cut up.

6. **Think Critically** Write a paragraph describing the characteristics of the cut-up photograph that helped you put the image back together. Think of other examples in which characteristics of objects are used to match them up with other objects.

Science Online Preview this chapter's content and activities at fl6.msscience.com

Plate Tectonics Make the following Foldable to help identify what you already know, what you want to know, and what you learned about plate tectonics. LA.A.1.3.4

STEP 1 **Fold** a sheet of paper vertically from side to side. Make the front edge about 1.25 cm shorter than the back edge.

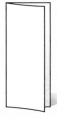

STEP 2 **Turn** lengthwise and fold into thirds.

STEP 3 **Unfold and cut** only the layer along both folds to make three tabs.

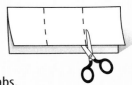

STEP 4 **Label** each tab.

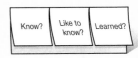

Identify Questions Before you read the chapter, write what you already know about plate tectonics under the left tab of your Foldable, and write questions about what you'd like to know under the center tab. After you read the chapter, list what you learned under the right tab.

Benchmarks—SC.D.1.3.3 (pp. 385–386): The student knows how conditions that exist in one system influence the conditions that exist in other systems; SC.H.1.3.1 Annually Assessed (pp. 384–387): The student knows that scientific knowledge is subject to modification as new information challenges prevailing theories and as a new theory leads to looking at old observations in a new way.

Also covers: SC.D.1.3.2 Annually Assessed (pp. 384–387), SC.D.1.3.5 (p. 384), SC.H.1.3.2 (pp. 384–387), SC.H.1.3.6 (p. 384), SC.H.2.3.1 (pp. 384–386), SC.H.3.3.5 (pp. 384, 387)

Continental Drift

as you read

What **You'll Learn**

- **Describe** the hypothesis of continental drift.
- **Identify** evidence supporting continental drift.

Why **It's Important**

The hypothesis of continental drift led to plate tectonics—a theory that explains many processes in Earth.

Review Vocabulary

continent: one of the six or seven great divisions of land on the globe

New Vocabulary

- continental drift
- Pangaea

Evidence for Continental Drift

If you look at a map of Earth's surface, you can see that the edges of some continents look as though they could fit together like a puzzle. Other people also have noticed this fact. For example, Dutch mapmaker Abraham Ortelius noted the fit between the coastlines of South America and Africa more than 400 years ago.

Pangaea German meteorologist Alfred Wegener (VEG nur) thought that the fit of the continents wasn't just a coincidence. He suggested that all the continents were joined together at some time in the past. In a 1912 lecture, he proposed the hypothesis of continental drift. According to the hypothesis of **continental drift,** continents have moved slowly to their current locations. Wegener suggested that all continents once were connected as one large landmass, shown in **Figure 1,** that broke apart about 200 million years ago. He called this large landmass **Pangaea** (pan JEE uh), which means "all land."

Reading Check *Who proposed continental drift?*

Figure 1 This illustration represents how the continents once were joined to form Pangaea. This fitting together of continents according to shape is not the only evidence supporting the past existence of Pangaea.

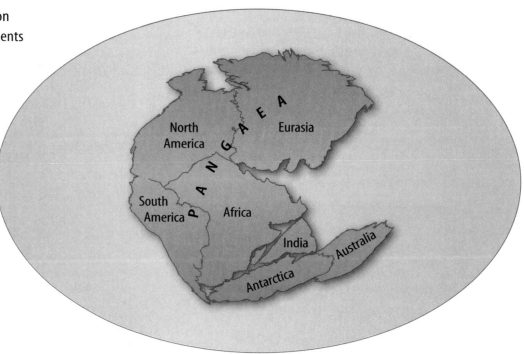

A Controversial Idea Wegener's ideas about continental drift were controversial. It wasn't until long after Wegener's death in 1930 that his basic hypothesis was accepted. The evidence Wegener presented hadn't been enough to convince many people during his lifetime. He was unable to explain exactly how the continents drifted apart. He proposed that the continents plowed through the ocean floor, driven by the spin of Earth. Physicists and geologists of the time strongly disagreed with Wegener's explanation. They pointed out that continental drift would not be necessary to explain many of Wegener's observations. Other important observations that came later eventually supported Wegener's earlier evidence.

Fossil Clues Besides the puzzlelike fit of the continents, fossils provided support for continental drift. Fossils of the reptile *Mesosaurus* have been found in South America and Africa, as shown in **Figure 2.** This swimming reptile lived in freshwater and on land. How could fossils of *Mesosaurus* be found on land areas separated by a large ocean of salt water? It probably couldn't swim between the continents. Wegener hypothesized that this reptile lived on both continents when they were joined.

Reading Check *How do* Mesosaurus *fossils support the past existence of Pangaea?*

LA.A.1.3.4

LA.B.2.3.4

Science Online

Topic: Continental Drift
Visit fl6.msscience.com for Web links to information about the continental drift hypothesis.

Activity Research and write a brief report about the initial reactions, from the public and scientific communities, toward Wegener's continental drift hypothesis.

Figure 2 Fossil remains of plants and animals that lived in Pangaea have been found on more than one continent.
Evaluate *How do the locations of Glossopteris, Mesosaurus, Kannemeyerid, Labyrinthodont, and other fossils support Wegener's hypothesis of continental drift?*

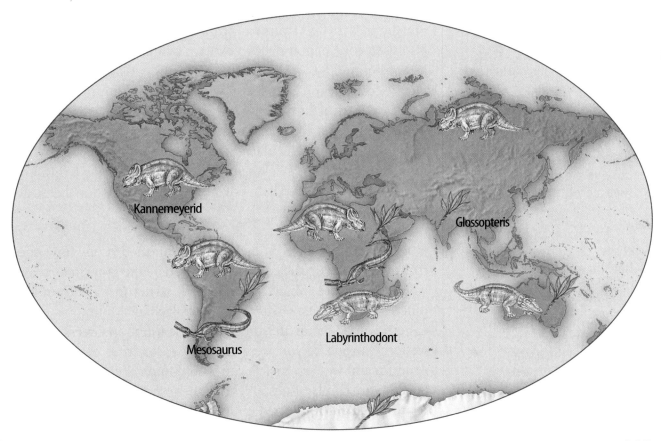

Figure 3 This fossil plant, *Glossopteris,* grew in a temperate climate.

A Widespread Plant Another fossil that supports the hypothesis of continental drift is *Glossopteris* (glahs AHP tur us). **Figure 3** shows this fossil plant, which has been found in Africa, Australia, India, South America, and Antarctica. The presence of *Glossopteris* in so many areas also supported Wegener's idea that all of these regions once were connected and had similar climates.

Climate Clues Wegener used continental drift to explain evidence of changing climates. For example, fossils of warm-weather plants were found on the island of Spitsbergen in the Arctic Ocean. To explain this, Wegener hypothesized that Spitsbergen drifted from tropical regions to the arctic. Wegener also used continental drift to explain evidence of glaciers found in temperate and tropical areas. Glacial deposits and rock surfaces scoured and polished by glaciers are found in South America, Africa, India, and Australia. This shows that parts of these continents were covered with glaciers in the past. How could you explain why glacial deposits are found in areas where no glaciers exist today? Wegener thought that these continents were connected and partly covered with ice near Earth's south pole long ago.

Rock Clues If the continents were connected at one time, then rocks that make up the continents should be the same in locations where they were joined. Similar rock structures are found on different continents. Parts of the Appalachian Mountains of the eastern United States are similar to those found in Greenland and western Europe. If you were to study rocks from eastern South America and western Africa, you would find other rock structures that also are similar. Rock clues like these support the idea that the continents were connected in the past.

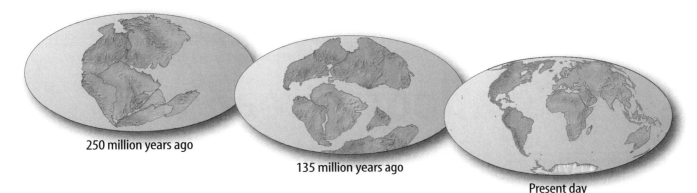

250 million years ago

135 million years ago

Present day

How could continents drift?

Although Wegener provided evidence to support his hypothesis of continental drift, he couldn't explain how, when, or why these changes, shown in **Figure 4,** took place. The idea suggested that lower-density, continental material somehow had to plow through higher-density, ocean-floor material. The force behind this plowing was thought to be the spin of Earth on its axis—a notion that was quickly rejected by physicists. Because other scientists could not provide explanations either, Wegener's idea of continental drift was initially rejected. The idea was so radically different at that time that most people closed their minds to it.

Rock, fossil, and climate clues were the main types of evidence for continental drift. After Wegener's death, more clues were found, largely because of advances in technology, and new ideas that related to continental drift were developed. You'll learn about a new idea, seafloor spreading, in the next section.

Figure 4 These computer models show the probable course the continents have taken. On the far left is their position 250 million years ago. In the middle is their position 135 million years ago. At right is their current position.

---

section 1 review

Summary

Evidence for Continental Drift

- Alfred Wegener proposed in his hypothesis of continental drift that all continents were once connected as one large landmass called Pangaea.

- Evidence of continental drift came from fossils, signs of climate change, and rock structures from different continents.

How could continents drift?

- During his lifetime, Wegener was unable to explain how, when, or why the continents drifted.

- After his death, advances in technology permitted new ideas to be developed to help explain his hypothesis.

Self Check

1. **Explain** how Wegener used climate clues to support his hypothesis of continental drift. SC.H.3.3.5

2. **Describe** how rock clues were used to support the hypothesis of continental drift.

3. **Summarize** the ways that fossils helped support the hypothesis of continental drift. SC.D.1.3.5

4. **Think Critically** Why would you expect to see similar rocks and rock structures on two landmasses that were connected at one time?

Applying Skills   SC.D.1.3.3

5. **Compare and contrast** the locations of fossils of the temperate plant *Glossopteris,* as shown in **Figure 2,** with the climate that exists at each location today.

Benchmarks—SC.D.1.3.3 (pp. 389–391): The student knows how conditions that exist in one system influence the conditions that exist in other systems; SC.H.1.3.2 (pp. 389–391): The student knows that the study of the events that led scientists to discoveries can provide information about the inquiry process and its effects.

Also covers: SC.D.1.3.5 (p. 389), SC.H.1.3.6 (p. 389), SC.H.2.3.1 (p. 391), SC.H.3.3.5 (p. 389)

section 2

Seafloor Spreading

as you read

What You'll Learn

- **Explain** seafloor spreading.
- **Recognize** how age and magnetic clues support seafloor spreading.

Why It's Important

Seafloor spreading helps explain how continents moved apart.

Review Vocabulary

seafloor: portion of Earth's crust that lies beneath ocean waters

New Vocabulary

- seafloor spreading

Mapping the Ocean Floor

If you were to lower a rope from a boat until it reached the seafloor, you could record the depth of the ocean at that particular point. In how many different locations would you have to do this to create an accurate map of the seafloor? This is exactly how it was done until World War I, when the use of sound waves was introduced by German scientists to detect submarines. During the 1940s and 1950s, scientists began using sound waves on moving ships to map large areas of the ocean floor in detail. Sound waves echo off the ocean bottom—the longer the sound waves take to return to the ship, the deeper the water is.

Using sound waves, researchers discovered an underwater system of ridges, or mountains, and valleys like those found on the continents. In some of these underwater ridges are rather long rift valleys where volcanic eruptions and earthquakes occur from time to time. Some of these volcanoes actually are visible above the ocean surface. In the Atlantic, the Pacific, and in other oceans around the world, a system of ridges, called the mid-ocean ridges, is present. These underwater mountain ranges, shown in **Figure 5,** stretch along the center of much of Earth's ocean floor. This discovery raised the curiosity of many scientists. What formed these mid-ocean ridges?

✔ Reading Check *How were mid-ocean ridges discovered?*

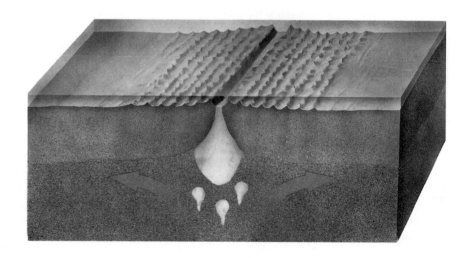

Figure 5 As the seafloor spreads apart at a mid-ocean ridge, new seafloor is created. The older seafloor moves away from the ridge in opposite directions.

The Seafloor Moves In the early 1960s, Princeton University scientist Harry Hess suggested an explanation. His now-famous theory is known as **seafloor spreading.** Hess proposed that hot, less dense material below Earth's crust rises toward the surface at the mid-ocean ridges. Then, it flows sideways, carrying the seafloor away from the ridge in both directions, as seen in **Figure 5.**

As the seafloor spreads apart, magma is forced upward and flows from the cracks. It becomes solid as it cools and forms new seafloor. As new seafloor moves away from the mid-ocean ridge, it cools, contracts, and becomes denser. This denser, colder seafloor sinks, helping to form the ridge. The theory of seafloor spreading was later supported by the following observations.

 **Reading Check** *How does new seafloor form at mid-ocean ridges?*

Evidence for Spreading

In 1968, scientists aboard the research ship *Glomar Challenger* began gathering information about the rocks on the seafloor. *Glomar Challenger* was equipped with a drilling rig that allowed scientists to drill into the seafloor to obtain rock samples. Scientists found that the youngest rocks are located at the mid-ocean ridges. The ages of the rocks become increasingly older in samples obtained farther from the ridges, adding to the evidence for seafloor spreading.

Using submersibles along mid-ocean ridges, new seafloor features and life-forms also were discovered there, as shown in **Figure 6.** As molten material is forced upward along the ridges, it brings heat and chemicals that support exotic life-forms in deep, ocean water. Among these are giant clams, mussels, and tube worms.

INTEGRATE Physics **Magnetic Clues** Earth's magnetic field has a north and a south pole. Magnetic lines, or directions, of force leave Earth near the south pole and enter Earth near the north pole. During a magnetic reversal, the lines of magnetic force run the opposite way. Scientists have determined that Earth's magnetic field has reversed itself many times in the past. These reversals occur over intervals of thousands or even millions of years. The reversals are recorded in rocks forming along mid-ocean ridges.

Figure 6 Many new discoveries have been made on the seafloor. These giant tube worms inhabit areas near hot water vents along mid-ocean ridges.

LA.A.2.3.5
LA.B.2.3.1

INTEGRATE Chemistry

Curie Point Find out what the Curie point is and describe in your Science Journal what happens to iron-bearing minerals when they are heated to the Curie point. Explain how this is important to studies of seafloor spreading.

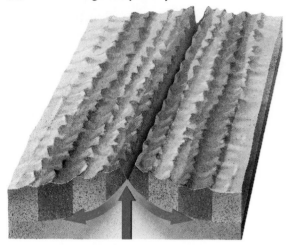

■ Normal magnetic polarity
■ Reverse magnetic polarity

Figure 7 Changes in Earth's magnetic field are preserved in rock that forms on both sides of mid-ocean ridges.
Explain *why this is considered to be evidence of seafloor spreading.*

Magnetic Time Scale Iron-bearing minerals, such as magnetite, that are found in the rocks of the seafloor can record Earth's magnetic field direction when they form. Whenever Earth's magnetic field reverses, newly forming iron minerals will record the magnetic reversal.

Using a sensing device called a magnetometer (mag nuh TAH muh tur) to detect magnetic fields, scientists found that rocks on the ocean floor show many periods of magnetic reversal. The magnetic alignment in the rocks reverses back and forth over time in strips parallel to the mid-ocean ridges, as shown in **Figure 7.** A strong magnetic reading is recorded when the polarity of a rock is the same as the polarity of Earth's magnetic field today. Because of this, normal polarities in rocks show up as large peaks. This discovery provided strong support that seafloor spreading was indeed occurring. The magnetic reversals showed that new rock was being formed at the mid-ocean ridges. This helped explain how the crust could move—something that the continental drift hypothesis could not do.

section 2 review

Summary

Mapping the Ocean Floor

- Mid-ocean ridges, along the center of the ocean floor, have been found by using sound waves, the same method once used to detect submarines during World War I.

- Harry Hess suggested, in his seafloor spreading hypothesis, that the seafloor moves.

Evidence for Spreading

- Scientists aboard *Glomar Challenger* provided evidence of spreading by discovering that the youngest rocks are located at ridges and become increasingly older farther from the ridges.

- Magnetic alignment of rocks, in alternating strips that run parallel to ridges, indicates reversals in Earth's magnetic field and provides further evidence of seafloor spreading.

Self Check

1. **Summarize** What properties of iron-bearing minerals on the seafloor support the theory of seafloor spreading? `SC.D.1.3.3`

2. **Explain** how the ages of the rocks on the ocean floor support the theory of seafloor spreading. `SC.D.1.3.5`

3. **Summarize** How did Harry Hess's hypothesis explain seafloor movement?

4. **Explain** why some partly molten material rises toward Earth's surface.

5. **Think Critically** The ideas of Hess, Wegener, and others emphasize that Earth is a dynamic planet. How is seafloor spreading different from continental drift?

Applying Math

6. **Solve One-Step Equations** North America is moving about 1.25 cm per year away from a ridge in the middle of the Atlantic Ocean. Using this rate, how much farther apart will North America and the ridge be in 200 million years?

Benchmark—SC.D.1.3.3: The student knows how conditions that exist in one system influence the conditions that exist in other systems; **SC.D.1.3.5:** The student understands concepts of time and size relating to the interaction of Earth's processes (e.g., lightning striking in a split second as opposed to the shifting of the Earth's plates altering the land-scape, distance between atoms measured in Angstrom units as opposed to distance between stars measured in light-years).

Seafloor Spreading Rates

How did scientists use their knowledge of seafloor spreading and magnetic field reversals to reconstruct Pangaea? Try this lab to see how you can determine where a continent may have been located in the past.

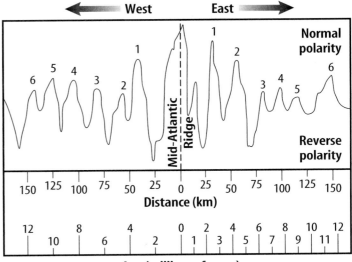

Age (millions of years)

Real-World Problem

Can you use clues, such as magnetic field reversals on Earth, to help reconstruct Pangaea?

Goals

■ **Interpret** data about magnetic field reversals. Use these magnetic clues to reconstruct Pangaea.

Materials

metric ruler
pencil

Procedure

1. Study the magnetic field graph above. You will be working only with normal polarity readings, which are the peaks above the baseline in the top half of the graph.

2. Place the long edge of a ruler vertically on the graph. Slide the ruler so that it lines up with the center of peak 1 west of the Mid-Atlantic Ridge.

3. **Determine** and record the distance and age that line up with the center of peak 1 west. Repeat this process for peak 1 east of the ridge.

4. **Calculate** the average distance and age for this pair of peaks.

5. Repeat steps 2 through 4 for the remaining pairs of normal-polarity peaks.

6. **Calculate** the rate of movement in cm per year for the six pairs of peaks. Use the formula *rate = distance/time*. Convert kilometers to centimeters. For example, to calculate a rate using normal-polarity peak 5, west of the ridge:

$$\text{rate} = \frac{125 \text{ km}}{10 \text{ million years}} = \frac{12.5 \text{ km}}{\text{million years}} =$$

$$\frac{1{,}250{,}000 \text{ cm}}{1{,}000{,}000 \text{ years}} = 1.25 \text{ cm/year}$$

Conclude and Apply

1. **Compare** the age of igneous rock found near the mid-ocean ridge with that of igneous rock found farther away from the ridge.

2. If the distance from a point on the coast of Africa to the Mid-Atlantic Ridge is approximately 2,400 km, calculate how long ago that point in Africa was at or near the Mid-Atlantic Ridge.

3. How could you use this method to reconstruct Pangaea?

section 3

Also covers: SC.D.1.3.5 (p. 401), SC.H.1.3.1 Annually Assessed (pp. 392–401), SC.H.1.3.2 (pp. 392–401), SC.H.1.3.6 (p. 399), SC.H.2.3.1 (pp. 402–403)

Theory of Plate Tectonics

as you read

What You'll Learn

- **Compare and contrast** different types of plate boundaries.
- **Explain** how heat inside Earth causes plate tectonics.
- **Recognize** features caused by plate tectonics.

Why It's Important

Plate tectonics explains how many of Earth's features form.

Review Vocabulary

converge: to come together
diverge: to move apart
transform: to convert or change

New Vocabulary

✷ **plate tectonics**
- plate
- lithosphere
- asthenosphere
- convection current

✷ FCAT Vocabulary

Plate Tectonics

The idea of seafloor spreading showed that more than just continents were moving, as Wegener had thought. It was now clear to scientists that sections of the seafloor and continents move in relation to one another.

Plate Movements In the 1960s, scientists developed a new theory that combined continental drift and seafloor spreading. According to the theory of **plate tectonics,** Earth's crust and part of the upper mantle are broken into sections. These sections, called **plates,** move on a plasticlike layer of the mantle. Plates can be thought of as rafts that float and move on this layer. Plate movements cause seismic activity along plate borders.

Composition of Earth's Plates Plates are made of the crust and a part of the upper mantle, as shown in **Figure 8.** These two parts combined are the **lithosphere** (LIH thuh sfihr). This rigid layer is about 100 km thick and generally is less dense than material underneath. The plasticlike layer below the lithosphere is called the **asthenosphere** (as THE nuh sfihr). The rigid plates of the lithosphere float and move around on the asthenosphere.

Concepts in Motion fl6.msscience.com

Figure 8 Plates of the lithosphere are composed of oceanic crust, continental crust, and part of the rigid upper mantle.

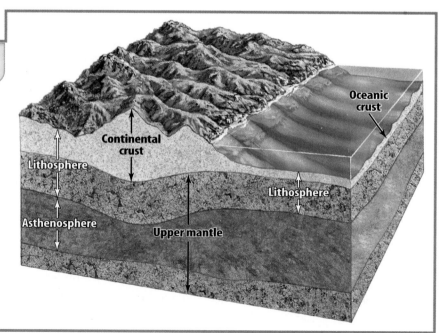

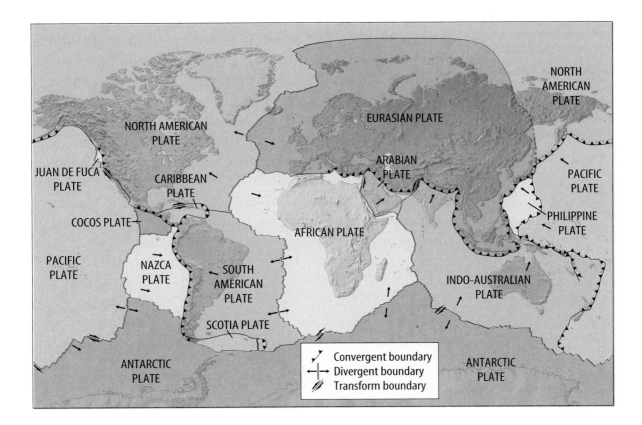

Plate Boundaries

When plates move, they can interact in several ways. They can move toward each other and converge, or collide. They also can pull apart or slide alongside one another. When the plates interact, the result of their movement is seen at the plate boundaries, as in **Figure 9.**

Reading Check *What are the general ways that plates interact?*

Movement along any plate boundary means that changes must happen at other boundaries. What is happening to the Atlantic Ocean floor between the North American and African Plates? Compare this with what is happening along the western margin of South America.

Plates Moving Apart The boundary between two plates that are moving apart is called a divergent boundary. You learned about divergent boundaries when you read about seafloor spreading. In the Atlantic Ocean, the North American Plate is moving away from the Eurasian and the African Plates, as shown in **Figure 9.** That divergent boundary is called the Mid-Atlantic Ridge. The Great Rift Valley in eastern Africa might become a divergent plate boundary. There, a valley has formed where a continental plate is being pulled apart. **Figure 10** shows a side view of what a rift valley might look like and illustrates how the hot material rises up where plates separate.

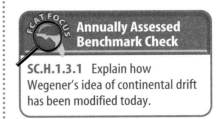

Annually Assessed Benchmark Check

SC.H.1.3.1 Explain how Wegener's idea of continental drift has been modified today.

Plates Moving Together If new crust is being added at one location, why doesn't Earth's surface keep expanding? As new crust is added in one place, it disappears below the surface at another. The disappearance of crust can occur where two plates move together at a convergent boundary.

When an oceanic plate converges with a less dense continental plate, the denser oceanic plate sinks under the continental plate. The area where an oceanic plate subducts, or goes down, into the mantle is called a subduction zone. Some volcanoes form above subduction zones. **Figure 10** shows how this type of convergent boundary creates a deep-sea trench where one plate bends and sinks beneath the other. High temperatures cause rock to melt around the subducting slab as it goes under the other plate. The newly formed magma is forced upward along these plate boundaries, forming volcanoes. Extreme pressure can build up between two colliding plates. Rapid release of the pressure can cause very large earthquakes. If this occurs under water, a giant wave called a tsunami can be formed.

Applying Science

How well do the continents fit together?

Recall the Launch Lab you performed at the beginning of this chapter. While you were trying to fit pieces of a cut-up photograph together, what clues did you use?

Identifying the Problem

Take a copy of a map of the world and cut out each continent. Lay them on a tabletop and try to fit them together, using techniques you used in the Launch Lab. You will find that the pieces of your Earth puzzle—the continents—do not fit together well. Yet, several of the areas on some continents fit together extremely well.

Take out another world map—one that shows the continental shelves as well as the continents. Copy it and cut out the continents, this time including the continental shelves.

Solving the Problem

1. Does including the continental shelves solve the problem of fitting the continents together?

2. Why should continental shelves be included with maps of the continents?

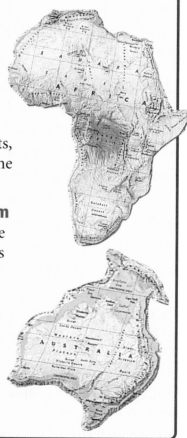

Figure 10

By diverging at some boundaries and converging at others, Earth's plates are continually—but gradually—reshaping the landscape around you. The Mid-Atlantic Ridge, for example, was formed when the North and South American Plates pulled apart from the Eurasian and African Plates (see globe). Some features that occur along plate boundaries— rift valleys, volcanoes, and mountain ranges—are shown on the right and below.

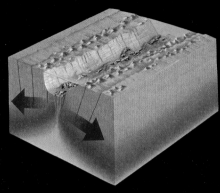

A RIFT VALLEY When continental plates pull apart, they can form rift valleys. The African continent is separating now along the East African Rift Valley.

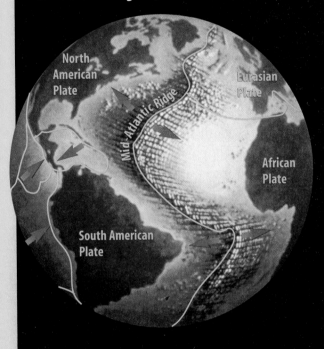

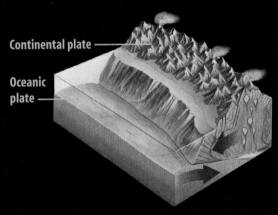

SUBDUCTION Where oceanic and continental plates collide, the oceanic plate plunges beneath the less dense continental plate. As the plate descends, molten rock (yellow) forms and rises toward the surface, creating volcanoes.

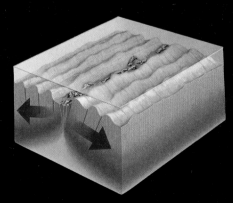

SEAFLOOR SPREADING A mid-ocean ridge, like the Mid-Atlantic Ridge, forms where oceanic plates continue to separate. As rising magma (yellow) cools, it forms new oceanic crust.

CONTINENTAL COLLISION Where two continental plates collide, they push up the crust to form mountain ranges such as the Himalaya.

Where Plates Collide A subduction zone also can form where two oceanic plates converge. In this case, the colder, older, denser oceanic plate bends and sinks down into the mantle. The Mariana Islands in the western Pacific are a chain of volcanic islands formed where two oceanic plates collide.

Usually, no subduction occurs when two continental plates collide, as shown in **Figure 10.** Because both of these plates are less dense than the material in the asthenosphere, the two plates collide and crumple up, forming mountain ranges. Earthquakes are common at these convergent boundaries. However, volcanoes do not form because there is no, or little, subduction. The Himalaya in Asia are forming where the Indo-Australian Plate collides with the Eurasian Plate.

Where Plates Slide Past Each Other The third type of plate boundary is called a transform boundary. Transform boundaries occur where two plates slide past one another. They move in opposite directions or in the same direction at different rates. When one plate slips past another suddenly, earthquakes occur. The Pacific Plate is sliding past the North American Plate, forming the famous San Andreas Fault in California, as seen in **Figure 11.** The San Andreas Fault is part of a transform plate boundary. It has been the site of many earthquakes.

Figure 11 The San Andreas Fault in California occurs along the transform plate boundary where the Pacific Plate is sliding past the North American Plate. Overall, the two plates are moving in roughly the same direction.

Explain *Why, then, do the red arrows show movement in opposite directions?*

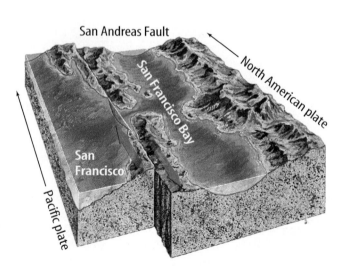

This photograph shows an aerial view of the San Andreas Fault.

Causes of Plate Tectonics

Many new discoveries have been made about Earth's crust since Wegener's day, but one question still remains. What causes the plates to move? Scientists now think they have a good idea. They think that plates move by the same basic process that occurs when you heat soup.

Convection Inside Earth Soup that is cooking in a pan on the stove contains currents caused by an unequal distribution of heat in the pan. Hot, less dense soup is forced upward by the surrounding, cooler, denser soup. As the hot soup reaches the surface, it cools and sinks back down into the pan. This entire cycle of heating, rising, cooling, and sinking is called a **convection current.** A version of this same process, occurring in the mantle, is thought to be the force behind plate tectonics. Scientists suggest that differences in density cause hot, plasticlike rock to be forced upward toward the surface.

Moving Mantle Material Wegener wasn't able to come up with an explanation for why plates move. Today, researchers who study the movement of heat in Earth's interior have proposed several possible explanations. All of the hypotheses use convection in one way or another. It is, therefore, the transfer of heat inside Earth that provides the energy to move plates and causes many of Earth's surface features. One hypothesis is shown in **Figure 12.** It relates plate motion directly to the movement of convection currents. According to this hypothesis, convection currents cause the movements of plates.

Mini LAB

Modeling Convection Currents

Procedure

1. Complete a safety worksheet.
2. Pour **water** into **a clear, colorless casserole dish** until it is 5 cm from the top.
3. Center the dish on a **hot plate** and heat it. **WARNING:** *Wear thermal mitts to protect your hands.*
4. Add a few **grains of rice** to the water above the center of the hot plate.
5. Looking from the side of the dish, observe what happens in the water.
6. Illustrate your observations in your **Science Journal.**

Analysis

1. Determine whether any currents form in the water.
2. Infer what causes the currents to form.

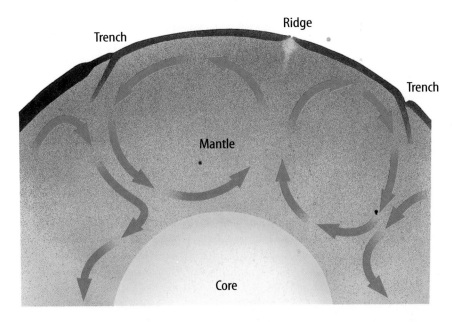

Figure 12 In one hypothesis, convection currents occur throughout the mantle. Such convection currents (see arrows) are the driving force of plate tectonics.

Features Caused by Plate Tectonics

Earth is a dynamic planet with a hot interior. This heat leads to convection, which powers the movement of plates. As the plates move, they interact. The interaction of plates produces forces that build mountains, create ocean basins, and cause volcanoes. When rocks in Earth's crust break and move, energy is released in the form of seismic waves. Humans feel this release as earthquakes. You can see some of the effects of plate tectonics in mountainous regions, where volcanoes erupt, or where landscapes have changed from past earthquake or volcanic activity.

✓ Reading Check *What happens when seismic energy is released as rocks in Earth's crust break and move?*

Normal Faults and Rift Valleys Tension forces, which are forces that pull apart, can stretch Earth's crust. This causes large blocks of crust to break and tilt or slide down the broken surfaces of crust. When rocks break and move along surfaces, a fault forms. Faults interrupt rock layers by moving them out of place. Entire mountain ranges can form in the process, called fault-block mountains, as shown in **Figure 13.** Generally, the faults that form from pull-apart forces are normal faults—faults in which the rock layers above the fault move down when compared with rock layers below the fault.

Rift valleys and mid-ocean ridges can form where Earth's crust separates. Examples of rift valleys are the Great Rift Valley in Africa, and the valleys that occur in the middle of mid-ocean ridges. Examples of mid-ocean ridges include the Mid-Atlantic Ridge and the East Pacific Rise.

Figure 13 Fault-block mountains can form when Earth's crust is stretched by tectonic forces. The arrows indicate the directions of moving blocks.

Name *the type of force that occurs when Earth's crust is pulled in opposite directions.*

Mountains and Volcanoes Compression forces squeeze objects together. Where plates come together, compression forces produce several effects. As continental plates collide, the forces that are generated cause massive folding and faulting of rock layers into mountain ranges such as the Himalaya, shown in **Figure 14,** or the Appalachian Mountains. The type of faulting produced is generally reverse faulting. Along a reverse fault, the rock layers above the fault surface move up relative to the rock layers below the fault.

As you learned earlier, when two oceanic plates converge, the denser plate is forced beneath the other plate. Curved chains of volcanic islands called island arcs form above the sinking plate. If an oceanic plate converges with a continental plate, the denser oceanic plate slides under the continental plate. Folding and faulting at the continental plate margin can thicken the continental crust to produce mountain ranges. Volcanoes also typically are formed at this type of convergent boundary.

Reading Check *What features occur where plates converge?*

Figure 14 Three general types of plate convergence can occur. These different events can change Earth's features in different ways.

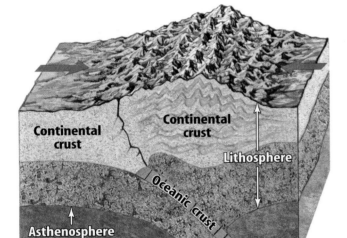

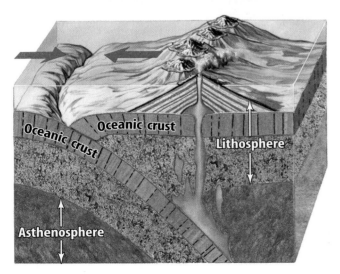

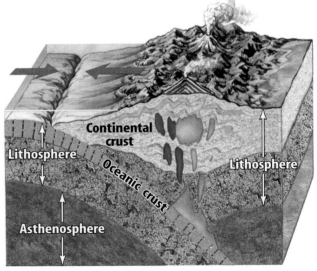

Figure 15 Most of the movement along a strike-slip fault is parallel to Earth's surface. When movement occurs, human-built structures along a strike-slip fault are offset, as shown here in this road.

Direction of Forces In which directions do forces act at convergent, divergent, and transform boundaries? Demonstrate these forces using wooden blocks or your hands.

Strike-Slip Faults At transform boundaries, two plates slide past one another without converging or diverging. The plates stick and then slide, mostly in a horizontal direction, along large strike-slip faults. In a strike-slip fault, rocks on opposite sides of the fault move in opposite directions, or in the same direction at different rates. This type of fault movement is shown in **Figure 15.** One such example is the San Andreas Fault. When plates move suddenly, vibrations are generated inside Earth that are felt as an earthquake.

Earthquakes, volcanoes, and mountain ranges are evidence of plate motion. Plate tectonics explains how activity inside Earth can affect Earth's crust differently in different locations. You've seen how plates have moved since Pangaea separated. Is it possible to measure how far plates move each year?

Testing for Plate Tectonics

Until recently, the only tests scientists could use to check for plate movement were indirect. They could study the magnetic characteristics of rocks on the seafloor. They could study volcanoes and earthquakes. These methods supported the theory that the plates have moved and still are moving. However, they did not provide proof—only support—of the idea.

New methods had to be discovered to be able to measure the small amounts of movement of Earth's plates. One method, shown in **Figure 16,** uses lasers and a satellite. Now, scientists can measure exact movements of Earth's plates of as little as 1 cm per year.

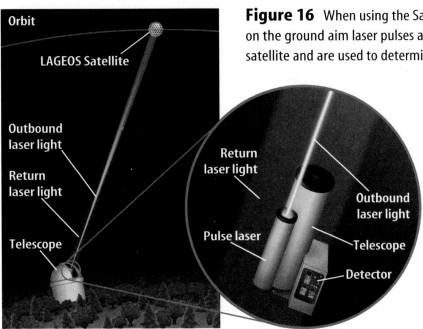

Figure 16 When using the Satellite Laser Ranging System, scientists on the ground aim laser pulses at a satellite. The pulses reflect off the satellite and are used to determine a precise location on the ground.

Orbit

LAGEOS Satellite

Outbound laser light

Return laser light

Telescope

Return laser light

Pulse laser

Outbound laser light

Telescope

Detector

Current Data Satellite Laser Ranging System data show that Hawaii is moving toward Japan at a rate of about 8.3 cm per year. Maryland is moving away from England at a rate of 1.7 cm per year. Using such methods, scientists have observed that the plates move at rates ranging from about 1 cm to 12 cm per year.

section 3 review

Summary

Plate Tectonics

- The theory of plate tectonics states that sections of the seafloor and continents move as plates on a plasticlike layer of the mantle.

Plate Boundaries

- The boundary between two plates moving apart is called a divergent boundary.
- Plates move together at a convergent boundary.
- Transform boundaries occur where two plates slide past one another.

Causes of Plate Tectonics

- Convection currents are thought to cause the movement of Earth's plates.

Features Caused by Plate Tectonics

- Tension forces cause normal faults, rift valleys, and mid-ocean ridges at divergent boundaries.
- At convergent boundaries, compression forces cause folding, reverse faults, and mountains.
- At transform boundaries, two plates slide past one another along strike-slip faults.

Self Check

1. **Describe** what occurs at plate boundaries that are associated with seafloor spreading.
2. **Describe** three types of plate boundaries where volcanic eruptions can occur.
3. **Explain** how convection currents are related to plate tectonics. `SC.D.1.3.3`
4. **Think Critically** Using **Figure 9** and a world map, determine what natural disasters might occur in Iceland. Also determine what disasters might occur in Tibet. Explain why some Icelandic disasters are not expected to occur in Tibet. `SC.D.1.3.3`

Applying Skills

5. **Predict** Plate tectonic activity causes many events that can be dangerous to humans. One of these events is a seismic sea wave, or tsunami. Learn how scientists predict the arrival time of a tsunami in a coastal area.
6. **Use a Word Processor** Write three separate descriptions of the three basic types of plate boundaries—divergent boundaries, convergent boundaries, and transform boundaries. Then draw a sketch of an example of each boundary next to your description.

LAB

Use the Internet

Benchmark—SC.D.1.3.3: The student knows how conditions that exist in one system influence the conditions that exist in other systems; SC.H.1.3.6: The student recognizes the scientific contributions that are made by individuals of diverse backgrounds, interests, talents, and motivations.

Predicting Tectonic Activity

Goals

■ **Research** the locations of earthquakes and volcanic eruptions around the world.

■ **Plot** earthquake epicenters and the locations of volcanic eruptions.

■ **Predict** locations that are tectonically active based on a plot of the locations of earthquake epicenters and active volcanoes.

Data Source

Internet Lab

Visit fl6.msscience.com for more information about earthquake and volcano sites, and data from other students.

▶ Real-World Problem

The movement of plates on Earth causes forces that build up energy in rocks. The release of this energy can produce vibrations in Earth that you know as earthquakes. Earthquakes occur every day. Many of them are too small to be felt by humans, but each event tells scientists something more about the planet. Active volcanoes can do the same and often form at plate boundaries.

Can you predict tectonically active areas by plotting locations of earthquake epicenters and volcanic eruptions?

Think about where earthquakes and volcanoes have occurred in the past. Make a hypothesis about whether the locations of earthquake epicenters and active volcanoes can be used to predict tectonically active areas.

ⓞ *Make a Plan*

1. Make a data table in your Science Journal like the one shown.

2. Collect data for earthquake epicenters and volcanic eruptions for at least the past two weeks. Your data should include the longitude and latitude for each location. For help, refer to the Web sources provided.

Locations of Epicenters and Eruptions			
Earthquake Epicenter/ Volcanic Eruption	Longitude	Latitude	Magnitude
Do not write in this book.			

ⓞ *Follow Your Plan*

1. Make sure your teacher approves your plan before you start.

2. **Plot** the locations of earthquake epicenters and volcanic eruptions on a map of the world. Use an overlay of tissue paper or plastic.

ⓞ *Analyze Your Data*

1. After you have collected the necessary data, predict where the tectonically active areas on Earth are.

2. **Compare and contrast** the areas that you predicted to be tectonically active with the plate boundary map shown in **Figure 9.**

ⓞ *Conclude and Apply*

1. What areas on Earth do you predict to be the locations of tectonic activity?

2. How close did your prediction come to the actual location of tectonically active areas?

3. How could you make your predictions closer to the locations of actual tectonic activity?

4. Would data from a longer period of time help? Explain.

5. What types of plate boundaries were close to your locations of earthquake epicenters? Volcanic eruptions?

6. **Explain** which types of plate boundaries produce volcanic eruptions. Be specific.

𝒞ommunicating Your Data

Find this lab using the link below. Post your data in the table provided. **Compare** your data to those of other students. Combine your data with those of other students and plot these combined data on a map to recognize the relationship between plate boundaries, volcanic eruptions, and earthquake epicenters.

Internet Lab
fl6.msscience.com

Listening In
by Gordon Judge

I'm just a bit of seafloor on this mighty solid sphere.
With no mind to be broadened, I'm quite content
    down here.
The mantle churns below me, and the sea's in turmoil, too;
But nothing much disturbs me, I'm rock solid through
    and through.

I do pick up occasional low-frequency vibrations –
(I think, although I can't be sure, they're sperm whales'
    conversations).
I know I shouldn't listen in, but what else can I do?
It seems they are all studying for degrees from the OU.

They've mentioned me in passing, as their minds begin
    improving:

I think I've heard them say
    "The theory says the sea-
    floor's moving...".
They call it "Plate Tectonics", this
    new theory in their noddle.
If they would only ask me, I
    could tell them it's all
    twaddle....

But, how can I be moving, when I know full well myself
That I'm quite firmly anchored to a continental shelf?
"Well, the continent is moving, too; you're *pushing* it,
    you see,"
I hear those OU whales intone, hydro-acoustically....

Well, thank you very much, OU. You've upset my
    composure.
Next time you send your student whales to look at
    my exposure
I'll tell them it's a load of tosh: it's *they* who move,
    not me,
Those arty-smarty blobs of blubber, clogging up the sea!

Understanding Literature LA.E.1.3.3

Point of View Point of view refers to the perspective from which an author writes. This poem begins, "I'm just a bit of seafloor...." Right away, you know that the poem, or story, is being told from the point of view of the speaker, or the "first person." What effect does the first-person narration have on the story?

LA.E.1.3.3

Respond to the Reading

1. Who is narrating the poem?
2. Why might the narrator think he or she hasn't moved?
3. **Linking Science and Writing** Using the first-person point of view, write an account from the point of view of a living or nonliving thing.

INTEGRATE Earth Science Volcanoes can occur where two plates move toward each other. When an oceanic plate and a continental plate collide, a volcano will form. Subduction zones occur when one plate sinks under another plate. Rocks melt in the zones where these plates converge, causing magma to move upward and form volcanic mountains.

Reviewing Main Ideas

Section 1 Continental Drift

1. Alfred Wegener suggested that the continents were joined together at some point in the past in a large landmass he called Pangaea. Wegener proposed that continents have moved slowly, over millions of years, to their current locations.

2. The puzzlelike fit of the continents, fossils, climatic evidence, and similar rock structures support Wegener's idea of continental drift. However, Wegener could not explain what process could cause the movement of the landmasses.

Section 2 Seafloor Spreading

1. Detailed mapping of the ocean floor in the 1950s showed underwater mountains and rift valleys.

2. In the 1960s, Harry Hess suggested seafloor spreading as an explanation for the formation of mid-ocean ridges.

3. The theory of seafloor spreading is supported by magnetic evidence in rocks and by the ages of rocks on the ocean floor.

Section 3 Theory of Plate Tectonics

1. In the 1960s, scientists combined the ideas of continental drift and seafloor spreading to develop the theory of plate tectonics. The theory states that the surface of Earth is broken into sections called plates that move around on the asthenosphere.

2. Currents in Earth's mantle called convection currents transfer heat in Earth's interior. It is thought that this transfer of heat energy moves plates.

3. Earth is a dynamic planet. As the plates move, they interact, resulting in many of the features of Earth's surface.

Visualizing Main Ideas

Copy and complete the concept map below about continental drift, seafloor spreading, and plate tectonics.

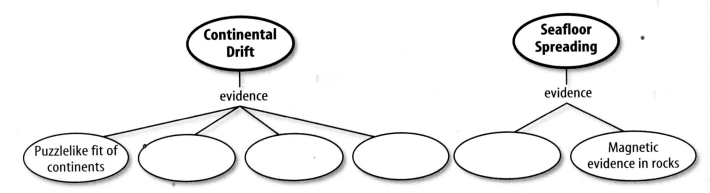

Using Vocabulary

asthenosphere p. 392
continental drift p. 384
convection current p. 397
lithosphere p. 392

Pangaea p. 384
plate p. 392
✷ plate tectonics p. 392
seafloor spreading p. 389

✷ FCAT Vocabulary

Each phrase below describes a vocabulary term from the list. Write the term that matches the phrase describing it.

1. plasticlike layer below the lithosphere

2. idea that continents move slowly across Earth's surface

3. large, ancient landmass that consisted of all the continents on Earth

4. composed of oceanic or continental crust and upper mantle

5. explains locations of mountains, trenches, and volcanoes

6. theory proposed by Harry Hess that includes processes along mid-ocean ridges

Checking Concepts

Choose the word or phrase that best answers the question.

7. Which layer of Earth contains the asthenosphere?
   A) crust
   B) mantle
   C) outer core
   D) inner core

8. What type of plate boundary is the San Andreas Fault part of?
   A) divergent
   B) subduction
   C) convergent
   D) transform

9. What hypothesis states that continents slowly moved to their present positions on Earth?
   A) subduction
   B) erosion
   C) continental drift
   D) seafloor spreading

Use the illustration below to answer question 10.

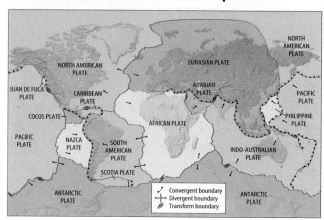

10. Which plate is subducting beneath the South American Plate?
    A) Nazca
    B) African
    C) North American
    D) Indo-Australian

11. Which of the following features is evidence that many continents were at one time near Earth's south pole? `SC.D.1.3.3`
    A) glacial deposits
    B) earthquakes
    C) volcanoes
    D) mid-ocean ridges

12. What evidence in rocks supports the theory of seafloor spreading? `SC.D.1.3.3`
    A) plate movement
    B) magnetic reversals
    C) subduction
    D) convergence

13. Which type of plate boundary is the Mid-Atlantic Ridge a part of?
    A) convergent
    B) divergent
    C) transform
    D) subduction

14. What theory states that plates move around on the asthenosphere?
    A) continental drift
    B) seafloor spreading
    C) subduction
    D) plate tectonics

Vocabulary PuzzleMaker fl6.msscience.com

Thinking Critically

15. Infer Why do many earthquakes but few volcanic eruptions occur in the Himalaya? SC.D.1.3.3

16. Explain Glacial deposits often form at high latitudes near the poles. Explain why glacial deposits have been found in Africa.

17. Describe how magnetism is used to support the theory of seafloor spreading. SC.D.1.3.3

18. Explain why volcanoes do not form along the San Andreas Fault. SC.D.1.3.3

19. Explain why the fossil of an ocean fish found on two different continents would not be good evidence of continental drift.

20. Form Hypotheses Mount St. Helens in the Cascade Range is a volcano. Use **Figure 9** and a U.S. map to hypothesize how it might have formed.

21. Concept Map Make an events-chain concept map that describes seafloor spreading along a divergent plate boundary. Choose from the following phrases: *magma cools to form new seafloor, convection currents circulate hot material along divergent boundary,* and *older seafloor is forced apart.*

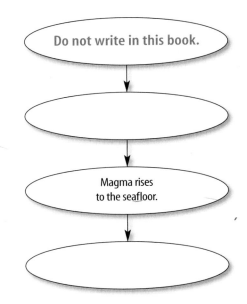

Do not write in this book.

Magma rises to the seafloor.

Performance Activities

22. Observe and Infer In the MiniLAB called "Modeling Convection Currents," you observed convection currents produced in water as it was heated. Repeat the experiment, placing sequins, pieces of wood, or pieces of rubber bands into the water. How do their movements support your observations and inferences from the MiniLab?

Applying Math

23. A Growing Rift Movement along the African Rift Valley is about 2.1 cm per year. If plates continue to move apart at this rate, how much larger will the rift be (in meters) in 1,000 years? In 15,500 years? SC.D.1.3.5

Use the illustration below to answer questions 24 and 25.

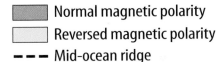

Normal magnetic polarity
Reversed magnetic polarity
--- Mid-ocean ridge

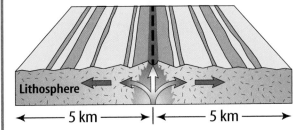

Lithosphere
←— 5 km —→|←— 5 km —→

24. New Seafloor 10 km of new seafloor has been created in 50,000 years, with 5 km on each side of a mid-ocean ridge. What is the rate of movement, in km per year, of each plate? In cm per year? SC.D.1.3.5

25. Use a Ratio If 10 km of seafloor were created in 50,000 years, how many kilometers of seafloor were created in 10,000 years? How many years will it take to create a total of 30 km of seafloor? SC.D.1.3.5

FCAT FOCUS

The assessed Florida Benchmark appears above each question.
Record your answers on the answer sheet provided by your teacher or on a sheet of paper.

Multiple Choice

SC.D.1.3.3

1 Which hypothesis or theory is best supported by the evidence presented in the diagram below?

A. continental drift

B. seafloor spreading

C. reversals in Earth's magnetic field

D. high temperatures in Earth's interior

SC.D.1.3.3

2 Which of the following observations best supports the hypothesis of continental drift?

F. Blue whales can be found in every ocean on Earth.

G. Limestone often contains fossils of animals that lived in the sea.

H. Some mammal species in Australia are found nowhere else on Earth.

I. Fossils of the same species of land lizard are found on continents separated by an ocean.

SC.D.1.3.3

3 The map shows the major plates near South America, their direction of movement, and the type of boundary between them.

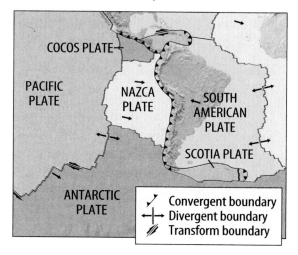

What boundary feature most likely occurs along the Nazca and South American plates?

A. rift valleys

B. volcanoes

C. a strike-slip fault

D. new oceanic crust

SC.H.1.3.2

4 Alfred Wegener described continental drift in 1912. Why weren't Wegener's ideas accepted by scientists until the 1950s?

F. Wegener was not respected because he was not a geologist.

G. The fossil evidence of the time did not support Wegener's ideas.

H. The continents Wegener proposed do not actually line up very well.

I. Wegener could not explain how or why the continents moved.

SC.D.1.3.3

5 What is the main cause of convection currents in Earth's mantle?

A. Energy from the Sun heats the upper part of the mantle more than the lower part.

B. Earthquakes produce cracks in Earth's crust, allowing hot, plasticlike rock to rise up from the mantle.

C. Heat released by volcanoes melts rock at the surface, and the molten rock sinks through cracks in the mantle.

D. Warmer, less dense rock rises toward the surface and cooler, denser rock sinks back toward the core.

Gridded Response

SC.D.1.3.5

6 The graph shows the relationship between the average depth and age of the seafloor in one particular area of the ocean.

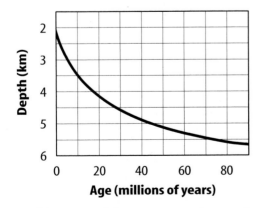

Relationship Between Depth and Age of Seafloor

For this area of the ocean, estimate the average depth, in kilometers, of seafloor that is 70 million years old.

Short Response

SC.H.1.3.1

7 In 1968, scientists measured the age of rocks taken from mid-ocean ridges and nearby areas. Explain how this information helped to support the idea of seafloor spreading.

Extended Response

SC.D.1.3.3

8 The arrows in the diagram below represent heat transfer in Earth's mantle.

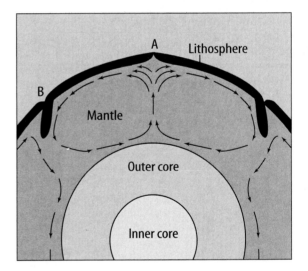

PART A What type of plate boundary is most likely to occur along the region labeled "A"? Describe what happens to Earth's plates at this boundary and what features may form as a result.

PART B What type of plate boundary is most likely to occur along the region labeled "B"? Describe what happens to Earth's plates at this boundary and what features may form as a result.

How Are
Arms &
Centimeters
Connected?

About 5,000 years ago, the Egyptians developed one of the earliest recorded units of measurement—the cubit, which was based on the length of the arm from elbow to fingertip. The Egyptian measurement system probably influenced later systems, many of which also were based on body parts such as arms and feet. Such systems, however, could be problematic, since arms and feet vary in length from one person to another. Moreover, each country had its own system, which made it hard for people from different countries to share information. The need for a precise, universal measurement system eventually led to the adoption of the meter as the basic international unit of length. A meter is defined as the distance that light travels in a vacuum in a certain fraction of a second—a distance that never varies. Meters are divided into smaller units called centimeters, which are seen on the rulers here.

unit ⚡ projects

Visit unit projects at **fl6.msscience.com** for project ideas and resources. Projects include:

- **History** Design a ceiling tile all about a specific chemical element. Name, symbol, who and when discovered will be displayed to promote interest in the periodic table.
- **Technology** Convert a family recipe from English measurement to SI units of measurement. Enjoy a classroom bake-off!
- **Model** Create a character in an SI world. Develop a picture storybook or comic book to demonstrate your knowledge of SI measurement.

Web Quest *Chemistry of Fireworks* explores the chemical compounds of fireworks, what chemicals are used, and how firework displays are created.

411

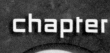
Sunshine State Standards—**SC.A.1:** The student understands that all matter has observable, measurable properties; **SC.H.1:** The student uses the scientific processes and habits of mind to solve problems.

Measurement

The Checkered Flag

Race car drivers win or lose by tenths of a second. The driver must monitor his fuel usage, speed, and oil temperature to win the race. In this chapter, you will learn how scientists measure things like distance, time, volume, and temperature.

Science Journal As a pit crew member, how can you determine how far the car travels per liter of fuel? Explain in your Science Journal how you would do this.

Start-Up Activities

SC.A.1.3.1
SC.H.1.3.4
SC.H.1.3.7

Communicating Measurements

You often make measurements. If you want to share your measurements with others, how do you communicate exactly what you mean? The lab below demonstrates the importance of using standard unit measurements.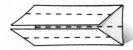

1. Complete a safety worksheet.

2. As a class, choose six objects to measure.

3. Measure the length of each object using the width of your hand. Record your measurements in your Science Journal.

4. Measure and record each object's length using a meterstick.

5. Compare your measurements to those of your classmates. Explain any differences in your measurements.

6. **Think Critically** Explain in your Science Journal the benefit of using standardized units when communicating measurements to others.

Preview this chapter's content and activities at
fl6.msscience.com

Measurement Make the following Foldable to help you organize information about measurements.

STEP 1 Fold a sheet of paper in half two times lengthwise. Unfold.

STEP 2 Fold the paper widthwise in equal thirds and then in half.

STEP 3 Unfold, lay the paper lengthwise, and draw lines along the folds. Label your table as shown.

	Estimate It	Measure It	Round It
Length of			
Volume of			
Mass of			
Temperature of			
Rate of			

Estimates Before you read the chapter, select objects to measure and estimate their measurements. As you read the chapter, complete the table.

Benchmarks—SC.A.1.3.1 Annually Assessed (pp. 413–420): The student identifies various ways in which substances differ; SC.A.1.3.2 Annually Assessed (p. 419): The student understands the difference between weight and mass.

Also covers: SC.A.1.3.3 (p. 420), SC.H.1.3.4 Annually Assessed (p. 416), SC.H.1.3.5 Annually Assessed (p. 418), SC.H.1.3.7 (p. 413)

Description and Measurement

as you read

What You'll Learn

- **Distinguish** between qualitative and quantitative descriptions.
- **Identify** the SI units of length, volume, mass, temperature, and time.
- **Recognize** tools used to measure each property listed above.

Why It's Important

SI units are found on products and signs you see every day.

Review Vocabulary

description: a statement that gives a mental image of an experience

New Vocabulary

- measurement
- estimation
- SI
- meter
- ✳ **volume**
- ✳ **mass**
- kilogram
- weight
- kelvin
- rate

 FCAT Vocabulary

Describing Properties

How would you describe the properties of the clothes you are wearing today? You might start with the colors or texture of the material. Then you might mention sizes—size-7 pants or size-14 shirt. Using numbers is another way to describe properties. These are examples of the two ways you can describe properties—qualitatively and quantitatively.

Qualitative and Quantitative Descriptions Qualitative descriptions provide information on properties or characteristics. You describe a property using words such as clear or cloudy, soft or hard, green or blue. On the other hand, quantitative descriptions use numbers. Quantitative descriptions also are called measurements. **Measurement** is a way to describe the world with numbers. Measurements tell us how much, how long, or how far. The circular device in **Figure 1** measures the performance of an automobile in a crash test. Engineers use this information to design safer vehicles. These measurements are numbers that give specific information about the safety of a car's occupant.

Figure 1 This device measures the range of motion of a seat-belted mannequin in a simulated accident.

Figure 2 Both quantitative and qualitative descriptions are necessary to completely describe events, like this one at the 2004 Olympic Games.
Describe *this event using both quantitative and qualitative descriptions.*

Both Types of Descriptions are Needed Usually, both qualitative and quantitative descriptions are needed to completely describe events, like the one shown in **Figure 2.** Suppose someone told you that runner Stefano Baldini from Italy won a race at the Athens Summer Olympics. Is this qualitative information enough to describe the event? Wouldn't it be important to know that he ran 26.2 miles in an official time of 2 h, 10 min, 55 sec? Likewise, knowing the distance and time doesn't mean much if you don't know the name of the athlete.

✓ Reading Check *Compare and contrast the terms* qualitative *and* quantitative.

Figure 3 This student is about 1.5 m tall.
Estimate *the height of the tree in the photo.*

Estimation

What happens when you want to know the size of an object but you can't measure it? Maybe it is too large to measure or you don't have the correct measurement tool. **Estimation** can help you make a rough measurement of an object. When you estimate, you can use your knowledge of something familiar to guess an object's measurement. For example, the tree in **Figure 3** is too tall to measure easily. Because you know the height of the student next to the tree, you can estimate the height of the tree. Estimation is a skill based on previous experience and saves time when exact numbers are not needed.

Estimation also is used to check that an answer is reasonable. Suppose you calculate your friend's running speed as 50 m/s (meters per second). You are familiar with how long a second is and how long a meter is. Can your friend really run a 50-m dash in one second? Estimation tells you that 50 m/s is unrealistically fast and you need to check your calculation.

Table 1 SI Prefixes	
Prefix	**Multiplier**
giga-	1,000,000,000
mega-	1,000,000
kilo-	1,000
hecto-	100
deka-	10
[unit]	1
deci-	0.1
centi-	0.01
milli-	0.001
micro-	0.000 001
nano-	0.000 000 001

INTEGRATE
Astronomy

Unit Confusion How important is it to use the same system of units when communicating data? In 1999, the *Mars Climate Orbiter* disappeared as it was to begin orbiting Mars. NASA later discovered that a unit system error caused a flight path error. This costly error may have been prevented if scientists had kept accurate records of their work. Research the error and determine what systems of units were involved.

Units of Measurement

Suppose you were asked to run in a race. Would you know how far to run if you were told to run a "ten"? Is it ten feet, ten yards, ten meters, or ten kilometers? Feet, yards, meters, and kilometers are examples of units. Units compare measured values to a known standard quantity. The units of a number are needed in order for it to make sense. There are many units for every kind of measurement. As you read earlier, length can be described using units of feet, yards, meters, or kilometers. How are these units different? Units are organized into systems. A system of units is a group of units that are related and can be used together.

The SI Unit System There are many systems of units being used today. However, sharing data and ideas is complicated when people use different measuring systems to describe the same types of measurements. To avoid this confusion, scientists established the International System of Units, or SI, in 1960 as the accepted measurement system. **SI** units are related by multiples of ten, as shown in **Table 1,** and provide a worldwide standard of physical measurement for science, industry, and commerce. In this book, we use only SI measurements.

SI Base Units The SI system contains seven base units shown in **Table 2.** All other SI units can be obtained from these base units. SI units are different from English or other types of units because they are related by multiples of ten. For example, 100 centimeters equals one meter, and 1,000 grams equals one kilogram. The meanings of the SI prefixes are shown in **Table 1.**

Table 2 SI Base Units		
Quantity	**Unit**	**Symbol**
length	meter	m
mass	kilogram	kg
temperature	kelvin	K
time	second	s
electric current	ampere	A
amount of substance	mole	mol
intensity of light	candela	cd

Length

Length is the distance between two points. Tools can measure very small lengths, like the thickness of a human hair, and very long lengths, like the distance to a planet.

Common Units of Length The **meter** (m) is the SI unit of length. One meter is about the length of a baseball bat. The size of a room or a building's height would be measured in meters. For example, the height of the towers over Tampa's Sunshine-Skyway bridge is 84 meters.

Objects smaller than a meter might be measured in centimeters (cm) or millimeters (mm). The prefix *centi-* means "one hundredth." There are 100 centimeters in a meter. A dollar bill is about 15.5 cm long. The prefix *milli-* means "one thousandth." There are 1,000 millimeters in a meter. The height of the letter *t* on this page is about 3 mm.

Kilometers are used to measure long distances such as the distance between cities or between Earth and the Moon. The prefix *kilo-* means "one thousand." There are one thousand meters in a kilometer. You may be most familiar with kilometers as the measure of long-distance races, such as a 10K, or 10-km race. A 10-km race is about 6.2 miles.

Measuring Tools Lengths in millimeters and centimeters often are measured using a metric ruler or meterstick. On a metric ruler, centimeters are marked with longer, numbered lines. The distance between two of these long lines is one centimeter. One centimeter is divided into ten millimeters, marked by the shorter lines. To measure the length of an object, place one end of the object at the zero mark of the ruler, as shown in **Figure 4.** Write down the number of centimeters just below the other end of the object, in this case, eight. Then, count the number of millimeters between the centimeter mark and the end of the object. In this case, there is one millimeter between the 8-cm mark and the end of the object. The length of this object is 8.1 cm.

To measure very long distances, lasers can be used to measure the time it takes for light to travel to an object. The distance is then calculated based on the distance that light travels in one second.

Annually Assessed Benchmark Check

SC.A.1.3.1 What part of a written measurement identifies the property being measured?

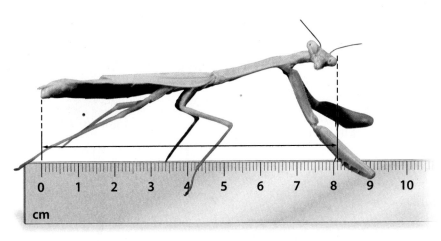

Figure 4 You can see from this metric ruler that the body of this praying mantis is about 8.1 cm long.

Figure 5 A cubic meter equals the volume of a cube 1 m by 1 m by 1 m.
Calculate *how many cubic centimeters are in a cubic meter.*

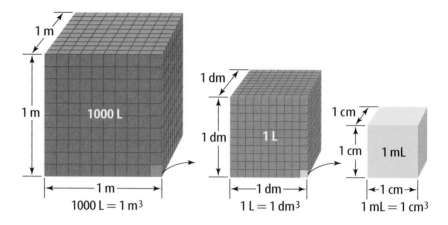

1000 L = 1 m³ 1 L = 1 dm³ 1 mL = 1 cm³

SC.A.1.3.1
SC.H.1.3.5

Mini LAB

Measuring Volume

Procedure

1. Find a square or rectangular **object** that fits into a **liquid measuring cup.**
2. Measure the object's length, width, and height. Calculate the volume. Record this in your Science Journal.
3. Fill the measuring cup halfway with **water.** Record the volume.
4. Lower the object into the water. If it floats, push it just under the surface with a **pencil.**
5. Record the new volume.

Analysis

1. How many milliliters of water were displaced? What does this represent?
2. What was the volume in cubic centimeters you calculated using a ruler?
3. Would you expect the two values to be the same? Why or why not?

Try at Home

Volume

The amount of space an object occupies is its **volume.** The cubic meter (m³), shown in **Figure 5,** is the SI unit of volume. You can measure smaller volumes with the cubic centimeter (cm³ or cc). To find the volume of a square or rectangular object, such as a brick or your textbook, measure its length, width, and height and multiply them together. What is the volume of a compact disc case in cm³?

You are probably familiar with a 2-L bottle. A liter is a measurement of liquid volume. A cube that is 10 cm by 10 cm by 10 cm holds 1 L (1,000 cm³) of water. A cube that is 1 cm on each side holds 1 mL (1 cm³) of water.

Measuring Volume There are two ways to measure the volume of an object. The dimensions of objects of regular shapes can be measured, and volume can be calculated from these measurements. How can you find the volume of something irregular, like a rock? To measure the volume of an irregular object, start with a known volume of water in a beaker or graduated cylinder like the one shown in **Figure 6.** Immerse the object in the water. The increase in volume is equal to the volume of the object.

Figure 6 A graduated cylinder is one tool used to measure volume.

Figure 7 A triple-beam balance compares an unknown mass to known masses.

Mass and Weight

The **mass** of an object measures the amount of matter in the object. The **kilogram** (kg) is the SI unit for mass. One liter of water has a mass of about 1 kg. Smaller masses are measured in grams (g). One gram is about the mass of a large paper clip.

You can determine mass with a triple-beam balance, shown in **Figure 7.** The balance compares an object to a known mass. It is balanced when the known standard mass of the slides on the balance is equal to the object on the pan.

Why use the word *mass* instead of *weight*? Weight and mass are not the same. Mass depends only on the amount of matter in an object. If you ride in an elevator in the morning and then ride in the space shuttle later that afternoon, your mass is the same. Mass does not change when your location changes.

Weight The measure of the gravitational force exerted on a body is **weight.** The SI unit for weight is the newton (N). Weight depends on gravity, which can change depending on where the object is located. Spring scales measure how a planet's gravitational force pulls on objects as shown in **Figure 8.**

If you were to travel to other planets, your weight would change, even though you would still be the same size and have the same mass. This is because gravitational force is different on each planet. If you could take your bathroom scale, which uses a spring, to each of the planets in this solar system, you would find that you weigh much less on Mars and much more on Jupiter. A mass of 75 pounds, or 34 kg, on Earth is a weight of 332 N. The same mass weighs 126 N on Mars and 782 N on Jupiter.

✔️ **Reading Check** *What does weight measure?*

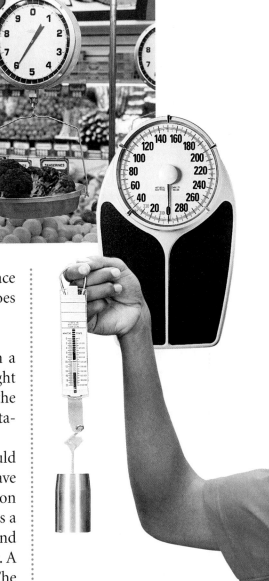

Figure 8 A spring scale measures an object's weight by how much it stretches a spring.

Figure 9 A comparison of three common temperature scales is shown below.

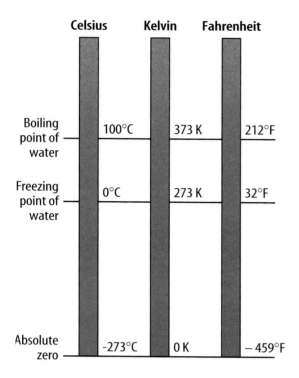

Celsius | Kelvin | Fahrenheit

Boiling point of water — 100°C | 373 K | 212°F

Freezing point of water — 0°C | 273 K | 32°F

Absolute zero — -273°C | 0 K | −459°F

Temperature

Temperature is a measure of the average kinetic energy, or energy of motion, of the particles that make up matter. It is related to how hot or cold an object is.

Temperature is measured in SI with the **kelvin** (K) scale. The Fahrenheit and Celsius temperature scales are the most common scales used throughout the world. All three temperature scales are used in scientific laboratories. A comparison of the temperature scales is shown in **Figure 9.** It is important to know that the difference in 1°F and 1°C is not the same temperature change. One degree Fahrenheit represents a smaller temperature difference than one degree Celsius. However, a 1 K difference in temperature is the same as a 1°C difference in temperature.

Time and Rate

Time is the interval between two events. The SI unit of time is the second (s). Time also is measured in hours (h). Although the hour is not an SI unit, it is easier to use to measure longer periods of time.

A **rate** is the amount of change of one measurement in a given amount of time. One rate that you are familiar with is speed, which is the distance traveled in a given time. Speed often is measured in kilometers per hour (km/h).

---

section review

Summary

Description and Measurement

- Quantitative descriptions answer questions such as how much, how long, or how far.

Estimation

- Estimates are based on previous knowledge and comparisons with familiar items.

The International System

- The SI units are accepted as the standard for physical measurements around the world.

Measurement

- Length is the distance between two points.
- Volume is the space an object occupies.
- Mass is the amount of matter in an object.
- Celsius is a common temperature scale.

Self Check

1. **Explain** the difference between qualitative and quantitative descriptions. `SC.A.1.3.1`

2. **Explain** how you could estimate the length of a parking space if you did not have a measuring device available.

3. **List** the SI base units and the quantities they measure. `SC.A.1.3.1`

4. **Explain** how you could find the volume of an irregularly shaped object. `SC.A.1.3.1`

Applying Math

5. **Measure** A block of wood is 0.2 m by 0.1 m by 0.5 m. Find its dimensions in centimeters, then find its volume in cubic centimeters.

6. **Thinking Critically** Why would it be important to write °C or °F when stating a temperature difference?

section 2

Mathematics and Measurement

Calculations

Suppose you want to determine the speed Justin Gatlin ran in Athens when he won the 100.0-m dash in 9.85 s. To determine his speed, divide the distance he ran, 100.0 m, by his time, 9.85 s. If this calculation is performed on a calculator, you get 10.15228426, as shown in **Figure 10.** The answer that should be recorded is 10.2 m/s. How were the units determined? Why weren't all the digits recorded? In this section, you'll learn what to do with units and how to determine how many digits to record.

Why does the number of digits matter? Recording too many digits in an answer implies that the scale on the measuring tool was divided into smaller units than it actually was. This is misleading and might be considered dishonest when doing scientific research. In the example above, writing all ten digits implies that the time clock measured the time as 9.850000000 s. However, the clock used in Athens measured the time as 9.85 s. How are the numbers 9.850000000 s and 9.85 s different? They have a different number of significant digits.

as you read

***What* You'll Learn**
- **Determine** the number of digits to record in a calculation.
- **Determine** the units recorded in a calculation.

***Why* It's Important**
Many FCAT questions require that answers be written with the correct units and significant digits.

Review Vocabulary
unit: a quantity adopted as a standard of measurement

New Vocabulary
- significant digits
- precision
- accuracy

Figure 10 The calculator usually gives the answer in too many digits. It is important to know how many digits to record for your answer.

Figure 11 The clock measures time to the nearest hour, but the stop watch measures time to the nearest hundredth second. **Explain** *why time measured with the stop watch has more significant digits.*

Significant Digits

The number of **significant digits** in a measurement indicates the uncertainty of the measuring tool used. Not all numbers in a measurement are considered significant. The number of significant digits is counted as follows:

Determining Significant Digits

- Digits other than zero (1, 2, 3, 4, 5, 6, 7, 8, 9) are always significant.
- Final zeros after a decimal point or between two other digits (601.04560) are significant.
- Initial zeros before any other digit (0.004010) are NOT significant.
- Final zeros in a whole number (1650) might or might not be significant. The measuring tool determines significant digits.
- All counted numbers are significant.

Measurements like 15.3 cm, 0.0203 mL, and 1.00 s have three significant digits. Measurements like 0.1 m, 2 g, and 0.004 mL have one significant digit. In the last example, 9.850000000 s has ten significant digits and 9.85 s has only three.

Measuring Tools and Significant Digits The number of significant digits in a measurement depends on the tool used to make a measurement. To measure the time it takes to run a 5-kilometer race, the clock in **Figure 11** might provide a time of 0.5 h. The stopwatch might provide a time of 0.591197 h. The timer that measures smaller units provides more significant digits.

Multiplication and Division The number of significant digits in a product or quotient is determined by the multiplier or divisor with the fewest significant digits.

$$6.14 \times 5.6 = \boxed{34}.384$$

3 digits   2 digits   2 digits

Because 5.6 has the fewest significant digits, 34.384 must be rounded to 2 significant digits to the ones place.

Rounding To round a number, look at the digit to the right of the digit in the place being rounded.

$$\underline{34}.384$$
↑

If this digit is less than five, the digit in the place being rounded—the number 4 in this case—remains the same and the numbers following are dropped. If the digit is five or greater, the digit in the place being rounded is increased by one. In the number 34.384, the number 3 is less than the number 5. Therefore, the answer is 34 and the .384 is dropped.

In the earlier example, when 100.0 m is divided by 9.85 s, the calculator reads 10.15228426. The number of significant digits recorded is determined by the measurement with the fewest significant digits. Since 100.0 has four significant digits and 9.85 has three significant digits, the answer is rounded to three significant digits—the tenths place.

$$\begin{array}{l} \text{(4 digits)} \\ \text{(3 digits)} \end{array} \frac{100.0 \text{ m}}{9.85 \text{ s}} = \boxed{10.1}5228426$$

3 digits ↑

Since the digit in the hundredths place, 5, is five or greater, the digit in the tenths place, 1 is increased by one. The remaining digits are dropped. The answer is 10.2 m/s.

Addition and Subtraction The number of significant digits in a sum or difference is determined by the number being added or subtracted with the fewest decimal places.

$$\begin{array}{ll} 6.14 & \text{hundredths} \\ + \ 5.6 \quad & \text{tenths} \\ \hline \boxed{11.7}4 & \text{tenths} \end{array}$$

Because 5.6 has the fewest decimal places—the tenths place—11.74 must be rounded to the tenths place. Because the digit in the hundredths place is less than five, the digit in the tenths place remains the same and the four is dropped. The rounded answer is 11.7. Another example of rounding a calculator answer is shown in **Figure 12.**

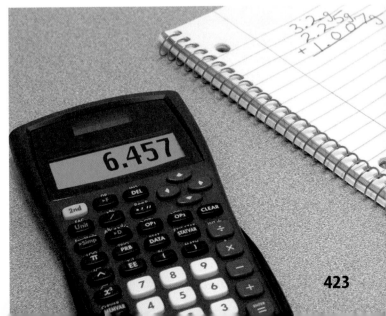

Figure 12 In this example, the calculator gives an answer with too many digits. You must use the significant digit rules and round your answer.

Evaluate *What is the correct answer to this problem?*

423

Calculations with Units

You've learned how to determine the number of digits to record in a sum, difference, product, or quotient. Now you'll learn what to do with the units in these calculations. When adding or subtracting measurements with the same units, the units of the sum or difference match the units of the measurements. When multiplying measurements, the units are multiplied. For example, to determine the volume of a cube with sides 10 cm long, the length, width, and height of the cube are multiplied.

$$10 \text{ cm} \times 10 \text{ cm} \times 10 \text{ cm} = 1000 \text{ cm} \times \text{cm} \times \text{cm} = 1000 \text{ cm}^3$$

When dividing measurements, the units are divided. If the units are different, they are written on either side of a "/" symbol. If the units being divided are the same, they can be cancelled.

Applying Math — Significant Figures and Units

VEHICLE SPEED If a vehicle can travel 3.46 km in 32 s, what is its speed in kilometers per second? Speed equals distance ÷ time. Use the correct significant digits and units.

Solution

1 *This is what you know:*

- speed = $\dfrac{\text{distance}}{\text{time}}$
- distance = 3.46 km
- time = 32 s

2 *This is what you need to find out:*

- the quotient of 3.46 km and 32 s
- the significant digits in 3.46 km and 32 s
- the units of the quotient

3 *This is the procedure you need to use:*

- use a calculator to calculate
  speed = $\dfrac{3.46}{32}$ = 0.108125
- 3.46 has three significant digits, 32 has two significant digits
- Round $\boxed{0.10}$8125 to two significant digits.
- The digit following the 0 is 8. Round the 0 to 1.
- The units are divided. The answer is 0.11 km/s.

Practice Problems

1. A person walks 12.5 km in 2.5 hours. Calculate this rate and write your answer using the correct significant digits and units.

Math Practice | For more practice, visit fl6.msscience.com

Figure 13

From golf to gymnastics, many sports require precision and accuracy. Archery—a sport that involves shooting arrows into a target—clearly shows the relationship between these two factors. An archer must be accurate enough to hit the bull's-eye and precise enough to do it repeatedly.

A The archer who shot these arrows is neither accurate nor precise—the arrows are scattered all around the target.

C Here we have a winner! All of the arrows have hit the bull's-eye, a result that is both precise and accurate.

B This archer's attempt demonstrates precision but not accuracy—the arrows were shot consistently to the left of the target's center.

Mini LAB

Measuring Accurately

Procedure

1. Complete a safety worksheet.
2. Fill a **400-mL beaker** with **ice** and **cold water**.
3. Measure the temperature of the ice water three times using a **computer temperature probe**. Dry the probe and allow it to warm to room temperature between measurements. Record the measurements.
4. Repeat Step 2 using an **alcohol thermometer**.

Analysis

1. Average the measurements.
2. Which measuring device is more precise? Explain. Can you determine which is more accurate? How?

Precision and Accuracy

One way to evaluate measurements is to determine whether they are precise. **Precision** is a description of how close measurements in a group are to each other. A group with measurements that are close together is more precise than a group that is spread apart. However, precise measurements don't necessarily mean they are accurate. **Accuracy** is how close a measurement is to a real, actual, or accepted value. **Figure 13** illustrates the difference between precision and accuracy.

INTEGRATE Health

Precision and accuracy are important in many medical procedures. One of these procedures is the delivery of radiation in the treatment of cancerous tumors. Because radiation damages cells, it is important to limit the radiation to only the cancerous cells that are to be destroyed. A technique called Stereotactic Radiotherapy (SRT) allows doctors to be accurate and precise in delivering radiation to areas of the brain. The patient makes an impression of his or her teeth on a bite plate that is attached to the radiation machine. This same bite plate is used for every treatment to position the patient precisely the same way each time. A CAT scan locates the tumor in relation to the bite plate, and the doctors can pinpoint where the radiation should go.

section 2 review

Summary

Significant Digits and Units

- The number of significant digits in a product or quotient is determined by the multiplier or divisor with fewest significant digits.
- The number of significant digits in a sum or difference is determined by the number of significant digits in the numbers being added or subtracted.
- When adding or subtracting, the units match the units of the measurements.
- When multiplying measurements, the units are multiplied. When dividing measurements, the units are divided.

Precision and Accuracy

- Precision describes how close measurements in a group are to each other. Accuracy compares a measurement to the real value.

Self Check

1. **Explain** why using correct significant digits in measurements and calculations is important.
2. **Round** the following numbers to three significant digits: 0.03256 g, 12.46 s, and 10.56 ml.
3. **Calculate** the area of a room with a length of 4.45 m and a width of 8.5 m using correct units and significant digits. Area equals length $\times$ width.
4. **Think Critically** Hannah obtained the following values in an experiment to find the boiling point of water: 99°C, 101°C, and 95°C. Are these numbers accurate or precise? Explain.

Applying Skills

5. **Calculate Density** Find the density of a rock sample that has a mass of 5.526 g and a volume of 1.2 cm³. Density is mass divided by volume.

section 3

Also covers: SC.H.1.3.4 Annually Assessed (pp. 427, 434–435), SC.H.1.3.5 Annually Assessed (pp. 428–429, 433)

Tables and Graphs

Tables and Graphs

Data must be presented in a way that helps others identify important facts quickly. Two ways of displaying data are tables and graphs. You will find data presented in tables and graphs every day in books, magazines, newspapers, and on television.

Tables A **table** displays information in rows and columns. The data in a table could be presented in a paragraph, but it would be harder to pick out the facts or make comparisons. Listing data in a table puts it all in one place. For example, **Table 3** lists information on endangered species in the United States.

Graphs A **graph** is used to collect, organize, and summarize data in a visual way. The relationships between the data often are seen more clearly when shown in a graph. Graphs are a good way to show how the smallest values compare with the largest. Three common types of graphs are line, bar, and circle graphs.

as you read

What You'll Learn

- **Describe** how to use tables and graphs to give information.
- **Identify** and use three types of graphs.
- **Distinguish** the correct use of each type of graph.

Why It's Important

Tables and graphs help you communicate data about the world around you in an organized and efficient way.

Review Vocabulary

✷ **axis:** a reference line in a coordinate system or graph

New Vocabulary

- table
- graph
- line graph
- bar graph
- circle graph
- ✷ variable
- ✷ independent variable
- ✷ dependent variable

✷ FCAT Vocabulary

Table 3 Endangered Species in the United States	
Year	**Species**
1986	327
1988	398
1990	442
1992	579
1994	741
1996	837
1998	924
2000	971
2002	988

Creating Line Graphs

A **line graph** shows the relationship between two variables—how one variable affects another. A **variable** is an event, condition, or factor that changes in a study or test. Examples include temperature and time. Both variables must be numbers. Often, data in tables can be used to create graphs.

Axes and Variables An **independent variable** is placed along the horizontal axis, or *x*-axis, and is a factor that is controlled or changed—for example, time or year. A **dependent variable** is placed along the vertical axis, or *y*-axis, and is a factor that is measured or observed. The value of a dependent variable is affected by changes to an independent variable.

Drawing and Labeling Axes To create a line graph using the data from **Table 3,** first determine the dependent and independent variables. Then determine the best scale for each axis. For example, if the value of the largest dependent variable is 988 species, each mark on the *y*-axis might be a multiple of 150 species—300, 450, 600, etc. The year or independent variable could be marked in multiples of 2—1986, 1988, 1990, etc. **Figure 14** shows how the axes and labels may be drawn.

The scale on the *y*-axis of the graph in **Figure 14** starts at 300. The graph would have to be much larger if the axis started at 0. Sometimes it's better to start a scale with a value other than 0 to keep your graph from becoming too large.

Figure 14 When making a line graph, you must choose the best scale for each axis. Then, you must label and mark your axes.

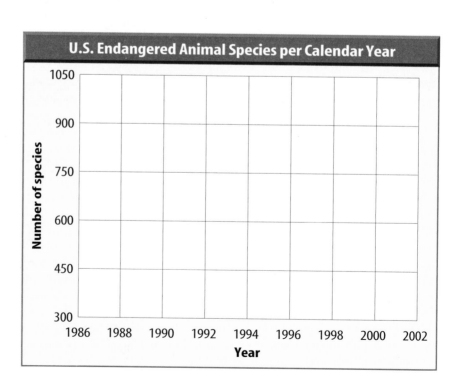

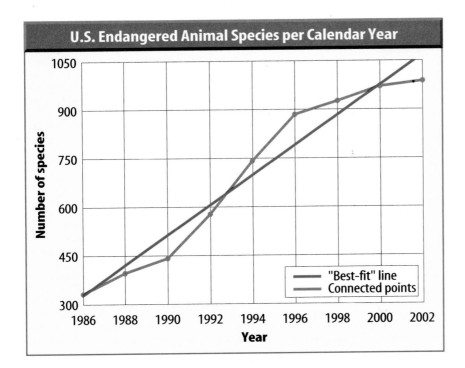

U.S. Endangered Animal Species per Calendar Year

"Best-fit" line
Connected points

Figure 15 This line graph shows the data points plotted from **Table 3**.
Explain *what the red and blue lines represent.*

Plotting Data To plot data on a line graph, draw a point at the intersection of a value on the *x*-axis and the corresponding value on the *y*-axis as shown in **Figure 15.** Draw a point for each pair of values you intend to plot. Then, connect the points as shown with the red line above. The data from **Table 3** is shown graphed above.

Reading Check *How do you plot a point on a line graph?*

Fitting a Line to the Data Sometimes the data points you plot on a graph do not fall on a straight line as shown with the red line above. This means that the value of the dependent variable does not change evenly as the value of the independent variable changes. When this happens, there are different ways to draw a line that best represents the data points. The first way is to simply draw short lines between each data point, as was done in **Figure 15.** The resulting line may be a zigzag or curved.

Another way is to draw a straight line through the data points, trying to center the line on as many points as possible. The blue line in **Figure 15** is drawn in this way. This line shows a line that best "fits" the data points. A line drawn this way shows the average change in the dependent variable over time. Many times, this is the most accurate way to represent the data points in a graph.

Reading Check *What does a "best-fit" line show?*

SC.H.1.3.5

Mini LAB

Making Predictions

Procedure
1. Half fill a **drinking glass** with **water**. Measure the height of the water.
2. Place five marbles in the glass and measure the water level again. Record the information in a table. Repeat this step until **20 marbles** are in the glass. Set the glass aside.
3. Draw a line graph using the data in your table. Use the graph to predict the water level for 30 marbles.
4. Test your prediction by adding ten more marbles to the glass and measuring the water level.

Analysis
1. How does your predicted value compare with the measured value for 30 marbles?
2. Could you make a good prediction for 50 or 100 marbles? Explain.

Try at Home

Figure 16 This line graph can be used to predict values by extending the line and the axes.

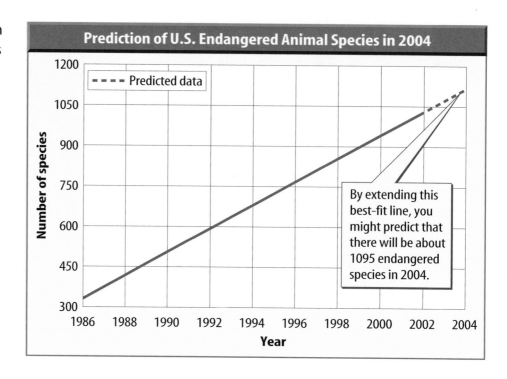

Prediction of U.S. Endangered Animal Species in 2004

- - - - Predicted data

By extending this best-fit line, you might predict that there will be about 1095 endangered species in 2004.

Number of species

Year

Using Line Graphs to Predict Line graphs not only represent data, they can help you make predictions. This is done by extending the line beyond the last data point on the graph. **Figure 16** shows the *x*- and *y*-axes extended. The number of endangered species in 2004 can be predicted from the graph.

Bar Graphs

A **bar graph** uses rectangular blocks, or bars, of varying heights to show the relationships among variables. One variable is divided into parts. It can be numbers, such as the time of day, or a category, such as an animal. The second variable must be a number. The bars show the size of the second variable. An example of a bar graph is shown in **Figure 17.**

Figure 17 Bar graphs allow you to compare results easily.
Infer *which group has the most endangered species.*

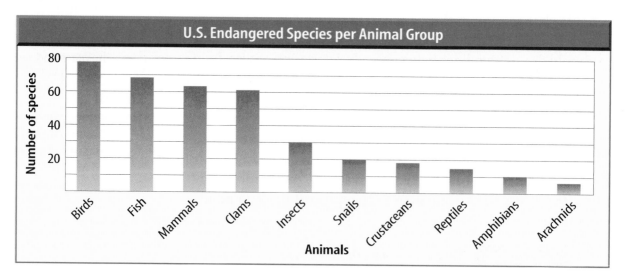

U.S. Endangered Species per Animal Group

Number of species

Birds   Fish   Mammals   Clams   Insects   Snails   Crustaceans   Reptiles   Amphibians   Arachnids

Animals

Circle Graphs

A **circle graph** is used to show how parts of a whole are related to each other. Circle graphs are sometimes called pie charts. In a circle graph, each wedge represents a fraction of the whole. Looking at the graph in **Figure 18,** you quickly see which animal groups have the highest number of endangered species by comparing the sizes of the pieces.

Reading Check *What is another name for a circle graph?*

A circle has 360°. To make a circle graph, you must find what fraction of 360° each part should be. For example, **Table 4** shows the number of endangered species by group for 2002. Suppose you want to construct a graph showing the percentage of endangered animals by group. For this graph you would not include the number of endangered plants because your graph should include only animals.

First, determine the total number of parts, or endangered animals in **Table 4.** The total number of parts is 389. One fraction of the total, *Mammals,* is 65 of 389 species. What fraction of 360° is this? To determine this, set up a ratio and solve for *x*:

$$\frac{65}{389} = \frac{x}{360°} \qquad x = 60.2°$$

Mammals will have an angle of 60.2° in the graph. The other angles in the circle are determined the same way. To draw the circle graph, use a compass to draw a circle. Then draw a line from the center of the circle to the edge. Use a protractor and the angles you calculated to divide the circle into parts. At times, the sum of all of the angles may not equal exactly 360° due to rounding.

Table 4 U.S. Endangered Species in 2002

Birds	78
Fish	71
Mammals	65
Clams	62
Snails	21
Insects	35
Crustaceans	18
Reptiles	14
Amphibians	13
Arachnids	12
Plants	599

U.S. Endangered Species per Animal Group

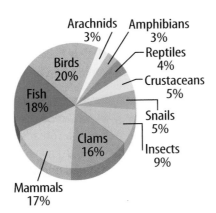

Figure 18 This circle graph shows the percentage of endangered species made up by each animal group in 2002.

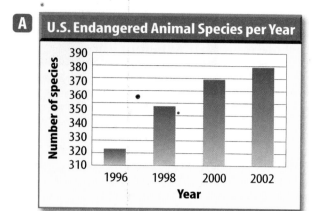

A U.S. Endangered Animal Species per Year

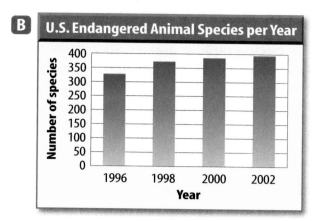

B U.S. Endangered Animal Species per Year

Figure 19 Careful reading of graphs is important. **A** This graph does not start at zero, which makes it appear that the number of species has more than quadrupled from 1996 to 2002. **B** The actual increase is about 20 percent, as you can see from this full graph. The broken scale must be noted in order to interpret the results correctly.

Reading Graphs When you use or make graphs to display data, be careful—the scale of a graph can be misleading. The way the scale on a graph is marked can create the wrong impression, as seen in **Figure 19A.** Until you see that the *y*-axis doesn't start at zero, it appears that the number of endangered species has quadrupled in just six years.

This is called a broken scale and is used to highlight small but significant changes, just as an inset on a map draws attention to a small area of a larger map. **Figure 19B** shows the same data on a graph that does not have a broken scale. The number of species has only increased 20 percent from 1996 to 2002. Both graphs have correct data, but they must be read carefully. Always analyze the measurements and graphs that you come across. If there is a surprising result, look closer at the scale.

section 3 review

Summary

Tables and Graphs

- Tables display information in rows and columns, while graphs are used to summarize data visually.

- A line graph shows the relationship between two variables, a bar graph shows the relationship among variables, and a circle graph shows the parts of a whole.

- Independent variables are changed. Dependent variables are observed.

- The line in a graph must be drawn carefully to represent the data accurately.

- Line graphs can be used to predict values beyond the data plotted in the graph.

- It is important to pay close attention to the scale on graphs in order to analyze the information.

Self Check

1. **Explain** how to use **Figure 19** to find the number of endangered species in 1998.

2. **Infer** what type of graph you would use to display data gathered in a survey about students' after-school activities.

3. **Think Critically** Why is it important to be careful when making or using graphs?

4. **Describe** when it is better to draw a straight line through data rather than just connect the dots.

5. **Identify** when you would use a broken scale.

Applying Skills

6. **Use a Spreadsheet** Make a spreadsheet to display how the total mass of a 500-kg elevator changes as 50-kg passengers are added one at a time.

PACE YOURSELF

◉ Real-World Problem

In long-distance running, the winner often is the one who sets the right pace. Hikers also learn how many steps it takes to go certain distances. But how do you estimate pace in SI units?

Goals
- ■ **Measure** using SI units.
- ■ **Graph** data in SI units.
- ■ **Calculate** speed and pace in SI units.

Materials
meterstick
stopwatch
*watch with a second hand
*Alternate materials

Safety Precautions
Complete a safety worksheet before you begin.

◉ Procedure

1. Make a data table that will keep track of time and number of steps through 5, 10, 15, and 20 meters for each student in the class.

Data Table for One Student

Distance (m)	Time (s)	Number of Steps
0–5		
5–10	Do not write in this book.	
10–15		
15–20		

2. Have students measure out a 20-m course, marking every five meters.

3. Have students arrange themselves by height.

4. Station students each with a stopwatch at 5, 10, 15, and 20 meters. Have another student at each of these marks count the steps of the walker.

5. Each student will walk the 20-m course as quickly as possible. Each timekeeper will record the time for a student to walk from one point to the next on the course. The step-counter will count the number of steps taken from one point to the next on the course. Record the data in the table.

6. Make sure you have all of the data from the class, including your own data.

◉ Analyze Your Data

Make two graphs for your walk. Both will have distance on the y-axis. One will have time on the x-axis, and the other will have steps on the x-axis. Draw a line that best fits the data points.

◉ Conclude and Apply

1. **Calculate** your speed (m/s) and pace (m/step) at 5, 10, 15, and 20 m. Were these numbers consistent, or did they change?

2. **Compare and contrast** your calculations to those of taller and shorter classmates. Explain any differences.

3. **Infer** how your results would be different if you ran the course.

𝒞ommunicating Your Data

Make a graph of the pace of each student at 20 m on the y-axis and height on the x-axis.

Benchmark—SC.A.1.3.1: The student identifies various ways in which substances differ (e.g., mass, volume, shape, density, texture, and reaction to temperature and light); **SC.H.1.3.4:** The student knows that accurate record keeping, openness, and replication are essential to maintaining an investigator's credibility with other scientists and society.

Design Your Own

Thinking in SI

▶ Real-World Problem

If you live in the United States, you are probably more familiar with English units than with SI units. How can you begin to train yourself to think of measurements in SI units? In this lab, you will be making measurements of a number of properties. For each property, you will first make an estimate in SI units, and then make a measurement. See how your skills improve with each measurement, and which properties are easiest to estimate.

▶ Form a Hypothesis

Certain measurements can be more difficult to estimate than others, especially in an unfamiliar unit system. Predict which will be most difficult to estimate in SI units—length, mass, volume, or temperature. Develop a hypothesis to explain why some estimates will be easier than others.

▶ Test Your Hypothesis

Make a Plan

1. Gather the materials necessary to measure in SI units. How will you measure length? What about mass, volume, and temperature?

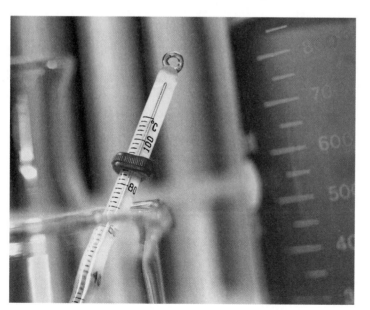

2. Choose some readily-available items for estimating and measuring. How many things will you use? How large should items be? Should the items vary a lot or very little?

3. How will you test both your hypothesis and your predictions? Do you need to collect other data?

4. How will you record estimates and measurements? Create a data table that includes both.

Goals

- **Estimate** various properties in SI units.
- **Develop** a better sense of the magnitudes of SI units

Possible Materials

ruler
meterstick
balance
graduated cylinder
thermometer

Safety Precautions

Complete a safety worksheet before you begin.

Data Table

Item Name	Property Evaluated	Estimated Value	Actual Value	Difference
		Do not write in this book.		

Follow Your Plan

1. Make sure that your teacher approves your plan before you start.

2. Carefully measure the property of each item immediately after you estimate it.

3. Record your data as you go.

⏵ Analyze Your Data

1. **Calculate** the differences between your estimates and your actual measurements.

2. **Graph** the differences against the sequence of measurements. Label the *x*-axis first measurement, second measurement, and so forth. Make one graph for each property.

3. **Graph** the differences against the actual measurements. Make one graph for each property.

⏵ Conclude and Apply

1. **Evaluate** the trends in your sequence graph. Did your estimates improve? Why or why not?

2. Did the size of the object affect the accuracy of your estimates? If so, how?

3. **Discuss** which estimates were most and least accurate. Why were some easier and others harder to estimate?

Communicating Your Data

Combine your graph of error versus size with the graphs from the rest of the class.

SCIENCE Stats

Biggest, Tallest, Loudest

Did you know...

... The world's most massive flower belongs to a species called *Rafflesia* (ruh FLEE zhee uh) and has a mass of up to 11 kg. The diameter, or the distance across the flower's petals, can measure up to 1 m.

... The world's tallest building is the Petronus Towers in Kuala Lumpur, Malaysia. It is 452 m tall. The tallest building in the United States is Chicago's Sears Tower, shown here, which measures 442 m.

Applying Math How many of the largest rafflesia petals would you have to place side by side to equal the height of the Sears Tower?

...One of the loudest explosions on Earth was the 1883 eruption of Krakatau (krah kuh TAHEW), an Indonesian volcano. It was heard from more than 3,500 km away.

Write About It

Visit fl6.msscience.com to find facts that describe some of the shortest, smallest, or fastest things on Earth. Create a class bulletin board with the facts you and your classmates find.

Reviewing Main Ideas

Section 1 **Description and Measurement**

1. Estimation is used to make an educated guess at a measurement.

2. The SI unit of length is the meter. Volume—the amount of space an object occupies—can be measured in cubic meters. The mass of an object is measured in kilograms.

Section 2 **Mathematics and Measurement**

1. Measurements should be recorded using the correct units and number of significant digits to avoid misrepresenting the data.

2. Accuracy describes how close a measurement is to the true value. Precision describes how close measurements are to each other.

Section 3 **Tables and Graphs**

1. Tables and graphs are used to collect, organize, summarize, and display data in a way that is easy to use and understand.

2. Line graphs show the relationship between two variables that are numbers on an *x*-axis and a *y*-axis. Bar graphs divide a variable into parts to show a relationship. Circle graphs show the parts of a whole like pieces of a pie.

Visualizing Main Ideas

Copy and complete the following concept map.

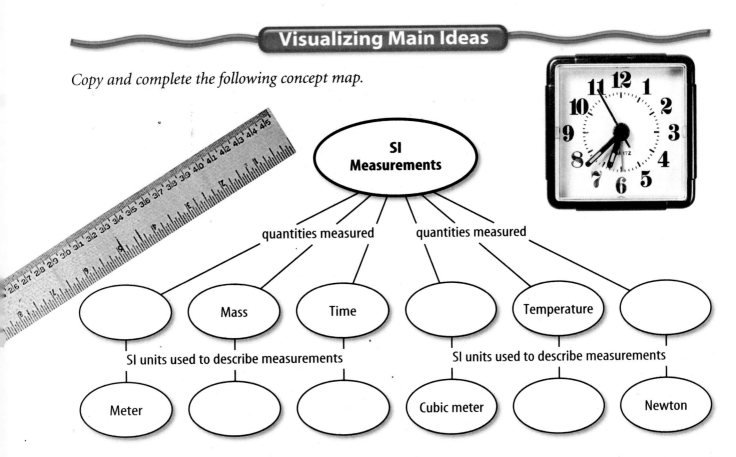

Using Vocabulary

Each phrase below describes a vocabulary word. Write the word that matches the phrase describing it.

1. the SI unit for length

2. a description with numbers

3. a method of making a rough measurement

4. the amount of matter in an object

5. a graph that shows parts of a whole

6. a description of how close measurements are to each other

7. the SI unit for temperature

8. an international system of units

9. the amount of space an object occupies

Checking Concepts

Choose the word or phrase that best answers the question.

10. The measurement 25.81 g was measured to the nearest
A) gram.
B) kilogram.
C) tenth of a gram.
D) hundredth of a gram.

11. What is the SI unit of mass?
A) kilometer
C) liter
B) meter
D) kilogram

12. What would you use to measure length?
A) graduated cylinder
B) balance
C) meterstick
D) spring scale

13. The cubic meter is the SI unit of what?
A) volume
C) mass
B) weight
D) distance

14. Which term describes how close measurements are to the actual value?
A) significant digits
B) estimation
C) accuracy
D) precision

15. Which is a temperature scale?
A) volume
C) Celsius
B) mass
D) Mercury

16. Which is used to organize data?
A) table
C) precision
B) rate
D) meterstick

17. To show the number of wins for each football team in your district, which would you use?
A) photograph
C) bar graph
B) line graph
D) SI

18. To show 25 percent on a circle graph, the section must measure what angle?
A) 25°
C) 180°
B) 90°
D) 360°

Thinking Critically

19. Infer How would you estimate the volume your backpack could hold?

20. Explain Why do scientists in the United States use SI rather than the English system (feet, pounds, pints, etc.) of measurement?

21. List the following in order from smallest to largest: 1 m, 1 mm, 10 km, 100 mm.

22. Describe an instance when you would use a line graph. Could you use a bar graph for the same purpose?

23. Compare and contrast volume, length, and mass. How are they similar? Different? Give several examples of units that are used to measure each quantity. Which units are SI? `SC.A.1.3.1`

24. Infer Computer graphics artists can specify the color of a point on a monitor by using characters for the intensities of three colors of light. Why was this method of describing color invented?

Use the photo below to answer question 25.

25. Interpreting Scientific Illustrations If you used this scale to weigh something, what is the smallest place value you would record?

Performance Activities

26. Newspaper Search Find a graph in a magazine or newspaper. What variable is plotted on the *x*-axis? What variable is plotted on the *y*-axis?

Applying Math

Use the table below to answer question 27.

Areas of Bodies of Water	
Body of Water	**Area (km²)**
Currituck Sound (North Carolina)	301
Pocomoke Sound (Maryland/Virginia)	286
Chincoteague Bay (Maryland/Virginia)	272
Core Sound (North Carolina)	229

27. Make and Use Graphs The table shows the area of several bodies of water. Make a bar graph of the data.

Use the illustration below to answer question 28.

Distance = 2,859.85 km

New York

Denver

28. Travel Distances The map above shows the driving distance from New York City to Denver, Colorado in kilometers. Convert the distance to meters.

29. Round Digits Calculate the products of the following equations and round each product to the correct number of significant digits.

$$42.86 \text{ kg} \times 38.703 \text{ kg} =$$
$$10 \text{ g} \times 25.05 \text{ g} =$$
$$5.8972 \text{ nm} \times 34.15731 \text{ nm} =$$

The assessed Florida Benchmark appears above each question.

Record your answers on the answer sheet provided by your teacher or on a sheet of paper.

Multiple Choice

SC.A.1.3.2

1 Mass and weight are different properties of matter. What does the mass of an object measure?

A. the volume and density of the object

B. the amount of matter in the object

C. the pull of gravity on the object

D. the size and shape of the object

SC.A.1.3.2

2 Kellie wants to make some measurements on a piece of wood. She finds the instrument shown below in the classroom.

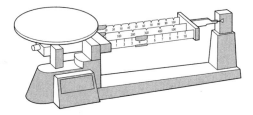

Which characteristic of the piece of wood could Kellie measure using this tool?

F. length

G. mass

H. volume

I. weight

SC.H.1.3.4

3 Measurements must be accurate and precise to make an experiment valid. Which is the **best** way to describe measurements that are accurate?

A. They are based on an estimate.

B. They are not based on numbers.

C. They are almost the same value.

D. They are very close to an accepted value.

SC.H.1.3.4

4 Mrs. Horton's class heated ice until it melted and continued heating the water (H_2O) until it became steam. The graph below shows the data the class collected.

Phase Changes of H_2O

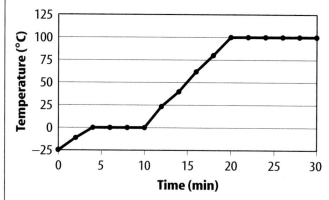

What is the next step that should be taken to make sure the results are dependable?

F. make a conclusion

G. report the conclusion

H. repeat the experiment

I. modify the experiment

SC.A.1.3.1

5 Greg has a box that measures 4 centimeters (cm) deep, 12 cm wide, and 12 cm long. How many cubes that measure 2 cm on each side, can he use to completely fill the box?

A. 72

B. 144

C. 288

D. 576

Gridded Response

SC.A.1.3.1

6 Maria mixed 35.77 g of Solid A with 95.3 g of Solid B. How would she write the mass of the mixture with the correct number of significant digits?

Short Response

SC.H.1.3.4

7 Ling has just completed a scientific investigation on the effects of fertilizers on plant stem growth. She plans to use the type of graph below to communicate her results.

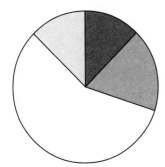

Is this graph appropriate for the kind of data Ling will collect? Justify your answer.

Extended Response

SC.A.1.3.2

8 Suppose that Patel has been traveling through the solar system. He has just landed on a planet, but he is lost. He decides to get on a scale to figure out where he is. Patel has a mass of 60 kilograms (kg). On Earth, he weighs about 588 Newtons (N). On this planet, he weighs about 42 Newtons (N).

Weight of 1 kg of Mass on Different Planets	
Planet	**Weight (in N)**
Mercury	3.7
Venus	8.9
Earth	9.8
Mars	4.0
Jupiter	23.2
Saturn	9.0
Uranus	8.7
Neptune	11.0
Pluto	0.7

PART A Use the table above to predict on which planet Patel has landed.

PART B Explain why Patel's weight on Earth is different from his weight on another planet.

FCAT Tip

Think Positively Some questions might seem hard to you, but you might be able to figure out what to do if you reread the question carefully.

Sunshine State Standards—SC.A.1: The student understands that all matter has observable, measurable properties.

Understanding Matter

An Underwater Flame?

Wendy Craig Duncan carried the Olympic flame underwater on the way to the 2000 Summer Olympics in Sydney, Australia. How many different states of matter can you find in this picture? In this chapter, you will learn about the four states of matter, and the physical and chemical properties of matter.

Science Journal How many states of matter do you see in this photo? List as many as you can.

Start-Up Activities

 SC.H.2.3.1
SC.H.1.3.4

Can you classify pennies by their properties?

Your teacher has given you a collection of pennies. It is your task to separate these pennies into groups. In this chapter, you will learn how to identify things based on their physical and chemical properties. With an understanding of these principles of matter, you will discover how things are classified or put into groups.

1. Complete a safety worksheet.

2. Choose a property that will allow you to separate the pennies into groups.

3. Classify and sort each penny based on the chosen property.

4. Explain how you classified the pennies. Compare your system of classification with those of others in the classroom.

5. **Think Critically** Write a paragraph in your Science Journal explaining how your group classified its pennies. What other properties could have been used to classify the pennies?

 **Preview this chapter's content and activities at** fl6.msscience.com

Properties of Matter Make the following Foldable to help you organize your thoughts into clear categories about properties of matter.

LA.A.1.3.4

STEP 1 Draw a mark at the midpoint of a sheet of paper along the side edge. Then **fold** the top and bottom edges in to touch the midpoint.

STEP 2 Fold in half from side to side.

STEP 3 Turn the paper vertically. **Open and cut** along the inside fold lines to form four tabs.

STEP 4 Label each tab as shown.

Classify Before you read the chapter, define each term on the front of the tabs. As you read the chapter, correct your definitions and write about each under the appropriate tab. Use the information in your Foldable to compare and contrast physical and chemical properties of matter. Write about each on the back of the tabs.

443

Benchmarks—SC.A.1.3.1 Annually Assessed (pp. 444–453): The student identifies various ways in which substances differ; SC.A.1.3.5 (p. 450): The student knows the difference between a physical change in a substance and a chemical change; SC.A.1.3.6 Annually Assessed (p. 448): The student knows that equal volumes of different substances may have different masses.

Also covers: SC.A.1.3.4 (p. 449), SC.H.1.3.4 Annually Assessed (p. 443), SC.H.1.3.5 Annually Assessed (p. 448), SC.H.1.3.7 Annually Assessed (p. 443), SC.H.2.3.1 (pp. 445–447, 451–452)

section 1

Physical Properties and Changes

as you read

What You'll Learn

- **Identify** physical properties of matter.
- **Explain** why materials with different masses have different densities.
- **Observe** water displacement to determine volume.
- **Describe** the states of matter.
- **Determine** how temperature changes affect substances.
- **Classify** matter using physical properties.

Why It's Important

Observing physical properties will help you interpret the world around you.

Review Vocabulary

✳ **mass:** amount of matter in an object

New Vocabulary

- physical property
- ✳ density
- states of matter
- melting point
- boiling point
- ✳ physical change

✳ FCAT Vocabulary

Using Your Senses

As you look in your empty wallet and realize that your allowance isn't coming anytime soon, you decide to get an after-school job. You've been hired at the new grocery store that will open next month. They are getting everything ready for the grand opening, and you will be helping make decisions about where things will go and how they will be arranged.

When you come into a new situation or have to make any kind of decision, what do you usually do first? Most people would make some observations. Observing involves seeing, hearing, tasting, touching, and smelling.

Whether in a new job or in the laboratory, you use your senses to observe materials. It is important to never taste, touch, or smell any of the materials being used in the lab without guidance, as noted in **Figure 1.** In the laboratory, you will rely mostly on other observations.

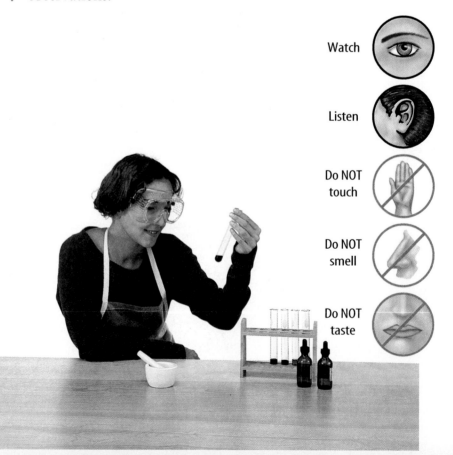

Watch

Listen

Do NOT touch

Do NOT smell

Do NOT taste

Figure 1 In the laboratory, you usually use only two of your senses—sight and hearing. It is unsafe to touch, taste, or smell any chemicals.

Figure 2 Color, shape, and texture are physical properties of matter.
Describe *the physical properties of an apple.*

Physical Properties

On the first day of your new job, the boss gives you an inventory list and a drawing of the store layout. She explains that every employee is going to help to create a system to organize the merchandise. Where will you begin?

You decide to go to an existing grocery store to observe the physical properties of the items on your list. A **physical property** is any characteristic of a material that can be observed or measured without changing the identity of the material.

Color and Shape What patterns do you observe on your inventory list? The list is organized by similarity of products, so you go to an aisle to make observations.

In the laundry product aisle, color is the first physical property that you notice. The detergent packages come in a variety of colors. You also notice that each package has a different shape. Some packages are rectangular, some are square, and some are more rounded. Shape and color are both physical properties of matter. You could arrange the detergent packages according to these properties.

Texture The next area that you investigate is the produce section. You notice a wide variety of fruits and vegetables. As you pick up the different types of produce, you notice the way they feel. Some fruits have smooth skin, while others have prickly or fuzzy skin. Texture is a physical property that describes the way something feels when you touch it. **Figure 2** shows the wide variety of physical properties in produce. Each item has a unique combination of color, shape, and texture.

Figure 3 These windows illustrate the difference between transparent, translucent, and opaque.

Transparent, Translucent, and Opaque The next area to be observed is the dairy section. There are rows of milk containers in various packaging. Some milk brands are packaged in cardboard containers, while others are packaged in plastic containers.

In one glass container, you notice that chocolate milk is visible through the glass. However, the same type of milk is not visible through some plastic containers. Why can you see through one container and not another? The glass container is transparent—you can see through it. The plastic container is opaque—meaning that no light passes through it. Some plastic containers are neither opaque nor transparent. They allow some light to pass through, but you can't see through them like you can see through the glass container. The plastic in these containers is translucent. Examples of a translucent, transparent, and opaque windows are shown in **Figure 3.** Transparency, translucency, and opaqueness are physical properties.

Metallic Properties As you continue your walk through the store, you observe canned food items. The cans are made of metal. What are the physical properties of metals? Metals are relatively hard. They can be hammered, pressed, or rolled into thin sheets. This is a physical property called malleability (ma lee uh BIH luh tee). Many metals can be drawn into wires, as shown in **Figure 4.** This property is called ductility (duk TIH luh tee).

At the grocery store, your employer might consider the properties of metals when purchasing grocery carts and shelves. Metal grocery carts can be dented more easily than plastic carts, but might be less likely to break. The metal in shelves attracts magnets which can be used to post prices and weekly specials.

Figure 4 This artist used the ductility of metal to create this sculpture.

Length Some properties of matter can be identified by using your senses, such as color, shape, and texture. Other properties can be measured. How much is there? How much space does it take up? One measurable physical property is length. Length is measured using a ruler, meterstick, or tape measure. Objects can be classified by their length. For example, you could choose to organize the bread in the bakery section of your store by the length of the loaf.

Mass Back in the laundry aisle, you notice a child struggling to lift one of the boxes of detergent. That raises a question. How much detergent is in each box? Mass is a physical property that describes the amount of material in an object. The larger detergent boxes are heavier than the smaller boxes. In other words, the larger boxes have more mass than the smaller boxes. Organizing the boxes by mass is another option. You might place the boxes with more mass on the bottom shelves.

Volume Another physical property that describes how much of something you have is volume. Volume measures the amount of space an object takes up. Liquids usually are measured by volume. The juice bottles on your list could be organized by volume.

 **Reading Check** *What term describes the amount of material in an object?*

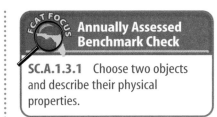
Annually Assessed Benchmark Check

SC.A.1.3.1 Choose two objects and describe their physical properties.

Figure 5 Water displacement is used to determine the volume of irregularly shaped objects. **Explain** *how you would determine the volume of a brick.*

Measuring Volume There are two methods used for measuring the volume of a solid, such as a cube. The first method is by measuring the length (ℓ), width (w), and height (h) of the cube. The volume is then determined by multiplying length, width, and height ($V = \ell \times w \times h$). Another method for determining the volume of a solid is by immersion. The object is placed in a known volume of water. The difference in the volume of water before and after the object is added equals the object's volume.

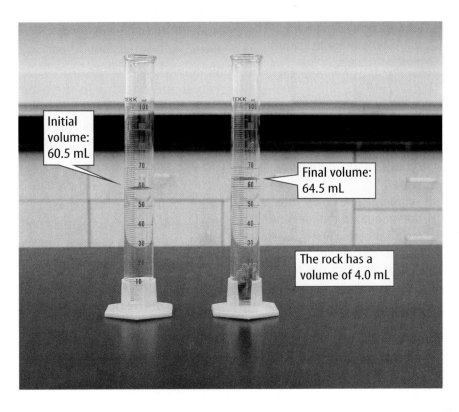

Initial volume: 60.5 mL

Final volume: 64.5 mL

The rock has a volume of 4.0 mL

Figure 6 These balls take up about the same space, but the bowling ball has more mass than the kickball. The bowling ball is more dense.

Bowling ball   **Kickball**

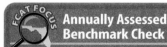
SC.A.1.3.6
SC.H.1.3.5

Mini LAB

Determining Density

Procedure
1. Complete a safety worksheet.
2. Find **three objects of the same size.** For example: a marble, a rubber ball, and a wood sphere.
3. Measure the mass of each object using a **balance.** Record the mass in your **Science Journal.**
4. Fill a **100-mL graduated cylinder** with 50 mL of **water.**
5. Submerge one object into the graduated cylinder and record the new water level. Empty the cylinder.
6. Repeat steps 3 and 4 for the remaining two objects.

Analysis
1. Create a data table.
2. Determine the volume and density for each object.

Density Another measurable physical property related to mass and volume is **density**—the amount of mass a material has in a given volume. If two objects have the same volume, the more massive object is more dense. Density is a physical property of a substance that does not change. Therefore, you can determine the identity of an unknown substance by calculating its density. Density is calculated by dividing the mass of a substance by its volume.

$$\text{Density} = \frac{\text{mass}}{\text{volume}} \quad \text{or} \quad D = \frac{m}{V}$$

Same Volume, Different Mass **Figure 6** shows two balls that are the same size but not the same mass. The bowling ball is more dense than the kickball. The customers of your grocery store will notice the density of their bags of groceries if the baggers load all of the canned goods in one bag and put all of the cereal and napkins in the other.

Reading Check *What two properties are related in the measurement of density?*

Liquid Layers Some salad dressings are made with oil and water. Before you use these types of dressings, you are advised to shake the bottle vigorously. Why is this? If you look closely at the bottle before shaking it, you will notice two liquid layers. One layer is oil and the other is water. Oil and water form two separate layers because their densities are different. The density of oil is less than the density of water. Therefore, the oil is the top layer. When two or more substances are mixed, they will form layers in order of density. The substance with the greatest density will form the bottom layer. The one with the lowest density will form the top layer.

States of Matter

What happens to ice cream if you leave it out on the kitchen counter? It melts into a soupy mess. Its state of matter changes from a solid to a liquid. The four **states of matter** are solid, liquid, gas, and plasma (PLAZ muh). When you organize the products in your grocery store, you probably should understand something about each product's state of matter. You might be familiar with three of these—solids, liquids, and gases. However, you might not be familiar with plasma. While very common in the universe, plasma is less common on Earth. Plasma exists in lightening, fluorescent bulbs, and neon signs. Besides their appearance, how do the states of matter differ?

Moving Particles Matter is made up of moving particles. The state of matter is determined by how much energy the particles have. Molecular motion increases as matter changes from a solid to a liquid and to a gas. The particles of a solid vibrate in a fixed position. They remain close together and give the solid a definite shape and volume. The particles of a liquid are moving much faster and have enough energy to slide past one another. This allows a liquid to take the shape of its container. The particles of a gas are moving so quickly that they have enough energy to move freely away from other particles. The particles of a gas take up as much space as possible and will spread out to fill any container. **Figure 7** illustrates the differences in the states of water.

Figure 7 The molecules in ice are tightly packed and vibrate in place. In liquid water they can slip past each other because they have more energy to move. In water vapor, they fill the entire container and move with even more energy.

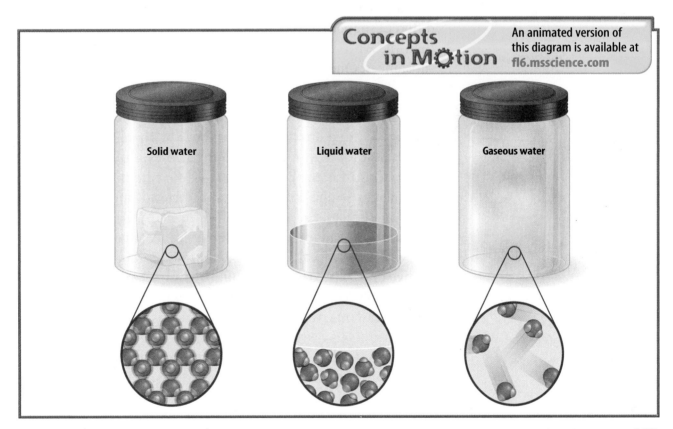

Concepts in Motion

An animated version of this diagram is available at fl6.msscience.com

Solid water

Liquid water

Gaseous water

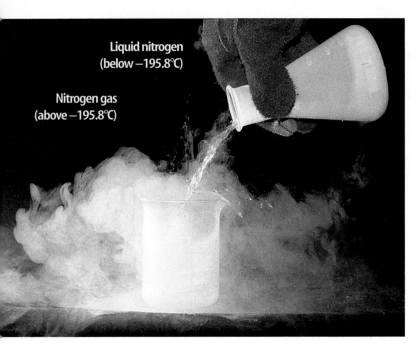

Liquid nitrogen
(below −195.8°C)

Nitrogen gas
(above −195.8°C)

Melting and Boiling Points The temperature at which a solid becomes a liquid at a given pressure is its **melting point.** The temperature at which a liquid becomes a gas at a given pressure is its **boiling point.** Melting and boiling points are physical properties that can be used to identify an unknown substance. At atmospheric pressure, water always melts at 0°C and boils at 100°C. Nitrogen boils at −195.8°C at atmospheric pressure. The change of liquid nitrogen to gaseous nitrogen is shown in **Figure 8.**

✓ **Reading Check**   *What physical change takes place at the boiling point?*

Figure 8 When liquid nitrogen is poured from a flask, you see an instant change to gas because nitrogen's boiling point is −195.8°C, which is much lower than room temperature.

Physical Changes

You have learned about several physical properties that you can observe with your senses and that you can measure. Now you will learn about changes in these properties. In a **physical change,** the physical properties of a substance change but the identity of the substance does not change. For example, if you cut an apple in half, many of its physical properties change. Each half has a different shape, a different mass, and takes up a different volume than the whole. However, the halves are still made of the same substances. One type of physical change is a change of state.

Changes of State You have already read about melting and boiling. Melting and boiling are physical changes. Freezing, or the change of a liquid to a solid, also is a physical change. Condensation is the change of a gas to a liquid. For example, water vapor in the air condenses into clouds and into droplets on cold surfaces such as a bathroom mirror. Boiling, condensing, freezing, and melting all are physical changes.

Another physical change is sublimation. Sublimation is the change of a solid to a gas without becoming a liquid. One example of sublimation is the change of solid carbon dioxide—dry ice—to gaseous carbon dioxide. Dry ice is used to keep things cold.

For your job at the grocery store, you will need to consider changes of state when organizing products. Some items must be kept frozen while others must be kept at room temperature.

Using Physical Properties

In the previous pages, many physical properties were discussed. These physical properties—such as appearance, state, shape, length, mass, volume, texture, density, melting point, boiling point, malleability, and ductility—can be used to help you identify, separate, and classify substances.

For example, salt can be described as a white solid. Each salt crystal, if you look at it under a microscope, could be described as having a three-dimensional cubic structure. You can measure the density, melting point, and boiling point of a sample of salt. These physical properties can be used to identify an unknown substance.

Figure 9 Coins can be sorted by their physical properties. Sorting by size is used here.
Identify *three other properties that can be used to sort coins.*

Sorting and Separating When you do laundry, you sort according to physical properties. Perhaps you sort by color. When you select a heat setting on an iron, you classify the clothes by the type of fabric. When miners during the Gold Rush panned for gold, they separated the dirt and rocks by the density of the particles. **Figure 9** shows a coin sorter that separates the coins based on their size. Iron filings can be separated from sand by using a magnet.

Scientists who work with animals use physical properties or characteristics to determine the identity of a specimen. They do this by using a system called a dichotomous (di KAH tuh mus) key. The term *dichotomous* refers to two parts or divisions. Part of a dichotomous key for identifying hard-shelled crabs is shown on the next page in **Figure 10.** To begin the identification of your unknown animal, you are given two choices. Your animal will match only one of the choices. In the key in **Figure 10,** you are to determine whether or not your crab lives in a borrowed shell. Based on your answer, you are either directed to another set of choices or given the name of the crab you are identifying.

LA.A.2.3.5
LA.B.2.3.1

INTEGRATE
Career

Field Biologists Scientists who investigate plants and animals in their environment are field biologists. These scientists work and sometime live in the environment that they are studying. Field biologists are employed by government agencies, industries, and private business. In your Science Journal, research and describe what careers are available to field biologists.

Figure 10

Whether in the laboratory or in the field, scientists often encounter substances or organisms that they cannot immediately identify. One approach to tracking down the identity of such "unknowns" is to use a dichotomous key, such as the one shown. The key is designed so a user can compare physical properties or characteristics of the unknown substance or organism—in this case, a crab—with characteristics of known organisms in a stepwise manner. With each step, a choice must be made. Each choice leads to subsequent steps that guide the user through the key until a positive identification is made.

Dichotomous Key

1.	A. Lives in a "borrowed" shell (usually some type of snail shell)	Hermit Crab
	B. Does not live in a "borrowed" shell	go to #2
2.	A. Shell completely overlaps the walking legs	Box Crab
	B. Walking legs are exposed	Kelp Crab

Can you identify the three crabs shown here by following this dichotomous key?

Everyday Examples Identification by physical properties is a subject in science that is easy to observe in the real world. Suppose you volunteer to help your friend choose a family pet. While visiting the local animal shelter, you spot a cute dog. The dog looks like the one in **Figure 11.** You look at the sign on the cage. It says that the dog is male, one to two years old, and its breed is unknown. You and your friend wonder what breed of dog he is. What kind of information do you and your friend need to figure out the dog's breed? First, you need a thorough description of the physical properties of the dog. What does the dog look like? Second, you need to know the descriptions of various breeds of dogs. Then you can match up the description of the dog with the correct breed. The dog you found is a white, medium-sized dog with large black spots on his back. He also has black ears and a black mask around his eyes. The manager of the shelter tells you that the dog is close to full-grown. What breed is the dog?

Narrowing the Options To find out, you may need to research the various breeds of dogs and their descriptions. Often, determining the identity of something that is unknown is easiest by using the process of elimination. You figure out all of the breeds the dog can't be. Then your list of possible breeds is smaller. Upon looking at the descriptions of various breeds, you eliminate small dog and large dog breeds. You also eliminate breeds that do not contain white dogs. With the remaining breeds, you might look at photos to see which ones most resemble your dog. Scientists use similar methods to determine the identities of living and nonliving things.

Figure 11 Physical descriptions are used to determine the identities of unknown things.
Observe *What physical properties can be used to describe this dog?*

---

section ① review

Summary

Physical Properties

- Physical properties include color, shape, length, mass, volume, and density.

States of Matter

- There are four states of matter.
- Matter can change from one state of matter to another.
- State of matter is determined by how much energy the particles have.

Using Physical Properties

- Substances can be classified according to their physical properties.

Self Check

1. **Identify** the physical properties of this textbook. `SC.A.1.3.1`
2. **List** the three states of water in order from fastest to slowest particle movement. `SC.A.1.3.4`
3. **Explain** how water might have two different densities.
4. **Think Critically** Which evaporates more quickly—rubbing alcohol that has been refrigerated or unrefrigerated?

Applying Math

5. **Solve One-Step Equations** Nickel has a density of 9.8 g/cm^3. Lead has a density of 11.3 g/cm^3. If both samples have a volume of 4 cm^3, what are the masses of each? `MA.D.2.3.1`

---

section
2

Chemical Properties and Changes

as you read

What You'll Learn

- **Recognize** chemical properties.
- **Identify** chemical changes.
- **Classify** matter according to chemical properties
- **Describe** the law of conservation of mass.

Why It's Important

Knowing the chemical properties will allow you to distinguish differences in matter.

Review Vocabulary

✳ **heat:** a form of energy that flows from a warmer object to a cooler object

New Vocabulary

- chemical property
- ✳ chemical change
- law of conservation of mass

✳ FCAT Vocabulary

Ability to Change

It is time to celebrate. You and your coworkers have cooperated in classifying all of the products and setting up the shelves in the new grocery store. The store manager agrees to a celebration party and campfire at the nearby park. Several large pieces of firewood and some small pieces of kindling are needed to start the campfire. After the campfire, all that remains of the wood is a small pile of ash. Where did the wood go? What property of the wood is responsible for this change?

All of the properties that you observed and used for classification in the first section were physical properties that you could observe easily. In addition, even when those properties changed, the identity of the object remained the same. Something different seems to have happened in the bonfire example.

Some properties do indicate a change of identity for the substances involved. A **chemical property** is any characteristic that gives a substance the ability to undergo a change that results in a new substance. **Figure 12** shows some properties of substances that can be observed only as they undergo a chemical change.

✔ **Reading Check** *What does a chemical property give a substance the ability to do?*

Figure 12 These are four examples of chemical properties.

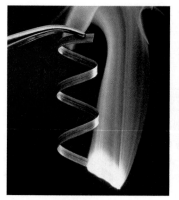

Flammability

Reacts with oxygen

Reacts with light

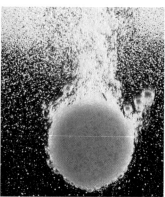

Reacts with water

An untreated iron gate will rust.

Silver dishes develop tarnish.

Common Chemical Properties

You don't have to be in a laboratory to see the changes that take place because of chemical properties. These are called chemical changes. A **chemical change** is a change in the identity of a substance due to the chemical properties of that substance. A new substance or substances are formed as a result of such a change.

The campfire you enjoyed to celebrate the opening of the grocery store resulted in chemical changes. The oxygen in the air reacted with the wood to form a new substance called ash. Wood can burn. This chemical property is called flammability. Some products have warnings on their labels about keeping them away from heat and flame because of the flammability of the materials. Sometimes after a campfire you see stones that didn't burn around the edge of the ashes. These stones have the chemical property of being incombustible.

Common Reactions An unpainted iron gate, such as the one shown in **Figure 13,** will rust in time. The rust is a result of oxygen in the air reacting with the iron and causing corrosion. The corrosion produces a new substance called iron oxide, also known as rust. Other chemical reactions occur when metals interact with other elements. The middle photo shows tarnish, the grayish-brown film that develops on silver when it reacts with sulfur in the air. The ability to react with oxygen or sulfur is a chemical property. The photo on the right shows another example of this chemical property.

Have you ever sliced an apple or banana and left it sitting on the table? The brownish coloring that you notice is a chemical change that occurs between the fruit and the oxygen in the air. Those who work in the produce department at the grocery store must be careful with any fruit they slice to use as samples. Although nothing is wrong with brown apples, they don't look appetizing.

Figure 13 Many kinds of interactions with oxygen can occur. Copper sculptures develop a green patina, which is a mixture of copper compounds.

LA.B.2.3.1

Enzyme Research Researchers have discovered an enzyme in fruit that is involved in the browning process. They are doing experiments to try to grow grapevines in which the level of this enzyme, polyphenol oxidase (PPO), is reduced. This could result in grapes that do not brown as quickly. Write a paragraph in your Science Journal about why this would be helpful to fruit growers, store owners, and customers.

Heat and Light Vitamins often are dispensed in dark-brown bottles. Do you know why? Many vitamins will change when exposed to light. This is a chemical property. They are protected in those colored bottles from undergoing a chemical change with light.

Some substances are sensitive to heat and will undergo a chemical change when heated or cooled. One example is limestone. Limestone is generally unreactive. Some limestone formations have been around for centuries without changing. However, if limestone is heated, it undergoes a chemical change and produces carbon dioxide and lime, a chemical used in many industrial processes. The chemical property in this case is the ability to change when heated.

Another chemical property is the ability to change with electrical contact. Electricity can cause a change in some substances and decompose some compounds. Water is one of those compounds that can be separated into its components of hydrogen and oxygen using electricity.

Something New

The important difference in a chemical change is that a new substance is formed. Because of chemical changes, you can enjoy many things in life that you would not have experienced without them. What about that perfect, browned marshmallow you roasted at the campfire? A chemical change occurred as a result of the fire to make the taste and the appearance different.

Sugar is normally a white, crystalline substance, but after you heat it over a flame, it turns to a dark-brown caramel. A new substance has been formed. Sugar also can undergo a chemical change when sulfuric acid is added to it. The new substance has obviously different properties from the original, as shown in **Figure 14.**

If eggs, sugar, flour, and other ingredients didn't change chemically through baking, you couldn't enjoy birthday cake. Cake begins as liquid and ends as solid. The baked cake clearly has different properties.

Figure 14 When sugar and sulfuric acid combine, a chemical change occurs and a new substance forms. During this reaction, the mixture foams and a toxic gas is released, leaving only water and air-filled carbon behind.

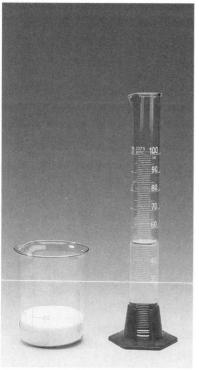

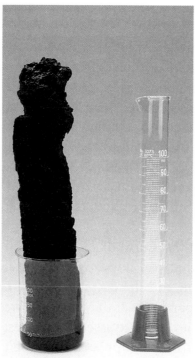

Signs of Change How do you know that you have a new substance? Is it just because it looks different? You could put a salad in a blender and it would look different, but a chemical change would not have occurred. You still would have lettuce, carrots, and any other vegetables that were there to begin with.

You can look for signs when evaluating whether you have a new substance as a result of a chemical change. Look at the piece of birthday cake in **Figure 15.** When a cake bakes, gas bubbles form and grow within the ingredients. Bubbles are a sign that a chemical change has taken place. When you look closely at a piece of cake, you can see the airholes left from the bubbles.

Other signs of change include the production of heat, light, smoke, change in color, and sound. Which of these signs of change would you have seen or heard during the campfire?

Is it reversible? One other way to determine whether a physical change or a chemical change has occurred is to decide whether or not you can reverse the change by simple physical means. Physical changes usually can be reversed easily. For example, melted butter can become solid again if it is placed in the refrigerator. A figure made of modeling clay, like the one in **Figure 16,** can be smashed to fit back into a container. However, chemical changes can't be reversed using physical means. For example, the ashes in a fireplace cannot be put back together to make the logs that you had to start with. Can you find the egg in a cake? Where is the white flour?

✔ **Reading Check** *What kind of change can be reversed easily?*

Figure 15 The evidence of a chemical change in the cake is the holes left by the air bubbles that were produced during baking. **Identify** *other examples of a chemical change.*

Figure 16 A change such as molding clay can be undone easily.

Table 1 Comparing Properties	
Physical Properties	color, shape, length, mass, volume, density, state, ability to attract a magnet, melting point, boiling point, malleability, ductility
Chemical Properties	flammability; ability to react with oxygen, water, vinegar; ability to react in the presence of electricity, light, heat, etc.

SC.A.1.3.5
SC.H.1.3.5

Mini LAB

Observing Yeast

Procedure

1. Observe a **tablespoon** of **dry yeast** with a **magnifying lens.** Draw and describe what you observe.
2. Put the yeast in 50 mL of **warm,** not hot, **water.**
3. Compare your observations of the dry yeast with those of the wet yeast.
4. Put a pinch of **sugar** in the water and observe for 15 minutes.
5. Record your observations.

Analysis

1. Are new substances formed when sugar is added to the water and yeast? Explain.
2. Do you think this is a chemical change or a physical change? Explain.

Try at Home

Classifying According to Chemical Properties

Classifying according to physical properties is often easier than classifying according to chemical properties. **Table 1** summarizes the two kinds of properties. The physical properties of a substance are easily observed, but the chemical properties can't be observed without changing the substance. However, once you know the chemical properties, you can classify and identify matter based on those properties. For example, if you try to burn what looks like a piece of wood but find that it won't burn, you can rule out the possibility that it is wood.

In a grocery store, the products sometimes are separated according to their flammability or sensitivity to light or heat. You don't often see the produce section in front of big windows where heat and light come in. The fruit and vegetables would undergo a chemical change and ripen too quickly. You also won't find the lighter fluid and rubbing alcohol near the bakery or other places where heat and flame could be present.

Architects and product designers have to take into account the chemical properties of materials when they design buildings and merchandise. For example, children's sleepwear and bedding can't be made of a flammable fabric. Also, some of the architects designing the most modern buildings are choosing materials like titanium because it does not react with oxygen like many other metals do.

The Law of Conservation of Mass

It was so convenient to turn the firewood into the small pile of ash left after the campfire. You began with many kilograms of flammable substances but ended up with just a few kilograms of ash. Could this be a solution to the problems with landfills and garbage dumps? Why not burn all the trash? If you could make such a reduction without creating undesirable materials, this would be a great solution.

Mass Is Not Destroyed Before you celebrate your discovery, think this through. Did mass really disappear during the fire? It appears that way when you compare the mass of the pile of ashes to the mass of the firewood you started with. The **law of conservation of mass** states that the mass of what you end with is always the same as the mass of what you start with.

This law was first investigated about 200 years ago, and many investigations since then have proven it to be true. One experiment done by French scientist Antoine Lavoisier was a small version of a campfire. He determined that a fire does not make mass disappear or truly get rid of anything. The question, however, remains. Where did the mass go? The ashes aren't heavy enough to account for the mass of all of the pieces of firewood.

Where did the mass go? If you look at the campfire example more closely, you see that the law of conservation of mass is true. When flammable materials burn, they combine with oxygen. Ash, smoke, and gases are produced. The smoke and gases escape into the air. If you could measure the mass of the oxygen and all of the original firewood that was burned and compare it to the remaining mass of the ash, smoke, and gas, they would be equal.

LA.B.2.3.1

LA.B.2.3.4

Science nline

Topic: Antoine Lavoisier
Visit fl6.msscience.com for Web links to information about Antoine Lavoisier, the founder of modern chemistry.

Activity Research the nonscientific portion of Lavoisier's life. Write a 2-paragraph magazine article from your findings.

Applying Science

Do light sticks conserve mass?

Light sticks often are used on Halloween to light the way for trick-or-treaters. They make children visible to drivers. They also are used as toys, for camping, marking trails, emergency traffic problems, and by the military. They work well underwater. A light stick contains two chemicals in separate tubes. When you break the inner tube, the two chemicals react producing a greenish light. The chemicals are not toxic, and they will not catch fire.

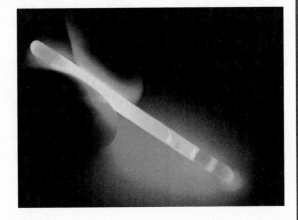

Identifying the Problem

In all reactions that occur in the world, mass is never lost or gained. This is the law of conservation of mass. An example of this phenomenon is the light stick. How can you prove this?

Solving the Problem

Describe how you could show that a light stick does not gain or lose mass when you allow the reaction to take place. Is this reaction a chemical or physical change? What is your evidence?

Figure 17 This reaction demonstrates the law of conservation of mass. Although a chemical change has occurred and new substances were made, the mass remained constant.

Before and After Mass is not destroyed or created during any chemical change. The law of conservation of mass is demonstrated in **Figure 17.** In the first photo, you see one substance in the flask and a different substance contained in a test tube inside the flask. The total mass is 16.150 g. In the second photo, the flask is turned upside down. This allows the two substances to mix and react. Because the flask is sealed, nothing is allowed to escape. In the third photo, the flask is placed on the balance again and the total mass is determined to be 16.150 g. If no mass is lost or gained, what happens in a reaction? Instead of disappearing or appearing, the particles in the substances rearrange into different combinations with different properties.

section 2 review

Summary

Common Chemical Properties

- A new substance, or substances, form(s) as a result of a chemical change.
- Exposure to oxygen, heat, and light can cause chemical reactions.

Something New

- Physical changes can be reversed. Chemical changes cannot be reversed.
- Substances can be classified according to their chemical properties.

The Law of Conservation of Mass

- Mass is not gained or lost during a chemical reaction.

Self Check

1. **Define** What is a chemical property? Give four examples. `SC.A.1.3.5`

2. **Identify** some of the signs that a chemical change has occurred. `SC.A.1.3.5`

3. **Think Critically** You see a bright flash and then flames during a class demonstration. Is this an example of a physical change or a chemical change? Explain. `SC.A.1.3.5`

Applying Math

4. **Solving One-Step Equations** A student heats 4.00 g of a blue compound, which reacts completely to produce 2.56 g of a white compound and an unknown amount of colorless gas. What is the mass of this gas? `MA.D.2.3.1`

Benchmark—SC.A.1.3.5: The student knows the difference between a physical change in a substance (i.e., altering the shape, form, volume, or density) and a chemical change (i.e., producing new substances with different characteristics); **SC.A.1.3.1:** identifies various ways in which substances differ; **SC.H.1.3.5:** knows that a change in one or more variables may alter the outcome of an investigation.

Different Changes

The products of both chemical and physical changes appear different from the starting materials. How can you tell these two types of changes apart? If a change is not reversible using physical processes, it is a chemical change. If a change can be reversed by physical processes, it is a physical change. In this lab you will investigate chemical and physical changes.

▶ Real-World Problem

How can we distinguish physical and chemical changes?

Goals
- **Observe** the properties of substances.
- **Examine** changes in properties of substances.
- **Determine** which changes are physical and which are chemical.

Materials
250-mL beaker (3)	borax
water	balance
table sugar	graduated cylinder
shallow pan (2)	stirring rod
white glue	

Safety Precautions
Complete a safety worksheet before you begin.

▶ Procedure

1. Describe the physical properties of sugar, borax, water, and glue in your Science Journal.
2. In a beaker, dissolve 15 g of sugar to 100 mL of water. Record your observations. Set the beaker aside.
3. In another beaker, dissolve 4 mL of borax in 100 mL of water to make a borax solution.
4. In a third beaker, stir 50 mL of glue into 50 mL of water to make a glue solution.
5. Slowly add 50 mL of borax solution to the glue solution and stir the mixture.
6. Record the properties of the mixture.
7. Place both the sugar solution and the mixture into separate shallow pans and leave them out overnight.
8. Record the properties of the substances the next day.

▶ Conclude and Apply

1. **Compare and contrast** the properties of the substances before and after they were mixed.
2. **Describe** the differences between the two solutions after left overnight.
3. **Infer** which changes were physical and which were chemical. Explain the reasons for your conclusions.

*C*ommunicating Your Data

Try making the glue-borax polymer with different amounts of borax solution or the glue-water mix. Describe any differences in the properties of the polymers. **For more help, refer to the** Science Skill Handbook.

LAB

Design Your Own

Liquid Layers

Goals

■ **Design** an experiment to observe whether liquids float or sink in other liquids.

■ **Predict** whether a liquid will float or sink on another liquid.

Possible Materials

100 mL beaker (2)
graduated cylinder (3)
20–30 mL each of liquids A, B, and C prepared by your teacher

Safety Precautions

Complete a safety work-sheet before you begin.

◉ Real-World Problem

Oil and other liquids often have to be transported across vast oceans. What if the tanker carrying these liquids leaks or sinks? Liquids that escape the tanker must be removed from the ocean quickly to minimize the danger to humans and ocean-dwelling organisms. Will cleanup crews be removing the liquids from the bottom of the ocean or from its surface?

◉ Form a Hypothesis

Using what you've learned about density, predict whether equal volumes of three different liquids will have equal or different masses. Predict what will happen when these liquids are mixed. Also, predict whether the same mass of three different liquids will have equal or different volumes. Predict what will happen when these liquids are mixed. Form a hypothesis to explain your predictions.

◉ Test Your Hypothesis

Make a Plan

1. As a group, discuss your four predictions. Agree on a hypothesis that will explain your predictions.

2. **Identify** the results that will confirm your predictions and your hypothesis.

3. **Choose and organize** the steps you will take to confirm each of the four predictions your group made. For each group of liquids tested, select the variable that your group will change. Determine constants. Determine which variables will be measured. What calculations will need to be made to confirm your hypothesis?

4. **Construct** data tables for each group of liquids tested. Determine column headings, row headings, and units of measurements.

5. Think through each step of your plan to make sure you haven't forgotten anything.

Follow Your Plan

1. Make sure your teacher approves your plan before you start.

2. Carry out the experiment according to your approved plan. When making measurements, write possible sources of error in your Science Journal.

3. Record all observations and complete your data table in your Science Journal.

▶ Analyze Your Data

1. Complete any calculations necessary to confirm your hypothesis.

2. Write a statement that summarizes the result of each test.

3. Identify at least 3 sources of error in your experiment. Explain how each source of error could have affected your results.

▶ Conclude and Apply

1. Did your results support your hypothesis? If so, **explain** how your hypothesis was supported. If not, **determine** whether you would change your experimental plan or modify your hypothesis and explain your choice.

2. **Explain** why the substances formed the layers in the order that they did.

3. **Predict** what would happen if you combined three different substances of equal mass together with the same three substances of equal volume.

4. **Predict** Would you expect the density of 15 mL of water to be the same as the density of 10 g of water? Explain.

5. **Predict** Would you expect the density of 15 g of water to sink or float on 10 g of corn oil? What data would you need to make a prediction?

6. **Apply** Would you expect crude oil in an oil tanker to float or sink in the salty ocean water? What data would you need to answer this question?

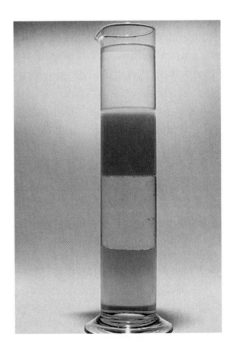

Communicating
Your Data

As a group, create a diagram of each group of liquids you combined. Label each layer with its density. Compare your diagrams with those of other groups. Discuss any differences.

The Road to Understanding Matter

What a Ride!

Front wheel drive, a powerful motor, and a smooth ride are characteristics to look for in an automobile. This car, developed by Nippondenso, packs it all under a gold plated hood. At 4.78 mm long, this car is about the size of a grain of rice! Created to show the power and potential of technology applied to unimaginably small objects, this car demonstrates a fraction of the knowledge scientists have gained in exploring matter on a very small scale.

Matter Mileposts

Philosophers and scientists have speculated about the building blocks of matter for centuries. Around 425 B.C., the Greek Democritis used the term "atomos" to describe the indivisible particles making up matter of all types.

While early thinkers typically lacked the ability to test their theories, later technological advances applied to the study of matter moved science from the realm of the philosophical to the quantitative. In the 1700s, scientists experimented with gases, a type of matter difficult to confine and hard to study. Their findings eliminated the last of the old Greek notions and laid the foundation for modern chemistry.

It was the work of French scientist Antoine Lavoisier (1743–1794) which earned him the title "Father of Modern Chemistry." By focusing on measurable, quantifiable data, he forever changed the way science was conducted. Lavoisier's experiments with gases led to the development of the law of conservation of mass, a cornerstone of modern chemistry which helps explain what happens to matter during chemical change.

A Changing Road Map

In the 1930s, scientists used the first particle accelerators to reveal the composition of the atom. These machines accelerate subatomic particles, like electrons, to speeds close to the speed of light. Collisions at this speed cause these particles to shatter, and provide the opportunity to detect and analyze the smaller particles which comprise them.

Once thought to be the smallest building blocks, the proton, neutron, and electron are now joined by other subatomic particles groups, including quarks. Scientists currently believe the quark is the most fundamental particle. Studying particles created in particle accelerators is difficult because most exist for less than a billionth of a second.

As the technology behind these powerful machines advances, current hypotheses will undergo revision. The nature of scientific study is to build upon and extend, while sometimes uprooting, commonly held theories. Experimentation to discover the building blocks of matter is no exception.

Investigate Research the two types of particle accelerators. Compare how they work and their sizes. Describe what scientists learn about atomic structure using these machines. Use the link to the right or your school's media center to get started. LA.A.2.3.5 LA.B.2.3.1

TIME

For more information, visit fl6.msscience.com

Reviewing Main Ideas

Section 1 **Physical Properties and Changes**

1. Any characteristic of a material that can be observed or measured is a physical property.

2. The four states of matter are solid, liquid, gas, and plasma. The state of matter is determined by the energy the particles have.

3. Color, shape, length, mass, volume, density, texture, melting point, and boiling point are common physical properties.

4. In a physical change the properties of a substance change, but the identity of the substance always stays the same.

5. You can classify materials according to their physical properties.

Section 2 **Chemical Properties and Changes**

1. Chemical properties give a substance the ability to undergo a chemical change.

2. Common chemical properties include: ability to burn, reacts with oxygen, reacts in the presence of heat or light, and breaks down with electricity.

3. In a chemical change, substances combine to form a new material.

4. The mass of the products of a chemical change is always the same as the mass of what you started with.

5. A chemical change results in a substance with a new identity, but matter is not created or destroyed.

Visualizing Main Ideas

Copy and complete the following table comparing properties of different objects.

Properties of Matter		
Type of Matter	**Physical Properties**	**Chemical Properties**
Log		
Pillow		
Bowl of cookie dough	Do not write in this book.	
Book		
Glass of orange juice		

Using Vocabulary

boiling point p. 450
✳ chemical change p. 455
chemical property p. 454
✳ density p. 448
law of conservation
of mass p. 459

melting point p. 450
✳ physical change p. 450
physical property p. 445
states of matter p. 449

✳ FCAT Vocabulary

Fill in the blanks with the correct vocabulary word or words.

1. The _____ is the temperature at which matter in a solid state changes to a liquid.

2. _____ is a measure of the mass of an object in a given volume.

3. A(n) _____ is easily observed or measured without changing the object.   SC.A.1.3.1

4. A _____ results in a new substance and cannot be reversed by physical means.   SC.A.1.3.5

5. Solid, liquid, and gas are all examples of _____.   SC.A.1.3.4

Checking Concepts

Choose the word or phrase that best answers the question.

6. Which is an example of a physical change?
   A) burning   **C)** rusting   SC.A.1.3.5
   B) melting   **D)** tarnishing

7. Which is a sign that a chemical change has occurred?   SC.A.1.3.5
   A) smoke   **C)** change in shape
   B) broken pieces   **D)** change in state

8. Particles in which state of matter vibrate in a fixed position?   SC.A.1.3.4
   A) gas   **C)** steam
   B) ice   **D)** water

9. What is density?
   A) the amount of mass for a given volume
   B) the amount of space an object takes up
   C) the distance between two points
   D) how light is reflected from an object's surface

Use the table below to answer question 10.

Physical Properties of Liquids		
Liquid	**Mass (g)**	**Volume (cm³)**
Corn syrup	15.3	14.2
Milk	12.5	12.1
Orange juice	27.5	25.0
Vinegar	8.3	8.2

10. Which liquid below has the greatest density?
    A) corn syrup   SC.A.1.3.1
    B) milk
    C) orange juice
    D) vinegar

11. Which is a chemical property?   SC.A.1.3.5
    A) density
    B) flammability
    C) size
    D) volume

12. What change results in a new substance being produced?   SC.A.1.3.5
    A) chemical
    B) change of state
    C) mass
    D) physical

13. What is conserved during any change?
    A) color   **C)** mass
    B) identity   **D)** volume

Thinking Critically

14. **Explain** Use the law of conservation of mass to explain what happens to atoms when they combine to form a new substance.

15. **Describe** the four states of matter. How are they different? SC.A.1.3.4

16. **Observe** A globe is placed on your desk and you are asked to identify its physical properties. How would you describe the globe? SC.A.1.3.5

17. **Evaluate** What information do you need to know about a material to find its density?

18. **Classify** the following as a chemical or physical change: an egg breaks, a newspaper burns in the fireplace, a dish of ice cream is left out and melts, and a loaf of bread is baked. SC.A.1.3.5

19. **Draw Conclusions** The densities of three liquids are 0.85 g/mL, 1.13 g/mL, and 0.96 g/mL. Which liquid would be on the top, middle, and bottom if they were combined? Explain. SC.A.1.3.1

20. **Infer** Concrete is formed through a chemical reaction of sand, gravel, crushed stones, and water. Do the starting materials have the same properties as the end materials? Give two examples to support your response. SC.A.1.3.1

21. **Describe** In terms of particle movement, explain how increasing temperature changes water in the solid state. SC.A.1.3.4

22. **Concept Map** Use a spider map to organize and define physical properties of matter. Include the concepts of color, shape, length, density, mass, states of matter, volume, density, melting point, and boiling point. SC.A.1.3.1

Performance Activities

23. **Comic Strip** Create a comic strip demonstrating a chemical change in a substance. Include captions and drawings that demonstrate your understanding of the law of conservation of mass. SC.A.1.3.5

Applying Math

24. **Measure in SI** Find the density of the piece of lead that has a mass of 49.01 g and a volume of 4.5 cm^3. MA.D.2.3.1

Use the table below to answer question 25.

| Density | | | |
Sample	Mass	Volume	Density
A	3.0 g	6.5 cm^3	
B	1.2 g	1.1 cm^3	
C	4.5 g		0.88 g/cm^3
D	125 g		0.36 g/cm^3
E		85 cm^3	2.3 g/cm^3
F		10 cm^3	0.75 g/cm^3

25. **Density** Copy and complete the table by supplying the missing information. MA.E.1.3.1

26. **Density** Using the formula for density, evaluate if two samples with the same volume, but different densities, will have the same mass. Give two sample calculations to support your answer. SC.A.1.3.6 MA.E.1.3.1

The assessed Florida Benchmark appears above each question.

Record your answers on the answer sheet provided by your teacher or on a sheet of paper.

Multiple Choice

SC.A.1.3.5

1 Making a cake involves mixing butter, eggs, sugar, and flour in a bowl and then baking the mixture. As the mixture bakes, the liquid turns brown and changes to a solid. Which step in the process of making a cake results in a chemical change?

  A. melting butter

  B. baking the mixture

  C. breaking egg shells

  D. adding sugar and flour

SC.A.1.3.6

2 Pam and Reggie were asked to make observations of the bowling ball and kickball shown below.

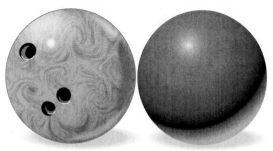

Bowling ball   Kickball

Which is an observation they might have made by looking at the two balls?

  F. They have nearly equal masses.

  G. They have nearly equal weights.

  H. They have nearly equal volumes.

  I. They have nearly equal densities.

SC.A.1.3.4

3 Which is not a physical property of matter?

  A. density

  B. flammability

  C. mass

  D. volume

SC.A.1.3.4

4 Models can be used to compare the different states of matter. The diagram below shows models of the three states of water (H_2O).

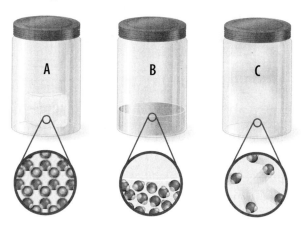

What state of matter do the particles in jar **A** represent?

  F. gas

  G. liquid

  H. plasma

  I. solid

SC.A.1.3.5

5 Which **most** likely describes a chemical change in a substance?

   A. Frozen water melts and becomes a liquid.

   B. A lump of clay is reshaped to become a statue.

   C. A nail exposed to water and air becomes rusty.

   D. Milk and chocolate syrup are mixed to make a drink.

Gridded Response

SC.A.1.3.1

6 When Ahmad heated mercury(II) oxide, HgO, liquid mercury (Hg) and oxygen (O_2) were produced. The table below shows some of the data from his experiment.

$2HgO \rightarrow 2Hg + O_2$	
Beginning mass of HgO	216 grams
Mass of Hg after heating	200 grams
Mass of O_2 after heating	? grams

According to the law of conservation of mass, what mass of O_2, in grams, is generated?

Short Response

SC.A.1.3.6

7 A dry sponge has a mass of 60 grams (g). A moist sponge has a mass of 90 grams (g). The volume of each sponge is 180 cubic centimeters (cm^3). Compare and contrast the densities of the two sponges.

Extended Response

SC.H.2.3.1

8 The graph below shows the relationship of mass to volume for iron (Fe).

Iron Samples

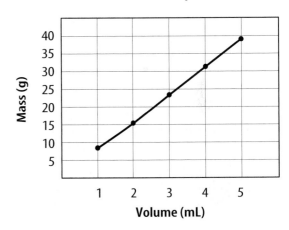

   PART A According to the graph, what are the mass and density of 5.0 milliliters (mL) of iron?

   PART B What is the mass of an iron sample that has a volume of 9.0 mL? Explain your answer.

chapter

16

Sunshine State Standards—SC.A.1: The student understands that all matter has observable, measurable properties; SC.A.2: The student understands the basic principles of atomic theory; SC.H.2.

Atoms, Elements, and the Periodic Table

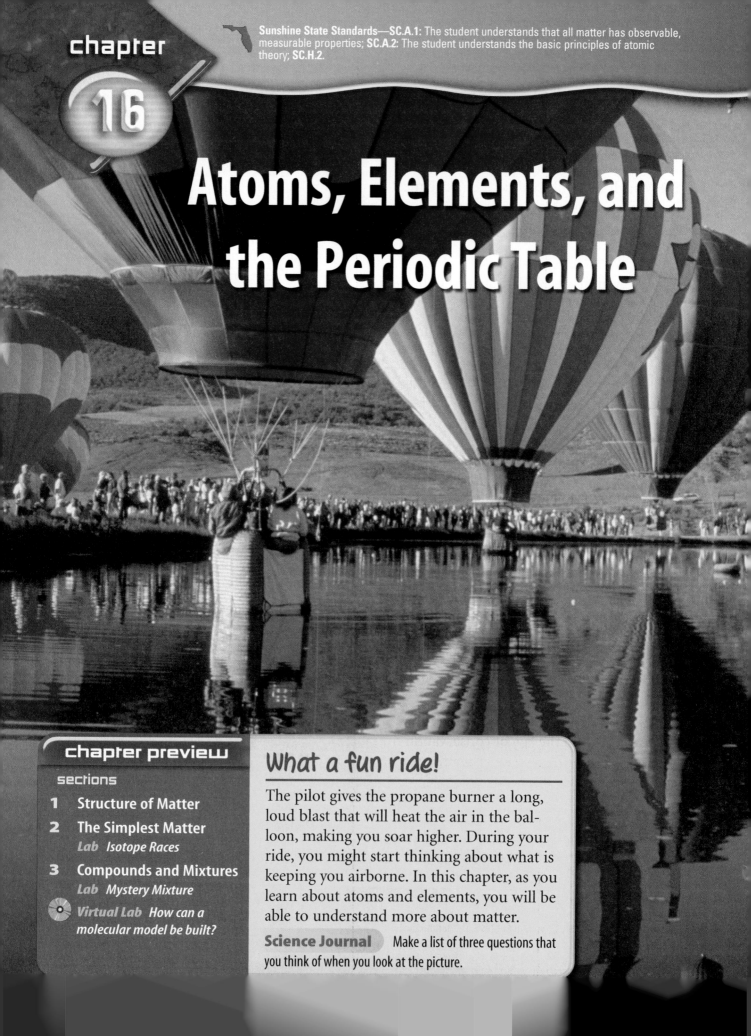

What a fun ride!

The pilot gives the propane burner a long, loud blast that will heat the air in the balloon, making you soar higher. During your ride, you might start thinking about what is keeping you airborne. In this chapter, as you learn about atoms and elements, you will be able to understand more about matter.

Science Journal Make a list of three questions that you think of when you look at the picture.

Start-Up Activities

 SC.H.1.3.5

What is matter?

You've just finished playing basketball. You're hot and thirsty. You reach for your bottle of water and take a drink. Releasing your grip, you notice that the bottle is nearly empty. According to the dictionary, *empty* means "containing nothing." When you have finished the water in the bottle, is it really empty?

1. Complete a safety worksheet.
2. Inflate two balloons equally. Attach 6 cm of tape along the center of a meterstick. Attach one balloon to each end of the meterstick using tape.
3. Balance the meterstick and balloons on top of a ring stand. On the tape, mark the location where the meterstick is balanced.
4. Put a small hole in one balloon using a pin. Allow the balloon to deflate. Balance the meterstick. Mark the location where the meterstick balances.
5. **Think Critically** Describe your observations in your Science Journal. Explain your observations.

FOLDABLES Study Organizer

Atoms, Elements, and the Periodic Table Make the following Foldable to help you identify the main ideas about atoms, elements, compounds, and mixtures.

LA.A.1.3.4

STEP 1 Draw a mark at the midpoint of a sheet of paper along the side edge. Then **fold** the top and bottom edges in to touch the midpoint.

STEP 2 Fold in half from side to side.

STEP 3 Open and cut along the inside fold lines to form four tabs.

STEP 4 Label each tab as shown.

Read and Write As you read the chapter, list several everyday examples of atoms, elements, compounds, and mixtures on the back of the appropriate tab.

 **Science Online**

Preview this chapter's content and activities at fl6.msscience.com

471

section
1

Structure of Matter

as you read

What You'll Learn

- **Describe** characteristics of matter.
- **Identify** what makes up matter.
- **Identify** the parts of an atom.
- **Compare** the models that are used for atoms.

Why It's Important

Matter makes up almost everything we see—and much of what we can't see.

Review Vocabulary

☀ **density:** the mass of an object divided by its volume

New Vocabulary

☀ **matter**
☀ **atom**
● **law of conservation of matter**
☀ **electron**
☀ **nucleus**
☀ **proton**
☀ **neutron**

☀ FCAT Vocabulary

What is matter?

Is a glass with some water in it half empty or half full? Actually, neither is correct. The glass is completely full—half full of water and half full of air. What is air? Air is a mixture of several gases, including nitrogen and oxygen, which are kinds of matter. **Matter** is anything that has mass and takes up space. So, even though you can't see it or hold it in your hand, air is matter. What about all the things you can see, taste, smell, and touch? Most are made of matter, too. Look at the things pictured in **Figure 1** and determine which of them are matter.

What isn't matter?

You can see the words on this page because of the light from the Sun or from a fixture in the room. Does light have mass or take up space? What about the warmth from the Sun or the heat from the heater in your classroom? Light and heat do not take up space, and they have no mass. Therefore, they are not forms of matter. Emotions, thoughts, and ideas are not matter either. Does this information change your mind about the items in **Figure 1**?

✔ **Reading Check** *Why is air matter, but light is not?*

Figure 1 A rainbow is formed when light filters through the raindrops, a plant grows from a seed in the ground, and a statue is sculpted from bronze.
Identify *which are matter.*

Table 1 Early Beliefs About the Composition of Matter

Many Indian Philosophers (1000 B.C.)	Kashyapa, an Indian Philosopher (1000 B.C.)	Many Greek Philosophers (500–300 B.C.)	Democritus (380 B.C.)	Aristotle (330 B.C.)	Chinese Philosophers (300 B.C.)
• Ether—an invisible substance that filled the heavens • Earth • Water • Air • Fire	• Five elements broken down into smaller units called parmanu • Parmanu of earth elements are heavier than air elements	• Earth • Water • Air • Fire	• Tiny individual particles he called *atomos* • Empty space through which atoms move • Each substance composed of one type of *atomos*	• Empty space could not exist • Earth • Water • Air • Fire	• Metal • Earth • Water • Air • Fire

What makes up matter?

Suppose you cut a chunk of wood into smaller and smaller pieces. Do the pieces seem to be made of the same matter as the large chunk you started with? If you could cut a small enough piece, would it still have the same properties as the first chunk? Is there a limit to how small a piece can be? For centuries, people have asked questions like these and wondered what matter is made of. Studying how people have made these discoveries will help you understand the inquiry process.

An Early Idea Democritus, who lived from about 460 B.C. to 370 B.C., was a Greek philosopher who thought the universe was made of empty space and tiny bits of stuff. He believed that the bits of stuff were so small they could not be divided into smaller pieces. He called these tiny pieces *atomos*. The term *atom*, which is used today, comes from a Greek word that means "cannot be divided." An **atom** is a small particle that makes up most types of matter. An atom is too small to be seen even with a powerful microscope. **Table 1** shows Democritus's ideas and those of other early scientists and philosophers. Democritus thought that different types of atoms existed for every type of matter and that the atom's identity explained the characteristics of each type of matter. Democritus's ideas about atoms were a first step toward understanding matter. However, his ideas were not accepted for over 2,000 years. In the early 1800s, scientists built upon the concept of atoms to form the current atomic theory of matter.

INTEGRATE History

Atomism Historians note that Leucippus developed the idea of the atom around 440 B.C. He and his student, Democritus, refined the idea of the atom years later. Their concept of the atom was based on five major points: (1) all matter is made of atoms, (2) there are empty spaces between atoms, (3) atoms are complete solids, (4) atoms do not have internal structure, and (5) atoms are different in size, shape, and weight.

Figure 2 When wood burns, matter is not lost. The total mass of the wood and the oxygen it combines with during a fire equals the total mass of the ash, water vapor, carbon dioxide, and other gases produced.
Infer *When you burn wood in a fireplace, what is the source of oxygen?*

wood + oxygen = ash + gases + water vapor

Lavoisier's Contribution Lavoisier (la VWAH see ay), a French chemist who lived about 2,000 years after Democritus, also was curious about matter—especially when it changed form. Before Lavoisier, people thought matter could appear and disappear because of the changes they saw as matter burned or rusted. You might have thought that matter can disappear if you've ever watched wood burn in a fireplace or at a bonfire. Lavoisier showed that wood and the oxygen it combines with during burning have the same mass as the ash, water vapor, carbon dioxide, and other gases that are produced, as shown in **Figure 2.** In a similar way, an iron bar, oxygen, and water have the same mass as the rust that forms when they interact. From Lavoisier's work came the **law of conservation of matter,** which states that matter is not created or destroyed—it only changes form.

Models of the Atom

Models often are used for things that are too small or too large to be observed, or that are too difficult to be understood easily. One way to make a model is to make a smaller version of something large. If you wanted to design a new sailboat, would you build a full-sized boat and hope it would float? It would be more efficient, less expensive, and safer to build and test a smaller version first. Then, if it didn't float, you could change your design and build another model. You could keep trying until the model worked.

In the case of atoms, scientists use large models to explain something that is too small to be seen. These models of the atom were used to explain data or facts that were gathered experimentally. As a result, these models also are theories.

Dalton's Atomic Model In the early 1800s, an English schoolteacher and chemist named John Dalton studied the experiments of Lavoisier and others. Dalton thought he could design an atomic model that explained the results of those experiments. Dalton's atomic model was a set of ideas—not a physical object. Dalton believed that matter was made of atoms that were too small to be seen by the human eye. He also thought that each type of matter was made of only one kind of atom. For example, gold atoms make up a gold nugget and give a gold ring its shiny appearance. Likewise, iron atoms make up an iron bar and give it unique properties, and so on. Because predictions using Dalton's model were supported by data, the model became known as the atomic theory of matter.

Sizes of Atoms Atoms are so small it would take about 1 million of them lined up in a row to equal the thickness of a human hair. For another example of how small atoms are, look at **Figure 3.** Imagine you are holding an orange in your hand. If you wanted to be able to see the individual atoms on the orange's surface, the size of the orange would have to be increased to the size of Earth. Then, imagine the Earth-sized orange covered with billions and billions of marbles. Each marble would represent one of the atoms on the skin of the orange. No matter what kind of model you use to picture it, the result is the same—an atom is an extremely small particle of matter.

Figure 3 If this orange were as large as Earth, each of its atoms would be marble-sized.

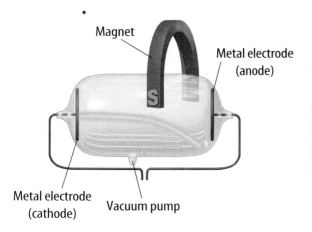

Magnet

Metal electrode
(anode)

S

Metal electrode
(cathode) Vacuum pump

Figure 4 In Thomson's experiment, the magnet caused the cathode rays inside the tube to bend. **Describe** *what you think would happen to the cathode rays if the magnet were removed.*

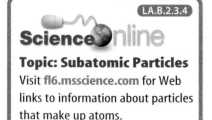

LA.B.2.3.4

Science nline

Topic: Subatomic Particles
Visit fl6.msscience.com for Web links to information about particles that make up atoms.

Activity Can any of the particles be divided further? Display your data in a table.

Discovering the Electron One of the many pioneers in the development of today's atomic model was J.J. Thomson, an English scientist. He conducted experiments using a cathode-ray tube, which is a glass tube sealed at both ends, out of which most of the air has been pumped. Thomson's tube had a metal plate at each end. The plates were connected to a high-voltage electrical source that gave one of the plates—the anode—a positive charge and the other plate—the cathode—a negative charge. During his experiments, Thomson observed rays that traveled from the cathode to the anode. These cathode rays were bent by a magnet, as seen in **Figure 4,** showing that they were made up of particles that had mass and charge. Thomson knew that like charges repel each other and opposite charges attract each other. When he saw that the rays traveled toward a positively charged plate, he concluded that the cathode rays were made up of negatively charged particles. These invisible, negatively charged particles are called **electrons.**

✔ **Reading Check** *Why were the cathode rays in Thomson's cathode-ray tube bent by a magnet?*

Try to imagine Thomson's excitement at this discovery. He had shown that atoms are not too tiny to divide after all. Rather, they are made up of even smaller subatomic particles. Other scientists soon built upon Thomson's results and found that the electron had a small mass. In fact, an electron is 1/1,837 the mass of the lightest atom, the hydrogen atom. In 1906, Thomson received the Nobel Prize in Physics for his work on the discovery of the electron.

Matter that has an equal amount of positive and negative charge is said to be neutral—it has no net charge. Because most matter is neutral, Thomson pictured the atom as a ball of positive charge with electrons embedded in it. It was later determined that neutral atoms contained an equal number of positive and negative charges.

Thomson's Model Thomson's model, shown in **Figure 5,** can be compared to chocolate chips spread throughout a ball of cookie dough. However, the model did not provide all the answers to the questions that puzzled scientists about atoms.

Rutherford—The Nucleus Scientists still had questions about how the atom was arranged and about the presence of positively charged particles. In about 1910, a team of scientists led by Ernest Rutherford worked on these questions. In their experiment, they bombarded an extremely thin piece of gold foil with alpha particles. Alpha particles are tiny, high-energy, positively charged particles that he predicted would pass through the foil. Most of the particles passed straight through the foil as if it were not there at all. However, other particles changed direction, and some even bounced back. Rutherford thought the result was so remarkable that he later said, "It was almost as incredible as if you had fired a 15-inch shell at a piece of tissue paper, and it came back and hit you."

Positive Center Rutherford concluded that because so many of the alpha particles passed straight through the gold foil, the atoms must be made of mostly empty space. However, because some of the positively charged alpha particles bounced off something, the gold atoms must contain some positively charged object concentrated in the midst of this empty space. Rutherford called the positively charged, central part of the atom the **nucleus** (NEW klee us). He named the positively charged particles in the nucleus **protons**. He also suggested that electrons were scattered in the mostly empty space around the nucleus, as shown in **Figure 6.**

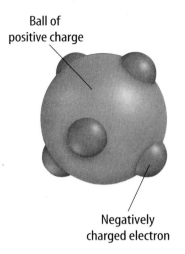

Ball of positive charge

Negatively charged electron

Figure 5 Thomson's model shows the atom as electrons embedded in a ball of positive charge.
Explain *how Thomson knew atoms contained positive and negative charges.*

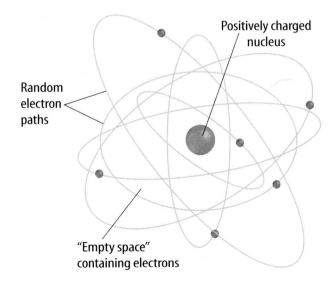

Positively charged nucleus

Random electron paths

"Empty space" containing electrons

Figure 6 Rutherford concluded that the atom must be mostly empty space, in which electrons travel in random paths around the nucleus. He also thought the nucleus of the atom must be small and positively charged.
Identify *where most of the mass of an atom is concentrated.*

Discovering the Neutron Rutherford had been puzzled by one observation from his experiments with nuclei. After the collisions, the nuclei seemed to be heavier. Where did this extra mass come from? James Chadwick, a student of Rutherford's, answered this question. The alpha particles themselves were not heavier. The atoms that had been bombarded had given off new particles. Chadwick experimented with these new particles and found that, unlike electrons, the paths of these particles were not affected by an electric field. To explain his observations, he said that these particles came from the nucleus and had no charge. Chadwick called these uncharged particles **neutrons** (NEW trahnz). His proton-neutron model of the atomic nucleus is still accepted today.

Improving the Atomic Model

Early in the twentieth century, a scientist named Niels Bohr found evidence that electrons in atoms are arranged according to energy levels. The lowest energy level is closest to the nucleus and can hold only two electrons. Higher energy levels are farther from the nucleus and can contain more electrons. To explain these energy levels, some scientists thought that the electrons might orbit an atom's nucleus in paths that are specific distances from the nucleus, as shown in **Figure 7.** This is similar to how the planets orbit the Sun.

The Modern Atomic Model As a result of continuing research, scientists now realize that because electrons have characteristics that are similar to waves and particles, their energy levels are not defined, planet-like orbits around the nucleus. Rather, it seems most likely that electrons move in what is called the atom's electron cloud, as shown in **Figure 8.**

Physicists and Chemists
Physicists generally study the physical atom. The physical atom includes the inner components of an atom, neutrons and protons. Chemists, on the other hand, study the chemical atom. The chemical atom refers to how different elements combine to form new substances.

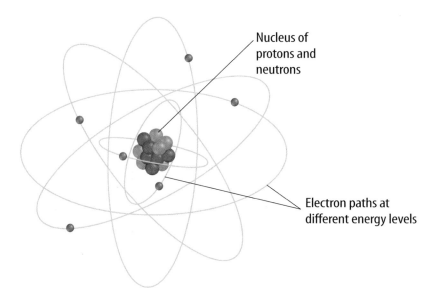

Nucleus of protons and neutrons

Electron paths at different energy levels

Figure 7 This simplified Bohr model shows a nucleus of protons and neutrons and electron paths based on energy levels.
Determine *how many electrons this atom contains.*

The Electron Cloud A spherical cloud of varying density surrounding the nucleus is the electron cloud. The varying density shows where an electron is more or less likely to be. Atoms with electrons in higher energy levels have electron clouds of different shapes that also show where those electrons are likely to be. Generally, the electron cloud has a radius 10,000 times that of the nucleus.

Further Research By the 1930s, it was recognized that matter was made up of atoms. The mass of an atom is concentrated in its nucleus, which is made of protons and neutrons. Electrons, which exist in areas outside of the nucleus, account for only a very small fraction of an atom's mass. But scientists continued to study the basic parts of this atom. Today, they have succeeded in breaking down protons and neutrons into even smaller particles called quarks. Quarks have fractional electric charges of $+2/3$ or $-1/3$, unlike the $+1$ charge of a proton or the -1 charge of an electron. Research will continue as new discoveries are made about the structure of matter.

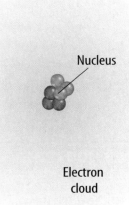

Nucleus

Electron cloud

Figure 8 This model of the atom shows the electrons moving around the nucleus in a region called the electron cloud. The dark cloud of color represents the area where the electron is more likely to be found.
Infer *What does the intensity of color near the nucleus suggest?*

section 1 review

Summary

What is matter?

- Matter is anything that has mass and takes up space.
- Matter is composed of atoms.

Models of the Atom

- Democritus introduced the idea of an atom. Lavoisier showed matter is neither created nor destroyed, just changed.
- Dalton's ideas led to the atomic theory of matter.
- Thomson discovered the electron.
- Rutherford discovered protons exist in the nucleus.
- Chadwick discovered the neutron.

Improving the Atomic Model

- Niels Bohr suggested electrons move in energy levels.
- More recent physicists introduced the idea of the electron cloud and were able to break down protons and neutrons into smaller particles called quarks.

Self Check

1. **List** five examples of matter and five examples that are not matter. Explain your answers.
2. **Describe** and name the parts of the atom. `SC.A.2.3.2`
3. **Explain** why the word *atom* was an appropriate term for Democritus's idea.
4. **Describe** the conclusions that Rutherford obtained from the gold-foil experiment. `SC.A.2.3.2`
5. **Explain** the law of conservation of matter using your own examples.
6. **Think Critically** When neutrons were discovered, were these neutrons created in the experiment? How does Lavoisier's work help answer this question?

Applying Skills

7. **Classify** each scientist and his contribution according to the type of discovery each person made. Explain why you grouped certain scientists together. `SC.H.3.3.5`
8. **Evaluate Others' Data and Conclusions** Analyze, review, and critique the strengths and weaknesses of Thomson's "cookie dough" theory using the results of Rutherford's gold-foil experiment.

Benchmarks—SC.A.2.3.2 (pp. 483–484); SC.H.2.3.1 (pp. 480–482, 484–485): The student recognizes that patterns exist within and across systems.

section 2

Also covers: SC.A.1.3.1 Annually Assessed (pp. 483–485), SC.H.1.3.1 Annually Assessed (p. 482), SC.H.3.3.5 (p. 482)

The Simplest Matter

as you read

What You'll Learn

- **Describe** the relationship between elements and the periodic table.
- **Explain** the meaning of atomic mass and atomic number.
- **Identify** what makes an isotope.
- **Contrast** metals, metalloids, and nonmetals.

Why It's Important

Everything on Earth is made of the elements that are listed on the periodic table.

Review Vocabulary

✹ **mass:** a measure of the amount of matter an object has

New Vocabulary

- ✹ **element**
- **atomic number**
- **isotope**
- **mass number**
- **atomic mass**
- **metal**
- **nonmetal**
- **metalloid**

✹ FCAT Vocabulary

The Elements

Have you watched television today? TV sets are common, yet each one is a complex system. The outer case is made mostly of plastic, and the screen is made of glass. Many of the parts that conduct electricity are metals or combinations of metals. Other parts in the interior of the set contain materials that barely conduct electricity. All of the different materials have one thing in common: they are made up of even simpler materials. In fact, if you had the proper equipment, you could separate the plastics, glass, and metals into these simpler materials.

One Kind of Atom Eventually, though, you would separate the materials into groups of atoms. At that point, you would have a collection of elements. An **element** is matter made of only one kind of atom. At least 111 elements are known and about 90 of them occur naturally on Earth. These elements combine to form all living and most nonliving things. Examples of naturally occurring elements include the oxygen and nitrogen in the air you breathe and the metals gold, silver, aluminum, and iron. The other elements are known as synthetic elements. These elements have been made in nuclear reactions by scientists with machines called particle accelerators, like the one shown in **Figure 9.** Some synthetic elements have important uses in medical testing and are found in smoke detectors and heart pacemaker batteries.

Figure 9 The Tevatron has a circumference of 6.3 km—a distance that allows particles to accelerate to high speeds. These high-speed collisions can create synthetic elements.

Figure 10 When you look for information in the library, a system of organization called the Dewey Decimal Classification System helps you find a book quickly and efficiently.

Dewey Decimal Classification System	
000	Computers, information, and general reference
100	Philosophy and psychology
200	Religion
300	Social sciences
400	Languages
500	Science
600	Technology
700	Arts and recreation
800	Literature
900	History and geography

The Periodic Table

Suppose you go to a library, like the one shown in **Figure 10,** to look up information for a school assignment. How would you find the information? You could look randomly on shelves as you walk up and down rows of books, but the chances of finding your book would be slim. To avoid such haphazard searching, some libraries use the Dewey Decimal Classification System to categorize and organize their volumes to help you find books quickly and efficiently.

Charting the Elements Chemists have created a chart called the periodic table of the elements to help them organize and display the elements. **Figure 11** shows how scientists changed their model of the periodic table over time.

On the inside back cover of this book, you will find a modern version of the periodic table. Each element is represented by a chemical symbol that contains one to three letters. The symbols are a form of chemical shorthand that chemists use to save time and space—on the periodic table as well as in written formulas. The symbols are an important part of an international system that is understood by scientists everywhere.

The elements are organized on the periodic table by their properties. There are rows and columns that represent relationships between the elements. The rows in the table are called periods. The elements in a row have the same number of energy levels. The columns are called groups. The elements in each group have similar properties related to their structure. They also tend to form similar bonds.

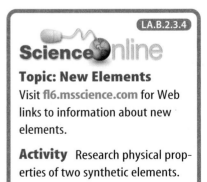

LA.B.2.3.4

Science Online

Topic: New Elements
Visit fl6.msscience.com for Web links to information about new elements.

Activity Research physical properties of two synthetic elements.

Figure 11

The familiar periodic table that adorns many science classrooms is based on a number of earlier efforts to identify and classify the elements. In the 1790s, one of the first lists of elements and their compounds was compiled by French chemist Antoine-Laurent Lavoisier, who is shown in the background picture with his wife and assistant, Marie Anne. Three other tables are shown here.

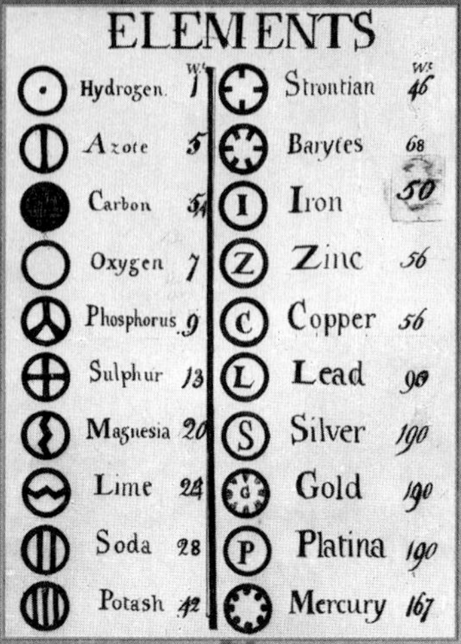

John Dalton (Britain, 1803) used symbols to represent elements. His table also assigned masses to each element.

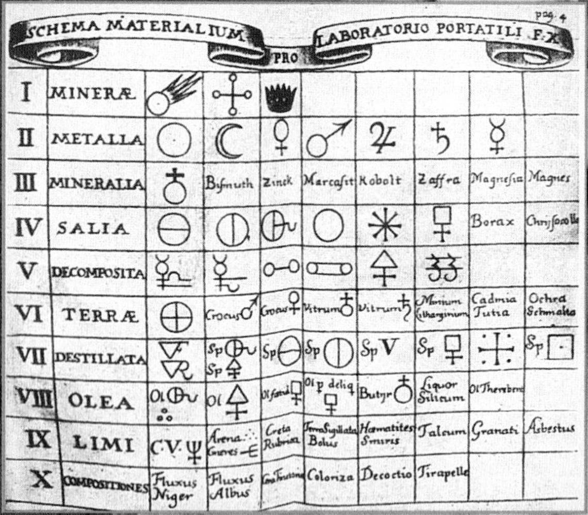

An early alchemist put together this table of elements and compounds. Some of the symbols have their origin in astrology.

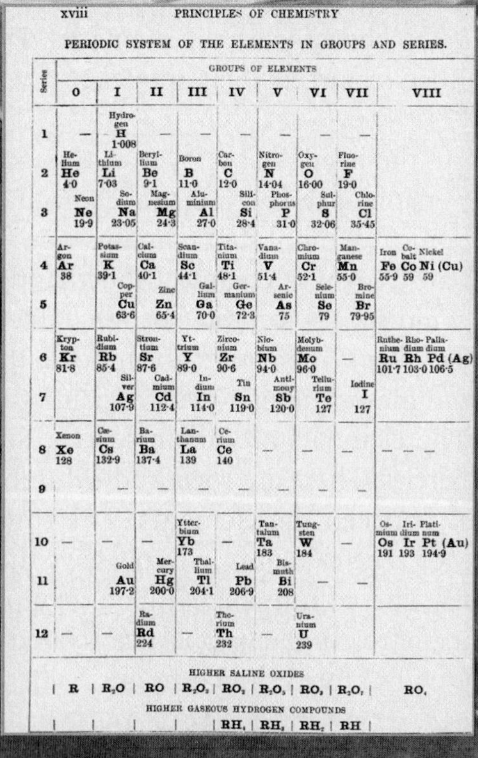

Dmitri Mendeleev (Russia, 1869) arranged the 63 elements known to exist at that time into groups based on their chemical properties and atomic weights. He left gaps for elements he predicted were yet to be discovered.

Identifying Characteristics

Each element is different and has unique properties. These differences can be described in part by looking at the relationships between the atomic particles in each element. The periodic table contains numbers that describe these relationships.

Atomic Number and Protons Look at the element block for chlorine, shown in **Figure 12.** Cl is the symbol for chlorine. The number above the symbol, 17, is the element's atomic number. The **atomic number** of an element is the number of protons in each atom of that element. For example, every atom of chlorine has 17 protons. Its atomic number is 17. Every atom of uranium contains 92 protons. Its atomic number is 92.

Isotopes and Neutrons Atoms of the same element have the same number of protons. However, atoms of the same element might have different numbers of neutrons. For example, some chlorine atoms contain 18 neutrons while others contain 20 neutrons. Atoms of the same element that contain different numbers of neutrons are called **isotopes** (I suh tohps).

Mass Number An atom's **mass number** is the number of protons plus the number of neutrons it contains.

$$\text{mass number} = \text{protons} + \text{neutrons}$$

The mass number of a chlorine atom with 18 neutrons is 35 (18 neutrons + 17 protons). The mass number of a chlorine atom with 20 neutrons is 37 (20 neutrons + 17 protons). An isotope of an element is written with the element symbol followed by its mass number. The isotopes of chlorine are written as Cl-35 and Cl-37. **Table 2** shows the numbers of particles that make up these two isotopes.

Determining the Number of Neutrons If you know the mass number of an atom and the type of element it is, you can determine the number of neutrons in that atom using the following equation:

$$\text{neutrons} = \text{mass number} - \text{protons}$$

Likewise, the number of protons—and thus the element—can be determined if the number of neutrons and the mass number of an atom are known.

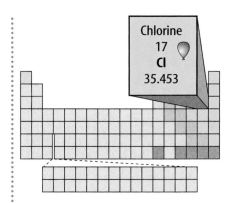

Figure 12 The periodic table block for chlorine shows its symbol, atomic number, and atomic mass.
Determine *if chlorine atoms are more or less massive than carbon atoms.*

Table 2 Chlorine Isotopes		
Atomic Property	**Cl-35**	**Cl-37**
Mass number	35	37
Atomic number	17	17
Number of protons	17	17
Number of neutrons	18	20
Number of electrons in a neutral atom	17	17

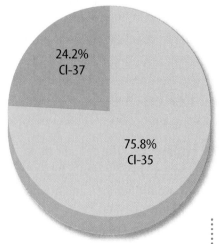

24.2%
Cl-37

75.8%
Cl-35

Figure 13 If you have 1,000 atoms of chlorine, about 758 will be chlorine-35 and have a mass of 34.97 u each. About 242 will be chlorine-37 and have a mass of 36.97 u each. The total mass of the 1,000 atoms is 35,454 u.
Calculate *the average mass of one chlorine atom.*

Atomic Mass The **atomic mass** is the weighted average mass of the isotopes of an element. The atomic mass is the number found below the element symbol in **Figure 12.** The unit that scientists use for atomic mass is called the atomic mass unit, which is given the symbol u. It is defined as 1/12 the mass of a carbon-12 atom.

The calculation of atomic mass takes into account the different isotopes of the element. Chlorine's atomic mass of 35.45 u could be confusing because there aren't any chlorine atoms that have that exact mass. About 76 percent of chlorine atoms are chlorine-35 and about 24 percent are chlorine-37, as shown in **Figure 13.** The weighted average mass of all chlorine atoms is 35.45 u.

 **Reading Check** *Where is the atomic mass of each element located on the periodic table?*

Classification of Elements

Elements fall into three general categories—metals, metalloids (ME tuh loydz), and nonmetals. The elements in each category have similar properties.

Metals generally have a shiny or metallic luster and are good conductors of heat and electricity. All metals, except mercury, are solids at room temperature. Metals are malleable (MAL yuh bul), which means they can be bent and pounded into various shapes. The beautiful form of the shell-shaped basin in **Figure 14** is a result of this characteristic. Metals are also ductile, which means they can be drawn into wires without breaking. If you look at the periodic table, you can see that most of the elements are metals.

Figure 14 The artisan is chasing, or chiseling, the malleable metal into the desired form.

Other Elements **Nonmetals** are elements that usually are dull in appearance. Most are poor conductors of heat and electricity. Many are gases at room temperature, and bromine is a liquid. The solid nonmetals generally are brittle, meaning they cannot change shape easily without breaking. The nonmetals are essential to the chemicals of life. More than 97 percent of your body is made up of various nonmetals, as shown in **Figure 15.** You can see that, except for hydrogen, the nonmetals are found on the right side of the periodic table.

Metalloids are elements that have characteristics of metals and nonmetals. On the periodic table, metalloids are found between the metals and nonmetals. All metalloids are solids at room temperature. Some metalloids are shiny and many are conductors, but they are not as good at conducting heat and electricity as metals are. Some metalloids, such as silicon, are used to make the electronic circuits in computers, televisions, and other electronic devices.

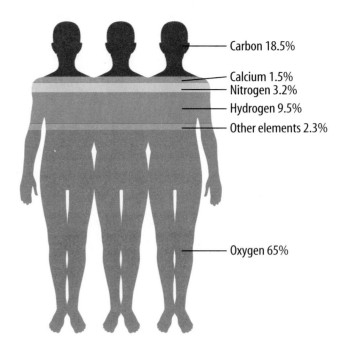

- Carbon 18.5%
- Calcium 1.5%
- Nitrogen 3.2%
- Hydrogen 9.5%
- Other elements 2.3%
- Oxygen 65%

Figure 15 You are made up of mostly nonmetals.
Calculate *How many kilograms of oxygen are in a person that weighs 68 kg?*

✓ **Reading Check** *What is a metalloid?*

section 2 review

Summary

The Elements

- An element is matter made of only one type of atom.
- Some elements occur naturally on Earth. Synthetic elements are made in nuclear reactions in particle accelerators.
- Elements are divided into three categories based on certain properties.

The Periodic Table

- The periodic table arranges and displays all known elements in an orderly way.
- Each element has a chemical symbol.

Identifying Characteristics

- Each element has a unique number of protons, called the atomic mass number.
- Isotopes of an element are important when determining the atomic mass of an element.

Self Check

1. **Explain** some of the uses of metals based on their properties. SC.A.1.3.1
2. **Describe** the difference between atomic number and atomic mass. SC.A.2.3.2
3. **Define** the term *isotope.* Explain how two isotopes of an element are different. SC.A.2.3.2
4. **Describe** how the periodic table is organized. SC.A.1.3.1
5. **Think Critically** Describe how to find the atomic number for the element oxygen. Explain what this information tells you about oxygen.

Applying Math

6. **Solve Simple Equations** An atom of niobium has a mass number of 93. How many neutrons are in the nucleus of this atom? An atom of phosphorus has 15 protons and 15 neutrons in the nucleus. What is the mass number of this isotope? SC.A.2.3.2

Isotope Races

Isotopes of the same element often have very different properties and therefore very different uses. This lab will introduce you to a number of isotopes used in science and the information available in the periodic table.

▶ Real-World Problem

How can you use the periodic table to learn isotope information?

Goals
- **Practice** using the periodic table to find information.
- **Calculate** atomic number and neutron number from an isotope name.

Materials
periodic table
Science Journal
pen or pencil

▶ Procedure

1. Divide into teams of four students and get in lines facing forward. The first one in line should have a periodic table.

2. Your teacher will show the first person in line an isotope name.

3. The first person in line will find the element on the periodic table and show the second person in line what it is.

4. The second person in line will find the atomic number of the isotope and show the third person in line both the element and the atomic number.

5. The third person in line will then calculate the number of neutrons in the isotope and tell the last person in line the element, atomic number, and number of neutrons.

6. The last person in line will report the element name, atomic number, number of neutrons, and mass number of the isotope.

7. Repeat this race with four more isotopes.

▶ Conclude and Apply

1. **Calculate** the percentage of the atomic mass number of chlorine-35 that is composed of neutrons.

2. **Determine** the error in the following: Americium-241 has 146 neutrons and 98 protons.

3. **Identify** the isotope with a mass number of 60 and 33 neutrons.

Communicating Your Data

Prepare a graph of atomic number versus number of neutrons. Place the isotopes in the graph with stable and radioactive isotopes in different colors. Discuss any pattern you detect.

section 3

Compounds and Mixtures

Substances

Scientists classify matter in several ways that depend on what it is made of and its pattern of behavior. For example, matter that has the same composition and properties throughout is called a **substance.** Elements, such as a bar of gold or a sheet of aluminum, are substances. When different elements combine, other substances are formed.

Compounds What do you call the colorless liquid that flows from the kitchen faucet? You probably call it water, but maybe you've seen it written H_2O. The elements hydrogen and oxygen exist as separate, colorless gases. These two elements can combine, as shown in **Figure 16,** to form the compound water, which is different from the elements that make it up. A **compound** is a substance whose smallest unit is made up of atoms of more than one element bonded together.

Compounds often have properties that are different from the elements that make them up. Water is distinctly different from the elements that make it up. It also is different from another compound made from the same elements. Have you ever used hydrogen peroxide (H_2O_2) to disinfect a cut? This compound is a different combination of hydrogen and oxygen and has different properties from those of water.

Water is a nonirritating liquid that is used for bathing, drinking, cooking, and much more. In contrast, hydrogen peroxide carries warnings on its labels such as *Keep Hydrogen Peroxide Out of the Eyes.* Although it is useful in solutions for cleaning contact lenses, it is not safe for your eyes directly from the bottle.

Figure 16 A space shuttle is powered by the reaction between liquid hydrogen and liquid oxygen. The reaction produces a large amount of energy and the compound water.
Explain *why a car that burns hydrogen rather than gasoline would be friendly to the environment.*

as you read

What You'll Learn
- **Identify** the characteristics of a compound.
- **Compare and contrast** different types of mixtures.

Why It's Important
The food you eat, the materials you use, and all matter can be classified by compounds or mixtures.

Review Vocabulary
formula: shows which elements and how many atoms of each make up a compound

New Vocabulary
- substance
- ✹ mixture
- ✹ compound

✹ FCAT Vocabulary

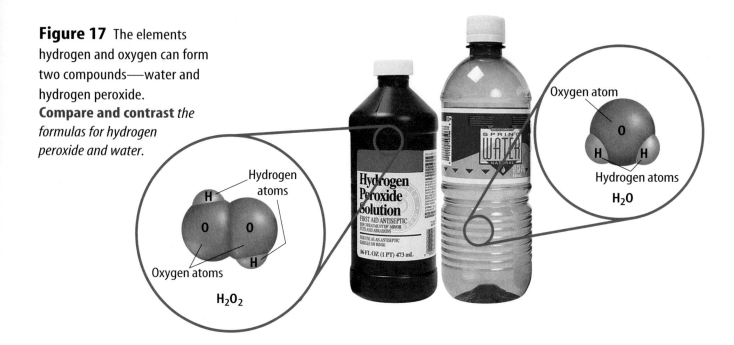

Figure 17 The elements hydrogen and oxygen can form two compounds—water and hydrogen peroxide. **Compare and contrast** *the formulas for hydrogen peroxide and water.*

Hydrogen atoms

H

O   O

Oxygen atoms

H_2O_2

Oxygen atom

O

H   H

Hydrogen atoms

H_2O

Comparing Compounds

Procedure

1. Collect the following substances—**granular sugar, rubbing alcohol, salad oil,** and **spoons.**
2. Observe the color, appearance, and state of each substance. Note the thickness or texture of each substance.
3. Stir a spoonful of each substance into separate **containers** of **hot tap water** and observe.

Analysis

1. Compare the different properties of the substances.
2. The three substances are made of only carbon, hydrogen, and oxygen. Infer how they can have different properties.

Try at Home

Compounds Have Formulas What's the difference between water and hydrogen peroxide? H_2O is the chemical formula for water, and H_2O_2 is the formula for hydrogen peroxide. The formula tells you which elements make up a compound as well as how many atoms of each element are present. Look at **Figure 17.** The subscript number written below and to the right of each element's symbol tells you how many atoms of that element exist in one unit of that compound. For example, hydrogen peroxide has two atoms of hydrogen and two atoms of oxygen. Water is made up of two atoms of hydrogen and one atom of oxygen.

Carbon dioxide, CO_2, is another common compound. Carbon dioxide is made up of one atom of carbon and two atoms of oxygen. Carbon and oxygen also can form the compound carbon monoxide, CO, which is a gas that is poisonous to all warm-blooded animals. As you can see, no subscript is used when only one atom of an element is present. A given compound always is made of the same elements in the same proportion. For example, water always has two hydrogen atoms for every oxygen atom, no matter what the source of the water is. No matter what quantity of the compound you have, the formula of the compound always remains the same. If you have 12 atoms of hydrogen and six atoms of oxygen, the compound is still written H_2O, but you have six molecules of H_2O (6 H_2O), not $H_{12}O_6$. The formula of a compound communicates its identity and makeup to any scientist in the world.

✓ **Reading Check** *Propane has three carbon and eight hydrogen atoms. What is its chemical formula?*

Mixtures

When two or more substances (elements or compounds) come together but don't combine to make a new substance, a **mixture** results. Unlike compounds, the proportions of the substances in a mixture can be changed without changing the identity of the mixture. For example, if you put some sand into a bucket of water, you have a mixture of sand and water. If you add more sand or more water, it's still a mixture of sand and water. Its identity has not changed. Air is another mixture. Air is a mixture of nitrogen, oxygen, and other gases, which can vary at different times and places. Whatever the proportion of gases, it is still air. Even your blood is a mixture that can be separated, as shown in **Figure 18,** by a machine called a centrifuge.

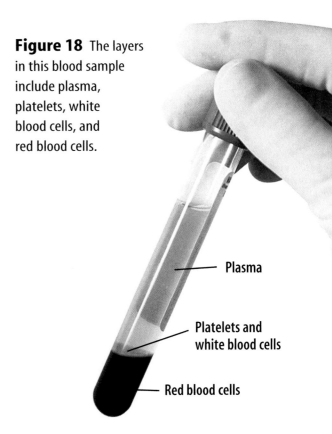

Figure 18 The layers in this blood sample include plasma, platelets, white blood cells, and red blood cells.

— Plasma

— Platelets and white blood cells

— Red blood cells

 **Reading Check** *How do the proportions of a mixture relate to its identity?*

Applying Science

What's the best way to desalt ocean water?

You can't drink ocean water because it contains salt and other suspended materials. Or can you? In many areas of the world, drinking water is in short supply. Methods for getting the salt out of salt water are being used to meet the demand for freshwater. Use your problem-solving skills to find the best method to use in a particular area.

Methods for Desalting Ocean Water			
Process	Amount of Water a Unit Can Desalt in a Day (m^3)	Special Needs	Number of People Needed to Operate
Distillation	1,000 to 200,000	lots of energy to boil the water	many
Electrodialysis	10 to 4,000	stable source of electricity	1 to 2 persons

Identifying the Problem

The table above compares desalting methods. In distillation, the ocean water is heated. Pure water boils off and is collected, and the salt is left behind. Electrodialysis uses an electric current to pull salt particles out of water.

Solving the Problem

1. What method(s) might you use to desalt the water for a large population where energy is plentiful?
2. What method(s) would you choose to use in a single home?

Figure 19 Mixtures are part of your everyday life.

Science Online

Topic: Mixtures
Visit fl6.msscience.com for Web links to information about separating mixtures.

Activity Describe the difference between mixtures and compounds.

Your blood is a mixture made up of elements and compounds. It contains white blood cells, red blood cells, water, and a number of dissolved substances. The different parts of blood can be separated and used by doctors in different ways. The proportions of the substances in your blood change daily, but the mixture does not change its identity.

Separating Mixtures Sometimes you can use a liquid to separate a mixture of solids. For example, if you add water to a mixture of sugar and sand, only the sugar dissolves in the water. The sand then can be separated from the sugar and water by pouring the mixture through a filter. Heating the remaining solution will separate the water from the sugar.

At other times, separating a mixture of solids of different sizes might be as easy as pouring them through successively smaller sieves or filters. A mixture of marbles, pebbles, and sand could be separated in this way.

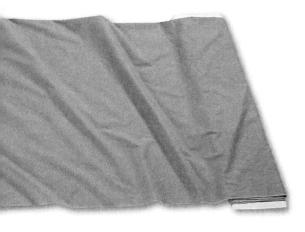

Homogeneous or Heterogeneous Mixtures, such as the ones shown in **Figure 19,** can be classified as homogeneous or heterogeneous. *Homogeneous* means "the same throughout." You can't see the different parts in this type of mixture. In fact, you might not always know that homogeneous mixtures are mixtures because you can't tell by looking. Which mixtures in **Figure 19** are homogeneous? No matter how closely you look, you can't see the individual parts that make up air or the parts of the mixture called brass in the lamp shown. Homogeneous mixtures can be solids, liquids, or gases.

A heterogeneous mixture has larger parts that are different from each other. You can see the different parts of a heterogeneous mixture, such as sand and water. How many heterogeneous mixtures are in **Figure 19?** A pepperoni and mushroom pizza is a tasty kind of heterogeneous mixture. Other examples of this kind of mixture include tacos, vegetable soup, a toy box full of toys, or a toolbox full of nuts and bolts.

INTEGRATE Earth Science

Rocks and Minerals
Scientists called geologists study rocks and minerals. A mineral is composed of a pure substance. Rocks are mixtures and can be described as being homogeneous or heterogeneous. Research to learn more about rocks and minerals and note some examples of homogeneous and heterogeneous rocks in your Science Journal.

---

section 3 review

Summary

Substances

- A substance can be either an element or a compound.
- A compound contains more than one kind of element bonded together.
- A chemical formula shows which elements and how many atoms of each make up a compound.

Mixtures

- A mixture contains substances that are not chemically bonded together.
- There are many ways to separate mixtures based on their physical properties.
- Homogeneous mixtures are those that are the same throughout. These types of mixtures can be solids, liquids, or gases.
- Heterogeneous mixtures have larger parts that are different from each other.

Self Check

1. **List** three examples of compounds and three examples of mixtures. Explain your choices.
2. **Determine** A container contains a mixture of sand, salt, and pebbles. How can each substance be separated from the others? SC.A.1.3.1
3. **Think Critically** Explain whether your breakfast was a compound, a homogeneous mixture, or a heterogeneous mixture. SC.A.1.3.1

Applying Skills

4. **Compare and contrast** compounds and mixtures based on what you have learned from this section.
5. **Use a Database** Use a computerized card catalog or database to find information about one element from the periodic table. Include information about the properties and uses of the mixtures and/or compounds in which the element is frequently found.

Mystery Mixture

◉ *Real-World Problem*

You will encounter many compounds that look alike. For example, a laboratory stockroom is filled with white powders. It is important to know what each is. In a kitchen, cornstarch, baking powder, and powdered sugar are compounds that look alike. To avoid mistaking one for another, you can learn how to identify them. Different compounds can be identified by using chemical tests. For example, some compounds react with certain liquids to produce gases. Other combinations produce distinctive colors. Some compounds have high melting points. Others have low melting points. How can the compounds in an unknown mixture be identified by experimentation?

Goals

■ **Test** for the presence of certain compounds.

■ **Decide** which of these compounds are present in an unknown mixture.

Materials

test tubes (4)
cornstarch
powdered sugar
baking soda
small scoops (4)
dropper bottles (2)
iodine solution
white vinegar
hot plate
250-mL beaker
water (125 mL)
test-tube holder
small pie pan

Safety Precautions

Complete a safety worksheet before you begin.

WARNING: *Use caution when handling hot objects. Substances could stain or burn clothing. Be sure to point the test tube away from your face and your classmates while heating.*

Procedure

1. Copy the data table below into your Science Journal. Record your results carefully for each of the following steps.

2. Place a small scoopful of cornstarch on the pie pan. Do the same for the sugar and baking soda, making separate piles. Add a drop of vinegar to each. Wash and dry the pan after you record your observations.

3. Place a small scoopful of cornstarch, sugar, and baking soda on the pie pan. Add a drop of iodine solution to each one. Wash and dry the pan after you record your observations.

4. Place a small scoopful of each compound in a separate test tube. Use only enough solid to fill the bottom, rounded portion of the test tubes. Hold the test tubes with the test-tube holder. Gently heat each test tube in a beaker of boiling water on a hot plate. Record your observations.

5. Follow steps 2 through 4 to test your mystery mixture for each compound.

Identifying Presence of Compounds

Substance to Be Tested	Fizzes with Vinegar	Turns Blue with Iodine	Melts when Heated
Cornstarch			
Sugar		Do not write in this book.	
Baking soda			
Mystery mix			

Analyze Your Data

Identify from your data table which compound(s) you have as your mystery mixture.

Conclude and Apply

1. **Describe** how you decided which substances were in your mystery mixture.

2. **Explain** how you would be able to tell if none of the three compounds were in your mystery mixture.

3. **Draw a Conclusion** What would you conclude if you tested baking powder from your kitchen and found that it fizzed with vinegar, turned blue with iodine, and did not melt when heated?

4. **Identify** possible sources of error in your results.

Communicating Your Data

Make a different data table to display your results in a new way. **For more help, refer to the** Science Skill Handbook.

Ancient Views of Matter

air

water

Two cultures observed the world around them differently

The world's earliest scientists were people who were curious about the world around them and who tried to develop explanations for the things they observed. This type of observation and inquiry flourished in ancient cultures such as those found in India and China. Read on to see how the ancient Indians and Chinese defined matter.

Indian Ideas

To Indians living about 3,000 years ago, the world was made up of five elements: fire, air, earth, water, and ether, which they thought of as an unseen substance that filled the heavens. Building upon this concept, the early Indian philosopher Kashyapa (kah SHI ah pah) proposed that the five elements could be broken down into smaller units called parmanu (par MAH new). Parmanu were similar to atoms in that they were too small to be seen but still retained the properties of the original element. Kashyapa also believed that each type of parmanu had unique physical and chemical properties.

metal

Parmanu of earth elements, for instance, were heavier than parmanu of air elements. The different properties of the parmanu determined the characteristics of a substance. Kashyapa's ideas about matter are similar to those of the Greek philosopher Democritus, who lived centuries after Kashyapa.

fire

Chinese Ideas

The ancient Chinese also broke matter down into five elements: fire, wood, metal, earth, and water. Unlike the early Indians, however, the Chinese believed that the elements constantly changed form. For example, wood can be burned and thus changes to fire. Fire eventually dies down and becomes ashes, or earth. Earth gives forth metals from the ground. Dew or water collects on these metals, and the water then nurtures plants that grow into trees, or wood.

This cycle of constant change was explained in the fourth century B.C. by the philosopher Tsou Yen. Yen, who is known as the founder of Chinese scientific thought, wrote that all changes that took place in nature were linked to changes in the five elements.

earth

Research Write a brief paragraph that compares and contrasts the ancient Indian and Chinese views of matter. How are they different? Similar? Which is closer to the modern view of matter? Explain.

LA.B.2.3.1

Reviewing Main Ideas

Section 1 Structure of Matter

1. Matter is anything that occupies space and has mass.

2. Matter is made up of atoms.

3. Atoms are made of smaller parts called protons, neutrons, and electrons.

4. Many models of the atom have been created as scientists try to discover and define the atom's internal structure. Today's model has a central nucleus with the protons and neutrons, and an electron cloud surrounding it.

Section 2 The Simplest Matter

1. Elements are the building blocks of matter.

2. An element's atomic number tells how many protons its atoms contain, and its atomic mass tells the average mass of its atoms.

3. Isotopes are two or more atoms of the same element that have different numbers of neutrons.

Section 3 Compounds and Mixtures

1. Compounds are substances that are produced when elements combine. Compounds contain specific proportions of the elements that make them up.

2. Mixtures are combinations of compounds and elements that have not formed new substances. Their proportions can change.

Visualizing Main Ideas

Copy and complete the following concept map.

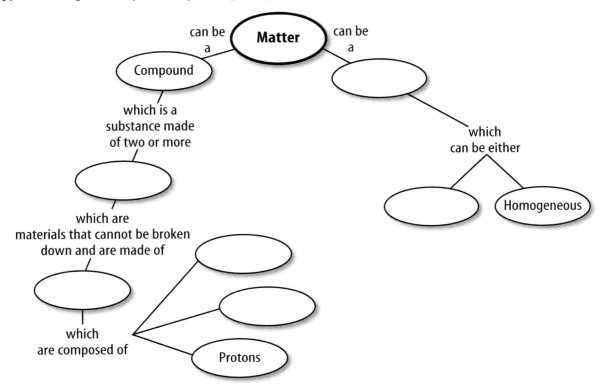

Using Vocabulary

atom p. 473
atomic mass p. 484
atomic number p. 483
compound p. 487
electron p. 476
element p. 480
isotope p. 483
law of conservation
   of matter p. 474
mass number p. 483

matter p. 472
metal p. 484
metalloid p. 485
mixture p. 489
neutron p. 478
nonmetal p. 485
nucleus p. 477
proton p. 477
substance p. 487

✳ FCAT Vocabulary

Fill in the blanks with the correct vocabulary word or words.

1. The _____ is the particle in the nucleus of the atom that carries a positive charge and is counted to identify the atomic number. SC.A.2.3.2

2. The new substance formed when elements combine chemically is a(n) _____.

3. Anything that has mass and takes up space is _____.

4. The particles in the atom that account for most of the mass of the atom are protons and _____. SC.A.2.3.2

5. Elements that are shiny, malleable, ductile, good conductors of heat and electricity, and make up most of the periodic table are _____. SC.A.1.3.1

Checking Concepts

Choose the word or phrase that best answers the question.

6. What is a solution an example of?
   A) element
   B) heterogeneous mixture
   C) compound
   D) homogeneous mixture

7. The nucleus of one atom contains 12 protons and 12 neutrons, while the nucleus of another atom contains 12 protons and 16 neutrons. What are the atoms? SC.A.1.3.1
   A) chromium atoms
   B) two different elements
   C) two isotopes of an element
   D) negatively charged

8. Copper (Cu) has 29 protons and 39 neutrons. What is the atomic number for copper? SC.A.2.3.2
   A) 10   C) 39
   B) 29   D) 68

9. What does the atom consist of? SC.A.2.3.2
   A) electrons, protons, and alpha particles
   B) neutrons and protons
   C) electrons, protons, and neutrons
   D) elements, protons, and electrons

10. In an atom, where is an electron located? SC.A.2.3.2
    A) in the nucleus with the proton
    B) on the periodic table of the elements
    C) with the neutron
    D) in a cloudlike formation surrounding the nucleus

11. How is matter defined?
    A) the negative charge in an atom
    B) anything that has mass and occupies space
    C) the mass of the nucleus
    D) sound, light, and energy

12. What are two atoms that have the same number of protons called? SC.A.2.3.2
    A) metals
    B) nonmetals
    C) isotopes
    D) metalloids

13. Which is a heterogeneous mixture? SC.A.1.3.1
    A) air   C) a salad
    B) brass   D) apple juice

Use the illustration below to answer questions 14 and 15.

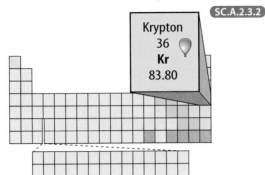

SC.A.2.3.2

Krypton
36
Kr
83.80

14. Using the figure above, krypton has
    A) an atomic number of 84.
    B) an atomic number of 36.
    C) an atomic mass of 36.
    D) an atomic mass of 72.

15. From the figure, the element krypton is
    A) a solid.   C) a mixture.
    B) a liquid.   D) a gas.

Thinking Critically

16. **Analyze Information** A chemical formula is written to indicate the makeup of a compound. What is the ratio of sulfur atoms to oxygen atoms in SO_2?

17. **Determine** which element contains seven electrons and seven protons. SC.A.2.3.2

18. **Determine** Using the periodic table, what are the atomic numbers for carbon (C), sodium (Na), and nickel (Ni)? SC.A.2.3.2

19. **Explain** how cobalt-60 and cobalt-59 can be the same element but have different mass numbers. SC.A.1.3.1

20. **Analyze Information** What did Rutherford's gold-foil experiment tell scientists about atomic structure?

21. **Predict** Suppose Rutherford had bombarded aluminum foil with alpha particles instead of the gold foil he used in his experiment. What observations do you predict Rutherford would have made? Explain your prediction.

22. **Draw Conclusions** You are shown a liquid that looks the same throughout. You're told that it contains more than one type of element and that the proportion of each varies throughout the liquid. Is this an element, a compound, or a mixture?

Use the illustrations below to answer question 23.

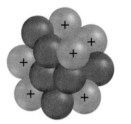 

23. **Interpret Scientific Illustrations** Look at the two carbon atoms above. Explain whether or not the atoms are isotopes. SC.A.1.3.1

24. **Explain** how the atomic mass of krypton was determined. SC.A.2.3.2

Performance Activities

25. **Newspaper Article** As a newspaper reporter in the year 1896, you have heard about the discovery of the electron. Research and write a newspaper article about the scientist and the discovery.

Applying Math

SC.A.2.3.2

26. **Atomic Mass** Krypton (Kr) has six naturally occurring isotopes with atomic masses of 78, 80, 82, 83, 84, and 86. Make a table of the number of protons, electrons, and neutrons in each isotope.

27. **Atomic Ratio** A researcher is analyzing two different compounds, sulfuric acid (H_2SO_4) and hydrogen peroxide (H_2O_2). What is the ratio of hydrogen to oxygen in sulfuric acid? What is the ratio of hydrogen to oxygen in hydrogen peroxide? SC.A.1.3.1

The assessed Florida Benchmark appears above each question.
Record your answers on the answer sheet provided by your teacher or on a sheet of paper.

Multiple Choice

SC.A.2.3.2

1 The diagram below shows some properties of chlorine.

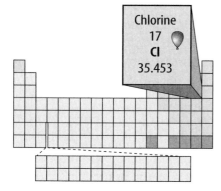

What does the number 35.453 represent?

A. the average atomic mass of a chlorine atom

B. the number of neutrons in every chlorine atom

C. the number of protons in every chlorine atom

D. the number of neutrons and protons in every chlorine atom

SC.A.1.3.1

2 Which characteristic is typical of a solid, nonmetal element?

F. shiny

G. brittle

H. good heat conductor

I. good electrical conductor

SC.H.2.3.1

3 How are the elements in the periodic table organized?

A. by atomic weight

B. by their structures

C. by their properties

D. by name

SC.A.2.3.2

4 The illustration below shows three different atoms.

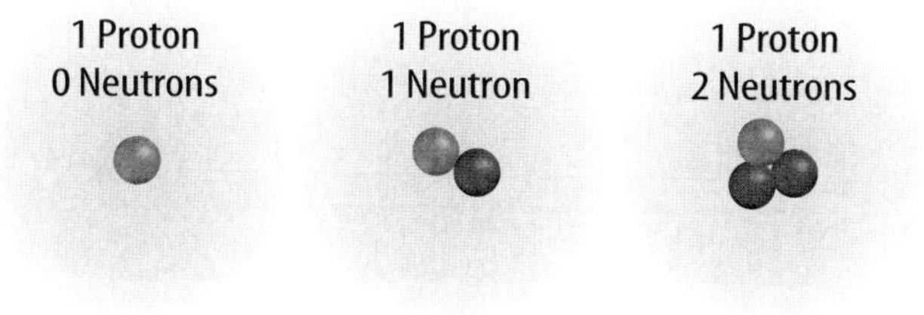

| 1 Proton | 1 Proton | 1 Proton |
| 0 Neutrons | 1 Neutron | 2 Neutrons |

Which correctly identifies the three atoms shown in the diagram?

F. They are all isotopes of chlorine.

G. They are all isotopes of helium.

H. They are all isotopes of hydrogen.

I. They are all isotopes of lithium.

SC.A.1.3.1

5 What state of matter are metalloids at room temperature?

A. gas

B. liquid

C. plasma

D. solid

SC.H.1.3.2

6 Democritus first proposed that matter is made up of tiny particles called atoms. Which term **best** describes Democritus's proposal about matter?

   F. It was an experiment.

   G. It was a hypothesis.

   H. It was a law.

   I. It was a theory.

Gridded Response

SC.A.1.3.1

7 Carbon-14 is an isotope of the element carbon. How many protons does Carbon-14 have?

Short Response

SC.H.1.3.1

8 The diagram below shows examples of Bohr's atomic model and the modern atomic model. Explain how these two models are similar and how they are different.

Bohr's Atomic Model   Modern Atomic Model

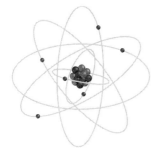   

Extended Response

SC.H.1.3.5

9 The diagram below shows Ernest Rutherford's gold foil experiment.

Source of positively charged particles

A few of the particles ricochet back toward the source.

Most of the particles pass through the foil with little or no deflection.

Positively charged particle beam

Gold foil

Detector screen

   PART A Describe the setup shown. What did Rutherford expect to happen in the experiment?

   PART B What actually occurred during the experiment and what did Rutherford conclude?

FCAT Tip

Calculators When working with calculators, use careful and deliberate keystrokes. Calculators will display an incorrect answer if you press the wrong keys or press keys too quickly. Remember to check your answer to make sure that it is reasonable.

How Are
Cone-Bearing
Trees &
Static Electricity
Connected?

When the bark of a cone-bearing tree is broken it secretes resin, which hardens and seals the tree's wound. The resin of some ancient trees fossilized over time, forming a golden, gemlike substance called amber. The ancient Greeks prized amber highly, not only for its beauty, but also because they believed it had magical qualities. They had noticed that when amber was rubbed with wool or fur, small bits of straw or ash would stick to it. Because of amber's color and its unusual properties, some believed that amber was solidified sunshine. The Greek name for amber was *elektron*, which means "substance of the Sun."

By the seventeenth century, the behavior of amber had sparked the curiosity of a number of scientists, and an explanation of amber's behavior finally emerged. When amber is rubbed by wool or fur, static electricity is produced. Today, a device called a Van de Graaff generator, like the one shown above, can produce static electricity involving millions of volts, and has been used to explore the nature of matter in atom-smashing experiments.

unit projects

Visit unit projects at fl6.msscience.com for project ideas and resources. Projects include:

- **History** Design a creative bookmark depicting a variety of aspects of Ben Franklin's contributions to science and his country.
- **Career** Discover how magnetic-resonance imaging is used in the medical field and how it compares to traditional X rays.
- **Model** Design an electrifying review game demonstrating your new understanding of electricity and magnetism.

 Maglev Trains: Floating Locomotives encourages understanding of magnets and their application in the transportation field. Design a maglev train and present it to the class.

Sunshine State Standards—**SC.A.1:** The student understands that all matter has observable, measurable properties; **SC.C.1:** understands that types of motion may be described, measured, and predicted; **SC.C.2:** understands that the types of force that act on an object and the effect of that force can be described. . . .

Motion, Forces, and Simple Machines

Catching Some Air

This skateboarder pauses briefly in the air as he changes direction and begins his descent. How does his motion change as he reaches the bottom of the halfpipe and starts up the other side? In this chapter, you'll learn how forces affect motion.

Science Journal   Write a paragraph comparing the motion of a ball and a paper airplane being thrown high in the air and returning to the ground.

Start-Up Activities

  SC.H.1.3.5

Forces in Motion

You see forces in motion every day. Milk pours from a jug into your glass. Your pencil rolls across a desk and falls to the ground. Your friend tosses a flying disc that rises up on a draft of wind before floating down to you. During most of these events, more than one force is acting on an object. In this lab, you will observe and compare the motion of a falling object with different forces acting upon it.

1. Complete a safety worksheet.
2. Set a softball on the edge of a table and push it off so that it drops to the floor. Use a stopwatch to time how long it takes the ball to fall.
3. Tie one end of a 50-cm length of string around the softball and tie the other end around a tennis ball. Place the softball at the edge of the table and stretch out the string so that the tennis ball is at the other end of the table. Let the softball drop and time its fall.
4. Repeat step 2, replacing the tennis ball with a second softball.
5. **Think Critically** In your science journal, describe how the motion of the softball changed. How would the motion of the falling softball change if it were tied to two softballs?

FOLDABLES™
Study Organizer

Describing and Explaining Motion Make the following Foldable to help you understand motion, forces, and simple machines.

LA.A.1.3.4

STEP 1 **Fold** a vertical sheet of paper from side to side. Make the front edge about 1 cm shorter than the back edge.

STEP 2 **Turn** lengthwise and **fold** into thirds.

STEP 3 **Unfold and cut** only the top layer along both folds to make three tabs.

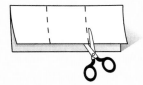

STEP 4 Label each tab. Know? Like to know? Learned?

Identify Questions Before you read the chapter, write what you already know about motion, forces, and simple machines under the left tab of your Foldable, and write questions about what you'd like to know under the center tab. After you read the chapter, list what you learned under the right tab.

Science online Preview this chapter's content and activities at fl6.msscience.com

Also covers: SC.H.1.3.5 Annually Assessed (p. 503)

Describing Motion

What You'll Learn

- **Identify** when motion occurs.
- **Recognize** a reference point.
- **Compare** speed, velocity, and acceleration.

Why It's Important

Understanding motion will help you understand why objects move.

Review Vocabulary

✷ **galaxy:** a large group of stars, gases, and dust held together by gravity

New Vocabulary

✷ speed
✷ velocity
✷ acceleration

✷ FCAT Vocabulary

Figure 1 One of these two cars has moved.
Explain *how you know which car has moved.*

Motion

Every day you see objects and people in motion. A car driving down the street slows down and stops at a stop sign, then speeds up and turns left. Students leave your school building when classes are over and head home in different directions. You move from room to room in your house.

Sometimes it can be hard to tell if something is moving. For example, when you lie in your bed, you seem to be motionless. Yet you are moving as Earth spins on its axis and moves around the Sun. When you are on a bus or in a car, you see other cars going past you. Are you moving or are they moving?

Motion Is Relative

This might have happened to you. You are sitting in a car in a parking lot and are startled when you notice the car seems to be rolling backward. After looking around, you realize that it is the car beside you that is moving forward. Why did you seem to be moving backward?

You noticed motion when you saw your car getting farther away from the car beside you. At first you thought the car beside you wasn't moving. You thought your car had to be moving for the two cars to get farther apart. But after you looked around, you saw that your car was in the same place in the parking lot. You knew then that your car hadn't moved backward. It was the other car that had moved forward. Look at **Figure 1.** How can you tell which car has moved?

A person sitting on a moving bus is not moving if the reference point is the seat. The person is moving if the reference point is the ground.

A person walking in the aisle of the bus is moving if the reference point is the seat and if the reference point is the ground.

Motion Depends on a Reference Point Motion always is described relative to an object that is assumed to be not moving. Something that is not moving is sometimes said to be at rest. A reference point is an object that is assumed to be at rest.

In the previous example, your car seemed to be moving when you thought the other car was not moving. You chose that car as your reference point. Then your car seemed to be moving. But when you chose the parking lot as your reference point, your car was at rest and the other car was moving.

Reading Check *What is a reference point?*

Choosing a Reference Point You can choose a reference point depending on the motion of the object you want to describe. If you are walking on a bus that is moving, as shown in **Figure 2,** you might describe your motion relative to the bus. Then the bus would be your reference point. You could also describe your motion relative to the ground, so the ground would be your reference point. Depending on the reference point that you choose, how would your motion be different?

A Reference Point for Earth's Motion How does Earth move through space? The answer to that question depends on the reference point that is chosen. Look at **Figure 3** on the next page. If the Sun is the reference point, Earth is moving in a nearly circular path around the Sun. However, the Sun is moving relative to the center of the Milky Way galaxy. This causes Earth's motion relative to the Milky Way galaxy to be different from its motion relative to the Sun, as shown in **Figure 3.** The motion of Earth through space depends on the reference point chosen.

Figure 2 The motion of a person on a bus depends on the reference point that is chosen.

Figure 3

In the vastness of space, Earth's motion can be described only in relation to other objects, such as stars and galaxies. The illustration here shows how Earth moves relative to the Sun and to the Milky Way galaxy, which is part of a cluster of galaxies called the Local Group.

A Imagine you are looking down on the Sun's north pole. From this perspective, Earth traces out a nearly circular path, moving counterclockwise in its orbit around the Sun.

B The Sun belongs to a collection of several billion stars that make up the Milky Way galaxy. Viewed from the "top" of the galaxy, the Sun moves clockwise in a nearly circular orbit around the galaxy's center. Earth's orbit around the Sun is not in the same plane as the galaxy. As a result, Earth's motion traces out a corkscrew path* as it moves with the Sun relative to the center of the galaxy.

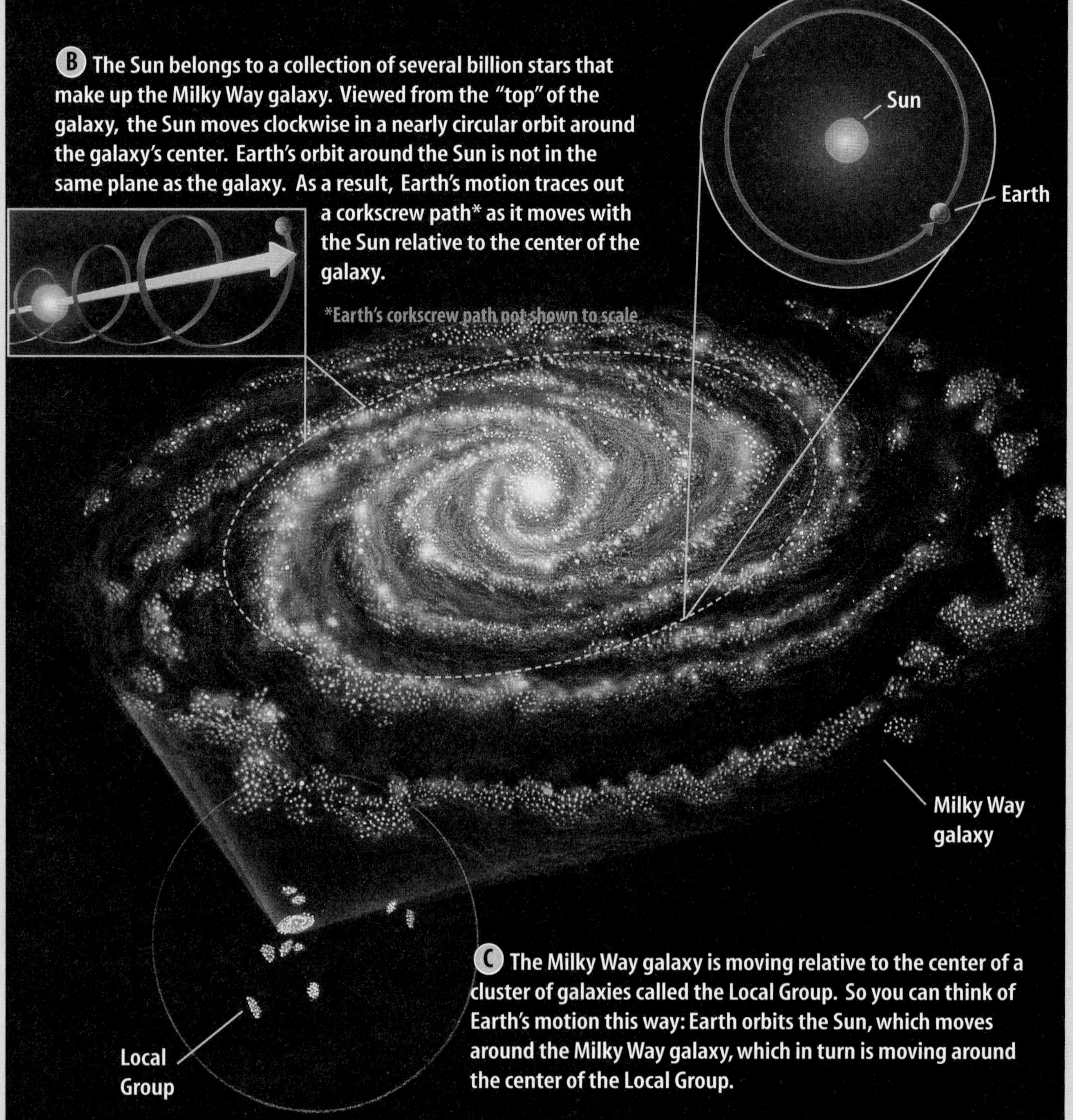

*Earth's corkscrew path not shown to scale

Sun

Earth

Milky Way galaxy

Local Group

C The Milky Way galaxy is moving relative to the center of a cluster of galaxies called the Local Group. So you can think of Earth's motion this way: Earth orbits the Sun, which moves around the Milky Way galaxy, which in turn is moving around the center of the Local Group.

Motion is a Change in Position

When you ride a bike, you are in motion relative to the ground. That motion can be described in different ways. How far did you travel? What direction did you move? How long were you moving? How fast were you riding? Did you speed up or slow down?

Motion occurs when the position of an object changes. The position of an object is how far the object is from a reference point, as shown in **Figure 4.** When something is moving relative to a reference point, its position relative to the reference point is changing. If the position of an object doesn't change, then it is not moving. The position of an object is measured in meters, which is a unit of length.

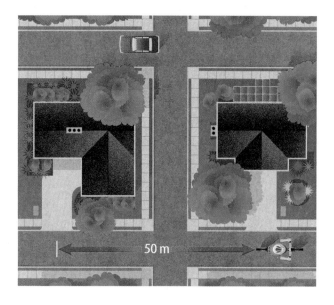

Figure 4 The reference point is the middle of the driveway of the house on the left.
Determine *the position of the bike rider.*

Distance One way to describe your motion is to tell how far you went or the distance you traveled. Suppose you traveled in a straight line and didn't change direction. Then the distance you traveled equals your final position minus your initial position.

For example, suppose your house is the reference point. You start pedaling your bike and ride in a straight line. When you start moving you are 50 m from your house, as shown in **Figure 5.** This is your initial position. When you stop, you are 150 m from your house. This is your final position. Then the distance you traveled is 150 m − 50 m = 100 m.

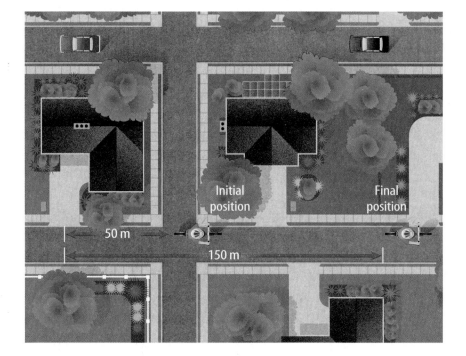

Figure 5 The distance the bike rider has traveled is the final position minus the initial position.
Determine *the distance the bike rider has traveled.*

Movement of Earth's Crust
The outer part of Earth is the crust. Earth's crust is broken into huge pieces called plates that move slowly. Research how fast plates can move. In your Science Journal, make a table showing the speeds of some plates.

Speed

How fast are you moving when you walk down a hallway at school or ride in a car? The answer to how fast you are moving is your speed. **Speed** is the distance traveled divided by the time it takes to travel that distance.

When you're riding in a car on a trip, the speed of the car changes as it slows down and speeds up. If your speed changes, what speed would describe how fast you traveled for the entire trip? If your speed isn't constant, you can determine your average speed for the trip using the equation below.

Average Speed Equation

$$\text{average speed (m/s)} = \frac{\text{total distance (m)}}{\text{total time (s)}}$$

$$\overline{v} = \frac{d}{t}$$

In this equation, the symbol $\overline{v}$ stands for average speed. Average speed can be measured in units other than m/s. For example, the speed of a car usually is given in units of km/h.

Applying Math Solve a Simple Equation

BICYCLE SPEED A bicycle travels a total distance of 12 m in 4 s. What is its average speed?

Solution

1 *This is what you know:*
- total distance: $d = 12$ m
- total time: $t = 4$ s

2 *This is what you need to find:*
average speed: $\overline{v} = ?$ m/s

3 *This is the procedure you need to use:*
Substitute the known values for total distance and total time into the average speed equation and calculate the average speed:

$$\overline{v} = \frac{d}{t} = \frac{12\text{ m}}{4\text{ s}} = 3\text{ m/s}$$

4 *Check your answer:*
Multiply your answer by the time. You should calculate the distance that was given.

Practice Problems

1. What is the average speed of a sprinter who runs 100 m in 10 s? MA.D.2.3.1

2. If an airplane travels 1,350 km in 3 h, what is its average speed? MA.D.2.3.1

Math Practice | For more practice, visit fl6.msscience.com

Velocity

Suppose you are walking at a constant speed headed north on a street. You turn when you reach an intersection, and continue walking at the same speed. Now you are headed east, as shown in **Figure 6.** Your motion has changed, even though your speed has stayed constant. To describe how your motion changed, you would tell how fast you are going and your direction.

The direction and speed of an object is given by the object's velocity. The **velocity** of an object is the speed of an object and its direction of motion. If you were walking north at a speed of 2 m/s, your velocity would be 2 m/s north. When you were walking east at the same speed, your velocity was 2 m/s east.

Figure 6 The person's motion changed because the direction of motion changed from north to east.

Changing Velocity How does the velocity of something change? Velocity changes when speed changes or direction of motion changes. Suppose you are riding your bike to a friend's house, as shown in **Figure 7.** Your velocity is 5 m/s north. You slow down as you reach a corner, and your velocity changes to 3 m/s north. Your velocity changed because your speed decreased. After you turn the corner, your velocity is 3 m/s east. Your velocity changed because your direction changed. Then you speed up so your velocity is 5 m/s east. This time your velocity changed because your speed increased.

Reading Check *When does the velocity of an object change?*

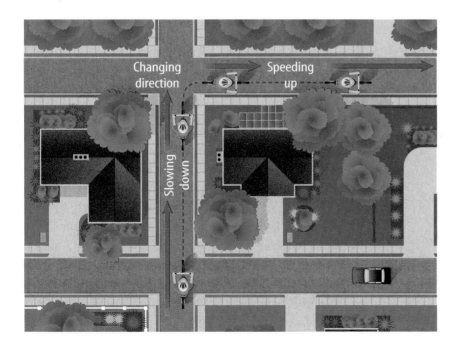

Figure 7 A bike rider slows down, turns a corner, and speeds up. The arrows show the bike rider's velocity at different times. The direction of the arrow shows the direction of motion. The length of the arrow shows the bike rider's speed.

Acceleration

Distance, speed, and velocity describe motion by telling how far, how fast, and in what direction. Sometimes it is important to know how motion is changing. Is an approaching car speeding up or slowing to a stop? Is the skater coming at you on a sidewalk changing direction? The acceleration of an object tells how velocity is changing. **Acceleration** is the change in velocity divided by the time needed for the change to occur.

A change in velocity can be due to a change in speed, a change in direction, or both. When velocity is changing, an object is accelerating. This means that something is accelerating if it is speeding up, slowing down, or turning. The runners in **Figure 8** are accelerating when they go around the turns in the track.

Figure 8 These runners are changing direction as they go around the turn. Because their velocity is changing, the runners are accelerating.

✔ **Reading Check** *When does acceleration occur?*

---

section ① review

Summary

Motion

● The description of an object's motion depends upon the reference point chosen.

● The distance traveled is the final position minus the initial position of an object.

Speed, Velocity, and Acceleration

● The speed of an object is the distance traveled divided by the time it takes to travel that distance.

● The average speed can be calculated from this equation:

$$\bar{v} = \frac{d}{t}$$

● The velocity of an object is the speed of an object and its direction of motion.

● The acceleration of an object is the change in velocity divided by the time needed for the change to occur.

Self Check

1. **Describe** a situation in which motion is described in terms of a reference point. `SC.C.1.3.1`

2. **Evaluate** In a model of the solar system, the planets are shown revolving around the Sun. What is the reference point in this model? `SC.C.1.3.1`

3. **Explain** If you are traveling around a curve at a constant speed of 30 km/h, is your velocity changing? Explain. `SC.C.1.3.1`

4. **Think Critically** A jet airliner is flying with a constant speed of 700 km/h. Can the airliner be accelerating if its speed is constant? Explain. `SC.C.1.3.1`

Applying Math

5. **Calculate** If you traveled 50 m in 25 s, what is your distance traveled and average speed? `SC.C.1.3.1`

6. **Average Speed** Kyla and David travel 25 km to their grandmother's house after school. The trip takes 0.6 h. What was their average speed in km/h? `SC.C.1.3.1`

More Section Review fl6.msscience.com

Benchmarks—SC.A.1.3.2 Annually Assessed (p. 517): The student understands the difference between weight and mass; SC.C.2.3.2 Annually Assessed (pp. 514–515): The student knows common contact forces; SC.C.2.3.3 Annually Assessed (pp. 512–513): The student knows that if more than one force acts on an object, then the forces can reinforce or cancel each other....

Also covers: SC.C.2.3.1 (pp. 515–516), SC.C.2.3.5 Annually Assessed (p. 513), SC.C.2.3.6 Annually Assessed (p. 513), SC.C.2.3.7 (p. 516), SC.H.1.3.4 Annually Assessed (p. 518), SC.H.1.3.5 Annually Assessed (p. 518), SC.H.1.3.7 Annually Assessed (p. 518)

section 2

Forces and Motion

What is a force?

It's finally lunchtime, and you head to your school's lunchroom. In the lunchroom, you pull a chair away from a table so you can sit down. After you finish lunch, you push the chair back under the table before you leave. In both cases you exerted a force on the chair. A **force** is a push or a pull.

Forces are exerted by one object on another. When you pulled the chair away from the lunch table, one object—you—exerted a force on another object—the chair.

Force has Size and Direction Just like velocity and acceleration, a force has both a size and a direction. The size of a force is sometimes called the strength of the force. In SI units, the strength of a force is measured in newtons (N). A force of one newton is about the force it takes to lift a quarter-pound hamburger. To lift a two-liter bottle of water requires a force of about 20 N.

The direction of a force is the direction of the push or pull. When you pulled the chair away from the table in the lunchroom, the force exerted on the chair was in the direction away from the table. When you pushed the chair under the table, the direction of the force on the chair was toward the table. **Figure 9** shows the direction of the force exerted by pulling on a grocery cart and pushing on a door.

as you read

What You'll Learn

- **Evaluate** forces acting on an object.
- **Recognize** contact and non-contact forces acting on an object.
- **Identify** the difference between weight and mass.

Why It's Important

The changes in the motions of all objects are due to the forces that act on them.

Review Vocabulary

✴ **gravitation:** the attractive force that acts between all objects due to their mass

New Vocabulary

- ✴ **force**
- ● **balanced force**
- ● **unbalanced force**
- ✴ **inertia**
- ● **contact force**
- ✴ **friction**
- ✴ **gravity**

✴ FCAT Vocabulary

Force exerted by girl on door

Motion of door

Force exerted by man pulling on cart

Motion of cart

Figure 9 A force is a push or a pull that one object exerts on another. Pulling on the grocery cart exerts a force on the cart. Pushing on the door exerts a force on the door.

Force and Muscles
When you push or pull on something, muscles in your body contract. This contraction is caused by chemical reactions in muscle tissue. These chemical reactions make certain molecules in your muscles slide past each other. Research how a muscle contracts and describe what you learn in your Science Journal.

Figure 10 The net force on an object depends on the strength and direction of the forces acting on the object.
Infer *how the net force in the photo on the left would change if one person stopped pushing.*

Combining Forces

Suppose you are trying to move a heavy piece of furniture, like the dresser shown in **Figure 10.** You don't have to push as hard if a friend helps and you both push together in the same direction. When more than one force acts on an object, the forces combine. The combination of all the forces acting on an object is called the net force. The net force on the dresser was the combination of your push and your friend's push. The way that forces combine depends on the direction of the forces.

Forces in the Same Direction If both you and a friend push on the same side of the dresser, the forces that you both exert are in the same direction. When the forces acting on an object are in the same direction, they add together to form the net force, as shown on the left in **Figure 10.** The net force is in the same direction as the individual forces. When you both push on the dresser in the same direction, the net force is in the same direction that both of you are pushing.

Forces in the Opposite Direction Suppose you push on one side of the dresser and a friend pushes on the other side, as shown on the right in **Figure 10.** Then the two forces are in opposite directions. When two forces are in opposite directions, the net force equals the larger force minus the smaller force. Then the net force is in the same direction as the larger force. If you push on the dresser harder than your friend, the net force is in the direction of your push.

Balanced and Unbalanced Forces

If you and a friend push on the dresser in **Figure 11** in opposite directions with the same size force, then the forces combine to make the net force zero. When the net force is zero, the forces on an object are **balanced forces.** If the net force is not zero, the forces on an object are **unbalanced forces.** The forces on the dresser were unbalanced when you both pushed on the dresser in the same direction. The forces also were unbalanced when different-sized forces acted on the dresser in opposite directions.

Unbalanced Forces Cause Motion to Change

No matter how hard you push, the dresser won't move if your friend pushes just as hard in the opposite direction. When the forces acting on it are balanced, the dresser doesn't move. But when you both push in the same direction, you can make the dresser move. The dresser only moves when the forces acting on it are unbalanced.

You might think that unbalanced forces cause objects only to move. But unbalanced forces also can cause objects to stop moving. When you catch a basketball pass, you exert an unbalanced force on the ball with your hands. The basketball quickly slows down and stops. The motion of an object changes only if unbalanced forces are acting on it.

✔ Reading Check *When does the motion of an object change?*

Unbalanced Forces Cause Change in Speed One way the motion of an object changes is when it speeds up or slows down. When you and a friend pushed on the dresser and it moved, you changed its motion. The unbalanced forces acting on the dresser made it speed up. When you caught the basketball, the unbalanced force acting on the ball caused it to slow down. Unbalanced forces can change the speed of an object.

Unbalanced Forces Cause Change in Direction An object's motion also changes when the direction of its motion changes. Unbalanced forces can change the direction of an object's motion. For example, an unbalanced force is exerted on the ball in **Figure 12** when it is hit by the hockey stick. This unbalanced force causes the ball to change direction, as well as to change speed.

Figure 11 The forces acting on an object are balanced when the net force is zero.
Compare and contrast *the forces exerted on each side of the dresser.*

FCAT FOCUS **Annually Assessed Benchmark Check**

SC.C.2.3.3 Sam pushes on a door with a force of 15 N to the left and Maria pushes with a force of 25 N to the right. What force should Tamika exert to make the forces on the door balanced?

Figure 12 The unbalanced force exerted on the ball by the hockey stick changed the direction in which the ball was moving.

Figure 13 Inertia is the reason that it is easier to move a toy truck than a car.
Explain *how inertia depends on mass.*

Inertia

Objects resist having their motion changed. Only when unbalanced forces act on an object does its motion change. **Inertia** is the tendency of an object to resist a change in its motion. Because of inertia, the tendency for an object that is not moving is to stay at rest.

Inertia also causes a moving object to resist a change in its motion. The motion of a moving object changes if the object changes speed or direction. This means that inertia causes a moving object to tend to move in a straight line with constant speed. You've felt the effects of inertia when you're riding in a car that comes to a sudden stop. Even with a seat belt on, you can feel yourself continue to move forward. Your inertia resisted a change in motion.

Inertia and Mass The more mass an object has, the more inertia it has. It is harder to change the motion of an object that has more mass. Imagine pushing a toy truck and a car, as in **Figure 13.** A car might have a thousand times more mass than the toy truck. It's easy to start, stop, and turn the toy truck. But more than one person usually is needed to push a car and start it moving.

Contact Forces

You could push on the dresser only while your hand was touching it. A force exerted only when two objects are touching each other is called a **contact force.** The force exerted by your hand on the dresser is a contact force because your hand had to touch the dresser to exert the force.

Friction Suppose you push a book so it slides on a table. **Figure 14** shows that besides the force exerted by your hand, another contact force called friction acts on the book as it slides on the table top. **Friction** is a force that opposes the relative motion of two surfaces that are in contact. The frictional force on the sliding book is exerted on the book by the table.

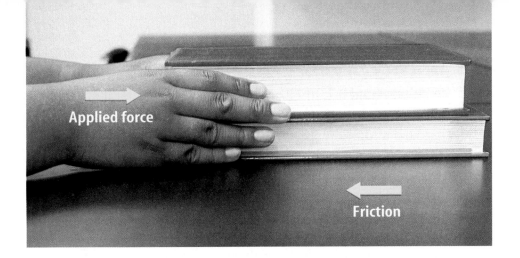

Applied force

Friction

The Size and Direction of Friction Like all forces, friction has a size and a direction as shown in **Figure 14.** The size of a frictional force depends on the surfaces that are in contact. The strength of the frictional force usually depends on the roughness of the surfaces. The frictional force usually becomes smaller as the surfaces become smoother. The surface of a concrete sidewalk is rougher than the surface of an ice rink. So there is less friction on a hockey puck sliding on ice than on a puck sliding on a concrete sidewalk.

What is the direction of a frictional force? Look at **Figure 14** again. The force of friction on the sliding book is in the opposite direction to the direction in which the book is moving. The direction of the frictional force on a sliding object is always opposite to the direction of the object's motion.

Air Resistance A contact force that is exerted by air on an object moving in the air is air resistance. You can feel the force of air resistance pushing against you when you ride a bike. Just like friction, the direction of the air resistance force on an object is always opposite to the direction of the object's motion. The strength of the air resistance force depends on the shape of the object and how fast it is moving.

Non-contact Forces

You might have used a magnet to pick up objects such as paper clips. Suppose you place a paperclip on your desktop and slowly bring one end of a bar magnet close to it. When the magnet gets close enough, the paper clip will be pulled toward the magnet and finally stick to it. The magnet exerted a force on the paper clip that pulled it toward the magnet.

You might have noticed that the paper clip was pulled toward the magnet even though the magnet wasn't touching the clip. The force exerted by the magnet is a non-contact force. A non-contact force is a force exerted by one object on another when the objects are not touching.

Figure 14 Friction opposes the motion of one surface sliding on another surface. The frictional force on the book is opposite to the direction in which the book is moving.
Determine *the direction of the frictional force on a book that is sliding to the left.*

Annually Assessed Benchmark Check

SC.A.1.3.2 A ball falls from a high cliff. How do the ball's mass and weight change as the ball falls?

SC.C.2.3.1

Mini LAB

Determining Weights in Newtons

Procedure
1. Stand on a **bathroom scale** and measure your weight.
2. Hold a **large book,** stand on the scale, and measure the combined weight of you and the book.

Analysis
1. Find the weight of the book by subtracting your weight from the combined weight.
2. Multiply your weight and the weight of the book by 4.4 to calculate the weights in newtons.

Try at Home

Gravity

If you hold a softball above the ground and let it go, the ball falls to the ground. The motion of the ball changed after you let it go, so a force was acting on it. Earth exerted the force, called gravity, that pulled the ball downward. **Gravity** is the pull that every object always exerts on every other object due to their masses. The force due to gravity usually is called the gravitational force.

A gravitational force exists between any two objects that have mass. As a result, they always exert gravitational forces on each other. The softball exerts a force on the Earth and the Earth exerts a force on the softball. Two objects don't have to be touching to exert a gravitational force on each other. Just like the magnetic force, the gravitational force is a non-contact force that acts at a distance.

Gravity Depends on Mass and Distance The gravitational force that one mass exerts on another, such as the force that Earth exerts on you, depends on two things as shown in **Figure 15.** One is the masses of the objects. The more mass the objects have, the stronger the gravitational force each object exerts on the other. The other is the distance between the objects. As the objects get closer together, the gravitational force the objects exert on each other becomes stronger.

✓ **Reading Check** *What does the gravitational force depend on?*

An astronaut in the space shuttle orbiting Earth usually is about 400 km above Earth's surface. When the astronaut and Earth are this far apart, the force of gravity on the astronaut is about 90 percent as strong as when the astronaut is standing on the ground.

Figure 15 Gravitational force depends on the masses of the objects and the distance between them.

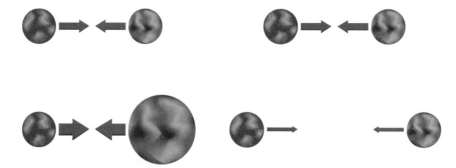

The gravitational force increases if the mass of one of the balls gets larger.

The gravitational force decreases as the balls move farther apart.

Mass and Weight

Do you know how much you weigh? You might think that your weight is the same thing as your mass. However, weight and mass are different. Your mass is the amount of matter in you. Recall that mass is measured in kilograms. On Earth, your weight is the strength of the gravitational force that Earth exerts on you. The strength of the gravitational force depends on your mass. As your mass changes, the gravitational force that Earth exerts on you also changes. As a result, your weight changes.

When you stand on a scale to measure your weight, as shown in **Figure 16,** you are measuring the strength of this gravitational force. Because weight is a force, it is measured in newtons. In the United States, force usually is measured in units called pounds. A force of 1 pound is the same as a force of about 4.4 N. A person that weighs 100 pounds weighs about 440 N in SI units.

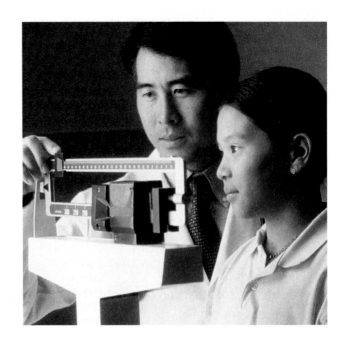

Figure 16 When you weigh yourself on a scale, you are measuring the gravitational force exerted on you.

section 2 review

Summary

Force

- A force is a push or a pull that is exerted by one object on another object.
- A force has a size and a direction.
- The net force is the combination of all the forces acting on an object.

Forces and Motion

- The forces on an object are balanced if the net force is zero.
- The forces on an object are unbalanced if the net force is not zero.
- Unbalanced forces cause motion to change.

Types of Forces

- Contact forces, such as friction, are exerted when objects are touching each other.
- Non-contact forces can act at a distance.
- Gravity is the attractive force that objects exert on each other because they have mass.

Self Check

1. **Explain** How would the gravitational force between Earth and the Moon change if the distance between them increased? SC.C.2.3.7

2. **Explain** how the inertia of an object is related to the object's mass.

3. **Compare** an astronaut's weight in orbit with the astronaut's weight on Earth, assuming the mass of the astronaut doesn't change. SC.A.1.3.2

4. **Determine** the net force on a car moving in a straight line at constant speed. SC.C.2.3.6

5. **Think Critically** A book sliding across a table slows down and comes to a stop. Explain whether the forces acting on the book are balanced or unbalanced. SC.C.2.3.3

Applying Math

6. **Net Force** One person pushes on a piano that is at rest with a force of 40 N to the left. Another person pushes with a force of 55 N to the right. In what direction is the net force on the piano? SC.C.2.3.3 MA.A.3.3.1

Benchmark—**SC.C.2.3.3:** The student knows that if more than one force acts on an object, then the forces can reinforce or cancel each other . . .; **SC.C.2.3.6:** explains and shows the ways in which a net force can act on an object; **SC.H.1.3.4; SC.H.1.3.5; SC.H.1.3.7**

Combining Forces

When you lift your backpack, how does its motion depend on the force that you exert? What other forces are acting on the backpack?

▶ Real-World Problem

How do the forces acting on an object combine to affect its motion?

Goals
- ■ **Determine** the net force acting on an object.
- ■ **Observe** how changing the net force on an object affects its motion.

Materials
spring scale
500-g weight with hook

Safety Precautions
Complete a safety worksheet before you begin.

▶ Procedure

1. Make a data table similar to the table shown.
2. Hook the weight to the spring scale. Measure the force exerted by the spring scale. Record the measurement in your data table.
3. Slowly raise the weight upward. Measure the force exerted by the spring scale as the weight moves upward. Record the measurement in your data table.

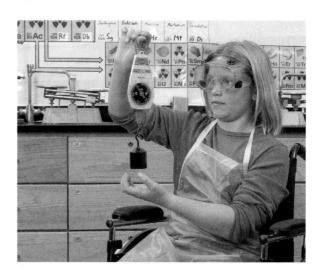

4. Quickly raise the weight upward. Measure the force exerted by the spring scale as the weight moves upward. Record the measurement in your data table.

▶ Conclude and Apply

1. **Diagram** the forces acting on the weight.
2. **Infer** the force of gravity on the weight.
3. **Calculate** the net force on the weight for each trial. For which trial was the net force on the weight greatest?
4. How did the motion of the weight depend on the net force on the weight?

Communicating
Your Data

Compare your measurements with the measurements collected by your classmates. Discuss and explain any major differences you observe in the collected data.

Data Table	
Motion of Weight	**Force Exerted by Spring Scale (N)**
Not moving	
Slowly rising	**Do not write in this book.**
Quickly rising	

section

3

Simple Machines

What is a machine?

How many machines have you used today? A machine is a device that makes doing work easier. A can opener like the one in **Figure 17** is a machine that changes the force applied by your hand into a larger force that opens the can.

A **simple machine** is a machine that uses only one movement to do work. A screwdriver is an example of a simple machine. It does work with only one motion—turning. Simple machines include the pulley, lever, wheel and axle, inclined plane, wedge, and screw. A compound machine is a combination of simple machines. A can opener is a compound machine that combines a wedge, a lever, and a wheel and axle.

Making Work Easier

How do machines make doing work easier? When you think of doing work, you might think of doing household chores or homework. In science, work is done when a force causes an object to move. When you push on a wall, you don't do any work if the wall doesn't move.

When you use a machine, you apply a force on the machine. The force applied on the machine is the input force. The machine then applies a force on some object. This force is the output force. One way a machine makes work easier is by making the output force greater than the input force. The **mechanical advantage** of a machine equals the output force divided by the input force.

as you read

What **You'll Learn**

- **Explain** how machines make doing work easier.
- **Define** mechanical advantage.
- **Distinguish** the different types of simple machines.

Why **It's Important**

Machines make doing work easier.

Review Vocabulary

✷ **force:** a push or a pull that one object exerts on another

New Vocabulary

- simple machine
- mechanical advantage
- ✷ **pulley**
- ✷ **lever**
- ✷ **inclined plane**

✷ FCAT Vocabulary

Figure 17 A can opener is a machine that applies a force to the lid of the can. This force is larger than the force applied to the can opener by the person's hand.

Observing Mechanical Advantage—Pulleys

Procedure 🥽
1. Complete a safety worksheet.
2. Tie a **3-m-long rope** to the middle of a **broomstick** or **dowel** and hold this stick horizontally. Another student should hold another stick horizontally. Wrap the rope around both sticks four times, leaving about 0.5 m between the sticks.
3. A third student should pull on the rope while the other two students try to keep the sticks from coming closer together.
4. Observe what happens. Repeat using only two wraps of the rope and then using eight wraps.

Analysis
1. Describe what you observed. Could the students hold the sticks apart?
2. Compare and contrast the results with two, four, and eight turns of the rope around the sticks.

Input Work and Output Work When a machine is used, the input force and the output force do work. When you use a screwdriver, you apply the input force on the screwdriver's handle. The input work is the work you do as you turn the handle. The output force is applied by the screwdriver's blade. The output work is the work done by the screwdriver as the blade turns the screw.

Even though a machine can make the output force greater than the input force, it can't make the output work greater than the input work. In fact, the output work is always less than the input work. Friction between the moving parts in a machine always converts some of the input work into thermal energy. The output work would equal the input work only if there were no friction.

The Pulley

To raise a window blind, you pull down on a cord. The blind uses a pulley to change the direction of the force. A **pulley** is an object, like a wheel, that has a groove with a rope or cable running through it. For a fixed pulley, such as the one in **Figure 18,** the output force is in a different direction than the input force. However, the sizes of the output force and the input force are the same. As a result, a fixed pulley has a mechanical advantage of 1.

A combination of pulleys can make the output force greater than the input force. The double-pulley system shown in **Figure 18** has a mechanical advantage of 2. Each supporting rope holds half of the weight, so the input force needed to lift the weight is half as large as for a single pulley.

Figure 18 A pulley changes the direction of the input force and can make the output force greater than the input force.

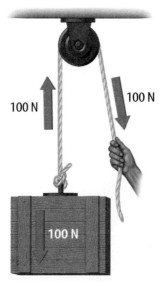

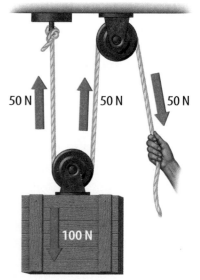

A single pulley changes the direction of the input force.

A combination of pulleys decreases the input force that has to be applied to lift the weight.

Figure 19 A lever is classified according to the locations of the input force, output force, and fulcrum.

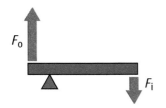

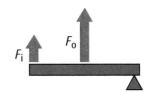

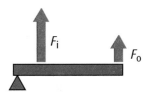

Sometimes a screwdriver is used as a first-class lever. The fulcrum is between the input and output forces.

A wheelbarrow is a second-class lever. The fulcrum is the wheel, and the input force is applied on the handles. The load, which is where the output force is applied, is between the input force and the fulcrum.

A hockey stick is a third-class lever. The fulcrum is your upper hand, and the input force is applied by your lower hand. The output force is applied at the bottom end of the stick.

The Lever

A **lever** is a rod or plank that pivots about a fixed point called the fulcrum. There are three types, or classes, of levers. The different classes depend on the positions of the input force, output force, and the fulcrum, as shown in **Figure 19.**

In a first-class lever, the fulcrum is between the input force and the output force. The output force can be greater or less than the input force, depending on the location of the fulcrum. As a result, the mechanical advantage of a first-class lever can be greater than 1 or less than 1. For example, if the fulcrum is closer to the output force than to the input force, the output force is greater than the input force. Then the mechanical advantage is greater than 1.

In a second-class lever, the output force is applied between the input force and the fulcrum, as in a wheelbarrow. The output force is always greater than the input force for this type of lever, so the mechanical advantage is always greater than 1.

In a third-class lever, the input force is applied between the output force and the fulcrum. The output force is always less than the input force for this type of lever. Instead, a third-class lever increases the distance over which the output force is applied.

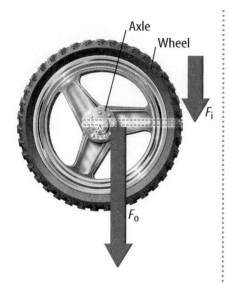

Figure 20 The radius of the wheel is greater than the radius of the axle. The mechanical advantage of the wheel and axle is greater than 1 if the input force is applied to the wheel.

The Wheel and Axle Try turning a doorknob by holding the narrow base of the knob. It's much easier to turn the larger knob. A doorknob is an example of a wheel and axle. Look at **Figure 20.** A wheel and axle is made of two round objects that are attached and rotate together about the same axis. The larger object is called the wheel, and the smaller object is the axle. The mechanical advantage of a wheel and axle can be calculated by dividing the radius of the wheel by the radius of the axle.

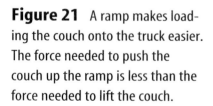 **Reading Check** *How do the lever, pulley, and wheel and axle make work easier?*

The Inclined Plane

An **inclined plane** is a flat, sloped surface. A ramp, such as the one in **Figure 21,** is an example of an inclined plane. An inclined plane makes doing work easier by reducing the amount of force that has to be applied to lift an object. Imagine trying to lift a heavy couch onto the back of a truck. Pushing the couch up the ramp, as in **Figure 21,** requires less force than lifting the couch straight upward. However, when the ramp is used, the force applied to the couch is exerted over a longer distance than when the couch is lifted upward.

The mechanical advantage of an inclined plane is the length of the inclined plane divided by its height. The longer the ramp is, the less force it takes to move the object. Ramps might have enabled the ancient Egyptians to build their pyramids. To move limestone blocks having a mass of more than 1,000 kg each, archaeologists hypothesize that the Egyptians built enormous ramps.

Figure 21 A ramp makes loading the couch onto the truck easier. The force needed to push the couch up the ramp is less than the force needed to lift the couch.

The Wedge When you take a bite out of an apple, you are using wedges. A wedge is a moving inclined plane with one or two sloping sides. Your front teeth are wedges. A wedge changes the direction of the input force. As you push your front teeth into the apple, the downward input force is changed by your teeth into a sideways force that pushes the skin of the apple apart. Knives and axes also are wedges that are used for cutting.

Figure 22 shows that the teeth of meat-eaters, or carnivores, are more wedge-shaped than the teeth of plant-eaters, or herbivores. The teeth of carnivores are used to cut and rip meat, whereas herbivores' teeth are used for grinding plant material. Scientists can determine what a fossilized animal ate when it was living by examining its teeth.

The Screw A road going up a mountain usually wraps around the mountain. Such a road is less steep than a road straight up the side of the mountain, so it's easier to climb. However, you travel a greater distance to climb the mountain on the mountain road. The mountain road is similar to a screw. A screw is an inclined plane wrapped around a post. The inclined plane forms the screw threads. Just like a wedge, a screw also changes the direction of the force you apply. When you turn a screw, the input force is changed by the threads to an output force that pulls the screw into the material. Friction between the threads and the material holds the screw tightly in place.

Figure 22 Plant-eaters and meat-eaters have different teeth.

These wedge-shaped teeth enable a meat-eater to tear meat.

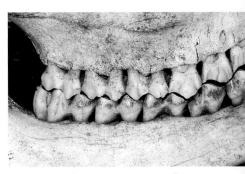

The teeth of a plant-eater are flatter and used for grinding.

section 3 review

Summary

Using Machines

- Machines make doing work easier.
- A machine can make the output force larger than the input force.
- A machine can apply the output force in a different direction than the input force.
- The mechanical advantage of a machine is the output force divided by the input force.

Simple Machines

- A simple machine is a device that does work with only one motion.
- The six simple machines are the pulley, lever, wheel and axle, inclined plane, wedge, and screw.

Self Check

1. **Describe** two ways that using a machine makes doing work easier. `SC.C.2.3.4`
2. **Explain** why the output work is always less than the input work in a real machine.
3. **Compare** a wheel and axle to a lever. `SC.C.2.3.4`
4. **Think Critically** Compare and contrast a second-class lever and a third-class lever. `SC.C.2.3.4`

Applying Math

5. **Mechanical Advantage** What is the mechanical advantage of a wheel and axle if the radius of the wheel is 12 cm and the radius of the axle is 2 cm?
6. **Inclined Plane** If the mechanical advantage of a 2-m long ramp is 2, what is the height of the ramp?

Design Your Own

Stretched to the Limit

Goals

- **Observe** the effect of different amounts of mass on a rubber band.
- **Measure** the effect of different masses on a rubber band.
- **Identify** the forces acting on the different masses.

Possible Materials

rubber bands
assorted weights with hooks
ring stand and bar
meterstick

Safety Precautions

Complete a safety worksheet becore you begin.

▶ Real-World Problem

Bungee jumping is a sport that involves jumping off buildings and bridges with only an elastic cord attached to your body to prevent you from falling to the ground. The physics of bungee jumping involves the conversion of gravitational potential energy into the elastic energy of the stretched cord. Your team is preparing for a bungee jump and you want to maximize each team member's freefall distance without making contact with the ground. However, your team members vary in body mass. Using the materials available to you, design an experiment that models bungee jumping and helps your team prepare for a safe jump.

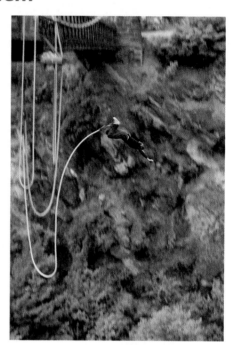

▶ Form a Hypothesis

Form a hypothesis to predict the effect of various masses on your bungee cord model.

▶ Test Your Hypothesis

Make a Plan

1. As a group, decide upon the materials you will need to test your hypothesis. Also decide upon any safety equipment you will need to ensure the safety of your group members during the experiment.

2. Devise an experiment to test your hypothesis. List the steps of your experiment in logical order. Be specific. State exactly what you will do during each step.

3. Create a data table in your Science Journal to record your data. Be certain your data table contains enough rows to record the results of all your planned trials.

4. Reread your entire experiment to make certain you have all needed materials and that your experimental steps can be easily followed and are in logical order.

▶ Follow Your Plan

1. Show your experiment steps and data table to your teacher and include any changes in your plan that your teacher suggests.

2. Carry out your experiment as planned and approved taking all the necessary safety precautions.

3. Record your results in your data table as you complete each trial.

▶ Analyze Your Data

1. **Graph** the results of your experiment.

2. **Interpret Data** Using your graph, explain how the distance the rubber band stretched depended on the mass.

3. **Draw Conclusions** Were the forces acting on the mass balanced or unbalanced? Explain your answer.

▶ Conclude and Apply

1. **Identify** the force that causes the rubber band to stretch.

2. **Infer** how the force exerted on the rubber band changed as the amount of mass hanging from the rubber band increased.

3. **Infer** how the distance the rubber band stretched depended on the force pulling on the rubber band.

4. **Think Critically** How well does your model compare to actual bungee jumping? How could you improve your model?

Communicating
Your Data

Compare your data and results with those of other students. Discuss any differences in the data and infer reasons for these differences.

SCIENCE Stats

Fastest Facts

Did you know...

...**Nature's fastest creature** is the peregrine falcon. It swoops down on its prey, traveling at speeds of more than 300 km/h. That tremendous speed enables the peregrine falcon to catch and kill other birds, which are its main prey.

...**The Supersonic Transport (SST),** was the world's fastest passenger jet, and cruised at twice the speed of sound. Traveling at 2,150 km/h, the SST could travel from New York to London—a distance of about 5,600 km—in 2 h 55 min 45 s.

Applying Math How long would it take a peregrine falcon moving at top speed to fly from New York to London?

...**The fastest animal on land** is the cheetah. This large cat can sprint at speeds of over 100 km/h. That is about as fast as a car traveling at freeway speeds, though the cheetah can only maintain top speed for a few hundred meters.

Graph It

Visit fl6.msscience.com to find the top speeds of four or five land animals. Create a bar graph that compares the speeds.

Reviewing Main Ideas

Section 1 **Describing Motion**

1. Motion depends on the reference point.

2. Average speed equals the total distance divided by the total time:

$$\bar{v} = \frac{d}{t}$$

3. The velocity of an object is the speed of an object and its direction of motion.

Section 2 **Forces and Motion**

1. A force is a push or pull.

2. The net force is the combination of all the forces acting on an object.

3. The forces on an object are balanced if the net force is zero.

4. The forces on an object are unbalanced if the net force is not zero.

5. Unbalanced forces cause motion to change.

Section 3 **Simple Machines**

1. Machines make work easier.

2. A simple machine is a machine that does work with one movement.

3. The six simple machines are the pulley, lever, wheel and axle, incline plane, wedge, and screw.

Visualizing Main Ideas

Copy and complete the following concept map on simple machines.

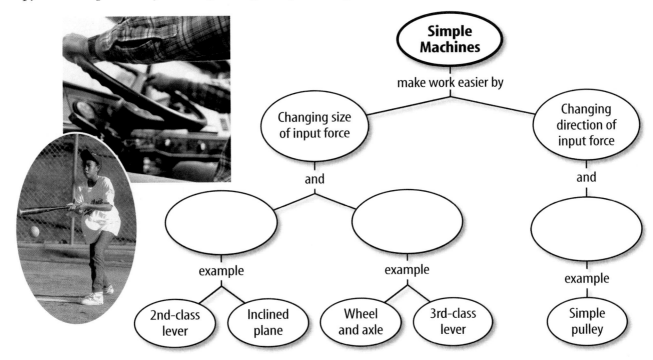

Simple Machines

make work easier by

Changing size of input force

Changing direction of input force

and

and

example

example

example

2nd-class lever

Inclined plane

Wheel and axle

3rd-class lever

Simple pulley

Using Vocabulary

* acceleration p. 510
  balanced forces p. 513
  contact force p. 514
* force p. 511
* friction p. 514
* gravity p. 516
* inclined plane p. 522
* inertia p. 514

* lever p. 521
  mechanical advantage
    p. 519
* pulley p. 520
  simple machine p. 519
* speed p. 508
  unbalanced forces p. 513
* velocity p. 509

* FCAT Vocabulary

Complete each statement using a word or phrase from the list above.

1. The _____ is equal to the output force divided by the input force.

2. The force due to _____ always opposes the sliding motion of two surfaces in contact.

3. When _____ act on an object, the motion of the object doesn't change.

4. An example of a non-contact force is _____ .

5. The _____ of an object includes the speed and direction of motion.

6. The output force exerted by a _____ depends on the position of the fulcrum.

Checking Concepts

Choose the word or phrase that best answers the question.

7. What decreases friction? SC.C.2.3.2
   A) a rougher surface
   B) a smoother surface
   C) increasing speed
   D) increasing inertia

8. What happens when an unbalanced force is applied to an object? SC.C.2.3.3
   A) The object accelerates.
   B) The object moves with constant velocity.
   C) The object remains at rest.
   D) The force of friction increases.

9. Which is an example of a simple machine?
   A) baseball bat   C) can opener SC.C.2.3.4
   B) scissors   D) car

10. What simple machines make up an ax?
    A) a lever and a wedge SC.C.2.3.4
    B) two levers
    C) a wedge and a pulley
    D) a lever and a screw

11. A car is driving at constant velocity. Which of the following is **NOT** true? SC.C.2.3.5
    A) All the forces acting are balanced.
    B) A net force keeps it moving.
    C) The car is moving in a straight line with constant speed.
    D) The car is not accelerating.

12. What are the units for acceleration?
    A) m/s^2 C) m/s
    B) $kg\, m/s^2$ D) N

13. What is inertia related to?
    A) speed   C) mass
    B) gravity   D) work

14. Which of the following is a force? SC.C.2.3.2
    A) inertia   C) speed
    B) acceleration   D) friction

15. How does a fixed pulley make doing work easier? SC.C.2.3.4
    A) It decreases the distance over which the input force needs to be applied.
    B) It changes the direction of the input force.
    C) It increases the input force.
    D) It decreases the input force.

16. Which of the following statements is **NOT** true about mass and weight? SC.A.1.3.2
    A) Mass varies with your location.
    B) Weight can be measured in pounds.
    C) Weight is the measure of the strength of gravitational force.
    D) Weight can be measured in newtons.

Thinking Critically

17. Infer Pulley system A has a mechanical advantage of 4 and pulley system B has a mechanical advantage of 6. Which pulley system would require a smaller input force to lift a piano? Explain. `SC.C.2.3.4`

18. Determine whether the forces acting on a car are balanced or unbalanced if the car is turning while moving at a constant speed. Explain your answer. `SC.C.2.3.5`

19. Explain If a bus is traveling at a constant speed around a curve, is the bus also traveling at a constant velocity? `SC.C.1.3.1`

Use the illustration below to answer question 20.

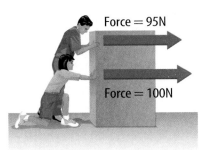

Force = 95N

Force = 100N

20. Calculate Sam and Lee Ann are pushing a heavy box across the floor. What is the net force on the box? `SC.C.2.3.3`

21. Infer Two teams in a tug-of-war pull on the rope. The rope is moving with a constant speed in a straight line to the left. What is the net force on the rope? `SC.C.2.3.3`

22. Explain whether an object is accelerating when it slows down. `SC.C.1.3.1`

23. Identify Give an example in which gravity speeds up a moving object and an example in which gravity slows down a moving object. `SC.C.2.3.6`

Performance Activities

24. Invention Design a human-powered compound machine to do a specific job. Identify the simple machines used in your design, and describe what each of the simple machines does. `SC.C.2.3.4`

25. Simple Machines Find or draw pictures of common simple machines. Identify and label the type of simple machine each picture represents. `SC.C.2.3.4`

Applying Math

Use the graph below to answer question 26.

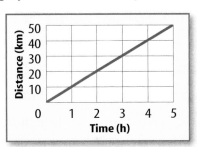

26. Speed and Time The graph above is a distance-time graph of Marion's bicycle ride. What is Marion's average speed? How long did it take her to travel 20 km? `SC.C.1.3.1` `MA.E.1.3.1`

27. Net Force Joey pushes on a refrigerator with a force of 300 N east. Juan pushes in the same direction with a force of 150 N and Amanda pushes in the opposite direction with a force of 250 N. What is the net force on the refrigerator? `SC.C.2.3.3`

28. Mechanical Advantage A ramp is 8.0 m long and 2.0 m high. What is the mechanical advantage of the ramp? `SC.C.2.3.4`

29. Distance Traveled How far does a car travel in 1.5 h if its average speed is 80 km/h?

30. Weight in SI Maria weighed herself on her bathroom scales. She weighed 115 pounds. What is her weight in SI units?

The assessed Florida Benchmark appears above each question.
Record your answers on the answer sheet provided by your teacher or on a sheet of paper.

Multiple Choice

SC.A.1.3.2

1 What factors give an object weight?

A. mass and inertia

B. mass and gravity

C. size and velocity

D. size and acceleration

SC.C.2.3.2

2 Edwin pulls his book bag across the floor. Which of these acts against the motion of the book bag?

F. the acceleration of the bag

G. the work done by the floor

H. the force exerted on Edwin by the bag

I. the friction between the bag and floor

SC.C.2.3.3

3 The diagram shows two forces being applied to a box of books.

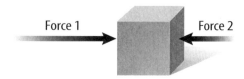

Force 1 → □ ← Force 2

What will be the result of the forces acting on the box?

A. The box will not move.

B. The box will move to the left.

C. The box will move to the right.

D. The box will move downward.

SC.C.2.3.4

4 Look at the diagram below. Which of the following is a second-class lever?

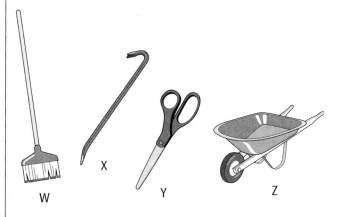

W   X   Y   Z

F. W

G. X

H. Y

I. Z

SC.C.2.3.4

5 Hannah is using a shovel as a lever to lift a rock in her garden. She is using a second rock as the fulcrum and pushing down on the handle of the shovel. She is not able to lift the rock. How can she increase the mechanical advantage of the lever?

A. She can place the fulcrum closer to the rock she is lifting.

B. She can move the fulcrum away from the rock she is lifting.

C. She can remove the fulcrum and lift on the end of the shovel instead.

D. She can push down on the shovel between the fulcrum and the rock.

SC.C.2.3.3

6 A book is sitting on a desk. Which describes the forces acting on the book?

   F. The forces are balanced.

   G. The forces are unbalanced.

   H. There are no forces acting on the book.

   I. Only contact forces act on the book.

SC.C.2.3.7

7 Which of the following would NOT cause the gravitational force between object A and object B to increase?

   A. The objects move closer together.

   B. The objects move farther apart.

   C. The mass of object A increases.

   D. The mass of object B decreases.

 Gridded Response

SC.C.1.3.1

8 The diagram below shows the distance a train traveled between two points on a track.

375 m

If the train traveled 375 m in 15 seconds (s), what was the average speed of the train in meters per second (m/s)?

 Short Response

SC.C.2.3.3

9 A skydiver with an open parachute falls through the air with a constant velocity. Identify the contact and non-contact forces acting on the skydiver and the direction in which these forces are acting. What is the net force on the skydiver?

 Extended Response

SC.C.2.3.5

10 Car manufacturers often use crash-test dummies to test the safety of their cars. The diagram shows what happens to such a dummy when a car crashes into a wall.

   PART A The car moves forward until it hits the wall. The crash-test dummy moves forward within the car until it hits the windshield. Explain why the dummy keeps moving after the car hits the wall.

   PART B Explain how the force exerted by a seat belt keeps the dummy from hitting the windshield.

FCAT Tip

Be Careful For each question, double-check that you are filling in the correct answer bubble for the question number you are working on.

Sunshine State Standards—SC.A.2: The student understands the basic principles of atomic theory; **SC.B.1:** recognizes that energy may be changed in form with varying efficiency.

Energy

Snow Surfing

With no more than a board, a lot of snow, and a slope, this snowboarder goes from standing to moving at speeds greater than 50 km/h. The snowboarder's speed increases because energy is changing form. In fact, energy changing form causes all the changes that occur around you every day.

Science Journal List three changes that you have seen occur today, and describe what changed.

Start-Up Activities

SC.B.1.3.1

Changing Forms of Energy

Think of all the things you do every day, such as riding to school, walking to class, and listening to music. All the things you do every day involve changing energy from one form to another. When energy changes from one form to another, changes occur.

1. Add sand to a plastic cup with a tight-fitting lid until it is about one-fourth full.

2. Using a thermometer, measure and record the temperature of the sand to the nearest tenth of a degree.

3. Place the lid on the cup. Hold the lid tightly in place and shake the cup vigorously for five minutes.

4. Remove the lid and immediately measure the temperature of the sand.

5. **Think Critically** How did the temperature of the sand change? Describe the changes that occurred in the sand as you shook the cup.

Science Online Preview this chapter's content and activities at fl6.msscience.com

Energy Make the following Foldable to help you understand the different ways energy can be transformed.

LA.A.1.3.4
LA.B.2.3.1

STEP 1 Fold a sheet of paper in half lengthwise.

STEP 2 Fold paper down 2.5 cm from the top. (Hint: From the tip of your index finger to your middle knuckle is about 2.5 cm.)

STEP 3 Open and draw lines along the 2.5 cm fold. Label as shown.

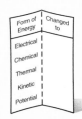

Cause and Effect As you read the chapter, write answers to what each form of energy can be changed to under the *Changed To* heading on your Foldable. On the back of your Foldable, describe what caused each form of energy to change and explain the effects of the change.

section
1

Benchmarks—SC.A.2.3.3 Annually Assessed (pp. 539–541): The student knows that radiation, light, and heat are forms of energy used to cook food, treat diseases, and provide energy; SC.B.1.3.1 Annually Assessed (pp. 535–540, 543): identifies forms of energy and explains that they can be measured and compared; SC.B.1.3.2 (pp. 541, 543); SC.B.1.3.4 (p. 542); SC.B.2.3.1 (p. 542)

Also covers: SC.H.1.3.7 Annually Assessed (p. 543)

Energy Changes

as you read

What **You'll Learn**

- **Explain** what energy is.
- **Describe** the forms energy takes.
- **Describe** how energy is used.

Why **It's Important**

Energy causes all the changes that take place around you.

Review Vocabulary

✴ **energy transfer:** a change in energy from one form to another

New Vocabulary

✴ **energy**
✴ **kinetic energy**
✴ **potential energy**
✴ **thermal energy**
✴ **calorie**
✴ **law of conservation of energy**

✴ FCAT Vocabulary

Figure 1 Lightning causes dramatic change as it lights up the sky.

Energy

Energy is a term you probably use every day. You might say that eating a plate of spaghetti gives you energy, or that a gymnast has a lot of energy. Do you realize that a burning fire, a bouncing ball, and a tank of gasoline also have energy?

What is energy? The word *energy* comes from the ancient Greek word *energos,* which means "active." You probably have used the word *energy* in the same way. When you say you have a lot of energy, what does this mean? **Energy** is the ability to cause change. For example, energy can change the temperature of a pot of water, or it can change the direction and speed of a baseball. The energy in a thunderstorm, like the one shown in **Figure 1,** produces lightning that lights up the sky and thunder that can rattle windows. Energy can change the arrangement of atoms in molecules and cause chemical reactions to occur. You use energy when you change the speed of a bicycle by pedaling faster or when you put on the brakes.

Reading Check *What does energy do?*

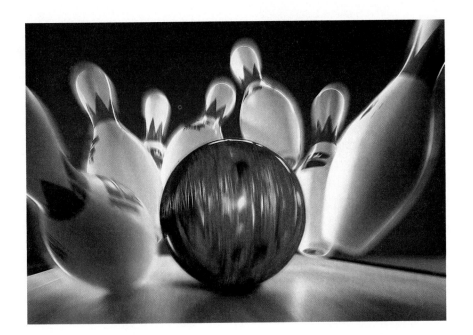

Figure 2 Any moving object has energy because it can cause change.
Identify *a change that the bowling ball is causing.*

Kinetic Energy

One soccer ball is sitting on the ground and another is rolling toward the net. How does the energy of the moving ball compare to the one at rest? A moving ball certainly has the ability to cause change. For example, a moving bowling ball shown in **Figure 2** causes the bowling pins to fall. A moving ball has energy due to its motion. The energy an object has due to its motion is called **kinetic energy.** A football thrown by a quarterback has kinetic energy. A sky diver or a leaf falling toward Earth also has kinetic energy.

Mass, Speed, and Kinetic Energy Although moving objects have kinetic energy, not all moving objects have the same amount of kinetic energy. What determines the amount of kinetic energy in a moving object? The amount of kinetic energy an object has depends on the mass and speed of the object, as shown in **Figure 3** on the next page. Imagine a small rock and a large boulder rolling down a hillside at the same speed. Which would have more kinetic energy? Think about the damage the rock and the boulder could do if they hit something at the bottom of the hill. The large boulder could cause more damage, so it has more kinetic energy. Even though the rock and the boulder were moving at the same speed, the boulder had more kinetic energy than the rock because it had more mass.

Kinetic energy also depends on speed. The faster a bowling ball moves, the more pins it can knock down. When more pins are knocked down, a greater change has occured. So the faster the bowling ball moves, the more kinetic energy it has. Kinetic energy increases as speed increases.

INTEGRATE Life Science

Food Contains Chemical Energy You transform energy every time you eat and digest food. The food you eat contains chemical energy. Your body changes this form of energy into other forms of energy that keep your body warm and move your muscles. The amount of chemical energy contained in food is measured in Calories. Check some food labels to see how many Calories your food contains.

Figure 3

The amount of kinetic energy of a moving object depends on the mass and the speed of the object. Energy is measured in units called joules (J). For example, the fastest measured speed a baseball has been thrown is about 45 m/s. The kinetic energy of a baseball traveling at that speed is about 150 J.

▲ There is evidence that a meteorite 10 km in diameter collided with Earth about 65 million years ago and might have caused the extinction of dinosaurs. The meteorite may have been moving 400 times faster than the baseball and would have a tremendous amount of kinetic energy due to its enormous mass and high speed—about a trillion trillion joules.

▼ A 600-kg race car, traveling at about 50 m/s, has about 5,000 times the kinetic energy of the baseball.

▼ Earth's atmosphere is continually bombarded by particles called cosmic rays, which are mainly high-speed protons. The mass of a proton is about a 100 trillion trillion times smaller than the mass of the baseball. Yet, some of these particles travel so fast, they have nearly the same kinetic energy as the baseball.

◀ A sprinter with a mass of about 55 kg and running at 9 m/s has kinetic energy about 15 times greater than the baseball.

Potential Energy

Suppose the ski lift in **Figure 4** takes a skier to the top of a hill. The skier has no kinetic energy when she is standing at the top of the hill. But as she skis down and moves faster, her kinetic energy increases. Where does this kinetic energy come from? Gravity pulls the skier down the hill. If the skier were standing at the bottom of the hill, gravity would not start her moving, as it does when she is at the top of the hill. When the skier's position is at the top of the hill, she has a form of energy called potential energy. **Potential energy** is energy that is stored because of an object's position. By using the ski lift to take her to the top of the hill, the skier increased her potential energy by changing her position.

Increasing Potential Energy When you raise an object above its original position, it has the potential to fall. If it does fall, it has kinetic energy. To raise an object, you have to transfer energy to the object. The ski lift uses energy when it takes a skier up a hill and transfers some of that energy to the skier. This energy becomes stored as potential energy in the skier. As the skier goes down the hill, the potential energy she had at the top of the hill is converted to kinetic energy.

If the skier were lifted higher, her potential energy would increase. The higher an object is lifted above Earth, the greater its potential energy.

Reading Check *Why did the skier's potential energy increase as she was carried up the hill?*

Figure 4 Potential and kinetic energy change as the skier moves up and down the slope.

Her potential energy is largest at the top of the hill.

The skier's potential energy increases as the ski lift carries her up the hill.

As she skis down the hill, potential energy transforms into kinetic energy.

Here her kinetic energy is greatest and her potential energy is smallest.

Mini LAB

Comparing Potential Energy

Procedure

1. Hold a **tennis ball** about 1.5 m above a hard surface.
2. Before the ball is dropped, estimate the height the ball will reach on each of its first three bounces.
3. Drop the ball and have a partner use a **meterstick** to measure the height of the ball's first three bounces.

Analysis

1. When did the ball have the greatest and least amount of potential energy? Explain.
2. Infer why the height of the ball differed in each bounce.
3. How did the mechanical energy of the ball change after each bounce?

Converting Potential and Kinetic Energy

When a skier skis down a hill, potential energy is transformed to kinetic energy. Kinetic energy also can be transformed into potential energy. Suppose you throw a ball straight up into the air. The muscles in your body cause the ball to move upward when it leaves your hand. Because it is moving, the ball has kinetic energy. Look at **Figure 5.** As the ball gets higher and higher, its potential energy is increasing. At the same time, the ball is slowing down and its kinetic energy is decreasing.

What happens when the ball reaches its highest point? The ball comes to a stop for an instant before it starts to fall downward again. At its highest point the ball has no kinetic energy because it isn't moving. All the kinetic energy the ball had when it left your hand has been converted to potential energy. As a result, the ball will go no higher. As the ball falls downward, its potential energy is converted back into kinetic energy.

Mechanical Energy The sum of the kinetic and potential energy of an object is the mechanical energy of the object. The mechanical energy of the ball wouldn't change if potential energy is converted only into kinetic energy, and if kinetic energy is converted only into potential energy. However, as the ball moves through the air, the force due to air resistance acts on the ball. This force converts a small amount of the ball's mechanical energy into another form of energy—thermal energy. As a result, the mechanical energy of the ball when you catch it is slightly less than when you threw it upward.

✔ **Reading Check** *What is the mechanical energy of an object?*

Figure 5 Energy is transformed as a ball rises and falls.

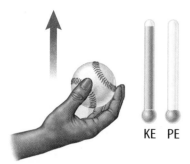

As the ball leaves the person's hand, it is moving the fastest and has maximum kinetic energy.

As the ball moves upward, it slows down as its kinetic energy is transformed into potential energy.

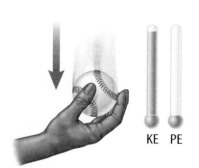

As the ball moves downward, it speeds up as its potential energy is transformed into kinetic energy.

Forms of Energy

Besides kinetic energy and potential energy, there are other forms of energy. Some of these energy forms are due to motion and are a type of kinetic energy. Other energy forms are stored energy and are a type of potential energy. Some of these forms of energy can be transferred from one object to another.

Thermal Energy All matter contains particles, such as atoms or molecules. The particles in matter are always moving. As a result, these particles have energy that is due to their motion. The energy of the particles in matter due to their continual motion is **thermal energy.** The thermal energy in an object increases when the object's temperature increases.

✔ **Reading Check** *How does the thermal energy of an object change when its temperature increases?*

Electrical Energy When you plug a hair dryer into an electrical outlet and turn it on, another form of energy is being used—electrical energy. When the hair dryer is turned on, electrically charged particles called electrons flow in various parts of the hair dryer. The energy of these flowing electrons is electrical energy. As electrons flow in a hair dryer, their electrical energy is used to make an electric motor spin and to make parts of the hair dryer hot.

Chemical Energy The food that you eat is a source of energy that is used by your body. Food contains chemical compounds. Chemical compounds are made of atoms that are bonded together. The bonds between atoms store chemical energy. Because chemical energy is energy that is stored, it is a type of potential energy. Chemical energy is released when chemical reactions occur. The chemical reactions that occur as your body digests food release chemical energy. This energy is used by your body to grow, to move, and in many other ways.

Radiant Energy When you sit in sunlight, you can feel the warmth of the Sun on your skin. You feel warm because the Sun gives off, or emits, a form of energy called radiant energy. The radiant energy that comes from the Sun sometimes is called solar energy. Radiant energy is energy that is transferred by waves from one place to another. The waves emitted by the Sun transfer radiant energy. These waves travel through space and strike your skin, making it feel warm. Light also is a type of wave that transfers radiant energy. **Figure 6** shows examples of other objects that give off radiant energy.

A campfire is used to provide light and warmth. A fire emits radiant energy that you see as light and feel as warmth.

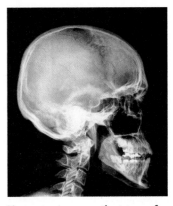

X rays are waves that transfer radiant energy as they move from place to place. The radiant energy transferred by X rays is used to form images of the human body.

A microwave oven uses the radiant energy transferred by microwaves to cook food.

Figure 6 Campfires, X-ray images, and microwave ovens all use radiant energy.
Identify *other objects that emit radiant energy.*

Annually Assessed Benchmark Check

SC.B.1.3.1 Compare and contrast chemical energy and nuclear energy.

Figure 7 An electric fan converts electrical energy into other forms of energy.

Mechanical energy

Thermal energy

Electrical energy

Nuclear Energy The Sun emits an enormous amount of radiant energy every second. This energy is produced by reactions that occur in the Sun. However, these reactions aren't chemical reactions. Instead, the Sun's radiant energy is produced by reactions that involve the nuclei of atoms. Nuclear energy is energy stored in the nucleus of an atom. This energy is released when changes occur in an atom's nucleus.

Measuring Energy

Recall that in the SI system of units, time is measured in seconds and distance is measured in meters. In the SI system of units, energy is measured using a unit called the joule (J). A student with a mass of 50 kg walking at a speed of 2 m/s has 100 J of kinetic energy. The same student sitting on a ledge 1 m above the ground has about 500 J of potential energy.

Sometimes it is more convenient to measure energy using other units. Another unit for energy is the calorie. One **calorie** is the amount of energy needed to warm one gram of water by 1°C. One calorie (cal) is equal to about 4.19 J. A different energy unit is used to measure the energy content of food. This unit is the Calorie (with a capital C) and is equal to 1,000 cal, or 4,190 J. A candy bar that has 200 Calories supplies your body with almost 838,000 J of energy.

Changing Forms of Energy

When you throw a ball into the air, the kinetic energy of the ball changes into potential energy as the ball moves upward. As the ball falls, potential energy changes into kinetic energy as the ball speeds up. As the ball rises and falls, one form of energy changes into another form of energy.

Every day, all around you and inside you, energy is changing from one form to another. Changes in forms of energy make a car move and make headphones produce sound. Inside your body chemical energy is changed to thermal energy, electrical energy, and mechanical energy. All the events that you see around you involve energy changing form.

Changing Electrical Energy Many of the devices you use every day, like the one shown in **Figure 7,** change electrical energy to other forms of energy. For example, hair dryers, CD players, and refrigerators contain electric motors. In an electric motor, electrical energy makes the shaft of the motor spin, so that electrical energy is changed to mechanical energy. Hair dryers and electric stoves contain heating elements that change electrical energy into thermal energy. A lightbulb produces light by changing electrical energy to radiant energy.

Changing Chemical Energy A different energy transfer is used by a stove that burns natural gas. When a fuel like wood, gasoline, or natural gas is burned, chemical energy is changed into thermal energy and light, or radiant energy. **Figure 8** shows another example of chemical energy changing form. When you light a candle, wax is burned to produce thermal energy and light. In a car's engine, gasoline is burned to produce thermal energy. The car converts this thermal energy to mechanical energy that enables the car to move. Your body uses food as fuel. Chemical reactions in your body change the chemical energy stored in food to thermal energy and mechanical energy.

Using Energy

When you use a hair dryer, or toast bread in a toaster, or listen to a CD, you are using energy. In each case, you used electrical energy to do something—dry your hair, cook food, and make sound. When you burn a candle or heat water on the stove you are using chemical energy to do something—provide light or heat water. Energy that is used to do something or perform a task is useful energy.

The Law of Conservation of Energy

Where does energy come from? Even though energy changes from one form to another when it is used, energy never is created or destroyed. According to the **law of conservation of energy**, energy never can be created or destroyed, but only can be changed from one form to another.

Sometimes it might seem that energy is being lost. A book sliding on a table slows down and stops. The book's kinetic energy decreased as it slowed down. **Figure 9** shows what happens to this energy. The kinetic energy of the book is not destroyed, but is changed into another form of energy—thermal energy. Friction causes the kinetic energy of the book to be changed into thermal energy. This thermal energy makes the book, the table, and the surrounding air slightly warmer.

Figure 8 Fireworks are a spectacular display of chemical energy changing to thermal energy and radiant energy.

FCAT FOCUS **Annually Assessed Benchmark Check**

SC.B.1.3.2 How much thermal energy is produced in an electric motor if 100 J of electrical energy are converted into 92 J of mechanical energy?

Figure 9 As the book slides along the table, kinetic energy is changed into thermal energy. When the book stops, all of its kinetic energy has been changed into thermal energy.

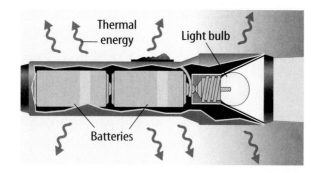

Figure 10 The energy conversions in a flashlight produce some thermal energy that is not useful energy.

Annually Assessed Benchmark Check

SC.B.2.3.1 Why does the amount of useful energy decrease when energy changes from one form into another?

Useful Energy Always Decreases

When energy is used, it usually is changed from one form to another. For example, a battery in a flashlight converts chemical energy into electrical energy. This electrical energy is changed into useful radiant energy by the flashlight bulb. However, some of the electrical energy also is changed to thermal energy, as shown in **Figure 10.** When energy changes form, some thermal energy is produced. Not all of this thermal energy can be used to do something useful. As a result, when energy changes form, the amount of useful energy is always less than the initial amount of energy. Some energy always is changed into thermal energy that cannot be used to perform useful work.

When energy is changed from one form to another, it becomes less concentrated and more spread out. For example, the electrical energy in a flashlight is concentrated in the batteries. When the flashlight is used, the light and thermal energy produced is transferred to the air surrounding the flashlight. Compared to the energy in the batteries, the light and thermal energy transferred to the air is spread out, and is less concentrated. All energy conversions that occur cause energy to become more spread out and less concentrated.

section 1 review

Summary

Energy
- Energy is the ability to cause change.
- Kinetic energy is the energy an object has because of its motion. Potential energy is stored energy.

Forms of Energy
- Energy comes in different forms. Some of these forms are thermal energy, electrical energy, chemical energy, radiant energy, and nuclear energy.
- One form of energy can be changed into another form of energy.

Using Energy
- According to the law of conservation of energy, energy cannot be created or destroyed, but only can change form.
- When energy changes form, some thermal energy is produced and the amount of useful energy decreases.

Self Check

1. **Describe** the energy transformations that occur when a lightbulb is turned on. SC.B.1.3.1
2. **Explain** how the total energy changes when a falling rock hits the ground. SC.B.1.3.2
3. **Infer** on which part of a roller coaster a roller coaster car has the greatest potential energy. SC.B.1.3.1
4. **Determine** which has the greater kinetic energy if both are traveling at the same speed—a fully loaded truck or a motorcycle. SC.B.1.3.1
5. **Think Critically** When a ball is thrown upward, how does the height reached by the ball depend on its initial speed? SC.B.1.3.2

Applying Skills

6. **Diagram** the energy transformations that occur when you eat breakfast, walk to the bus stop, and ride the bus to school. SC.B.1.3.2

Benchmark—SC.B.1.3.1: The student identifies forms of energy and explains that they can be measured and compared; **SC.B.1.3.2:** The student knows that energy cannot be created or destroyed, but only changed from one form to another; **SC.H.1.3.7:** The student knows that when similar investigations give different results, the scientific challenge is to verify whether the differences are significant by further study.

Energy Conversions

Have you ever watched one ball strike another ball that is sitting still? What happens to the energy of the first ball? Is all of the energy transferred to the second ball?

▶ Real-World Problem

What are the energy conversions that occur when one ball strikes another ball?

Goals
- **Measure** the height changes in two balls that are transferring energy.
- **Observe** the change in potential energy of the two balls.

Materials
metersticks (2)
ring stand
hook collar
string (about 80 cm long)
duct tape
tennis balls (2)

Safety Precautions 🥽
Complete a safety worksheet before you begin.

▶ Procedure

1. Make a data table in your Science Journal.

2. Assemble your ring stand, hook collar, string, and tennis balls as shown in the figure. Secure the tennis balls to the ends of the string by tying and taping them.

3. Drape the string over the hook collar as shown in the figure. The string should touch the hook at the halfway point on the string. Shorten the string if either ball touches the ring stand or lab table.

4. Allow one ball to fall straight down. Make sure it is completely still.

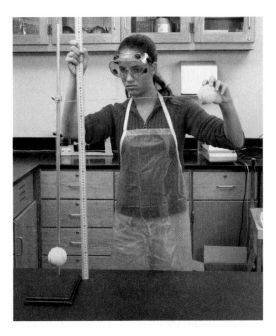

5. Hold the other ball out at a 90° angle. Measure the height of the ball.

6. Drop the ball allowing it to strike the other ball. Record the height that each ball reaches for 5 passes.

▶ Conclude and Apply

1. How did the maximum height reached by each ball change after each collision?

2. How did the mechanical energy of the ball change?

3. Why did the mechanical energy of the ball change after each collision?

*C*ommunicating
Your Data

Compare your data to the data collected by your classmates. Discuss and explain any differences you observe in the collected data.

Benchmarks—SC.A.1.3.3 (pp. 544–545, 550, 552–553): The student knows that temperature measures the average energy of motion of the particles that make up the substance; SC.B.1.3.5 (pp. 548–551): The student knows the processes by which thermal energy tends to flow from a system of higher temperature to a system of lower temperature.

Also covers: SC.H.1.3.4 Annually Assessed (pp. 552–553), SC.H.1.3.5 Annually Assessed (pp. 550, 552–553), SC.H.1.3.7 Annually Assessed (pp. 552–553)

section 2

Thermal Energy

as you read

What You'll Learn

- **Distinguish** between temperature, heat, and thermal energy.
- **Explain** how thermal energy moves.

Why It's Important

The flow of thermal energy warms Earth, produces weather, cooks your food, and warms and cools your home.

Review Vocabulary

molecule: a particle formed when two or more atoms bond together

New Vocabulary

- temperature
- ✹ heat
- ✹ conduction
- ✹ convection
- ✹ radiation

✹ FCAT Vocabulary

Figure 11 In gases, atoms or molecules are free to move in all directions.

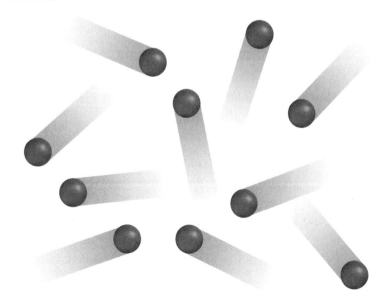

Temperature

What's today's temperature? If you looked at a thermometer, listened to a weather report on the radio, or saw a weather map on television, you probably used the air temperature to help you decide what to wear. Some days are so hot you don't need a jacket. Others are so cold you want to bundle up.

Hot and *cold* are words used in everyday language to describe temperature. However, they are not scientific words because they mean different things to different people. A summer day that seems hot to one person might seem just right to another. If you grew up in Florida but moved to Minnesota, you might find the winters unbearably cold. Have you ever complained that a classroom was too cold when other students insisted that it was too warm?

Particles are in Random Motion What is temperature? Remember that any material or object is made up of atoms or molecules. These particles are moving constantly, even if the object appears to be perfectly still. Every object you can think of—your hand, the pencil on your desk, or even the desktop—contains particles that are in constant motion. In solids, liquids, and gases particles do not move in a single direction. Instead they move in all directions. In a gas, particles are far apart and can move, as shown in **Figure 11.** In liquids, atoms are close together and can't move as far as in a gas. In solids, particles are bound more tightly together than in a liquid. Instead of moving freely as shown in **Figure 11,** atoms or molecules in a solid vibrate back and forth. The motion of particles in all directions in solids, liquids, and gases is called random motion. Because the particles are moving, they have kinetic energy. The faster the particles are moving, the more kinetic energy they have.

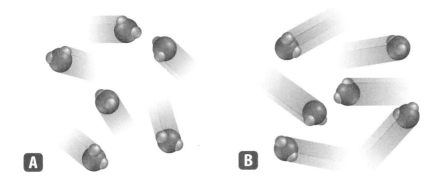

<figure>**Figure 12** Temperature depends on the average kinetic energy of the atoms or molecules. **A** The gas molecules move slower on average at a lower temperature. **B** Gas molecules move faster on average at a higher temperature.</figure>

Temperature and Kinetic Energy **Temperature** is a measure of the average kinetic energy of the particles in an object. When an object's temperature is higher, its atoms or molecules have more kinetic energy. **Figure 12** shows gas molecules at two temperatures. At the higher temperature, the molecules are moving faster and have more kinetic energy.

Applying Science

Can you be fooled by temperature?

On a cold morning, you might have heard a meteorologist give the wind chill index, as well as the temperature. Although wind cannot lower the temperature of the outside air, it can make you feel as if the temperature were lower.

Wind Chill Index

Temperature (°C)	Wind Speed (km/h)							
	10	20	30	40	50	60	70	80
20	18°C	16°C	14°C	13°C	13°C	12°C	12°C	12°C
12	9°C	5°C	3°C	1°C	0°C	0°C	−1°C	−1°C
0	−4°C	−10°C	−14°C	−17°C	−18°C	−19°C	−20°C	−21°C
−20	−26°C	−36°C	−43°C	−47°C	−49°C	−51°C	−52°C	−53°C
−36	−44°C	−57°C	−65°C	−71°C	−74°C	−77°C	−78°C	−79°C

Identifying the Problem

A wind chill index of −29°C presents little danger to you if you are properly dressed. Below this temperature, however, your skin can become frostbitten within minutes. Use the table to find wind chill values for conditions that present the greatest dangers.

Solving the Problem

1. Assuming you live in an area where wind speeds in the winter rarely reach 50 km/h, at which air temperature should you be certain to take extra precautions?
2. What happens to the wind chill index as wind speeds get higher and temperatures get lower?

Measuring Temperature

Some people might say that the water in a swimming pool feels warm, although others might say it feels cool. Because the temperature of the water feels different to different people, you cannot describe or measure temperature accurately by how it feels. Remember that temperature is related to the kinetic energy of all the atoms in an object. You might think that to measure temperature, you must measure the kinetic energy of the atoms. But atoms are so small that even a tiny piece of material consists of trillions and trillions of atoms. Because they are so small and objects contain so many of them, it is impossible to measure the kinetic energy of all the individual atoms. However, a practical way to measure temperature is to use a thermometer.

Reading Check *Why can't the kinetic energy of all the atoms in an object be measured?*

The Celsius Scale A temperature scale that is used widely throughout the world is the Celsius (SEL see us) scale. On the Celsius temperature scale, the freezing point of water is given the temperature 0°C and the boiling point is given the temperature 100°C as shown in **Figure 13.**

Reading Check *What are the boiling and freezing points of water on the Celsius temperature scale?*

Figure 13 This thermometer uses the height of a liquid in a tube to measure temperature. The liquid height changes with temperature because the liquid expands as its temperature increases. The thermometer is calibrated by marking the liquid height at two known temperatures.

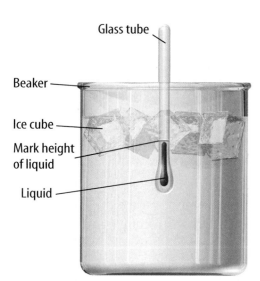

The height of the liquid is marked when the thermometer is placed in water at 0°C.

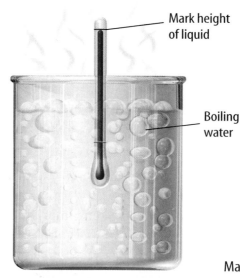

The height of the liquid is marked when the thermometer is placed in boiling water at 100°C.

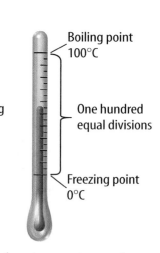

Make a temperature scale by dividing the distance between the two marks into equal degrees.

The Fahrenheit Scale One temperature scale you might be familiar with is the Fahrenheit (FAYR un hite) scale. The Fahrenheit scale currently is used mainly in the United States. On the Fahrenheit scale, the freezing point of water is given the temperature 32°F, and the boiling point is 212°F. The space between the boiling point and the freezing point is divided into 180 equal degrees. Because there are only 100 Celsius degrees between the boiling and freezing points of water, a temperature change of one Celsius degree is bigger than a change of one Fahrenheit degree.

Thermal Energy and Heat

Recall that thermal energy is the energy of the particles in an object due to their random motion. As the temperature of the object increases, the particles move faster and the thermal energy of the object increases. Thermal energy can be transferred between objects at different temperatures.

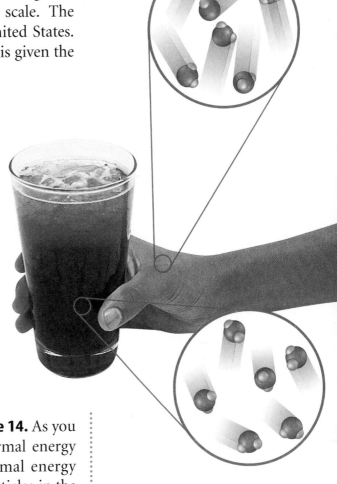

For example, thermal energy is transferred when you hold a glass of iced tea, as shown in **Figure 14.** As you hold the glass of iced tea, the tea warms up. Thermal energy moves from your hand to the iced tea. The thermal energy added to the tea causes the kinetic energy of the particles in the tea to increase. As a result, the temperature of the tea increases.

A transfer of thermal energy from a substance at a higher temperature to a substance at a lower temperature is **heat**. Thermal energy will stop moving from your hand to the iced tea only when both are at the same temperature.

Temperature Changes Depend on the Material

When the temperature of a material changes, thermal energy has been transferred to the material or from the material. The temperature change depends on the amount of thermal energy transferred. It also depends on the amount of material and the type of material. For example, water is an unusual material. Compared to equal amounts of other materials, the temperature of water rises more slowly as it absorbs thermal energy. As a result, water is often used as a coolant. Water is used in a car's cooling system to absorb thermal energy produced by the engine, as shown in **Figure 15.** This keeps the engine temperature low enough to prevent damage from overheating.

Figure 14 Your hand is warmer than the iced tea. The particles in your hand are moving faster and have more thermal energy than the particles in the tea.

Figure 15 A car overheats when the cooling system doesn't absorb enough thermal energy from the engine.

Winter

During the winter, the lake is warmer than the surrounding land.

Summer

During the summer, the lake is cooler than the surrounding land.

Figure 16 Water can absorb and lose a great deal of heat without a large temperature change.

LA.A.2.3.5

INTEGRATE
History

The Caloric Theory At one time heat was thought to be a fluid called caloric. In the late eighteenth century, Benjamin Thompson noticed that large amounts of thermal energy were generated during the boring of the holes in cannons. He concluded the amount of thermal energy produced depended only on the work done by the drill. James Joule later showed that other forms of energy could be converted into thermal energy. Research how the work of Thompson and Joule disproved the caloric theory.

Lakes and Air Temperature How does the temperature of water in a lake compare to the temperature of the surrounding air on a hot summer day? You might have noticed that the water is cooler than the air during the day and warmer than the air at night. This is because it takes longer for a large body of water to warm up or cool down than it does for the surrounding air and land to change temperature. Even from season to season, a large body of water can change temperature less than the surrounding land, as shown in **Figure 16.**

Thermal Energy on the Move

A transfer of thermal energy occurs if there is a temperature difference between two areas in contact. Thermal energy is transferred from warm places to cooler ones. This transfer can take place in three ways—radiation, conduction, and convection. Conduction transfers thermal energy mainly through solids and liquids. Convection transfers thermal energy through liquids and gases. Radiation can transfer thermal energy through space.

Conduction Have you ever picked up a metal spoon that was in a pot of boiling water? The spoon handle became hot because of conduction. **Conduction** (kun DUK shun) is the transfer of thermal energy by collisions between the atoms and molecules in a material.

As the part of the spoon in the boiling water became warmer, its atoms and molecules moved faster. These particles then collided with slower-moving particles in the spoon. In these collisions, thermal energy was transferred from the faster-moving to the slower-moving particles farther up the spoon's handle.

Conduction in a Solid When conduction occurs, thermal energy is transferred. However, in a solid, the particles don't move from place to place. Instead, they vibrate back and forth, bumping into each other. These collisions transfer energy from particle to particle, while the particles stay in place.

✓ Reading Check *How is energy transferred by conduction?*

Conductors Conduction transfers thermal energy from one place to another. However, thermal energy moves at different speeds in different materials. Materials in which thermal energy moves easily are called thermal conductors. Most metals are good conductors of thermal energy. Metals such as gold, silver, and copper are the best thermal conductors. Copper is a widely used conductor because it is less expensive than gold or silver. Copper often is used in cooking pans. A pan with a copper bottom conducts thermal energy more evenly. It helps spread thermal energy across the bottom surface of the pan to prevent hot spots from forming. Some cooking pans are made of steel but have copper bottoms. This allows food to cook evenly.

Insulators Some materials are poor conductors of thermal energy. These materials can be used as thermal insulators. When you are cold, for example, you can put on a sweater or a jacket or add another blanket to your bed. You are keeping yourself warm by adding insulation. The clothes and the blanket are poor conductors of thermal energy. In fact, they make it more difficult for thermal energy to escape from your body. By trapping the thermal energy your body produces, you feel warmer.

Blankets and clothes help keep you warm because they are made of materials that contain many air spaces, as shown in **Figure 18.** Air is a good insulator. Materials that contain air also are good insulators. For example, building insulation is made from materials that contain air spaces.

Materials made of plastics also are often good insulators. If you put a plastic spoon in boiling water, it takes a long time for it to get hot. Many cooking pans have plastic handles that won't melt instead of metal ones. These handles remain at a comfortable temperature while the pans are used for cooking. Other examples of insulators include wood, rubber, and ceramic materials such as tiles.

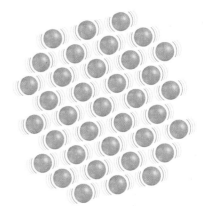

Figure 17 In a solid, particles collide with each other as they vibrate back and forth.

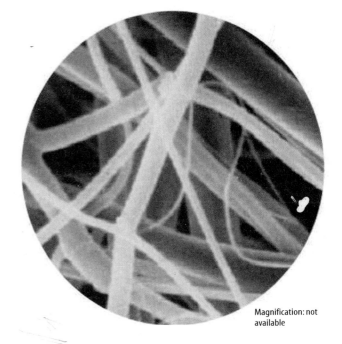

Figure 18 Under high magnification, this insulating material is seen to contain many air spaces. **Explain** *how increasing the number of air spaces in a material affects the movement of thermal energy.*

Magnification: not available

Figure 19 The furnace's fan helps circulate hot air through your home. Warmer air moves upward while cooler air moves downward. **Explain** *why the hot air ducts are placed near the floor.*

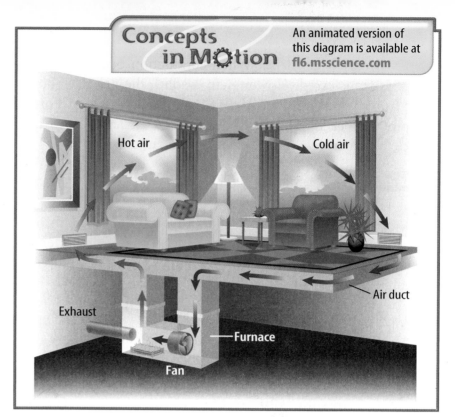

Concepts in Motion

An animated version of this diagram is available at fl6.msscience.com

Hot air

Cold air

Air duct

Exhaust

Furnace

Fan

SC.A.1.3.3
SC.H.1.3.5

Comparing Energy Content

Procedure

1. Pour equal amounts of **hot, cold, and room-temperature water** into each of **three transparent, labeled containers.**
2. Measure and record the temperature of the water in each container.
3. Use a **dropper** to gently put a drop of **food coloring** in the center of each container.
4. After 5 min, observe each container.

Analysis

1. Based on the speed at which the food coloring spreads through the water, rank the containers from fastest to slowest.
2. Infer how water temperature affected the movement of the food coloring.
3. In which container do the water particles have the most kinetic energy?

Try at Home

Some Materials Feel Hotter Think about getting into a car that has been sitting in sunlight on a hot day. Would you rather sit on a vinyl-covered seat or a fabric-covered seat? Even if the temperatures of the seats are the same, the vinyl seat feels hotter than the fabric seat. How hot something feels depends on how quickly thermal energy moves in the material, as well as the temperature of the material. Vinyl is a better thermal conductor than fabric, so thermal energy flows to your skin more rapidly from the vinyl seat than from the fabric seat. As a result, the vinyl feels hotter than the fabric does.

Convection Thermal energy also can be transferred by particles that move from one place to another. **Convection** transfers thermal energy when particles move between objects or areas that have different temperatures. This type of energy transfer is most common in gases and liquids. As temperature increases, particles move around more quickly, and the distance between particles increases. This causes density to decrease as temperature increases. Cooler, denser material then forces the warmer, less dense material to move upward.

Some homes are heated by convection. Look at **Figure 19.** Air is warmed in the furnace. The warm, less dense air is then forced up through the air duct by the furnace fan. The warm air gets pushed up through the room by the cooler air around it. As the warm air cools, it becomes more dense. Cool, dense air sinks and is then pulled into the return air duct by the furnace fan to be warmed again and recirculated.

Examples of Convection

Eagles and hawks float effortlessly high in the air. Sometimes a bird can stay in the air without flapping its wings because it is held up by a thermal.

As shown in **Figure 20,** a thermal is a column of warm air that is forced up as cold air around it sinks. It is a convection current in the air.

Convection also occurs in liquids. In a pot of boiling water, the warmer, less dense water is forced up as the cooler, denser water sinks. Convection currents on a larger scale are formed in oceans by cold water flowing from the poles and warm water flowing from tropical regions.

Radiation The transfer of thermal energy by waves is **radiation** (ray dee AY shun). These waves can be visible light waves or types of waves that you cannot see. When these waves strike an object, their energy can be absorbed and the object's temperature rises. Radiation can travel through air and even through a vacuum.

The Sun transfers energy to Earth by radiation. When you stand by a fire, radiation makes you feel warm. Thermal energy is transferred by radiation from the fire and you become warmer. You also can use radiation to cook food. A microwave oven cooks food by using microwave radiation to transfer energy to the food.

Cool, dense air

Hot, less dense air

Cool, dense air

Light from the Sun

Air heats up near the surface, expands, and is pushed upward.

Light energy heats up the ground.

Figure 20 Thermals form when hot, less-dense air is pushed upward by cooler, denser air.

---

section 2 review

Summary

Temperature

- The particles that make up an object are in constant random motion.
- The temperature of an object is a measure of the average kinetic energy of the particles in the object.

Thermal Energy and Heat

- Heat is a transfer of thermal energy due to a difference in temperature.
- Thermal energy always flows from a higher temperature to a lower temperature.
- Conduction, convection, and radiation are ways thermal energy is transferred.
- Insulators are materials in which thermal energy does not flow easily.

Self Check

1. **Explain** how the motion of particles in an object changes when its temperature increases. SC.A.1.3.3

2. **Explain** why some insulating materials contain small air spaces. SC.B.1.3.5

3. **Identify** the type of thermal energy transfer that can take place with little or no matter present. Explain. SC.B.1.3.5

4. **Think Critically** Popcorn is cooked in a hot-air popper, in a microwave oven, or in a pan on a stove. Identify how thermal energy is transferred in each case. SC.B.1.3.5

Applying Math

5. **Convert Temperature** To change a temperature from Fahrenheit to Celsius, subtract 32 from the Fahrenheit temperature, then multiply by 5/9. If the temperature is 77°F, what is the Celsius temperature? MA.B.2.3.2

Benchmark—SC.A.1.3.3: The student knows that temperature measures the average energy of motion of the particles that make up the substance; **SC.H.1.3.4:** knows that accurate record keeping, openness, and replication are essential to maintaining an investigator's credibility with other scientists and society; **SC.H.1.3.5:** knows that a change in one or more variables may alter the outcome of an investigation; **SC.H.1.3.7:** knows that when similar investigations give different results, the scientific challenge is to verify whether the differences are significant by further study.

Temperature Changes

▶ Real-World Problem

Sometimes a bowl of soup can be too hot to eat, and you have to wait for the soup to cool. How long does it take for hot soup to cool? Does the soup cool faster if it isn't as hot? In this lab, you will investigate how the temperature of water changes over time.

▶ Procedure

1. Copy the data table into your Science Journal. Work in teams of three. Decide who will be the timekeeper, who will read the thermometers and stir the beakers, and who will record observations.

2. Fill one beaker with the ice and 100 mL of water. Add 100 mL of water to another beaker.

3. Heat 100 mL of water in the third beaker until it is about 70°C. Remove the beaker from the heat source.

4. Remove the ice from the first beaker and put a thermometer in each of the three beakers. Record the beginning temperatures of the three beakers of water.

5. Predict what will happen to the temperatures of each of the three beakers of water as they sit at room temperature for 15 minutes. Record your predictions in your Science Journal.

Goals

■ **Predict** how cold and warm water will change over time in a room-temperature environment.

■ **Measure** the temperature changes that occur over time.

Materials

thermometers (3)
stirring rods (3)
400-mL beakers (3)
300 mL of water
stop watch or clock with
    second hand
hot plate
ice
paper towels
graph paper

Safety Precautions

Complete a safety worksheet before you begin.

WARNING: *Do not use mercury thermometers. Use caution when heating water with a hot plate.*

Data Table

Time	Cold Water (°C)	Warm Water (°C)	Room Temp. Water (°C)
Start			
1 min			
2 min			
3 min		Do not write in this book.	
4 min			
5 min			
6 min			
7 min			
8 min			

6. At one minute intervals, have the timekeeper notify the thermometer reader to take a reading. The reader should read the temperature of each beaker of water in the same order every minute. Continue taking readings for 15 minutes.

7. Graph your data. Using a different color pencil for each beaker, plot the time and temperature data from the cold, lukewarm, and hot water on one *x*-axis and *y*-axis. Connect the points for each graph with a curve.

8. Extend the curve for each graph to predict how the temperature in each beaker would change if you took temperature readings for five additional minutes.

◉ Analyze Your Data

1. **Explain** what the extended temperature curves appear to do.

2. **Describe** how your predictions compare to your results.

◉ Conclude and Apply

1. **Predict** what would happen if you combined the warm water with the room temperature water.

2. **Infer** what you could do to slow the change in temperature among the beakers. How could you speed it up?

Communicating Your Data

Compare your results with other students in your class. Discuss any differences in the data and infer reasons for these differences.

Hiroshima
by Lawrence Yep

On August 6, 1945, an American B-29 bomber dropped a new weapon called the atom bomb on the Japanese city of Hiroshima. The bomb destroyed 60 percent of the city, killing between 90,000 and 140,000 people.

Everything is made up of tiny particles called atoms. They are so small they are invisible to the eye. Energy holds these parts together like glue. When the atom breaks up into its parts, the energy goes free and there is a big explosion.

Inside the bomb, one uranium atom collides with another. Those atoms both break up. Their parts smash into more atoms and split them in turn.

This is called a chain reaction. There are millions and millions of atoms inside the bomb. When they all break up, it is believed that the atom bomb will be equal to 20,000 tons of dynamite. In 1945, it is the most powerful weapon ever made....

Up until then, no single bomb has ever caused so much damage or so many deaths.

The wind mixes their dust with the dirt and debris. Then it sends everything boiling upward in a tall purple-gray column. When the top of the dust cloud spreads out, it looks like a strange, giant mushroom.

The bomb goes off 580 meters above the ground. The temperature reaches several million degrees Celsius immediately.

One mile away, the fierce heat starts fires.

Even two miles away, people are burned by the heat.

Understanding Literature

Summarize When you summarize something, you mention only the main ideas and necessary supporting details. The author of *Hiroshima* has chosen to summarize the events. He briefly explains the science behind the atom bomb. He also gives some details about the destruction after the bomb was dropped on Hiroshima, Japan. How are summaries useful?

Respond to the Reading

1. What was the author's reason for writing this piece? **LA.B.2.3.1**
2. How is the atom bomb different from other bombs?
3. **Linking Science and Writing** Write a one- or two-paragraph summary of one of the sections in this chapter.

INTEGRATE Physics Energy can be released by chemical reactions when the bonds between atoms are broken. In this excerpt from *Hiroshima*, Lawrence Yep describes the effects of the energy released in a different process—the energy released when the nuclei of atoms are split. This reaction released an enormous amount of energy that destroyed a city.

Reviewing Main Ideas

Section 1 Energy Changes

1. Energy is the ability to cause change.

2. Energy can be transformed from one form into another.

3. Kinetic energy is the energy an object has due to its motion. Kinetic energy increases as the speed of an object increases.

4. Potential energy is stored energy that increases as an object's height increases.

5. According to the law of conservation of energy, energy is never created or destroyed, but only changes form.

6. When energy is changed from one form to another, some thermal energy is produced and the amount of useful energy decreases.

Section 2 Thermal Energy

1. The temperature of a material is a measure of the average kinetic energy of the particles in the material.

2. The most widely used temperature scale is the Celsius scale. The Fahrenheit temperature scale is used in the United States.

3. Thermal energy is the energy contained in an object that depends on the object's temperature.

4. Heat is the transfer of thermal energy from a higher temperature to a lower temperature.

5. Thermal energy can be transferred from one place to another by conduction, convection, and radiation.

Visualizing Main Ideas

Copy and complete the following concept map on energy.

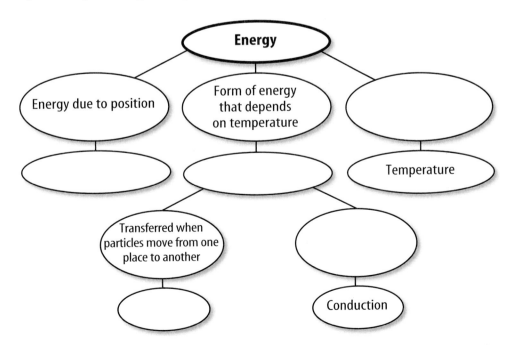

Using Vocabulary

* calorie p. 540
* conduction p. 548
* convection p. 550
* energy p. 534
* heat p. 547
* kinetic energy p. 535
* FCAT Vocabulary

* law of conservation of energy p. 541
* potential energy p. 537
* radiation p. 551
* temperature p. 545
* thermal energy p. 539

Fill in the blanks with the correct vocabulary word or words.

1. A(n) _____ is a unit of energy.

2. The energy due to motion is _____.

3. The movement of thermal energy from warm to cool objects is _____.

4. Energy that is due to the random motion of the particles in a material is _____.

5. _____ is energy that is stored.

6. _____ is the transfer of thermal energy by collisions between the particles in a material.

7. The transfer of thermal energy by waves is called _____.

8. The transfer of thermal energy by particles moving from one place to another is _____.

9. _____ is the ability to cause change.

Checking Concepts

Choose the word or phrase that best answers the question.

10. Which of the following correctly describes energy? `SC.B.1.3.2`
A) can be created
B) can be destroyed
C) cannot change form
D) can change form

11. The average kinetic energy of the particles in an object is related to which of the following? `SC.A.1.3.3`
A) chemical energy   C) temperature
B) heat   D) useful energy

12. The transfer of thermal energy due to the movement of warm air in a room is an example of which process? `SC.B.1.3.5`
A) convection
B) temperature
C) conduction
D) potential energy

13. Which of the following describes how the total amount of energy changes during an energy transformation? `SC.B.1.3.2`
A) It increases.
B) It decreases.
C) It stays the same.
D) It all becomes thermal energy.

14. How is energy from the Sun transferred to Earth? `SC.B.1.3.5`
A) It is transferred by conduction.
B) It is transferred by convection.
C) It is transferred by radiation.
D) It is transferred by contact.

15. When would you have the most potential energy? `SC.B.1.3.1`
A) walking up the hill
B) sitting at the top of the hill
C) running up the hill
D) sitting at the bottom of the hill

16. What form of energy is always produced when energy changes from one form to another? `SC.B.1.3.4`
A) radiant   C) thermal
B) chemical   D) electrical

17. Thermal energy moves most easily in which of these materials? `SC.B.1.3.5`
A) plastic   C) air
B) wood   D) copper

Vocabulary PuzzleMaker fl6.msscience.com

Thinking Critically

18. **Concept Map** Below is a concept map on the energy changes that occur when a person jumps upward. Copy and complete the map by indicating the type of energy—kinetic, potential, or both—the person has at each of the following stages: halfway up, the highest point, halfway down, and just before hitting the ground. `SC.B.1.3.1`

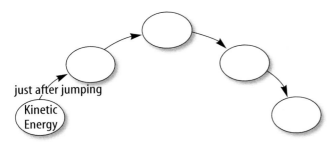

just after jumping
Kinetic Energy

19. **Infer** When a ball falls and hits the ground, how does the initial potential energy of the ball compare with the amount of thermal energy produced? `SC.B.1.3.2`

Use the table below to answer question 20.

Kinetic Energy of a Ball	
Speed of Ball (m/s)	Kinetic Energy (J)
5	2.5
10	10.0
15	22.5
20	40.0
25	62.5
30	90.0

20. **Make a Graph** Using the data in the table above, graph the kinetic energy of the ball on the y-axis and the speed of the ball on the x-axis. Describe the shape of your graph. How does the kinetic energy change when the speed doubles? `SC.B.1.3.1`

21. **Explain** why the amount of useful energy always decreases when energy is changed from one form to another. `SC.B.1.3.4`

22. **Explain** why the walls of houses often are filled with fiberglass insulation. `SC.B.1.3.5`

23. **Determine** the energy transformations that occur in each of the following situations—a log burns in a fireplace, a ball is dropped, a slice of pizza is heated in a microwave oven. `SC.B.1.3.2`

24. **Explain** why a blanket is a better conductor of heat when it is wet than when it is dry. `SC.B.1.3.5`

Performance Activities

25. **Design an Experiment** to determine how quickly the temperature of different materials changes as they absorb radiant energy. Use the following items—three different colors of construction paper, three thermometers, and a sunny window or a heat lamp. `SC.A.2.3.3`

Applying Math

Use the table below to answer question 26.

Fahrenheit and Celsius Temperatures	
Celsius Temperature (°C)	Fahrenheit Temperature (°F)
100	212
50	122
0	32
−25	−13
−50	−58

26. **Temperature Scales** Graph the data in the table with the Celsius temperature on the x-axis and the Fahrenheit temperature on the y-axis. From your graph, determine the temperature that has the same value on both temperature scales. `MA.E.1.3.1`

The assessed Florida Benchmark appears above each question.

Record your answers on the answer sheet provided by your teacher or on a sheet of paper.

Multiple Choice

SC.B.1.3.5

1 The illustration below shows how a room is heated by a furnace.

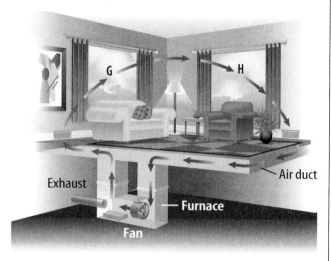

How does the air at point G compare to the air at point H?

A. The air at point G is warmer but has the same density.

B. The air at point G is cooler and is more dense.

C. The air at point G is cooler but has a greater density.

D. The air at point G is warmer and less dense.

SC.B.1.3.2

2 Which of the following is an example of an object with kinetic energy?

F. a ball lying in the grass

G. a pencil resting on a desk

H. an apple falling to the ground

I. a skier waiting at the top of a hill

SC.B.1.3.5

3 How does thermal energy flow as you hold a glass of iced tea?

A. by radiation from the ice to your hand

B. by convection from the ice to your hand

C. by conduction from your hand to the glass

D. by convection from your hand to the glass

SC.B.1.3.4

4 The illustration below shows the energy transformations that occur in a flashlight.

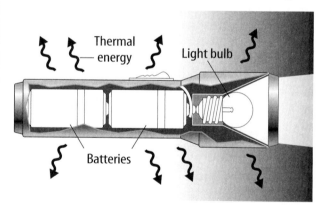

How much thermal energy is produced by the bulb if 42.0 joules (J) of electrical energy are changed into 4.2 J of radiant energy?

F. 4.2 J

G. 37.8 J

H. 42.0 J

I. 46.2 J

SC.B.1.3.1

5 Shaun is using a ball to experiment with potential energy. Which should Shaun do to increase the ball's potential energy?

A. The ball should be rolled down a ramp.

B. The ball should be cooled.

C. The ball should be dropped.

D. The ball should be lifted higher.

SC.A.1.3.3

6 At which temperature is the average kinetic energy of molecules the largest?

F. 30°C

G. 20°C

H. 10°C

I. −5°C

Gridded Response

SC.B.1.3.5

7 The diagram below shows a wind chill index.

Wind Chill Index					
Temperature (°C)	Wind Speed (km/h)				
	20	30	40	50	60
20	16°C	14°C	13°C	13°C	12°C
12	5°C	3°C	1°C	0°C	0°C
0	−10°C	−14°C	−17°C	−18°C	−19°C
−20	−36°C	−43°C	−47°C	−49°C	−51°C
−36	−57°C	−65°C	−71°C	−74°C	−77°C

If the outside temperature is 12°C, at what wind speed in kilometers per hour (km/h) will the wind chill be the same as the freezing point of water?

Short Response

SC.B.1.3.5

8 Explain why when foods are placed in a refrigerator, the temperature of frozen foods increases, while the temperature of hot foods decreases.

Extended Response

SC.B.1.3.1

9 The illustration below shows a roller coaster. The labels show different positions of the roller-coaster car as it travels over the tracks.

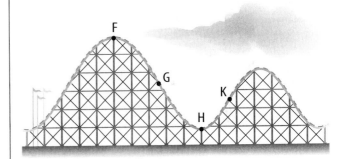

PART A Describe how the energy in a roller-coaster car is continually transformed as it moves from left to right along the track.

PART B Compare and contrast the kinetic and potential energy of the roller-coaster car at points F, G, H, and K.

FCAT Tip

Be Prepared Bring at least two sharpened No. 2 pencils and a good eraser to the test. Before the test, check to make sure that your eraser erases completely.

Sunshine State Standards—**SC.B.1:** The student recognizes that energy may be changed in form with varying efficiency; **SC.C.2:** The student understands that the types of force that act on an object and the effect of that force can be described, measured, and predicted.

Electricity and Magnetism

Lightning in a Bottle

These lacy streamers in the plasma globe and lightning have something in common. They are sparks, caused by the rapid movement of electric charges. Here, the charges move from the metal ball in the center to the inner wall of a surrounding glass ball.

Science Journal List five electrical devices you used today and describe what each device did.

Start-Up Activities

SC.H.1.3.5
SC.C.2.3.1

Electric and Magnetic Forces

You exert a force on a skateboard when you give it a push. But forces can be exerted between objects even when they are not touching. When you throw a ball up into the air, Earth's gravity exerts a force on the ball that pulls it downward. Electric and magnetic forces also can be exerted on objects that are not in contact with each other.

1. Complete a safety worksheet.

2. Inflate a rubber balloon and rub it against your hair or a piece of wool.

3. Bring the balloon close to a small bit of paper. Then bring the balloon close to a paper clip. Record your observations.

4. Bring a bar magnet close to a small bit of paper. Then bring the bar magnet close to a paper clip. Record your observations.

5. **Think Critically** Describe how the forces exerted by the balloon and the magnet were similar and how they were different. Compare the force exerted by the balloon and the force exerted by gravity on the paper. Compare the force exerted by the magnet and the force exerted by gravity on the paper clip.

FOLDABLES™ Study Organizer

Electric and Magnetic Forces
Make the following Foldable to help you understand the properties of electric forces and magnetic forces.

LA.A.1.3.4

STEP 1 Fold a sheet of paper in half lengthwise.

STEP 2 Fold paper down about 2 cm from the top.

STEP 3 Open and draw lines along the horizontal fold. Label as shown.

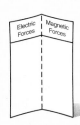

Electric Forces | Magnetic Forces

Summarize in a Table As you read the chapter, summarize the properties of electric forces in the left column and properties of magnetic forces in the right column.

Preview this chapter's content and activities at
fl6.msscience.com

561

Benchmarks—**SC.C.2.3.1 (pp. 563–565):** The student knows that many forces (e.g., gravitational, electrical, and magnetic) act at a distance (i.e. without contact).

Also covers: **SC.A.2.3.2** (p. 562), **SC.D.1.3.5** (p. 567), **SC.H.1.3.5 Annually Assessed** (p. 561), **SC.H.1.3.6** (p. 566)

Electric Charge and Forces

What You'll Learn

- **Describe** how electric charges exert forces on each other.
- **Define** an electric field.
- **Explain** how objects can become electrically charged.
- **Describe** how lightning occurs.

Why It's Important

Most of the changes that occur around you and inside you are the result of forces between electric charges.

Review Vocabulary

atom: the smallest particle of an element; contains protons, neutrons, and electrons

New Vocabulary

✳ **neutral**
● electric field
● insulator
● conductor
● static charge
● electric discharge

✳ FCAT Vocabulary

Electric Charges

Does a clock radio wake you up in the morning? Do you use a toaster or a microwave oven to help make breakfast? All of these devices use electrical energy to operate. The source of this energy lies in the forces between the electric charges found in atoms.

Positive and Negative Charge The matter around you is made of atoms. Atoms are particles less than a billionth of a meter in size—much too small to be seen, even with tremendous magnification. Every atom contains electrons that move around a nucleus, as shown in **Figure 1.** The nucleus contains protons and neutrons. An atom has the same number of protons and electrons.

Protons and electrons have electric charge. Electrons have negative charge and protons have positive charge. The amount of positive charge on a proton equals the amount of negative charge on an electron. Neutrons have no electric charge.

Neutral and Charged Objects Because an atom has equal numbers of protons and electrons, it contains equal amounts of positive and negative charge. The amounts of positive charge and negative charge balance out so that the total charge on an atom is zero. Something that has zero total charge is **neutral.** An object is electrically charged if the amounts of positive and negative charge it contains are not equal.

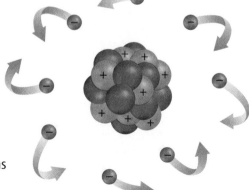

Figure 1 In an atom, negatively charged electrons move around a nucleus that contains neutrons and positively charged protons.

The Forces Between Charges

When you drop a ball and it falls to the ground, the ball and Earth exert an attractive force on each other—the gravitational force. Just as two masses, such as Earth and the ball, exert forces on each other, two objects that are electrically charged exert forces on each other.

The gravitational force is always attractive. The forces exerted by charged objects on each other can be attractive or repulsive, as shown in **Figure 2.** If two objects are positively charged, they repel each other. If two objects are negatively charged, they also repel each other. If one object is positively charged and the other is negatively charged, they attract each other. In other words, like charges repel and unlike charges attract.

Electric Force Depends on Distance The electric force between two charged objects depends on the distance between the objects. The electric force decreases as the distance between the objects increases. For example, as two electrons move farther apart, the repulsive force between them decreases.

Electric Force Depends on Charge The electric force between two charged objects also depends on the amount of charge on each object. As the amount of charge on either object increases, the electric force between the objects also increases.

Electric Forces and Electric Fields

Charged objects don't have to be touching to exert electric forces on each other. Another way to say this is that electric forces act at a distance. An example of this, as shown in **Figure 3,** is when you rub a balloon on a cat's fur and hold the balloon above the cat. The balloon and the fur exert electric forces on each other even though they aren't touching. This means the electric forces act on each other when they are some distance apart.

A positive and a negative charge attract.

Two positive charges repel.

Two negative charges repel.

Figure 2 Electric charges exert forces on each other. The forces can be attractive or repulsive. The arrows show the direction of the electric force acting on each charge. **Describe** *how the forces change if the charges move closer together.*

Figure 3 Rubbing a balloon on a cat's fur causes the balloon and the fur to be electrically charged. Electric forces exerted by the balloon cause the cat's fur to stand on end.

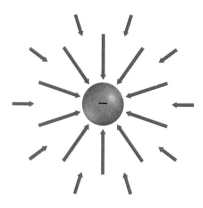

Figure 4 The electric field around a positive charge points away from the charge. The electric field around a negative charge points toward the charge.

Figure 5 Clothes that have been tumbling in a dryer become electrically charged by contact. Articles of clothing that have opposite charges stick together when they come out of the dryer.

An Electric Field Surrounds a Charge How do electric charges exert forces on each other if they are not touching? Any electric charge, such as a proton or an electron, is surrounded by an electric field. An **electric field** is the region of space surrounding an electric charge where a force is exerted on other electric charges. All objects that are electrically charged, like the balloon and the cat's fur, are surrounded by an electric field. An electric force is exerted on any charged object that is in an electric field. The electric field surrounding a charged object becomes weaker as the distance from the object increases.

Visualizing an Electric Field The electric field surrounding an electric charge is invisible. **Figure 4** shows one way to visualize the electric field around a charge. The electric field is represented by arrows. The arrows point in the direction a positive charge would move. Also, the arrows are shorter where the field is weaker. **Figure 4** shows the electric field at some of the points in the space surrounding a positive charge and a negative charge.

Making Objects Electrically Charged

When you rubbed a balloon on the cat's fur, it became electrically charged. The balloon no longer contained equal numbers of protons and electrons. The balloon became electrically charged because electric charges were transferred from the fur to the surface of the balloon.

Charging by Contact When you rubbed the balloon on the fur, the surface of the balloon came in contact with the surfaces of strands of fur. As atoms in the fur and in the balloon came close to each other, electrons were transferred from atoms in the fur to atoms in the balloon. This is an example of charging by contact, which is the transfer of electric charge between objects in contact.

Because the balloon gained electrons after rubbing, it had more electrons than protons and was negatively charged. Because the fur lost electrons, it had more protons than electrons and was positively charged. The amount of negative charge gained by the balloon equaled the amount of positive charge left on the fur.

Another example of charging by contact is shown in **Figure 5.** As clothes tumble in a clothes dryer, they rub against each other. Charging by contact occurs and electrons are transferred from one article of clothing to another. This can cause articles of clothing to stick to each other when you take them out of the dryer.

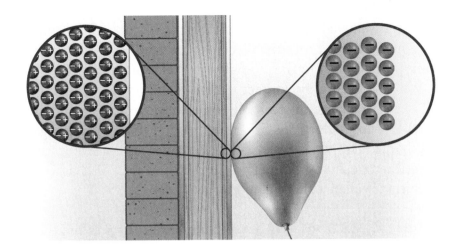

Figure 6 Charging by polarization causes a negatively charged balloon to stick to a wall. The balloon's electric field pushes electrons in the wall to one side of their atoms. The surface of the wall becomes positively charged and attracts the negatively charged balloon.

Infer *whether a positively charged balloon would stick to the wall.*

Charging by Polarization Have you ever rubbed a balloon on your sweater or your hair and then stuck the balloon to a wall? Charging by contact caused the balloon to become negatively charged. Bringing the balloon close to the wall caused the part of the wall next to the balloon to become positively charged, as shown in **Figure 6.** The negatively charged balloon then was attracted to this positively charged area of the wall.

How did the balloon make that part of the wall positively charged? The electric field around the balloon repelled the electrons in the atoms of the wall. The force exerted by the electric field pushed some of the electrons in these atoms to the side of the atom away from the balloon.

This process is called charge polarization. When charge polarization occurs, an electric field causes one side of an atom to be positively charged and the other side to be negatively charged. Because some of the negatively charged electrons in the wall have been pushed away from the balloon, that part of the wall becomes positively charged.

Conductors and Insulators

The wall in the example above was made of materials in which electrons were held tightly by their atoms. As a result, electrons do not move easily in these materials. **Insulators** are materials in which electric charges do not move easily. Plastics, rubber, and wood are examples of materials that are insulators.

In other materials, some electrons are held so loosely by atoms that they can move in the material easily. Materials in which electric charges can move easily are **conductors.** The best conductors are metals such as gold, silver, and copper. Because electrons can move easily in copper, it is widely used in electric wires.

SC.C.2.3.1

Mini LAB

Observing Charging by Polarization

Procedure
1. Turn on a **water faucet.** Adjust the flow so that the water stream is as slow as possible without producing drops.
2. Rub a **balloon** or a **comb** on your hair or on **wool cloth.**
3. Bring the charged end of the balloon or comb near the stream of water, and observe the result.

Analysis
1. Explain the behavior of the stream of water using the concept of charging by polarization.
2. How does the total charge of the water change?

Try at Home

Static Charge

If you walk across a carpet wearing shoes with rubber soles, charging by contact occurs. Electrons are transferred from the atoms in the carpet to the atoms on the soles of your shoes.

When charging by contact occurs, the amount of positive and negative charge on each object is no longer balanced. The object that loses electrons has more positive charge than negative charge. The object that gains electrons has more negative charge than positive charge. The imbalance of electric charge on an object is called a **static charge.**

Electric Discharge When you walk across a carpet and then touch a metal doorknob, sometimes you might feel an electric shock. Perhaps you see a spark jump between your hand and the doorknob. The spark is an example of an electric discharge. An **electric discharge** is the movement of static charge from one place to another. The spark you saw was the result of a static charge moving between your hand and the doorknob.

Figure 7 shows why a spark occurs when you touch the doorknob. Electrons that are transferred from the carpet to your shoes spread over your skin. As you reach toward the metal doorknob, the electric field around your hand repels electrons in the doorknob. They move away, leaving the surface of the doorknob nearest your hand with a positive charge. If the attractive electric force on the excess electrons is strong enough, these electrons can be pulled from your hand toward the doorknob. This rapid movement of charge causes the spark you see and the shock you feel.

Figure 7 Static charge on your hand causes a spark to jump from your hand to the doorknob.

The excess negative charge on your hand repels electrons in the doorknob, leaving positive charges on the surface of the doorknob.

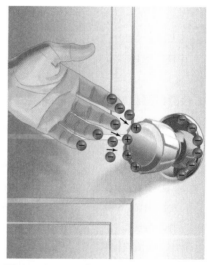

The attractive force between the charges on your hand and the doorknob can cause electrons to move to the doorknob.

The electric field between the cloud and the ground causes charges to move, forming the lightning flash.

Air currents cause the bottom of the cloud to become negatively charged.

Charging by polarization causes the ground beneath the cloud to become positively charged.

Lightning A spectacular example of an electric discharge is lightning. **Figure 8** shows how lightning is produced. During a storm, air currents in a storm cloud sometimes cause electrons to be transferred from the top to the bottom of the storm cloud. The electric field surrounding the bottom of the storm cloud repels electrons in the ground. This makes the ground positively charged. The attractive electric forces cause charges to move between the cloud and the ground. This produces a flash of lightning that lasts for about one ten-thousandth of a second.

Air currents in a storm cloud can cause other parts of the storm cloud to become positively and negatively charged. As a result, lightning flashes often occur between one storm cloud and another, and also within a storm cloud.

INTEGRATE Health

Lightning Safety A lightning flash can be dangerous. On average, lightning strikes about 400 people a year in the United States, and causes about 80 deaths. You should always take lightning seriously, particularly if you are outside and a thunderstorm is in sight. You can help protect yourself by following the 30-30 rule. If the time between the lightning and the thunder is 30 seconds or less, the storm is dangerously close. Seek shelter in an enclosed building or a car, and avoid touching any metal surfaces. Wait 30 minutes after the last flash of lightning before leaving the shelter—even if the Sun comes out. One in ten lightning strikes occurs when no storm clouds are visible.

Figure 8 Lightning occurs when the static charge on a storm cloud causes charging by polarization on the ground or another cloud.

LA.A.1.3.4

LA.B.2.3.4

Science Online

Topic: Lightning
Visit fl6.msscience.com for Web links to information about different types of lightning that occur in Earth's atmosphere.

Activity Make a table listing different types of lightning in one column and a description of the lightning type in a second column.

Figure 9 A lightning rod provides a path to conduct the charge in a lightning strike into the ground.

Grounding A lightning flash can transfer an enormous amount of electrical energy. When lightning strikes trees in a forest, it can spark a forest fire. If lightning strikes a building, the building can be damaged or set on fire.

One way to protect buildings from the damaging effects of lightning is to attach a metal lightning rod to the top of the building. A thick wire is connected to the lightning rod, and the other end of the wire is connected to the ground.

When lightning strikes the lightning rod, the electric charges in the lightning flash flow through the connecting wire into the ground. Earth can be a conductor, and because Earth is so large, it can absorb large quantities of excess electric charge. The process of providing a path to drain excess charge into Earth is called grounding. Because the lightning rod in **Figure 9** is grounded, the excess charge in the lightning strike flows harmlessly into the ground without damaging the building.

section 1 review

Summary

Electric Charges and Forces

- Electrons are negatively charged and protons are positively charged.
- An electric charge is surrounded by an electric field that exerts a force on other charges.
- Like charges repel each other; unlike charges attract each other.

Making Objects Charged

- The transfer of electric charges between two objects that touch is charging by contact.
- Charging by polarization occurs when an electric field rearranges the charges in an object.
- Static charge is an imbalance of electric charge on an object.

Lightning

- Lightning is an electric discharge between a storm cloud and the ground, or within or between storm clouds.
- Grounding can prevent damage caused to buildings by lightning strikes.

Self Check

1. **Explain** why an atom is electrically neutral. `SC.A.2.3.2`
2. **Describe** how a balloon becomes electrically charged after you rub the balloon on a cat's fur.
3. **Predict** Suppose the air currents in a storm cloud caused the bottom of the cloud to become positively charged. Predict whether lightning could occur between the cloud and the ground. Explain your reasoning.
4. **Infer** When charging by contact occurs, how is the amount of positive charge on one object related to the amount of negative charge on the other object?
5. **Describe** how the electric force between two objects depends on the amount of charge on the objects and the distance between them.
6. **Think Critically** Sometimes, just before a lightning strike occurs nearby, the hair on a person's head will stand up. Explain why this happens. `SC.C.2.3.1`

Applying Skills

7. **Sequence** Make an events-chain concept map that shows the sequence of events that occurs when a flash of lightning is produced.

More Section Review fl6.msscience.com

section 2

Also covers: SC.B.1.3.4 (pp. 572–574), SC.H.1.3.4 Annually Assessed (p. 577), SC.H.1.3.5 Annually Assessed (p. 577)

Electric Current

Electric Current

When you turn on a TV, images appear on the screen and sound comes out of the speakers. The TV produces light waves that carry energy to your eyes, and sound waves that carry energy to your ears. Where does this energy come from? You know that unless the TV is plugged into an electrical outlet, nothing happens when you turn it on. The electrical outlet provides electrical energy that the TV transforms into sound and light. This electrical energy becomes available only when an electric current flows in the TV.

What is an electric current? An **electric current** is the flow of electric charges. In some ways an electric current is like the flow of water in a pipe. In the pipe, water flows as water molecules move along the pipe. In a wire, there is an electric current when electrons in the wire move along the wire.

In a wire, the numbers of protons and electrons are equal and the wire is electrically neutral, as shown in **Figure 10.** When current flows in the wire, these electrons move along the wire. At the same time, electrons flow into one end of the wire and flow out of the other end. **Figure 10** shows that the number of electrons that flow out one end of the wire is equal to the number of electrons that flow into the other end. As a result, the wire remains electrically neutral.

The Unit for Current

The amount of electric current in a wire is the amount of charge that flows into and out of the wire every second. The SI unit for current is the ampere, which has the symbol A. One ampere of electric current means an enormous number of electrons—about six billion billion—are flowing into and out of the wire every second.

Copper wire

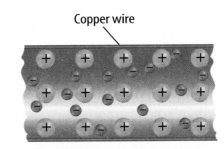

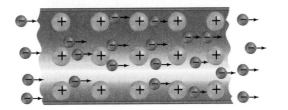

Figure 10 When a current flows in a wire, the same number of charges flow into and out of the wire. The wire remains electrically neutral.

as you read

What **You'll Learn**

■ **Describe** how an electric current flows.
■ **Explain** how electrical energy is transferred to a circuit.
■ **Explain** how current, voltage, and resistance are related in a circuit.
■ **Distinguish** between series and parallel circuits.

Why **It's Important**

Electrical appliances you use every day transform the electrical energy in an electric current into other useful forms of energy.

Review Vocabulary

✳ **kinetic energy:** the energy an object has due to its motion

New Vocabulary

● electric current
✳ circuit
● electric resistance
● voltage
● series circuit
● parallel circuit

✳ FCAT Vocabulary

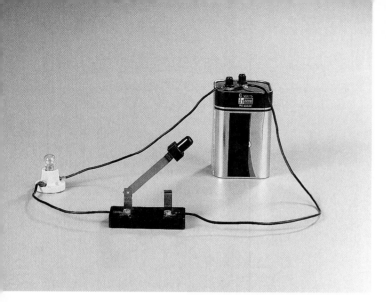
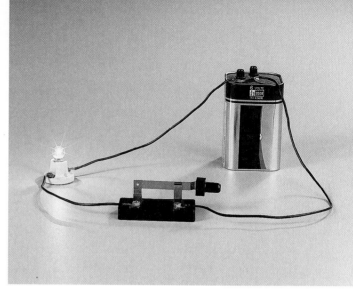

Figure 11 A battery, lightbulb, and connecting wires form a simple electric circuit. Current flows as long as the switch is closed. When the switch is open, current no longer flows.
Explain *whether current would flow if the lightbulb were disconnected.*

A Simple Electric Circuit

When a lightning flash occurs, electrical energy is transformed into heat, sound, and light in an instant. But to watch your favorite shows on TV, electrical energy must be transformed into light and sound for as long as your shows last. This means that an electric current must be kept flowing in your TV as you watch it.

Electric current will flow continually only if the charges can flow in a closed path. A closed path in which electric charges can flow is a **circuit.** A simple electric circuit is shown in **Figure 11.** Current will flow in this circuit as long as the conducting path between the battery, wires, and lightbulb is not broken. If the switch is open, current will not flow.

Making Electric Charges Flow

Water flows in a pipe when there is a force exerted on the water. For example, a pump can exert a force on water that pushes it through a pipe. A force must be exerted on electric charges to make them flow. Remember that a force is exerted on an electric charge by an electric field. To make electric charges flow in a circuit, there must be an electric field in the circuit.

A Battery Makes Charges Flow The battery in **Figure 11** produces the electric field in the circuit that causes electrons to flow. When the battery is connected in a circuit, chemical reactions occur in the battery. These chemical reactions cause the negative terminal to become negatively charged, and the positive terminal to become positively charged. The negative and positive charges on the battery terminals produce the electric field in the circuit that causes electrons to flow. The battery makes electrons flow in the direction from the negative terminal toward the positive terminal.

Electric Resistance It can be slow going when you try to walk to class through a crowded hallway. You are constantly speeding up and slowing down, as well as changing direction. Even though you might change speed and direction many times, you keep getting closer and closer to your classroom.

In some ways, the flow of electrons in a circuit is similar to walking down a crowded hallway. Electrons are constantly speeding up, slowing down, and changing direction as they flow. These changes in speed and direction occur because electrons are constantly colliding with atoms, as shown in **Figure 12.** An electron flowing in a wire may be involved in trillions of collisions each second.

Reading Check *Why do electrons constantly change direction as they flow in a circuit?*

The measure of how difficult it is for electrons to flow in an object is called the **electric resistance** of the object. The resistance of insulators usually is much higher than the resistance of conductors. The unit for electric resistance is the ohm, symbolized by Ω. An electric resistance of 20 ohms would be written as 20 Ω.

A Model for Electron Flow One way to picture how electrons flow in a circuit is to imagine a tennis ball bouncing down a flight of stairs, as shown in **Figure 13.** In this model the ball is like an electron moving through a circuit, and the steps are like the atoms it bumps into. When you drop the ball, it speeds up as gravity pulls it downward. When it hits a step, it changes direction. The ball also slows down as it bounces upward because the force of gravity continues to pull it downward. After the ball reaches the top of its bounce, it falls downward toward the next step and speeds up again. This process is repeated as the ball bounces from step to step.

Even though the ball changes direction after it hits each step, the overall motion of the ball is downward. In the same way, an electron in a circuit changes direction after each collision. However, its overall motion is in the direction of the current flow.

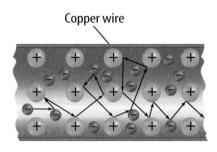

Figure 12 Collisions with atoms and other charges cause electrons in a wire to change direction many times each second.

Figure 13 The motion of an electron flowing in an electric circuit is similar to the motion of a ball bouncing down the stairs. The force of gravity keeps the ball moving downward. An electric field keeps an electron moving in the direction of the current.

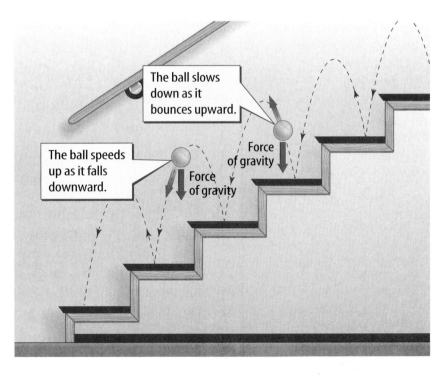

The ball slows down as it bounces upward.

The ball speeds up as it falls downward.

Force of gravity

Force of gravity

The Speed of Electric Current Because the ball changes direction and slows down after each collision with a step, the time it takes the ball to reach the bottom of the stairs is much longer than if the ball had fallen without bouncing. In the same way, the electric resistance in a wire causes electrons to flow slowly. It may take several minutes for an electron in a circuit to travel one centimeter.

If electrons travel so slowly, why does a lightbulb light up the instant you flip a switch? When you flip the switch you close a circuit and an electric field travels through the circuit at the speed of light. The electric field causes electrons in the lightbulb to start flowing almost immediately after the switch is flipped. It is the electrons flowing in the lightbulb that cause it to glow.

Transferring Electrical Energy

As the ball bounces down a flight of stairs, it transfers energy to the stairs. Each time the ball collides with a step, some of the ball's kinetic energy is transferred to the step. Electrons flowing in a circuit also have kinetic energy. When a current flows in a material, the repeated collisions between electrons and atoms cause a continual transfer of kinetic energy to the material. The energy that flowing electrons transfer to the circuit also is called electrical energy. As electrons bump into atoms, electrical energy is converted into other forms of energy, such as thermal energy and light.

For example, a lightbulb contains a filament that is a small coil of narrow wire, as shown in **Figure 14.** When current flows in the filament, electrical energy is converted into thermal energy and light. The filament becomes hot and glows, giving off light that enables you to see in the dark.

Figure 14 A lightbulb filament is a coil of thin wire. The electric resistance in the filament converts electrical energy into thermal energy and light.

Electrical Energy and the Electric Field As electrons flow in a circuit, the electrical energy transferred to the circuit depends on the strength of the electric field. If the electric field becomes stronger, the electric force exerted on electrons increases as they move from one point to another in the circuit. This causes electrons to move faster between collisions. You might recall that the kinetic energy of an object increases as its speed increases. So the kinetic energy of flowing electrons increases as the electric field gets stronger. As a result, increasing the electric field causes more electrical energy to be transferred to the circuit.

The voltage across the ends of this wire is small. Only a small amount of electrical energy is transferred to this wire.

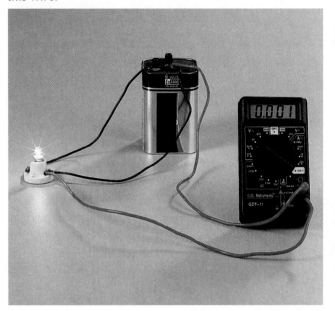

The voltage across the connections to the lightbulb is large. A large amount of electrical energy is transferred to the lightbulb.

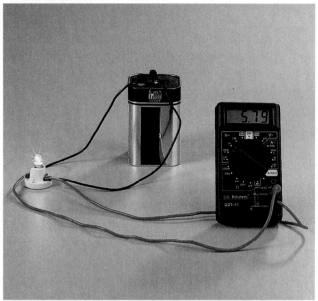

Voltage

You might have seen signs on electrical equipment that read "Danger! High Voltage." What is voltage? Voltage depends on the electrical energy of the electrons flowing in a circuit. As electrons flow in a circuit, they transfer electrical energy. The amount of electrical energy transferred between any two points in a circuit depends on the voltage between the points. **Voltage** is a measure of the amount of electrical energy transferred by an electric charge as it moves from one point to another in a circuit.

One way to measure the voltage between two points in a circuit is with a voltmeter. **Figure 15** shows how the voltage measured between two points in a circuit can be different depending on the location of the points in the circuit. The SI unit for voltage is the volt, which has the symbol V.

Battery Voltage The voltage between the positive and negative terminals of a battery usually is called the battery voltage. As the battery voltage increases, the electrical energy transferred to the circuit by the electrons flowing in the circuit also increases. A battery's voltage depends on the chemical reactions that occur in the battery. **Figure 16** shows some different types of batteries and the chemicals they contain. A battery converts chemical energy into electrical energy. This electrical energy then can be transformed into other forms of energy in the circuit.

 *What form of energy is transformed into electrical energy in a battery?*

Figure 15 A voltmeter measures the voltage between different points in this electric circuit.
Determine *To which part of the circuit is most of the electrical energy transferred?*

Figure 16

Many electrical devices use batteries to supply electrical energy. Every battery consists of one or more cells. The chemical reactions in a cell produce a voltage when the cell is connected in a circuit. Each cell has three parts—an electrolyte, a positive electrode, and a negative electrode. The electrolyte contains chemicals that cause chemical reactions to occur at the positive and negative electrodes. There are two types of cells—dry cells and wet cells.

Dry-Cell Batteries Flashlight batteries and the batteries that run portable CD players are dry-cell batteries. This type of cell is called a dry cell because the electrolyte is a paste, and not a liquid. The cells commonly used in dry-cell batteries have a voltage of 1.5 V. The most inexpensive dry-cell batteries are zinc-carbon batteries, shown on the right.

The positive electrode is a porous carbon rod. Chemical reactions occur in the rod that remove electrons that enter the rod from the circuit.

Positive terminal

Plastic insulator

In a zinc-carbon battery, the electrolyte is a moist paste containing the chemicals ammonium chloride, zinc chloride, and manganese dioxide.

The negative electrode is a zinc container. Here, chemical reactions remove electrons from the zinc atoms.

Negative terminal

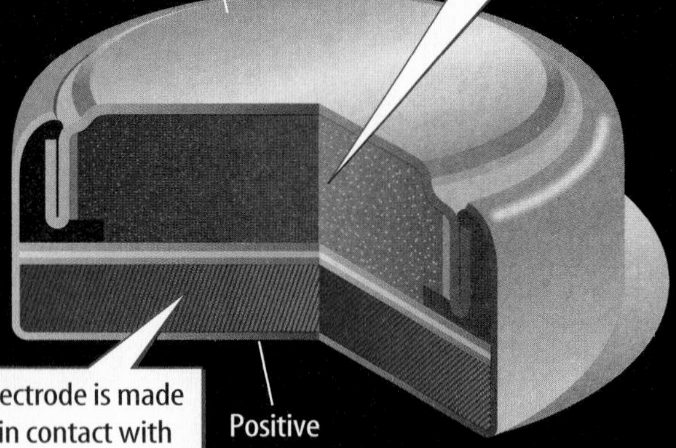

Negative terminal

The negative electrode is a gel containing powdered zinc metal and an electrolyte.

A silver oxide battery is a button-shaped or coin-shaped battery, often used in a camera or a calculator. This type of battery also is a dry-cell battery, and usually has a voltage of 1.5 V.

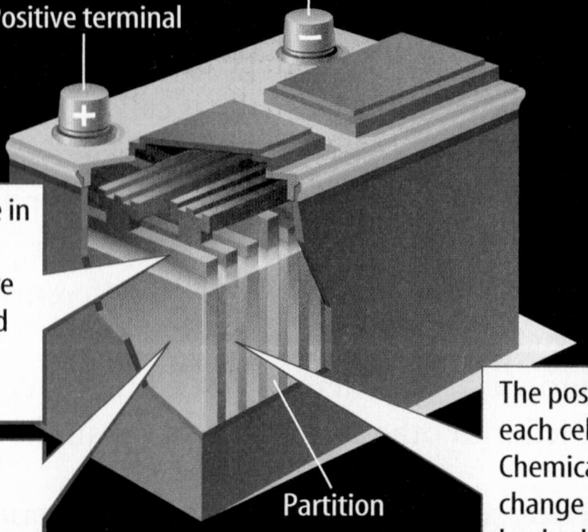

The positive electrode is made of silver oxide in contact with an electrolyte paste. Chemical reactions here change the silver oxide to silver metal.

Positive terminal

Wet-Cell Batteries In a wet cell the electrolyte is a liquid. The most common wet-cell battery is a car battery. A 12-V car battery contains six wet cells connected in series. Each wet cell produces 2 V. Unlike the dry-cell batteries shown above, a wet-cell battery is rechargeable.

The negative electrode in each cell is lead metal. Chemical reactions here change the lead to lead sulfate and produce electrons.

Positive terminal

The electrolyte in a car battery is a solution of sulfuric acid.

Partition

The positive electrode in each cell is lead dioxide. Chemical reactions here change lead dioxide to lead sulfate.

Ohm's Law The voltage, current, and resistance in a circuit are related. What happens if the voltage in a circuit is increased? As the voltage in a circuit increases, the electric field in the circuit increases and causes electrons to speed up more between collisions. As a result, the current in the circuit increases. Increasing the resistance in the circuit increases the number of collisions that occur every second as electrons flow. This makes it more difficult for electrons to flow in the circuit. As a result, increasing the resistance reduces the current.

The relationship between the voltage, current, and resistance in a circuit is known as Ohm's law. Ohm's law can be written as the following equation.

Ohm's Law
voltage (in volts) = **current** (in amperes) $\times$ **resistance** (in ohms)
$$V = IR$$

Applying Math   Solve a Simple Equation

FLASHLIGHT VOLTAGE When a flashlight is turned on, the current that flows in the flashlight circuit is 0.10 A. If the resistance of the circuit is 30.0 Ω, what is the voltage in the circuit?

Solution

1 *This is what you know:*
- current: $I = 0.10$ A
- resistance: $R = 30.0$ Ω

2 *This is what you need to find:*
voltage: $V = ?V$

3 *This is the procedure you need to use:*
Substitute the known values for current and resistance into Ohm's law, and calculate the voltage:

$V = IR = (0.10$ A$)(30.0$ $\Omega) = 3.0$ V

4 *Check your answer:*
Divide your answer by the given resistance, 30.0 Ω. The result should be the given current, 0.10 A.

Practice Problems

1. When a portable radio is playing, the current in the radio is 0.3 A. If the resistance of the radio is 30.0 Ω, what is the voltage supplied by the radio battery? **MA.D.2.3.1**

2. The batteries in a portable CD player supply a voltage of 6.0 V. If the resistance in the CD player is 24 Ω, what is the current in the CD player when it's turned on? **MA.D.2.3.1**

Math Practice | For more practice, visit fl6.msscience.com

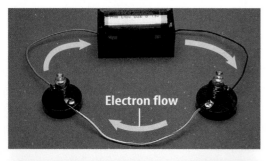

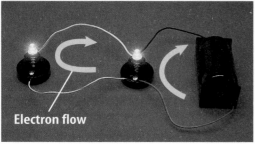

Figure 17 A series circuit (top) has only one path for current to follow. A parallel circuit (bottom) has more than one path for current to follow.

Series and Parallel Circuits

There usually are a number of devices and appliances connected to the circuits in your house. There are two ways that devices can be connected in a circuit. One way is a series circuit, shown in the upper part of **Figure 17,** and the other way is a parallel circuit, shown in the lower part of **Figure 17.**

In a **series circuit,** devices are connected so there is only one closed path for current to follow. However, if any part of this path is broken, current will no longer flow in the circuit.

In a **parallel circuit,** devices are connected so there is more than one closed path for current to follow. If the current flow is broken in one path, current will continue to flow in the other paths. The electric circuits in your house are parallel circuits. As a result, you can switch off a light in one room without turning off all the other lights in the house.

section **2** review

Summary

Electric Current

- An electric current is the flow of electric charges, such as electrons.
- Electric current will flow continually only in a closed path called a circuit.
- A battery produces an electric field in a circuit that causes electrons to flow.

Electric Resistance

- A measure of how difficult it is for electrons to flow in a material is electric resistance.
- Electric resistance results from the collisions between electrons flowing in a current and the atoms and other charges in the circuit.

Electrical Energy and Voltage

- An electric current transfers electrical energy to a circuit.
- A battery transforms chemical energy into electrical energy.
- Voltage is a measure of the electrical energy transferred by an electron as it moves from one point to another in a circuit.

Self Check

1. **Describe** how the charge on a wire changes when an electric current flows in the wire. `SC.C.2.3.1`
2. **Explain** what causes electrons in an electric current to flow slowly in a circuit. `SC.A.2.3.2`
3. **Describe** the process that causes electrical energy to be transformed into thermal energy and light energy as a current flows in a lightbulb. `SC.B.1.3.4`
4. **Determine** how the current in a circuit changes if the voltage in the circuit is decreased and the resistance remains the same.
5. **Think Critically** Two lightbulbs are connected in a series circuit. If the current flowing in one lightbulb is 0.5 A, what is the current flowing in the other lightbulb? Explain. `SC.B.1.3.4`

Applying Math

6. **Calculate Voltage** A hairdryer with a resistance of 10.0 Ω is plugged into an electrical outlet. If the current in the hairdryer is 11 A, what is the voltage? `MA.D.2.3.1`
7. **Calculate Resistance** What is the resistance of a loudspeaker connected to a 9.0-V battery if the current in the speaker is 0.3 A? `MA.D.2.3.1`

Benchmark—SC.H.1.3.4: The student knows that accurate record keeping, openness, and replication are essential to maintaining an investigator's credibility with other scientists and society; **SC.H.1.3.5:** The student knows that a change in one or more variables may alter the outcome of an investigation.

Batteries in Series and Parallel

Many battery-powered devices use more than one battery to supply electrical energy. Why are these batteries usually connected so that a positive terminal is in contact with a negative terminal?

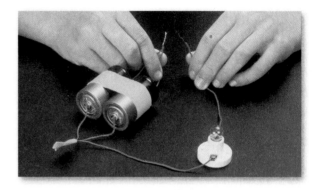

⊙ Real-World Problem

How does the way that batteries are connected affect the voltage they provide?

Goals
- **Infer** how the voltage produced by two batteries in a circuit depends on how they are connected.

Materials
1.5-V lightbulbs (2)
1.5-V batteries (3)
minibulb sockets (2)
10-cm lengths of insulated wire (8)
tape

Safety Precautions 🥽 🧤 🔥

Complete a safety worksheet before you begin.

⊙ Procedure

1. Make a brightness tester by connecting one battery to a lightbulb. Disconnect one wire after you've made the lightbulb glow.

2. Tape two batteries together in series so that the positive terminal of one battery touches the negative terminal of the other battery.

3. Connect the batteries to a lightbulb. Close the circuit in the brightness tester and compare the brightness of the lightbulbs. Record your observations.

4. Tape two batteries together in parallel side-by-side with positive terminals on one end and negative terminals on the other end.

5. Tape a wire to each battery terminal. Twist together the ends of the wires connected to both negative terminals. Do the same for the wires connected to the positive terminals.

6. Repeat step 3.

⊙ Conclude and Apply

1. **Infer** If the brightness of a lightbulb increases as the current in a circuit increases, in which circuit was the current the largest?

2. **Apply** Ohm's law to determine in which circuit the voltage was the largest.

3. **Compare** the voltage provided by two batteries in series and in parallel.

*C*ommunicating Your Data

Compare your conclusions with those of other students in your class. **For more help, refer to the** Science Skill Handbook.

section 3

Magnetism

as you read

What You'll Learn

- **Describe** how magnets exert forces on each other.
- **Explain** why some materials are magnetic.
- **Describe** how objects become temporary magnets.
- **Explain** how an electric generator produces electrical energy.

Why It's Important

Magnetism helps produce the electrical energy you obtain from electrical outlets.

Review Vocabulary

* **magnetic:** able to exert a non-contact force that can attract iron, cobalt, nickel, and certain other materials

New Vocabulary

* **magnetic field**
• magnetic domain
• electromagnet
• electromagnetic induction

* FCAT Vocabulary

Magnets

Did you use a magnet today? If you've watched TV, listened to a CD, dried your hair with a hairdryer, or used a computer, the answer is yes. Magnets are a part of all these devices and many others. Magnets can exert forces on objects that are made from, or contain, magnetic materials. Magnets also exert forces on other magnets. It is the forces exerted by magnets that make them so useful.

Magnetic Poles Every magnet has two ends or sides. Each of the ends or sides is a magnetic pole. There are two types of magnetic poles. One is a north pole and the other is a south pole. Every magnet has a north pole and a south pole. For example, one end of a bar magnet is a south pole and the other end is a north pole. For a magnet in the shape of a disc or a ring, one side is a north pole and the other side is a south pole.

✔ **Reading Check** *Where would the poles of a magnet shaped like a horseshoe be located?*

The Forces Between Magnetic Poles The magnetic poles of a magnet exert forces on the magnetic poles of other magnets, as shown in **Figure 18.** If two north poles or two south poles are moved toward each other, they repel. If the north pole of one magnet is brought toward the south pole of another magnet, the magnets attract each other. In other words, like poles repel and unlike poles attract. The magnetic forces between two magnets become stronger as the magnets move closer together, and weaker as they move farther apart.

Figure 18 The magnetic forces between magnetic poles are attractive between unlike poles and repulsive between like poles. **Compare** *the forces between magnetic poles to the forces between electric charges.*

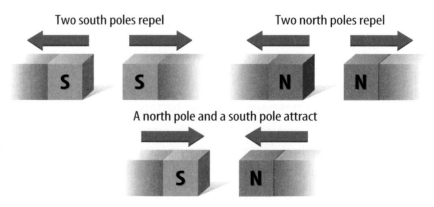

Two south poles repel   Two north poles repel

A north pole and a south pole attract

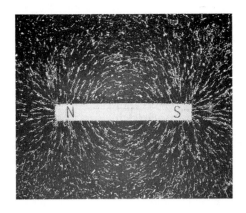
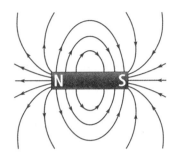

Figure 19 Iron filings sprinkled around a bar magnet show the magnetic field lines. Magnetic field lines always connect the north and south poles of a magnet.

Magnetic Field If you hold two like poles of two magnets near each other, you can feel them push each other apart, even though they are not touching. Recall that electric charges exert forces on each other even if they are not touching. This is because an electric charge is surrounded by an electric field.

In a similar way, a magnet is surrounded by a magnetic field that exerts forces on other magnets. However, not only is a magnet surrounded by a magnetic field but so is a moving electric charge. A **magnetic field** is the region of space surrounding a magnet or a moving charge where a magnetic force is exerted on other magnets and moving charges.

The magnetic field around a bar magnet is shown in **Figure 19.** Iron filings sprinkled around a bar magnet line up to form a pattern of curved lines. These lines are called magnetic field lines. Magnetic field lines help show the direction of the magnetic field around a magnet.

Magnetic Materials

A paper clip will stick to a magnet, but a piece of aluminum foil won't stick. Both the paper clip and the aluminum are metal. Why is one attracted to the magnet and the other is not?

Only metals that contain the elements iron, nickel, cobalt, and a few other rare-earth elements are attracted to magnets. Materials that contain these elements are magnetic materials. Magnets also contain one or more of these metals. The steel paper clip contains iron and therefore is a magnetic material.

Why are some materials magnetic? All atoms contain moving electrons. These moving charges are surrounded by magnetic fields. In the atoms of most elements these magnetic fields cancel. As a result, atoms of these elements are not surrounded by a magnetic field and are not magnets. However, in atoms of magnetic materials, such as iron, cobalt, and nickel, these magnetic fields do not cancel. The atoms of these elements are tiny magnets with a north pole and a south pole.

Earth's Magnetic Field
Earth is surrounded by a magnetic field that is similar to the magnetic field around a bar magnet. Earth's magnetic poles are located near the geographic north pole and south pole. A compass uses Earth's magnetic field to help determine direction. Because a compass needle is a magnet, it rotates so it points toward Earth's magnetic poles. As a result, the north end of a compass needle points north.

Figure 20 This spoon is made of a magnetic alloy. The spoon is not a magnet because the magnetic poles of the magnetic domains point in random directions.
Explain *why the spoon is not surrounded by a magnetic field.*

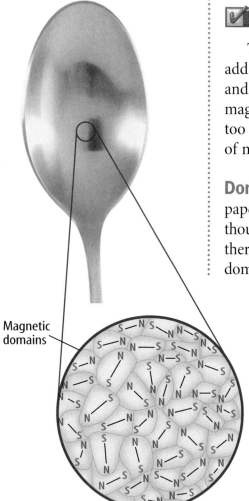

Magnetic domains

Magnetic Domains In a magnetic material, forces that atoms exert on each other cause the magnetic fields surrounding atoms to point in the same direction. As a result, large numbers of atoms have their like magnetic poles pointing in the same direction. A group of atoms that have their like magnetic poles pointing in the same direction is called a **magnetic domain. Figure 20** shows how the atoms in a magnetic material form magnetic domains.

Reading Check *What are magnetic domains?*

The magnetic fields of all the atoms in a magnetic domain add together. As a result, each magnetic domain has a north pole and a south pole and is surrounded by a magnetic field. A single magnetic domain may contain trillions of atoms, but it is still too small to see. Even a small piece of iron may contain billions of magnetic domains.

Domains Line Up in Permanent Magnets Why do the paper clips stick to a bar magnet but not to each other? Even though they both are made of magnetic material, iron, they neither attract nor repel each other. In a paper clip the magnetic domains are oriented in random directions, as shown in **Figure 21.**

Because the magnetic fields around the domains are in random directions, they cancel out. As a result, the paper clip is not surrounded by a magnetic field.

Figure 21 shows that in a permanent magnet, such as a bar magnet, most of the domains are oriented in a single direction. As a result, the magnetic fields around the domains don't cancel out. Instead, these magnetic fields add together to form a stronger magnetic field. The magnetic field that surrounds the magnet is the combination of the magnetic fields around the magnetic domains.

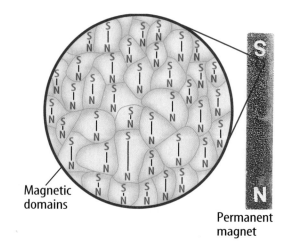

Magnetic domains

Permanent magnet

Figure 21 In a permanent magnet, most of the like poles of the magnetic domains point in the same direction.
Explain *why the magnet is surrounded by a magnetic field.*

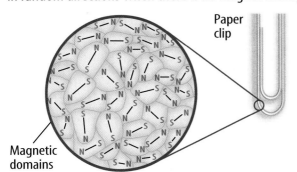

The poles of the magnetic domains in the paper clip point in random directions when there is no magnet nearby.

Paper clip

Magnetic domains

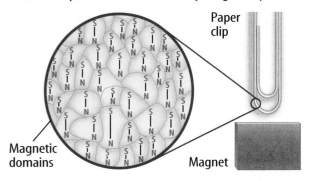

The force exerted by the magnet on the domains causes them to point toward the nearby magnetic pole.

Paper clip

Magnetic domains

Magnet

Why are magnetic materials attracted to a magnet?

A paper clip is not a magnet, but it contains magnetic domains that are small magnets. Usually, these domains point in all directions. However, when a permanent magnet comes close to the paper clip, the magnetic field of the magnet exerts forces on the magnetic domains of the paper clip. These forces cause the magnetic poles of the domains to line up and point in a single direction when a permanent magnet is nearby, as shown in **Figure 22.** The nearby pole of the permanent magnet is always next to the opposite poles of the magnetic domains. This causes the paper clip to be attracted to the magnet.

Because the domains are lined up, their magnetic fields no longer cancel out. As long as the domains in the paper clip are lined up, the paper clip is a temporary magnet with a north pole and a south pole.

Electromagnetism

Even though they might seem to be different, electricity and magnetism are related. Recall that a moving electric charge is surrounded by a magnetic field. As a result, magnetic fields are produced by electric charges in motion. This connection between electricity and magnetism often is called electromagnetism. Electrons are flowing in a current-carrying wire, and this produces a magnetic field around the wire.

Electromagnets The magnetic field produced by a current-carrying wire can be made much stronger by wrapping the wire around an iron core. A current-carrying wire wrapped around an iron core is an **electromagnet.** Just like a bar magnet, one end of an electromagnet is a north magnetic pole and the other end is a south magnetic pole, as **Figure 23** shows. However, if the direction of current flow in the wire coil of an electromagnet is reversed, then the north and south poles switch places.

Figure 22 A paper clip that contains iron becomes a temporary magnet when a permanent magnet is nearby.

Mini LAB

Observing Magnetic Force on a Wire

Procedure
1. Complete a safety worksheet.
2. Connect one end of a **50-cm piece of 22-gauge wire** to one terminal of a **D-cell battery.**
3. Form the wire into a loop and place one pole of a **bar magnet** about 2 cm outside the loop.
4. Touch the wire's free end to the other battery terminal. Record your observations.
5. Repeat step 4 with the connections to the battery terminals reversed.

Analysis
1. Explain how your observations show that a current in the wire produces a magnetic field.
2. Infer how the magnetic field around the wire depends on the direction of current in the wire.

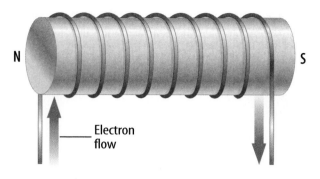

Figure 23 An electromagnet has north and south magnetic poles, and can be attracted or repelled by a permanent magnet. **Describe** *how the magnetic field around the electromagnet changes if the current in the coil is decreased.*

Figure 24 When the wire loop rotates in the magnetic field of the permanent magnet, an electric current flows in the lightbulb.

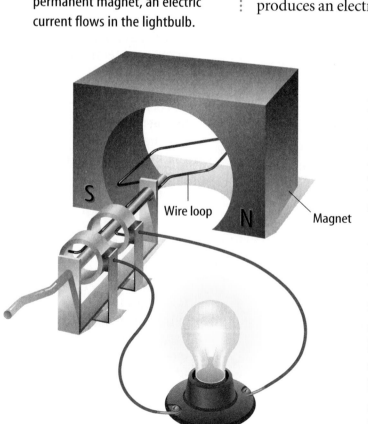

Using Electromagnets The strength of the magnetic field produced by an electromagnet depends on the amount of current flowing in the wire coil. Increasing the amount of current increases the magnetic field strength. However, the magnetic field disappears if no current flows in the coil. As a result, an electromagnet is a temporary magnet whose magnetic properties can be controlled. Because of this, electromagnets are used in many devices, including doorbells, telephones, CD players, and computers.

Generating Electric Current

If an electric current produces a magnetic field, can a magnetic field be used to produce an electric current? The answer is yes. If a magnet is moved through a wire loop that is part of a circuit, an electric current flows in the circuit. The current flows only as long as the magnet is moving. A current also flows in the circuit if it is the wire loop that moves and the magnet that is at rest. The production of an electric current by moving a magnet and a loop relative to each other is called **electromagnetic induction.**

Remember that a battery produces an electric field in a circuit that causes electrons to flow. Electromagnetic induction also produces an electric field in a circuit that causes electrons to flow.

Electric Generators You plug a lamp into an electrical outlet and turn the switch on. Immediately, an electric current flows in the lamp, causing the lightbulb to glow. Electrical energy is supplied to the lamp through the electric field created in the lamp. However, when you plug a device into an electrical outlet, the electrical energy used is produced by an electric generator instead of a battery.

Figure 24 shows a simple electrical generator. A loop of wire is rotated within a magnetic field. The motion of the wire loop with respect to the magnetic field produces an electrical field in the wire. This electrical field causes a current to flow. Current continues to flow as long as the wire loop is kept rotating. To keep the wire loop rotating, mechanical energy must be continually supplied to the generator. As a result, a generator converts mechanical energy into electrical energy.

Power Plants The electrical energy you obtain from an electrical outlet is produced by generators in electric power plants. In these generators electromagnets are rotated past wire coils. To rotate the magnets, power plants use mechanical energy in the form of the kinetic energy of moving steam or moving water into electrical energy.

In some power plants fossil fuels are burned to heat water and produce steam that is used to spin generators. In hydroelectric power plants, the flow of water from behind a dam provides the mechanical energy that is transformed into electrical energy, as shown in **Figure 25.**

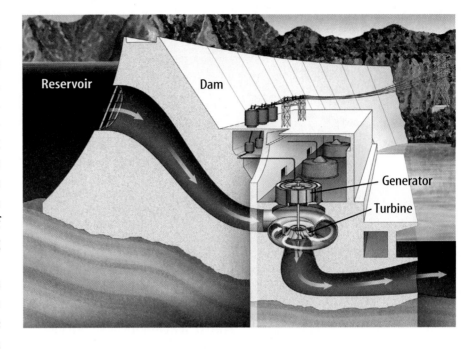

Figure 25 In a hydroelectric plant, the kinetic energy of falling water is converted into electrical energy by a generator.

section 3 review

Summary

Magnets

- All magnets have a north pole and a south pole.
- Like magnetic poles repel each other and unlike magnetic poles attract each other.
- A magnet is surrounded by a magnetic field that exerts a force on other magnets.

Magnetic Materials

- Individual atoms are magnets in magnetic materials such as iron, cobalt, and nickel.
- Magnetic domains contain atoms with their like magnetic poles pointing in the same direction.
- The magnetic domains in a permanent magnet have their magnetic poles aligned.

Electromagnetism

- An electric current is surrounded by a magnetic field.
- An electric current can be produced by the relative motion of a magnet and a wire loop.

Self Check

1. **Compare and contrast** a permanent magnet and a temporary magnet made from a magnetic material.
2. **Explain** why an object made from aluminum will not stick to a magnet.
3. **Compare and contrast** an electric generator and a battery.
4. **Identify** the circumstances that would cause an aluminum wire to be attracted or repelled by a magnet. SC.H.1.3.5
5. **Compare and contrast** an electromagnet and a permanent magnet.
6. **Think Critically** The north pole of one magnet is attracted only to the south pole of another magnet. However, a paper clip will stick to either the north pole or the south pole of a bar magnet. Explain.

Applying Math

7. **Solve a Simple Equation** A certain power plant generates enough electrical energy to supply 100,000 homes. How many of these power plants would be needed to generate enough energy for 2,000,000 homes? MA.D.2.3.1

Benchmark—**SC.C.2.3.1:** The student knows that many forces (e.g., gravitational, electrical, and magnetic) act at a distance (i.e., without contact); **SC.H.1.3.5:** The student knows that a change in one or more variables may alter the outcome of an investigation.

Magnets and Electric Current

▶ Real-World Problem

Have you ever used a compass? The needle in a compass is a small bar magnet with a north pole and a south pole. Because a compass needle is a magnet, other magnets and magnetic fields can cause a compass needle to move. As a result, a compass can be used to detect the presence of a magnetic field. An electric current flowing in a wire is surrounded by a magnetic field. How does an electric current affect a compass needle?

Goals

- **Observe** the effects of a bar magnet on a compass.
- **Observe** the effects of a current-carrying wire on a compass.
- **Observe** how the relative motion of a magnet and a wire coil affects a compass.

Materials

bar magnet
compass
D-cell batteries (2)
3-m length of insulated wire
50-cm length of insulated wire
tape

Safety Precautions

Complete a safety worksheet before you begin.

▶ Procedure

1. Make a data table similar to the one below.

Effects of Magnets and Current on a Compass

Situation	Effect on Compass
Bar magnet nearby	
Current-carrying wire nearby	**Do not write in this book.**
Magnet moves in coil	
Coil moves past magnet	

2. Place a compass on the table top. Place one pole of a bar magnet next to the compass. Record your observations.

3. Make a battery pack by taping two D-cell batteries together so the negative terminal of one battery is in contact with the positive terminal of the other battery.

4. Tape one end of the 50-cm wire to the exposed positive terminal of the battery pack.

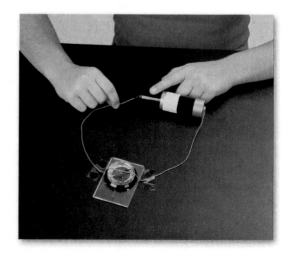

5. Place the wire on top of the compass and position the wire so it lines up with the compass needle. Touch the free end of the wire to the other terminal of the battery pack for a few seconds. Record your observations.

6. Wrap the long piece of wire around three fingers about 25 times so there is about 3 cm of wire left at each end. Tape the coil so it doesn't unravel.

7. Wrap the 50-cm wire around the compass several times so there is about 3 cm of wire left at each end. Connect the ends of the wire from the compass with the ends of the wire from the coil.

8. Hold the bar magnet in the center of the coil. Keeping the coil stationary, move the magnet quickly back and forth. Record your observations.

9. Hold the bar magnet in the center of the coil. Keeping the magnet stationary, move the coil quickly back and forth. Record your observations.

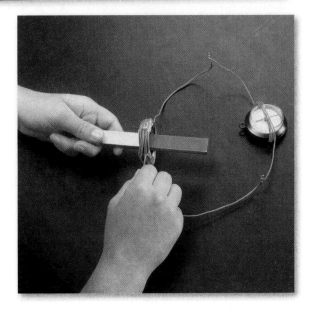

◉ *Analyze Your Data*

1. **Describe** how the bar magnet affected the compass when the magnet was placed next to it.

2. **Describe** how the compass was affected when an electric current flowed in the wire that had been placed on top of the compass.

3. **Compare** how the compass was affected when the magnet was moved inside the stationary wire coil and when the wire coil was moved past the stationary magnet.

◉ *Conclude and Apply*

1. **Compare** the effect of the bar magnet on the compass and the effect of the current-carrying wire on the compass.

2. **Infer** why the current-carrying wire had the effect on the compass that you observed.

3. **Infer** whether a current flowed in the wire coil when the coil and the magnet were moving relative to each other. Which observations support your conclusion?

*C*ommunicating

Compare your observations with those of other students in your class. Which actions caused the compass needle to move the most?

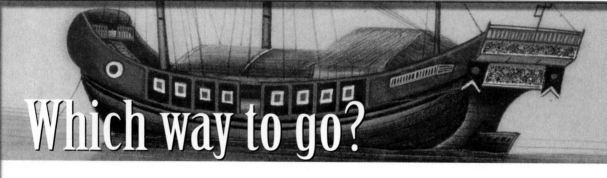

Which way to go?

The first record of boats large enough to carry trade goods is around 3500 B.C. The first navigators sailed close to shore and navigated by land characteristics that they could see by day. Sailing at night was impossible. Eventually, sailors learned to find their way by using the position of the Sun and stars. Using their knowledge of the heavens and the ocean currents, Vikings and Polynesians traveled remarkable distances, far from the sight of land. But what happened on cloudy nights?

Kissing Rocks

The Chinese had discovered the solution more than 2,000 years ago. They found interesting rocks that they called *tzhu shih*—loving stones, because they liked to "kiss." These rocks contained magnetite, a mineral containing magnetic iron oxide.

The compass on the right was used by sailors during the 18th century. The compass on the left is a modern compass.

The Chinese realized that they could use the magnetite to magnetize iron needles. When the needles floated in water, they always pointed north and south. They had made the first compass!

Earth's Magnetic Field

Earth's iron core produces a magnetic field similar to the field of a huge bar magnet. A compass needle rotates until its north and south poles point toward Earth's opposite magnetic poles, which are close to the geographic north and south poles. So whether it was clear or cloudy, the compass allowed sailors to travel great distances and to return home safely!

A modern GPS receiver uses a system of satellites to determine its position on Earth's surface.

The World Opens Up

Between the 13th and 19th centuries, there were many improvements to the compass. The ability to travel the seas opened trade between distant cultures. Goods and customs were exchanged, leading to the development of new ideas and tools. Knowing which way to go in rain or shine opened up the world.

Brainstorm Imagine that you are an early sailor before the invention of the compass. What would limit your knowledge of the world? How far could you travel by boat? What kinds of trips might you take? How would the compass change your lifestyle and your culture?

TIME

For more information, visit
fl6.msscience.com

Reviewing Main Ideas

Section 1 Electric Charge and Forces

1. Positive and negative charges are surrounded by an electric field that exerts forces on other charges.

2. Two positive or two negative charges repel each other; a positive and a negative charge attract each other.

3. Charges can be transferred from one object to another. Charges in an object can be rearranged by an electric field.

Section 2 Electric Current

1. An electric current is the flow of electric charges. A current will flow continually in a closed path called a circuit.

2. An electric field in a circuit causes charges to flow and transfer electrical energy.

3. Resistance is a measure of how difficult it is for electrons to flow in a material.

4. Voltage is a measure of the energy transferred by an electron as it flows in a circuit.

Section 3 Magnetism

1. A magnet has a north pole and a south pole and is surrounded by a magnetic field.

2. Like magnetic poles repel each other and unlike poles attract each other.

3. Some materials are magnetic because their atoms behave like magnets.

4. An electric current is surrounded by a magnetic field. Moving a wire loop and a magnet past each other produces a current.

Visualizing Main Ideas

Copy and complete the following concept map on electric current.

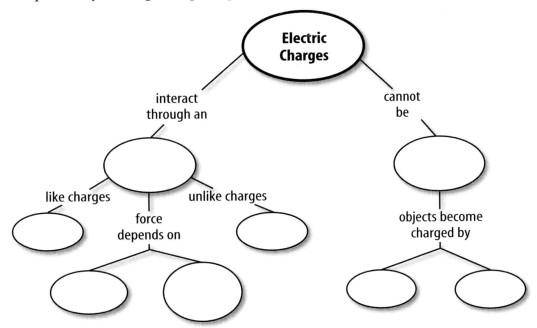

Using Vocabulary

✱ circuit p. 570	insulator p. 565
conductor p. 565	magnetic domain p. 580
electric current p. 569	✱ magnetic field p. 579
electric discharge p. 566	✱ neutral p. 562
electric field p. 564	parallel circuit p. 576
electric resistance p. 571	series circuit p. 576
electromagnet p. 581	static charge p. 566
electromagnetic induction p. 582	voltage p. 573

✱ FCAT Vocabulary

Complete each statement using a word(s) from the vocabulary list above.

1. A(n) _____ is a closed path that electric current can follow.

2. In a(n) _____, electric charges can move easily.

3. A(n) _____ has more than one path for electric current to follow.

4. An object that does not contain equal amounts of positive charge and negative charge has a(n) _____.

5. A(n) _____ is the flow of electric charges.

6. _____ is a measure of the energy electrons transfer to a circuit as they flow.

7. A(n) _____ is made of a current-carrying wire wrapped around an iron core.

8. A measure of how difficult it is for current to flow in an object is its _____.

Checking Concepts

Choose the word or phrase that best answers the question.

9. Which of the following causes current to flow in a wire?   SC.C.2.3.1
   A) electric field
   B) electric circuit
   C) electric resistance
   D) magnetic domains

10. Which of the following energy conversions occurs inside a battery?
    A) electrical to chemical
    B) chemical to electrical
    C) thermal to electrical
    D) thermal to chemical

11. How does the electric force between two electrons change as they get farther apart?
    A) The force stays the same.
    B) The force increases.
    C) The force decreases.
    D) The force switches direction.

12. Every electric charge is surrounded by which of the following?   SC.C.2.3.1
    A) electric field
    B) electric resistance
    C) electric current
    D) magnetic domains

13. Which of the following is true about a permanent magnet?
    A) Its domains are lined up.
    B) It contains an iron core.
    C) Its domains are randomly oriented.
    D) It contains a current-carrying wire.

14. What does a simple generator rotate in a magnetic field to produce current?
    A) a battery   C) a magnet
    B) a wire loop   D) domains

15. Increasing the voltage in a circuit increases which of the following in the circuit?
    A) the electric resistance
    B) the energy transferred to the circuit
    C) the static charge
    D) the number of charges

16. Which of the following does **NOT** describe the magnetic force between two magnets?
    A) Like poles repel.
    B) Like poles attract.
    C) It decreases as the magnets move apart.
    D) Unlike poles attract.

Vocabulary PuzzleMaker fl6.msscience.com

Thinking Critically

17. Compare the force of gravity to the forces between electric charges. `SC.C.2.3.1`

18. Explain why an electron can push another electron even though both electrons are not touching. `SC.C.2.3.1`

19. Explain why a charged balloon does not attract a person's hair if the balloon is far from the person's head.

20. Determine how the total charge on a doorknob changes when the doorknob is charged by an electric field.

Use the table below to answer questions 21–23.

Effect of Battery Voltage on Current

Battery	Battery Voltage (V)	Current in Circuit (A)
A	2	0.2
B	4	0.4
C	6	0.6
D	10	1.0

21. Make a Graph The table above shows the current measured in a circuit when different batteries are connected in the circuit. For each battery, plot the current on the vertical axis and the battery voltage on the horizontal axis. Describe the shape of the plotted line.

22. Infer from your graph the current in the circuit if the battery voltage is 8 V.

23. Predict from the table above the current in the circuit if the battery voltage is 12 V.

24. Explain why even though aluminum and iron are both metals, aluminum is not a magnetic material, but iron is. `SC.A.2.3.2`

25. Predict whether a generator that is designed to rotate a permanent magnet around a wire loop that doesn't move, will produce electric current. `SC.C.2.3.1`

26. Concept Map Copy and complete the following concept map on magnets.

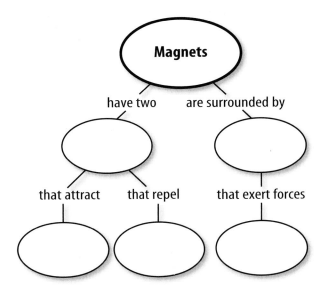

Performance Activities

27. Electricity Usage Determine the number of hours in a week that you and your family spend using certain electrical appliances. Choose three appliances. Put paper and a pencil by each one so that each person can write down the amount of time they are used. Which appliance is used the most?

Applying Math

28. Lightbulb A 100-W lightbulb has a resistance of 120 Ω. If the lightbulb is connected into a circuit in which the voltage is 110 V, what is the current in the lightbulb? `MA.D.2.3.1`

29. Battery The voltage of a battery in a circuit is increased from 3 V to 4.5 V. If the resistance in the circuit is 5 Ω, calculate the percentage change in the current. `MA.D.2.3.1`

 The assessed Florida Benchmark appears above each question.
Record your answers on the answer sheet provided by your teacher or on a sheet of paper.

Multiple Choice

SC.A.2.3.2

1 Which of the following is **true** of an object that is negatively charged?

A. It has more neutrons than protons.

B. It has more protons than electrons.

C. It has more protons than neutrons.

D. It has more electrons than protons.

SC.A.2.3.2

2 Which will cause the electric force between two charged objects to become stronger?

F. The objects getting smaller.

G. The objects moving faster.

H. The objects moving closer together.

I. The objects losing some of their charge.

SC.B.1.3.1

3 The table below shows the currents and voltages for four circuits.

Current and Voltage in Circuits		
Circuit Number	Voltage (volts)	Current (amps)
1	6	0.1
2	9	0.05
3	12	0.075
4	15	0.25

Which circuits have the same resistance?

A. circuits 1 and 2

B. circuits 1 and 4

C. circuits 2 and 3

D. circuits 3 and 4

SC.B.1.3.1

4 Kenneth is investigating electromagnets. He made the three electromagnets shown in the diagram below.

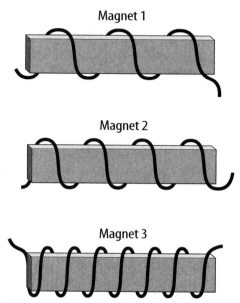

Magnet 1

Magnet 2

Magnet 3

If the amount of electrical current flowing through the coils of each electromagnet is the same, which statement is **true** about Kenneth's electromagnets?

F. Magnet 1 will produce the strongest magnetic field.

G. Magnet 3 will produce the strongest magnetic field.

H. Magnet 2 will produce the weakest magnetic field.

I. All three electromagnets have the same magnetic field.

 SC.C.2.3.1

5 Which of the following is **true** of the electric force between two electric charges?

  A. It is always attractive.

  B. It is always repulsive.

  C. It is a contact force.

  D. It can act at a distance.

 SC.C.2.3.1

6 What happens when an object with a positive charge is brought near an object with a negative charge?

  F. The objects repel one another.

  G. The objects become magnets.

  H. The objects lose their charges.

  I. The objects attract one another.

 Gridded Response

SC.B.1.3.1

7 An electric circuit is shown in the diagram below.

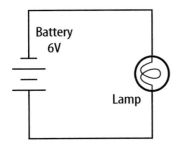

Battery
6V

Lamp

If the resistance of the circuit is 3 ohms, what is the current, in amperes, of the circuit?

READ INQUIRE EXPLAIN **Short Response**

SC.H.1.3.5

8 Explain why the current stops flowing in a lightbulb when the filament breaks.

READ INQUIRE EXPLAIN **Extended Response**

SC.H.2.3.1

9 The diagram below shows the electrical circuit inside a flashlight.

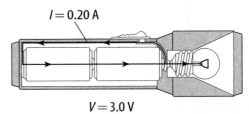

$I = 0.20$ A

$V = 3.0$ V

  PART A Based on the information in the diagram, what is the resistance (in ohms) of the flashlight circuit?

  PART B Explain the transformations in energy that occur in the circuit of the flashlight.

FCAT Tip

Clear Your Calculator When using a calculator, always press clear before starting a new problem.

Sunshine State Standards—**SC.A.2:** The student understands that the types of force that act on an object and the effect of that force can be described, measured, and predicted; **SC.B.1:** The student recognizes that energy may be changed in form with varying efficiency; **SC.C.1:** The student understands that types of motion may be described. . . .

Waves

Catch A Wave

On a breezy day in Maui, Hawaii, wind-surfers ride the ocean waves. Waves transfer energy. You can see the ocean waves in this picture, but there are other waves you cannot see, such as microwaves, radio waves, and sound waves.

Science Journal Write a paragraph about some places where you have seen water waves.

Start-Up Activities

 SC.B.1.3.6

Wave Properties

If you drop a pebble in a pool of water, you notice how the water forms peaks and valleys as the waves spread out in all directions. How could you describe these waves? In this lab you'll make a model of one type of wave.

1. Complete a safety worksheet.
2. Place a piece of thick string about 50 cm long on a table. Form the string into a series of peaks and valleys, where each peak is followed by a valley.
3. Compare your wave model with those of other students. Notice how many peaks you have in your wave model.
4. Reform the string so that you have a different number of peaks.
5. **Think Critically** Write a description of your wave model. How did the distance between peaks change as the number of peaks changed?

 Preview this chapter's content and activities at fl6.msscience.com

 Waves Make the following Foldable to compare and contrast the characteristics of transverse and compressional waves.

LA.A.1.3.4

STEP 1 **Fold** one sheet of paper lengthwise.

STEP 2 **Fold** into thirds.

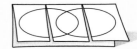

STEP 3 **Unfold and draw** overlapping ovals. **Cut** the top sheet along the folds.

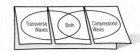

STEP 4 **Label** the ovals as shown.

Construct a Venn Diagram As you read the chapter, list the characteristics unique to transverse waves under the left tab, those unique to compressional waves under the right tab, and those characteristics common to both under the middle tab.

Benchmarks—SC.A.2.3.1 (pp. 595–597): The student describes and compares the properties of particles and waves; SC.C.1.3.2 Annually Assessed (p. 597): The student knows that vibrations in materials set up wave disturbances that spread away from the source (e.g., sound and earthquake waves).

Also covers: SC.B.1.3.3 Annually Assessed (p. 598), SC.B.1.3.6 Annually Assessed (p. 598), SC.H.1.3.5 Annually Assessed (p. 597), SC.H.2.3.1 (p. 594)

section 1

What are waves?

as you read

What You'll Learn

- **Explain** the relationship among waves, energy, and matter.
- **Describe** the difference between transverse waves and compressional waves.

Why It's Important

Waves enable you to see and hear the world around you.

Review Vocabulary

✷ **energy:** the ability to cause change

New Vocabulary

- wave
- ✷ vibration
- transverse wave
- ✷ crest
- ✷ trough
- compressional wave
- electromagnetic wave

✷ FCAT Vocabulary

What is a wave?

When you are relaxing on an air mattress in a pool and someone does a cannonball dive off the diving board, you suddenly might find yourself bobbing up and down. You can make something move by giving it a push or pull, but the person jumping didn't touch your air mattress. How did the energy from the dive travel through the water and move your air mattress? The up-and-down motion was caused by the peaks and valleys of the ripples that spread out from the splash. This pattern of peaks and valleys makes up water waves.

Waves Transfer Energy A **wave** is a disturbance that transfers energy from one place to another without transferring matter. For example, when the student in **Figure 1** throws the ball, the ball has kinetic energy as it moves from place to place. A ball is made of matter, and when the ball is thrown, matter as well as energy moves from place to place. The waves in **Figure 1** also transfer energy as they make the water move up and down. However, even though the waves travel outward from the boat, the water does not travel outward along with the wave. Instead, the wave causes water to move up and down as the wave passes. After the wave passes, the water returns to its initial position.

Figure 1 Water waves and a moving ball both transfer energy from one place to another.

Water waves produced by a boat travel outward, but matter does not move along with the waves.

When the ball is thrown, energy is transferred as matter moves from place to place.

Figure 2 When the people in a stadium do the wave, a disturbance travels around the stadium, but the people in the stadium don't move along with the wave.

A Model For Waves

Have you ever been in a stadium or an arena when the crowd does the wave? In some ways, the stadium wave is like a wave that travels in water. In a stadium wave, a group of people in one part of the stadium stands up, raises their arms, and then sits down. As they sit down, other people nearby stand up, raise their arms, and sit down.

As this process continues, a disruption or disturbance seems to travel around the stadium. The disruption is the change that occurs when people stand up and sit down. Energy is transferred when people stand up and sit down as the wave moves around the stadium. However, even though energy moves from place to place, people don't move along with the wave. After the stadium wave passes, people are sitting in the same seats that they were before the wave reached them. Their positions haven't changed.

 **Reading Check** *What is transferred as a wave moves?*

Annually Assessed Benchmark Check

SC.C.1.3.2 When a guitar is played, sound waves are produced by the vibrations of what objects?

Mechanical Waves

Without the people in the stadium, a stadium wave could not exist. It is the people that enable energy to be transferred from place to place. In a water wave, water molecules transfer energy just as the people transfer energy in a stadium wave. Energy is transferred in a water wave as water molecules exert forces on each other. The types of waves that can travel only through matter are called mechanical waves. The matter through which a mechanical wave travels is called the medium.

Mechanical waves are produced by something that is vibrating. A **vibration** is a repeating back and forth motion. For example, your hand is vibrating when you shake the end of a rope back and forth. The vibrating motion of your hand produces a wave that travels along the rope.

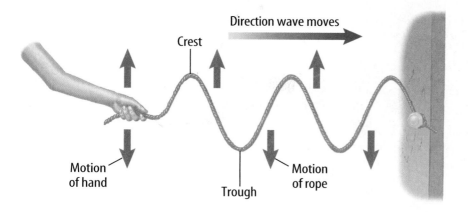

Figure 3 Shaking one end of a rope makes a transverse wave. The rope moves vertically up and down, while the wave moves horizontally to the right.

Transverse Waves In a mechanical **transverse wave,** the wave makes the matter in the medium move at right angles to the direction the wave moves. An example of a transverse wave is shown in **Figure 3.** A person shakes the end of the rope up and down. This causes any part of the rope to move up and down.

The up-and-down motion of the rope produces a transverse wave that travels from the person's hand to the doorknob. The rope is moving vertically up and down, while the wave is traveling horizontally. The motion of the rope is at right angles, or perpendicular, to the motion of the wave.

Shaking one end of the rope up and down makes a transverse wave with a series of peaks and valleys. As **Figure 3** shows, on a transverse wave the high points, or peaks, are called **crests** and the low points, or valleys, are called **troughs.**

Reading Check *What are the highest points of transverse waves called?*

Figure 4 A piece of yarn tied to a coil on a spring shows how a compressional wave causes the coil to move.

The compressional wave starts moving toward the coil with the yarn.

The wave makes the coil move in the direction the wave is traveling.

After the wave passes, the coil moves back to its original position.

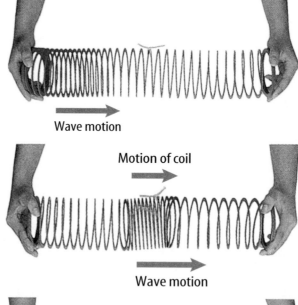

Compressional Waves The other type of mechanical wave is a compressional wave. Another name for a compressional wave is a longitudinal wave. In a **compressional wave,** matter in the medium moves back and forth along the same direction that the wave travels. **Figure 4** shows a compressional wave traveling along a spring. In this example, the coils of the spring are the medium in which the wave travels.

As a compressional wave travels along the spring, the coils of the spring move back and forth. After the compressional wave passes, the coils are in the same place that they were before the wave reached them, as shown in **Figure 4.** Only energy is transferred as the wave moves along the spring.

Sound Waves

Sound waves are compressional waves. Like all waves, sound waves are made by something that is vibrating. If you touch your throat with your fingers when you hum, you can feel vibrations. These vibrations are caused by the vibrations of your vocal cords. If you touch a stereo speaker while it's playing, you can feel the speaker vibrating, too.

Making Sound Waves Something that vibrates in air produces a sound wave. Look at the stereo speaker in **Figure 5.** An electric current causes the speaker cone to vibrate back and forth. As the speaker cone moves outward, air molecules next to it are pushed closer together. This group of air molecules that are closer together is a compression. The compression moves away from the speaker, just as the closely spaced coils moved along the spring.

As the speaker cone moves inward, the air molecules near it have more room and spread farther apart. This group of molecules that are farther apart is a rarefaction (rair eh FAK shun). The rarefaction also moves away from the speaker cone. As the speaker cone vibrates back and forth, it forms a series of compressions and rarefactions that move away and spread out in all directions. This series of compressions and rarefactions is a sound wave.

SC.H.1.3.5
SC.C.1.3.2

Mini LAB

Comparing Sounds

Procedure
1. Complete a safety worksheet.
2. Hold a **wooden ruler** firmly on the edge of your **desk** so that most of it extends off the edge of the desk.
3. Pluck the free end of the ruler so that it vibrates up and down. Pluck the ruler again, using more force.
4. Repeat step 2, moving the ruler about 1 cm further onto the desk each time until only about 5 cm extends off the edge.

Analysis
1. Describe how the sound changed when the ruler was plucked harder.
2. Describe the differences in the sound as the end of the ruler extended farther from the desk.

Figure 5 A speaker cone vibrating in air produces a series of compressions and rarefactions that form a sound wave.
Describe *how compressions and rarefactions are different.*

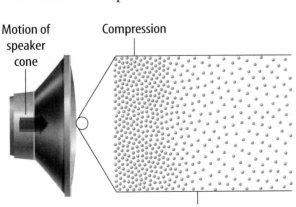

Motion of speaker cone — Compression

Molecules in air

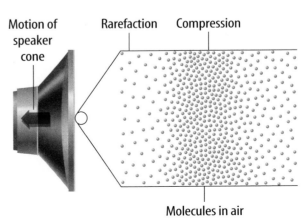

Motion of speaker cone — Rarefaction — Compression

Molecules in air

Global Positioning Systems
Maybe you've used a global positioning system (GPS) receiver to determine your location while driving, boating, or hiking. Earth-orbiting satellites send electromagnetic radio waves that transmit their exact locations and times of transmission. The GPS receiver uses information from four of these satellites to determine your location to within about 16 m.

Electromagnetic Waves

Waves that can travel through space where there is no matter are **electromagnetic waves.** There are different types of electromagnetic waves, including radio waves, infrared waves, visible light waves, ultraviolet waves, X rays, and gamma rays. These waves can travel in matter or in space. Radio waves from TV and radio stations travel through air, and may be reflected from a satellite in space. They then travel through air, through the walls of your house, and to your TV or radio.

Radiant Energy from the Sun The Sun emits electromagnetic waves that travel through space and reach Earth. The energy carried by electromagnetic waves is called radiant energy. Almost 92 percent of the radiant energy that reaches Earth from the Sun is carried by infrared and visible light waves. Infrared waves make you feel warm when you sit in sunlight, and visible light waves enable you to see. A small amount of the radiant energy that reaches Earth from the Sun is carried by ultraviolet waves. These are the waves that can cause sunburn if you are exposed to sunlight for too long.

section 1 review

Summary

What is a wave?

● A wave is a disturbance that transfers energy but not matter.

Mechanical Waves

● Mechanical waves require a medium in which to travel.

● When a transverse wave travels, particles of the medium move at right angles to the direction the wave is traveling.

● When a compressional wave travels, particles of the medium move back and forth along the same direction the wave is traveling.

● Sound is a compressional wave.

Electromagnetic Waves

● Electromagnetic waves can travel through empty space.

● The Sun emits different types of electromagnetic waves, including infrared, visible light, and ultraviolet waves.

Self Check

1. **Describe** the movement of a floating object on a pond when struck by a wave. SC.C.1.3.2

2. **Explain** why a sound wave can't travel from a satellite to Earth. SC.B.1.3.6

3. **Compare and contrast** a transverse wave and a compressional wave. How are they similar and different?

4. **Compare and contrast** a mechanical wave and an electromagnetic wave.

5. **Think Critically** How is it possible for a sound wave to transmit energy but not matter? SC.A.2.3.1

Applying Skills

6. **Concept Map** Create a concept map that shows the relationships among the following: *waves, mechanical waves, electromagnetic waves, compressional waves,* and *transverse waves.*

7. **Use a Word Processor** Use word-processing software to write short descriptions of the waves you encounter during a typical day.

section 2

Also covers: SC.H.1.3.5 Annually Assessed (p. 604), SC.H.2.3.1 (p. 602)

Wave Properties

Amplitude

Imagine that you are shaking one end of a rope tied to a doorknob. How could you describe the waves that you make? One way is to tell how high the crests are or how low the troughs are. The height of the crests or depth of the troughs is measured from the rest position of the rope. The rope's rest position is its position when no wave is moving on the rope. **Figure 6** shows the rest position for the rope tied to the doorknob. The **amplitude** of a transverse wave is the distance of a crest or a trough from the rest position, as shown in **Figure 6.** The amplitude of a transverse wave increases as the crests become higher and the troughs become deeper.

Amplitude and Energy Waves transfer energy from one place to another. The amount of energy transferred by a wave is related to the amplitude of the wave. Waves with larger amplitudes transfer more energy than waves with smaller amplitudes. For example, you might have stood at the ocean shore and felt small waves break against your legs. These waves have only a small amplitude and don't carry enough energy to push you around. But a higher ocean wave can crash into you and knock you over. The higher ocean wave has a larger amplitude and carries more energy than the smaller wave.

as you read

What **You'll Learn**

■ **Describe** the relationship between the frequency and wavelength of a wave.
■ **Explain** why waves travel at different speeds.

Why **It's Important**

The properties of a wave determine whether the wave is useful or dangerous.

Review Vocabulary
✳ **speed:** the distance traveled divided by the time needed to travel the distance

New Vocabulary
✳ **amplitude**
✳ **wavelength**
✳ **frequency**

✳ FCAT Vocabulary

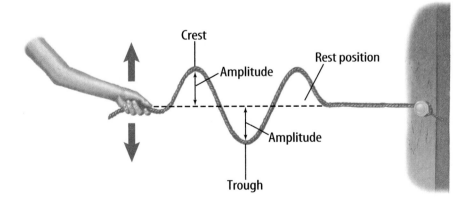

Crest
Amplitude
Rest position
Amplitude
Trough

Figure 6 The position of the rope before the wave reaches it is the rest position. The distance of a crest or a trough from the rest position is the amplitude of the wave.
Compare *the distance of a crest and a trough from the rest position.*

For transverse waves, wavelength is the distance from crest to crest or trough to trough.

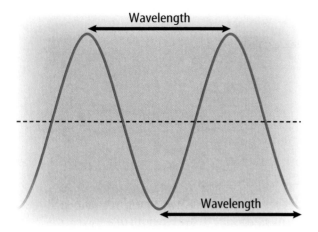

For compressional waves, wavelength is the distance from compression to compression or rarefaction to rarefaction.

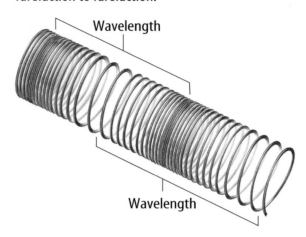

Figure 7 A transverse or a compressional wave has a wavelength.

Figure 8 The range of wavelengths of electromagnetic waves is the electromagnetic spectrum.

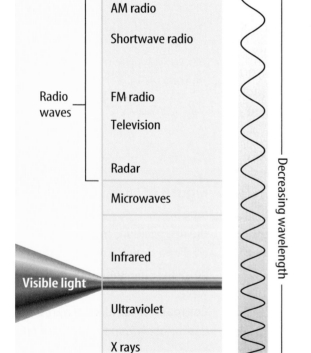

INTEGRATE Earth Science

The devastating effect that a wave with large amplitude can have is seen in the aftermath of tsunamis. Tsunamis are huge sea waves that are caused by underwater earthquakes along faults on the seafloor. The movement of the seafloor along a fault produces the wave. As the wave moves toward shallow water and slows down, the amplitude of the wave grows. The tremendous amounts of energy tsunamis carry cause great damage when they move ashore.

Wavelength

Another way to describe a wave is by its wavelength. **Figure 7** shows the wavelength of a transverse wave and a compressional wave. For a transverse wave, **wavelength** is the distance from one crest to the next crest, or from one trough to the next trough. For a compressional wave, the wavelength is the distance between the center of one compression and the center of the next compression, or from the center of one rarefaction to the center of the next rarefaction.

Electromagnetic waves have wavelengths that range from kilometers, for radio waves, to less than the diameter of an atom, for X rays and gamma rays. This range is called the electromagnetic spectrum. **Figure 8** shows the names given to different parts of the electromagnetic spectrum. Visible light is only a small part of the electromagnetic spectrum. It is the wavelength of visible light waves that determines their color. For example, the wavelength of red light waves is longer than the wavelength of green light waves.

Frequency

The **frequency** of a wave is the number of wavelengths that pass a given point in 1 s. The unit of frequency is the number of wavelengths per second, or hertz (Hz). If the number of wavelengths that pass by a point is known, the frequency of the wave can be calculated from this equation:

Frequency Equation

$$\text{frequency (in Hz)} = \frac{\text{number of wavelengths}}{\text{time (in s)}}$$

$$f = \frac{n}{t}$$

For example, if five wavelengths pass by a point in 1 s, the frequency is

$$f = \frac{n}{t} = \frac{5}{1\ \text{s}} = 5\ \text{Hz}$$

A Sidewalk Model For waves that travel with the same speed, frequency and wavelength are related. To model this relationship, imagine people on two parallel moving sidewalks in an airport, as shown in **Figure 9.** The left sidewalk has four travelers spaced 4 m apart. The right sidewalk has 16 travelers spaced 1 m apart.

Now imagine that both sidewalks are moving at the same speed and approaching a pillar between them. On which sidewalk will more people go past the pillar? On the right sidewalk, four people will pass the pillar for each one person on the other sidewalk. When four people pass the pillar on the left sidewalk, 16 people pass the pillar on the right sidewalk.

Figure 9 When people are farther apart on a moving sidewalk, fewer people pass the pillar every minute.
Infer *how the number of people passing the pillar each minute would change if the sidewalk moved slower.*

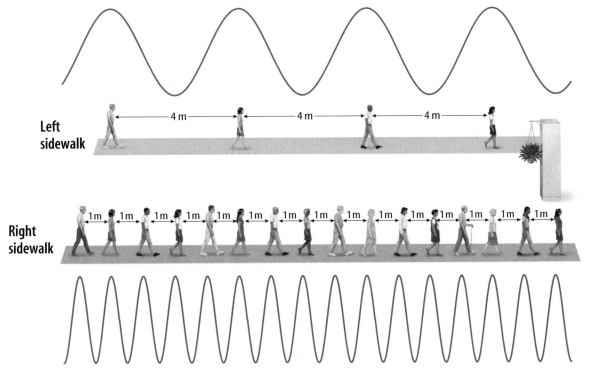

LA.A.1.3.4

INTEGRATE Health

Ultrasonic Waves Sound waves with ultra-high frequencies cannot be heard by the human ear, but they are used by medical professionals in several ways. They are used to perform echocardiograms of the heart, produce ultrasound images of internal organs, break up blockages in arteries, and sterilize surgical instruments. Describe how the wavelengths of these sound waves compare to sound waves you can hear.

Figure 10 The frequency of the notes on a musical scale increases as the notes get higher in pitch, but the wavelength of the notes decreases.

Frequency and Wavelength Suppose that each person in **Figure 9** represents the crest of a wave. Then the pattern of movement of people on the left sidewalk is like a wave with a wavelength of 4 m. For the right sidewalk, the wavelength would be 1 m. On the left sidewalk, where the wavelength is longer, the people pass the pillar *less* frequently. Smaller frequencies result in longer wavelengths. On the right sidewalk, where the wavelength is shorter, the people pass the pillar *more* frequently. Higher frequencies result in shorter wavelengths. This is true for all waves that travel at the same speed. As the frequency of a wave increases, its wavelength decreases.

✔ **Reading Check** *How are frequency and wavelength related?*

Color and Pitch Because frequency and wavelength are related, either the wavelength or frequency of a light wave determines the color of the light. For example, blue light has a larger frequency and shorter wavelength than red light.

Either the wavelength or frequency determines the pitch of a sound wave. Pitch is how high or low a sound seems to be. When you sing a musical scale, the pitch and frequency increase from note to note. Wavelength and frequency are also related for sound waves traveling in air. As the frequency of sound waves increases, their wavelength decreases. **Figure 10** shows how the frequency and wavelength change for notes on a musical scale.

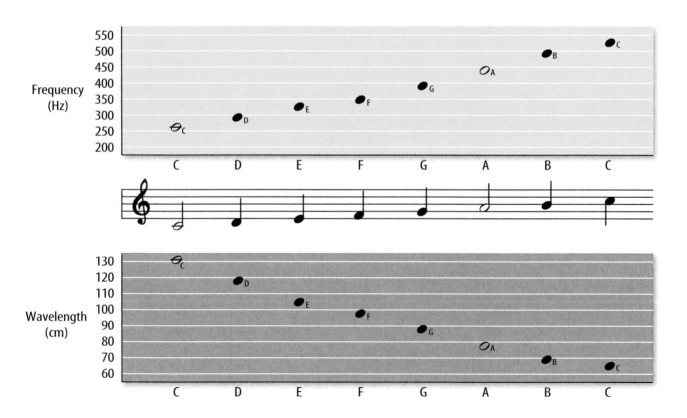

Wave Speed

You've probably watched a thunderstorm on a hot summer day and seen the flashes of lightning. If the storm is several kilometers away, you usually hear the thunder seconds after you see the lightning. This happens because light travels much faster in air than sound does. In air, light travels at a speed of about 300 million m/s and sound travels at about 340 m/s. Light from the lightning bolt may reach your eyes in millionths of a second. However, it will take several seconds for the thunder to reach your ears.

Wave Speed Depends on the Medium The speed of a wave depends on the medium in which it travels. Sound travels at about 340 m/s in air, but travels at a speed of about 1,500 m/s in water. Mechanical waves, such as sound, usually travel fastest in solids and slowest in gases. On the other hand, electromagnetic waves, such as light, travel fastest in a vacuum where there is no matter at all. When electromagnetic waves travel in matter, they usually move fastest in gases and slowest in solids.

The speed of a wave also depends on the temperature of the medium. For example, sound waves travel faster as the temperature of the medium increases. Sound travels at 331 m/s in air at 0°C and 346 m/s in air at 25°C.

LA.B.2.3.1

LA.B.2.3.4

Science Online

Topic: Wave Speed
Visit fl6.msscience.com for Web links to information about wave speed in different materials.

Activity Make a chart showing the speed of light in different materials.

section 2 review

Summary

Amplitude

- In a transverse wave, the amplitude is one-half the distance between a crest and a trough.
- The larger the amplitude, the greater the energy carried by the wave.

Wavelength

- For a transverse wave, wavelength is the distance from crest to crest, or from trough to trough.
- For a compressional wave, wavelength is the distance from compression to compression, or from rarefaction to rarefaction.

Frequency

- The frequency of a wave is the number of wavelengths that pass a given point in 1 s.
- For waves that travel at the same speed, as the frequency of the wave increases, its wavelength decreases.

Self Check

1. **Describe** how the frequency of a wave changes as its wavelength changes. SC.B.1.3.6

2. **Explain** why a sound wave with a large amplitude is more likely to damage your hearing than one with a small amplitude.

3. **Explain** the time difference between seeing and hearing a fireworks display? SC.B.1.3.6

4. **Explain** why the statement "The speed of light is 300 million m/s" is not always correct. SC.B.1.3.6

5. **Think Critically** Explain the differences between the waves that make up bright, green light and dim, red light.

Applying Math

6. **Wavelength** If three crests of a wave pass by a point, how many complete wavelengths have passed by the point? SC.B.1.3.6 MA.D.2.3.1

7. **Frequency** Find the frequency of a wave if ten wavelengths pass a point in 2 s. SC.B.1.3.6 MA.D.2.3.1

Waves on a Spring

Mechanical waves can be compressional or transverse waves. Both types of waves can be made to travel on a coiled spring toy. How are compressional and transverse waves different?

◯ *Real-World Problem*

What are some of the properties of transverse and compressional waves on a coiled spring?

Goals

- **Create** transverse and compressional waves on a coiled spring toy.
- **Investigate** wave properties such as speed and amplitude.

Materials

long, coiled spring toy
colored yarn (5 cm)
meterstick
stopwatch

Safety Precautions 🥽 ✋

Complete a safety worksheet before you begin.

WARNING: *Avoid overstretching or tangling the spring to prevent injury or damage.*

◯ *Procedure*

1. Prepare a data table such as the one shown.

Wave Data	
Length of stretched spring toy	
Average time for a wave to travel from end to end—step 4	Do not write in this book.
Average time for a wave to travel from end to end—step 5	

2. Work in pairs or groups and clear a place on an uncarpeted floor about 6 m by 2 m.

3. Stretch the springs between two people to the length suggested by your teacher. Measure the length.

4. Create a wave with a quick, sideways snap of the wrist. Time several waves as they travel the length of the spring. Record the average time in your data table.

5. Repeat step 4 using waves that have slightly larger amplitudes.

6. Squeeze together about 20 of the coils. Observe what happens to the unsqueezed coils. Release the coils and observe.

7. Quickly push the spring toward your partner, then pull it back.

8. Tie the yarn to a coil near the middle of the spring. Repeat step 7, observing the string.

9. **Calculate** and compare the speeds of the waves in steps 4 and 5.

◯ *Conclude and Apply*

1. **Classify** the wave pulses you created in each step as compressional or transverse.

2. **Classify** the unsqueezed coils in step 6 as a compression or a rarefaction.

3. **Compare and contrast** the motion of the yarn in step 8 with the motion of the wave.

𝒞ommunicating Your Data

Write a summary paragraph of how this lab demonstrated any of the vocabulary words from the first two sections of the chapter. **For more help, refer to the** Science Skill Handbook.

Benchmarks—**SC.A.2.3.1 (p. 611):** The student describes and compares the properties of particles and waves. **Also covers:** SC.B.1.3.6 Annually Assessed (pp. 611, 612–613), **SC.C.1.3.2** Annually Assessed (p. 611), **SC.H.1.3.4** Annually Assessed (pp. 612–613), **SC.H.1.3.5** Annually Assessed (p. 606), **SC.H.1.3.6** (p. 614), **SC.H.1.3.7** Annually Assessed (pp. 612–613), **SC.H.2.3.1** (pp. 609–610), SC.H.3.3.5 (p. 614)

section 3

Wave Behavior

Reflection

What causes the echo when you yell across an empty gymnasium or down a long, empty hallway? Why can you see your face when you look in a mirror? The echo of your voice and the face you see in the mirror are caused by wave reflection.

Reflection occurs when a wave strikes an object or surface and bounces off. An echo is reflected sound. Sound reflects from all surfaces. Your echo bounces off the walls, floor, ceiling, furniture, and people. You see your face in a mirror or a still pond, as shown in **Figure 11,** because of reflection. Light waves produced by a source of light such as the Sun or a lightbulb bounce off your face, strike the mirror, and reflect back to your eyes.

When a surface is flat and very smooth, a reflected image is sharp and clear, as shown in **Figure 11.** However, if a surface is rough and uneven, like the water surface on the right in **Figure 11,** the reflected image is no longer clear and sharp. If the surface is too rough, like a piece of paper, no reflected image can be seen.

☑ **Reading Check** *What causes reflection?*

as you read

What **You'll Learn**

- **Explain** how waves can reflect from some surfaces.
- **Explain** how waves change direction when they move from one material into another.
- **Describe** how waves are able to bend around barriers.
- **Compare** waves and particles.

Why **It's Important**

The reflection of light waves enables you to see objects around you.

Review Vocabulary

echo: the repetition of a sound caused by the reflection of sound waves

New Vocabulary

- ✳ **reflection**
- ✳ **refraction**
- ✳ **prism**
- ✳ **diffraction**
- ● **interference**

✳ FCAT Vocabulary

The smooth surface of a still pond enables you to see a sharp, clear image of yourself.

If the surface of the pond is rough and uneven, your reflected image is no longer clear and sharp.

Figure 11 The image formed by reflection depends on the smoothness of the surface.

Observing Refraction

Procedure

1. Complete a safety worksheet.
2. Fill a **clear drinking glass** about half full with **water.**
3. Place a **pencil** in the glass and look at the glass from the side. Describe how the pencil looks.
4. Slowly add **water** to the glass. Describe how the appearance of the pencil changes.

Analysis

1. How does the appearance of the pencil depend on the level of water in the glass?
2. Through what materials do light waves from the lower part and the upper part of the pencil travel to reach your eyes?
3. If light travels faster in air than in water, how did the change in speed of light waves affect the appearance of the pencil?

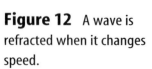

Refraction

A wave changes direction when it reflects from a surface. Waves also can change direction in another way. Perhaps you have tried to grab a sinking object when you are in a swimming pool, only to come up empty-handed. Yet you were sure you grabbed right where you saw the object. You missed grabbing the object because the light waves from the object changed direction as they passed from the water into the air. The bending of a wave as it moves from one medium into another is called **refraction.**

Refraction and Wave Speed Remember that the speed of a wave can be different in different materials. For example, light waves travel faster in air than in water. Refraction occurs when the speed of a wave changes as it passes from one substance to another, as shown in **Figure 12.** A line that is perpendicular to the water's surface is called the normal. When a light wave passes from air into water, it slows down and bends toward the normal. When the wave passes from water into air, it speeds up and bends away from the normal. The more the light wave speeds up or slows down, the larger the change in direction.

When you look into a fishbowl, a fish you see is not where it seems to be. Refraction makes the fish appear to be closer to the surface and farther away from you than it really is, as shown in **Figure 13.** Light waves reflected from the fish are bent away from the normal as they pass from water to air. Your brain interprets the light that enters your eyes by assuming that light waves always travel in straight lines. As a result, the light waves seem to be coming from a fish that is closer to the surface.

Figure 12 A wave is refracted when it changes speed.

Explain *how the direction of the light wave changes if it doesn't change speed.*

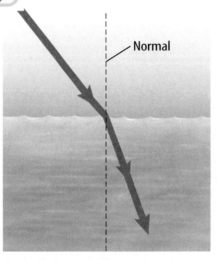

As the light wave slows down, it bends toward the normal.

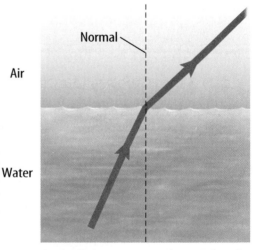

As the light wave speeds up, it bends away from the normal.

Refraction by a Prism What color is a beam of sunlight? You might say that a beam of sunlight seems to be white. **Figure 14** shows what happens when a beam of white light passes through a **prism,** which is a wedge-shaped piece of glass. The light coming out of the prism is made of bands of different colors. How did the prism change white light into light with different colors?

Recall that the color of light waves depends on the wavelength of the waves. For example the wavelength of blue light waves is shorter than the wavelength of red light waves. Light that looks white is a mixture of light waves with different wavelengths. These light waves are refracted, or bent, as they go into and out of the prism.

The amount of bending of a light wave by the prism increases as the wavelength decreases. As a result, blue light waves are bent the most, and red light waves are bent the least. This causes light waves with different colors to be separated when they leave the prism.

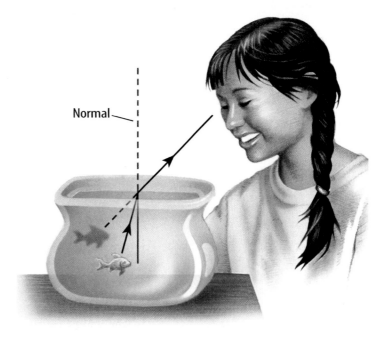

Figure 13 When you look at the goldfish in the water, the fish is in a different position than it appears.
Infer *how the location of the fish would change if light traveled faster in water than in air.*

Diffraction

Why can you hear music from the band room when you are down the hall? You can hear the music because the sound waves bend as they pass through an open doorway. This bending isn't caused by refraction. Instead, the bending is caused by diffraction. **Diffraction** is the bending of waves around a barrier. The sound waves bend when they reach the corners of the doorway.

Light waves from the band room also bend around the edges of the open door. However, for an opening as wide as a door, the amount the light bends is much too small to be noticed. This is why you can't see into the room until you reach the open door.

Figure 14 White light is a mixture of light waves with different wavelengths. When these light waves pass through a prism, they are bent by different amounts, forming bands of color.

Diffraction and Wavelength The reason that light waves don't diffract much when they pass through an open door is that the wavelengths of visible light are much smaller than the width of the door. Light waves have wavelengths between about 400 and 700 billionths of a meter, while the width of a doorway is about one meter. Sound waves that you can hear have wavelengths between a few millimeters and about 10 m. They bend more easily around the corners of an open door. A wave is diffracted more when its wavelength is similar in size to the barrier or opening.

Reading Check *Under what conditions would more diffraction of a wave occur?*

Diffraction of Water Waves Perhaps you have noticed water waves bending around barriers. For example, when water waves strike obstacles such as the islands shown in **Figure 15,** they don't stop moving. Here the size and spacing of the islands is not too different from the wavelength of the water waves. So the water waves bend around the islands, and keep on moving. They also spread out after they pass through openings between the islands. If the islands were much larger than the water wavelength, less diffraction would occur.

What happens when waves meet?

Suppose you throw two pebbles into a still pond. Ripples spread from the impact of each pebble and travel toward each other. What happens when two of these ripples meet? Do they collide like billiard balls and change direction? Waves behave differently from billiard balls when they meet. Waves pass right through each other and continue moving.

Figure 15 Water waves bend or diffract around these islands. More diffraction occurs when the object is closer in size to the wavelength.

Wave Interference During the time the two waves overlap with each other, they combine and form a new wave. **Interference** occurs when two waves overlap and combine to form a new wave. When the two waves finally pass each other and are no longer overlapping, they continue to move with the same wavelength and amplitude they had before they met.

The interference of two water waves is shown in **Figure 16** on the next page. Constructive interference occurs when a crest of one wave overlaps a crest of the other wave. The two waves combine to make a wave with a larger amplitude. Destructive interference occurs when a crest of one wave overlaps a trough of the other wave. Then the two waves combine to make a wave with a smaller amplitude.

Reducing Noise with Interference If you have heard a chain saw or a power mower in action, you know how loud these machines can be. The noise produced by many machines is loud enough to damage a person's hearing. This damage can be prevented by reducing the amount of energy that reaches the ear. Some types of ear protectors contain materials that absorb some of the sound energy so that less energy reaches the ear.

Another type of ear protector uses interference to reduce the sound energy reaching the ear. These ear protectors contain special electronic circuits. These circuits produce sound waves with wavelengths that destructively interfere with the noise. As a result, the amplitudes of the sound waves that reach the ear are reduced.

LA.B.2.3.1

LA.B.2.3.4

Topic: Interference
Visit fl6.msscience.com for Web links to information about wave interference.

Activity Write a paragraph about the kinds of interference you found in your research.

Applying Science

Can you create destructive interference?

Your brother is vacuuming and you can't hear the television. Is it possible to diminish the sound of the vacuum so you can hear the TV? Can you eliminate some sound waves and keep the sounds you do want to hear?

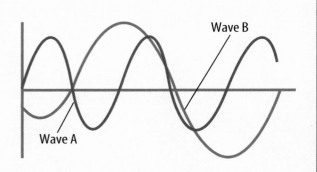

Identifying the Problem

It is possible to create a wave that will destructively interfere with one wave, but will not destructively interfere with another wave. The graph shows two waves with different wavelengths.

Solving the Problem

1. Create the graph of a wave that will eliminate wave **A** but not wave **B**.
2. Create the graph of a wave that would amplify wave **A**.

Figure 16

Whether they are ripples on a pond or huge ocean swells, when water waves meet they can combine to form new waves in a process called interference. As shown below, wave interference can be constructive or destructive.

Constructive Interference

In constructive interference, a wave with greater amplitude is formed.

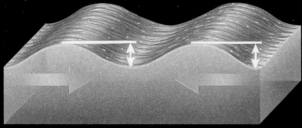

A   **B**

The crests of two waves—A and B—approach each other.

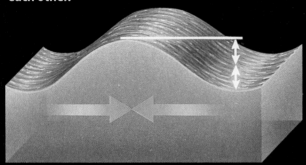

The two waves form a wave with a greater amplitude while the crests of both waves overlap.

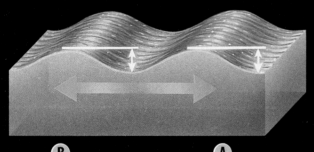

B   **A**

The original waves pass through each other and go on as they started.

Destructive Interference

In destructive interference, a wave with a smaller amplitude is formed.

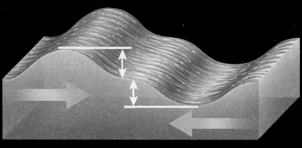

A   **B**

The crest of one wave approaches the trough of another.

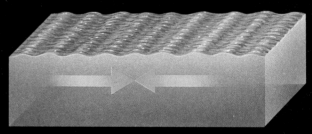

If the two waves have equal amplitude, they momentarily cancel when they meet.

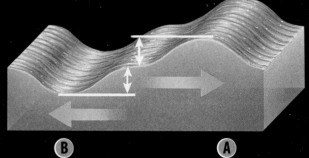

B   **A**

The original waves pass through each other and go on as they started.

Comparing Waves and Particles

If you try to pick up the waves moving on a water surface, you'll end up with only a wet hand. But you can grab an object that has mass. The difference is that objects you can grab are matter, while a wave is not matter. Instead, a wave is a disturbance.

A wave and a particle of matter are different in other ways. **Table 1** shows some of the properties of waves and particles. Besides having mass, a particle takes up space and has volume. A particle also can have an electric charge. A wave doesn't have volume or electric charge. However, waves have properties that particles don't have, such as amplitude, wavelength and frequency.

Another difference is that a wave moves with a certain speed in a given material. For example, in air at 25°C, sound has a speed of 346 m/s. However, a ball moving through the same air can have various speeds, depending on the forces acting on it.

Waves and particles have some similarities. The motion of both can be described by speed and direction. Also, both a wave and a particle can transfer energy from place to place.

Table 1 Wave and Particle Properties

Properties of Particles	Properties of Waves	Properties of Waves and Particles
Mass	Amplitude	Speed
Volume	Wavelength	Direction
Electric charge	Frequency	Transfers energy
Speed doesn't depend on surrounding material.	Speed depends on material it moves in.	

section 3 review

Summary

Reflection

- Reflected sound waves can produce echoes.
- Reflected light rays produce images in a mirror.

Refraction

- The bending of waves as they pass from one medium to another is refraction.
- Refraction occurs when the wave's speed changes.
- A prism separates sunlight into the colors of the visible spectrum.

Diffraction and Interference

- The bending of waves around barriers is diffraction.
- Interference occurs when waves combine to form a new wave while they overlap.
- Destructive interference can reduce noise.

Self Check

1. **Explain** why you don't see your reflection in a building made of rough, white stone.
2. **Explain** how you are able to hear the siren of an ambulance on the other side of a building. `SC.C.1.3.2`
3. **Describe** the behavior of light that enables magnifying lenses and contact lenses to bend light rays. `SC.B.1.3.6`
4. **Define** the term *diffraction*. How does the amount of diffraction depend on wavelength? `SC.B.1.3.6`
5. **Think Critically** Why don't light rays that stream through an open window into a darkened room spread evenly through the entire room? `SC.B.1.3.6`

Applying Skills

6. **Infer** When light waves move from water into glass, the waves change direction and refract toward the normal. Infer how the speed of light in water compares with the speed of light in glass. `SC.B.1.3.6`

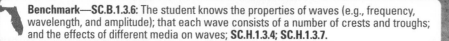
Benchmark—SC.B.1.3.6: The student knows the properties of waves (e.g., frequency, wavelength, and amplitude); that each wave consists of a number of crests and troughs; and the effects of different media on waves; **SC.H.1.3.4; SC.H.1.3.7.**

Use the Internet

The Speed of Sound in Different Materials

Goals

- **Organize** collected information about the speed of sound waves in different materials into a data table.
- **Research** how the speed of sound waves changes in different materials.
- **Research** how the speed of sound waves changes in air at different temperatures.

Data Source

Internet Lab

Visit **fl6.msscience.com** for more information about sound waves traveling in different materials and at different temperatures, and for data collected by other students.

◉ Real-World Problem

Have you ever been underwater and heard a sound? A sound that is made underwater usually sounds different than when the same sound is made in air. One reason that the sounds are different is that sound waves travel with different speeds in different materials, such as water and air. The speed of sound waves also changes when they are traveling through the same material but at a different temperature. How does the speed of sound waves change when they travel in different materials? How does a change in temperature cause the speed of sound waves to change?

Make a Plan

1. Read general information about changes in the speed of sound waves as they travel through different materials or temperatures.

2. **Research** the speed of sound waves in different materials and in air and water at different temperatures by visiting the Web site on the left.

3. Check the Web site to the left to see what others have learned about how different materials and temperatures affect the speed of sound waves.

Follow Your Plan

1. Show your teacher your plan and make any changes suggested by your teacher.

2. **Research** information about the affect of different materials and temperatures on the speed of sound waves.

3. **Organize** your information in a data table like the one shown.

Analyze Your Data

1. **Compare** the speed of sound waves when they are traveling through different materials.

2. **Graph** the data you collected on the speed of sound waves traveling in air at different temperatures.

3. **Graph** the data you collected about the changes in sound wave speeds as they travel through different materials.

Speed of Sound Data		
Material	Temperature (°C)	Speed of Sound (m/s)
Do not write in this book.		

Conclude and Apply

1. **Infer** how the state of matter through which a sound wave is traveling affects the wave's speed.

2. **Infer** how the temperature of the air through which a sound wave is traveling affects the wave's speed.

3. **Infer** how the temperature of the water through which a sound wave is traveling affects the wave's speed.

4. **Infer** whether the speed of sound in air or in water changes more if temperature is increased.

Communicating Your Data

Find this lab using the link below. **Post** your data in the table provided. **Compare** your data to those collected by other students. **Discuss** any differences in your data.

Internet Lab
fl6.msscience.com

SCIENCE Stats

Waves, Waves, and More Waves

Did you know...

. . . Radio waves from space were discovered in 1932 by Karl G. Jansky, an American engineer. His discovery led to the creation of radio astronomy, a field that explores parts of the universe that can't be seen with telescopes.

. . . The highest recorded ocean wave was 34 meters high, which is comparable to the height of a ten-story building. This super wave was seen in the North Pacific Ocean and recorded by the crew of the naval ship *USS Ramapo* in 1933.

Applying Math A tsunami formed by an earthquake on the ocean floor travels at 900 km/h. How long will it take the tsunami to travel 4,500 km?

. . . Waves let dolphins see with their ears! A dolphin sends out ultrasonic pulses, or clicks, at rates of 800 pulses per second. These sound waves are reflected back to the dolphin after they hit an obstacle or a meal. This process is called echolocation.

Graph It

Go to fl6.msscience.com to learn about discoveries by radio astronomers. Make a time line showing some of these discoveries. LA.B.2.3.2 LA.B.2.3.4

Reviewing Main Ideas

Section 1 What are waves?

1. A wave is a disturbance that transfers energy but not matter.

2. Mechanical waves can travel only through matter. Electromagnetic waves can travel through matter and space.

3. In a mechanical transverse wave, matter in the medium moves back and forth at right angles to the direction the wave travels.

4. In a compressional wave, matter in the medium moves forward and backward in the same direction as the wave.

Section 2 Wave Properties

1. The amplitude of a transverse wave is the distance between the rest position and a crest or a trough.

2. The energy carried by a wave increases as the amplitude increases.

3. Wavelength is the distance between neighboring crests or neighboring troughs.

4. The frequency of a wave is the number of wavelengths that pass a given point in 1 s.

5. Waves travel through different materials at different speeds.

Section 3 Wave Behavior

1. Reflection occurs when a wave strikes an object or surface and bounces off.

2. The bending of a wave as it moves from one medium into another is called refraction. A wave changes direction, or refracts, when the speed of the wave changes.

3. The bending of waves around a barrier is called diffraction.

4. Interference occurs when two or more waves combine and form a new wave while they overlap.

Visualizing Main Ideas

LA.A.2.3.7

Copy and complete the following spider map about waves.

Refraction

Interference

Behavior

Transverse

Water waves

Mechanical waves

Waves

Properties

Wavelength

Frequency

Speed

Electromagnetic waves

Move through matter and space

Radio waves

Ultraviolet waves

Visible light

X rays

Using Vocabulary

amplitude p. 599
compressional
   wave p. 597
crest p. 596
diffraction p. 607
electromagnetic
   wave p. 598
frequency p. 601
interference p. 609

prism p. 607
reflection p. 605
refraction p. 606
transverse wave p. 596
trough p. 596
vibration p. 595
wave p. 594
wavelength p. 600

FCAT Vocabulary

Fill in the blanks with the correct word or words.

1. _____ is the change in direction of a wave going from one medium to another.

2. The type of wave that has rarefactions is a _____.

3. The distance between two adjacent crests of a transverse wave is the _____.

4. The more energy a wave carries, the greater its _____ is.

5. A(n) _____ can travel through space without a medium.

Checking Concepts

Choose the word or phrase that best answers the question.

6. What is the material through which mechanical waves travel?
   A) charged particles
   B) space
   C) a vacuum
   D) a medium

7. What is transferred by a water wave?
   A) speed   C) energy
   B) amplitude   D) matter

8. What are the lowest points on a transverse wave called?
   A) crests   C) compressions
   B) troughs   D) rarefactions

9. What determines the pitch of a sound wave?
   A) amplitude   C) speed
   B) frequency   D) refraction

10. What is the distance between adjacent wave compressions?
    A) one wavelength
    B) 1 km
    C) 1 m/s
    D) 1 Hz

11. What occurs when a wave strikes an object or surface and bounces off?
    A) diffraction
    B) refraction
    C) interference
    D) reflection

12. What is the name for a change in the direction of a wave when it passes from one medium into another?
    A) refraction   C) reflection
    B) interference D) diffraction

Use the figure below to answer question 13.

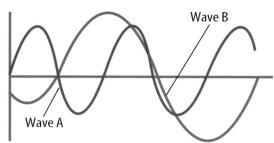
Wave B
Wave A

13. What occurs when waves A and B overlap?
    A) diffraction
    B) refraction
    C) interference
    D) reflection

14. Light waves of what color have the shortest wavelength and the highest frequency?
    A) red   C) orange
    B) green   D) blue

Thinking Critically

15. **Explain** what kind of wave—transverse or compressional—is produced when an engine bumps into a string of coupled railroad cars on a track.

16. **Infer** Is it possible for an electromagnetic wave to travel through a vacuum? Through matter? Explain your answers. SC.B.1.3.6

17. **Draw a Conclusion** Why does the frequency of a wave decrease as the wavelength increases? SC.B.1.3.6

18. **Explain** why you don't see your reflected image when you look at a white, rough surface?

19. **Infer** If a cannon fires at a great distance from you, why do you see the flash before you hear the sound? SC.B.1.3.6

20. **Form a Hypothesis** Form a hypothesis that can explain this observation. Waves A and B travel away from Earth through Earth's atmosphere. Wave A continues on into space, but wave B does not. SC.B.1.3.6

Use the figure below to answer question 21.

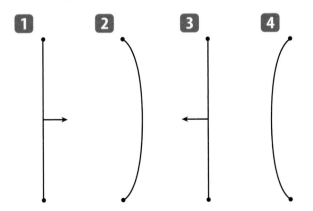

21. **Explain** how the drum head shown above causes compressions and rarefactions as it vibrates in air.

22. **Explain** why you can hear a person talking even if you can't see them. SC.C.1.3.2

23. **Compare and Contrast** AM radio waves have wavelengths between about 200 m and 600 m, and FM radio waves have wavelengths of about 3 m. Why can AM radio signals often be heard behind buildings and mountains but FM radio signals cannot?

24. **Infer** how the wavelength of a wave would change if the speed of the wave increased, but the frequency remained the same. SC.B.1.3.6

25. **Explain** You are motionless on a rubber raft in the middle of a pool. A friend sitting on the edge of the pool tries to make the raft move to the other edge of the pool by slapping the water every second to form a wave. Explain whether the wave produced will cause you to move to the edge of the pool. SC.C.1.3.2

Performance Activities

26. **Make Flashcards** Work with a partner to make flashcards for the bold-faced terms in the chapter. Illustrate each term on the front of the cards. Write the term and its definition on the back of the card. Use the cards to review the terms with another team.

Applying Math

Use the equation below to answer questions 27–29.

frequency = (number of wavelengths) / (time)

27. **Frequency** In a wave pool, you count four wavelengths go past you in 8 s. What is the frequency of the waves?

28. **Wavelengths** A sound wave has a frequency of 40 Hz. How many wavelengths of the sound wave pass a given point in 10 s?

29. **Time** A water wave on the ocean has a frequency of 10 Hz. How much time will it take for 30 wavelengths to pass a given point?

The assessed Florida Benchmark appears above each question.
Record your answers on the answer sheet provided by your teacher or on a sheet of paper.

Multiple Choice

SC.A.2.3.1

1 Which property of a sound wave changes as its energy decreases?

A. amplitude

B. frequency

C. pitch

D. wavelength

SC.A.2.3.1

2 The diagram below shows four different waves.

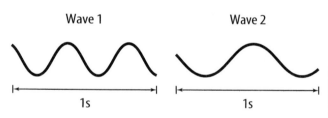

Wave 1   Wave 2

1s   1s

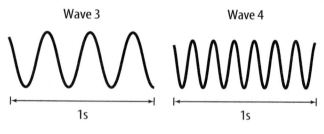

Wave 3   Wave 4

1s   1s

Which wave has the greatest frequency?

F. wave 1

G. wave 2

H. wave 3

I. wave 4

SC.A.2.3.1

3 The table below shows the speed of sound through different mediums.

Speed of Sound		
Material	**State**	**Speed (m/s)**
Air	gas	346
Water	liquid	1,497
Glass	solid	4,540
Iron	solid	5,200

Based on the information in the table, which statement is **true** about sound?

A. Sound travels faster through gases than liquids.

B. Sound travels faster through liquids than solids.

C. Sound travels faster through solids than through gases.

D. Sound travels faster through gases than through solids.

SC.C.1.3.2

4 When Heather looked into a pond, she saw an unclear image of herself. Which of the following explains why Heather's image was unclear?

F. The light waves changed speed when they struck the water.

G. The light waves scattered in many different directions.

H. There were no light waves striking the water's surface.

I. The light waves bounced off the surface in only one direction.

SC.C.1.3.2

5 Jaime's brother is listening to music in his bedroom. Which wave behavior explains why Jaime can hear the music in the living room, which is down the hall from his brother's bedroom?

    A. reflection

    B. diffraction

    C. interference

    D. refraction

SC.H.1.3.3

6 What is the speed of a wave that has a wavelength of 6 m and a frequency of 72 Hz?

    F. 12 m/s

    G. 80 m/s

    H. 432 m/s

    I. 444 m/s

Gridded Response

SC.A.2.3.1

7 What is the wavelength, in meters, of the wave shown in the diagram below?

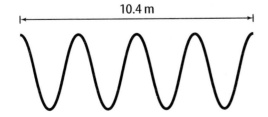

10.4 m

Short Response

SC.C.1.3.2

8 Zoë used a spring to make a transverse wave. Jason used a spring to make a compressional wave. How are these waves alike and how are they different?

Extended Response

SC.B.1.3.6

9 The diagram below shows one light ray entering a fish tank and another light ray leaving the tank.

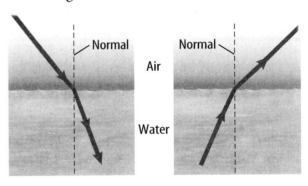

  PART A What wave behavior is displayed in the diagram?

  PART B Explain what causes this bending of the light waves.

FCAT Tip

Practice Remember that test-taking skills can improve with practice. If possible, take at least one practice test to familiarize yourself with the test format and instructions.

How Are Eyeglasses & the Moon Connected?

It's said that in 1608, a Dutch eyeglass maker held two eyeglass lenses, one in front of the other, looked through them, and discovered that distant objects suddenly looked larger and closer. Realizing the importance of the discovery, the eyeglass maker mounted the lenses in a tube that held them at a fixed distance apart. The first telescope had been invented! Before long, scientists all over Europe were using this new device. Until that time, the Moon had been seen as a polished globe of light in the night sky. In 1609, a telescope revealed for the first time that the Moon was a world in some ways like our own, with a rugged surface marked by mountains and craters. Over the first few decades after the telescope was invented, astronomers not only mapped the surface of the Moon, but discovered that other planets have moons of

chapter

21

Sunshine State Standards—**SC.D.1:** The student recognizes that processes in the lithosphere, atmosphere, hydrosphere, and biosphere interact to shape the Earth; **SC.E.1:** understands the interaction and organization in the Solar System and the universe . . . ; **SC.H.1:** uses the scientific processes . . . to solve problems.

The Moon, Planets, and Stars

Why study comets?

Comets, like the one in the photograph, contain ice, rock, and dust that are as old as the solar system. By studying comets, scientists learn more about how the solar system formed.

Science Journal   Write a short story about what it would be like to ride on a comet as it orbits the Sun.

Start-Up Activities

How do planets shine?

On a clear night you might see a bright planet like Venus, Mars, or Jupiter. Planets may look like stars, but they're different. Learn how light comes from a planet in the following lab.

1. Complete a safety worksheet.
2. Tape a sheet of white construction paper to a stack of books so that it stands upright.
3. Tape a sheet of plain white paper vertically to another stack of books. Position the books so that the plain paper faces the construction paper and is about 30 cm from it.
4. Hold a flashlight next to the sheet of plain white paper and direct the light toward the white construction paper.
5. Darken the room and observe the sheet of plain white paper with the flashlight on and off.
6. **Think Critically** Describe in your Science Journal how the appearance of the plain white paper changes. Diagram the path of the light waves from the flashlight to this paper.

FOLDABLES™ **Study Organizer**

Planets in the Solar System Make the following Foldable to compare and contrast the inner planets and the outer planets.

LA.A.1.3.4

STEP 1 Fold one sheet of paper lengthwise.

STEP 2 Fold into thirds.

STEP 3 Unfold and draw overlapping ovals. Cut the top sheet along the folds.

STEP 4 Label the ovals as shown.

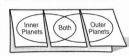

Construct a Venn Diagram As you read the chapter, list the characteristics unique to the inner planets under the left tab. List those unique to the outer planets under the right tab. List characteristics that are common to both inner and outer planets under the middle tab.

 **Preview this chapter's content and activities at fl6.msscience.com**

623

section

1

Benchmarks—SC.E.1.3.1 Annually Assessed (pp. 625–626, 631): The student understands the vast size of our Solar System and the relationship of the planets and their satellites; SC.H.1.3.4 Annually Assessed (p. 631): The student knows that accurate record keeping, openness, and replication are essential to maintaining an investigator's credibility . . . .

Also covers: SC.D.1.3.5 (p. 626), SC.H.1.3.1 Annually Assessed (pp. 625–626, 631), SC.H.1.3.6 (p. 626), SC.H.1.3.7 Annually Assessed (p. 631), SC.H.2.3.1 (pp. 626–627, 629, 631), SC.H.3.3.5 (p. 630)

Earth's Place in Space

as you read

What You'll Learn

- **Explain** Earth's rotation and revolution.
- **Explain** why Earth has seasons.
- **Model** the relative positions of Earth, the Moon, and the Sun during different lunar phases.

Why It's Important

You'll understand night and day and the seasons.

Review Vocabulary

☀ **axis:** the imaginary line around which a planet or moon rotates

New Vocabulary

- ● rotation
- ● orbit
- ● revolution
- ● lunar highlands
- ● maria
- ● eclipse
- ● tide
- ☀ spring tide
- ☀ neap tide

☀ FCAT Vocabulary

Figure 1 Earth's rotation causes night and day.

Axis

Earth's rotation

Earth Moves

You wake up, stretch and yawn, then glance out your window to see the first rays of dawn. By lunchtime, the Sun is high in the sky. As you sit down to dinner in the evening, the Sun appears to sink below the horizon. Although it seems like the Sun moves across the sky, it is Earth that is moving.

Earth's Rotation Earth spins in space like a twirling figure skater. Your planet spins around an imaginary line running through its center, called an axis. **Figure 1** shows how Earth spins around its axis.

The spinning of Earth around its axis is called Earth's **rotation** (roh TAY shun). Earth rotates once every 24 h. The Sun appears each morning due to Earth's rotation. Throughout the day, Earth continues to rotate and the Sun appears to move across the sky. In the evening, the Sun seems to go down because the place where you are on Earth is rotating away from the Sun.

You can see how this works by standing and facing a lamp. Pretend you are Earth and the lamp is the Sun. Now, without pivoting your head, turn around slowly in a counterclockwise direction. The lamp seems to move across your vision, then disappear. You rotate until you finally see the lamp again. The lamp didn't move—you did. When you rotated, you were like Earth rotating in space, causing different parts of the planet to face the Sun at different times. The rotation of Earth—not movement of the Sun—causes night and day.

✓ Reading Check *Why does the Sun appear to move across the sky?*

Because the Sun only appears to move across the sky, this movement is called apparent motion. Stars, planets, and the Moon also appear to move across the sky. You might have observed the Moon rise and set, just like the Sun. How can you recognize apparent motion that results from Earth's rotation?

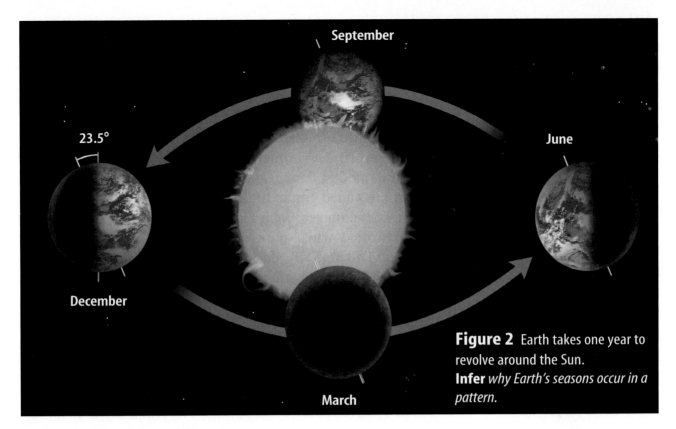

Figure 2 Earth takes one year to revolve around the Sun.
Infer why Earth's seasons occur in a pattern.

September

June

23.5°

December

March

Earth's Revolution Earth rotates in space, but it also moves in other ways. Like an athlete running around a track, Earth moves around the Sun in a regular, curved path called an **orbit.** The movement of Earth around the Sun is known as Earth's **revolution** (reh vuh LEW shun). A year on Earth is the time it takes for Earth to complete one revolution, as seen in **Figure 2.**

Seasons Who doesn't love summer? The long, warm days are great for swimming, biking, and relaxing. Why can't summer last all year? Blame it on Earth's axis and revolution around the Sun. The axis is not straight up and down like a skyscraper—it is slightly tilted. It's because of this tilt and Earth's revolution that you experience seasons.

Look at **Figure 2.** Summer occurs when your part of Earth is tilted toward the Sun. During summer, sunlight strikes at a higher angle than it does during winter. You might have noticed that when you go outside at noon, your shadow is shorter during summer than during winter. Because summer sunlight strikes at a higher angle, it is more intense than winter sunlight. There also are more hours of daylight during summer than during winter. These two factors cause summer to be warm. Six months later, when the part of Earth that you live on is tilted away from the Sun, you have winter. During winter, sunlight strikes at a lower angle than during summer. The days are short, and the nights are long. Autumn and spring begin when Earth is neither tilted toward nor away from the Sun.

SC.E.1.3.1

Mini LAB

Modeling Earth's Seasons

Procedure
1. Complete a safety worksheet.
2. Place a **shaded lamp** on a **table** in your classroom. The lamp represents the Sun. Turn on the lamp, and turn off the overhead lights.
3. Using a **globe,** model Earth's position during each of the four seasons. Remember to tilt the globe so that its axis makes an angle of about 23.5° from straight up.

Analysis
During which season did the light shine most intensely on the northern hemisphere of the globe? During which season did it shine the least?

Figure 3 When you ride on a merry-go-round, it takes the same amount of time for you to rotate as it does for you to revolve around the center.
Explain *how this pattern is similar to the way the Moon rotates and revolves.*

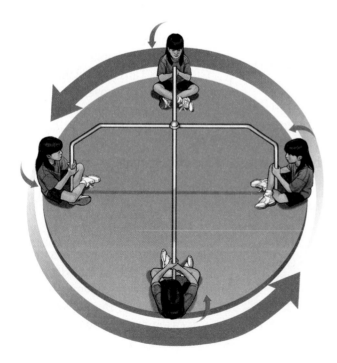

Earth's Moon

Does the Moon look perfect to you? Many ancient people thought that the Moon's surface was perfectly smooth. This belief was common until about 400 years ago when a scientist named Galileo looked at the Moon through his telescope. Galileo saw large, mountainous regions with many craters. He also saw smooth, dark regions. The mountainous areas of the Moon are called **lunar highlands.** The lunar highlands are about 4.5 billion years old. The many craters on the lunar highlands formed when meteorites hit the Moon just after it formed. The smooth, dark regions of the Moon are called **maria,** which is the Latin word for *sea.* The maria formed when lava erupted from the Moon's interior and cooled in low areas on its surface.

Orbiting Earth While Earth revolves around the Sun, the Moon and a variety of human-made objects orbit Earth. The Moon revolves around Earth once every 27.3 days. It has an average distance from Earth of 384,400 km. This is like traveling from Los Angeles to New York and back again 49 times. Other objects orbit much closer to Earth than the Moon does. These objects include the *International Space Station,* a wide variety of satellites, and much debris. The debris, often called space junk, consists of parts from old rockets and a variety of discarded tools and equipment.

Rotation and Revolution How long does it take for the Moon to rotate one time? The answer is 27.3 days—exactly the same amount of time that it takes for the Moon to revolve around Earth one time. Because the Moon rotates and revolves at the same rate, the same side of the Moon always faces Earth. The side of the Moon that faces Earth is called the near side. The opposite side of the Moon is called the far side. If you've ever ridden on a playground merry-go-round, you rotated and revolved somewhat like the Moon. Look at **Figure 3.** When you ride on a merry-go-round, your body rotates at exactly the same rate as it revolves. You always face the center of the merry-go-round, just like the Moon always keeps the same face toward Earth.

Moon Phases How many different moon shapes have you seen? Have you seen the Moon look round or maybe like a half circle? Although the Moon looks different at different times of the month, it doesn't change. What does change is the way the Moon appears from Earth. These changes are called phases of the Moon. **Figure 4** shows the various phases of the Moon.

Light from the Sun The Moon does not produce its own light. The light that comes to Earth from the Moon is reflected sunlight. Also, just as half of Earth experiences day while the other half experiences night, one half of the Moon is lit by the Sun while the other half is dark.

The Lunar Cycle The phase of the Moon that you see on any given night depends on the relative positions of the Moon, the Sun, and Earth in space. These positions change because the Moon is continually revolving around Earth as Earth revolves around the Sun. It takes the Moon about one month to go through its phases. During that time, called a lunar cycle, you see different portions of the daylight side of the Moon.

The lunar cycle begins with new moon. During new moon, the Moon is between Earth and the Sun. Half of the Moon is lit by the Sun, but this half can't be seen from Earth. For about two weeks after new moon, the portion of the lit side of the Moon that can be seen from Earth increases. At first, only a small crescent is visible. Then, you see the first quarter moon followed by the gibbous moon. Finally, the Moon is full. At full moon, Earth is between the Moon and the Sun, and the entire near side of the Moon is visible from Earth. For about two weeks after full moon, the moon phase appears to get smaller. The phase gradually changes from a gibbous moon, to a third quarter moon, crescent moon, and finally new moon again.

Reading Check *What is the lunar cycle?*

Recall that the near side of the Moon always faces Earth. This means that during the new moon phase, the far side of the Moon is lighted by the Sun. The far side of the Moon is lighted just as much as the near side is. The far side can't be seen from Earth because it is always facing away from it.

Figure 4 When the moon phases get larger, they are said to be waxing. When the moon phases get smaller, they are waning. **Explain** *the difference between a waxing crescent and a waning crescent.*

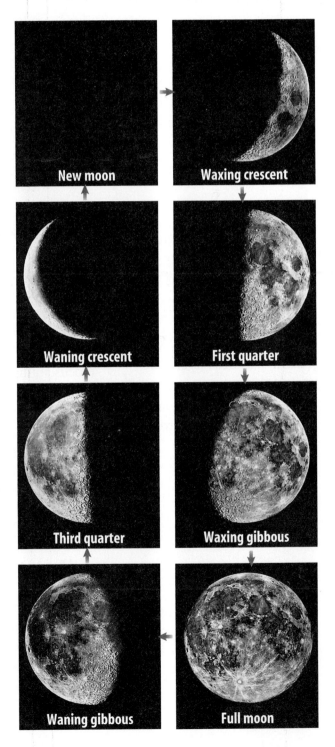

New moon | Waxing crescent

Waning crescent | First quarter

Third quarter | Waxing gibbous

Waning gibbous | Full moon

Figure 5 During a solar eclipse, the Moon moves directly between the Sun and Earth. The Sun's corona is visible during a total solar eclipse. **Identify** *the phase that the Moon must be in for a solar eclipse to occur.*

Sun's corona

Area of partial eclipse

Sun

Moon

Area of total eclipse

Earth

LA.B.2.3.4

Science Online

Topic: Eclipse Data

Visit fl6.msscience.com for Web links to information about future solar and lunar eclipses.

Activity Find out when you will next be able to observe an eclipse in your area.

Solar Eclipse Have you ever tried to watch TV with someone standing between you and the screen? You can't see a thing. The picture from the screen can't reach your eyes because someone is blocking it. Sometimes the Moon is like that person standing in front of the TV. It moves directly between the Sun and Earth and blocks sunlight from reaching Earth. The Moon's shadow travels across parts of Earth. This event, shown in **Figure 5,** is an example of an **eclipse** (ih KLIHPS). Because it is an eclipse of the Sun, it is known as a solar eclipse. The Moon is much smaller than the Sun, so it casts a small shadow on Earth. Sunlight is blocked completely only on the small area of Earth where the Moon's darker shadow falls. In that area, the eclipse is said to be a total solar eclipse.

✓ Reading Check *What causes solar eclipses?*

Due to the small size of the shadow—about 269 km wide—only a lucky few get to experience each solar eclipse. For the few minutes the total eclipse lasts, the sky darkens, flowers close, and some planets and brighter stars become visible. The Sun's spectacular corona, its pearly white, outermost layer, can be observed. Far more people will be in the lighter part of the Moon's shadow and will experience a partial solar eclipse. **WARNING:** *Never look at the Sun during an eclipse. You might damage your eyes.*

Figure 6 During a lunar eclipse, Earth is between the Sun and the Moon. The Moon often appears red during a lunar eclipse.
Infer why lunar eclipses are observed more frequently than solar eclipses.

Lunar eclipse

Lunar Eclipse Sometimes Earth is directly between the Sun and the Moon. When Earth's shadow falls on the Moon, an eclipse of the Moon occurs. This is called a lunar eclipse. Everyone on the nighttime side of Earth, weather permitting, can see a lunar eclipse. When eclipsed, the full moon becomes dim and sometimes turns deep red, as shown in **Figure 6.**

Tides The Moon's gravity pulls on Earth. One effect of the Moon's gravity is tides. **Tides** are an alternate rise and fall in sea level. They are most noticeable along a beach. At high tide, water moves farther onto the beach. At low tide, water moves off the beach.

Tides occur because the Moon's gravity decreases with distance from the Moon. Places on Earth closer to the Moon are pulled harder than places that are farther from the Moon. The Moon's gravity holds Earth in its path around the center of mass of the Earth-Moon system. At places on Earth that are closer to the Moon, the Moon's gravity is a bit stronger than it needs to be to hold Earth. At places on Earth that are farther from the Moon, the Moon's gravity is a bit weaker than it needs to be.

The small differences in the Moon's gravity cause the water in Earth's oceans to form two bulges, shown in **Figure 7.** One bulge is on the side of Earth toward the Moon, and one is on the opposite side. These bulges of water are the high tides. The areas of Earth that are neither toward nor away from the Moon are the low tides. As Earth rotates, different places pass through high and low tide.

Figure 7 Tides form because the Moon's gravity pulls harder on parts of Earth that are closer to it. Two tidal bulges occur—one on the side of Earth closest to the Moon, and one on the opposite side of Earth.

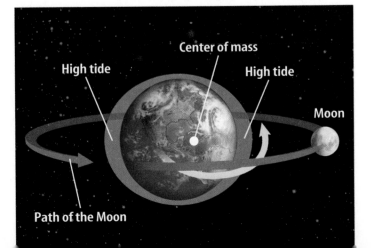

High tide

Center of mass

High tide

Moon

Path of the Moon

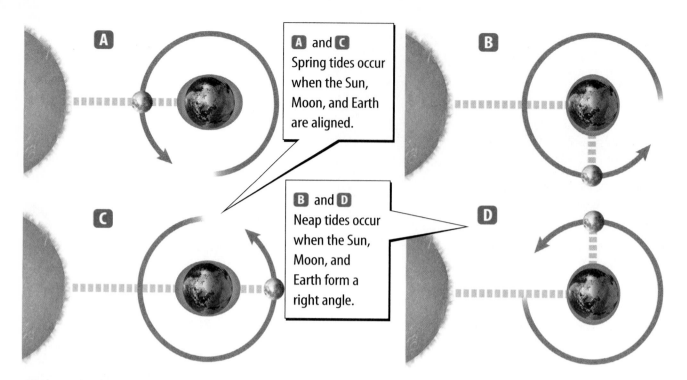

A and **C**
Spring tides occur when the Sun, Moon, and Earth are aligned.

B and **D**
Neap tides occur when the Sun, Moon, and Earth form a right angle.

Figure 8 Because the Moon revolves around Earth, spring tides and neap tides each occur about twice each month.

The Sun's Effect on Tides Because the Sun is much farther from Earth, it has about half as much tide-generating force as the Moon. **Spring tide** occurs when the Sun, Earth, and the Moon are lined up at the new and full phases of the Moon, as shown in **Figure 8.** High tides are higher and low tides are lower during spring tide because the Moon's gravity and the Sun's gravity combine to produce a greater effect. **Neap tide** occurs twice monthly when the Sun, Earth, and the Moon are at right angles to each other. In this arrangement, also shown in **Figure 8,** the Sun's gravity reduces the tide-generating effect of the Moon's gravity. At these times, tides are less extreme.

section 1 review

Summary

Earth Moves
- Seasons occur because of Earth's tilted axis and Earth's revolution around the Sun.

Earth's Moon
- The Moon has many surface features including craters, maria, and lunar highlands.
- Different moon phases occur depending on the positions of Earth, the Sun, and the Moon.

Tides
- The Moon has the greatest effect on Earth's tides. The Sun has a lesser effect.

Self Check

1. **Define** Earth's revolution and rotation. `SC.E.1.3.1`
2. **Explain** why lunar eclipses occur during a full moon. `SC.E.1.3.1`
3. **Compare and contrast** spring tides and neap tides. `SC.E.1.3.1`
4. **Think Critically** What would seasons be like if Earth's axis were tilted at a greater angle (more than 23.5°)? `SC.E.1.3.1`

Applying Skills

5. **Research Information** Some scientific knowledge is very old, yet it still is correct today. Do research to learn how much the ancient Mayan civilization knew about the length of a year. `SC.H.3.3.5`

Benchmark—**SC.E.1.3.1:** The student understands the vast size of our Solar System and the relationship of the planets and their satellites; **SC.H.1.3.4:** knows that accurate record keeping, openness, and replication are essential to maintaining an investigator's credibility with other scientists and society; **SC.H.1.3.7:** knows that when similar investigations give different results, the scientific challenge is to verify whether the differences are significant by further study; **SC.H.2.3.1:** recognizes that patterns exist within and across systems.

Moon Phases

The Moon is Earth's nearest neighbor in space. The Sun, which is much farther away, is the source of light that reflects off of the Moon. In this lab, you'll observe how the positions of the Sun, the Moon, and Earth cause the different phases of the Moon.

◉ Real-World Problem

How do the positions of the Sun, the Moon, and Earth affect the phases of the Moon?

Goals

■ **Model and observe** moon phases.

■ **Record and label** phases of the Moon.

■ **Infer** how the positions of the Sun, the Moon, and Earth affect phases of the Moon.

Materials

drawing paper (several sheets)
softball
flashlight

Safety Precautions

Complete a safety worksheet before you begin.

◉ Procedure

1. Turn on the flashlight and darken other lights in the room. Select a member of your group to hold the flashlight. This person will be the Sun. Select another member of your group to hold up the softball so that the light shines directly on the ball. The softball will be the Moon in your experiment.

2. Everyone else represents Earth and should sit between the Sun and the Moon.

3. **Observe** how light shines on the Moon. Draw the Moon, being careful to add shading to represent its dark portion.

4. The student who is holding the Moon should begin to walk in a slow circle around the group, stopping at least seven times at different spots. Each time the Moon stops, observe it, draw it, and shade in its dark portion.

◉ Conclude and Apply

1. **Compare and contrast** your drawings with those of other students. Discuss similarities and differences in the drawings.

2. In your own words, explain how the positions of Earth, the Sun, and the Moon affect the phase of the Moon that is visible from Earth.

3. **Compare** your drawings with **Figure 4.** Which phase is the Moon in for each drawing? Label each drawing with the correct moon phase.

*C*ommunicating Your Data

Use your drawings to make a poster explaining phases of the Moon. **For more help, refer to the** Science Skill Handbook.

Benchmarks—SC.D.1.3.5 (p. 633): The student understands concepts of time and size relating to the interaction of Earth's processes; SC.E.1.3.1 Annually Assessed (pp. 632, 634): The student understands the vast size of our Solar System and the relationship of the planets and their satellites.

Also covers: SC.E.1.3.2 Annually Assessed (p. 634)

section 2

The Solar System

Distances in Space

Imagine that you are an astronaut living in the future, doing research on a space station in orbit around Earth. You've been working hard for a long time and need a vacation. Where will you go? How about a tour of the solar system? The **solar system,** shown in **Figure 9,** is made up of the Sun, the nine planets, and many other objects that orbit the Sun. These all are kept in orbit over a vast distance by the Sun's immense gravity.

✔ **Reading Check** *What holds the solar system together?*

The planets in the solar system revolve around the Sun in elliptical orbits. The orbits of most of the planets are only slightly elliptical. They are almost circular. Pluto and Mercury have orbits that are more elliptical. Their orbits are similar to a slightly flattened circle.

Figure 9 The Sun is the center of the solar system, which is made up of the nine planets and other objects that orbit the Sun.
Compare and contrast *the sizes of the different planets.*

Pluto

Neptune

Uranus

Saturn

Jupiter

Measuring Space Distances in space are hard to imagine because space is so vast. Suppose you had to measure your pencil, the hallway outside your classroom, and the distance from your home to school. Would you use the same unit for each measurement? No. You probably would measure your pencil in centimeters. You would use something bigger to measure the length of the hallway, such as meters. You might measure the trip from your home to school in kilometers. Larger units are used to measure longer distances. Imagine trying to measure the trip from your home to school in centimeters. If you didn't lose count, you'd end up with a huge number.

Astronomical Unit Kilometers are fine for measuring long distances on Earth, such as the distance from New York to Chicago (about 1,200 km). Even bigger units are needed to measure vast distances in space. One such measure is the astronomical (as truh NAH mih kul) unit. An **astronomical unit** equals 150 million km, which is the average distance from Earth to the Sun. Astronomical unit is abbreviated *AU*. If something is 3 *AU* away from the Sun, then the object is three times farther from the Sun than Earth is. The *AU* is a convenient unit for measuring distances in the solar system.

Reading Check *Why is the astronomical unit useful for measuring distances in the solar system?*

LA.A.1.3.4
LA.B.2.3.4

Science online

Topic: Space Technology
Visit fl6.msscience.com for Web links about technology that is used to explore space.

Activity Create a concept map that explains why technology is essential to science.

FCAT FOCUS Annually Assessed Benchmark Check

SC.E.1.3.1 What type of orbit do planets and their moons follow in the solar system?

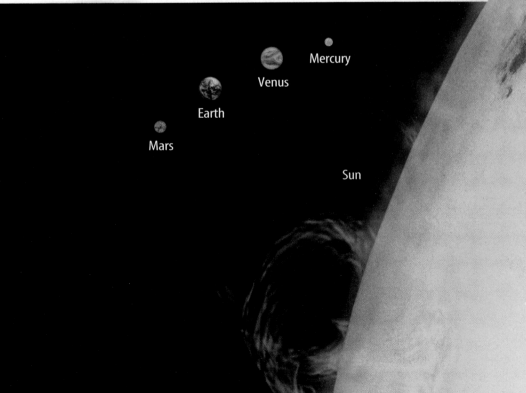

Mercury

Venus

Earth

Mars

Sun

Touring the Solar System

Now you know a little more about how to measure distances in the solar system. Next, you can travel outward from the Sun and take a look at the objects in the solar system. Maybe you can find a nice destination for your next vacation. Strap yourself into your spacecraft and get ready to travel. It's time to begin your journey. What will you see first?

Inner Planets

The first group of planets you pass is the inner planets. These planets are mostly solid, with minerals similar to those on Earth. As with all the planets, much of what is known comes from space probes that send data back to Earth. Various space probes took the photographs shown in **Figure 10** and the rest of this section. Some were taken while in space and others upon landing.

Mercury The first planet that you will visit is the one that is closest to the Sun. Mercury, shown in **Figure 10,** is the second-smallest planet. Its surface has many craters. Craters form when meteorites, which are chunks of rock or metal that fall from the sky, strike a planet's surface. You will read about meteorites later in this section. Because of Mercury's small size and low gravity, gases that could form an atmosphere escape into space. The lack of an atmosphere and the closeness of this planet to the Sun cause great extremes in temperature. Mercury's surface temperature can reach 425°C during the day and drop to −170°C at night, making the planet unfit for life.

Reading Check *Why do surface temperatures on Mercury vary so much?*

Figure 10 Mercury and Venus are closer to the Sun than Earth is.

Like the Moon, Mercury's surface is scarred by craters.

Earth's closest neighbor, Venus, is covered in clouds.

Venus You won't be able to see much at your next stop, also shown in **Figure 10.** Venus, the second-closest planet to the Sun, is hard to see because its surface is surrounded by thick clouds. These clouds trap the solar energy that reaches the surface of Venus. That energy causes surface temperatures to hover around 472°C—hot enough to bake a clay pot.

Earth Home sweet home. You've reached Earth, the third planet from the Sun. You didn't realize how unusual your home planet was until you saw other planets. Earth's surface temperatures allow water to exist as a solid, a liquid, and a gas. The degree of tilt of Earth's axis and Earth's distance from the Sun are necessary to maintain the complex ecosystem we see. Also, ozone in Earth's atmosphere works like a screen to limit the number of ultraviolet (ul truh VI uh lut) rays that reach the planet's surface. Ultraviolet rays are harmful rays from the Sun. Because of Earth's atmosphere, life can thrive on the planet. You would like to linger on Earth, shown in **Figure 11,** but you have six more planets to explore.

Mars Has someone else been here? You see signs of earlier visits to Mars, the fourth of the inner planets. Tiny robotic explorers have been left behind. However, it wasn't a person who left them here. Spacecraft that were sent from Earth to explore Mars's surface left the robots. If you stay long enough and look around, you might notice that Mars, shown in **Figure 12,** has seasons and polar ice caps. Signs indicate that the planet once had abundant liquid water. Water might even be shaping the surface of Mars today. You'll also notice that the planet looks red. That's because the sediment on its surface contains iron oxide, which is rust. Two small moons, Phobos and Deimos, orbit Mars.

Figure 11 Earth is the only planet known to support life.

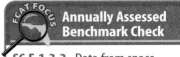

Annually Assessed Benchmark Check

SC.E.1.3.2 Data from space probes show that water was once abundant on which planet?

Figure 12 Mars often is called the Red Planet.
Explain *what causes Mars's surface to appear red.*

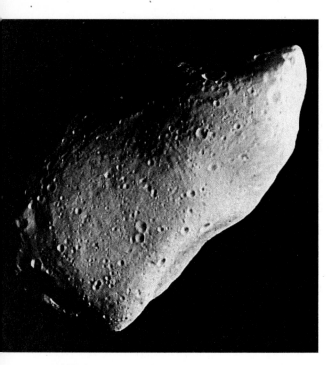

Asteroid Belt Look out for asteroids. On the next part of your trip, you must make your way through the asteroid belt that lies between Mars and the next planet, Jupiter. As you can see in **Figure 13,** asteroids are pieces of rock made of minerals similar to those that formed the rocky planets and moons. In fact, these asteroids might have become a planet if it weren't for the giant planet, Jupiter. Jupiter's huge gravitational force might have prevented a small planet from forming in the area of the asteroid belt. The asteroids also might be the remains of larger bodies that broke up in collisions. The asteroid belt separates the solar system's planets into two groups—the inner planets, which you've already visited, and the outer planets, which are coming next.

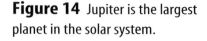 **Reading Check** *What are asteroids?*

Figure 13 This close-up of the asteroid Gaspra was taken by the *Galileo* space probe in 1991. **Describe** *Gaspra's surface features.*

Outer Planets

Moving past the asteroids, you come to the outer planets. The outer planets are Jupiter, Saturn, Uranus, Neptune, and Pluto. Let's hope you aren't looking for places to stop and rest. Trying to stand on most of these planets would be like trying to stand on a cloud. That's because all of the outer planets, except Pluto, are huge balls of gas called gas giants. Each might have a solid core, but none of them has a solid surface. The gas giants have lots of moons that orbit the planets just like Earth's Moon orbits Earth. They have rings surrounding them that are made of dust and ice. The only outer planet that doesn't have rings is Pluto. Pluto also differs from the other outer planets because it is composed of ice and rock.

Figure 14 Jupiter is the largest planet in the solar system.

Jupiter If you're looking for excitement, you'll find it on Jupiter, which is the largest planet in the solar system and the fifth from the Sun. It also has the shortest day—less than 10 h long—which means this giant planet is spinning faster than any other planet. Watch out for a huge, red whirlpool near the middle of the planet! That's the Great Red Spot, a giant storm on Jupiter's surface. Jupiter, shown in **Figure 14,** looks like a miniature solar system. It has 63 moons. The largest moon, called Ganymede (GA nih meed), is larger than the planet Mercury. The moon Europa might have liquid water under its icy crust. Another of Jupiter's moons, Io, has more active volcanoes than any other object in the solar system.

Saturn You might have thought that Jupiter was unusual. Wait until you see Saturn, the sixth planet from the Sun. You'll be dazzled by its rings, shown in **Figure 15.** Saturn's several broad rings are made up of hundreds of smaller rings, which are made up of pieces of ice and rock. Some of these pieces are like specks of dust. Others are many meters across. Saturn is orbited by at least 33 moons, the largest of which is Titan. Titan has an atmosphere that is thought to resemble Earth's atmosphere during primitive times. Some scientists hypothesize that Titan's atmosphere might provide clues about how life formed on Earth.

Uranus After Saturn, you come to Uranus, the seventh planet from the Sun. Uranus warrants a careful look because of the interesting way it spins around its axis. The axis of most planets is tilted just a little, somewhat like the handle of a broom that is leaning against a wall. Uranus, also shown in **Figure 15,** is nearly lying on its side. Its axis is tilted almost even with the plane of its orbit like a broomstick lying on the floor. Uranus's atmosphere is made mostly of hydrogen with smaller amounts of helium and methane. The methane gives Uranus its distinctive bluish-green color. Uranus has a system of rings and at least 27 moons.

Figure 15 Saturn and Uranus are two of the four gas giant planets.

Applying Science

How can you model distances in the solar system?

The distances between the planets and the Sun are unimaginably large but definitely measurable. Astronomers have developed a system of measurement to describe these distances in space. Could you represent these vast distances in a simple classroom model? Use your knowledge of SI and your ability to read a data table to find out.

Identifying the Problem

The table shows the distances of the planets and asteroid belt from the Sun. Notice that the inner planets are fairly close together, and the outer planets are far apart. Study the distances carefully, then answer the questions.

Solving the Problem
1. How can you make a scale model of the solar system that will fit in your classroom? What unit will you use to show the distances?
2. Show the conversion between astronomical units and the unit you use for your model.

Solar System Data	
Planet	**Distance from the Sun (AU)**
Mercury	0.39
Venus	0.72
Earth	1.00
Mars	1.52
Asteroid belt	2–4
Jupiter	5.20
Saturn	9.54
Uranus	19.19
Neptune	30.07
Pluto	39.48

Neptune

Pluto

Figure 16 The outermost planets are Neptune and Pluto. This is the best image available of Pluto, which has not yet been visited by spacecraft.

Figure 17 Solar wind is a stream of charged particles moving away from the Sun. Comet tails point away from the Sun because they are pushed by solar wind.

Neptune Neptune is the next stop in your space travel. Neptune, shown in **Figure 16,** is the eighth planet from the Sun. Neptune's atmosphere is composed of hydrogen, helium, and methane. The methane gives the planet a blue color. In 1989, *Voyager 2* sent pictures of Neptune showing a Great Dark Spot in its atmosphere. The spot was gone when observations were made using the *Hubble Space Telescope* in 1994. Neptune is the last of the big, gas planets with rings around it. It has 13 known moons. Triton, the largest of these, has geysers that shoot gaseous nitrogen into space. The low number of craters on Triton indicates that lava still flows onto its surface.

Pluto The last planet that you come to on your tour is Pluto, a small, rocky planet with a frozen crust. Pluto was discovered in 1930 and is farthest from the Sun. It is the smallest planet in the solar system—smaller even than Earth's moon—and the one scientists know the least about. It is the only planet in the solar system that has never been visited by a spacecraft. Pluto, shown in **Figure 16,** has one moon, Charon, which is nearly half the size of the planet itself.

Comets

A **comet** is a large body of ice and rock that travels around the Sun in an elliptical orbit. These objects are like dirty snowballs that often are between one and fifty kilometers across. Comets might originate in a cloud of objects far beyond the orbit of Pluto known as the Oort Cloud. This belt is 50,000 AU from the Sun. Some comets also originate in the Kuiper Belt, which lies just beyond the orbit of Neptune. As a comet approaches the Sun, solar radiation changes some of the ice into gas. Solar winds blow gas and dust away from the comet, forming what appears from Earth as a bright tail, shown in **Figure 17.**

✓ **Reading Check** *Why do comets have tails?*

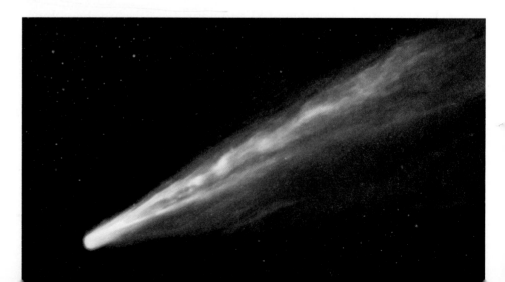

Meteorites Occasionally, chunks of extraterrestrial rock and metal fall to Earth. **Meteorites** are any fragments from space that survive their plunge through the atmosphere and land on Earth's surface. Small ones are no bigger than pebbles. The one in **Figure 18** has a mass of 14.5 metric tons. Hundreds of meteorites fall to Earth each year. Luckily, strikes on buildings or other human-made objects are rare. In fact, only a tiny fraction of the meteorites that fall are ever found. Scientists are extremely interested in those that are, because they yield important clues from space. For example, many seem to be about 4.5 billion years old, which provides a rough estimate of the age of the solar system. Several thousand meteorites have been collected in Antarctica, where moving ice sheets concentrate them in certain areas. Any rock seen on an ice sheet in Antarctica is probably a meteorite, because few other rocks are exposed. Meteorites can be one of three types—irons, stones, and stoney-irons. Irons are almost all iron, with some nickel mixed in. Stones are rocky. The rarest, stoney-irons, are a mixture of metal and rock.

Figure 18 This meteorite on display at the American Museum of Natural History in New York has a mass of 14.5 metric tons.
Explain *why meteorites are rare.*

section 2 review

Summary

Distances in Space

- The planets in the solar system orbit around the Sun.
- Distances in the solar system are vast. Scientists measure these distances using the astronomical unit (AU).

Inner Planets

- The inner planets are solid, rocky planets.
- Earth is the only planet known to support life.

Outer Planets

- Jupiter, Saturn, Uranus, and Neptune are gas giants that have ring systems.
- Pluto is a small planet made up of ice and rock.

Comets

- Comets are bodies of ice and rock that orbit the Sun.

Self Check

1. **Explain** why the planets and other objects in the solar system orbit around the Sun. SC.E.1.3.1
2. **List** the planets in the solar system in order starting with the planet that is closest to the Sun. SC.E.1.3.1
3. **Compare and contrast** the moons that were discussed in this chapter. SC.E.1.3.1
   SC.E.1.3.1
4. **Infer** why carbon dioxide ice exists on Mars but not Earth.
5. **Think Critically** Earth has abundant life. Do you think that other planets or moons might support life? If so, which ones? Which characteristics of the planets or moons might be conducive to life?

Applying Skills

6. **Compare and contrast** Earth to other planets in terms of size, composition, distance from the Sun, and surface features. You might want to make a table to record your data. SC.E.1.3.1

section 3

Also covers: SC.E.1.3.1 Annually Assessed (p. 648), SC.E.1.3.4 (p. 642), SC.E.2.3.1 (p. 643), SC.H.1.3.5 Annually Assessed (p. 248), SC.H.1.3.6 (pp. 645, 648), SC.H.1.3.7 Annually Assessed (p. 648), SC.H.2.3.1 (pp. 641–644), SC.H.3.3.4 (p. 648), SC.H.3.3.5 (p. 645)

Stars and Galaxies

as you read

What You'll Learn

- **Explain** why stars appear to move across the sky.
- **Describe** some constellations.
- **Explain** the life cycle of stars.

Why It's Important

Understanding the vastness of the universe will help you to appreciate Earth's place in space.

Review Vocabulary

✳ **star:** a large, spherical mass of gas that is held together by gravity and gives off light and other types of radiation; the Sun is a typical star

New Vocabulary

✳ constellation ✳ galaxy
- supernova • light-year

✳ FCAT Vocabulary

Stars

Every night, a new world opens to you as the stars come out. Stars are always in the sky. You can't see them during the day because the Sun's light makes Earth's atmosphere so bright that it hides them. The Sun is a star, too. It is the closest star to Earth. Each night the stars appear to move across the sky. This happens because Earth is rotating around its axis. The stars that can be seen in the sky also change with the season as Earth revolves around the Sun.

Constellations Ursa Major, Ursa Minor, Orion, Taurus—do these names sound familiar? They are **constellations** (kahn stuh LAY shunz), or groups of stars that form patterns in the sky. **Figure 19** shows some constellations.

Constellations are named after animals, objects, and people—real or imaginary. Many of the names that early Greek astronomers gave to the constellations are still in use. However, throughout history, different groups of people have seen different things in the constellations. In early England, people thought the Big Dipper and the constellation Ursa Major looked like a plow. Native Americans saw a horse and rider. To the Chinese, it looked like a governmental official and his helpers moving on a cloud. What image does the Big Dipper bring to your mind?

Figure 19 Find the Big Dipper in the constellation Ursa Major.
Explain why people call it the Big Dipper.

Starry Colors Although they look similar from Earth, stars are different colors. The color of a star is a clue about its temperature. Just as the red flames in a campfire are cooler, red stars are the coolest visible stars. Yellow stars have medium temperature. Bluish-white stars, like the blue flames on a gas stove, are the hottest.

✓ Reading Check *How is a star's color related to its temperature?*

Stars also vary in size. Most of the stars in the universe are small. The Sun is a yellow, medium-sized star. Betelgeuse (BEE tul joos) is much bigger than the Sun. If this huge star were in the same place as the Sun, it would swallow Mercury, Venus, Earth, and Mars.

Apparent Magnitude Look at the sky on a clear night and you can easily notice that some stars are brighter than others. A system called apparent magnitude is used for classifying how bright a star appears from Earth. The dimmest stars that are visible to the unaided eye measure 6 on the apparent magnitude scale. A star with an apparent magnitude of 5 is 2.5 times brighter. The smaller the number is, the brighter the star is. The brightest star in the sky, Sirius, has an apparent magnitude of −1.5, and the Sun's apparent magnitude is −26.7.

Compared to other stars, the Sun is medium in size and temperature. It looks so bright because it is so close to Earth. Apparent magnitude is a measure of how bright a star looks from Earth but not a measure of its actual brightness, known as absolute magnitude. As **Figure 20** shows, a small, close star might look brighter than a giant star that is far away.

Figure 20 This flashlight looks brighter than the car headlights because it is closer. In a similar way, a small but close star can appear brighter than a more distant, giant star.

An animated version of this diagram is available at fl6.msscience.com

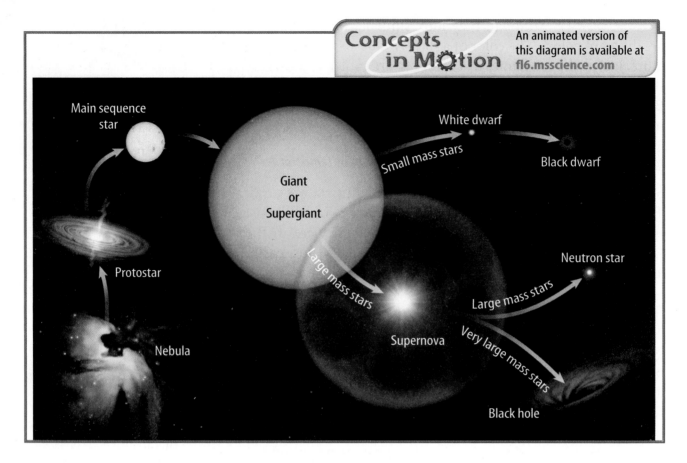

Figure 21 illustrates the lifetime of a star:

Main sequence star → Giant or Supergiant

Small mass stars → White dwarf → Black dwarf

Protostar ← Nebula

Large mass stars → Supernova → Large mass stars → Neutron star

Very large mass stars → Black hole

Figure 21 The events in the lifetime of a star depend on the star's mass.

Describe *what happens to giant stars when their cores collapse.*

INTEGRATE Physics

Determining the Age of Stars Some groups of stars, called clusters, contain stars that all formed at the same time. Scientists study these stars through a telescope to determine their color and brightness. This information can be used to find out how far along each star is in its life cycle. Because scientists know how long it takes for different stars to go through their life cycles, the age of the star cluster can be estimated.

The Lives of Stars

Scientists hypothesize that stars begin their lives as huge clouds of gas and dust. They are made of similar chemical elements. The force of gravity, which causes attraction between objects, causes the gases to move closer together. When this happens, temperatures within the cloud begin to rise. A star forms when this cloud gets so dense and hot that the atoms within it merge. This process is called fusion, and it changes matter to the energy that powers the star.

After a star has formed, it continues to evolve. When a medium-sized star like the Sun uses up some of the gases in its center, it expands to become a giant star. Giants are large, cool stars that have a red color. The Sun will become a giant in about five billion years. At this time, it will expand to cover the orbits of Mercury, Venus, and possibly Earth. It will remain that way for about a billion years. Then, the Sun will lose its outer shell, and the core will shrink to become a white dwarf star. A white dwarf is a hot, small star. Eventually, the white dwarf will cool and stop shining to become a black dwarf.

How long a star lives depends on how massive it is. Stars more massive than the Sun complete their life cycles in shorter amounts of time. The smallest stars shine the longest. **Figure 21** illustrates how the course of a star's life is determined by its size.

Supergiants When a large star begins to use up the fuel in its core, it expands to become a supergiant. These stars are similar to giant stars, except they are much larger. Eventually, the core of the supergiant will collapse. A huge shock wave moves through the star, and the star explodes and becomes bright. This exploding star is called a **supernova.** For a few brief days, the supernova might shine more brightly than a whole galaxy. The dust and gas released by this explosion, shown in **Figure 22,** might eventually become part of a new star.

 Meanwhile, the core of the supergiant is still around. If the core isn't too large, it becomes a neutron star. These are small objects that are extremely dense. However, if the core is more than about three times as massive as the Sun, the force of gravity is so great that the core collapses rapidly to form a black hole, shown in **Figure 23.** Light shone into a black hole disappears, and no light can escape from a black hole.

Galaxies

If you are away from city lights and look at the sky through a telescope, you might see faint patches of light. Some of these faint patches are galaxies. A **galaxy** is a large group of stars, gas, and dust held together by gravity. Galaxies have the same elements, forces, and forms of energy that occur in our solar system.

Types of Galaxies Galaxies come in different shapes and sizes. The four major types of galaxies are elliptical, spiral, barred spiral, and irregular. They are distinguished by their shapes. Elliptical galaxies are very common. They're shaped like huge footballs or spheres. Spiral galaxies have arms radiating outward from the center, somewhat like a giant pinwheel. As shown in **Figure 24,** some spiral galaxies have bar-shaped centers. Irregular galaxies are just that—irregular. They come in many different shapes and can't be classified easily. Irregular galaxies usually are smaller than other galaxies.

Figure 22 This photo shows the remains of a supernova.

Figure 23 A black hole has such strong gravity that not even light can escape. This drawing shows a black hole stripping gas from a nearby star.
Explain *how black holes form.*

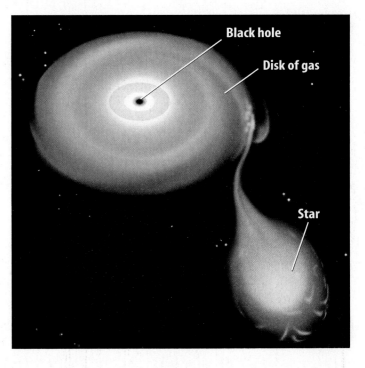

Black hole

Disk of gas

Star

NATIONAL GEOGRAPHIC VISUALIZING GALAXIES

Figure 24

Most stars visible in the night sky are part of the Milky Way Galaxy. Other galaxies, near and far, vary greatly in size and mass. The smallest galaxies are just a few thousand light-years in diameter and a million times more massive than the Sun. Large galaxies—which might be more than 100,000 light-years across—have a mass several trillion times greater than the Sun. Astronomers group galaxies into four general categories, as shown here.

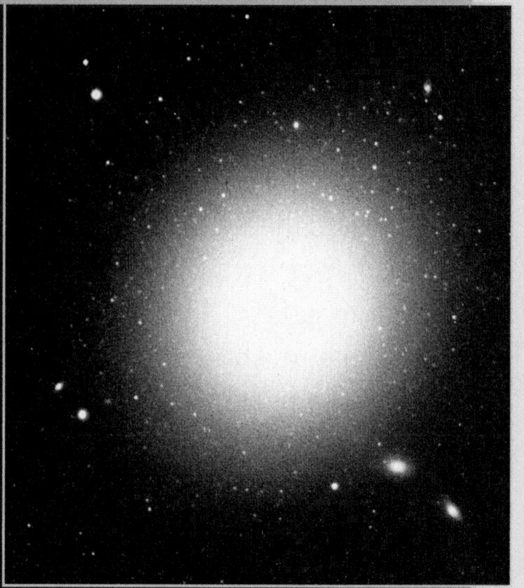

▲ **ELLIPTICAL GALAXIES** They are nearly spherical to oval in shape and consist of a tightly packed group of relatively old stars.

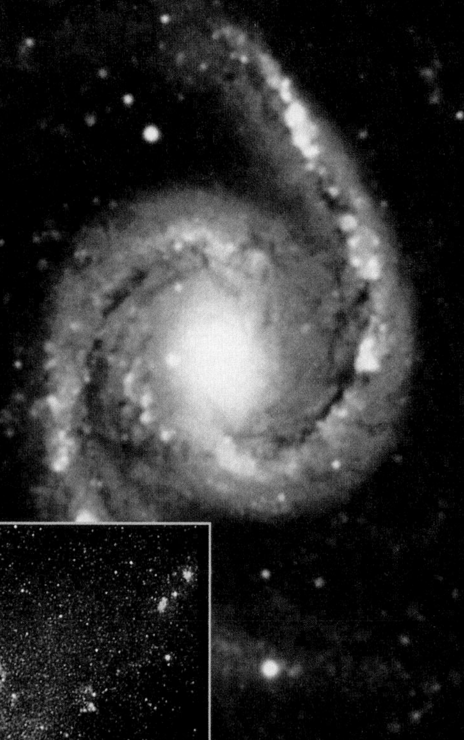

▶ **SPIRAL GALAXIES** Spiral galaxies consist of a large, flat disk of interstellar gas and dust with arms of stars extending from the disk in a spiral pattern. The Andromeda Galaxy, one of the Milky Way Galaxy's closest neighbors, is a spiral galaxy.

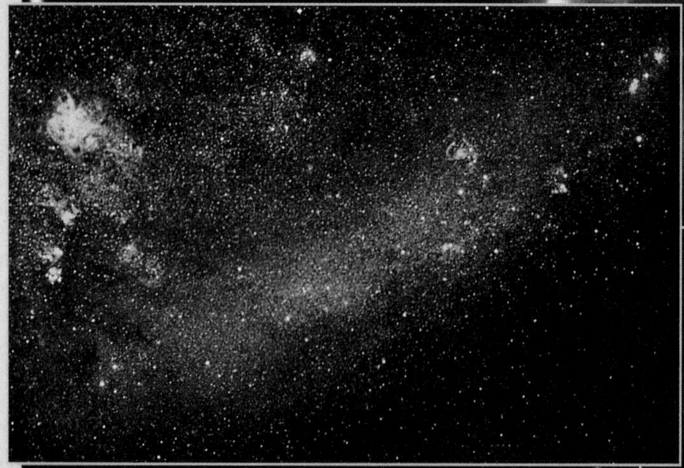

▲ **IRREGULAR GALAXIES** Some galaxies are neither spiral nor elliptical. Their shape seems to follow no set pattern, so astronomers have given them the general classification of irregular.

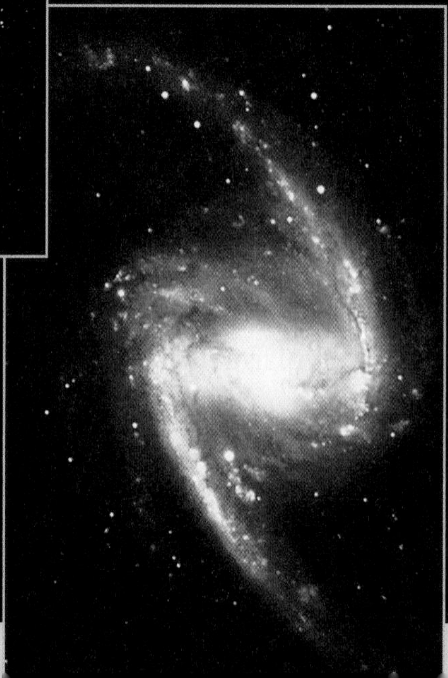

◀ **BARRED SPIRAL GALAXIES** Sometimes the flat disk that forms the center of a spiral galaxy is elongated into a bar shape. Two arms containing many stars swirl out from either end of the bar, forming what is known as a barred spiral galaxy.

Cygnus arm

Perseus arm

Centaurus arm

Orion arm

Sagittarius arm

Location of the Sun

The Milky Way Galaxy Which type of galaxy do you live in? Look at **Figure 25.** You live in the Milky Way, which is a giant spiral galaxy. Hundreds of billions of stars are in the Milky Way, including the Sun. Just as Earth revolves around the Sun, stars revolve around the centers of galaxies. The Sun revolves around the center of the Milky Way about once every 225 million years.

A View from Within You can see part of the Milky Way as a band of light across the night sky. However, you can't see the whole Milky Way. To understand why, think about boarding a Ferris wheel and looking straight up. Can you really tell what the ride looks like? Because you are at the bottom looking up, you get a limited view. Your view of the Milky Way from Earth is like the view of the Ferris wheel from the bottom. As you can see in **Figure 26,** you can view only parts of this galaxy because you are within it.

Reading Check *Why can't you see the entire Milky Way from Earth?*

The faint band of light across the sky that gives the Milky Way its name is the combined glow of stars in the galaxy's disk. In 1609, when the Italian astronomer Galileo looked at the Milky Way with a telescope, he showed that the band was actually made of countless individual stars. The galaxy is vast—bigger and brighter than most of the galaxies in the universe. Every star you see in the sky with your naked eye is a member of the Milky Way Galaxy.

Figure 25 The Sun is located toward the edge of the Milky Way.

Figure 26 This is the view of the Milky Way from inside the galaxy. **Infer** *why it is called the Milky Way.*

645

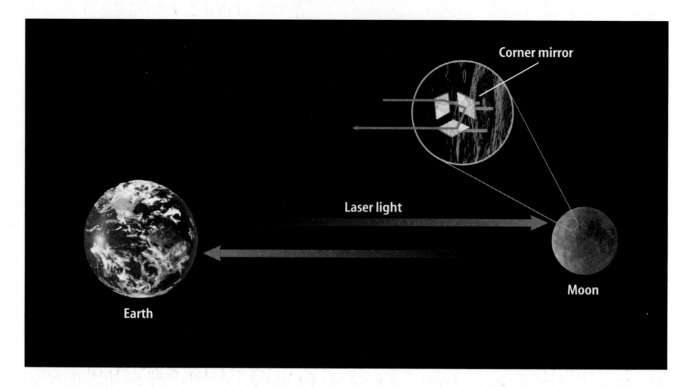

Corner mirror

Laser light

Moon

Earth

Figure 27 The constant speed of light through space helps astronomers in many ways. For example, the distance to the Moon has been determined by bouncing a laser beam off mirrors left by *Apollo 11* astronauts.

LA.A.2.3.5

Red Shift The Milky Way belongs to a cluster of galaxies called the Local Group. Scientists have determined that galaxies outside of the Local Group are moving away from Earth. Based on this, what can you infer about the size of the universe? Research the phenomenon known as red shift and describe to the class how it has helped astronomers learn about the universe.

Speed of Light The speed of light is unique. Light travels through space at about 300,000 km/s—so fast it could go around Earth seven times in 1 s. You can skim across ocean waves quickly on a speedboat, but no matter how fast you go, you can't gain on light waves. It's impossible to go faster than light. Most galaxies are moving away from the Milky Way and a few are moving closer, but the light from all galaxies travels toward Earth at the same speed. The constant speed of light is useful to astronomers, as shown in **Figure 27.**

Light-Years Earlier you learned that distances between the planets are measured in astronomical units. However, distances between galaxies are vast. Measuring them requires an even bigger unit. Scientists often use light-years to measure distances between galaxies. A **light-year** is the distance light travels in one year—about 9.5 trillion km.

✔ **Reading Check** *Why is a light-year better than an astronomical unit for measuring distances between galaxies?*

Would you like to travel back in time? In a way, that's what you're doing when you look at a galaxy. The galaxy might be millions of light-years away. The light that you see started on its journey long ago. You are seeing the galaxy as it was millions of years ago. On the other hand, if you could look at Earth from this distant galaxy, you would see events that happened here millions of years ago. That's how long it takes the light to travel the vast distances through space.

The Universe

Each galaxy contains billions of stars. Some might have as many stars as the Milky Way, and a few might have more. As many as 100 billion galaxies might exist. All these galaxies with all of their countless stars make up the universe.

Look at **Figure 28.** The *Hubble Space Telescope* spent ten days in 1995 photographing a tiny sector of the sky to produce this image. More than 1,500 galaxies were discovered. Astronomers think a similar picture would appear if they photographed any other sector of the sky. In this great vastness of exploding stars, black holes, star-filled galaxies, and empty space is one small planet called Earth. If you reduced the Sun to the size of a period on this page, the next-closest star would be more than 16 km away. Earth looks even lonelier when you consider that the universe also seems to be expanding. Most other galaxies are moving away at speeds as fast as 20,000 km/s. In relation to the immensity of the universe, Earth is an insignificant speck of dust. Could it be the only place where life exists?

Figure 28 The *Hubble* Deep Field image shows hundreds of galaxies in one tiny sector of the sky. **Explain** *what this image indicates about the sky.*

Reading Check *How do other galaxies move relative to Earth?*

section 3 review

Summary

Stars
- Constellations consist of stars that form patterns in the sky.

The Lives of Stars
- Stars evolve through time.
- How stars evolve depends on how massive they are.

Galaxies
- A galaxy is a large group of stars, gas, and dust held together by gravity.
- You live in the Milky Way Galaxy.

The Universe
- The universe might include 100 billion galaxies.

Self Check

1. **Explain** why stars appear to move across the sky each night. Why are some stars only visible during certain seasons?
2. **List and describe** some constellations. `SC.E.1.3.3`
3. **Describe** the life cycle of a star like the Sun. `SC.E.1.3.4`
4. **Think Critically** Some stars might no longer be in existence, but you still see them in the night sky. Why?

Applying Math

5. **Convert Units** A light-year is about 9.5 trillion kilometers. Alpha Centauri is a star that is 4.3 light-years from Earth. How many trillion kilometers away is this star? `SC.D.1.3.5` `MA.A.3.3.1`

Design Your Own

Space Colony *Inquiry*

Goals

- **Infer** what a space colony might look like on another planet.
- **Classify** planetary surface conditions.
- **Draw** a space colony for a planet.

Possible Materials

drawing paper
markers
books about the planets

Real-World Problem

Many fictional movies and books describe astronauts from Earth living in space colonies on other planets. Some of these make-believe societies seem far-fetched. So far, humans haven't built a space colony on another planet. However, if it happens, what would it look like?

Form a Hypothesis

Research a planet. Review conditions on the surface of the planet. Make a hypothesis about the things that would have to be included in a space colony to allow humans to survive on the planet.

⦿ Test Your Hypothesis

Make a Plan

1. Select a planet and study the conditions on its surface.
2. **Classify** the surface conditions in the following ways.
   a. solid or gas
   b. hot, cold, or a range of temperatures
   c. heavy atmosphere, thin atmosphere, or no atmosphere
   d. bright or dim sunlight
   e. unique conditions
3. **List** the things that humans need to survive. For example, humans need air to breathe. Does your planet have air that humans can breathe, or would your space colony have to provide the air?
4. Make a table for the planet showing its surface conditions and the features the space colony would have to have so that humans could survive on the planet.
5. **Discuss** your decisions as a group to make sure they make sense.

Follow Your Plan

1. Make sure your teacher approves your plan before you start.
2. **Draw** a picture of the space colony. Draw another picture showing the inside of the space colony. Label the parts of the space colony and explain how they aid in the survival of its human inhabitants.

⦿ Analyze Your Data

1. **Compare and contrast** your space colony with those of other students who researched the same planet you did. How are they alike? How are they different?
2. Would you change your space colony after seeing other groups' drawings? If so, what changes would you make? Explain your reasoning.

⦿ Conclude and Apply

1. **Describe** the most interesting thing you learned about the planet you studied.
2. Was your planet a good choice for a space colony?
3. Would humans want to live on your planet? Why or why not?
4. Could your space colony be built using present technology? Explain.

Communicating Your Data

Present your drawing and your table to the class. Make a case for why your planet would make a good home for a space colony. **For more help, refer to the** Science Skill Handbook.

Science and Language Arts

The Sun and the Moon
A Korean Folktale

The two children lived peacefully in the Heavenly Kingdom, until one day the Heavenly King said to them, "We can not allow anyone to sit here and idle away the time. So I have decided on duties for you. The boy shall be the Sun, to light the world of men, and the girl shall be the Moon, to shine by night." Then the girl answered, "Oh King, I am not familiar with the night. It would be better for me not to be the Moon." So the King made her the Sun instead, and made her brother the Moon.

It is said that when she became the Sun, the people used to gaze up at her in the sky. But she was modest, and greatly embarrassed by this. So she shone brighter and brighter, so that is why the Sun is so bright, that her modesty might be forever respected.

Understanding Literature

Cause and Effect The folktale explains why the Sun and the Moon exist, as well as why you should never look directly at the Sun. No one is allowed to be idle in the Heavenly Kingdom. This is a cause. What is the effect?

Respond to the Reading

1. What was the purpose of this folktale?
2. What clues does the folktale give about the personalities of the girl and the King?
3. **Linking Science and Writing** Using the form of a folktale, explain what causes something that happens in the solar system. `LA.B.2.3.3`

INTEGRATE Astronomy The cause-and-effect relationships that astronomers use to explain the origin of the Sun and the Moon are different from what is told in this folktale. Astronomers hypothesize that the Sun formed from a collapsing cloud of ice, gas, and dust. As the cloud contracted, the temperature at its center became so high that nuclear fusion began, and the Sun was born. Many hypotheses about how the Moon formed have been suggested. The most favored of these suggests that the Moon formed from the matter that was blasted into space when a Mars-sized object struck Earth just after it formed.

Reviewing Main Ideas

Section 1 Earth's Place in Space

1. Day and night occur because Earth rotates around its axis.

2. Earth's axis is tilted about 23.5° from straight up.

3. Earth's revolution and Earth's tilted axis cause seasons to occur.

Section 2 The Solar System

1. The inner planets include Mercury, Venus, Earth, and Mars.

2. The outer planets are Jupiter, Saturn, Uranus, Neptune, and Pluto.

3. Meteorites are pieces of rock that fall to Earth from space.

Section 3 Stars and Galaxies

1. Apparent magnitude is a way to describe how bright stars appear from Earth. It is different from a star's actual brightness, or absolute magnitude.

2. Stars change throughout their lives. How they change depends on how massive they are.

3. There are four types of galaxies: elliptical, spiral, irregular, and barred spiral.

Visualizing Main Ideas

Copy and complete the concept map below using the following terms: asteroid belt, galaxy, universe, inner planets, comets and meteorites, *and* outer planets.

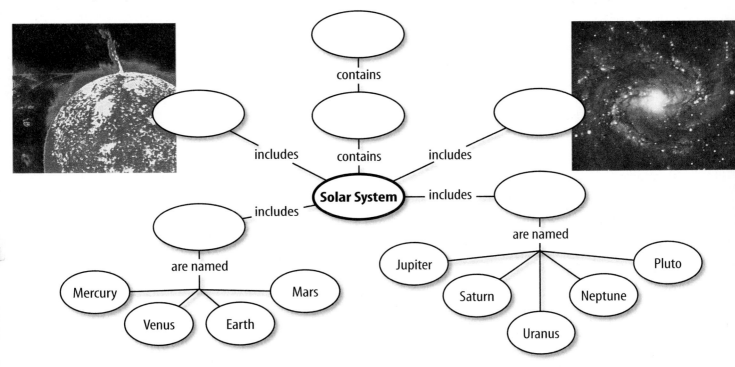

Using Vocabulary

astronomical unit p. 633	✴ **neap tide** p. 630
comet p. 638	orbit p. 625
✴ **constellation** p. 640	revolution p. 625
eclipse p. 628	rotation p. 624
✴ **galaxy** p. 643	✴ **solar system** p. 632
light-year p. 646	✴ **spring tide** p. 630
lunar highlands p. 626	supernova p. 643
maria p. 626	tides p. 629
meteorite p. 639	

✴ FCAT Vocabulary

Each question below asks about a vocabulary word from the list. Write the word that best answers each question.

1. What event occurs when Earth's shadow falls on the Moon? `SC.E.1.3.1`

2. Which Earth motion causes day and night?

3. What is a large group of stars, gas, and dust held together by gravity called? `SC.E.1.3.1`

4. What is a group of stars that forms a pattern in the sky called?

5. Which movement of Earth causes it to travel around the Sun? `SC.E.1.3.1`

Checking Concepts

Choose the word or phrase that best answers the question.

6. What is caused by the tilt of Earth's axis and its revolution? `SC.E.1.3.1`
   A) eclipses   C) tides
   B) phases   D) seasons

7. Which of the following is caused by the gravity of the Moon and the Sun? `SC.E.1.3.1`
   A) stars   C) comets
   B) tides   D) maria

8. An astronomical unit equals the distance from Earth to which of the following? `SC.E.1.3.1`
   A) the Moon   C) Mercury
   B) the Sun   D) Pluto

Use the photo below to answer question 9.

9. Why is Earth, shown above, a unique planet in the solar system? `SC.E.1.3.1`
   A) It is spherical.
   B) It has surface oceans.
   C) It has an elliptical orbit.
   D) It is the largest planet.

10. How many galaxies could be in the universe? `SC.E.2.3.1`
    A) 1 billion   C) 50 billion
    B) 10 billion   D) 100 billion

11. Which results from Earth's rotation? `SC.E.1.3.1`
    A) night and day   C) phases
    B) summer and   D) eclipses
       winter

12. What unit is often used to measure long distances in space, such as between stars and galaxies? `SC.D.1.3.5`
    A) kilometer   C) light-year
    B) astronomical   D) meter
       unit

13. How many planets are in the solar system? `SC.E.1.3.1`
    A) six   C) eight
    B) seven   D) nine

14. Which object's shadow travels across part of Earth during a solar eclipse? `SC.E.1.3.1`
    A) the Moon   C) an asteroid
    B) the Sun   D) a comet

15. If a star is massive enough, what can result after it produces a supernova?
    A) a galaxy   C) a black dwarf
    B) a black hole D) a white dwarf

Thinking Critically

16. Compare and Contrast Which of the planets in the solar system seems most like Earth? Which seems most different from Earth? Explain your answers using facts about the planets. `SC.E.1.3.1`

17. Predict How might a scientist predict the date and time of an eclipse? `SC.E.1.3.1`

18. Recognize Cause and Effect Which of the Moon's motions are real? Which are apparent? Explain each. `SC.E.1.3.1`

19. Make and Use Tables Research the size, composition, and surface features of each planet. Show this information in a table. How do tables help you to organize information? `SC.E.1.3.1`

20. Make a model of a lunar or solar eclipse based on what you have learned about Earth, the Sun, and the Moon. Use simple classroom materials. `SC.E.1.3.1`

21. Concept Map Copy and complete the following concept map using the following terms: *full, red surface, corona, solar,* and *few*. `SC.E.1.3.1`

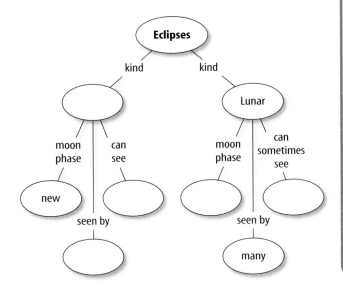

Performance Activities

22. Model Make a three-dimensional model showing the relative positions of Earth, the Sun, and the Moon during spring tides and neap tides. Which moon phase corresponds to each arrangement? `SC.E.1.3.1`

23. Poster Research the moons of Jupiter, Saturn, Uranus, or Neptune. Make a poster showing the characteristics of these moons. Display your poster for your class. `SC.E.1.3.1`

Applying Math

24. Distances in the Solar System `MA.A.3.3.1`
  a. Venus is 0.72 AU from the Sun. Neptune is 30.07 AU from the Sun. How many times farther from the Sun is Neptune than Venus?
  b. Jupiter is 5.20 AU from the Sun. Pluto is 39.48 AU from the Sun. How many times farther from the Sun is Pluto than Jupiter?

25. Earth's Circumference Earth's diameter at the equator is about 12,756 km. Using the equation $C = \pi d$, where C is circumference, d is diameter, and π is about 3.14, calculate Earth's circumference at the equator. `MA.B.1.3.1`

Use the graph below to answer question 26.

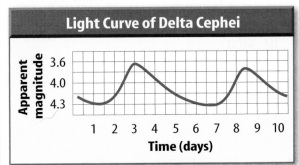

26. Variable Stars The brightness of some stars varies with time. The graph above shows how the apparent magnitude of a star named Delta Cephei varies with time. What is the period of this star's light curve? *Hint: The period is found by determining the time between apparent magnitude peaks.* `MA.D.1.3.1`

The assessed Florida Benchmark appears above each question.

Record your answers on the answer sheet provided by your teacher or on a sheet of paper.

Multiple Choice

SC.E.1.3.1

1 The table below lists how long it takes the planets in our solar system to complete their revolutions around the Sun.

Planetary Revolution	
Planet	**Period of revolution (Earth years)**
Mercury	0.241
Venus	0.615
Earth	1.00
Mars	1.88
Jupiter	11.9
Saturn	29.5
Uranus	84.0
Neptune	165
Pluto	248

Based on the data in the table, which of the following planets has the longest year?

A. Jupiter

B. Mars

C. Pluto

D. Saturn

SC.E.1.3.1

2 What formed when meteorites struck the Moon's surface?

F. craters

G. lunar highlands

H. maria

I. plateaus

SC.E.1.3.1

3 The diagram below shows Earth's revolution around the Sun.

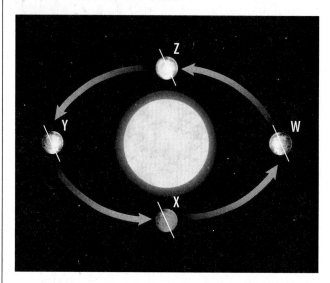

Assuming the top of the diagram represents north, which season occurs in the northern hemisphere when Earth is in position Z?

A. autumn

B. spring

C. summer

D. winter

SC.D.1.3.5

4 On Earth, distances between locations are commonly measured in miles or kilometers. Which of the following units are used to measure distances between galaxies?

F. astronomical units

G. decameters

H. light-years

I. nanometers

SC.E.1.3.1

5 The largest gap between the orbits of two neighboring planets is between Mars and Jupiter. A belt of smaller bodies that orbit the Sun is found in this gap. What name is given to the bodies in this belt?

A. asteroids

B. comets

C. meteors

D. stars

Gridded Response

SC.E.1.3.1

6 One lunar cycle takes about 28 days. If there are 365 days in a normal Earth year, how many lunar cycles occur in a year?

READ
INQUIRE
EXPLAIN

Short Response

SC.E.1.3.1

7 The diagram below shows the lunar cycle.

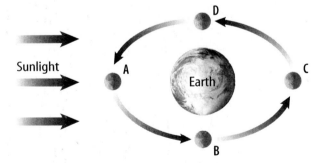

Explain how the positions of the Sun, the Moon, and Earth create the effect of lunar phases.

READ
INQUIRE
EXPLAIN

Extended Response

SC.E.1.3.1

8 The diagram below shows an outcome of the gravitational attraction between Earth and the Moon.

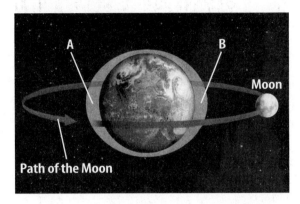

PART A What is occurring at points A and B?

PART B Describe how the gravitational attraction between the Moon and Earth affects Earth.

Sunshine State Standards—**SC.A.2**: The student understands . . . atomic theory; **SC.E.1**: understands the interaction and organization in the Solar System and the universe . . . ; **SC.H.1**: uses the scientific processes . . . to solve problems; **SC.H.3**: understands that science, technology, and society are interwoven . . . .

Exploring Space

Fiery end or new beginning?

These colorful streamers are the remains of a star that exploded in a nearby galaxy thousands of years ago. Eventually, new stars and planets may form from this material, just as our Sun and planets formed from similar debris billions of years ago.

Science Journal Do you think space exploration is worth the risk and expense? Explain.

Start-Up Activities

An Astronomer's View

You might think exploring space with a telescope is easy because the stars seem so bright and space is dark. But starlight passing through Earth's atmosphere, and differences in temperature and density of the atmosphere can distort images.

1. Complete a safety worksheet.

2. Cut off a piece of clear plastic wrap about 15 cm long.

3. Place an opened book in front of you and observe the clarity of the text.

4. Hold the piece of plastic wrap close to your eyes, keeping it stretched.

5. Look at the same text through the plastic wrap.

6. Fold the plastic wrap in half and look at the text again through both layers.

7. **Think Critically** Write a paragraph in your Science Journal comparing reading text through plastic wrap to an astronomer viewing stars through Earth's atmosphere. Predict what might occur if you increased the number of layers.

Science Online | Preview this chapter's content and activities at fl6.msscience.com

Exploring Space Make the following Foldable to help identify what you already know, what you want to know, and what you learned about exploring space.

LA.A.1.3.4

STEP 1 **Fold** a sheet of paper vertically from side to side. Make the front edge about 1.25 cm shorter than the back.

STEP 2 **Turn** lengthwise and **fold** into thirds.

STEP 3 **Unfold and cut** only the top layer along both folds to make three tabs. **Label** each tab.

Know? | Like to know? | Learned?

Identify Questions Before you read the chapter, write what you already know about exploring space under the left tab of your Foldable, and write questions about what you'd like to know under the center tab. After you read the chapter, list what you learned under the right tab.

Also covers: SC.H.1.3.1 Annually Assessed (p. 662), SC.H.1.3.4 Annually Assessed (p. 661), SC.H.1.3.5 Annually Assessed (p. 664), SC.H.1.3.7 Annually Assessed (p. 661), SC.H.3.3.5 (p. 661), SC.H.3.3.6 (p. 664)

Radiation from Space

as you read

What You'll Learn

- **Explain** the electromagnetic spectrum.
- **Identify** the differences between refracting and reflecting telescopes.
- **Recognize** the differences between optical and radio telescopes.

Why It's Important

Learning about space can help us better understand our own world.

Review Vocabulary

✴ **universe:** the total sum of all matter and energy that exists

New Vocabulary

✴ **radiation**
- electromagnetic spectrum
- refracting telescope
- reflecting telescope
- observatory
- radio telescope

✴ FCAT Vocabulary

Electromagnetic Waves

On a clear, dark night you might be able to see thousands of stars in the night sky. If you look at the night sky with binoculars or a telescope, you can see many more stars. You might even notice that some stars have different colors. However, stars are very far away. Even if you could travel at the speed of light, it would take many years to reach the nearest stars you see.

Even though stars are far from Earth, astronomers have measured the sizes, masses, and temperatures of different stars. Astronomers even have learned what stars are made of. To learn about stars and other objects in space, astronomers study the energy these objects give off.

Radiation from Stars Stars and other objects in the universe give off, or emit, energy in the form of waves. **Radiation** is energy that is transferred from one place to another by waves. When objects in the universe emit radiation, the waves that are given off are called electromagnetic waves. These waves can travel through vast regions of space and reach Earth. Electromagnetic waves travel through empty space and through matter.

Figure 1 The electromagnetic spectrum ranges from gamma rays with wavelengths of less than ten trillionths of a meter to radio waves with wavelengths of more than 100 km.
Observe *how frequency changes as wavelength shortens.*

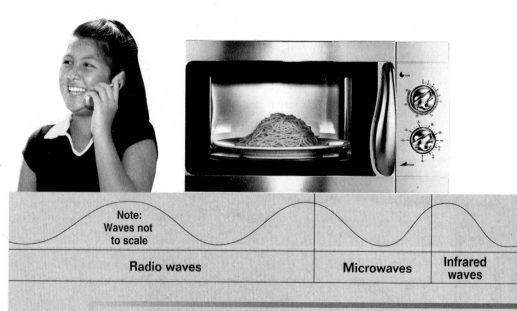

Note: Waves not to scale

| Radio waves | Microwaves | Infrared waves |

Increasing wavelength

The Electromagnetic Spectrum Electromagnetic waves are all around you. When you turn on the TV, warm up a pizza in the microwave, or have an X ray taken—you're using different types of electromagnetic waves. The light that enters your eyes also is a type of electromagnetic wave.

There is a wide range of electromagnetic waves. The main types are radio waves, microwaves, infrared waves, visible light, ultraviolet waves, X rays, and gamma rays. Each type of wave has a specific range of wavelengths and frequencies. The arrangement of electromagnetic waves according to their wavelengths and frequencies is called the **electromagnetic spectrum.**

The electromagnetic spectrum is shown in **Figure 1.** Radio waves have the longest wavelengths and lowest frequencies, and gamma rays have the shortest wavelengths and highest frequencies.

Effects of Electromagnetic Waves The different types of electromagnetic waves have different effects and are used in different ways. A TV uses radio waves broadcast by a TV station to make images and sounds. Infrared waves make your hands feel warm when you hold them by a fire. Ultraviolet waves emitted by the Sun can cause your skin to become sunburned. Gamma rays are emitted by the nuclei of some atoms and are used to treat cancer.

The Crab Nebula, shown in **Figure 1,** is a source of gamma radiation in space. This nebula was formed by an exploding star.

INTEGRATE Health

Ultraviolet Light Many newspapers include an ultraviolet (UV) index to urge people to minimize their exposure to the UV waves from the Sun. UV waves can damage living tissue. Compare the wavelengths and frequencies of visible light and ultraviolet waves.

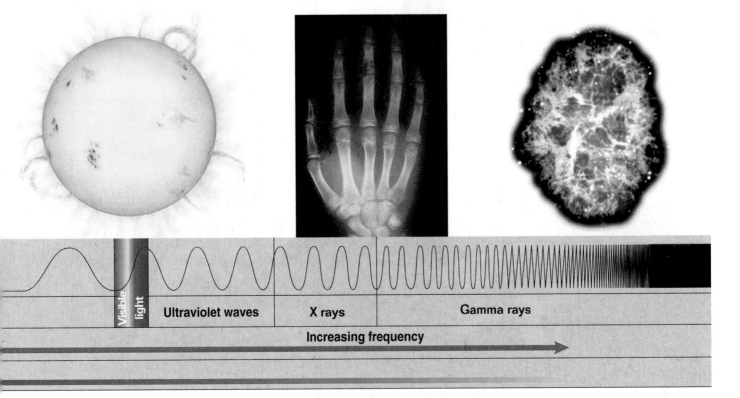

Visible light

Ultraviolet waves   X rays   Gamma rays

Increasing frequency

Optical Telescopes

Optical telescopes gather visible light, which is a type of electromagnetic wave, to produce magnified images of distant objects. Light is gathered by an objective lens or mirror, which redirects the light to form an image. An eyepiece lens then magnifies the image. The two types of optical telescopes are shown in **Figure 2.**

A **refracting telescope** uses a convex lens, which is curved outward like the surface of a ball, to gather light. Light from an object passes through a convex objective lens and is bent to form an image. The eyepiece lens magnifies the image for viewing.

A **reflecting telescope** uses a curved mirror to gather light and form an image. Light from the object being viewed passes through the open end of a reflecting telescope. This light strikes a concave mirror, which is curved inward like a bowl and is located at the base of the telescope. The light is reflected off the surface of the mirror and forms an image. A smaller, flat mirror reflects the image toward an eyepiece.

Using Optical Telescopes Most optical telescopes used by professional astronomers are housed in buildings called **observatories.** Observatories often have dome-shaped roofs that can be opened up for viewing. However, not all telescopes are located in observatories. The *Hubble Space Telescope* is an example.

Large optical telescopes often are used to photograph stars and other objects in space. To do this, the telescope's eyepiece usually is replaced with a camera.

Figure 2 These diagrams show how each type of optical telescope collects light and forms an image.

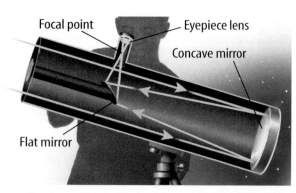

Convex lens · Eyepiece lens · Focal point

In a refracting telescope, a convex lens gathers light to form an image.

Focal point · Eyepiece lens · Concave mirror · Flat mirror

In a reflecting telescope, a concave mirror gathers light to form an image.

Optical telescopes are widely available for use by individuals.

Large Reflecting Telescopes Since the early 1600s, when the Italian scientist Galileo Galilei first turned a telescope toward the stars, people have been searching for better ways to study what lies beyond Earth's atmosphere. For example, the twin Keck reflecting telescopes, shown in **Figure 3,** have segmented mirrors 10 m wide. Until 2000, these mirrors were the largest reflectors ever used. To cope with the difficulty of building such huge mirrors, the Keck telescope mirrors are built out of many small mirrors that are pieced together. In 2000, the European Southern Observatory's telescope, in Chile, consisted of four 8.2-m reflectors. One of the mirrors in this telescope is shown in **Figure 4.**

 **Reading Check** *About how long have people been using telescopes?*

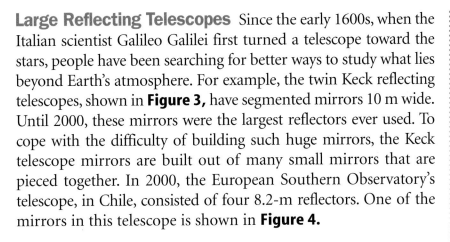

Figure 3 The twin Keck telescopes on Mauna Kea in Hawaii are used together. This more than doubles their light-gathering power.

SC.H.1.3.4
SC.H.1.3.7

Mini LAB

Observing Effects of Light Pollution

Procedure

1. Obtain a **cardboard tube** from an empty roll of paper towels.
2. Go outside on a clear night about two hours after sunset. Look through the cardboard tube at a specific constellation decided upon ahead of time.
3. Count the number of stars you can see without moving the observing tube. Repeat this three times.
4. Calculate the average number of observable stars at your location.

Analysis

1. Compare and contrast the number of stars visible from other students' homes.
2. Explain the causes and effects of your observations.

Try at Home

Figure 4 Large mirrors, like the one shown here, are housed in separate reflectors in the ESO telescope. Together, they can gather as much light as a single mirror 200 m across.

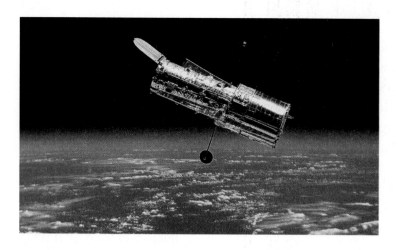

Hubble Space Telescope Earth's atmosphere absorbs and distorts light from stars. To see faint objects in space with much greater detail, the *Hubble Space Telescope*, shown in **Figure 5,** was launched into orbit in 1990 by the space shuttle *Discovery*. After astronauts repaired a problem with the telescope's mirrors in 1993, *Hubble* began sending images of distant objects to Earth that showed amazing detail. Using *Hubble's* images, astronomers have made important discoveries about a black hole at the center of our galaxy and clusters of galaxies far out in the universe.

Figure 5 The *Hubble Space Telescope* was designed to be repaired by astronauts in space every few years.
Explain *why many discoveries about our galaxy could not have been made before 1993.*

James Webb Space Telescope Plans are being made to launch a new space telescope that is capable of observing the earliest stars and galaxies. The *James Webb Space Telescope,* shown in **Figure 6,** will be the successor to the *Hubble Space Telescope*. As part of the Origins project, it will allow scientists to study the structure of galaxies, the production of elements by stars, and the process of star and planet formation. The telescope will be designed to see objects 400 times fainter than those currently studied with the twin Keck telescopes. The main mirror will be 6.5 m across. NASA hopes to launch the *James Webb Space Telescope* as early as 2011.

Figure 6 The *James Webb Space Telescope* honors the NASA administrator who contributed greatly to the Apollo Program. It will help scientists learn more about how galaxies form.

Radio Telescopes

Stars and other objects in space radiate electromagnetic energy of various types. For example, radio waves are emitted by stars, galaxies, and other objects. A **radio telescope,** such as the one shown in **Figure 7,** is used to study radio waves traveling through space. Unlike visible light, radio waves pass freely through Earth's atmosphere. Because of this, radio telescopes are useful 24 hours per day under most weather conditions.

Radio waves reaching Earth's surface strike the large, concave dish of a radio telescope. This dish reflects the waves to a point where a receiver is located. The information allows scientists to study certain types of stars, to map the universe, and to search for signs of intelligent life.

The largest radio telescope in 2005 was the Arecibo telescope in Puerto Rico. The 305-m reflector dish was built into a large limestone sinkhole. The huge dish allows faint radio signals to be received from distant galaxies.

Figure 7 This radio telescope is used to study radio waves traveling through space.

section 1 review

Summary

Electromagnetic Waves
- Light is a type of electromagnetic wave.
- The electromagnetic spectrum is made up of all the types of electromagnetic waves.
- Electromagnetic waves travel through empty space and through matter.

Optical Telescopes
- A refracting telescope uses lenses to collect, focus, and view light.
- A reflecting telescope uses a mirror to collect and focus light and a lens to view the image.
- Optical telescopes often are housed in domed buildings called observatories.
- Placing a telescope in space avoids problems caused by Earth's atmosphere.

Radio Telescopes
- Radio telescopes collect and measure radio waves coming from stars and other objects.

Self Check

1. **Identify** one advantage of radio telescopes over optical telescopes. SC.H.3.3.4

2. **Infer** If red light has a longer wavelength than blue light, which has the greater frequency?

3. **Explain** why your hands feel warm when you hold them in front of a hot oven. SC.A.2.2.3

4. **Describe** how Earth's atmosphere affects light from stars and other objects in space.

5. **Think Critically** How long would it take gamma rays from an exploding star to reach Earth if the star is 10.5 light-years away? SC.D.1.3.5

Applying Skills

6. **Sequence** these types of electromagnetic waves from longest wavelength to shortest wavelength: *gamma rays, visible light, X rays, radio waves, infrared waves, microwaves,* and *ultraviolet waves.*

Benchmark—**SC.H.1.3.5:** The student knows that a change in one or more variables may alter the outcome of an investigation; **SC.H.3.3.6:** The student knows that no matter who does science and mathematics or invents things, or when or where they do it, the knowledge and technology that result can eventually become available to everyone.

Building a Reflecting Telescope

Nearly four hundred years ago, Galileo Galilei saw what no human had ever seen. Using the telescope he built, he saw moons around Jupiter, details of lunar craters, and sunspots. What was it like to make these discoveries? Find out as you make your own reflecting telescope.

◉ Real-World Problem

How do you construct a reflecting telescope?

Goals
- **Construct** a reflecting telescope.
- **Observe** magnified images using the telescope and different magnifying lenses.

Materials
flat mirror
shaving or cosmetic mirror (a curved, concave mirror) on a stand
magnifying lenses of different magnifications (3–4)

Safety Precautions

WARNING: *Never observe the Sun directly or with mirrors.*

Complete a safety worksheet before you begin.

◉ Procedure

1. Position the cosmetic mirror so that it faces the object you want to look at. Choose the Moon, a planet, or an artificial light source.
2. Hold the flat mirror so that it is facing the cosmetic mirror.
3. Adjust the position of the flat mirror until

you can see the reflection of the object in it.

4. View the image of the object in the flat mirror with one of your magnifying lenses. Observe how the lens magnifies the image.
5. Use your other magnifying lenses to view the image of the object in the flat mirror. Observe how the different lenses change the image of the object.

◉ Analyze Your Data

1. **Describe** how the image changed when you used different magnifying lenses.
2. **Identify** the part or parts of your telescope that reflected the light of the image.
3. **Identify** the parts of your telescope that magnified the image.

◉ Conclude and Apply

1. **Explain** how the three parts of your telescope worked to reflect and magnify the light of the object.
2. **Infer** how the materials you used would have differed if you had constructed a refracting instead of a reflecting telescope.

*C*ommunicating
Your Data

Write an instructional pamphlet for amateur astronomers about how to construct a reflecting telescope.

Benchmarks—SC.E.1.3.2 Annually Assessed (p. 668): The student knows that available data from various satellite probes show the similarities and differences among planets and their moons in the Solar System.

Also covers: SC.C.2.3.5 Annually Assessed (p. 667), SC.D.1.3.5 (p. 670), SC.E.1.3.1 Annually Assessed (pp. 670–671), SC.H.1.3.3 (p. 668), SC.H.1.3.6 (pp. 668, 671–672), SC.H.3.3.5 (pp. 671–672), SC.H.3.3.6 (p. 669)

Early Space Missions

The First Missions into Space

You're offered a choice—front-row-center seats for this weekend's rock concert, or a copy of the video when it's released. Wouldn't you rather be right next to the action? Astronomers feel the same way about space. Even though telescopes have taught them a great deal about the Moon and planets, they want to learn more by going to those places or by sending spacecraft where humans can't go.

Rockets The space program would not have gotten far off the ground using ordinary airplane engines. To break free of gravity and enter Earth's orbit, spacecraft must travel at speeds greater than 11 km/s. The space shuttle and several other spacecrafts are equipped with special engines that carry their own fuel. **Rockets,** like the one in **Figure 8,** are engines that have everything they need for the burning of fuel. They don't even require air to carry out the process. Therefore, they can work in space, where there is no air. The simplest rocket engine is made of a burning chamber and a nozzle. More complex rockets have more than one burning chamber.

Rocket Types There are two types of rockets. One type is the liquid-fuel rocket and the other is the solid-fuel rocket. Solid-fuel rockets are generally simpler but they can't be shut down after they are ignited. Liquid-fuel rockets can be shut down after they are ignited and can be restarted. For this reason, liquid-fuel rockets are preferred for use in long-term space missions. Scientists on Earth can send signals that start and stop the spacecraft's engines whenever they want to modify its course or adjust its orbit. Liquid-fuel rockets successfully powered many space probes, including the early *Voyager* and *Galileo* missions.

Figure 8 Rockets differ according to the types of fuel used to launch them. Liquid oxygen is used often to support combustion. Many rockets have been launched from the Kennedy Space Center, shown here.

as you read

What **You'll Learn**

- **Compare and contrast** natural and artificial satellites.
- **Identify** the differences between artificial satellites and space probes.
- **Explain** the history of the race to the Moon.

Why **It's Important**

Early missions that sent objects and people into space began a new era of human exploration.

Review Vocabulary

✳ **gravity:** the force of attraction between two masses

New Vocabulary

- rocket
- satellite
- orbit
- space probe
- Project Mercury
- Project Gemini
- Project Apollo

✳ FCAT Vocabulary

Figure 9 The space shuttle uses both liquid and solid fuels. Here, the red liquid-fuel tank is visible behind a white, solid rocket booster.

Rocket Launching Solid-fuel rockets use a rubberlike fuel that contains its own oxidizer. The burning chamber of a rocket is a tube that has a nozzle at one end. As the solid fuel burns, hot gases exert pressure on all inner surfaces of the tube. The tube pushes back on the gas except at the nozzle where hot gases escape. The force exerted by the hot gases pushes the rocket forward.

Liquid-fuel rockets use a liquid fuel and an oxidizer, such as liquid oxygen, stored in separate tanks. To ignite the rocket, the oxidizer is mixed with the liquid fuel in the burning chamber. As the mixture burns, forces are exerted and the rocket is propelled forward. **Figure 9** shows the space shuttle, with both types of rockets, being launched.

Applying Math — Make and Use Graphs

DRAWING BY NUMBERS Points are defined by two coordinates, called an ordered pair. To plot an ordered pair, find the first number on the horizontal *x*-axis and the second on the vertical *y*-axis. The point is placed where these two coordinates intersect. Line segments are drawn to connect points. Draw a symmetrical house by using an *x-y* grid and these coordinates: (1,1), (5,1), (3,6), (5,5), (1,5)

Solution

1 On a piece of graph paper, label and number the x-axis 0 to 6 and the y-axis 0 to 6, as shown here.

2 Plot the above points and connect them with straight line segments, as shown here.

Section	Points
1	(1, −8) (3,−13) (6, −21) (9,−21) (9,−17) (8,−15) (8,−12) (6,−8) (5,−4) (4,−3) (4,−1) (5,1) (6,3) (8,3) (9,4) (9,7) (7,11) (4,14) (4,22) (−9,22) (−9,10) (−10,5) (−11,−1) (−11,−7) (−9,−8) (−8,−7) (−8,−1) (−6,3) (−6,−3) (−6,−9) (−7,−20) (−8,−21) (−4,−21) (−4,−18) (−3,−14) (−1,−8)
2	(0,11) (2,13) (2,17) (0,19) (−4,19) (−6,17) (−6,13) (−4,11)
3	(−4,9) (1,9) (1,5) (−1,5) (−2,6) (−4,6)

Practice Problems

1. Label and number the *x*-axis −12 to 10 and the *y*-axis −22 to 23. Draw an astronaut by plotting and connecting the points in each section. Do not draw segments to connect points in different sections. **MA.C.3.3.2**

2. Make your own drawing on graph paper and write its coordinates as ordered pairs. Then give it to a classmate to solve. **MA.C.3.3.2**

Math Practice | For more practice, visit fl6.msscience.com

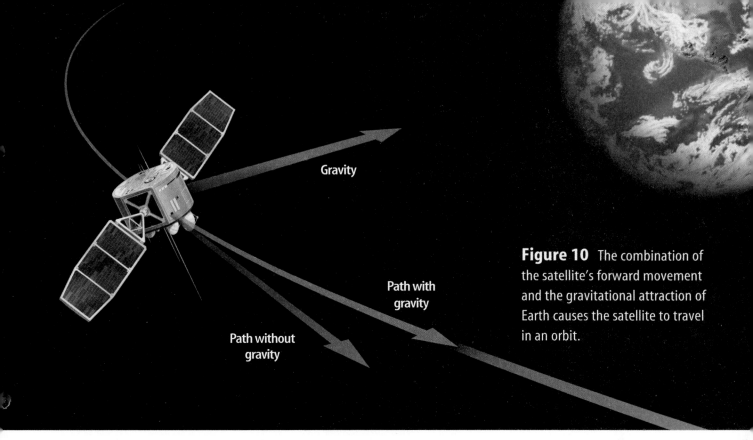

Gravity

Path with gravity

Path without gravity

Figure 10 The combination of the satellite's forward movement and the gravitational attraction of Earth causes the satellite to travel in an orbit.

Satellites The space age began in 1957 when the former Soviet Union used a rocket to send *Sputnik I* into space. *Sputnik I* was the first artificial satellite. A **satellite** is any object that revolves around another object. An object in motion travels in a straight line unless a force, such as gravity, makes it turn. Earth's gravity pulls a satellite toward Earth. The result of the satellite traveling forward while at the same time being pulled toward Earth is a curved path, called an **orbit**, around Earth. This is shown in **Figure 10.** *Sputnik I* orbited Earth for 57 days before gravity pulled it back into the atmosphere, where it burned up.

Figure 11 Data obtained from the satellite *Terra*, launched in 1999, illustrates the use of space technology to study Earth. This false-color image includes data on spring growth, sea-surface temperature, carbon monoxide concentrations, and reflected sunlight, among others.

Satellite Uses *Sputnik I* was an experiment to show that artificial satellites could be made and placed into orbit around Earth.

Today, thousands of artificial satellites orbit Earth. Communication satellites transmit radio and television programs to locations around the world. Other satellites gather scientific data, like those shown in **Figure 11,** which can't be obtained from Earth. Weather satellites constantly monitor Earth's global weather patterns.

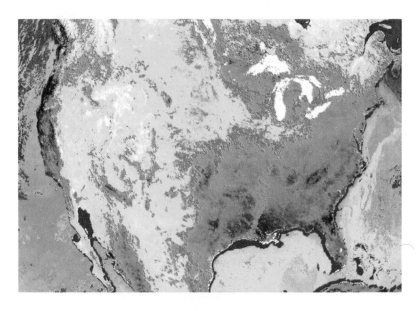

Astronomy Astronomers today have more choices than ever before. Some still use optical telescopes to study stars and galaxies. Others explore the universe using the radio, X-ray, infrared, or even gamma-ray regions of the electromagnetic spectrum. Still others deal with theory and work with physicists to understand the big bang and the nature of matter in the universe. Government, universities, and private industry offer jobs for astronomers.

Space Probes

Not all objects carried into space by rockets become satellites. Rockets also can be used to send instruments out into space to collect data. A **space probe** is an instrument that gathers information and sends it back to Earth. Unlike satellites that orbit Earth, space probes travel toward planets as shown in **Figure 12.** Some have traveled to the edge of the solar system, including *Pioneer 10,* launched in 1972. Although it stopped sending signals in 2003, it continues on through space. Also, the *Voyager* probes should continue to send data on the outer parts of the solar system until about 2020. Data from probes show the similarities and differences among the planets and their moons.

Space probes, like many satellites, carry cameras and other data-gathering equipment, as well as radio transmitters and receivers that allow them to communicate with scientists on Earth. **Table 1** shows some of the early space probes launched by the National Aeronautics and Space Administration (NASA).

Table 1 Some Early Space Missions				
Mission Name		**Date Launched**	**Destination**	**Data Obtained**
Mariner 2		August 1962	Venus	verified high temperatures in Venus's atmosphere
Pioneer 10		March 1972	Jupiter	sent back photos of Jupiter—first probe to encounter an outer planet
Viking 1		August 1975	Mars	orbiter mapped the surface of Mars; lander searched for life on Mars
Magellan		May 1989	Venus	mapped Venus's surface and returned data on the composition of Venus's atmosphere

Figure 12

Probes have taught us much about the solar system. As they travel through space, these car-size craft gather data with their onboard instruments and send results back to Earth via radio waves. Some data collected during these missions are made into pictures, a selection of which is shown here.

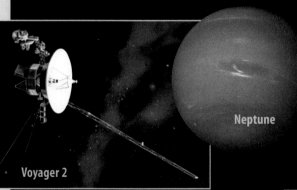
Mariner 10

Mercury

A In 1974, *Mariner 10* obtained the first good images of the surface of Mercury.

Venera 8

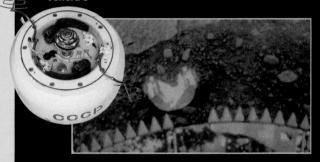

B A Soviet *Venera* probe took this picture of the surface of Venus on March 1, 1982. Parts of the spacecraft's landing gear are visible at the bottom of the photograph.

Magellan

D In 1990, *Magellan* imaged craters, lava domes, and great rifts, or cracks, on the surface of Venus.

Venus

Neptune

Voyager 2

C The *Voyager 2* mission included flybys of the outer planets Jupiter, Saturn, Uranus, and Neptune. *Voyager* took this photograph of Neptune in 1989 as the craft sped toward the edge of the solar system.

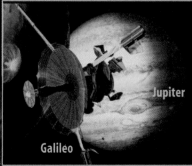
Jupiter

Galileo

E NASA's veteran space traveler *Galileo* nears Jupiter in this artist's drawing. The craft arrived at Jupiter in 1995 and sent back data, including images of Europa, one of Jupiter's 63 moons, seen below in a color-enhanced view.

Europa

Voyager and Pioneer Probes Space probes *Voyager 1* and *Voyager 2* were launched in 1977 and now are heading toward deep space. *Voyager 1* flew past Jupiter and Saturn. *Voyager 2* flew past Jupiter, Saturn, Uranus, and Neptune. These probes will explore beyond the solar system as part of the Voyager Interstellar Mission. Scientists expect these probes to continue to transmit data to Earth for at least 20 more years.

Pioneer 10, launched in 1972, was the first probe to survive a trip through the asteroid belt and encounter an outer planet, Jupiter. As of 2003, *Pioneer 10* was more than 12 billion km from Earth, and will continue beyond the solar system. The probe carries a gold medallion with an engraving of a man, a woman, and Earth's position in the galaxy.

Galileo Launched in 1989, *Galileo* reached Jupiter in 1995 and began orbiting the planet. *Galileo* then released a smaller probe that began a five-month trip toward the planet. The small probe took a parachute ride down through Jupiter's violent atmosphere in December 1995.

Before being crushed by the atmospheric pressure, the probe sent information about the atmosphere and its temperature and pressure to *Galileo* orbiting above. *Galileo* obtained data on Jupiter's moons, rings, and other features and relayed this information to excited scientists on Earth.

While making trips around Jupiter, *Galileo* surveyed the planet's largest moons. When *Galileo* studied Europa, scientists were surprised to discover that an ocean of water may be under the moon's surface. A cracked layer of ice makes up Europa's surface, shown in **Figure 13.**

Because water is necessary to support life, scientists are very anxious to find out more about Europa and its water. *Galileo* ended its study of Europa in 2000. A more advanced probe is being planned that will orbit this moon and survey its icy surface more closely.

✓ Reading Check *Why do scientists want to send another probe to Europa in the future?*

In October and November of 1999, *Galileo* approached Io, another one of Jupiter's moons. It came within 300 km and took photographs of a volcanic vent named Loki, which gives off more energy than all of Earth's volcanoes combined. *Galileo* also discovered jets on the surface that shoot out gas made of sulfur and oxygen.

Figure 13 Unlike Jupiter's other moons, Europa's surface has few craters. The markings may be caused by internal heat that cracks the icy surface.

Moon Quest

Throughout the world, people were shocked when they turned on their radios and television sets in 1957 and heard the radio transmissions from *Sputnik I* as it orbited Earth. All that *Sputnik I* transmitted was a sort of beeping sound, but people quickly realized that launching a human into space wasn't far off.

In 1961, Soviet cosmonaut Yuri A. Gagarin became the first human in space. He orbited Earth and returned safely. Soon, President John F. Kennedy called for the United States to send humans to the Moon and return them safely to Earth. His goal was to achieve this by the end of the 1960s. The race for space was underway.

The U.S. program to reach the Moon began with **Project Mercury.** The goals of Project Mercury were to orbit a piloted spacecraft around Earth and to bring it back safely. The program provided data and experience in the basics of space flight. On May 5, 1961, Alan B. Shepard became the first U.S. citizen in space. In 1962, *Mercury* astronaut John Glenn became the first U.S. citizen to orbit Earth. **Figure 14** shows Glenn preparing for liftoff.

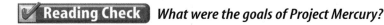

Reading Check *What were the goals of Project Mercury?*

Project Gemini The next step in reaching the Moon was called **Project Gemini.** Teams of two astronauts in the same *Gemini* spacecraft orbited Earth. One *Gemini* team met and connected with another spacecraft in orbit—a skill that would be needed on a voyage to the Moon.

The *Gemini* spacecraft was much like the *Mercury* spacecraft, except it was larger and easier for the astronauts to maintain. It was launched by a rocket known as a *Titan II,* which was a liquid fuel rocket.

In addition to connecting spacecraft in orbit, another goal of Project Gemini was to investigate the effects of space travel on the human body.

Along with the *Mercury* and *Gemini* programs, a series of robotic probes was sent to the Moon. *Ranger* proved that a spacecraft could be sent to the Moon. In 1966, *Surveyor* landed gently on the Moon's surface, indicating that the Moon's surface could support spacecraft and humans. The mission of *Lunar Orbiter* was to take pictures of the Moon's surface that would help determine the best future lunar landing sites.

Figure 14 An important step in the attempt to reach the Moon was John Glenn's first orbit around Earth.

SC.E.1.3.1

Mini LAB

Modeling a Satellite

WARNING: *Stand a safe distance away from classmates.*

Procedure
1. Complete a safety worksheet.
2. Tie one end of a strong, 50-cm-long **string** to a small **cork.**
3. Hold the other end of the string tightly with your arm fully extended.
4. Begin swinging the cork in a circular motion.
5. Gradually decrease the speed of the cork.

Analysis
1. What happened as the cork's motion slowed?
2. How does the cork resemble a satellite in orbit?

Figure 15 The Lunar Rover was first used during the *Apollo 15* mission. Riding in the moon buggy, *Apollo 15, 16,* and *17* astronauts explored the lunar surface.

Project Apollo The final stage of the U.S. program to reach the Moon was **Project Apollo.** On July 20, 1969, *Apollo 11* landed on the Moon's surface. Neil Armstrong was the first human to set foot on the Moon. His first words as he stepped onto its surface were, "That's one small step for man, one giant leap for mankind." Edwin Aldrin, the second of the three *Apollo 11* astronauts, joined Armstrong on the Moon, and they explored its surface for two hours. While they were exploring, Michael Collins remained in the Command Module; Armstrong and Aldrin then returned to the Command Module before beginning the journey home. A total of six lunar landings brought back more than 2,000 samples of moon rock and soil for study before the program ended in 1972. **Figure 15** shows an astronaut exploring the Moon's surface from the Lunar Rover vehicle.

section 2 review

Summary

First Missions into Space

- Rockets are engines that have everything they need to burn fuel.
- Rockets may be fueled with liquid or solid propellants.
- A satellite is any object that revolves around another object.

Space Probes

- A space probe is an instrument that gathers information and sends it back to Earth.
- *Voyager* and *Pioneer* are probes designed to explore the solar system and beyond.
- *Galileo* is a space probe that explored Jupiter and its moons.

Moon Quest

- Project Mercury sent the first piloted space-craft around Earth.
- *Ranger* and *Surveyor* probes explored the Moon's surface.
- *Gemini* orbited teams of two astronauts.
- Project Apollo completed six lunar landings.

Self Check

1. **Explain** how Neptune can have 13 satellites even though it is not orbited by human-made objects. `SC.E.1.3.1`
2. **Explain** why *Galileo* was considered a space probe as it traveled to Jupiter. However, once there, it became an artificial satellite. `SC.E.1.3.1`
3. **List** several discoveries made by the *Voyager 1* and *Voyager 2* space probes. `SC.E.1.3.2`
4. **Sequence** Draw a time line beginning with *Sputnik* and ending with Project Apollo. Include descriptions of important missions. `SC.E.1.3.2`
5. **Think Critically** Is Earth a satellite of any other body in space? Explain. `SC.E.1.3.1`
6. **Describe** the discovery that *Galileo* made when it photographed Io, one of Jupiter's moons. `SC.E.1.3.2`

Applying Math `MA.B.2.3.2`

7. **Solve Simple Equations** A measure of distance in the solar system is the astronomical unit, or AU. It equals about 0.15 billion km. In 2004, *Pioneer 10* was more than 86 AUs from Earth. How many billion km is this?

Benchmarks—SC.H.1.3.3 (p. 679): The student knows that science disciplines differ from one another in topic, techniques, and outcomes but that they share a common purpose, philosophy, and enterprise; SC.H.3.3.6 (p. 679): knows that no matter who does science . . . , or when or where they do it, the knowledge and technology that result can eventually become available to everyone.

Also covers: SC.E.1.3.2 Annually Assessed (pp. 677, 680), SC.H.1.3.4 Annually Assessed (p. 681), SC.H.1.3.6 (p. 674), SC.H.3.3.4 (p. 682), SC.H.3.3.5 (p. 674), SC.H.3.3.7 (p. 680)

Current and Future Space Missions

The Space Shuttle

Imagine spending millions of dollars to build a machine, sending it off into space, and watching its 3,000 metric tons of metal and other materials burn up after only a few minutes of work. That's exactly what NASA did with the rocket portions of spacecraft for many years. The early rockets were used only to launch a small capsule holding astronauts into orbit. Then sections of the rocket separated from the rest and burned when reentering the atmosphere.

A Reusable Spacecraft NASA administrators, like many others, realized that it would be less expensive and less wasteful to reuse resources. The reusable spacecraft that transports astronauts, satellites, and other materials to and from space is called the **space shuttle**, shown in **Figure 16,** as it is landing.

At launch, the space shuttle stands on end and is connected to an external liquid-fuel tank and two solid-fuel booster rockets. When the shuttle reaches an altitude of about 45 km, the emptied, solid-fuel booster rockets drop off and parachute back to Earth. These are recovered and used again. The external liquid-fuel tank separates and falls back to Earth, but it isn't recovered.

Work on the Shuttle After the space shuttle reaches space, it begins to orbit Earth. There, astronauts perform many different tasks. In the cargo bay, astronauts can conduct scientific experiments and determine the effects of spaceflight on the human body. When the cargo bay isn't used as a laboratory, the shuttle can launch, repair, and retrieve satellites. Then the satellites can be returned to Earth or repaired onboard and returned to space. After a mission, the shuttle glides back to Earth and lands like an airplane. A large landing field is needed because the landing speed of the shuttle is 335 km/h.

as you read

What You'll Learn

- **Explain** the benefits of the space shuttle.
- **Identify** the usefulness of orbital space stations.
- **Explore** space missions.
- **Identify** the applications of space technology to everyday life.

Why It's Important

Experiments performed on future space missions may benefit you.

Review Vocabulary
cosmonaut: astronaut of the former Soviet Union or present-day Russian space program

New Vocabulary
- space shuttle
- space station

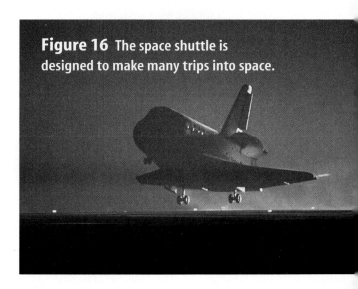

Figure 16 The space shuttle is designed to make many trips into space.

Figure 17 Astronauts performed a variety of tasks while living and working in space onboard *Skylab.*

Figure 18 Russian and American scientists have worked together to further space exploration.
Explain *why the docking of the space shuttle with* Mir *was so important.*

Space Stations

Astronauts can spend only a short time living in the space shuttle. Its living area is small, and the crew needs more room to live, exercise, and work. A **space station** has living quarters, work and exercise areas, and all the equipment and support systems needed for humans to live and work in space.

In 1973, the United States launched the space station *Skylab,* shown in **Figure 17.** Crews of astronauts spent up to 84 days there, performing experiments and collecting data on the effects on humans of living in space. In 1979, the abandoned *Skylab* fell out of orbit and burned up as it entered Earth's atmosphere.

Crews from the former Soviet Union have spent more time in space, onboard the space station *Mir,* than crews from any other country. Cosmonaut Dr. Valery Polyakov returned to Earth after 438 days in space studying the long-term effects of weightlessness.

Cooperation in Space

In 1995, the United States and Russia began an era of cooperation and trust in exploring space. Early in the year, American Dr. Norman Thagard was launched into orbit aboard the Russian *Soyuz* spacecraft, along with two Russian cosmonaut crewmates. Dr. Thagard was the first U.S. astronaut launched into space by a Russian booster and the first American resident of the Russian space station *Mir.*

In June 1995, Russian cosmonauts rode into orbit onboard the space shuttle *Atlantis,* America's 100th crewed launch. The mission of *Atlantis* involved, among other studies, a rendezvous and docking with the space station *Mir.* The cooperation that existed on this mission, as shown in **Figure 18,** continued through eight more space shuttle-*Mir* docking missions. Each of the eight missions was an important step toward building and operating the *International Space Station.* In 2001, the abandoned *Mir* space station fell out of orbit and burned up upon reentering the atmosphere. Cooperation continued as the *International Space Station* began to take form.

The _International Space Station_ The _International Space Station (ISS)_ will be a permanent laboratory designed for long-term research projects. Diverse topics will be studied, including research on the growth of protein crystals. This particular project will help scientists determine protein structure and function, which is expected to enhance work on drug design and the treatment of many diseases.

The _ISS_ will draw on the resources of 16 nations. These nations have built units for the space station, which are then transported into space onboard the space shuttle and Russian launch rockets. The station is constructed in space. **Figure 19** shows what the completed station will look like.

 _What is the purpose of the_ International Space Station?

Phases of _ISS_ NASA is planning the _ISS_ program in phases. Phase One, now concluded, involved the space shuttle-_Mir_ docking missions. Phase Two began in 1998 with the launch of the Russian-built _Zarya Module,_ also known as the Functional Cargo Block. In December 1998, the first assembly of _ISS_ occurred when a space shuttle mission attached the Unity module to _Zarya._ During this phase, crews of three people were delivered to the space station. Phase Two ended in 2001 with the addition of a U.S. laboratory.

Living in Space The project will continue with Phase Three when the Japanese Experiment Module, the European Columbus Orbiting Facility, and another Russian lab will be delivered.

It is hoped that the _International Space Station_ will be completed in 2010. Eventually, a seven-person crew should be able to work comfortably onboard the station. A total of 47 separate launches will be required to take all the components of the _ISS_ into space and prepare it for permanent habitation. NASA plans for crews of astronauts to stay onboard the station for several months at a time. NASA already has conducted numerous tests to prepare crews of astronauts for extended space missions. One day, the station could be a construction site for ships that will travel to the Moon and Mars.

Figure 19 This is a picture of what the proposed _International Space Station_ will look like when it is completed.

Topic: _International Space Station_
Visit fl6.msscience.com for Web links to information about the _International Space Station._

Activity You can watch the station travel across the sky. Find out the schedule and try to observe it.

Exploring Mercury

For 30 years *Mariner 10* was the only probe to have passed by Mercury. It gave scientists the first close-up look at this hot planet. Then, in August 2004, the *Messenger* probe was launched as part of NASA's Discovery Program. *Messenger* is traveling in a long, circular path that causes it to pass by Earth once and Venus twice. The gravitational pull of these planets speeds up the probe in its path around the Sun. Finally, in March 2011, the probe will become the first spacecraft to begin orbiting Mercury.

Messenger will use its seven instruments to study Mercury's metal core, its heavily cratered surface, and its thin atmosphere. The probe will also take pictures over the entire surface of the planet, including a dark polar area where ice may have formed.

Exploring the Moon

Does water exist in craters at the Moon's poles? This is one question NASA engineers explored with data gathered from the *Lunar Prospector* space probe shown in **Figure 20.** Launched in 1998, this probe's mission was to orbit the Moon for one year and map its structure and composition. Data from the probe seemed to indicate that large amounts of ice might be present in craters at the Moon's poles. It is thought that ice crystals may accumulate in dark areas that are never warmed by the Sun.

To look for this ice, the *Lunar Prospector* was deliberately crashed into a lunar crater. Astronomers on Earth carefully searched for signs of water vapor thrown up by the crash. However, none was found. Later tests showed that only a thin layer of ice may be mixed with lunar soil. Scientists are looking for a possible source of water to supply a future moon base.

LA.A.2.3.7

LA.B.2.3.4

Science  **nline**

Topic: Discovery Program
Visit fl6.msscience.com for Web links to information about NASA's Discovery Program.

Activity Prepare a table listing Discovery missions, projected launch dates, and the goals of each mission.

FCAT FOCUS **Annually Assessed Benchmark Check**

SC.E.1.3.2 What did the *Mariner 10* space probe discover about Mercury that is similar to the Moon?

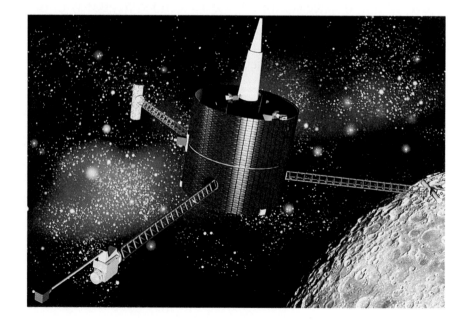

Figure 20 The *Lunar Prospector* analyzed the Moon's composition during its one-year mission.
Explain why Lunar Prospector *was deliberately crashed on the Moon.*

Figure 21 Gulleys, channels, and aprons of sediment photographed by the *Mars Global Surveyor* are similar to features on Earth known to be caused by flowing water. This water is thought to seep out from beneath the surface of Mars.

Exploring Mars

There have been several successful missions to Mars in recent years. In 1996 the *Mars Global Surveyor* and *Mars Pathfinder* were launched. *Surveyor* orbited Mars, taking detailed photos of the surface as shown in **Figure 21.** *Pathfinder* descended to the Martian surface using rockets and a parachute system to slow its landing. This probe carried a robot rover called *Sojourner* to study the surface. The photographs taken by *Surveyor* show that water had seeped to the surface of Mars in some areas.

Reading Check *What did scientists learn by studying photos from the* Mars Global Surveyor?

Another orbiting spacecraft, the *Mars Odyssey,* began mapping the surface of Mars in 2002. Its data confirmed what *Surveyor* had found—that Martian soil contains frozen water in the southern polar area. The next step was to send robots to explore the surface.

In 2003, the Mars Exploration Rovers named *Spirit* and *Opportunity* were launched and reached their separate destinations on Mars in January, 2004. Their main goals were to analyze Martian rocks and soils. Data and photographs sent back by these rovers have revealed much about Martian geology and the role of water on Mars. **Figure 22** shows a rock found by *Spirit.* A future mission is *Phoenix* in 2008, a robot lander capable of digging over a meter into the surface. The lander will look for ice in the frozen soil.

Figure 22 The Mars Rover *Spirit* studied this football-sized rock.

Figure 23 *Cassini* arrived at Saturn after traveling for more than six years. While en route, it photographed Jupiter and other objects.

Exploring Saturn

Launched in October 1997, the *Cassini* space probe arrived at Saturn in March 2004. *Cassini*, shown in **Figure 23,** will explore Saturn, its rings, and its moons until 2008. **Figure 24** shows a close-up view of the rings. A part of *Cassini's* mission was to deliver the *Huygens* probe to Titan, Saturn's largest moon. *Huygens*, which was built by the European Space Agency, landed on Titan in January 2005 using parachutes to slow its speed. As it landed it studied Titan's atmosphere and took pictures, which were sent back to Earth by *Cassini*. Some scientists theorize that Titan's atmosphere may be similar to the atmosphere of early Earth.

Planets Around Other Stars

Because stars are so far away, scientists cannot send probes to them to search for new planets. However, astronomers have developed ways of detecting planets around other stars by studying a star's light. Small, regular changes in brightness may mean that a planet is orbiting the star.

To further the search for Earth-sized planets—planets thought most likely to support life—NASA has planned the *Kepler* mission. *Kepler* will be a special orbiting telescope that will view many stars at the same time with an ultra-sensitive light detector. The launch of this satellite is planned for 2007.

Figure 24 *Cassini* captured spectacular photos of Saturn's rings and moons. The rings are made mainly of ice.

Everyday Space Technology

Many people have benefited from research done for space programs. Medicine especially has gained much from space technology. Space medicine led to better ways to diagnose and treat heart disease here on Earth and to better heart pacemakers. A screening system that works on infants is helping eye doctors spot vision problems early. Cochlear implants that help thousands of deaf people hear were developed using knowledge gained during the space shuttle program.

Space technology can even help catch criminals and prevent accidents. For example, a method to sharpen images that was devised for space studies is being used by police to read numbers on blurry photos of license plates. Equipment using space technology can be placed on emergency vehicles. This equipment automatically changes traffic signals as an emergency vehicle approaches intersections. A hand-held device used for travel directions is shown in **Figure 25.**

Figure 25 Global Positioning System (GPS) technology uses satellites to determine location on Earth's surface.

 **Reading Check** *How have research and technology developed for space benefited people here on Earth?*

---

section 3 review

Summary

The Space Station

- A space station is an orbiting laboratory.
- The *International Space Station (ISS)* has been built with the aid of 16 nations.
- The space shuttle can transport astronauts, satellites, and materials to and from the *ISS*.

Exploring Mars, the Moon, and Saturn

- The *Mars Global Surveyor* orbited Mars and the *Mars Pathfinder* studied its surface.
- *Lunar Prospector* orbited the Moon, mapping its structure and composition.
- The Mars Exploration Rovers *Spirit* and *Opportunity* studied Mars geology.
- The *Cassini* probe arrived at Saturn and explored Saturn's rings and moons.

Future Missions

- The *Messinger* probe was launched and will begin to orbit Mercury in 2011.

Self Check

SC.H.3.3.4

1. **Identify** the main advantage of the space shuttle.
2. **Describe** the importance of space shuttle-*Mir* docking missions. SC.H.3.3.6
3. **Explain** how the *International Space Station* is used.
4. **Identify** three ways in which space technology is a benefit to everyday life. SC.H.3.3.6
5. **Think Critically** What makes the space shuttle more versatile than earlier spacecraft? SC.H.3.3.4

Applying Math

6. **Use Percentages** *Voyager 1* had about 35 kg of hydrazine fuel left in 2003. If it started its trip with 105 kg of fuel, what percentage had been used?
7. **Use Percentages** Suppose you're in charge of assembling a crew of 50 people. Decide how many to assign each task, such as farming, maintenance, scientific experimentation, and so on. Calculate the percent of the crew assigned to each task. Justify your decisions.

Use the Internet

space probes

Goals

- **Organize** and understand information on a planet or moon that was collected by space probes.
- **Compare** the information and data you find with the information found by your classmates.
- **Communicate** your findings to other students.

Data Source
Internet Lab
Visit **fl6.msscience.com** for information about space probes and the data they sent back during their missions.

◉ *Real-World Problem*

Have you ever seen photographs of the eerie red surface of Mars or the spectacular rings of the planet Saturn? Have you ever wondered where the photographs came from? To the unaided eye, the planets appear to be nothing more than bright stars in the night sky. Even with a telescope, we cannot see features of planets close up. To view the planets and find out more about them, scientists have been launching probes into space for more than 40 years. How can you discover amazing photographs and interesting information about the planets in our solar system?

◉ *Make a Plan*

1. Read general information about past and present space probes sent on missions throughout our solar system.

2. Choose a planet or a moon you would like to learn more about that has been visited by space probes.

3. Use the Web link to the left to find out about space probe missions that have traveled to your chosen destination. Collect information from three of the sources listed on the Web page.

4. Write down your plan for researching the information on space probes.

▶ Follow Your Plan

1. Make sure your teacher approves your plan before you start.

2. **Research** information about the data and photographs collected by the space probes that have traveled to your chosen destination.

3. **Organize** your information in a chart or data table. List the space probe and mission name, the launch date, the destination, and the information it sent back.

4. Add your data to the table provided at the Web link below.

▶ Analyze Your Data

1. **Compare** the information from the different sources you used. How are some sources more understandable, reliable, or complete?

2. **Analyze** the photographs collected by the different space probes. Select which photographs were the most helpful in describing the planet or moon. Give examples.

3. **Infer** how the information gathered by the space probes you researched has helped people understand the planet or moon you have chosen to study.

▶ Conclude and Apply

1. **Compare** your findings with those of other students by visiting the link below. Design a chart to compare and contrast your findings with those of other students.

2. **Identify** questions about your chosen destination that you would like a future space probe mission to answer.

3. **Select** seven outstanding facts or photographs from your research. Explain how information from the space probes is able to show differences and similarities among the planets and moons in the solar system.

Communicating Your Data

Find this lab using the link below. Post your data in the table provided. Learn about other planets and moons by reviewing the data posted by other students.

Internet Lab
fl6.msscience.com

Cities in Space

Should the U.S. spend money to colonize space?

Humans have landed on the Moon, and spacecrafts have landed on Mars. But these space missions are just small steps that may lead to a giant new space program. As technology improves, humans may be able to visit and even live on other planets. But is it worth the time and money involved?

Those in favor of living in space point to the International Space Station that already is orbiting Earth. It's an early step toward establishing floating cities where astronauts can live and work. As Earth's population continues to increase and there is less room on this planet, why not expand to other planets or build a floating city in space? Also, the fact that there is little pollution in space makes the idea appealing to many.

Critics of colonizing space think we should spend the hundreds of billions of dollars that it would cost to colonize space on projects to help improve people's lives here on Earth. Building better housing, developing ways to feed the hungry, finding cures for diseases, and increasing funds for education should come first, these people say. And, critics continue, if people want to explore, why not explore right here on Earth, for example, the ocean floor.

Moon or Mars? If humans were to move permanently to space, the two most likely destinations would be Mars and the Moon, both bleak places. But those in favor of moving to these places say humans could find a way to make them livable as they have made homes in harsh climates and in many rugged areas here on Earth.

Photos suggest that Mars once had liquid water on its surface and that polar regions contain ice. If that water is frozen underground, humans may be able to access it. NASA is studying whether it makes sense to send astronauts and scientists to explore Mars.

Transforming Mars into an Earthlike place with breathable air and usable water will take much longer, but some small steps are being taken. Experimental plants are being developed that could absorb Mars's excess carbon dioxide and release oxygen. Solar mirrors that could warm Mars's surface are available.

Those for and against colonizing space agree on one thing—it will take large amounts of money, research, and planning. It also will take the same spirit of adventure that has led history's pioneers into so many bold frontiers—deserts, the poles, and the sky.

LA.C.3.3.3

Debate with your class the pros and cons of colonizing space. Do you think the United States should spend money to create space cities or use the money now to improve lives of people on Earth?

TIME

For more information, visit fl6.msscience.com

Reviewing Main Ideas

Section 1 Radiation from Space

1. The arrangement of electromagnetic waves according to their wavelengths is the electromagnetic spectrum.

2. Optical telescopes gather light to produce magnified images of distant objects.

3. Radio telescopes receive and record radio waves given off by some space objects.

Section 2 Early Space Missions

1. A satellite is an object that revolves around another object. The moons of planets are natural satellites. Artificial satellites are those made by people.

2. A space probe travels into the solar system, gathers data, and sends them back to Earth.

3. American-piloted space programs included the Gemini, Mercury, and Apollo Projects.

Section 3 Current and Future Space Missions

1. Space stations provide the opportunity to conduct research not possible on Earth. The *International Space Station* has been constructed in space with the cooperation of more than a dozen nations.

2. The space shuttle is a reusable spacecraft that carries astronauts, satellites, and other cargo to and from space.

3. Space technology is used to solve problems on Earth, too. Advances in engineering related to space travel have aided medicine, environmental sciences, and other fields.

Visualizing Main Ideas

Copy and complete the following concept map about the race to the Moon. Use the phrases: first satellite, Project Gemini, Project Mercury, team of two astronauts orbits Earth, Project Apollo.

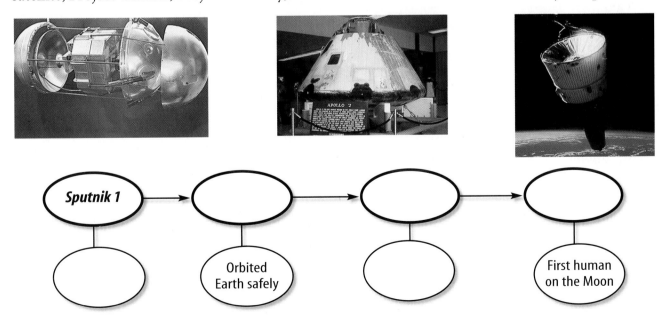

Sputnik 1 → ◯ → ◯ → ◯

◯   Orbited Earth safely   ◯   First human on the Moon

Using Vocabulary

electromagnetic
spectrum p.659
observatory p.660
orbit p.667
Project Apollo p.672
Project Gemini p.671
Project Mercury p.671
✳ radiation p.658

radio telescope p.663
reflecting telescope p.660
refracting telescope p.660
rocket p.665
satellite p.667
space probe p.668
space shuttle p.673
space station p.674

✳ FCAT Vocabulary

Fill in the blanks with the correct vocabulary word(s).

1. A(n) _____ telescope uses lenses to bend light.

2. A(n) _____ is an object that revolves around another object in space. `SC.E.1.3.1`

3. _____ was the first piloted U.S. space program.

4. A(n) _____ carries people and tools to and from space.

5. In the _____, electromagnetic waves are arranged, in order, according to their wavelengths.

Checking Concepts

Choose the word or phrase that best answers the question.

6. Which space probe has sent images of Venus to scientists on Earth? `SC.E.1.3.2`
   A) *Voyager*   C) *Apollo 11*
   B) *Viking*   D) *Magellan*

7. Which kind of telescope uses mirrors to collect light?
   A) radio
   B) electromagnetic
   C) refracting
   D) reflecting

8. What was *Sputnik I*?
   A) the first telescope
   B) the first artificial satellite
   C) the first observatory
   D) the first U.S. space probe

9. Which kind of telescope can be used during the day or night and during bad weather?
   A) radio
   B) electromagnetic
   C) refracting
   D) reflecting

10. When fully operational, what is the maximum number of people who will crew the *International Space Station?*
    A) 3   C) 15
    B) 7   D) 50

11. Which space mission's goal was to put a spacecraft into orbit and bring it back safely?
    A) Project Mercury
    B) Project Apollo
    C) Project Gemini
    D) *Viking I*

12. Which of the following is a natural satellite of Earth? `SC.E.1.3.1`
    A) *Skylab*
    B) the space shuttle
    C) the Sun
    D) the Moon

13. What does the space shuttle use to place a satellite into space?
    A) liquid-fuel tank
    B) booster rocket
    C) mechanical arm
    D) cargo bay

14. What part of the space shuttle is reused?
    A) liquid-fuel tanks
    B) *Gemini* rockets
    C) booster engines
    D) Saturn rockets

Vocabulary PuzzleMaker fl6.msscience.com

chapter 22 Review

Thinking Critically

15. Compare and contrast the advantages of a Moon-based telescope with an Earth-based telescope. **SC.H.3.3.4**

16. Infer how sensors used to detect toxic chemicals in the space shuttle could be beneficial to a factory worker. **SC.H.3.3.6**

17. Drawing Conclusions Which do you think is a wiser method of exploration—space missions with people onboard or robotic space probes? Why? **SC.H.3.3.4**

18. Explain Suppose two astronauts are outside the space shuttle orbiting Earth. The audio speaker in the helmet of one astronaut quits working. The other astronaut is 1 m away and shouts a message. Can the first astronaut hear the message? Support your reasoning.

19. Make and Use Tables Copy and complete the table below. Use information from several resources. **SC.E.1.3.2**

United States Space Probes

Probe	Launch Date(s)	Planets or Objects Visited
Vikings 1 and 2	Do not write in this book.	
Galileo		
Lunar Prospector		
Pathfinder		

20. Classify the following as a satellite or a space probe: *Cassini, Sputnik I, Hubble Space Telescope,* space shuttle, and *Voyager 2.* **SC.E.1.3.2**

21. Compare and contrast space probes and artificial satellites. **SC.E.1.3.2**

Performance Activities

22. Display Make a display showing some of the images obtained from the *Hubble Space Telescope.* Include samples of three types of galaxies, nebulae, and star clusters.

Applying Math

23. Space Distances The signal from a space probe takes 6 sec to reach Earth. If the speed of light is 300,000 km/s, how far away is the probe? **SC.E.1.3.1**

Use the graph below to answer question 24.

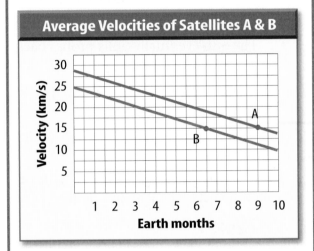

Average Velocities of Satellites A & B

24. Satellite Orbits The graph above predicts the average velocities of satellites A and B in orbit around a hypothetical planet. Because of contact with the planet's atmosphere, their velocities are decreasing. At a velocity of 15 km/s their orbits will decay and they will spiral downwards to the surface. Using the graph, determine how long will it take for each satellite to reach this point? **SC.E.1.3.1 MA.D.1.3.1**

25. Calculate Fuel The Cassini space probe began its mission with 90 kg of fuel. After five years, 89 percent of the fuel was used. How much was left? **MA.B.2.3.2**

26. Space Distances Find the distance in AUs to a star 8 light-years (LY) distant. (1 LY = 63,000 AUs) **SC.E.1.3.1 MA.B.2.3.2**

The assessed Florida Benchmark appears above each question.
Record your answers on the answer sheet provided by your teacher or on a sheet of paper.

Multiple Choice

SC.E.1.3.1

1 After traveling for 27 years, the *Voyager 1* space probe was about 90 AU from the Sun in late 2003. Which of the following does this indicate about space?

- **A.** The solar system spans tremendous distances.
- **B.** Probes travel slowly through the solar system.
- **C.** The Sun eventually pulls probes back toward itself.
- **D.** Probes cannot travel far beyond Earth's atmosphere.

SC.E.1.3.1

2 The table below compares the weights of several objects on Earth and on the Moon.

Comparison of Weight		
Object	Weight on Earth (kg)	Weight on the Moon (kg)
1	10	1.7
2	25	4.2
3	50	8.3
4	100	16.7
5	225	37.5

Which of the following is a conclusion that can be drawn from these data?

- **F.** Objects break apart on the Moon.
- **G.** There is less gravity on the Moon.
- **H.** There is no pressure on the Moon.
- **I.** Objects have less mass on the Moon.

SC.E.1.3.2

3 Data collected by *Mars Pathfinder* on the third Sol, or Martian day, of its operation are recorded in the table below.

Sol 3 Temperature Data from Mars Pathfinder			
	Temperature (°C)		
	Distance above surface		
Proportion of Sol	1.0 m	0.5 m	0.25 m
3.07	−70.4	−70.7	−73.4
3.23	−74.4	−74.9	−75.9
3.33	−53.0	−51.9	−46.7
3.51	−22.3	−19.2	−15.7
3.60	−15.1	−12.5	−8.9
3.70	−26.1	−25.7	−24.0

What conclusion can be drawn from these data?

- **A.** Heat is constantly being absorbed by the surface of Mars.
- **B.** Heat is constantly being released from the surface of Mars.
- **C.** There is no definite pattern to the temperature changes in Mars's atmosphere.
- **D.** There is a cycle of increases and decreases in temperature on Mars.

SC.E.1.3.1

4 What do the moons of all planets have in common?

- **F.** They all orbit at the space velocity.
- **G.** They all have at least one active volcano.
- **H.** They all have areas of ice and liquid water.
- **I.** They all stay in orbit due to the pull of gravity.

SC.H.3.3.4

5 Which of the following is an advantage of space telescopes over those used on Earth?

A. They are cheaper to build.

B. They have fewer technical problems.

C. They can be repaired easily.

D. They obtain higher quality images.

Gridded Response

SC.B.1.3.1

6 It took the *Cassini* space probe about seven years to travel 3,500,000 km to Saturn. If 1 AU is 150,000,000 km, how many AUs did *Cassini* travel? Round your answer to the nearest thousandth.

Short Response

SC.E.1.3.1

7 The diagram below shows a satellite near Earth.

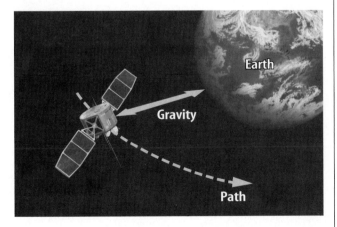

How is the motion of a satellite similar to the motion of the Moon?

Extended Response

SC.E.1.3.1

8 The diagram below shows a space shuttle being launched into space.

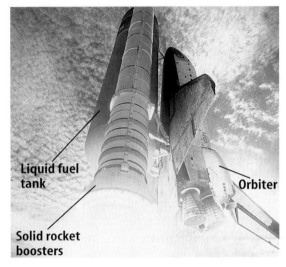

PART A Compare the size of the fuel tank to the size of the orbiter. What is the reason for this difference?

PART B How do space shuttles play a role in helping scientists learn about the solar system?

FCAT Tip

Pay Attention Listen carefully to the instructions from the teacher and carefully read the directions and each question.

Student Resources

CONTENTS

Scientific Methods

Scientists use an orderly approach called the scientific method to solve problems. This includes organizing and recording data so others can understand them. Scientists use many variations in this method when they solve problems.

Identify a Question

The first step in a scientific investigation or experiment is to identify a question to be answered or a problem to be solved. For example, you might ask which gasoline is the most efficient.

Gather and Organize Information

After you have identified your question, begin gathering and organizing information. There are many ways to gather information, such as researching in a library, interviewing those knowledgeable about the subject, testing, and working in the laboratory and field. Fieldwork is investigations and observations done outside of a laboratory.

Researching Information Before moving in a new direction, it is important to gather the information that already is known about the subject. Start by asking yourself questions to determine exactly what you need to know. Then you will look for the information in various reference sources, like the student is doing in **Figure 1.** Some sources may include textbooks, encyclopedias, government documents, professional journals, science magazines, and the Internet. Always list the sources of your information.

Figure 1 The Internet can be a valuable research tool.

Evaluate Sources of Information Not all sources of information are reliable. You should evaluate all your sources of information, and use only those you know to be dependable. For example, if you are researching ways to make homes more energy efficient, a site written by the U.S. Department of Energy would be more reliable than a site written by a company that is trying to sell a new type of weatherproofing material. Also, remember that research always is changing. Consult the most current resources available to you. For example, a 1985 resource about saving energy would not reflect the most recent findings.

Sometimes scientists use data that they did not collect themselves, or conclusions drawn by other researchers. These data must be evaluated carefully. Ask questions about how the data were obtained, if the investigation was carried out properly, and if it has been duplicated exactly with the same results. Would you reach the same conclusion from the data? Only when you have confidence in the data can you believe it is true and feel comfortable using it.

Interpret Scientific Illustrations As you research a topic in science, you will see drawings, diagrams, and photographs to help you understand what you read. Some illustrations are included to help you understand an idea that you can't see easily by yourself, like the tiny particles in an atom in **Figure 2.** A drawing helps many people to remember details more easily and provides examples that clarify difficult concepts or give additional information about the topic you are studying. Most illustrations have labels or a caption to identify or to provide more information.

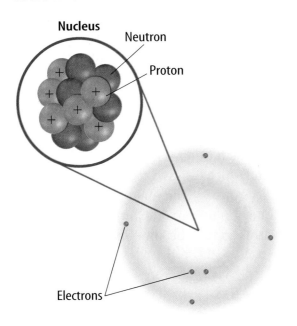

Figure 2 This drawing shows an atom of carbon with its six protons, six neutrons, and six electrons.

Concept Maps One way to organize data is to draw a diagram that shows relationships among ideas (or concepts). A concept map can help make the meanings of ideas and terms more clear, and help you understand and remember what you are studying. Concept maps are useful for breaking large concepts down into smaller parts, making learning easier.

Network Tree A type of concept map that not only shows a relationship, but how the concepts are related is a network tree, shown in **Figure 3.** In a network tree, the words are written in the ovals, while the description of the type of relationship is written across the connecting lines.

When constructing a network tree, write down the topic and all major topics on separate pieces of paper or notecards. Then arrange them in order from general to specific. Branch the related concepts from the major concept and describe the relationship on the connecting line. Continue to more specific concepts until finished.

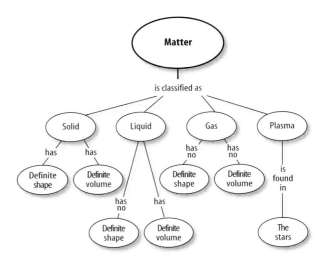

Figure 3 A network tree shows how concepts or objects are related.

Events Chain Another type of concept map is an events chain. Sometimes called a flow chart, it models the order or sequence of items. An events chain can be used to describe a sequence of events, the steps in a procedure, or the stages of a process.

When making an events chain, first find the one event that starts the chain. This event is called the initiating event. Then, find the next event and continue until the outcome is reached, as shown in **Figure 4.**

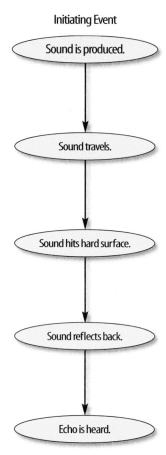

Figure 4 Events-chain concept maps show the order of steps in a process or event. This concept map shows how a sound makes an echo.

Cycle Map A specific type of events chain is a cycle map. It is used when the series of events do not produce a final outcome, but instead relate back to the beginning event, such as in **Figure 5.** Therefore, the cycle repeats itself.

To make a cycle map, first decide what event is the beginning event. This is also called the initiating event. Then list the next events in the order that they occur, with the last event relating back to the initiating event. Words can be written between the events that describe what happens from one event to the next. The number of events in a cycle map can vary, but usually contain three or more events.

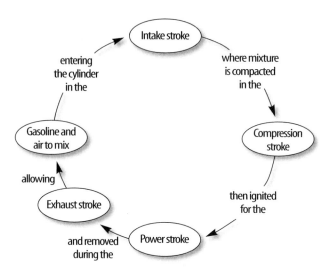

Figure 5 A cycle map shows events that occur in a cycle.

Spider Map A type of concept map that you can use for brainstorming is the spider map. When you have a central idea, you might find that you have a jumble of ideas that relate to it but are not necessarily clearly related to each other. The spider map on sound in **Figure 6** shows that if you write these ideas outside the main concept, then you can begin to separate and group unrelated terms so they become more useful.

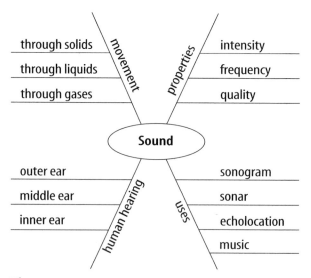

Figure 6 A spider map allows you to list ideas that relate to a central topic but not necessarily to one another.

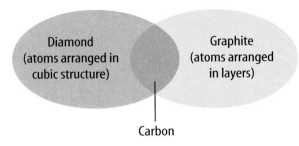

Figure 7 This Venn diagram compares and contrasts two substances made from carbon.

Venn Diagram To illustrate how two subjects compare and contrast you can use a Venn diagram. You can see the characteristics that the subjects have in common and those that they do not, shown in **Figure 7.**

To create a Venn diagram, draw two overlapping ovals that that are big enough to write in. List the characteristics unique to one subject in one oval, and the characteristics of the other subject in the other oval. The characteristics in common are listed in the overlapping section.

Make and Use Tables One way to organize information so it is easier to understand is to use a table. Tables can contain numbers, words, or both.

To make a table, list the items to be compared in the first column and the characteristics to be compared in the first row. The title should clearly indicate the content of the table, and the column or row heads should be clear. Notice that in **Table 1** the units are included.

Table 1 Recyclables Collected During Week			
Day of Week	**Paper (kg)**	**Aluminum (kg)**	**Glass (kg)**
Monday	5.0	4.0	12.0
Wednesday	4.0	1.0	10.0
Friday	2.5	2.0	10.0

Make a Model One way to help you better understand the parts of a structure, the way a process works, or to show things too large or small for viewing is to make a model. For example, an atomic model made of a plastic-ball nucleus and pipe-cleaner electron shells can help you visualize how the parts of an atom relate to each other. Other types of models can by devised on a computer or represented by equations.

Form a Hypothesis

A possible explanation based on previous knowledge and observations is called a hypothesis. After researching gasoline types and recalling previous experiences in your family's car you form a hypothesis—our car runs more efficiently because we use premium gasoline. To be valid, a hypothesis has to be something you can test by using an investigation.

Predict When you apply a hypothesis to a specific situation, you predict something about that situation. A prediction makes a statement in advance, based on prior observation, experience, or scientific reasoning. People use predictions to make everyday decisions. Scientists test predictions by performing investigations. Based on previous observations and experiences, you might form a prediction that cars are more efficient with premium gasoline. The prediction can be tested in an investigation.

Design an Experiment A scientist needs to make many decisions before beginning an investigation. Some of these include: how to carry out the investigation, what steps to follow, how to record the data, and how the investigation will answer the question. It also is important to address any safety concerns.

Test the Hypothesis

Now that you have formed your hypothesis, you need to test it. Using an investigation, you will make observations and collect data, or information. These data might either support or not support your hypothesis. Scientists collect and organize data as numbers and descriptions.

Follow a Procedure In order to know what materials to use, as well as how and in what order to use them, you must follow a procedure. **Figure 8** shows a procedure you might follow to test your hypothesis.

Procedure
1. Use regular gasoline for two weeks.
2. Record the number of kilometers between fill-ups and the amount of gasoline used.
3. Switch to premium gasoline for two weeks.
4. Record the number of kilometers between fill-ups and the amount of gasoline used.

Figure 8 A procedure tells you what to do step by step.

Identify and Manipulate Variables and Controls In any experiment, it is important to keep everything the same except for the item you are testing. The one factor you change is called the independent variable. The change that results is the dependent variable. Make sure you have only one independent variable, to assure yourself of the cause of the changes you observe in the dependent variable. For example, in your gasoline experiment the type of fuel is the independent variable. The dependent variable is the efficiency.

Many experiments also have a control—an individual instance or experimental subject for which the independent variable is not changed. You can then compare the test results to the control results. To design a control you can have two cars of the same type. The control car uses regular gasoline for four weeks. After you are done with the test, you can compare the experimental results to the control results.

Collect Data

Whether you are carrying out an investigation or a short observational experiment, you will collect data, as shown in **Figure 9.** Scientists collect data as numbers and descriptions and organize it in specific ways.

Observe Scientists observe items and events, then record what they see. When they use only words to describe an observation, it is called qualitative data. Scientists' observations also can describe how much there is of something. These observations use numbers, as well as words, in the description and are called quantitative data. For example, if a sample of the element gold is described as being "shiny and very dense" the data are qualitative. Quantitative data on this sample of gold might include "a mass of 30 g and a density of 19.3 g/cm^3."

Figure 9 Collecting data is one way to gather information directly.

Figure 10 Record data neatly and clearly so they are easy to understand.

When you make observations you should examine the entire object or situation first, and then look carefully for details. It is important to record observations accurately and completely. Always record your observations immediately as you make them, so you do not miss details or make a mistake when recording results from memory. Never put unidentified observations on scraps of paper. Instead they should be recorded in a notebook, like the one in **Figure 10.** Write your data neatly so you can easily read them later. At each point in the experiment, record your observations and label them. That way, you will not have to determine what the figures mean when you look at your notes later. Set up any tables that you will need to use ahead of time, so you can record any observations right away. Remember to avoid bias when collecting data by not including personal thoughts when you record observations. Record only what you observe.

Estimate Scientific work also involves estimating. To estimate is to make a judgment about the size or the number of something without measuring or counting. This is important when the number or size of an object or population is too large or too difficult to accurately count or measure.

Sample Scientists may use a sample or a portion of the total number as a type of estimation. To sample is to take a small, representative portion of the objects or organisms of a population for research. By making careful observations or manipulating variables within that portion of the group, information is discovered and conclusions are drawn that might apply to the whole population. A poorly chosen sample can be unrepresentative of the whole. If you were trying to determine the rainfall in an area, it would not be best to take a rainfall sample from under a tree.

Measure You use measurements every day. Scientists also take measurements when collecting data. When taking measurements, it is important to know how to use measuring tools properly. Accuracy also is important.

Length To measure length, the distance between two points, scientists use meters. Smaller measurements might be measured in centimeters or millimeters.

Length is measured using a metric ruler or meterstick. When using a metric ruler, line up the 0-cm mark with the end of the object being measured and read the number of the unit where the object ends. Look at the metric ruler shown in **Figure 11.** The centimeter lines are the long, numbered lines, and the shorter lines are millimeter lines. In this instance, the length would be 4.50 cm.

Figure 11 This metric ruler has centimeter and millimeter divisions.

Mass The SI unit for mass is the kilogram (kg). Scientists can measure mass using units formed by adding metric prefixes to the unit gram (g), such as milligram (mg). To measure mass, you might use a triple-beam balance similar to the one shown in **Figure 12.** The balance has a pan on one side and a set of beams on the other side. Each beam has a rider that slides on the beam.

When using a triple-beam balance, place an object on the pan. Slide the largest rider along its beam until the pointer drops below zero. Then move it back one notch. Repeat the process for each rider proceeding from the larger to smaller until the pointer swings an equal distance above and below the zero point. Sum the masses on each beam to find the mass of the object. Move all riders back to zero when finished.

Instead of putting materials directly on the balance, scientists often take a tare of a container. A tare is the mass of a container into which objects or substances are placed for measuring their masses. To mass objects or substances, find the mass of a clean container. Remove the container from the pan, and place the object or substances in the container. Find the mass of the container with the materials in it. Subtract the mass of the empty container from the mass of the filled container to find the mass of the materials you are using.

Figure 12 A triple-beam balance is used to determine the mass of an object.

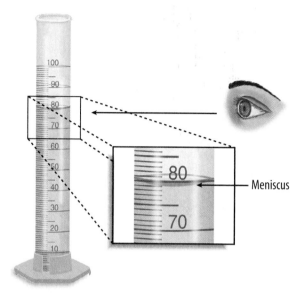

Figure 13 Graduated cylinders measure liquid volume.

Liquid Volume To measure liquids, the unit used is the liter (L). When a smaller unit is needed, scientists might use a milliliter (mL). Because a milliliter takes up the volume of a cube measuring 1 cm on each side it also can be called a cubic centimeter ($cm^3 = cm \times cm \times cm$).

You can use beakers and graduated cylinders to measure liquid volume. A graduated cylinder, shown in **Figure 13,** is marked from bottom to top in milliliters. In the lab, you might use a 10-mL graduated cylinder or a 100-mL graduated cylinder. When measuring liquids, notice that the liquid has a curved surface. Look at the surface at eye level, and measure the bottom of the curve. This is called the meniscus. The graduated cylinder in **Figure 13** contains 79.0 mL, or 79.0 cm^3, of a liquid.

Temperature Scientists often measure temperature using the Celsius scale. Pure water has a freezing point of 0°C and boiling point of 100°C. The unit of measurement is degrees Celsius. Two other scales often used are the Fahrenheit and Kelvin scales.

Figure 14 A thermometer measures the temperature of an object.

Scientists use a thermometer to measure temperature. Most thermometers in a laboratory are glass tubes with a bulb at the bottom end containing a liquid such as colored alcohol. The liquid rises or falls with a change in temperature. To read a glass thermometer like the thermometer in **Figure 14,** rotate it slowly until a red line appears. Read the temperature where the red line ends.

Form Operational Definitions An operational definition defines an object by how it functions, works, or behaves. For example, when you are playing hide and seek and a tree is home base, you have created an operational definition for a tree.

Objects can have more than one operational definition. For example, a ruler can be defined as a tool that measures the length of an object (how it is used). It can also be a tool with a series of marks used as a standard when measuring (how it works).

Analyze the Data

To determine the meaning of your observations and investigation results, you will need to look for patterns in the data. Then you must think critically to determine what the data mean. Scientists use several approaches when they analyze the data they have collected and recorded. Each approach is useful for identifying specific patterns.

Interpret Data The word *interpret* means "to explain the meaning of something." When analyzing data from an experiment, try to find out what the data show. Identify the control group and the test group to see whether or not changes in the independent variable have had an effect. Look for differences in the dependent variable between the control and test groups.

Classify Sorting objects or events into groups based on common features is called classifying. When classifying, first observe the objects or events to be classified. Then select one feature that is shared by some members in the group, but not by all. Place those members that share that feature in a subgroup. You can classify members into smaller and smaller subgroups based on characteristics. Remember that when you classify, you are grouping objects or events for a purpose. Keep your purpose in mind as you select the features to form groups and subgroups.

Compare and Contrast Observations can be analyzed by noting the similarities and differences between two more objects or events that you observe. When you look at objects or events to see how they are similar, you are comparing them. Contrasting is looking for differences in objects or events.

Recognize Cause and Effect A cause is a reason for an action or condition. The effect is that action or condition. When two events happen together, it is not necessarily true that one event caused the other. Scientists must design a controlled investigation to recognize the exact cause and effect.

Draw Conclusions

When scientists have analyzed the data they collected, they proceed to draw conclusions about the data. These conclusions are sometimes stated in words similar to the hypothesis that you formed earlier. They may confirm a hypothesis, or lead you to a new hypothesis.

Infer Scientists often make inferences based on their observations. An inference is an attempt to explain observations or to indicate a cause. An inference is not a fact, but a logical conclusion that needs further investigation. For example, you may infer that a fire has caused smoke. Until you investigate, however, you do not know for sure.

Apply When you draw a conclusion, you must apply those conclusions to determine whether the data support the hypothesis. If your data do not support your hypothesis, it does not mean that the hypothesis is wrong. It means only that the result of the investigation did not support the hypothesis. Maybe the experiment needs to be redesigned, or some of the initial observations on which the hypothesis was based were incomplete or biased. Perhaps more observation or research is needed to refine your hypothesis. A successful investigation does not always come out the way you originally predicted.

Avoid Bias Sometimes a scientific investigation involves making judgments. When you make a judgment, you form an opinion. It is important to be honest and not to allow any expectations of results to bias your judgments. This is important throughout the entire investigation, from researching to collecting data to drawing conclusions.

Communicate

The communication of ideas is an important part of the work of scientists. A discovery that is not reported will not advance the scientific community's understanding or knowledge. Communication among scientists also is important as a way of improving their investigations.

Scientists communicate in many ways, from writing articles in journals and magazines that explain their investigations and experiments, to announcing important discoveries on television and radio. Scientists also share ideas with colleagues on the Internet or present them as lectures, like the student is doing in **Figure 15.**

Figure 15 A student communicates to his peers about his investigation.

SAFETY SYMBOLS

SAFETY SYMBOLS	HAZARD	EXAMPLES	PRECAUTION	REMEDY
DISPOSAL	Special disposal procedures need to be followed.	certain chemicals, living organisms	Do not dispose of these materials in the sink or trash can.	Dispose of wastes as directed by your teacher.
BIOLOGICAL	Organisms or other biological materials that might be harmful to humans	bacteria, fungi, blood, unpreserved tissues, plant materials	Avoid skin contact with these materials. Wear mask or gloves.	Notify your teacher if you suspect contact with material. Wash hands thoroughly.
EXTREME TEMPERATURE	Objects that can burn skin by being too cold or too hot	boiling liquids, hot plates, dry ice, liquid nitrogen	Use proper protection when handling.	Go to your teacher for first aid.
SHARP OBJECT	Use of tools or glassware that can easily puncture or slice skin	razor blades, pins, scalpels, pointed tools, dissecting probes, broken glass	Practice common-sense behavior and follow guidelines for use of the tool.	Go to your teacher for first aid.
FUME	Possible danger to respiratory tract from fumes	ammonia, acetone, nail polish remover, heated sulfur, moth balls	Make sure there is good ventilation. Never smell fumes directly. Wear a mask.	Leave foul area and notify your teacher immediately.
ELECTRICAL	Possible danger from electrical shock or burn	improper grounding, liquid spills, short circuits, exposed wires	Double-check setup with teacher. Check condition of wires and apparatus.	Do not attempt to fix electrical problems. Notify your teacher immediately.
IRRITANT	Substances that can irritate the skin or mucous membranes of the respiratory tract	pollen, moth balls, steel wool, fiberglass, potassium permanganate	Wear dust mask and gloves. Practice extra care when handling these materials.	Go to your teacher for first aid.
CHEMICAL	Chemicals can react with and destroy tissue and other materials	bleaches such as hydrogen peroxide; acids such as sulfuric acid, hydrochloric acid; bases such as ammonia, sodium hydroxide	Wear goggles, gloves, and an apron.	Immediately flush the affected area with water and notify your teacher.
TOXIC	Substance may be poisonous if touched, inhaled, or swallowed.	mercury, many metal compounds, iodine, poinsettia plant parts	Follow your teacher's instructions.	Always wash hands thoroughly after use. Go to your teacher for first aid.
FLAMMABLE	Flammable chemicals may be ignited by open flame, spark, or exposed heat.	alcohol, kerosene, potassium permanganate	Avoid open flames and heat when using flammable chemicals.	Notify your teacher immediately. Use fire safety equipment if applicable.
OPEN FLAME	Open flame in use, may cause fire.	hair, clothing, paper, synthetic materials	Tie back hair and loose clothing. Follow teacher's instruction on lighting and extinguishing flames.	Notify your teacher immediately. Use fire safety equipment if applicable.

 Eye Safety
Proper eye protection should be worn at all times by anyone performing or observing science activities.

 Clothing Protection
This symbol appears when substances could stain or burn clothing.

 Animal Safety
This symbol appears when safety of animals and students must be ensured.

 Handwashing
After the lab, wash hands with soap and water before removing goggles.

Safety in the Science Laboratory

Introduction to Science Safety

Confucius, an ancient and well-known Chinese philosopher, is credited with a statement that could serve as a legacy of all types of human wisdom. It seems especially appropriate for the active learning you will experience in this science program.

> "I hear and I forget,
> I see and I remember,
> I do and I understand."

This is the basis for the safety routine that will be used in all the labs in this book. It is assumed that you will use all of your senses as you "experience" the labs. However, with such experience comes the potential for injury. The purpose of this section of the book is to help keep you safe by involving you in the safety process.

How will your teacher help?

It will be your teacher's responsibility to decide which science labs are safe and appropriate for you. Your teacher will identify the hazards involved in each activity and will ask for your assistance to reduce as much danger as possible. He or she will involve you in safety discussions about your understanding of the actual and potential dangers and the safety measures needed to keep everyone safe. Ideally, this will become a habit with each lab in which you take part.

Your teacher also will explain the safety features of your room as well as the most important safety equipment and routines for addressing safety issues. He or she also will require that you complete a *Student Lab-Safety Worksheet* for each lab to make certain you are prepared to perform the lab safely. **BEFORE** you may begin, your teacher will review your comments, make corrections, and sign or initial this form.

The ultimate purpose of the safety discussions and the *Student Lab-Safety Worksheet* will be to ***help you take some responsibility for your own safety*** and to help you to develop good habits when you prepare and perform science experiments and labs.

How can you help?

Since your teacher cannot anticipate every safety hazard that might occur and he or she cannot be everywhere in the room at the same time, you need to take some responsibility for your own safety. The following general information should apply to nearly every science lab.

Adapted from Gerlovich, et al. (2004). The Total Science Safety System CD, JaKel, Inc. Used with Permission.

Be able to locate and use all safety equipment as directed by your teacher, such as:

- fire extinguishers;
- fire blankets;
- eye protective equipment (goggles, safety glasses, face shield);
- eyewash;
- drench shower.

Complete the *Student Lab-Safety Worksheet* before starting any science lab.

Ask questions about any safety concerns that you might have BEFORE starting any lab of science investigation.

Remember! Your teacher will review your comments, make corrections, and sign or initial the *Student Lab-Safety Worksheet* **BEFORE** you will be permitted to begin the lab. A copy of this form appears below.

You must:

- Review any *Safety Symbols* in the labs and be certain you know what they mean.

- Follow all teacher instructions for safety and make certain you understand all the hazards related to the labs you are about to do.

- Be able to explain the purpose of the lab.

- Be able to explain, or demonstrate, all reasonable emergency procedures, such as:

  - how to evacuate the room during emergencies;
  - how to react to any chemical emergencies;
  - how to deal with fire emergencies;
  - how to perform a scientific investigation safely;
  - how to anticipate some safety concerns and be prepared to address them;
  - how to use equipment properly and safely.

Student Lab-Safety Worksheet

Student Name:_____
Date:_____
Lab Title:_____

Teacher Approval Initials

Date of Approval

In order to show your teacher that you understand the safety concerns of this lab, the following questions must be answered after the teacher explains the information to you. You must have your teacher initial this form before you can proceed with the lab.

1. How would you describe what you will be doing during this lab?

2. What are the safety concerns in this lab (explained by your teacher)?
   . _____
   . _____
   . _____
   . _____
   . _____

3. What additional safety concerns or questions do you have?

Adapted from Gerlovich, et al. (2004). The Total Science Safety System D, JaKel, Inc. Used with Permission

---

Adapted from Gerlovich, et al. (2004). The Total Science Safety System CD, JaKel, Inc. Used with Permission.

EXTRA  Labs

From Your Kitchen, Junk Drawer, or Yard

1 Your Daily Drink

▶ **Real-World Question**

How much liquid do you consume in a day?

Possible Materials
- 500-mL measuring cup
- calculator

▶ **Procedure**

1. When you drink a bottle or can of juice, soda, water, or other beverage, look on the label of the container to find the volume in milliliters.

2. Record the volumes of all the canned and bottled drinks you consume in one day in your Science Journal.
3. Use a measuring cup to measure the liquids that you pour from larger containers. Record these volumes in your Science Journal.
4. Add up the volumes of all the drinks you consumed during the day.

▶ **Conclude and Apply**

1. How much liquid did you drink during the day?
2. Infer how you would measure the mass of the foods you ate in one day.

2 Fungi Hunt

▶ **Real-World Question**

What types of fungi grow near your home?

Possible Materials
- camera
- film
- sketch pad
- colored pencils and markers
- poster board
- field guide to fungi

▶ **Procedure**

1. Take an adult with you to a nearby forest, stand of trees, or other shady spot.
2. Search for different types of fungi on dead logs, large trees, broken limbs, and in moist soil.
3. Take photographs or draw sketches of all the different types of fungi you discover.
4. Create a fungi poster board display with your photographs or sketches and a list of the places where you found them.
5. Use a fungi field guide to identify as many species as possible. Write the common and scientific names of the fungi you identify next to the matching picture or photograph on your poster.

▶ **Conclude and Apply**

1. List the types of fungi you discovered.
2. Infer why fungi grow rapidly in wet conditions.

Adult supervision required for all labs.

3 Guppies of All Colors

Real-World Question
How can the effects of selective breeding be observed?

Possible Materials
- metric ruler
- Science Journal
- pencil
- access to a pet store

Procedure
1. Go to a pet store with an adult and ask an employee if you would be able to observe the store's guppies for a school assignment.
2. Ask the employee to show you the aquaria housing plain guppies, which are sold as "feeder fish," and fancy tail guppies.
3. Observe the different varieties of plain guppies. Estimate their average body length and tail size. Describe their colors.
4. Observe all the fancy tail guppies. Estimate their average body length and tail size. Describe their colors.
5. Record any other differences in the traits of plain and fancy tail guppies you observe.

Conclude and Apply
1. Compare the traits of the plain guppies to the fancy tail guppies.
2. Infer why the fancy tail guppies have such a large variety of colors.

4 Spinning Like a Top

Real-World Question
How can you observe your inner ear restoring your body's balance?

Possible Materials
- large pillows
- stopwatch or watch

Procedure
1. Choose a carpeted location several meters away from any furniture.
2. Lay large pillows on the floor around you.
3. Spin around in a circle once, stare straight ahead, and observe what the room looks like. Have a friend spot you to prevent you from falling.
4. Spin around in circles continuously for 5 s, stare straight ahead, and observe what the room looks like. Have a friend spot you.
5. After you stop, use a stopwatch to time how long it takes for the room to stop spinning.
6. With a friend spotting you, spin for 10 s and time how long it takes for the room to stop spinning.

Conclude and Apply
1. How long did it take for the room to stop spinning after you spun in circles for 5 s and for 10 s?
2. Infer why the room appeared to spin even after you stopped spinning.

5 Vitamin Search

▶ Real-World Question

How many vitamins and minerals are in the foods you eat?

Possible Materials

- labels from packaged foods and drinks
- nutrition guidebook or cookbook

▶ Procedure

1. Create a data table to record the "% Daily Value" of important vitamins and minerals for a variety of foods.
2. Collect packages from a variety of packaged foods and check the Nutrition Facts chart for the "% Daily Value" of all the vitamins and minerals it contains. These values are listed at the bottom of the chart.
3. Use cookbooks or nutrition guidebooks to research the "% Daily Value" of vitamins and minerals found in several fresh fruits and vegetables such as strawberries, spinach, oranges, and lentils.

▶ Conclude and Apply

1. Infer why a healthy diet includes fresh fruits and vegetables.
2. Infer why a healthy diet includes a wide variety of nutritious foods.

Nutrition Facts

Serving Size 1 Meal

Amount Per Serving		
Calories 330	Calories from Fat 60	
		% Daily Value*
Total Fat 7g		10%
Saturated Fat 3.5g		17%
Polyunsaturated Fat 1g		
Monounsaturated Fat 2.5g		
Cholesterol 35mg		12%
Sodium 460mg		19%
Total Carbohydrate 52g		18%
Dietary Fiber 6g		24%
Sugars 17g		
Protein 15g		

Vitamin A 15%	•	Vitamin C 70%
Calcium 4%	•	Iron 10%

* Percent Daily Values are based on a 2,000 calorie diet. Your daily values may be higher or lower depending on your calorie needs.

	Calories	2,000	2,500
Total Fat	Less than	65g	80g
Sat Fat	Less than	20g	25g
Cholesterol	Less than	300mg	300mg
Sodium	Less than	2,400mg	2,400mg
Total Carbohydrate		300g	375g
Dietary Fiber		25g	30g

6 Acid Defense

▶ Real-World Question

How is stomach acid your internal first line of defense?

Possible Materials

- drinking glasses (2)
- milk
- cola or lemon juice
- masking tape
- marker
- measuring cup

▶ Procedure

1. Pour 100 mL of milk into each glass.
2. Pour 20 mL of cola into the second glass.
3. Using the masking tape and marker, label the first glass *No Acid* and the second glass *Acid*.
4. Place the glasses in direct sunlight and observe the mixture each day for several days.

▶ Conclude and Apply

1. Compare the odor of the mixture in both glasses after one or two days.
2. Infer how this experiment modeled one of your internal defenses against disease.

Adult supervision required for all labs.

7 Disappearing Energy

▶ Real-World Question
How much energy is transferred in a food chain?

Possible Materials 🔲 🔳
- sugar cubes
- picture or photograph of the Sun
- picture or photograph of grass
- picture or photograph of mouse
- picture or photograph of snake
- picture or photograph of red tailed hawk

▶ Procedure
1. Lay out your pictures or photographs as links in a food chain starting with the sun and ending with the hawk.
2. Pile 100 sugar cubes next to the picture of the sun. This represents all the Sun's energy reaching Earth.
3. Place ten sugar cubes next to the plant picture, which represents the Sun's energy captured by plants.
4. Place one sugar cube next to the mouse picture to represent the energy that passes from plants to herbivores.
5. Scrape a tenth of one sugar cube away and place the loose grains next to the picture of the snake.

▶ Conclude and Apply
1. Calculate the percentage of energy that is passed up each link in a food chain.
2. Infer how much sugar should be placed next to the red-tailed hawk picture.
3. Infer why there are no super predators that would eat tigers, hawks, or other top predators.

8 Echinoderm Hold

▶ Real-World Question
How do echinoderms living in intertidal ecosystems hold on to rocks?

Possible Materials 🔲 🔳
- plastic suction cup
- water
- paper towel or sponge

▶ Procedure
1. Moisten a paper towel or sponge with water.
2. Press a plastic suction cup on the moist towel or sponge until the entire bottom surface of the cup is wet.
3. Firmly press the suction cup down on a kitchen counter for 10 s.
4. Grab the top handle of the suction cup and try removing the cup from the counter by pulling it straight up.

▶ Conclude and Apply
1. Describe what happened when you tried to remove the cup from the counter.
2. Infer how echinoderms living in intertidal ecosystems withstand the constant pull of ocean waves and currents.

Adult supervision required for all labs.

9 Why recycle?

Real-World Question
What are the effects of throwing out aluminum cans instead of recycling them?

Possible Materials
- calculator
- an aluminum can

Procedure
1. An aluminum can has a mass of about 13 g.

2. Convert the can's mass from grams to kilograms by dividing the mass by 1,000.
3. Find the volume of the can (in milliliters) on the label.
4. Convert the volume from milliliters to liters by dividing it by 1,000.

Conclude and Apply
1. Calculate the mass of aluminum cans thrown out by Americans each year by multiplying the mass of the can in kilograms times 50,000,000,000.
2. Calculate the amount of fuel needed to remake the cans thrown out by Americans each year by multiplying the volume of the can in liters times 50,000,000,000 and dividing your total by 2.
3. Infer the environmental effects of throwing out aluminum cans instead of recycling them.

10 Cloud Watch

Real-World Question
What type of clouds will form over your home this week?

Possible Materials
- cloud chart
- Science Journal
- binoculars
- sunglasses

Procedure
1. Go outside and observe all the types of clouds in the sky. Use a cloud chart to identify the different types of clouds you find. In your Science Journal, record the name and the location in the sky (low, middle or high) of each type of cloud.

2. Observe the type of weather in your area during the hours following your cloud observation. Record your observations in your Science Journal.
3. Continue to make cloud and weather observations every day for seven days.

Conclude and Apply
1. List all the different clouds you identified during this lab.
2. Infer how the presence of different types of clouds can predict future patterns.

Adult supervision required for all labs.

11 Rock and Roll

Real-World Question
How can we model the weathering of rock?

Possible Materials 🔲 🔳
- white glue
- sand
- plastic bowl
- plastic spoon
- cookie tray
- barbecue brush
- aluminum foil
- cooking oil
- empty coffee can with lid
- water
- measuring cup
- transparent packing tape

Procedure
1. Make your own sedimentary rocks by adding equal amounts of white glue and sand to a bowl. Stir the sand and glue together until you make several small lumps.
2. Lay aluminum foil on the bottom of a cookie tray and coat the foil with cooking oil.
3. Lay your rocks on the tray in direct sunlight for three days until they dry.
4. Place your rocks in a coffee can and pour 50 mL of water into the can.
5. Place the lid on the can and secure the lid with thick transparent tape.
6. Shake the contents of the can for 4 min, open the lid, and observe your rocks.

Conclude and Apply
1. Describe what happened to your sedimentary rocks.
2. Infer how this activity modeled the weathering of rocks.

12 In Deep Water

Real-World Question
How can the water table and a well be modeled?

Possible Materials 🔳 🔳
- clear-plastic drink bottle (500-mL)
- aquarium gravel
- water
- blue food dye
- measuring cup
- long dropper

Procedure
1. Fill a clear-plastic bottle with aquarium gravel.
2. Pour 450 mL of water into the the measuring cup and add several drops of blue food dye.
3. Pour 300 mL of the blue water into the bottle with the gravel. Insert the dropper down into the gravel and try to suck out some of the water.
4. Pour another 150 mL of water into the bottle and try to suck out some of the water with the dropper.

Conclude and Apply
1. Describe how this lab models the water table and a well.
2. Infer how deep a well must be dug for it to yield water.
3. Infer why some wells only yield water at certain times of the year.

Extra Try at Home Labs

13 Measuring Movement

▶ Real-World Question
How can we model continental drift?

Possible Materials 🖼️ 🖼️
- flashlight, nail, rubber band or tape, thick circle of paper
- protractor
- mirror
- stick-on notepad paper
- marker
- metric ruler
- calculator

▶ Procedure
1. Cut a circle of paper to fit around the lens of the flashlight. Use a nail to make a hole in the paper. Fasten the paper with the rubber band or tape. You should now have a flashlight that shines a focused beam of light.
2. Direct the light beam of the flashlight on a protractor held horizontally so that the beam lines up to the 90° mark.
3. Darken a room and aim the light beam at a mirror from an angle. Measure the angle. Observe where the reflected beam hits the wall.
4. Have a partner place a stick-on note on the wall and mark the location of the beam on the paper with a marker.
5. Move the flashlight to a 100° angle and mark the beam's location on the wall with a second note.
6. Measure the distance between the two points on the wall and divide by ten to determine the distance per degree.

▶ Conclude and Apply
1. What was the distance per degree of your measurements?
2. Calculate what the distance would be between the first spot and a third spot marking the location of the flashlight at a 40° angle. Test your calculations.
3. Explain how this lab models measuring continental drift.

14 Disappearing Water?

▶ Real-World Question
How much difference does the type of measuring equipment make?

Possible Materials 🥽 🖼️
- scale
- water
- measuring cups of different sizes
- measuring spoons (1 tsp = 5 mL, 1 tbsp = 15 mL)

▶ Procedure
1. Measure out 83 mL of water using one of the measuring devices. Transfer this amount of water to the other measuring devices.
2. Record the readings for each measuring device for the same amount of water. Do they all give the same reading, or does it seem like the amount of water changed?
3. Remember, 1 mL of water weighs 1 g. Use the scale to find out what the true amount of water is in the container.
4. Repeat steps 1–3 for different amounts of water. Try 50 mL, 128 mL, and 12 mL.

▶ Conclude and Apply
1. Which measuring device was the most accurate? The least?
2. Which measuring device was the most precise? The least?
3. What problem came up when you had to use the small devices several times to get up to a larger amount of water?

Adult supervision required for all labs.

15 Materials Matter

▶ Real-World Question
Which materials will react together? How can materials change?

Possible Materials 🔲 🔲 🔲 🔲 🔲 🔲 🔲
- hotplate
- rusty nail
- shiny new nail
- baking soda
- vinegar
- flour
- water
- salt
- chalk
- aluminum foil

▶ Procedure
1. Experiment and record as many physical and chemical changes as possible in 45 min. Prepare your data charts in advance. Try to be efficient rather than speedy. Accurate observations are important.
2. Use at least three words to describe the physical properties of each material. If you know any chemical properties of the materials, add those to your chart.
3. Make physical changes to as many materials as you can. Combine materials to make chemical changes.
4. Describe your observations in the chart.

▶ Conclude and Apply
1. How is knowledge about physical and chemical properties used in building and manufacturing in the real world? Give examples.
2. Were you satisfied with your lab method? What would you do to make your work better next time?

16 Comparing Atom Sizes

▶ Real-World Question
How do the sizes of different types of atoms compare?

Possible Materials 🔲 🔲
- metric ruler or meterstick
- 1-m length of white paper
- transparent or masking tape
- colored pencils

▶ Procedure
1. Tape a 1-m sheet of paper on the floor.
2. Use a scale of 1 mm: 1 picometer for measuring and drawing the relative diameters of all the atoms.
3. Study the chart of atomic sizes.
4. Use your scale to measure the relative size of a hydrogen atom on the sheet of paper. Use a red pencil to draw the relative diameter of a hydrogen atom on your paper.
5. Use your scale to measure the relative sizes of an oxygen atom, iron atom, gold atom, and francium atom. Use four other colored pencils to draw the relative diameters of these atoms on the paper.
6. Compare the relative sizes of these different atoms.

Atomic Sizes (picometers)	
Element	**Diameter**
Hydrogen	50
Oxygen	146
Iron	248
Gold	288
Francium	540

▶ Conclude and Apply
1. Research the length of a picometer.
2. Using your scale, list the diameters of the atoms that you drew on your paper.

Extra Try at Home Labs

17 Mechanical Advantage

▶ **Real-World Question**

What are the mechanical advantages of the wheels and axles in your home?

Possible Materials
- handheld can opener
- several screwdrivers
- rolling pin
- pizza cutter
- doorknob
- metric ruler

▶ **Procedure**

1. Search your home's kitchen, closets, and toolbox to collect several wheels and axles such as a screwdriver, manual can opener, rolling pin, and pizza cutter.

2. Observe each wheel and axle and identify the wheel and the axle of each tool.

3. Measure the radius of the axle of each tool. Record your measurements in your Science Journal.

4. Measure the radius of the wheel of each tool. Record your measurements in your Science Journal. Be certain to use the same units for both measurements.

▶ **Conclude and Apply**

1. Calculate the mechanical advantage of each wheel and axle tool.

2. Infer why a wheel and axle gives you a mechanical advantage.

18 Thermal Propulsion

▶ **Real-World Question**

What has more molecular kinetic energy, hot air or cold air?

Possible Materials
- equal-size, oblong balloons (3)
- cotton thread
- desk lamp
- freezer
- scissors

▶ **Procedure**

1. Inflate each of the three balloons to the same length, but do not over-inflate them.

2. Knot the end of each balloon and tie it off tightly with a string. Tie a string around the middle of each balloon so it is snug, but not overly tight.

3. Overnight, leave one in a freezer, one under a desk lamp, and one in a dark place.

4. The next day, write down your observations of each of the balloons before taking them from their locations.

5. Do this step quickly. With the help of two friends, each of you take a balloon. Go to an indoor area with a high ceiling. Twist and pinch each balloon above the tied end and cut off the tied end, such that no air escapes. Hold the balloons pointing up in front of you and count down, "3, 2, 1, Go!" On the word *Go!*, everyone releases their balloons.

▶ **Conclude and Apply**

1. Which balloons flew for the longest amount of time?

2. Could you tell beforehand which balloons would have the most propulsion energy? What is the source of the propulsion energy?

Adult supervision required for all labs.

19 Magnetic Wires

Real-World Question

Which way does the magnetic field go around a current-carrying wire?

Possible Materials
- an electric circuit (battery, wire, lightbulb)
- compass
- paper
- iron filings or small bits of magnetic metal
- four textbooks
- four erasers or similar paperweights

Procedure
1. Hook up the electric circuit. You will know electricity is going through the wire if the lightbulb is on.

2. Hold the compass at several different points around the circuit. What do you notice?
3. Make a box around the circuit with the textbooks laid flat. Support the paper on the texts. Weight it down at the corners with erasers. Sprinkle iron filings on the paper while electricity is running through the circuit. What do you notice?

Conclude and Apply
1. Make a diagram of the magnetic field around the wire.
2. Would your results change if you changed the voltage of the battery?

20 Exploding Bag

Real-World Question

What happens when a bag pops?

Possible Materials
- paper bag or plastic produce bag

Procedure
1. Obtain a paper lunch bag. Smooth out the bag on a flat surface if it has any wrinkles.
2. Hold the neck of the bag and blow air into it until it is completely filled. The sides of the bag should be stretched out completely.

3. Twist the neck of the bag tightly to prevent air from escaping.
4. Pop the paper bag between your palms and observe what happens.
5. Examine the bag after you pop it. Observe any changes in the bag.

Conclude and Apply
1. Describe what happened when you popped the bag.
2. Infer why this happened to the bag.

21 Deep Space Distance

▶ Real-World Question
How can we compare the distances of objects in deep space?

Possible Materials 🖼️ 🧰
- meterstick
- metric ruler
- scissors
- masking tape
- tennis balls (2)
- thread

▶ Procedure
1. Go outside to a paved surface and place a piece of tape on the ground.
2. Lay a piece of thread next to the tape. This represents 1 A.U., the distance from the Sun to Earth.
3. Measure a distance of 3.9 mm from the tape and place a second piece of tape. This represents the distance from the Sun to Pluto.
4. Measure a distance of 5.0 mm from the first piece of tape and place a third piece of tape. This represents the distance from the Sun to Oort Cloud.
5. Measure a distance of 6.33 m from the first piece of tape and place a tennis ball. This represents the distance of one light-year.
6. Measure a distance of 26.71 m from the first piece of tape and place a tennis ball. This represents the distance from the Sun to the nearest star, Proxima Centuri.

▶ Conclude and Apply
1. The Milky Way galaxy is 90,000 light-years in diameter. Calculate the distance you would have to measure to represent the diameter of our galaxy.
2. Infer why space travel to other stars may not be possible.

22 Space Probe Flights

▶ Real-World Question
How can we compare the distances traveled by space probes to their destinations?

Possible Materials 🖼️ 🧰
- polystyrene balls (5)
- toothpicks (5)
- small stick-on labels (5)
- tennis ball
- meterstick

▶ Procedure
1. Write the names *Mariner 2, Pioneer 10, Mariner 10, Viking 1,* and *Voyager 2* on the five labels and stick each label on a toothpick. Stick a labeled toothpick into each of the polystyrene balls to represent these five United States space probes.
2. Place the tennis ball in an open space such as a basketball court or field.
3. Measure a distance of 0.42 m from the tennis ball and place the *Mariner 2* probe in that spot. Place the *Pioneer 10* probe 6.28 m away, the *Mariner 10* probe 0.92 m from the ball, the *Viking 1* probe 0.78 m away, and the *Voyager 2* probe 43.47 m from the tennis ball.

▶ Conclude and Apply
1. Create a timeline showing the year each probe was launched and its destination and relate this information to the distance traveled.
2. Mercury is 58 million km from the sun and Earth is 150 million km. Use this information to calculate the scale used for this activity.

Computer Skills

People who study science rely on computer technology to do research, record experimental data, analyze results from investigations, and communicate with other scientists. Whether you work in a laboratory or just need to write a lab report, good computer skills are necessary.

Figure 16 Students and scientists rely on computers to gather data and communicate ideas.

Hardware Basics

Your personal computer is a system consisting of many components. The parts you can see and touch are called hardware.

Monitor   Screen   System unit

Speaker   Speaker

Keyboard   Mouse

Figure 17 Most desktop computers consist of the components shown above. Notebook computers have the same components in a compact unit.

Desktop systems, like the one shown in **Figure 17,** typically have most of these components. Notebook and tablet computers have most of the same components as a desktop computer, but the components are integrated into a single, book-sized portable unit.

Storing Your Data

When you save documents created on computers at your school, they probably are stored in a directory on your school's network. However, if you want to take the documents you have created home, you need to save them on something portable. Removable media, like those shown in **Figure 18,** are disks and drives that are designed to be moved from one computer to another.

Figure 18 Removable data storage is a convenient way to carry your documents from place to place.

Removable media vary from floppy disks and recordable CDs and DVDs to small solid-state storage. Tiny USB "keychain" drives have become popular because they can store large amounts of data and plug into any computer with a USB port. Each of these types of media stores different amounts of data. Be sure that you save your data to a medium that is compatible with your computer.

Getting Started with Word Processing Programs

A word processor is used for the composition, editing, and formatting of written material. Word processors vary from program to program, but most have the basic functions shown in **Figure 19.** Most word processors also can be used to make simple tables and graphics.

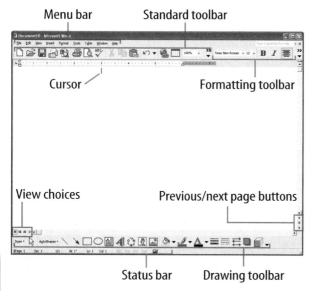

Figure 19 Word processors have functions that easily allow you to edit, format, view, and save text, tables, and images, making them useful for writing lab reports and research papers.

Word Processor Tips

- As you type, text will automatically wrap to the next line. Press *Enter* on your keyboard if you wish to start a new paragraph.
- You can move multiple lines of text around by using the *cut* and *paste* functions on the toolbar.
- If you make a typing or formatting error, use the *undo* function on the toolbar.
- Be sure to save your document early and often. This will prevent you from losing your work if your computer turns off unexpectedly.

- Use the *spell-check* function to check your spelling and grammar. Remember that *spell-check* will not catch words that are misspelled to look like other words, such as *cold* instead of *gold.* Reread your document to look for spelling and grammar mistakes.
- Graphics and spreadsheets can be added to your document by copying them from other programs and pasting them into your document.
- If you have questions about using your word processor, ask your teacher or use the program's *help* menu.

Getting Started with Spreadsheet Programs

A spreadsheet, like the one shown in **Figure 20,** helps you organize information into columns and rows. Spreadsheets are particularly useful for making data tables. Spreadsheets also can be used to perform mathematical calculations with your data. Then, you can use the spreadsheet to generate graphs and charts displaying your results.

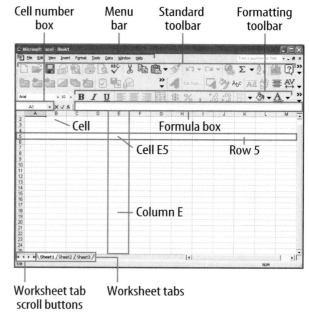

Figure 20 With formulas and graphs, spreadsheets help you organize and analyze your data.

Spreadsheet Tips

- Think about how to organize your data before you begin entering data.
- Each column (vertical) is assigned a letter and each row (horizontal) is assigned a number. Each point where a row and column intersect is called a cell, and is labeled according to where it is located. For example: column A, row 1 is cell A1.
- To edit the information in a cell, you must first activate the cell by clicking on it.
- When using a spreadsheet to generate a graph, make sure you use the type of graph that best represents the data. Review the *Science Skill Handbook* in this book for help with graphs.
- To learn more about using your spreadsheet program ask your teacher or use the program's Help menu.

Getting Started with Presentation Programs

There are many programs that help you orally communicate results of your research in an organized and interesting way. Many of these are slideshow programs, which allow you to organize text, graphs, digital photographs, sound, animations, and digital video into one multimedia presentation. Presentations can be printed onto paper or displayed on-screen. Slideshow programs are particularly effective when used with video projectors and interactive whiteboards, like the one shown in **Figure 21.** Although presentation programs are not the only way to communicate information publicly, they are an effective way to organize your presentation and remind your audience of major points.

Figure 21 Video projectors and interactive whiteboards allow you to present information stored on a computer to an entire classroom. They are becoming increasingly common in the classrooms.

Presentation Program Tips

- Often, color and strong images will convey a point better than words alone. But, be sure to organize your presentation clearly. Don't let the graphics confuse the message.
- Most presentation programs will let you copy and paste text, spreadsheets, art and graphs from other programs.
- Most presentation programs have built-in templates that help you organize text and graphics.
- As with any kind of presentation, familiarize yourself with the equipment and practice your presentation before you present it to an audience.
- Most presentation programs will allow you to save your document in html format so that you can publish your document on a Web site.
- If you have questions about using your presentation software or hardware, ask your teacher or use the program's Help menu.

Technology Skill Handbook

Doing Research with the World Wide Web

The Internet is a global network of computers where information can be stored and shared by anyone with an internet connection. One of the easiest ways to find information on the internet is by using the World Wide Web, a vast graphical system of documents written in the computer language, html (hypertext markup language). Web pages are arranged in collections of related material called "Web sites." The content on a Web site is viewed using a program called a Web browser. Web browsers, like the one shown in **Figure 22,** allow you to browse or surf the Web by clicking on highlighted hyperlinks, which move you from Web page to Web page. Web content can be searched by topic using a search engine. Search engines are located on Web sites which catalog key words on Web pages all over the World Wide Web.

Navigation buttons   Address bar   Loading indicator

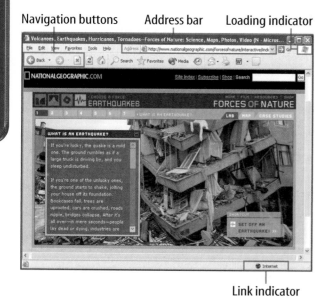

Link indicator

Figure 22 Web browsers have all the tools you need to navigate and view information on the Web.

World Wide Web Tips

- Search the Web using specific keywords. For example, if you want to research the element gold don't type *elements* into the search engine.

- When performing a Web search, enclose multiple keywords with quotes to narrow your results to the most relevant pages.

- The first hit your Web search results in is not always the best. Search results are arranged by popularity, not by relevance to your topic. Be patient and look at many links in your search results to find the best information.

- Think critically when you do science research on the Web. Compared to a traditional library, finding accurate information on the Web is not always easy because anyone can create a Web site. Some of the best places to start your research are websites for major newspapers and magazines, as well as U.S. government (*.gov*) and university (*.edu*) Web sites.

- Security is a major concern when browsing the Web. Your computer can be exposed to advertising software and computer viruses, which can hurt your computer's data and performance. *Do not download software at your school unless your teacher tells you to do so.*

- Cite information you find on the Web just as you would books and journals. An example of proper Web citation is the following:

  Menk, Amy J. (2004). *Urban Ecology.* Retrieved January 21, 2005, from McGraw-Hill Web site: http://www.mcgraw-hill.com/papers/urban.html

- The World Wide Web is a great resource for information, but don't forget to utilize local libraries, including your school library.

Math Review

Use Fractions

A fraction compares a part to a whole. In the fraction $\frac{2}{3}$, the 2 represents the part and is the numerator. The 3 represents the whole and is the denominator.

Reduce Fractions To reduce a fraction, you must find the largest factor that is common to both the numerator and the denominator, the greatest common factor (GCF). Divide both numbers by the GCF. The fraction has then been reduced, or it is in its simplest form.

Example Twelve of the 20 chemicals in the science lab are in powder form. What fraction of the chemicals used in the lab are in powder form?

Step 1 Write the fraction.

$$\frac{\text{part}}{\text{whole}} = \frac{12}{20}$$

Step 2 To find the GCF of the numerator and denominator, list all of the factors of each number.

Factors of 12: 1, 2, 3, 4, 6, 12 (the numbers that divide evenly into 12)

Factors of 20: 1, 2, 4, 5, 10, 20 (the numbers that divide evenly into 20)

Step 3 List the common factors.

1, 2, 4

Step 4 Choose the greatest factor in the list. The GCF of 12 and 20 is 4.

Step 5 Divide the numerator and denominator by the GCF.

$$\frac{12 \div 4}{20 \div 4} = \frac{3}{5}$$

In the lab, $\frac{3}{5}$ of the chemicals are in powder form.

Practice Problem At an amusement park, 66 of 90 rides have a height restriction. What fraction of the rides, in its simplest form, has a height restriction?

Add and Subtract Fractions To add or subtract fractions with the same denominator, add or subtract the numerators and write the sum or difference over the denominator. After finding the sum or difference, find the simplest form for your fraction.

Example 1 In the forest outside your house, $\frac{1}{8}$ of the animals are rabbits, $\frac{3}{8}$ are squirrels, and the remainder are birds and insects. How many are mammals?

Step 1 Add the numerators.

$$\frac{1}{8} + \frac{3}{8} = \frac{(1+3)}{8} = \frac{4}{8}$$

Step 2 Find the GCF.

$$\frac{4}{8} \quad (\text{GCF, 4})$$

Step 3 Divide the numerator and denominator by the GCF.

$$\frac{4 \div 4}{8 \div 4} = \frac{1}{2}$$

$\frac{1}{2}$ of the animals are mammals.

Example 2 If $\frac{7}{16}$ of the Earth is covered by freshwater, and $\frac{1}{16}$ of that is in glaciers, how much freshwater is not frozen?

Step 1 Subtract the numerators.

$$\frac{7}{16} - \frac{1}{16} = \frac{(7-1)}{16} = \frac{6}{16}$$

Step 2 Find the GCF.

$$\frac{6}{16} \quad (\text{GCF, 2})$$

Step 3 Divide the numerator and denominator by the GCF.

$$\frac{6 \div 2}{16 \div 2} = \frac{3}{8}$$

$\frac{3}{8}$ of the freshwater is not frozen.

Practice Problem A bicycle rider is riding at a rate of 15 km/h for $\frac{4}{9}$ of his ride, 10 km/h for $\frac{2}{9}$ of his ride, and 8 km/h for the remainder of the ride. How much of his ride is he riding at a rate greater than 8 km/h?

Unlike Denominators To add or subtract fractions with unlike denominators, first find the least common denominator (LCD). This is the smallest number that is a common multiple of both denominators. Rename each fraction with the LCD, and then add or subtract. Find the simplest form if necessary.

Example 1 A chemist makes a paste that is $\frac{1}{2}$ table salt (NaCl), $\frac{1}{3}$ sugar ($C_6H_{12}O_6$), and the remainder is water (H_2O). How much of the paste is a solid?

Step 1 Find the LCD of the fractions.

$$\frac{1}{2} + \frac{1}{3} \text{ (LCD, 6)}$$

Step 2 Rename each numerator and each denominator with the LCD.

Step 3 Add the numerators.

$$\frac{3}{6} + \frac{2}{6} = \frac{(3+2)}{6} = \frac{5}{6}$$

$\frac{5}{6}$ of the paste is a solid.

Example 2 The average precipitation in Grand Junction, CO, is $\frac{7}{10}$ inch in November, and $\frac{3}{5}$ inch in December. What is the total average precipitation?

Step 1 Find the LCD of the fractions.

$$\frac{7}{10} + \frac{3}{5} \text{ (LCD, 10)}$$

Step 2 Rename each numerator and each denominator with the LCD.

Step 3 Add the numerators.

$$\frac{7}{10} + \frac{6}{10} = \frac{(7+6)}{10} = \frac{13}{10}$$

$\frac{13}{10}$ inches total precipitation, or $1\frac{3}{10}$ inches.

Practice Problem On an electric bill, about $\frac{1}{8}$ of the energy is from solar energy and about $\frac{1}{10}$ is from wind power. How much of the total bill is from solar energy and wind power combined?

Example 3 In your body, $\frac{7}{10}$ of your muscle contractions are involuntary (cardiac and smooth muscle tissue). Smooth muscle makes $\frac{3}{15}$ of your muscle contractions. How many of your muscle contractions are made by cardiac muscle?

Step 1 Find the LCD of the fractions.

$$\frac{7}{10} - \frac{3}{15} \text{ (LCD, 30)}$$

Step 2 Rename each numerator and each denominator with the LCD.

$$\frac{7 \times 3}{10 \times 3} = \frac{21}{30}$$

$$\frac{3 \times 2}{15 \times 2} = \frac{6}{30}$$

Step 3 Subtract the numerators.

$$\frac{21}{30} - \frac{6}{30} = \frac{(21-6)}{30} = \frac{15}{30}$$

Step 4 Find the GCF.

$$\frac{15}{30} \text{ (GCF, 15)}$$

$$\frac{1}{2}$$

$\frac{1}{2}$ of all muscle contractions are cardiac muscle.

Example 4 Tony wants to make cookies that call for $\frac{3}{4}$ of a cup of flour, but he only has $\frac{1}{3}$ of a cup. How much more flour does he need?

Step 1 Find the LCD of the fractions.

$$\frac{3}{4} - \frac{1}{3} \text{ (LCD, 12)}$$

Step 2 Rename each numerator and each denominator with the LCD.

$$\frac{3 \times 3}{4 \times 3} = \frac{9}{12}$$

$$\frac{1 \times 4}{3 \times 4} = \frac{4}{12}$$

Step 3 Subtract the numerators.

$$\frac{9}{12} - \frac{4}{12} = \frac{(9-4)}{12} = \frac{5}{12}$$

$\frac{5}{12}$ of a cup of flour

Practice Problem Using the information provided to you in Example 3 above, determine how many muscle contractions are voluntary (skeletal muscle).

Math Skill Handbook

Multiply Fractions To multiply with fractions, multiply the numerators and multiply the denominators. Find the simplest form if necessary.

Example Multiply $\frac{3}{5}$ by $\frac{1}{3}$.

Step 1 Multiply the numerators and denominators.
$$\frac{3}{5} \times \frac{1}{3} = \frac{(3 \times 1)}{(5 \times 3)} = \frac{3}{15}$$

Step 2 Find the GCF.
$$\frac{3}{15} \quad (\text{GCF, 3})$$

Step 3 Divide the numerator and denominator by the GCF.
$$\frac{3 \div 3}{15 \div 3} = \frac{1}{5}$$

$\frac{3}{5}$ multiplied by $\frac{1}{3}$ is $\frac{1}{5}$.

Practice Problem Multiply $\frac{3}{14}$ by $\frac{5}{16}$.

Find a Reciprocal Two numbers whose product is 1 are called multiplicative inverses, or reciprocals.

Example Find the reciprocal of $\frac{3}{8}$.

Step 1 Inverse the fraction by putting the denominator on top and the numerator on the bottom.
$$\frac{8}{3}$$

The reciprocal of $\frac{3}{8}$ is $\frac{8}{3}$.

Practice Problem Find the reciprocal of $\frac{4}{9}$.

Divide Fractions To divide one fraction by another fraction, multiply the dividend by the reciprocal of the divisor. Find the simplest form if necessary.

Example 1 Divide $\frac{1}{9}$ by $\frac{1}{3}$.

Step 1 Find the reciprocal of the divisor.
The reciprocal of $\frac{1}{3}$ is $\frac{3}{1}$.

Step 2 Multiply the dividend by the reciprocal of the divisor.
$$\frac{\frac{1}{9}}{\frac{1}{3}} = \frac{1}{9} \times \frac{3}{1} = \frac{(1 \times 3)}{(9 \times 1)} = \frac{3}{9}$$

Step 3 Find the GCF.
$$\frac{3}{9} \quad (\text{GCF, 3})$$

Step 4 Divide the numerator and denominator by the GCF.
$$\frac{3 \div 3}{9 \div 3} = \frac{1}{3}$$

$\frac{1}{9}$ divided by $\frac{1}{3}$ is $\frac{1}{3}$.

Example 2 Divide $\frac{3}{5}$ by $\frac{1}{4}$.

Step 1 Find the reciprocal of the divisor.
The reciprocal of $\frac{1}{4}$ is $\frac{4}{1}$.

Step 2 Multiply the dividend by the reciprocal of the divisor.
$$\frac{\frac{3}{5}}{\frac{1}{4}} = \frac{3}{5} \times \frac{4}{1} = \frac{(3 \times 4)}{(5 \times 1)} = \frac{12}{5}$$

$\frac{3}{5}$ divided by $\frac{1}{4}$ is $\frac{12}{5}$ or $2\frac{2}{5}$.

Practice Problem Divide $\frac{3}{11}$ by $\frac{7}{10}$.

Use Ratios

When you compare two numbers by division, you are using a ratio. Ratios can be written 3 to 5, 3:5, or $\frac{3}{5}$. Ratios, like fractions, also can be written in simplest form.

Ratios can represent one type of probability, called odds. This is a ratio that compares the number of ways a certain outcome occurs to the number of possible outcomes. For example, if you flip a coin 100 times, what are the odds that it will come up heads? There are two possible outcomes, heads or tails, so the odds of coming up heads are 50:100. Another way to say this is that 50 out of 100 times the coin will come up heads. In its simplest form, the ratio is 1:2.

Example 1 A chemical solution contains 40 g of salt and 64 g of baking soda. What is the ratio of salt to baking soda as a fraction in simplest form?

Step 1 Write the ratio as a fraction.
$$\frac{salt}{baking\ soda} = \frac{40}{64}$$

Step 2 Express the fraction in simplest form.
The GCF of 40 and 64 is 8.
$$\frac{40}{64} = \frac{40 \div 8}{64 \div 8} = \frac{5}{8}$$

The ratio of salt to baking soda in the sample is 5:8.

Example 2 Sean rolls a 6-sided die 6 times. What are the odds that the side with a 3 will show?

Step 1 Write the ratio as a fraction.
$$\frac{number\ of\ sides\ with\ a\ 3}{number\ of\ possible\ sides} = \frac{1}{6}$$

Step 2 Multiply by the number of attempts.
$$\frac{1}{6} \times 6\ attempts = \frac{6}{6}\ attempts = 1\ attempt$$

1 attempt out of 6 will show a 3.

Practice Problem Two metal rods measure 100 cm and 144 cm in length. What is the ratio of their lengths in simplest form?

Use Decimals

A fraction with a denominator that is a power of ten can be written as a decimal. For example, 0.27 means $\frac{27}{100}$. The decimal point separates the ones place from the tenths place.

Any fraction can be written as a decimal using division. For example, the fraction $\frac{5}{8}$ can be written as a decimal by dividing 5 by 8. Written as a decimal, it is 0.625.

Add or Subtract Decimals When adding and subtracting decimals, line up the decimal points before carrying out the operation.

Example 1 Find the sum of 47.68 and 7.80.

Step 1 Line up the decimal places when you write the numbers.
$$\begin{array}{r} 47.68 \\ + \ 7.80 \\ \hline \end{array}$$

Step 2 Add the decimals.
$$\begin{array}{r} {\scriptstyle 1\ 1} \\ 47.68 \\ + \ 7.80 \\ \hline 55.48 \end{array}$$

The sum of 47.68 and 7.80 is 55.48.

Example 2 Find the difference of 42.17 and 15.85.

Step 1 Line up the decimal places when you write the number.
$$\begin{array}{r} 42.17 \\ - 15.85 \\ \hline \end{array}$$

Step 2 Subtract the decimals.
$$\begin{array}{r} {\scriptstyle 3\ 11} \\ 4\cancel{2}.17 \\ - 15.85 \\ \hline 26.32 \end{array}$$

The difference of 42.17 and 15.85 is 26.32.

Practice Problem Find the sum of 1.245 and 3.842.

Multiply Decimals To multiply decimals, multiply the numbers like numbers without decimal points. Count the decimal places in each factor. The product will have the same number of decimal places as the sum of the decimal places in the factors.

Example Multiply 2.4 by 5.9.

Step 1 Multiply the factors like two whole numbers.
$24 \times 59 = 1416$

Step 2 Find the sum of the number of decimal places in the factors. Each factor has one decimal place, for a sum of two decimal places.

Step 3 The product will have two decimal places.
14.16

The product of 2.4 and 5.9 is 14.16.

Practice Problem Multiply 4.6 by 2.2.

Divide Decimals When dividing decimals, change the divisor to a whole number. To do this, multiply both the divisor and the dividend by the same power of ten. Then place the decimal point in the quotient directly above the decimal point in the dividend. Then divide as you do with whole numbers.

Example Divide 8.84 by 3.4.

Step 1 Multiply both factors by 10.
$3.4 \times 10 = 34, 8.84 \times 10 = 88.4$

Step 2 Divide 88.4 by 34.

```
      2.6
 34)88.4
    -68
     204
    -204
       0
```

8.84 divided by 3.4 is 2.6.

Practice Problem Divide 75.6 by 3.6.

Use Proportions

An equation that shows that two ratios are equivalent is a proportion. The ratios $\frac{2}{4}$ and $\frac{5}{10}$ are equivalent, so they can be written as $\frac{2}{4} = \frac{5}{10}$. This equation is a proportion.

When two ratios form a proportion, the cross products are equal. To find the cross products in the proportion $\frac{2}{4} = \frac{5}{10}$, multiply the 2 and the 10, and the 4 and the 5. Therefore $2 \times 10 = 4 \times 5$, or $20 = 20$.

Because you know that both ratios are equal, you can use cross products to find a missing term in a proportion. This is known as solving the proportion.

Example The heights of a tree and a pole are proportional to the lengths of their shadows. The tree casts a shadow of 24 m when a 6-m pole casts a shadow of 4 m. What is the height of the tree?

Step 1 Write a proportion.
$$\frac{\text{height of tree}}{\text{height of pole}} = \frac{\text{length of tree's shadow}}{\text{length of pole's shadow}}$$

Step 2 Substitute the known values into the proportion. Let h represent the unknown value, the height of the tree.
$$\frac{h}{6} = \frac{24}{4}$$

Step 3 Find the cross products.
$h \times 4 = 6 \times 24$

Step 4 Simplify the equation.
$4h = 144$

Step 5 Divide each side by 4.
$$\frac{4h}{4} = \frac{144}{4}$$
$$h = 36$$

The height of the tree is 36 m.

Practice Problem The ratios of the weights of two objects on the Moon and on Earth are in proportion. A rock weighing 3 N on the Moon weighs 18 N on Earth. How much would a rock that weighs 5 N on the Moon weigh on Earth?

Use Percentages

The word *percent* means "out of one hundred." It is a ratio that compares a number to 100. Suppose you read that 77 percent of the Earth's surface is covered by water. That is the same as reading that the fraction of the Earth's surface covered by water is $\frac{77}{100}$. To express a fraction as a percent, first find the equivalent decimal for the fraction. Then, multiply the decimal by 100 and add the percent symbol.

Example Express $\frac{13}{20}$ as a percent.

Step 1 Find the equivalent decimal for the fraction.

$$
\begin{array}{r}
0.65 \\
20)\overline{13.00} \\
\underline{12\,0} \\
1\,00 \\
\underline{1\,00} \\
0
\end{array}
$$

Step 2 Rewrite the fraction $\frac{13}{20}$ as 0.65.

Step 3 Multiply 0.65 by 100 and add the % symbol.
$0.65 \times 100 = 65 = 65\%$

So, $\frac{13}{20} = 65\%$.

This also can be solved as a proportion.

Example Express $\frac{13}{20}$ as a percent.

Step 1 Write a proportion.
$$\frac{13}{20} = \frac{x}{100}$$

Step 2 Find the cross products.
$1300 = 20x$

Step 3 Divide each side by 20.
$$\frac{1300}{20} = \frac{20x}{20}$$
$65\% = x$

Practice Problem In one year, 73 of 365 days were rainy in one city. What percent of the days in that city were rainy?

Solve One-Step Equations

A statement that two expressions are equal is an equation. For example, $A = B$ is an equation that states that A is equal to B.

An equation is solved when a variable is replaced with a value that makes both sides of the equation equal. To make both sides equal the inverse operation is used. Addition and subtraction are inverses, and multiplication and division are inverses.

Example 1 Solve the equation $x - 10 = 35$.

Step 1 Find the solution by adding 10 to each side of the equation.
$x - 10 = 35$
$x - 10 + 10 = 35 + 10$
$x = 45$

Step 2 Check the solution.
$x - 10 = 35$
$45 - 10 = 35$
$35 = 35$

Both sides of the equation are equal, so $x = 45$.

Example 2 In the formula $a = bc$, find the value of c if $a = 20$ and $b = 2$.

Step 1 Rearrange the formula so the unknown value is by itself on one side of the equation by dividing both sides by b.

$a = bc$
$\frac{a}{b} = \frac{bc}{b}$
$\frac{a}{b} = c$

Step 2 Replace the variables a and b with the values that are given.

$\frac{a}{b} = c$
$\frac{20}{2} = c$
$10 = c$

Step 3 Check the solution.

$a = bc$
$20 = 2 \times 10$
$20 = 20$

Both sides of the equation are equal, so $c = 10$ is the solution when $a = 20$ and $b = 2$.

Practice Problem In the formula $h = gd$, find the value of d if $g = 12.3$ and $h = 17.4$.

Use Statistics

The branch of mathematics that deals with collecting, analyzing, and presenting data is statistics. In statistics, there are three common ways to summarize data with a single number—the mean, the median, and the mode.

The **mean** of a set of data is the arithmetic average. It is found by adding the numbers in the data set and dividing by the number of items in the set.

The **median** is the middle number in a set of data when the data are arranged in numerical order. If there were an even number of data points, the median would be the mean of the two middle numbers.

The **mode** of a set of data is the number or item that appears most often.

Another number that often is used to describe a set of data is the range. The **range** is the difference between the largest number and the smallest number in a set of data.

A **frequency table** shows how many times each piece of data occurs, usually in a survey. **Table 2** below shows the results of a student survey on favorite color.

Table 2 Student Color Choice		
Color	**Tally**	**Frequency**
red	||||	4
blue	卌	5
black	||	2
green	|||	3
purple	卌 ||	7
yellow	卌 |	6

Based on the frequency table data, which color is the favorite?

Example The speeds (in m/s) for a race car during five different time trials are 39, 37, 44, 36, and 44.

To find the mean:

Step 1 Find the sum of the numbers.
$$39 + 37 + 44 + 36 + 44 = 200$$

Step 2 Divide the sum by the number of items, which is 5.
$$200 \div 5 = 40$$

The mean is 40 m/s.

To find the median:

Step 1 Arrange the measures from least to greatest.
36, 37, 39, 44, 44

Step 2 Determine the middle measure.
36, 37, <u>39</u>, 44, 44

The median is 39 m/s.

To find the mode:

Step 1 Group the numbers that are the same together.
44, 44, 36, 37, 39

Step 2 Determine the number that occurs most in the set.
<u>44, 44</u>, 36, 37, 39

The mode is 44 m/s.

To find the range:

Step 1 Arrange the measures from greatest to least.
44, 44, 39, 37, 36

Step 2 Determine the greatest and least measures in the set.
<u>44</u>, 44, 39, 37, <u>36</u>

Step 3 Find the difference between the greatest and least measures.
$$44 - 36 = 8$$

The range is 8 m/s.

Practice Problem Find the mean, median, mode, and range for the data set 8, 4, 12, 8, 11, 14, 16.

Use Geometry

The branch of mathematics that deals with the measurement, properties, and relationships of points, lines, angles, surfaces, and solids is called geometry.

Perimeter The **perimeter** (P) is the distance around a geometric figure. To find the perimeter of a rectangle, add the length and width and multiply that sum by two, or $2(l + w)$. To find perimeters of irregular figures, add the length of the sides.

Example 1 Find the perimeter of a rectangle that is 3 m long and 5 m wide.

Step 1 You know that the perimeter is 2 times the sum of the width and length.
$P = 2(3\text{ m} + 5\text{ m})$

Step 2 Find the sum of the width and length.
$P = 2(8\text{ m})$

Step 3 Multiply by 2.
$P = 16\text{ m}$

The perimeter is 16 m.

Example 2 Find the perimeter of a shape with sides measuring 2 cm, 5 cm, 6 cm, 3 cm.

Step 1 You know that the perimeter is the sum of all the sides.
$P = 2 + 5 + 6 + 3$

Step 2 Find the sum of the sides.
$P = 2 + 5 + 6 + 3$
$P = 16$

The perimeter is 16 cm.

Practice Problem Find the perimeter of a rectangle with a length of 18 m and a width of 7 m.

Practice Problem Find the perimeter of a triangle measuring 1.6 cm by 2.4 cm by 2.4 cm.

Area of a Rectangle The **area** (A) is the number of square units needed to cover a surface. To find the area of a rectangle, multiply the length times the width, or $l \times w$. When finding area, the units also are multiplied. Area is given in square units.

Example Find the area of a rectangle with a length of 1 cm and a width of 10 cm.

Step 1 You know that the area is the length multiplied by the width.
$A = (1\text{ cm} \times 10\text{ cm})$

Step 2 Multiply the length by the width. Also multiply the units.
$A = 10\text{ cm}^2$

The area is 10 cm².

Practice Problem Find the area of a square whose sides measure 4 m.

Area of a Triangle To find the area of a triangle, use the formula:

$$A = \frac{1}{2}(\text{base} \times \text{height})$$

The base of a triangle can be any of its sides. The height is the perpendicular distance from a base to the opposite endpoint, or vertex.

Example Find the area of a triangle with a base of 18 m and a height of 7 m.

Step 1 You know that the area is $\frac{1}{2}$ the base times the height.
$A = \frac{1}{2}(18\text{ m} \times 7\text{ m})$

Step 2 Multiply $\frac{1}{2}$ by the product of 18×7. Multiply the units.
$A = \frac{1}{2}(126\text{ m}^2)$
$A = 63\text{ m}^2$

The area is 63 m².

Practice Problem Find the area of a triangle with a base of 27 cm and a height of 17 cm.

Circumference of a Circle The **diameter** (d) of a circle is the distance across the circle through its center, and the **radius** (r) is the distance from the center to any point on the circle. The radius is half of the diameter. The distance around the circle is called the **circumference** (C). The formula for finding the circumference is:

$$C = 2\pi r \ \ or \ \ C = \pi d$$

The circumference divided by the diameter is always equal to 3.1415926... This nonterminating and nonrepeating number is represented by the Greek letter π (pi). An approximation often used for π is 3.14.

Example 1 Find the circumference of a circle with a radius of 3 m.

Step 1 You know the formula for the circumference is 2 times the radius times π.
$$C = 2\pi(3)$$

Step 2 Multiply 2 times the radius.
$$C = 6\pi$$

Step 3 Multiply by π.
$$C \approx 19 \text{ m}$$

The circumference is about 19 m.

Example 2 Find the circumference of a circle with a diameter of 24.0 cm.

Step 1 You know the formula for the circumference is the diameter times π.
$$C = \pi(24.0)$$

Step 2 Multiply the diameter by π.
$$C \approx 75.4 \text{ cm}$$

The circumference is about 75.4 cm.

Practice Problem Find the circumference of a circle with a radius of 19 cm.

Area of a Circle The formula for the area of a circle is:
$$A = \pi r^2$$

Example 1 Find the area of a circle with a radius of 4.0 cm.

Step 1 $A = \pi(4.0)^2$

Step 2 Find the square of the radius.
$$A = 16\pi$$

Step 3 Multiply the square of the radius by π.
$$A \approx 50 \text{ cm}^2$$

The area of the circle is about 50 cm^2.

Example 2 Find the area of a circle with a radius of 225 m.

Step 1 $A = \pi(225)^2$

Step 2 Find the square of the radius.
$$A = 50625\pi$$

Step 3 Multiply the square of the radius by π.
$$A \approx 159043.1$$

The area of the circle is about 159043.1 m^2.

Example 3 Find the area of a circle whose diameter is 20.0 mm.

Step 1 You know the formula for the area of a circle is the square of the radius times π, and that the radius is half of the diameter.
$$A = \pi\left(\frac{20.0}{2}\right)^2$$

Step 2 Find the radius.
$$A = \pi(10.0)^2$$

Step 3 Find the square of the radius.
$$A = 100\pi$$

Step 4 Multiply the square of the radius by π.
$$A \approx 314 \text{ mm}^2$$

The area is about 314 mm^2.

Practice Problem Find the area of a circle with a radius of 16 m.

Volume The measure of space occupied by a solid is the **volume** (V). To find the volume of a rectangular solid multiply the length times width times height, or $V = l \times w \times h$. It is measured in cubic units, such as cubic centimeters (cm^3).

Example Find the volume of a rectangular solid with a length of 2.0 m, a width of 4.0 m, and a height of 3.0 m.

Step 1 You know the formula for volume is the length times the width times the height.
$$V = 2.0 \text{ m} \times 4.0 \text{ m} \times 3.0 \text{ m}$$

Step 2 Multiply the length times the width times the height.
$$V = 24 \text{ m}^3$$

The volume is 24 m^3.

Practice Problem Find the volume of a rectangular solid that is 8 m long, 4 m wide, and 4 m high.

To find the volume of other solids, multiply the area of the base times the height.

Example 1 Find the volume of a solid that has a triangular base with a length of 8.0 m and a height of 7.0 m. The height of the entire solid is 15.0 m.

Step 1 You know that the base is a triangle, and the area of a triangle is $\frac{1}{2}$ the base times the height, and the volume is the area of the base times the height.
$$V = \left[\frac{1}{2}(b \times h)\right] \times 15$$

Step 2 Find the area of the base.
$$V = \left[\frac{1}{2}(8 \times 7)\right] \times 15$$
$$V = \left(\frac{1}{2} \times 56\right) \times 15$$

Step 3 Multiply the area of the base by the height of the solid.
$$V = 28 \times 15$$
$$V = 420 \text{ m}^3$$

The volume is 420 m^3.

Example 2 Find the volume of a cylinder that has a base with a radius of 12.0 cm, and a height of 21.0 cm.

Step 1 You know that the base is a circle, and the area of a circle is the square of the radius times π, and the volume is the area of the base times the height.
$$V = (\pi r^2) \times 21$$
$$V = (\pi 12^2) \times 21$$

Step 2 Find the area of the base.
$$V = 144\pi \times 21$$
$$V = 452 \times 21$$

Step 3 Multiply the area of the base by the height of the solid.
$$V \approx 9{,}500 \text{ cm}^3$$

The volume is about 9,500 cm^3.

Example 3 Find the volume of a cylinder that has a diameter of 15 mm and a height of 4.8 mm.

Step 1 You know that the base is a circle with an area equal to the square of the radius times π. The radius is one-half the diameter. The volume is the area of the base times the height.
$$V = (\pi r^2) \times 4.8$$
$$V = \left[\pi\left(\frac{1}{2} \times 15\right)^2\right] \times 4.8$$
$$V = (\pi 7.5^2) \times 4.8$$

Step 2 Find the area of the base.
$$V = 56.25\pi \times 4.8$$
$$V \approx 176.71 \times 4.8$$

Step 3 Multiply the area of the base by the height of the solid.
$$V \approx 848.2$$

The volume is about 848.2 mm^3.

Practice Problem Find the volume of a cylinder with a diameter of 7 cm in the base and a height of 16 cm.

Math Skill Handbook

Science Applications

Measure in SI

The metric system of measurement was developed in 1795. A modern form of the metric system, called the International System (SI), was adopted in 1960 and provides the standard measurements that all scientists around the world can understand.

The SI system is convenient because unit sizes vary by powers of 10. Prefixes are used to name units. Look at **Table 3** for some common SI prefixes and their meanings.

Table 3 Common SI Prefixes			
Prefix	**Symbol**	**Meaning**	
kilo-	k	1,000	thousand
hecto-	h	100	hundred
deka-	da	10	ten
deci-	d	0.1	tenth
centi-	c	0.01	hundredth
milli-	m	0.001	thousandth

Example How many grams equal one kilogram?

Step 1 Find the prefix *kilo-* in **Table 3.**

Step 2 Using **Table 3,** determine the meaning of *kilo-*. According to the table, it means 1,000. When the prefix *kilo-* is added to a unit, it means that there are 1,000 of the units in a "kilounit."

Step 3 Apply the prefix to the units in the question. The units in the question are grams. There are 1,000 grams in a kilogram.

Practice Problem Is a milligram larger or smaller than a gram? How many of the smaller units equal one larger unit? What fraction of the larger unit does one smaller unit represent?

Dimensional Analysis

Convert SI Units In science, quantities such as length, mass, and time sometimes are measured using different units. A process called dimensional analysis can be used to change one unit of measure to another. This process involves multiplying your starting quantity and units by one or more conversion factors. A conversion factor is a ratio equal to one and can be made from any two equal quantities with different units. If 1,000 mL equal 1 L then two ratios can be made.

$$\frac{1{,}000 \text{ mL}}{1 \text{ L}} = \frac{1 \text{ L}}{1{,}000 \text{ mL}} = 1$$

One can convert between units in the SI system by using the equivalents in **Table 3** to make conversion factors.

Example 1 How many cm are in 4 m?

Step 1 Write conversion factors for the units given. From **Table 3,** you know that 100 cm = 1 m. The conversion factors are

$$\frac{100 \text{ cm}}{1 \text{ m}} \quad and \quad \frac{1 \text{ m}}{100 \text{ cm}}$$

Step 2 Decide which conversion factor to use. Select the factor that has the units you are converting from (m) in the denominator and the units you are converting to (cm) in the numerator.

$$\frac{100 \text{ cm}}{1 \text{ m}}$$

Step 3 Multiply the starting quantity and units by the conversion factor. Cancel the starting units with the units in the denominator. There are 400 cm in 4 m.

$$4 \text{ m} \times \frac{100 \text{ cm}}{1 \text{ m}} = 400 \text{ cm}$$

Practice Problem How many milligrams are in one kilogram? (Hint: You will need to use two conversion factors from **Table 3.**)

Math Skill Handbook

Table 4 Unit System Equivalents

Type of Measurement	Equivalent
Length	1 in = 2.54 cm
	1 yd = 0.91 m
	1 mi = 1.61 km
Mass and weight*	1 oz = 28.35 g
	1 lb = 0.45 kg
	1 ton (short) = 0.91 tonnes (metric tons)
	1 lb = 4.45 N
Volume	1 in^3 = 16.39 cm^3
	1 qt = 0.95 L
	1 gal = 3.78 L
Area	1 in^2 = 6.45 cm^2
	1 yd^2 = 0.83 m^2
	1 mi^2 = 2.59 km^2
	1 acre = 0.40 hectares
Temperature	$^\circ C = \dfrac{(^\circ F - 32)}{1.8}$
	$K = {}^\circ C + 273$

*Weight is measured in standard Earth gravity.

Convert Between Unit Systems **Table 4** gives a list of equivalents that can be used to convert between English and SI units.

Example If a meterstick has a length of 100 cm, how long is the meterstick in inches?

Step 1 Write the conversion factors for the units given. From **Table 4,** 1 in = 2.54 cm.

$$\frac{1\ in}{2.54\ cm}\quad and\quad \frac{2.54\ cm}{1\ in}$$

Step 2 Determine which conversion factor to use. You are converting from cm to in. Use the conversion factor with cm on the bottom.

$$\frac{1\ in}{2.54\ cm}$$

Step 3 Multiply the starting quantity and units by the conversion factor. Cancel the starting units with the units in the denominator. Round your answer to the nearest tenth.

$$100\ \cancel{cm} \times \frac{1\ in}{2.54\ \cancel{cm}} = 39.37\ in$$

The meterstick is about 39.4 in long.

Practice Problem A book has a mass of 5 lbs. What is the mass of the book in kg?

Practice Problem Use the equivalent for in and cm (1 in = 2.54 cm) to show how 1 in^3 = 16.39 cm^3.

Precision and Significant Digits

When you make a measurement, the value you record depends on the precision of the measuring instrument. This precision is represented by the number of significant digits recorded in the measurement. When counting the number of significant digits, all digits are counted except zeros at the end of a number with no decimal point such as 2,050, and zeros at the beginning of a decimal such as 0.03020. When adding or subtracting numbers with different precision, round the answer to the smallest number of decimal places of any number in the sum or difference. When multiplying or dividing, the answer is rounded to the smallest number of significant digits of any number being multiplied or divided.

Example The lengths 5.28 and 5.2 are measured in meters. Find the sum of these lengths and record your answer using the correct number of significant digits.

Step 1 Find the sum.

$$5.28 \text{ m} \quad \text{2 digits after the decimal}$$
$$+ \ 5.2 \ \text{ m} \quad \text{1 digit after the decimal}$$
$$\overline{10.48 \text{ m}}$$

Step 2 Round to one digit after the decimal because the least number of digits after the decimal of the numbers being added is 1.

The sum is 10.5 m.

Practice Problem How many significant digits are in the measurement 7,071,301 m? How many significant digits are in the measurement 0.003010 g?

Practice Problem Multiply 5.28 and 5.2 using the rule for multiplying and dividing. Record the answer using the correct number of significant digits.

Scientific Notation

Many times numbers used in science are very small or very large. Because these numbers are difficult to work with scientists use scientific notation. To write numbers in scientific notation, move the decimal point until only one non-zero digit remains on the left. Then count the number of places you moved the decimal point and use that number as a power of ten. For example, the average distance from the Sun to Mars is 227,800,000,000 m. In scientific notation, this distance is 2.278×10^{11} m. Because you moved the decimal point to the left, the number is a positive power of ten.

The mass of an electron is about 0.000 000 000 000 000 000 000 000 000 000 911 kg. Expressed in scientific notation, this mass is 9.11×10^{-31} kg. Because the decimal point was moved to the right, the number is a negative power of ten.

Example Earth is 149,600,000 km from the Sun. Express this in scientific notation.

Step 1 Move the decimal point until one non-zero digit remains on the left. 1.496 000 00

Step 2 Count the number of decimal places you have moved. In this case, eight.

Step 3 Show that number as a power of ten, 10^8.

Earth is 1.496×10^8 km from the Sun.

Practice Problem How many significant digits are in 149,600,000 km? How many significant digits are in 1.496×10^8 km?

Practice Problem Parts used in a high performance car must be measured to 7×10^{-6} m. Express this number as a decimal.

Practice Problem A CD is spinning at 539 revolutions per minute. Express this number in scientific notation.

Make and Use Graphs

Data in tables can be displayed in a graph—a visual representation of data. Common graph types include line graphs, bar graphs, and circle graphs.

Line Graph A line graph shows a relationship between two variables that change continuously. The independent variable is changed and is plotted on the *x*-axis. The dependent variable is observed, and is plotted on the *y*-axis.

Example Draw a line graph of the data below from a cyclist in a long-distance race.

Table 5 Bicycle Race Data	
Time (h)	Distance (km)
0	0
1	8
2	16
3	24
4	32
5	40

Step 1 Determine the *x*-axis and *y*-axis variables. Time varies independently of distance and is plotted on the *x*-axis. Distance is dependent on time and is plotted on the *y*-axis.

Step 2 Determine the scale of each axis. The *x*-axis data ranges from 0 to 5. The *y*-axis data ranges from 0 to 50.

Step 3 Using graph paper, draw and label the axes. Include units in the labels.

Step 4 Draw a point at the intersection of the time value on the *x*-axis and corresponding distance value on the *y*-axis. Connect the points and label the graph with a title, as shown in **Figure 20.**

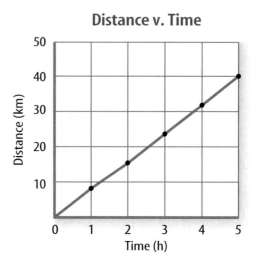

Distance v. Time

Figure 23 This line graph shows the relationship between distance and time during a bicycle ride.

Practice Problem A puppy's shoulder height is measured during the first year of her life. The following measurements were collected: (3 mo, 52 cm), (6 mo, 72 cm), (9 mo, 83 cm), (12 mo, 86 cm). Graph this data.

Find a Slope The slope of a straight line is the ratio of the vertical change, rise, to the horizontal change, run.

$$\text{Slope} = \frac{\text{vertical change (rise)}}{\text{horizontal change (run)}} = \frac{\text{change in } y}{\text{change in } x}$$

Example Find the slope of the graph in **Figure 23.**

Step 1 You know that the slope is the change in *y* divided by the change in *x*.
$$\text{Slope} = \frac{\text{change in } y}{\text{change in } x}$$

Step 2 Determine the data points you will be using. For a straight line, choose the two sets of points that are the farthest apart.
$$\text{Slope} = \frac{(40-0) \text{ km}}{(5-0) \text{ h}}$$

Step 3 Find the change in *y* and *x*.
$$\text{Slope} = \frac{40 \text{ km}}{5 \text{ h}}$$

Step 4 Divide the change in *y* by the change in *x*.
$$\text{Slope} = \frac{8 \text{ km}}{\text{h}}$$

The slope of the graph is 8 km/h.

Bar Graph To compare data that does not change continuously you might choose a bar graph. A bar graph uses bars to show the relationships between variables. The *x*-axis variable is divided into parts. The parts can be numbers such as years, or a category such as a type of animal. The *y*-axis is a number and increases continuously along the axis.

Example A recycling center collects 4.0 kg of aluminum on Monday, 1.0 kg on Wednesday, and 2.0 kg on Friday. Create a bar graph of this data.

Step 1 Select the *x*-axis and *y*-axis variables. The measured numbers (the masses of aluminum) should be placed on the *y*-axis. The variable divided into parts (collection days) is placed on the *x*-axis.

Step 2 Create a graph grid like you would for a line graph. Include labels and units.

Step 3 For each measured number, draw a vertical bar above the *x*-axis value up to the *y*-axis value. For the first data point, draw a vertical bar above Monday up to 4.0 kg.

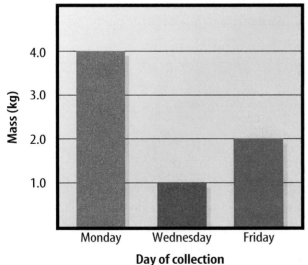

Aluminum Collected During Week

Practice Problem Draw a bar graph of the gases in air: 78% nitrogen, 21% oxygen, 1% other gases.

Circle Graph To display data as parts of a whole, you might use a circle graph. A circle graph is a circle divided into sections that represent the relative size of each piece of data. The entire circle represents 100%, half represents 50%, and so on.

Example Air is made up of 78% nitrogen, 21% oxygen, and 1% other gases. Display the composition of air in a circle graph.

Step 1 Multiply each percent by 360° and divide by 100 to find the angle of each section in the circle.

$$78\% \times \frac{360°}{100} = 280.8°$$

$$21\% \times \frac{360°}{100} = 75.6°$$

$$1\% \times \frac{360°}{100} = 3.6°$$

Step 2 Use a compass to draw a circle and to mark the center of the circle. Draw a straight line from the center to the edge of the circle.

Step 3 Use a protractor and the angles you calculated to divide the circle into parts. Place the center of the protractor over the center of the circle and line the base of the protractor over the straight line.

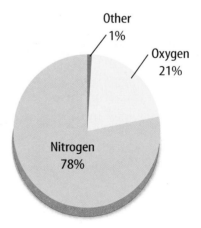

Other
1%

Oxygen
21%

Nitrogen
78%

Practice Problem Draw a circle graph to represent the amount of aluminum collected during the week shown in the bar graph to the left.

Using a Calculator

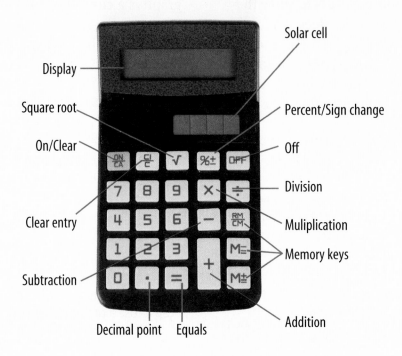

Display — Solar cell

Square root — Percent/Sign change

On/Clear — Off

Clear entry — Division

Multiplication

Memory keys

Subtraction — Addition

Decimal point   Equals

- Read the problem very carefully. Decide if you need the calculator to help you solve the problem.

- Clear the calculator by pressing the clear key when starting a new problem.

- If you see an E in the display, clear the error before you begin.

- If you see an M in the display, clear the memory and the calculator before you begin.

- If the number in the display is not one of the answer choices, check your work. You may have to round the number in the display.

- Your calculator will NOT automatically perform the correct order of operations.

- When working with calculators, use careful and deliberate keystrokes, and always remember to check your answer to make sure that it is reasonable. Calculators might display an incorrect answer if you press the keys too quickly.

- Check your answer to make sure that you have completed all of the necessary steps.

Science Reference Guide

Equations

Acceleration (ā) $= \dfrac{\text{change in velocity (m/s)}}{\text{time taken for this change (s)}}$ $\bar{a} = \dfrac{v_f - v_i}{t_f - t_i}$

Average speed (v̄) $= \dfrac{\text{distance}}{\text{time}}$ $\bar{v} = \dfrac{d}{t}$

Density (D) $= \dfrac{\text{mass (g)}}{\text{Volume (cm}^3)}$ $D = \dfrac{m}{V}$

Percent Efficiency (e) $= \dfrac{\text{Work out (J)}}{\text{Work in (J)}} \times 100$ $eff = \dfrac{W_{out}}{W_{in}} \times 100$

Force in newtons (F) $= \text{mass (kg)} \times \text{acceleration (m/s}^2)$ $F = ma$

Frequency in hertz (f) $= \dfrac{\text{number of events (waves)}}{\text{time (s)}}$ $f = \dfrac{n \text{ of events}}{t}$

Momentum (p) $= \text{mass (kg)} \times \text{velocity (m/s)}$ $p = mv$

Wavelength (λ) $= \dfrac{\text{velocity (m/s)}}{\text{frequency (Hz)}}$ $\lambda = \dfrac{v}{f}$

Work (W) $= \text{Force (N)} \times \text{distance (m)}$ $W = Fd$

Units of Measure

cm = centimeter   kg = kilogram
g = gram   m = meter
Hz = hertz   N = newton
J = joule (newton-meter)   s = second

Understanding Scientific Terms

This list of prefixes, suffixes, and roots is provided to help you understand science terms used throughout this textbook. The list identifies whether the prefix, suffix, or root is of Greek *(G)* or Latin *(L)* origin. Also listed is the meaning of the prefix, suffix, or root and a science word in which it is used.

ORIGIN	MEANING	EXAMPLE	ORIGIN	MEANING	EXAMPLE
A			dia (G)	apart	diaphragm
ad (L)	to, toward	adaxial	dorm (L)	sleep	dormancy
aero (G)	air	aerobic			
an (G)	without	anaerobic	**E**		
ana (G)	up	anaphase	echino (G)	spiny	echinoderm
andro (G)	male	androecium	ec (G)	outer	ecosystem
angio (G)	vessel	angiosperm	endo (G)	within	endosperm
anth/o (G)	flower	anthophyte	epi (G)	upon	epidermis
anti (G)	against	antibody	eu (G)	true	eukaryote
aqu/a (L)	of water	aquatic	exo (G)	outside	exoskeleton
archae (G)	ancient	archaebacteria			
arthro, artio (G)	jointed	arthropod	**F**		
askos (G)	bag	ascospore	fer (L)	to carry	conifer
aster (G)	star	Asteroidea			
autos (G)	self	autoimmune	**G**		
			gastro (G)	stomach	gastropod
B			gen/(e)(o) (G)	kind	genotype
bi (L)	two	bipedal	genesis (G)	to originate	oogenesis
bio (G)	life	biosphere	gon (G)	reproductive	archegonium
			gravi (L)	heavy	gravitropism
C			gymn/o (G)	naked	gymnosperm
carn (L)	flesh	carnivore	gyn/e (G)	female	gynoecium
cephalo (G)	head	cephalopod			
chlor (G)	light green	chlorophyll	**H**		
chroma (G)	pigmented	chromosome	hal(o) (G)	salt	halophyte
cide (L)	to kill	insecticide	hapl(o) (G)	single	haploid
circ (L)	circular	circadian	hemi (G)	half	hemisphere
cocc/coccus (G)	small and round	streptococcus	hem(o) (G)	blood	hemoglobin
con (L)	together	convergent	herb/a(i) (L)	vegetation	herbivore
cyte (G)	cell	cytoplasm	heter/o (G)	different	heterotrophic
			hom(e)/o (G)	same	homeostasis
D			hom (L)	human	hominid
de (L)	remove	decompose	hydr/o (G)	water	hydrolysis
dendron (G)	tree	dendrite			
dent (L)	tooth	edentate	**I**		
derm (G)	skin	epidermis	inter (L)	between	internode
di (G)	two	disaccharide	intra (L)	within	intracellular
			is/o (G)	equal	isotonic

ORIGIN	MEANING	EXAMPLE
K		
kary (G)	nucleus	eukaryote
kera (G)	hornlike	keratin
L		
leuc/o (G)	white	leukocyte
logy (G)	study of	biology
lymph/o (L)	water	lymphocyte
lysis (G)	break up	dialysis
M		
macr/o (G)	large	macromolecule
meg/a (G)	great	megaspore
meso (L)	in the middle	mesophyll
meta (G)	after	metaphase
micr/o (G)	small	microscope
mon/o (G)	only one	monocotyledon
morph/o (G)	form	morphology
N		
nema (G)	a thread	nematode
neuro (G)	nerve	neuron
nod (L)	knot	nodule
nomy(e) (G)	system of laws	taxonomy
O		
olig/o (G)	small, few	oligochaete
omni (L)	all	omnivore
orni(s) (G)	bird	ornithology
oste/o (G)	bone formation	osteocyte
ov (L)	an egg	oviduct
P		
pal(a)e/o (G)	ancient	paleontology
para (G)	beside	parathyroid
path/o (G)	suffering	pathogen
ped (L)	foot	centipede
per (L)	through	permeable
peri (G)	around, about	peristalsis
phag/o (G)	eating	phagocyte
phot/o (G)	light	photosynthesis
phyl (G)	race, class	phylogeny
phyll (G)	leaf	chlorophyll
phyte (G)	plant	epiphyte
Origin	Meaning	Example
pinna (L)	feather	pinnate

ORIGIN	MEANING	EXAMPLE
plasm/o (G)	to form	plasmodium
pod (G)	foot	gastropod
poly (G)	many	polymer
post (L)	after	posterior
pro (G) (L)	before	prokaryote
prot/o (G)	first	protocells
pseud/o (G)	false	pseudopodium
R		
re (L)	back to original	reproduce
rhiz/o (G)	root	rhizoid
S		
scope (G)	to look	microscope
some (G)	body	lysosome
sperm (G)	seed	gymnosperm
stasis (G)	remain constant	homeostasis
stom (G)	mouthlike opening	stomata
syn (G)	together	synapse
T		
tel/o (G)	end	telophase
terr (L)	of Earth	terrestrial
therm (G)	heat	endotherm
thylak (G)	sack	thylakoid
trans (L)	across	transpiration
trich (G)	hair	trichome
trop/o (G)	a change	gravitropism
trophic (G)	nourishment	heterotrophic
U		
uni (L)	one	unicellular
V		
vacc/a (L)	cow	vaccine
vore (L)	eat greedily	omnivore
X		
xer/o (G)	dry	xerophyte
Z		
zo/o (G)	living being	zoology
zygous (G)	two joined	homozygous

Diversity of Life: Classification of Living Organisms

A six-kingdom system of classification of organisms is used today. Two kingdoms—Kingdom Archaebacteria and Kingdom Eubacteria—contain organisms that do not have a nucleus and that lack membrane-bound structures in the cytoplasm of their cells. The members of the other four kingdoms have a cell or cells that contain a nucleus and structures in the cytoplasm, some of which are surrounded by membranes. These kingdoms are Kingdom Protista, Kingdom Fungi, Kingdom Plantae, and Kingdom Animalia.

Kingdom Archaebacteria

one-celled; some absorb food from their surroundings; some are photosynthetic; some are chemosynthetic; many are found in extremely harsh environments including salt ponds, hot springs, swamps, and deep-sea hydrothermal vents

Kingdom Eubacteria

one-celled; most absorb food from their surroundings; some are photosynthetic; some are chemosynthetic; many are parasites; many are round, spiral, or rod-shaped; some form colonies

Kingdom Protista

Phylum Euglenophyta   one-celled; photosynthetic or take in food; most have one flagellum; euglenoids

Phylum Bacillariophyta   one-celled; photosynthetic; have unique double shells made of silica; diatoms

Phylum Dinoflagellata   one-celled; photosynthetic; contain red pigments; have two flagella; dinoflagellates

Phylum Chlorophyta   one-celled, many-celled, or colonies; photosynthetic; contain chlorophyll; live on land, in freshwater, or salt water; green algae

Phylum Rhodophyta   most are many-celled; photosynthetic; contain red pigments; most live in deep, saltwater environments; red algae

Phylum Phaeophyta   most are many-celled; photosynthetic; contain brown pigments; most live in saltwater environments; brown algae

Phylum Rhizopoda   one-celled; take in food; are free-living or parasitic; move by means of pseudopods; amoebas

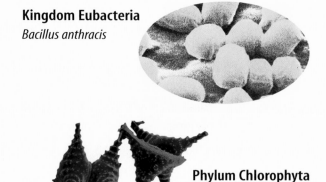

Kingdom Eubacteria
Bacillus anthracis

Phylum Chlorophyta
Desmids

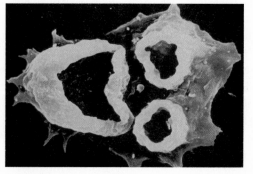

Amoeba

Phylum Zoomastigina one-celled; take in food; free-living or parasitic; have one or more flagella; zoomastigotes

Phylum Ciliophora one-celled; take in food; have large numbers of cilia; ciliates

Phylum Sporozoa one-celled; take in food; have no means of movement; are parasites in animals; sporozoans

Phylum Myxomycota
Slime mold

Phyla Myxomycota and Acrasiomycota one- or many-celled; absorb food; change form during life cycle; cellular and plasmodial slime molds

Phylum Oomycota many-celled; are either parasites or decomposers; live in freshwater or salt water; water molds, rusts and downy mildews

Kingdom Fungi

Phylum Zygomycota many-celled; absorb food; spores are produced in sporangia; zygote fungi; bread mold

Phylum Ascomycota one- and many-celled; absorb food; spores produced in asci; sac fungi; yeast

Phylum Basidiomycota many-celled; absorb food; spores produced in basidia; club fungi; mushrooms

Phylum Deuteromycota members with unknown reproductive structures; imperfect fungi; *Penicillium*

Phylum Mycophycota organisms formed by symbiotic relationship between an ascomycote or a basidiomycote and green alga or cyanobacterium; lichens

Phylum Oomycota
Phytophthora infestans

Lichens

Kingdom Plantae

Divisions Bryophyta (mosses), **Anthocerophyta** (hornworts), **Hepaticophyta** (liverworts), **Psilophyta** (whisk ferns) many-celled nonvascular plants; reproduce by spores produced in capsules; green; grow in moist, land environments

Division Lycophyta many-celled vascular plants; spores are produced in conelike structures; live on land; are photosynthetic; club mosses

Division Arthrophyta vascular plants; ribbed and jointed stems; scalelike leaves; spores produced in conelike structures; horsetails

Division Pterophyta vascular plants; leaves called fronds; spores produced in clusters of sporangia called sori; live on land or in water; ferns

Division Ginkgophyta deciduous trees; only one living species; have fan-shaped leaves with branching veins and fleshy cones with seeds; ginkgoes

Division Cycadophyta palmlike plants; have large, featherlike leaves; produces seeds in cones; cycads

Division Coniferophyta deciduous or evergreen; trees or shrubs; have needlelike or scalelike leaves; seeds produced in cones; conifers

Division Anthophyta
Tomato plant

Division Gnetophyta shrubs or woody vines; seeds are produced in cones; division contains only three genera; gnetum

Division Anthophyta dominant group of plants; flowering plants; have fruits with seeds

Kingdom Animalia

Phylum Porifera aquatic organisms that lack true tissues and organs; are asymmetrical and sessile; sponges

Phylum Cnidaria radially symmetrical organisms; have a digestive cavity with one opening; most have tentacles armed with stinging cells; live in aquatic environments singly or in colonies; includes jellyfish, corals, hydra, and sea anemones

Phylum Platyhelminthes bilaterally symmetrical worms; have flattened bodies; digestive system has one opening; parasitic and free-living species; flatworms

Division Bryophyta
Liverwort

Phylum Platyhelminthes
Flatworm

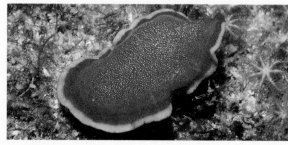

Phylum Chordata

Phylum Nematoda round, bilaterally symmetrical body; have digestive system with two openings; free-living forms and parasitic forms; roundworms

Phylum Mollusca soft-bodied animals, many with a hard shell and soft foot or footlike appendage; a mantle covers the soft body; aquatic and terrestrial species; includes clams, snails, squid, and octopuses

Phylum Annelida bilaterally symmetrical worms; have round, segmented bodies; terrestrial and aquatic species; includes earthworms, leeches, and marine polychaetes

Phylum Arthropoda largest animal group; have hard exoskeletons, segmented bodies, and pairs of jointed appendages; land and aquatic species; includes insects, crustaceans, and spiders

Phylum Echinodermata marine organisms; have spiny or leathery skin and a water-vascular system with tube feet; are radially symmetrical; includes sea stars, sand dollars, and sea urchins

Phylum Chordata organisms with internal skeletons and specialized body systems; most have paired appendages; all at some time have a notochord, nerve cord, gill slits, and a post-anal tail; include fish, amphibians, reptiles, birds, and mammals

Use and Care of a Microscope

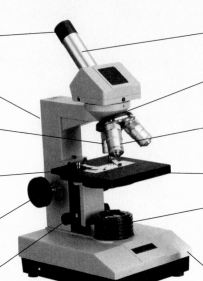

Eyepiece Contains magnifying lenses you look through.

Arm Supports the body tube.

Low-power objective Contains the lens with the lowest power magnification.

Stage clips Hold the microscope slide in place.

Coarse adjustment Focuses the image under low power.

Fine adjustment Sharpens the image under high magnification.

Body tube Connects the eyepiece to the revolving nosepiece.

Revolving nosepiece Holds and turns the objectives into viewing position.

High-power objective Contains the lens with the highest magnification.

Stage Supports the microscope slide.

Light source Provides light that passes upward through the diaphragm, the specimen, and the lenses.

Base Provides support for the microscope.

Caring for a Microscope

1. Always carry the microscope holding the arm with one hand and supporting the base with the other hand.

2. Don't touch the lenses with your fingers.

3. The coarse adjustment knob is used only when looking through the lowest-power objective lens. The fine adjustment knob is used when the high-power objective is in place.

4. Cover the microscope when you store it.

Using a Microscope

1. Place the microscope on a flat surface that is clear of objects. The arm should be toward you.

2. Look through the eyepiece. Adjust the diaphragm so light comes through the opening in the stage.

3. Place a slide on the stage so the specimen is in the field of view. Hold it firmly in place by using the stage clips.

4. Always focus with the coarse adjustment and the low-power objective lens first. After the object is in focus on low power, turn the nosepiece until the high-power objective is in place. Use ONLY the fine adjustment to focus with the high-power objective lens.

Making a Wet-Mount Slide

1. Carefully place the item you want to look at in the center of a clean, glass slide. Make sure the sample is thin enough for light to pass through.

2. Use a dropper to place one or two drops of water on the sample.

3. Hold a clean coverslip by the edges and place it at one edge of the water. Slowly lower the coverslip onto the water until it lies flat.

4. If you have too much water or a lot of air bubbles, touch the edge of a paper towel to the edge of the coverslip to draw off extra water and draw out unwanted air.

Weather Map Symbols

Sample Station Model

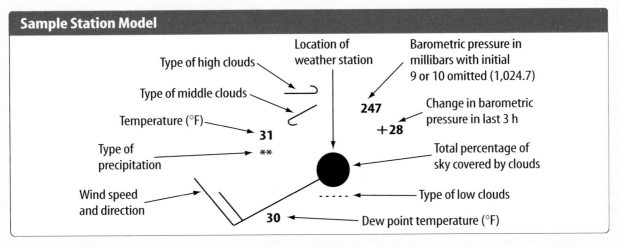

Type of high clouds

Type of middle clouds

Temperature (°F) — 31

Type of precipitation — **

Wind speed and direction

Location of weather station

Barometric pressure in millibars with initial 9 or 10 omitted (1,024.7) — 247

Change in barometric pressure in last 3 h — +28

Total percentage of sky covered by clouds

Type of low clouds — - - - -

Dew point temperature (°F) — 30

Sample Plotted Report at Each Station

Precipitation		Wind Speed and Direction		Sky Coverage		Some Types of High Clouds	
☰	Fog	○	0 calm	○	No cover	⌐⊃	Scattered cirrus
★	Snow	/	1–2 knots	◐	1/10 or less	⌐⊃	Dense cirrus in patches
●	Rain	⌐	3–7 knots	◕	2/10 to 3/10	⌐ʃ	Veil of cirrus covering entire sky
⟋⟍	Thunderstorm	⌐	8–12 knots	◕	4/10	⌐ʃ	Cirrus not covering entire sky
,	Drizzle	⌐	13–17 knots	◑	—		
▽	Showers	⌐	18–22 knots	◕	6/10		
		⌐	23–27 knots	◕	7/10		
		⌐	48–52 knots	◕	Overcast with openings		
		1 knot = 1.852 km/h		●	Completely overcast		

Some Types of Middle Clouds		Some Types of Low Clouds		Fronts and Pressure Systems	
∠	Thin altostratus layer	⌒	Cumulus of fair weather	(H) or High (L) or Low	Center of high- or low-pressure system
⫽	Thick altostratus layer	⌣	Stratocumulus	▲▲▲▲	Cold front
⌐	Thin altostratus in patches	- - - - -	Fractocumulus of bad weather	●●●●	Warm front
⌐	Thin altostratus in bands	——	Stratus of fair weather	▲●▲●	Occluded front
				●▲●▽	Stationary front

Physical Science Reference Tables

Standard Units

Symbol	Name	Quantity
m	meter	length
kg	kilogram	mass
Pa	pascal	pressure
K	kelvin	temperature
mol	mole	amount of a substance
J	joule	energy, work, quantity of heat
s	second	time
C	coulomb	electric charge
V	volt	electric potential
A	ampere	electric current
V	ohm	resistance

Physical Constants and Conversion Factors

Acceleration due to gravity	g	9.8 m/s/s or m/s^2
Avogadro's Number	N_A	6.02 3 10^{23} particles per mole
Electron charge	e	1.6 3 10^{219} C
Electron rest mass	m_e	9.11 3 10^{231} kg
Gravitation constant	G	6.67 3 10^{211} N 3 m^2/kg^2
Mass-energy relationship		1 u (amu) 5 9.3 3 10^2 MeV
Speed of light in a vacuum	c	3.00 3 108 m/s
Speed of sound at STP		331 m/s
Standard Pressure		1 atmosphere
		101.3 kPa
		760 Torr or mmHg
		14.7 lb/in.^{2}

Heat Constants

	Specific Heat (average) (kJ/kg 3 °C) (J/g 3 °C)	Melting Point (°C)	Boiling Point (°C)	Heat of Fusion (kJ/kg) (J/g)	Heat of Vaporization (kJ/kg) (J/g)
Alcohol (ethyl)	2.43 (liq.)	2117	79	109	855
Aluminum	0.90 (sol.)	660	2467	396	10500
Ammonia	4.71 (liq.)	278	233	332	1370
Copper	0.39 (sol.)	1083	2567	205	4790
Iron	0.45 (sol.)	1535	2750	267	6290
Lead	0.13 (sol.)	328	1740	25	866
Mercury	0.14 (liq.)	239	357	11	295
Platinum	0.13 (sol.)	1772	3827	101	229
Silver	0.24 (sol.)	962	2212	105	2370
Tungsten	0.13 (sol.)	3410	5660	192	4350
Water (solid)	2.05 (sol.)	0	–	334	–
Water (liquid)	4.18 (liq.)	–	100	–	–
Water (vapor)	2.01 (gas)	–	–	–	2260
Zinc	0.39 (sol.)	420	907	113	1770

Standard Units

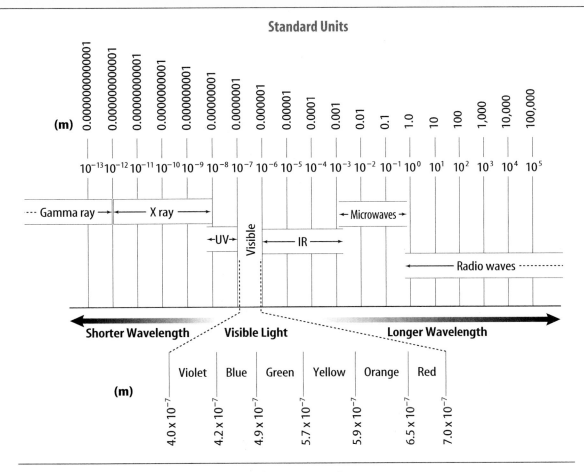

Uranium Decay Series

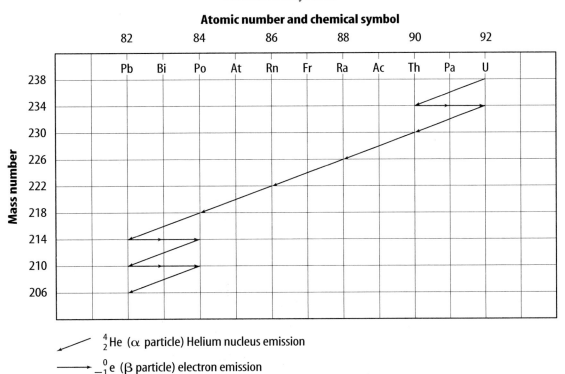

$^{4}_{2}$He (α particle) Helium nucleus emission

$^{0}_{-1}$e (β particle) electron emission

PERIODIC TABLE OF THE ELEMENTS

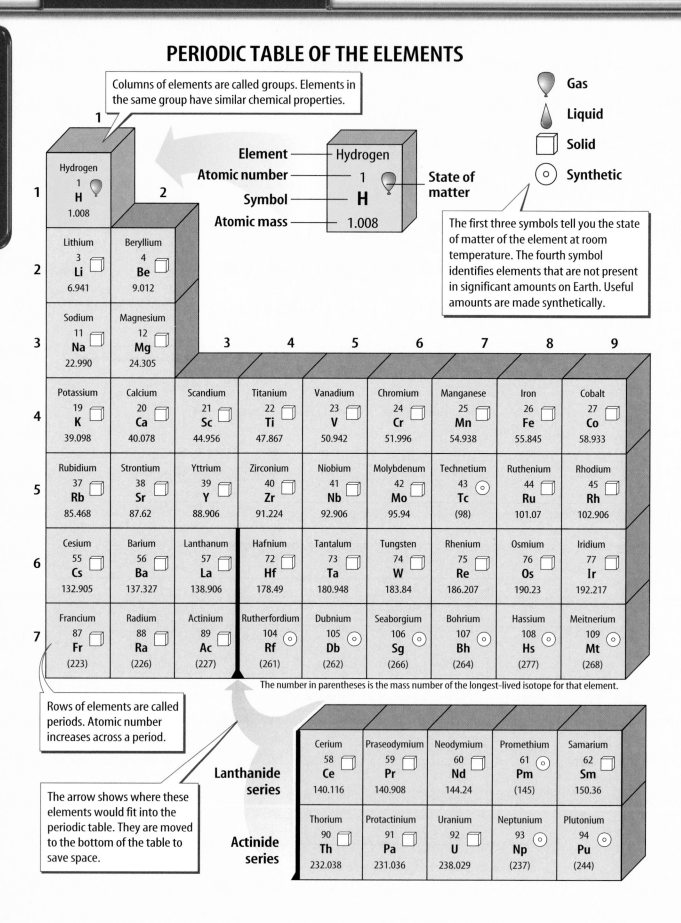

Columns of elements are called groups. Elements in the same group have similar chemical properties.

Gas

Liquid

Solid

Synthetic

Element — Hydrogen
Atomic number — 1
Symbol — H
Atomic mass — 1.008

State of matter

The first three symbols tell you the state of matter of the element at room temperature. The fourth symbol identifies elements that are not present in significant amounts on Earth. Useful amounts are made synthetically.

	1	2	3	4	5	6	7	8	9
1	Hydrogen 1 H 1.008								
2	Lithium 3 Li 6.941	Beryllium 4 Be 9.012							
3	Sodium 11 Na 22.990	Magnesium 12 Mg 24.305							
4	Potassium 19 K 39.098	Calcium 20 Ca 40.078	Scandium 21 Sc 44.956	Titanium 22 Ti 47.867	Vanadium 23 V 50.942	Chromium 24 Cr 51.996	Manganese 25 Mn 54.938	Iron 26 Fe 55.845	Cobalt 27 Co 58.933
5	Rubidium 37 Rb 85.468	Strontium 38 Sr 87.62	Yttrium 39 Y 88.906	Zirconium 40 Zr 91.224	Niobium 41 Nb 92.906	Molybdenum 42 Mo 95.94	Technetium 43 Tc (98)	Ruthenium 44 Ru 101.07	Rhodium 45 Rh 102.906
6	Cesium 55 Cs 132.905	Barium 56 Ba 137.327	Lanthanum 57 La 138.906	Hafnium 72 Hf 178.49	Tantalum 73 Ta 180.948	Tungsten 74 W 183.84	Rhenium 75 Re 186.207	Osmium 76 Os 190.23	Iridium 77 Ir 192.217
7	Francium 87 Fr (223)	Radium 88 Ra (226)	Actinium 89 Ac (227)	Rutherfordium 104 Rf (261)	Dubnium 105 Db (262)	Seaborgium 106 Sg (266)	Bohrium 107 Bh (264)	Hassium 108 Hs (277)	Meitnerium 109 Mt (268)

The number in parentheses is the mass number of the longest-lived isotope for that element.

Rows of elements are called periods. Atomic number increases across a period.

The arrow shows where these elements would fit into the periodic table. They are moved to the bottom of the table to save space.

Lanthanide series	Cerium 58 Ce 140.116	Praseodymium 59 Pr 140.908	Neodymium 60 Nd 144.24	Promethium 61 Pm (145)	Samarium 62 Sm 150.36
Actinide series	Thorium 90 Th 232.038	Protactinium 91 Pa 231.036	Uranium 92 U 238.029	Neptunium 93 Np (237)	Plutonium 94 Pu (244)

Reference Handbook

Metal

Metalloid

Nonmetal

The color of an element's block tells you if the element is a metal, nonmetal, or metalloid.

Science Online

Visit fl6.msscience.com for updates to the periodic table.

			13	**14**	**15**	**16**	**17**	**18**
								Helium 2 **He** 4.003
			Boron 5 **B** 10.811	Carbon 6 **C** 12.011	Nitrogen 7 **N** 14.007	Oxygen 8 **O** 15.999	Fluorine 9 **F** 18.998	Neon 10 **Ne** 20.180
10	**11**	**12**	Aluminum 13 **Al** 26.982	Silicon 14 **Si** 28.086	Phosphorus 15 **P** 30.974	Sulfur 16 **S** 32.065	Chlorine 17 **Cl** 35.453	Argon 18 **Ar** 39.948
Nickel 28 **Ni** 58.693	Copper 29 **Cu** 63.546	Zinc 30 **Zn** 65.409	Gallium 31 **Ga** 69.723	Germanium 32 **Ge** 72.64	Arsenic 33 **As** 74.922	Selenium 34 **Se** 78.96	Bromine 35 **Br** 79.904	Krypton 36 **Kr** 83.798
Palladium 46 **Pd** 106.42	Silver 47 **Ag** 107.868	Cadmium 48 **Cd** 112.411	Indium 49 **In** 114.818	Tin 50 **Sn** 118.710	Antimony 51 **Sb** 121.760	Tellurium 52 **Te** 127.60	Iodine 53 **I** 126.904	Xenon 54 **Xe** 131.293
Platinum 78 **Pt** 195.078	Gold 79 **Au** 196.967	Mercury 80 **Hg** 200.59	Thallium 81 **Tl** 204.383	Lead 82 **Pb** 207.2	Bismuth 83 **Bi** 208.980	Polonium 84 **Po** (209)	Astatine 85 **At** (210)	Radon 86 **Rn** (222)
Darmstadtium 110 **Ds** (281)	Roentgenium 111 **Rg** (272)	Ununbium * 112 **Uub** (285)		Ununquadium * 114 **Uuq** (289)				

* The names and symbols for elements 112–114 are temporary. Final names will be selected when the elements' discoveries are verified.

Europium 63 **Eu** 151.964	Gadolinium 64 **Gd** 157.25	Terbium 65 **Tb** 158.925	Dysprosium 66 **Dy** 162.500	Holmium 67 **Ho** 164.930	Erbium 68 **Er** 167.259	Thulium 69 **Tm** 168.934	Ytterbium 70 **Yb** 173.04	Lutetium 71 **Lu** 174.967
Americium 95 **Am** (243)	Curium 96 **Cm** (247)	Berkelium 97 **Bk** (247)	Californium 98 **Cf** (251)	Einsteinium 99 **Es** (252)	Fermium 100 **Fm** (257)	Mendelevium 101 **Md** (258)	Nobelium 102 **No** (259)	Lawrencium 103 **Lr** (262)

Reference Handbook

A science multilingual glossary is available at www.science.glencoe.com/multilingual_glossary. The glossary includes the following languages.

Arabic	Haitian Creole	Portuguese	Tagalog
Bengali	Hmong	Russian	Urdu
Chinese	Korean	Spanish	Vietnamese
English			

Cómo usar el glosario en español:
1. Busca el término en inglés que desees encontrar.
2. El término en español, junto con la definición, se encuentran en la columna de la derecha.

Pronunciation Key

Use the following key to help you sound out words in the glossary.

a . . . . ba**ck** (BAK)		**ew** . . . . f**oo**d (FEWD)	
ay . . . . d**ay** (DAY)		**yoo** . . . . p**u**re (PYOOR)	
ah . . . . f**a**ther (FAH thur)		**yew** . . . . f**ew** (FYEW)	
ow . . . . fl**ow**er (FLOW ur)		**uh** . . . . c**o**mma (CAH muh)	
ar . . . . c**ar** (CAR)		**u** (+ con) . . . . . . r**u**b (RUB)	
e . . . . l**e**ss (LES)		**sh** . . . . **sh**elf (SHELF)	
ee . . . . l**ea**f (LEEF)		**ch** . . . . na**t**ure (NAY chur)	
ih . . . . tr**i**p (TRIHP)		**g** . . . . **g**ift (GIHFT)	
i (i + con + e) . . **i**dea (i DEE uh)		**j** . . . . **g**em (JEM)	
oh . . . . g**o** (GOH)		**ing** . . . . s**ing** (SING)	
aw . . . . s**o**ft (SAWFT)		**zh** . . . . vi**s**ion (VIH zhun)	
or . . . . **or**bit (OR buht)		**k** . . . . ca**k**e (KAYK)	
oy . . . . c**oi**n (COYN)		**s** . . . . **s**eed, **c**ent (SEED, SENT)	
oo . . . . f**oo**t (FOOT)		**z** . . . . **z**one, rai**s**e (ZOHN, RAYZ)	

✳ FCAT Vocabulary

English — **A** — **Español**

✳ **abiotic (ay bi AH tihk) factors:** the nonliving parts of an ecosystem, including soil, temperature, water, and sunlight. (p. 202)

✳ **acceleration:** change in velocity divided by the amount of time needed for the change to take place; occurs when an object speeds up, slows down, or changes direction. (p. 510)

accuracy: compares a measurement to the true value. (p. 426)

active immunity: long-lasting immunity that results when the body makes its own antibodies in response to a specific antigen. (p. 175)

aerosols (ER uh sahls): solids, such as dust, salt, and pollen, and liquid droplets, such as acids, that are suspended in the atmosphere. (p. 291)

air mass: large body of air that develops over a particular region of Earth's surface. (p. 304)

algae (AL jee): one- or many-celled plantlike protists that usually are grouped based on their structure and the pigments they contain. (p. 53)

factores abióticos: partes inanimadas de un ecosistema; incluyen el suelo, la temperatura, el agua y la luz solar. (pág. 202)

aceleración: cambio en la velocidad dividido entre el tiempo necesario para que ocurra dicho cambio; sucede cuando un cuerpo viaja más rápida o más lentamente o cambia de dirección. (pág. 510)

exactitud: comparación de una medida con el valor real. (pág. 426)

inmunidad activa: inmunidad duradera que resulta cuando el cuerpo crea sus propios anticuerpos como respuesta a un antígeno específico. (pág. 175)

aerosoles: sólidos como el polvo, la sal, el polen y gotas de líquido, como los ácidos, que están suspendidos en la atmósfera. (pág. 291)

masa de aire: flujo enorme de aire que se forma sobre una región particular de la superficie terrestre. (pág. 304)

algas: protistas unicelulares o multicelulares similares a las plantas; se agrupan según su estructura y los pigmentos que contienen. (pág. 53)

allergen: substance that causes an allergic reaction. (p. 182)

alveoli (al VEE uh li): tiny, thin-walled, grapelike clusters at the end of each bronchiole that are surrounded by capillaries; carbon dioxide and oxygen exchange takes place. (p. 142)

amino acid: building block of protein. (p. 133)

✳ **amplitude:** for a transverse wave, the distance of a crest or a trough from the rest position of the particles in the medium. (p. 599)

antibiotic: chemical produced by a bacterium or fungus that limits or stops the growth of bacteria. (p. 52)

antibody: a protein made in response to a specific antigen that can attach to the antigen and cause it to be useless. (p. 174)

antigen (AN tih jun): complex molecule that is foreign to your body. (p. 174)

aquifer (AK wuh fur): layer of permeable rock that allows water to flow through. (p. 364)

artery: blood vessel that carries blood away from the heart. (p. 168)

✳ **asexual (ay SEK shul) reproduction:** a type of reproduction, such as budding or regeneration, in which a new organism is produced from a part of another organism by the process of mitosis. (p. 76)

asthenosphere (as THE nuh sfihr): plasticlike layer of Earth on which the lithospheric plates float and move around. (p. 392)

astronomical (as truh NAHM ih kul) unit: unit of measure that equals 150 million km, which is the average distance from Earth to the Sun. (p. 633)

✳ **atmosphere:** layer of gases surrounding Earth that protects living things from harmful doses of ultraviolet radiation and X-ray radiation and absorbs and distributes warmth. (p. 290)

✳ **atom:** a very small particle that makes up most kinds of matter and consists of smaller parts called protons, neutrons, and electrons. (p. 473)

atomic mass: average mass of an atom of an element; its unit of measure is the atomic mass unit (u), which is $\frac{1}{12}$ the mass of a carbon-12 atom. (p. 484)

atomic number: number of protons in the nucleus of each atom of a given element; the top number in the periodic table. (p. 483)

alérgeno: sustancia que produce una reacción alérgica. (pág. 182)

alvéolos: racimos parecidos a uvas, pequeños y de paredes finas que se encuentran en el extremo de cada bronquiolo y que están rodeados de capilares y en donde se realiza el intercambio de dióxido de carbono y oxígeno. (pág. 142)

aminoácido: elemento básico de las proteínas. (pág. 133)

amplitud: para una onda tranversal, la distancia de una cresta o un valle a partir de la posición de reposo de las partículas en el medio. (pág. 599)

antibiótico: sustancia química producida por una bacteria u hongo que limita o detiene el crecimiento de las bacterias. (pág. 52)

anticuerpo: proteína creada como respuesta a un antígeno específico y que se puede adherir al antígeno inutilizándolo. (pág. 174)

antígeno: molécula compleja extraña al cuerpo. (pág. 174)

acuífero: capa de roca permeable que permite que el agua fluya a través de ella. (pág. 364)

arteria: vaso sanguíneo que transporta la sangre fuera del corazón. (pág. 168)

reproducción asexual: tipo de reproducción, como el injerto o la regeneración, en la cual se produce un nuevo organismo a partir de una parte de otro organismo mediante el proceso de mitosis. (pág. 76)

astenosfera: capa flexible de la Tierra en que las placas litosféricas flotan y se mueven de un lugar a otro. (pág. 392)

unidad astronómica: unidad de medida que equivale a 150 millones de km, lo cual es la distancia promedio entre la Tierra y el Sol. (pág. 633)

atmósfera: capa de gases que rodea la Tierra y que protege a los seres vivos contra las dosis dañinas de radiación ultravioleta y rayos X. Absorbe y distribuye calor. (pág. 290)

átomo: partícula muy pequeña que constituye la mayoría de los tipos de materia y que está formada por partes más pequeñas llamadas protones, neutrones y electrones. (pág. 473)

masa atómica: masa promedio de un átomo de un elemento; su unidad de medida es la unidad de masa atómica (u), la cual es $\frac{1}{12}$ de la masa de un átomo de carbono-12. (pág. 484)

número atómico: número de protones en el núcleo de un átomo de determinado elemento; es el número superior en la tabla periódica. (pág. 483)

Glossary/Glosario

B

bacteria: smallest organisms on Earth, each of which is made up of only one cell. (p. 39)

balanced forces: forces on an object that cancel to make the net force on the object equal to zero. (p. 513)

bar graph: a type of graph that uses bars of varying sizes to show the relationship among variables. (p. 430)

beach: deposit of sediment whose materials vary in size, color, and composition; most commonly found on a smooth, gently sloped shoreline. (p. 371)

binomial nomenclature (bi NOH mee ul · NOH mun klay chur): two-word naming system that gives all organisms their scientific name. (p. 24)

biogenesis (bi oh JEN uh sus): theory that living things come only from other living things. (p. 19)

biomass energy: renewable energy derived from burning organic materials such as wood and alcohol. (p. 269)

biomes (BI ohmz): large geographic areas with similar climates and ecosystems; includes tundra, taiga, desert, temperate deciduous forest, temperate rain forest, tropical rain forest, and grassland. (p. 230)

biosphere: the part of Earth that supports life, including the top portion of Earth's crust, the atmosphere, and all the water on Earth's surface. (p. 200)

✳ **biotic factors:** the living parts of an ecosystem (p. 200)

bladder: elastic, muscular organ that holds urine until it leaves the body through the urethra. (p. 149)

boiling point: temperature at which a substance in a liquid state becomes a gas. (p. 450)

bronchi (BRAHN ki): two short tubes that branch off the lower end of the trachea and carry air into the lungs. (p. 142)

bacterias: los organismos más pequeños en la Tierra, cada uno de los cuales está formado por una sola célula. (pág. 39)

fuerzas equilibradas: fuerzas sobre un cuerpo que se cancelan para que la fuerza neta sobre el cuerpo sea igual a cero. (pág. 513)

gráfica de barras: tipo de gráfica que usa barras de diferentes tamaños para mostrar las diferencias entre las variables. (pág. 430)

playa: depósito de sedimentos cuyos materiales varían en tamaño, color y composición y que comúnmente se encuentran en litorales planos y poco inclinados. (pág. 371)

nomenclatura binaria: sistema de denominación de dos palabras que da a todos los organismos su nombre científico. (pág. 24)

biogénesis: teoría que sostiene que los seres vivos sólo provienen de otros seres vivos. (pág. 19)

energía de biomasa: energía renovable derivada de la combustión de materiales orgánicos, como la madera y el alcohol. (pág. 269)

biomas: grandes áreas geográficas con climas y ecosistemas similares; incluye la tundra, la taiga, el desierto, el bosque caducifolio templado, la pluviselva templada, la pluviselva tropical y las praderas. (pág. 230)

biosfera: parte de la Tierra que sustenta la vida; incluye la porción superior de la corteza terrestre, la atmósfera y toda el agua de la superficie terrestre. (pág. 200)

factores bióticos: partes vivas de un ecosistema. (pág. 200)

vejiga: órgano muscular elástico que retiene la orina hasta que ésta sale del cuerpo a través de la uretra. (pág. 149)

punto de ebullición: temperatura a la cual una sustancia en estado líquido se convierte en gas. (pág. 450)

bronquios: dos tubos cortos que salen del extremo inferior de la tráquea y llevan el aire a los pulmones. (pág. 142)

C

✳ **calorie:** a unit of energy; the amount of energy needed to raise the temperature of one gram of water by 1°C. (p. 540)

capillary (KAP uh ler ee): blood vessel that connects arteries and veins. (p. 168)

caloría: unidad de energía; la cantidad de energía necesaria para elevar la temperatura de un gramo de agua en 1°C. (pág. 540)

capilar: vaso sanguíneo que conecta las arterias y las venas. (pág. 168)

Glossary/Glosario

carbohydrate (kar boh HI drayt): nutrient that usually is the body's main source of energy. (p. 134)

cartilage: thick, smooth, flexible, and slippery tissue layer that covers the ends of bones, makes movement easier by reducing friction, and absorbing shocks. (p. 105)

cave: underground opening that can form when acidic groundwater dissolves limestone. (p. 367)

cell: smallest unit of an organism that can carry on life functions. (p. 14)

cell membrane: flexible structure that holds a cell together, forms a boundary between the cell and its environment, and helps control what enters and leaves the cell. (p. 41)

cell wall: structure of plants, algae, fungi, and many types of bacteria that supports and protects the cell membrane. (p. 41)

central nervous system: division of the nervous system, made up of the brain and spinal cord. (p. 112)

channel: groove created by water moving down the same path. (p. 354)

✳ **chemical change:** change in which the identity of a substance changes due to its chemical properties and forms a new substance or substances. (p. 455)

chemical property: any characteristic, such as the ability to burn, that allows a substance to undergo a change that results in a new substance. (p. 454)

✳ **chemical weathering:** occurs when chemical processes dissolve or alter the minerals in rocks, or change them into different minerals, at or near Earth's surface. (p. 327)

chloroplast (KLOR uh plast): green organelle in a plant's leaf cells where most photosynthesis takes place. (p. 43)

chyme (KIME): liquid product of digestion. (p. 131)

circle graph: a type of graph that shows the parts of a whole; sometimes called a pie graph, each piece of which represents a percentage of the total. (p. 431)

✳ **circuit:** closed conducting loop in which electric current can flow continually. (p. 570)

climate: average weather pattern in an area over a long period of time; can be classified by temperature, humidity, precipitation, and vegetation. (p. 328)

climax community: stable, end stage of ecological succession in which balance is in the absence of disturbance. (p. 229)

carbohidrato: nutriente que, por lo general, es la principal fuente de energía del cuerpo. (pág. 134)

cartílago: capa de tejido delgado, liso, flexible y resbaladizo que cubre los extremos de los huesos, facilita el movimiento al reducir la fricción y absorbe los golpes. (pág. 105)

caverna: apertura subterránea que puede formarse cuando el agua subterránea acidificada disuelve la piedra caliza. (pág. 367)

célula: la unidad más pequeña de un organismo que puede realizar funciones vitales. (pág. 14)

membrana celular: estructura flexible que mantiene unida la célula, constituye un límite entre la célula y su entorno y ayuda a controlar todo aquéllo que entra o sale de ésta. (pág. 41)

pared celular: estructura de las plantas, algas, hongos y varios tipos de bacterias, la cual sostiene y protege la membrana celular. (pág. 41)

sistema nervioso central: división del sistema nervioso compuesto por el encéfalo y la médula espinal. (pág. 112)

cauce: surco creado por el agua cuando se mueve cuesta abajo por el mismo curso. (pág. 354)

cambio químico: cambio en que la identidad de una sustancia cambia debido a sus propiedades químicas y forma una nueva sustancia o sustancias. (pág. 455)

propiedad química: cualquier característica, como la capacidad para quemarse, que permite que una sustancia sufra un cambio que da como resultado una nueva sustancia. (pág. 454)

meteorización química: ocurre cuando las reacciones químicas disuelven los minerales en las rocas o los convierten en diferentes minerales, en la superficie terrestre o cerca de ella. (pág. 327)

cloroplasto: organelo verde de la célula de las hojas de las plantas en donde tiene lugar la mayor parte de la fotosíntesis. (pág. 43)

quimo: líquido que se produce durante la digestión. (pág. 131)

gráfica circular: tipo de gráfica que muestra las partes de un todo; conocida también como gráfica de sectores, en la que cada sector representa un porcentaje del total. (pág. 431)

circuito: trayecto cerrado por el que puede fluir continuamente la corriente eléctrica. (pág. 570)

clima: patrón meteorológico promedio en un área durante un largo período de tiempo; puede clasificarse según la temperatura, la humedad, la precipitación y la vegetación. (pág. 328)

comunidad clímax: etapa final estable de la sucesión ecológica en la cual se da un equilibrio en ausencia de alteraciones. (pág. 229)

Glossary/Glosario

cloning: making copies of organisms; each of which is a clone that receives DNA from only one parent. (p. 72)

coal: sedimentary rock formed from decayed plant material; the world's most abundant fossil fuel. (p. 257)

comet: large body of ice and rock that orbits the Sun; develops a bright, glowing tail if it passes close to the Sun. (p. 638)

✳ **community:** all the populations that live in an ecosystem (p. 208)

✳ **compound:** a substance whose smallest unit is made up of atoms of more than one element bonded together. (p. 487)

compressional wave: a type of mechanical wave in which matter in the medium moves forward and backward along the direction the wave travels. (p. 597)

✳ **conduction:** transfer of thermal energy by collisions between the particles in a material. (p. 548)

conductor: material in which electric charges can move easily. (p. 565)

✳ **conservation:** the controlled use and maintenance of natural resources; the efforts to preserve or protect natural resources. (p. 263)

✳ **constellation (kan stuh LAY shun):** group of stars that form a pattern in the sky; often named after a real or imaginary animal, object, or person. (p. 640)

✳ **consumer:** an organism that obtains food by eating other organisms. (p. 213)

contact force: a force that is exerted by one object on another only when the objects are touching. (p. 514)

continental drift: Wegener's hypothesis that all continents were once connected in a single large landmass that broke apart about 200 million years ago and drifted slowly to their current positions. (p. 384)

contour farming: planting along the natural contours of the land to reduce soil erosion. (p. 341)

control: standard to which the outcome of a test is compared. (p. 9)

✳ **convection:** transfer of thermal energy that occurs when particles in a liquid or a gas move from one place to another. (p. 550)

convection current: current in Earth's mantle that transfers heat in Earth's interior and is the driving force for plate tectonics. (p. 397)

clonación: hacer copias de organismos; cada uno de los cuales es un clon que recibe DNA solamente de un progenitor. (pág. 72)

carbón: roca sedimentaria formada a partir de material vegetal descompuesto; es el combustible fósil más abundante en el mundo. (pág. 257)

cometa: cuerpo largo compuesto por hielo y roca, y que orbita el Sol; desarrolla una cola luminosa y brillante al pasar cerca del Sol. (pág. 638)

comunidad: todas las poblaciones que habitan en un ecosistema. (pág. 208)

compuesto: una substancia cuya unidad más pequeña está compuesta por átomos enlazados de más de un elemento (pág. 487)

onda de compresión: tipo de onda mecánica en que la materia en el medio realiza un movimiento oscilatorio en la dirección de la onda. (pág. 597)

conducción: transferencia de energía por medio de colisiones entre los átomos de un material. (pág. 548)

conductor: material en el cual las cargas eléctricas se pueden mover fácilmente. (pág. 565)

conservación: el uso y la conservación controlados de recursos naturales; los esfuerzos por preservar o proteger los recursos naturales. (pág. 263)

constelación: grupo de estrellas que forman un patrón en el firmamento y a las cuales a menudo se les da el nombre de un animal, objeto o personaje real o imaginario. (pág. 640)

consumidor: organismo que se alimenta de otros organismos. (pág. 213)

fuerza de contacto: fuerza que ejerce un cuerpo sobre otro cuerpo sólo cuando los cuerpos se tocan. (pág. 514)

deriva continental: hipótesis de Wegener que dice que todos los continentes estuvieron alguna vez conectados en una sola gran masa terrestre que se fragmentó hace cerca de 200 millones de años y que se desplazaron lentamente hasta sus posiciones actuales. (pág. 384)

cultivo de contorno: siembra a lo largo de los contornos naturales del terreno para reducir la erosión del suelo. (pág. 341)

control: estándar contra el cual se compara el resultado de una prueba. (pág. 9)

convección: transferencia de energía térmica que ocurre cuando las partículas de un líquido o gas se mueven de un lugar a otro. (pág. 550)

corriente de convección: corriente en el manto terrestre que transfiere calor en el interior de la Tierra y es la causa de la tectónica de placas. (pág. 397)

coral reef: diverse ecosystem formed from the calcium carbonate shells secreted by corals. (p. 243)

crest: a high point, or peak, on a transverse wave. (p. 596)

cytoplasm (SI tuh pla zum): gelatin-like substance inside the cell membrane that contains water, chemicals, and cell parts. (p. 41)

arrecife de coral: ecosistema diverso formado por las conchas de carbonato de calcio que secretan los corales. (pág. 243)

cresta: el punto más alto, o pico, de una onda transversal. (pág. 596)

citoplasma: sustancia gelatinosa en el interior de la membrana celular, la cual contiene agua, sustancias químicas y partes de la célula. (pág. 41)

D

decomposer: an organism that uses dead organisms or the wastes produced by other organisms as food. (p. 213)

density: measurable physical property that can be found by dividing the mass of an object by its volume. (p. 448)

dependent variable: a factor that can be changed or observed, placed on the vertical, or y-axis, of a table. (p. 428)

deposition: dropping of sediments that occurs when an agent of erosion loses its energy and can no longer carry its load. (p. 361)

dermis: skin layer below the epidermis that contains blood vessels, nerves, oil, sweat glands, and other structures. (p. 96)

desert: driest biome on Earth with less than 25 cm of rain each year; has dunes or thin soil with little organic matter, where plants and animals are adapted to survive extreme conditions. (p. 236)

dew point: temperature at which air is saturated with water vapor and condensation can occur. (p. 298)

diffraction: bending of waves around a barrier. (p. 607)

DNA (deoxyribonucleic acid): a chemical inside cells that contains hereditary information and controls how an organism will look and function by controlling which proteins a cell produces. (p. 68)

drainage basin: land area from which a river or stream collects runoff. (p. 356)

descomponedor: organismo que utiliza organismos muertos o los desechos producidos por otros organismos como alimento. (pág. 213)

densidad: propiedad física que se puede calcular al dividir la masa de un cuerpo entre su volumen. (pág. 448)

variable dependiente: un factor que se puede cambiar u observar, se puede trazar en el eje vertical, o el eje y, de una tabla. (pág. 428)

deposición: descarga de sedimentos que ocurre cuando un agente erosivo pierde su energía y es incapaz de transportar su carga. (pág. 361)

dermis: capa de piel debajo de la epidermis que contiene vasos sanguíneos, nervios, grasa y glándulas sudoríparas, además de otras estructuras. (pág. 96)

desierto: el bioma más seco sobre la Tierra con menos de 25 centímetros cúbicos de lluvia al año; tiene dunas o un suelo delgado con muy poca materia orgánica y aquí las plantas y animales están adaptados para sobrevivir en condiciones extremas. (pág. 236)

punto de rocío: temperatura a la cual el aire se satura con vapor del agua y a la cual puede ocurrir la condensación. (pág. 298)

difracción: desviación de las ondas alrededor de una barrera. (pág. 607)

DNA (ácido deoxirribonucléico): químico presente en el interior de las células, el cual contiene información genética y controla la futura apariencia y funcionamiento de un organismo a través del control de las proteínas que produce una célula. (pág. 68)

cuenca hidrográfica: terreno del cual un río o arroyo recoge escorrentía. (pág. 356)

E

eclipse (ih KLIHPS): event that occurs when the Moon moves between the Sun and Earth (solar eclipse), or when Earth moves between the Sun and the Moon (lunar eclipse), and casts a shadow. (p. 628)

eclipse: evento que ocurre cuando la Luna se mueve entre la Tierra y el Sol (eclipse solar) o cuando la Tierra se mueve entre el Sol y la Luna (eclipse lunar) y proyecta una sombra. (pág. 628)

Glossary/Glosario

ecology: study of the interactions that take place among organisms and their environment. (p. 200)

✹ **ecosystem (EE koh sihs tum):** all the living organisms living in an area, as well as the nonliving parts of their environment (p. 198)

electric current: flow of electric charge, measured in amperes (A). (p. 569)

electric discharge: movement of static charge from one place to another. (p. 566)

electric field: the region of space surrounding an electric charge where a force is exerted on other electric charges. (p. 564)

electric resistance: measure of how difficult it is for electrons to flow in a material; unit is the ohm (Ω). (p. 571)

electromagnet: a current-carrying wire wrapped around an iron core. (p. 581)

electromagnetic induction: production of electric current by moving a magnet and a wire coil relative to each other. (p. 582)

electromagnetic spectrum: arrangement of electromagnetic waves according to their wavelengths and frequencies. (p. 659)

electromagnetic waves: waves that can travel through matter or space; include radio waves, infrared waves, visible light waves, ultraviolet waves, X rays and gamma rays. (p. 598)

✹ **electron:** invisible, negatively charged particle located in a cloudlike formation that surrounds the nucleus of an atom. (p. 476)

✹ **element:** natural or synthetic material that is made of only one kind of atom; has unique properties and is generally classified as a metal, metalloid, or nonmetal. (p. 480)

✹ **energy:** ability to cause change; also the ability to do work. (p. 534)

✹ **environment:** all conditions, both living and nonliving, that surround and affect an organism. (p. 199)

enzyme: a type of protein that speeds up chemical reactions in the body without being changed or used up itself. (p. 128)

epidermis: outer, thinnest skin layer that constantly produces new cells to replace the dead cells that are rubbed off its surface. (p. 96)

✹ **erosion:** a combination of natural processes that wears away surface materials and moves them from one place to another. (p. 354)

estimation: method of making an educated guess at a measurement; using the size of something familiar to guess the size of a new object. (p. 415)

ecología: estudio de las interacciones entre los organismos y su medio ambiente. (pág. 200)

ecosistema: todos los organismos vivos que habitan en un área, así como las partes inanimadas de su ambiente. (pág. 198)

corriente eléctrica: flujo de cargas eléctricas; se mide en amperes (A). (pág. 569)

descarga eléctrica: movimiento de carga estática de un lugar a otro. (pág. 566)

campo eléctrico: la región alrededor de una carga eléctrica donde se ejerce una fuerza sobre otras cargas eléctricas. (pág. 564)

resistencia eléctrica: medida de la dificultad que presentan los electrones para fluir en un material; su unidad es el ohmio (Ω). (pág. 571)

electroimán: alambre envuelto alrededor de un núcleo de hierro que transporta corriente. (pág. 581)

inducción electromagnética: producción de corriente eléctrica moviendo un imán y una bobina de alambre relativos uno al otro. (pág. 582)

espectro electromagnético: arreglo de las ondas electromagnéticas según su longitud de onda y su frecuencia. (pág. 659)

ondas electromagnéticas: ondas que pueden viajar a través de la materia o del espacio; incluyen las ondas radiales, las ondas infrarrojas, las ondas de luz visible, las ondas ultravioletas, los rayos X y los rayos gama. (pág. 598)

electrón: partícula invisible con carga negativa, localizada en una formación parecida a una nube que rodea el núcleo de un átomo. (pág. 476)

elemento: materia natural o sintética que está hecho de sólo una clase de átomo; tiene propiedades únicas y se clasifica generalmente como un metal, un metaloide o un no metal. (pág. 480)

energía: capacidad de producir un cambio; también es la capacidad de realizar trabajo. (pág. 534)

ambiente: toda condición, tanto viva como inerte, que rodea y afecta un organismo (pág. 199)

enzima: tipo de proteína que acelera las reacciones químicas en el cuerpo sin que ésta sufra modificaciones o se agote. (pág. 128)

epidermis: la capa más delgada y externa de la piel que constantemente produce células nuevas para reemplazar a las células muertas que han sido eliminadas de la superficie. (pág. 96)

erosión: una combinación de los procesos naturales que desgasta los materiales superficiales y los mueve de un lugar a otro. (pág. 354)

estimación: método para hacer una suposición fundamentada de una medida, usando el tamaño de algo conocido para suponer el tamaño de un nuevo objeto. (pág. 415)

Glossary/Glosario

estuary: extremely fertile area where a river meets an ocean; contains a mixture of freshwater and salt water and serves as a nursery for many species of fish. (p. 244)

estuario: área extremadamente fértil donde un río desemboca en el océano; contiene una mezcla de agua dulce y salada y sirve como vivero para muchas especies de peces. (pág. 244)

fertilization: process in which sperm and egg join, resulting in a new organism. (p. 73)

fecundación: proceso en el cual un espermatozoide y un huevo se unen, dando como resultado un nuevo organismo. (pág. 73)

force: a push or a pull; SI unit is the newton. (p. 511)

fuerza: empuje o tracción; la unidad SI es el newton. (pág. 511)

fossil fuel: nonrenewable energy resource, such as oil and coal, formed over millions of years from the remains of dead plants and other organisms. (p. 256)

combustible fósil: recurso no renovable de energía, como el petróleo y el carbón, formado durante millones de años de los restos de plantas muertas y otros organismos. (pág. 256)

frequency: number of wavelengths that pass a given point in one second; measured in hertz (Hz). (p. 601)

frecuencia: número de longitudes de onda que pasan por un punto dado en un segundo; se mide en hertz (Hz). (pág. 601)

friction: force exerted on two surfaces in contact that resists the sliding motion between the two surfaces; always acts opposite to the direction of motion. (p. 514)

fricción: fuerza que opone resistencia al movimiento de deslizamiento entre dos superficies en contacto; siempre actúa en dirección opuesta al movimiento. (pág. 514)

front: boundary that develops where air masses of different temperatures collide; can be cold, warm, stationary, or occluded. (p. 305)

frente: límite que se forma en el lugar donde chocan masas de aire con diferentes temperaturas; puede ser frío, caliente, estacionario u ocluido. (pág. 305)

galaxy (GAL uk see): large group of stars, gas, and dust held together by gravity. (p. 643)

galaxia: grupo grande de estrellas, gas y polvo que se mantiene unido debido a la gravedad. (pág. 643)

gene: small section of DNA on a chromosome that carries information about a trait. (p. 78)

gene: pequeña sección de DNA en un cromosoma, la cual posee información referente a un rasgo. (pág. 78)

genetics (juh NET ihks): study of how traits are passed from parent to offspring. (p. 77)

genética: estudio acerca de cómo se transmiten los rasgos de padres a hijos. (pág. 77)

genus: first word of the two-word scientific name used to identify a group of similar species. (p. 24)

género: primera palabra, de las dos palabras del nombre científico, que se usa para identificar a un grupo de especies similares. (pág. 24)

geothermal energy: inexhaustible energy resource that uses hot magma or hot, dry rocks from below Earth's surface to generate electricity. (p. 268)

energía geotérmica: recurso energético inagotable que utiliza el magma caliente o las rocas secas y calientes que se encuentran debajo de la superficie terrestre para producir electricidad. (pág. 268)

geyser: hot spring that erupts periodically and shoots water and steam into the air—for example, Old Faithful in Yellowstone National Park. (p. 367)

géiser: aguas termales que hacen erupción periódicamente arrojando agua y vapor al aire; por ejemplo, Old Faithful en el parque nacional Yellowstone. (pág. 367)

graph: used to collect, organize, and summarize data in a visual way, making it easy to use and understand. (p. 427)

gráfica: se usa para recopilar, organizar y resumir información en forma visual, facilitando su uso y comprensión. (pág. 427)

Glossary/Glosario

grassland: temperate and tropical regions with 25 cm to 75 cm of precipitation each year that are dominated by climax communities of grasses; ideal for growing crops and raising cattle and sheep. (p. 237)

✹ **gravity:** the force every object exerts on every other object due to their masses; depends on the masses of the objects and the distance between them. (p. 516)

groundwater: water that soaks into the ground and collects in pores and empty spaces; an important source of drinking water. (p. 363)

praderas: regiones tropicales y templadas con 25 a 75 centímetros de lluvia al año; son dominadas por comunidades clímax de pastos y son ideales para la cría de ganado y ovejas. (pág. 237)

gravedad: la fuerza que ejerce todo cuerpo sobre otros cuerpos debido a sus masas; depende de la masa de los cuerpos y la distancia entre ellos. (pág. 516)

agua subterránea: agua que se difunde en el suelo y se acumula en poros y espacios vacíos; es una fuente importante de agua potable. (pág. 363)

H

✹ **habitat:** place where an organism lives; provides the food, shelter, moisture, temperature, and other factors required for the organism's survival. (p. 211)

✹ **heat:** transfer of thermal energy from one object to another due to a difference in temperature. (p. 547)

hemoglobin (HEE muh gloh bun): a molecule in red blood cells that carries oxygen and carbon dioxide. (p. 163)

heredity (huh RED uh tee): passing on of traits from parents to offspring. (p. 77)

homeostasis: regulation of an organism's internal, life-maintaining conditions. (p. 15)

horizon: each layer in a soil profile—horizon A (top layer of soil), horizon B (middle layer), and horizon C (bottom layer). (p. 332)

humidity: amount of water vapor in the atmosphere. (p. 298)

humus (HYEW mus): dark-colored, decayed organic matter that supplies nutrients to plants and is found mainly in topsoil. (p. 332)

hurricane: large storm, up to 970 km in diameter, that begins as a low-pressure area over tropical oceans, has sustained winds that can reach 250 km/h and gusts up to 300 km/h. (p. 309)

hydroelectric energy: electricity produced by waterpower using large dams in a river. (p. 268)

hypothesis: prediction that can be tested. (p. 8)

hábitat: lugar donde vive un organismo; provee alimento, refugio, humedad, temperatura y otros factores necesarios para la supervivencia del organismo. (pág. 211)

calor: transferencia de energía de un cuerpo a otro debido a una diferencia de temperatura; fluye de los cuerpos calientes a los fríos. (pág. 547)

hemoglobina: molécula en los glóbulos rojos que transporta oxígeno y dióxido de carbono. (pág. 163)

herencia: transmisión de los rasgos de padres a hijos. (pág. 77)

homeostasis: control de las condiciones internas que mantienen la vida de un organismo. (pág. 15)

horizonte: cada capa en un perfil del suelo: el horizonte A (capa superior del suelo), el horizonte B (capa media) y el horizonte C (capa inferior). (pág. 332)

humedad: cantidad de vapor de agua en la atmósfera. (pág. 298)

humus: materia orgánica en descomposición, de color oscuro, que suministra nutrientes a las plantas y se encuentra principalmente en la parte superior del suelo. (pág. 332)

huracán: enorme tormenta, de hasta 970 kilómetros de diámetro que comienza como un área de baja presión sobre los océanos tropicales y que tiene vientos sostenidos que pueden alcanzar hasta 250 km/h y ráfagas de hasta 300 km/h. (pág. 309)

energía hidroeléctrica: electricidad producida por la energía hidráulica generada mediante represas grandes construidas en los ríos. (pág. 268)

hipótesis: predicción que puede probarse. (pág. 8)

I

ice wedging: mechanical weathering process that occurs when water freezes in the cracks of rocks and expands, causing the rock to break apart. (p. 326)

cuñas de hielo: proceso de erosión mecánica que ocurre cuando el agua se congela en las grietas de las rocas y luego se expande, causando que la roca se fragmente. (pág. 326)

Glossary/Glosario

impermeable: describes materials that water cannot pass through. (p. 364)

inclined plane: a sloped surface or a ramp. (p. 522)

 independent variable: a factor that is changed in an experiment in order to study changes in the dependent variable. (p. 428)

 inertia: tendency of an object to resist a change in motion. (p. 514)

infectious disease: disease caused by a virus, bacterium, fungus, or protist that is spread from one person to another. (p. 178)

insulator: material in which electric charges cannot move easily. (p. 565)

interference: occurs when two or more waves combine and form a new wave when they overlap. (p. 609)

intertidal zone: part of the shoreline that is under water at high tide and exposed to the air at low tide. (p. 244)

involuntary muscle: muscle, such as heart muscle, that cannot be consciously controlled. (p. 101)

isotope (I suh tohps): two or more atoms of the same element that have different numbers of neutrons in their nuclei. (p. 483)

impermeable: describe materiales que impiden el paso del agua a través de ellos. (pág. 364)

plano inclinado: superficie inclinada o rampa. (pág. 522)

variable independiente: un factor que se cambia en un experimento para estudiar cambios en la variable dependiente. (pág. 428)

inercia: tendencia de un cuerpo a resistir cambios en movimiento. (pág. 514)

enfermedad infecciosa: enfermedad causada por un virus, bacteria, hongo o protista y que se propaga de una persona a otra. (pág. 178)

aislante: material en el cual las cargas eléctricas no se pueden mover fácilmente. (pág. 565)

interferencia: ocurre cuando dos o más ondas se combinan y al sobreponerse forman una nueva onda. (pág. 609)

zona intermareal: parte del litoral que está bajo el agua durante la marea alta y expuesta al aire durante la marea baja. (pág. 244)

músculo involuntario: músculo, como el músculo cardíaco, que no se puede controlar a voluntad. (pág. 101)

isótopo: dos o más átomos del mismo elemento que tienen diferente número de neutrones en su núcleo. (pág. 483)

J

joint: any place where two or more bones come together; can be movable or immovable. (p. 106)

articulación: todo lugar en donde se unen dos o más huesos; puede ser móvil o inmóvil. (pág. 106)

K

Kelvin (K): SI unit for temperature. (p. 420)

kilogram (kg): SI unit for mass. (p. 419)

 kinetic energy: energy an object has due to its motion. (p. 535)

kingdom: first and largest category used to classify organisms. (p. 23)

Kelvin (K): unidad del SI para temperatura. (pág. 420)

kilogramo (kg.): unidad del SI para masa. (pág. 419)

energía cinética: energía que posee un cuerpo en movimiento. (pág. 535)

reino: la primera categoría y la más grande que se usa para clasificar a los organismos. (pág. 23)

L

larynx: airway to which the vocal cords are attached. (p. 142)

law: statement about how things work in nature that seems to be true consistently. (p. 10)

laringe: pasaje aéreo al cual están adheridas las cuerdas vocales. (pág. 142)

ley: enunciado sobre cómo funciona todo en la naturaleza y el cual parece ser verdadero de manera consistente. (pág. 10)

✴ law of conservation of energy: states that energy cannot be created or destroyed but can only be transformed from one form into another. (p. 541)

law of conservation of mass: states that the mass of the products of a chemical change is always the same as the mass of what you started with. (p. 459)

law of conservation of matter: states that matter is not created or destroyed but only changes its form. (p. 474)

leaching: removal of minerals that have been dissolved in water. (p. 333)

✴ lever: a rod or plank that pivots about a fixed point. (p. 521)

lichen (LI kun): forms when a fungus and either a green alga or cyanobacterium live together in a close, beneficial association. (p. 56)

ligament: tough band of tissue that holds bones together at joints. (p. 106)

light-year: about 9.5 trillion km—the distance that light travels in one year—which is used to measure large distances between stars or galaxies. (p. 646)

limiting factors: anything that can restrict the size of a population, including living and nonliving features of an ecosystem, such as predators or drought. (p. 209)

line graph: a type of graph used to show the relationship between two variables that are numbers on an x-axis and a y-axis. (p. 428)

lithosphere (LIH thuh sfihr): rigid layer of Earth about 100 km thick, made of the crust and a part of the upper mantle. (p. 392)

litter: twigs, leaves, and other organic matter that help prevent erosion and hold water and may eventually be changed into humus by decomposing organisms. (p. 333)

longshore current: current that runs parallel to the shoreline, is caused by waves colliding with the shore at slight angles, and moves tons of loose sediment. (p. 370)

lunar highlands: mountainous areas on the Moon that are about 4.5 billion years old. (p. 626)

lymph: fluid that has diffused into the lymphatic capillaries. (p. 172)

ley de conservación de la energía: establece que la energía no se puede crear ni destruir, sino que solamente se pude transformar de una forma a otra. (pág. 541)

ley de conservación de la masa: establece que la masa de los productos de un cambio químico siempre es igual a la masa inicial. (pág. 459)

ley de conservación de la materia: establece que la materia no se crea ni se destruye, solamente cambia de forma. (pág. 474)

lixiviación: extracción de minerales que han sido disueltos en el agua. (pág. 333)

palanca: barra o tablón que gira sobre un punto fijo. (pág. 521)

liquen: se forma cuando un hongo y un alga verde o una cianobacteria viven juntos en una asociación estrecha y benéfica para ambos. (pág. 56)

ligamento: banda dura de tejido que mantiene los huesos unidos a las articulaciones. (pág. 106)

año luz: aproximadamente 9.5 trillones de kilómetros (la distancia que recorre la luz en un año), la cual se usa para medir largas distancias entre estrellas y galaxias. (pág. 646)

factores limitantes: cualquier factor que pueda restringir el tamaño de una población, incluyendo los elementos vivos e inanimados de un ecosistema, como los depredadores o las sequías. (pág. 209)

gráfica lineal: tipo de gráfica que se usa para mostrar la relación entre dos variables numéricas en un eje x y en un eje y. (pág. 428)

litosfera: capa rígida de la Tierra de unos 100 kilómetros de profundidad, comprende la corteza y una parte del manto superior. (pág. 392)

mantillo: ramitas, hojas y otro material orgánico que ayuda a prevenir la erosión y a retener el agua, y el cual, con el tiempo, los organismos descomponedores pueden transformarlo en humus. (pág. 333)

corriente costera: corriente que corre paralela al litoral; es causada por olas que chocan contra la orilla a ángulos ligeros y la cual mueve toneladas de sedimentos sueltos. (pág. 370)

relieves lunares: áreas montañosas lunares que tienen cerca de 4.5 billones de años de antigüedad. (pág. 626)

linfa: fluido que se encuentra difundido en los capilares linfáticos. (pág. 172)

M

magnetic domain: a group of atoms in a magnetic material with the magnetic poles of the atoms pointing in the same direction. (p. 580)

dominio magnético: grupo de átomos en un material magnético con los polos magnéticos de los átomos que apuntan en la misma dirección. (pág. 580)

✳ **magnetic field:** the region of space surrounding a magnet or a moving charge where a magnetic force is exerted on other magnets and moving charges. (p. 579)

maria: smooth, dark regions on the Moon that formed when lava flowed onto the Moon's surface. (p. 626)

✳ **mass:** amount of matter in an object. (p. 419)

mass number: sum of the number of protons and neutrons in the nucleus of an atom. (p. 483)

✳ **matter:** anything that has mass and takes up space and is made up of different kinds of atoms; includes all things that can be seen, tasted, smelled, or touched but does not include heat, sound, or light. (p. 472)

meander (mee AN dur): broad, C-shaped curve in a river or stream, formed by erosion of its outer bank. (p. 357)

measurement: way to describe objects and events with numbers; for example, length, volume, mass, weight, and temperature. (p. 414)

mechanical advantage: for a machine, the mechanical advantage equals the output force exerted by the machine divided by the input force applied to the machine. (p. 519)

mechanical weathering: physical processes that break rock apart without changing its chemical makeup; can be caused by ice wedging, animals, and plant roots. (p. 325)

✳ **meiosis (mi OH sus):** process in which sex cells are formed in reproductive organs; involves two divisions of the nucleus, producing four sex cells, each having half the number of chromosomes as the original cell. (p. 73)

melanin: pigment produced by the epidermis that protects skin and gives skin and eyes their color. (p. 97)

melting point: temperature at which a solid becomes a liquid. (p. 450)

metal: element that is malleable, ductile, a good conductor of electricity, and generally has a shiny or metallic luster. (p. 484)

metalloid: element that has characteristics of both metals and nonmetals and is a solid at room temperature. (p. 485)

meteorite: any rock from space that survives its plunge through the atmosphere and lands on Earth's surface. (p. 639)

meter (m): SI unit for length. (p. 417)

mineral resources: resources from which metals are obtained. (p. 273)

campo magnético: la región alrededor de un imán o una carga móvil en donde se ejerce una fuerza magnética sobre otros imanes y cargas móviles. (pág. 579)

mares lunares: regiones lisas y oscuras en la Luna que se formaron cuando la lava fluyó en la superficie lunar. (pág. 626)

masa: la cantidad de materia que posee un cuerpo. (pág. 419)

número de masa: suma del número de protones y neutrones en el núcleo de un átomo. (pág. 483)

materia: todo lo que posea masa, ocupe espacio y esté hecho de diferentes tipos de átomos; incluye todo lo que se puede ver, saborear, oler o tocar, pero no incluye el calor, el sonido o la luz. (pág. 472)

meandro: curva amplia en forma de C en un río o arroyo, formada por la erosión de su margen externo. (pág. 357)

medición: forma para describir cuerpos y eventos con números; por ejemplo, la longitud, el volumen, la masa, el peso y la temperatura. (pág. 414)

ventaja mecánica: para una máquina, la ventaja mecánica es igual a la fuerza de salida que ejerce la máquina dividida entre la fuerza de entrada que se le aplica a la máquina. (pág. 519)

meteorización mecánica: procesos físicos que fragmentan las rocas sin cambiar su composición química; pueden ser causada por las grietas de hielo, los animales y las raíces de las plantas. (pág. 325)

meiosis: proceso en que se forman las células sexuales en los órganos reproductores; implica dos divisiones nucleares que producen cuatro células sexuales, cada una de las cuales posee la mitad del número de cromosomas de la célula original. (pág. 73)

melanina: pigmento que produce la epidermis y el cual protege la piel y da el color a los ojos y a la piel. (pág. 97)

punto de fusión: temperatura a la cual un sólido se convierte en líquido. (pág. 450)

metal: elemento maleable, dúctil y buen conductor de electricidad que generalmente tiene un lustre brillante o metálico. (pág. 484)

metaloide: elemento que comparte características tanto de metales como de no metales y el cual es sólido a temperatura ambiente. (pág. 485)

meteorito: cualquier roca del espacio que sobrevive su incursión en la atmósfera y llega a la superficie terrestre. (pág. 639)

metro (m.): unidad del SI para longitud. (pág. 417)

recursos minerales: recursos a partir de los cuales pueden obtenerse metales. (pág. 273)

Glossary/Glosario

mineral: inorganic nutrient that regulates many chemical reactions in the body. (p. 136)

mitochondria (mi tuh KAHN dree uh): cell organelles in which cellular respiration takes place. (p. 42)

✳ **mitosis (mi TOH sus):** cell division process in which DNA in the nucleus is duplicated and the nucleus divides into two nuclei that contain the same genetic information. (p. 70)

✳ **mixture:** a combination of compounds and elements that has not formed a new substance and whose proportions can be changed without changing the mixture's identity. (p. 489)

mutation: change in a gene or chromosome that can result from something in the environment or an error in mitosis or meiosis; can be harmful, neutral, or beneficial, and adds variation to the genes of a species. (p. 182)

mineral: nutriente inorgánico que regula muchas reacciones químicas en el cuerpo. (pág. 136)

mitocondrias: organelos celulares en donde se lleva a cabo la respiración celular. (pág. 42)

mitosis: proceso de división celular en que se duplica el DNA en el núcleo y el núcleo se divide en dos núcleos que contienen la misma información genética. (pág. 70)

mezcla: combinación de compuestos y elementos que no han formado una nueva sustancia y cuyas proporciones pueden alterarse sin que se pierda la identidad de la mezcla. (pág. 489)

mutación: cambio en un gen o en un cromosoma que puede ser el resultado de un factor ambiental o un error de mitosis o meiosis; puede ser perjudicial, neutro o benéfico y añade variaciones a los genes de una especie. (pág. 182)

N

natural gas: fossil fuel formed from marine organisms that often is found in tilted or folded rock layers and is used for heating and cooking. (p. 259)

✳ **neap tide:** occurs twice monthly when Earth, the Sun, and the Moon are at right angles to each other to produce a smaller tidal effect. (p. 630)

nephron (NEF rahn): tiny filtering unit of the kidney. (p. 149)

neuron (NOO rahn): basic functioning unit of the nervous system, made up of a cell body, dendrites, and axons. (p. 111)

✳ **neutral:** something that has zero total electric charge. (p. 562)

✳ **neutron:** an uncharged particle located in the nucleus of an atom. (p. 478)

niche (NICH): the role of an organism in its ecosystem; refers to the unique ways an organism survives, obtains food and shelter, and avoids danger. (p. 210)

noninfectious disease: disease that is not caused by a pathogen. (p. 182)

nonmetal: element that usually is a gas or brittle solid and a poor conductor of electricity and heat; is the basis of the chemicals of life. (p. 485)

✳ **nonrenewable resource:** resource that is used faster than it can be replaced or restored. (p. 256)

gas natural: combustible fósil formado a partir de organismos marinos y que a menudo se encuentra en capas rocosas inclinadas o plegadas; se usa para la calefacción y para cocinar. (pág. 259)

marea muerta: ocurre dos veces al mes cuando el Sol, la Tierra y la Luna están en un ángulo recto de uno al otro y producen un menor efecto sobre la marea. (pág. 630)

nefrón: pequeña unidad de filtración del riñón. (pág. 149)

neurona: unidad de funcionamiento básico del sistema nervioso, formada por un cuerpo celular, dendritas y axones. (pág. 111)

neutro: algo con una carga eléctrica total de cero. (pág. 562)

neutrón: partícula sin carga, localizada en el núcleo de un átomo (pág. 478)

nicho: el papel que desempeña un organismo en su ecosistema; se refiere a las formas únicas en que un organismo sobrevive, obtiene alimento y refugio y evita los peligros. (pág. 210)

enfermedad no infecciosa: enfermedad que no es causada por un patógeno. (p. 182)

no metal: elemento que por lo general es un gas o sólido frágil y mal conductor de electricidad y calor; es la base de los compuestos químicos biológicos. (pág. 485)

recurso no renovable: recurso que se usa más rápidamente de lo que se puede reemplazar o reponer. (pág. 256)

no-till farming/parallel circuit

no-till farming: method for reducing soil erosion; plant stalks are left in the field after harvesting and the next year's crop is planted within the stalks without plowing. (p. 340)

nuclear energy: alternative energy source that is based on atomic fission. (p. 263)

nucleus (NEW klee us): positively charged, central part of an atom. (p. 477)

nutrient (NEW tree unt): substance in foods—proteins, carbohydrates, fats, vitamins, minerals, and water—that provides energy and materials for cell development, growth, and repair. (p. 128)

observatory: building that can house an optical telescope; often has a dome-shaped roof that can be opened for viewing. (p. 660)

oil: liquid fossil fuel formed from marine organisms that is burned to obtain energy and used in the manufacture of plastics. (p. 259)

orbit: curved path followed by a satellite as it revolves around an object. (pp. 625, 667)

ore: deposit in which a mineral exists in large enough amounts to be mined at a profit. (p. 273)

✳ **organ:** structure made of two or more different tissue types that work together to do a certain job. (p. 49)

organelles (or guh NELZ): specialized cell parts that perform a cell's activities. (p. 41)

✳ **organism:** any living thing. (p. 14)

organ system: group of organs that work together to perform a certain task. (p. 49)

oxidation (ahk sih DAY shun): chemical weathering process that occurs when some minerals are exposed to oxygen and water over time. (p. 328)

Pangaea (pan JEE uh): large, ancient landmass that was composed of all the continents joined together. (p. 384)

parallel circuit: circuit that has more than one path for electric current to follow. (p. 576)

agricultura de no-till/circuito en paralelo

agricultura de no-till: método para reducir la erosión del suelo; los tallos de las plantas se dejan en el terreno después de la cosecha y el cultivo del siguiente año se siembra entre los tallos sin arar la tierra. (pág. 340)

energía nuclear: fuente de energía alternativa que se basa en la fisión atómica. (pág. 263)

núcleo: parte central del átomo, cargada positivamente. (pág. 477)

nutriente: sustancia en los alimentos (proteínas, carbohidratos, grasas, vitaminas, minerales y agua) que suministra energía y materiales para el desarrollo, crecimiento y reparación de las células. (pág. 128)

observatorio: edificio que puede albergar un telescopio óptico; a menudo tiene un techo en forma de domo que puede abrirse para la observación. (pág. 660)

petróleo: combustible fósil líquido que se forma a partir de organismos marinos; se quema para obtener energía y se usa en la manufactura de plásticos. (pág. 259)

órbita: trayectoria curva y regular que sigue un satélite a medida que gira alrededor de un astro. (págs. 625, 667)

mena: depósito en que existen cantidades suficientes de un mineral para que la actividad minera sea lucrativa. (pág. 273)

órgano: estructura formada por dos o más tipos de tejidos que funcionan juntos para realizar una labor determinada. (pág. 49)

organelos: partes especializadas de las células que realizan las funciones celulares. (pág. 41)

organismo: cualquier ser vivo. (pág. 14)

sistema de órganos: grupo de órganos que funcionan en conjunto para realizar una labor determinada. (pág. 49)

oxidación: proceso de erosión química que ocurre cuando algunos minerales se exponen al oxígeno y al agua. (pág. 328)

Pangaea: masa terrestre extensa y antigua que estaba formada por todos los continentes unidos. (pág. 384)

circuito en paralelo: circuito en que la corriente eléctrica puede seguir más de una trayectoria. (pág. 576)

Glossary/Glosario

passive immunity: immunity that results when antibodies produced in one animal are introduced into another's body; does not last as long as active immunity. (p. 175)

pasteurization (pas chur ruh ZAY shun): process in which a liquid is heated to a temperature that kills most bacteria; increases the length of time foods can be stored without spoiling. (pp. 52, 177)

periosteum (pur ee AHS tee um): tough, tight-fitting membrane that covers a bone's surface and contains blood vessels that transport nutrients into the bone. (p. 105)

peripheral nervous system: division of the nervous system; includes all the nerves outside the CNS; connects the brain and spinal cord to other body parts. (p. 112)

peristalsis (per uh STAHL sus): waves of muscular contractions that move food through the digestive tract. (p. 130)

permeable (PUR mee uh bul): describes soil and rock with connecting pores through which water can flow. (p. 364)

✳ **photosynthesis (foh toh SIHN thuh sus):** process by which plants, algae, and many types of bacteria make their own food. (p. 43)

phylogeny (fi LAH juh nee): evolutionary history of an organism; used today to group organisms into six kingdoms. (p. 23)

✳ **physical change:** change in which the properties of a substance change but the identity of the substance always remains the same. (p. 450)

physical property: any characteristic of a material, such as state, color, and volume, that can be observed or measured without changing or attempting to change the material. (p. 445)

pioneer species: first organisms to grow in new or disturbed areas. (p. 226)

plasma: the liquid part of blood, which is made mostly of water. (p. 162)

plate: a large section of Earth's oceanic or continental crust and rigid upper mantle that moves around on the asthenosphere. (p. 392)

platelet: irregularly shaped cell fragments that help clot blood. (p. 163)

✳ **plate tectonics:** theory that Earth's crust and upper mantle are broken into plates that float and move around on a plasticlike layer of the mantle. (p. 392)

inmunidad pasiva: inmunidad que resulta cuando los anticuerpos que produce un animal se introducen en el cuerpo de otro animal; no es tan duradera como la inmunidad activa. (pág. 175)

pasteurización: proceso mediante el cual un líquido se calienta a una temperatura que destruye la mayoría de las bacterias; aumenta el período de tiempo durante el cual se pueden almacenar los alimentos sin que se echen a perder. (págs. 52, 177)

periostio: membrana fuerte y apretada que cubre la superficie de los huesos y contiene vasos sanguíneos que transportan nutrientes a los huesos. (pág. 105)

sistema nervioso periférico: parte del sistema nervioso compuesto por todos los nervios que no pertenecen al sistema nervioso central y que conecta el encéfalo y la médula espinal con otras partes del cuerpo. (pág. 112)

peristaltismo: ondas de contracciones musculares que mueven al alimento a través del sistema digestivo. (pág. 130)

permeable: describe el suelo y la roca que tienen poros conectados a través de los cuales puede fluir el agua. (pág. 364)

fotosíntesis: proceso mediante el cual las plantas, las algas y muchos tipos de bacterias producen su propio alimento. (pág. 43)

filogenia: historia evolutiva de un organismo; se usa actualmente para agrupar a los organismos en seis reinos. (pág. 23)

cambio físico: cambio en el cual las propiedades de una sustancia cambian, pero la identidad de la sustancia sigue siendo la misma. (pág. 450)

propiedad física: cualquier característica de un material, como estado, color y volumen, que se pueden observar o medir sin alterar o tratar de cambiar el material. (pág. 445)

especies pioneras: primeros organismos que crecen en áreas nuevas o alteradas. (pág. 226)

plasma: parte líquida de la sangre compuesta principalmente por agua. (pág. 162)

placa: enorme sección de la corteza terrestre u oceánica y del manto rígido superior que se mueve sobre la astenosfera. (pág. 392)

plaqueta: fragmentos celulares de forma irregular que ayudan a coagular la sangre. (pág. 163)

tectónica de placas: teoría que dice que la corteza terrestre y el manto superior están fragmentados en placas que flotan y se mueven sobre una capa viscosa del manto. (pág. 392)

❋ **population:** a group of the same type of organisms living in the same place at the same time. (p. 207)

❋ **potential energy:** energy that is stored in an object due to the object's position. (p. 537)

precipitation: occurs when drops of water or crystals of ice become too large to be suspended in a cloud and fall in the form of rain, freezing rain, sleet, snow, or hail. (p. 300)

precision: describes how closely measurements are to each other and how carefully measurements were made. (p. 426)

❋ **predator:** an organism that captures and eats other animals. (p. 213)

❋ **prey:** an organism that is hunted and caught for food. (p. 213)

❋ **prism:** a wedge-shaped piece of glass. (p. 607)

❋ **producer:** an organism that makes its own food using an energy source such as light. (p. 213)

Project Apollo: final stage in the U.S. program to reach the Moon in which Neil Armstrong was the first human to step onto the Moon's surface. (p. 672)

Project Gemini: second stage in the U.S. program to reach the Moon in which an astronaut team connected with another spacecraft in orbit. (p. 671)

Project Mercury: first step in the U.S. program to reach the Moon that orbited a piloted spacecraft around Earth and brought it back safely. (p. 671)

❋ **protist:** one- or many-celled eukaryotic organism that lives in moist or wet surroundings; can be plantlike, animal-like, or funguslike. (p. 53)

❋ **proton:** positively charged particle located in the nucleus of an atom that is counted to identify the atomic number. (p. 477)

protozoan: one-celled, animal-like protist that lives in water, soil, and living and dead organisms, and can move by using flagella, cilia, or pseudopods. (p. 53)

❋ **pulley:** grooved wheel with a rope or cable running through the groove. (p. 520)

población: grupo del mismo tipo de organismos que viven en el mismo lugar al mismo tiempo. (pág. 207)

energía potencial: energía almacenada en un cuerpo debido su posición. (pág. 537)

precipitación: ocurre cuando las gotas de agua o cristales de hielo adquieren un tamaño demasiado grande para estar suspendidos en una nube y caen en forma de lluvia, lluvia congelada, aguanieve, nieve o granizo. (pág. 300)

precisión: describe la cercanía entre una medición y otra y el cuidado con que fueron hechas dichas mediciones. (pág. 426)

depredador: un organismo que captura y come otros animales. (pág. 213)

presa: organismo que se captura como alimento. (pág. 213)

prisma: trozo de vidrio en forma de cuña. (pág. 607)

productor: organismo que produce su propio alimento al usar una fuente de energía como la luz. (pág. 213)

Proyecto Apolo: etapa final en el proyecto estadounidense para llegar a la Luna y en el cual Neil Armstrong fue el primer ser humano en caminar sobre la superficie lunar. (pág. 672)

Proyecto Géminis: segunda etapa del proyecto estadounidense para llegar a la Luna y en el cual un grupo de astronautas conectó dos naves espaciales en órbita. (pág. 671)

Proyecto Mercurio: primera etapa del proyecto estadounidense para llegar a la Luna y en el cual una nave espacial tripulada recorrió la órbita de la Tierra y regresó a ésta de manera segura. (pág. 671)

protista: organismo eucariota unicelular o multicelular que vive en ambientes húmedos o acuáticos; puede poseer características de plantas, animales u hongos. (pág. 53)

protón: partícula cargada positivamente, localizada en el núcleo de un átomo y que se cuenta para identificar el número atómico. (pág. 477)

protozoario: protista unicelular parecido a un animal, el cual vive en el agua, en la tierra o en organismos vivos o muertos y que se puede desplazar mediante flagelos, cilios o seudópodos. (pág. 53)

polea: rueda acanalada con una cuerda o cable que corre pasa por el canal. (pág. 520)

R

❋ **radiation:** energy that is transferred from one place to another by waves. (pp. 551, 658)

radiación: energía que se transfiere de un lugar a otro por ondas. (pág. 551, 658)

Glossary/Glosario

radio telescope: collects and records radio waves traveling through space; can be used day or night under most weather conditions. (p. 663)

rate: a ratio of two different kinds of measurements; the amount of change of one measurement in a given amount of time. (p. 420)

recycling: conservation method in which old materials are processed to make new ones through manufacturing processes. (p. 277)

reflecting telescope: optical telescope that uses a concave mirror to focus light and form an image at the focal point. (p. 660)

✳ **reflection:** occurs when a wave strikes an object or surface and bounces off. (p. 605)

refracting telescope: optical telescope that uses a double convex lens to bend light and form an image at the focal point. (p. 660)

refraction: bending of a wave as it moves from one medium into another medium. (p. 606)

relative humidity: measure of the amount of water vapor in the air compared with the amount that could be held at a specific temperature. (p. 298)

✳ **renewable resource:** a resource that can be replaced or restored as it is used or within a reasonable amount of time. (p. 266)

reserve: amount of a fossil fuel that can be extracted from Earth at a profit using current technology. (p. 261)

✳ **resource:** any material that can be used to satisfy a need. (p. 256)

revolution (rev uh LEW shun): movement of Earth around the Sun, which takes a year to complete. (p. 625)

rocket: special engine that can work in space and burns liquid or solid fuel. (p. 665)

rotation (roh TAY shun): spinning of Earth on its axis, which occurs once every 24 hours, produces day and night, and causes the planets and stars to appear to rise and set. (p. 624)

runoff: any rainwater that does not soak into the ground or evaporate but flows over Earth's surface; generally flows into streams and has the ability to erode and carry sediments. (p. 352)

radiotelescopio: recoge y registra ondas radiales que viajan a través del espacio; puede usarse de día o de noche en la mayoría de las condiciones del tiempo. (pág. 663)

tasa: relación de dos tipos de medidas diferentes; la cantidad de cambio en una medida en un tiempo determinado. (pág. 420)

reciclaje: método de conservación en que los materiales usados se procesan para producir otros nuevos. (pág. 277)

telescopio reflector: telescopio óptico que utiliza un espejo cóncavo para enfocar la luz y formar una imagen en el punto focal. (pág. 660)

reflexión: ocurre cuando una onda choca contra un cuerpo o superficie y rebota. (pág. 605)

telescopio refractor: telescopio óptico que utiliza una lente doble convexa para formar una imagen en el punto focal. (pág. 660)

refracción: desviación de una onda a medida que se mueve de un medio a otro. (pág. 606)

humedad relativa: medida de la cantidad de vapor de agua en el aire, comparada con la cantidad que éste podría mantener a una temperatura específica. (pág. 298)

recurso renovable: recurso que se puede reemplazar o reponer a medida que se utiliza o dentro de un período razonable de tiempo. (pág. 266)

reserva: depósito de un combustible fósil que se puede extraer de la Tierra y del cual, utilizando la tecnología actual, se obtienen utilidades. (pág. 261)

recurso: material que se puede utilizar para satisfacer una necesidad. (pág. 256)

traslación: movimiento de la Tierra alrededor del Sol, el cual tarda un año en completarse. (pág. 625)

cohete: máquina especial que puede funcionar en el espacio y quema combustible sólido o líquido. (pág. 665)

rotación: giro de la Tierra sobre su eje, el cual ocurre una vez cada 24 horas, produce el día y la noche y hace que los planetas y las estrellas parezcan salir y ponerse en el firmamento. (pág. 624)

escorrentía: agua de lluvia que no se filtra por el suelo ni se evapora, pero que fluye sobre la superficie terrestre; generalmente fluye hacia los arroyos y tiene la capacidad de causar erosión y transportar sedimentos. (pág. 352)

S

satellite: any natural or artificial object that revolves around another object. (p. 667)

satélite: cualquier cuerpo natural o artificial que gire alrededor de otro cuerpo. (pág. 667)

scientific methods: procedures used to solve problems and answer questions that can include stating the problem, gathering information, forming a hypothesis, testing the hypothesis with an experiment, analyzing data, and drawing conclusions. (p. 7)

seafloor spreading: Hess's theory that new seafloor is formed when magma is forced upward toward the surface at a mid-ocean ridge. (p. 389)

series circuit: circuit that has only one path for electric current to follow. (p. 576)

sex cell: specialized cells—female eggs and male sperm—that are produced by the process of meiosis, carry DNA, and join in sexual reproduction. (p. 72)

sexual reproduction: a type of reproduction in which a new organism is produced from the DNA of two sex cells (egg and sperm). (p. 72)

SI: International System of Units, related by multiples of ten, designed to provide a worldwide standard of physical measurement. (p. 416)

significant digits: the number of digits used to indicate the uncertainty of the measuring tool used. (p. 422)

simple machine: a device that uses only one movement to do work; includes the pulley, lever, wheel and axle, inclined plane, wedge, and screw. (p. 519)

soil: mixture of weathered rock and mineral fragments, decayed organic matter, water, and air that can take thousands of years to develop. (p. 330)

soil profile: vertical section of soil layers, each of which is a horizon. (p. 332)

solar energy: energy from the Sun that is clean, inexhaustible, and can be transformed into electricity by solar cells. (p. 266)

solar system: system of nine planets and numerous other objects that orbit our Sun, all held in place by the Sun's gravity. (p. 632)

space probe: instrument that gathers information and sends it back to Earth while traveling toward planets. (p. 668)

space shuttle: reusable spacecraft that can carry cargo, astronauts, and satellites to and from space. (p. 673)

métodos científicos: procedimientos que se usan para resolver problemas y responder preguntas; pueden incluir: enunciar un problema, recopilar datos, formular una hipótesis, comprobar la hipótesis mediante un experimento, analizar los datos y sacar conclusiones. (pág. 7)

expansión del suelo oceánico: teoría de Hess que dice que el nuevo suelo oceánico se forma cuando el magma se remonta hasta la superficie a través de una dorsal mediooceánica. (pág. 389)

circuito en serie: circuito en que la corriente eléctrica sólo puede seguir una trayectoria. (pág. 576)

células sexuales: células especializadas (óvulos y espermatozoides) que se producen mediante el proceso de meiosis, portan el DNA y forman parte de la reproducción sexual. (pág. 72)

reproducción sexual: tipo de reproducción en que se produce un nuevo organismo a partir del DNA de dos células sexuales (óvulo y espermatozoide) (pág. 72)

SI: Sistema Internacional de Unidades, relacionado en múltiplos de diez, diseñado como un estándar de medidas físicas a nivel mundial. (pág. 416)

dígitos significativos: el número de dígitos utilizados para indicar la incertidumbre del instrumento de la medición utilizó. (pág. 422)

máquina simple: dispositivo que facilita el trabajo con un solo movimiento; puede cambiar el tamaño o la dirección de una fuerza e incluye la cuña, el tornillo, la palanca, la rueda y el eje, la polea y el plano inclinado. (pág. 519)

suelo: mezcla de roca erosionada y fragmentos minerales, materia orgánica en descomposición, agua y aire que puede tardar miles de años en formarse. (pág. 330)

perfil del suelo: sección vertical de las capas del suelo, cada una de las cuales es un horizonte. (pág. 332)

energía solar: energía proveniente del Sol, la cual es limpia e inagotable y puede transformarse en electricidad mediante celdas solares. (pág. 266)

sistema solar: sistema de nueve planetas y numerosos otros cuerpos que giran alrededor del Sol, todos mantenidos en su lugar por la acción de la gravedad del Sol. (pág. 632)

sonda espacial: instrumento que reúne información y la envía a la Tierra mientras viaja hacia los planetas. (pág. 668)

transbordador espacial: nave espacial reutilizable que puede llevar carga, astronautas y satélites al espacio y regresarlos a la Tierra. (pág. 673)

space station: large facility with living quarters, work and exercise areas, and equipment and support systems for humans to live and work in space and conduct research. (p. 674)

✻ **speed:** equals the distance traveled divided by the amount of time it takes to travel that distance. (p. 508)

spontaneous generation: idea that living things come from nonliving things. (p. 19)

spring: forms when the water table meets Earth's surface; often found on hillsides and used as a freshwater source. (p. 367)

✻ **spring tide:** occurs when Earth, the Sun, and the Moon are lined up at the new and full phases of the Moon to produce a greater tidal effect. (p. 630)

state of matter: physical property that is dependent on both temperature and pressure and occurs in four forms—solid, liquid, gas, or plasma. (p. 449)

static charge: imbalance of electric charge on an object. (p. 566)

substance: matter that has the same composition and properties throughout. (p. 487)

succession: the pattern of gradual changes in the types of species that live in an area; can be primary or secondary. (p. 226)

supernova: very bright explosion of the outer part of a supergiant that takes place after its core collapses. (p. 643)

synapse (SIHN aps): small space across which an impulse moves from an axon to the dendrites or cell body of another neuron. (p. 111)

estación espacial: instalación grande con áreas para vivir, trabajar y hacer ejercicio; tiene equipos y sistemas de apoyo para que los seres humanos vivan, trabajen y lleven a cabo investigaciones en el espacio. (pág. 674)

rapidez: igual a la distancia viajada dividida entre la cantidad de tiempo que toma viajar esa distancia. (pág. 508)

generación espontánea: idea que sostiene que los seres vivos proceden de seres inertes. (pág. 19)

manantial: se forma cuando la capa freática alcanza la superficie terrestre; a menudo se encuentran en las laderas de montañas y se usan como fuente de agua potable. (pág. 367)

marea viva: ocurre cuando el Sol, la Tierra y la Luna se alinean en las fases de luna nueva y de luna llena para producir un mayor efecto sobre la marea. (pág. 630)

estados de la materia: propiedad física que depende de la temperatura y la presión, y que ocurre en cuatro formas: sólido, líquido, gas, o plasma. (pág. 449)

carga estática: desequilibrio de la carga eléctrica en un cuerpo. (pág. 566)

sustancia: materia que siempre tiene la misma composición y las mismas propiedades. (pág. 487)

sucesión: cambios graduales y naturales en los tipos de especies que viven en un área; puede ser primaria o secundaria. (pág. 226)

supernova: explosión muy brillante de la parte externa de una supergigante y la cual ocurre cuando se desintegra su núcleo. (pág. 643)

sinapsis: pequeño espacio a través del cual se mueve un impulso desde el axón hasta las dendritas o el cuerpo celular de otra neurona. (pág. 111)

T

table: presents information in rows and columns, making it easier to read and understand. (p. 427)

taiga (TI guh): world's largest biome, located south of the tundra between 50° N and 60° N latitude; has long, cold winters, precipitation between 35 cm and 100 cm each year, cone-bearing evergreen trees, and dense forests. (p. 232)

temperate deciduous forest: biome usually having four distinct seasons, annual precipitation between 75 cm and 150 cm, and climax communities of deciduous trees. (p. 233)

tabla: presentación de información en filas y columnas para facilitar su lectura y comprensión. (pág. 427)

taiga: el bioma más grande del mundo, localizado al sur de la tundra entre 50° y 60° de latitud norte; tiene inviernos prolongados y fríos, una precipitación que alcanza entre 35 y 100 centímetros al año, coníferas siempreverdes y bosques espesos. (pág. 232)

bosque caducifolio templado: bioma que generalmente tiene cuatro estaciones distintas, con una precipitación anual entre 75 y 150 centímetros cúbicos y un clímax de comunidades de árboles caducifolios. (pág. 233)

temperate rain forest: biome with 200 cm to 400 cm of precipitation each year, average temperatures between 9°C and 12°C, and forests dominated by trees with needlelike leaves. (p. 233)

temperature: measure of the average kinetic energy of the atoms in an object. (p. 545)

tendon: thick band of tissue that attaches bones to muscles. (p. 102)

terracing: farming method used to reduce erosion on steep slopes. (p. 341)

theory: explanation of things or events based on scientific knowledge resulting from many observations and experiments. (p. 10)

✳ **thermal energy:** the energy due to the continual motion of the particles in matter. (p. 539)

tides: the alternate rise and fall of sea level caused by the gravitational attractions of the Moon and the Sun. (p. 629)

✳ **tissue:** group of similar cells that all do the same work. (p. 49)

tornado: violent, whirling wind, usually less than 200 m in diameter, that travels in a narrow path over land and can be highly destructive. (p. 308)

trachea (TRAY kee uh): air-conducting tube that connects the larynx with the bronchi, is lined with mucous membranes and cilia, and contains strong cartilage rings. (p. 142)

transverse wave: a type of mechanical wave in which the wave energy causes matter in the medium to move up and down or back and forth at right angles to the direction the wave travels. (p. 596)

tropical rain forest: most biologically diverse biome; has an average temperature of 25°C and receives between 200 cm and 600 cm of precipitation each year. (p. 234)

troposphere (TROPH uh sfihr): layer of the atmosphere that is closest to Earth's surface and contains nearly all of its clouds and weather. (p. 292)

✳ **trough:** a low point, or valley, on a transverse wave. (p. 596)

tundra: cold, dry, treeless biome with less than 25 cm of precipitation each year, a short growing season, permafrost, and winters that can be six to nine months long. Tundra is separated into two types: arctic tundra and alpine tundra. (p. 231)

pluviselva templada: bioma con 200 a 400 centímetros de precipitación al año; tiene una temperatura promedio entre 9 y 12°C y bosques dominados por árboles de hojas en forma de aguja. (pág. 233)

temperatura: medida de la energía cinética promedio de los átomos de un cuerpo. (pág. 545)

tendón: banda de tejido grueso que une los huesos y los músculos. (pág. 102)

terrazas: método de siembra que se usa para reducir la erosión en laderas inclinadas. (pág. 341)

teoría: explicación de cosas o eventos basada en el conocimiento científico y que resulta de muchas observaciones y experimentos. (pág. 10)

energía térmica: energía que se debe al movimiento continuo de las partículas en la materia. (pág. 539)

mareas: el ascenso y descenso regulares del nivel del mar causados por las atracciones gravitatorias de la Luna y el Sol. (pág. 629)

tejido: grupo de células similares que desempeñan la misma función. (pág. 49)

tornado: violento remolino de viento, por lo general con menos de 200 metros de diámetro, que sigue una trayectoria estrecha sobre la tierra y puede ser altamente destructivo. (pág. 308)

tráquea: tubo conductor de aire que conecta la laringe con los bronquios, está forrada con membranas mucosas y cilios y contiene fuertes anillos de cartílago. (pág. 142)

onda transversal: tipo de onda mecánica en el cual la energía de la onda hace que la materia en el medio se mueva hacia arriba y hacia abajo o en forma oscilante en ángulos rectos respecto a la dirección en que viaja la onda. (pág. 596)

pluviselva tropical: el bioma más diverso biológicamente; tiene una temperatura promedio de 25°C y recibe entre 200 y 600 centímetros de precipitación al año. (pág. 234)

troposfera: capa de la atmósfera más cercana a la superficie terrestre y que contiene casi todas sus nubes y tiempo. (pág. 292)

valle: un punto bajo, o el depresión, en una onda transversal. (pág. 596)

tundra: bioma sin árboles, frío y seco, con menos de 25 centímetros de precipitación al año; tiene una estación corta de crecimiento, permafrost e inviernos que pueden durar entre 6 y 9 meses. La tundra se divide en dos tipos: tundra ártica y tundra alpina. (pág. 231)

unbalanced forces: forces on an object that do not cancel so that the net force on the object is not equal to zero. (p. 513)

ureter: tube that carries urine from each kidney to the bladder. (p. 149)

fuerzas desequilibradas: fuerzas sobre un cuerpo que no se cancelan de modo que la fuerza neta sobre el cuerpo no sea igual a cero. (pág. 513)

uréter: conducto que transporta la orina desde cada uno de los riñones hasta la vejiga. (pág. 149)

vacuole (VAK yew ohl): balloonlike cell organelle in the cytoplasm that can store food, water, and other substances. (p. 42)

variable: an event, condition, or factor that can be changed in a study or test. (pp. 9, 428)

variation: different ways that a trait can appear—for example, differences in height, hair color, or weight. (p. 81)

vein: blood vessel that carries blood to the heart. (p. 168)

velocity: speed of an object and its direction of motion; changes when speed changes, direction of motion changes, or both change. (p. 509)

vibration: a repeated back-and-forth motion (p. 595)

villi (VIHL I): fingerlike projections covering the wall of the small intestine that increase the surface area for food absorption. (p. 131)

vitamin: water-soluble or fat-soluble organic nutrient needed in small quantities for growth, preventing some diseases, and regulating body functions. (p. 135)

voltage: a measure of the amount of electrical potential energy transferred by an electric charge as it moves from one point to another in a circuit. (p. 573)

volume (m^3): the amount of space an object occupies measured in cubic meters. (p. 418)

voluntary muscle: muscle, such as a leg or arm muscle, that can be consciously controlled. (p. 101)

vacuola: organelo celular en forma de balón que se encuentra en el citoplasma y que puede almacenar alimentos, agua y otras sustancias. (pág. 42)

variable: un acontecimiento, la condición, o el factor que puede ser cambiado en un estudio o la prueba. (págs. 9, 428)

variación: diferentes formas en que puede aparecer un rasgo. Por ejemplo, diferencias de tamaño, color del cabello o peso. (pág. 81)

vena: vasos sanguíneos que llevan la sangre al corazón. (pág. 168)

velocidad: rapidez de un cuerpo y su dirección de movimiento; varía cuando cambian la rapidez, la dirección de movimiento o ambas. (pág. 509)

vibración: movimiento rítmico oscilante. (pág. 595)

microvellosidades: proyecciones digitales que cubren las paredes del intestino delgado y aumentan el área de superficie para la absorción de los alimentos. (pág. 131)

vitamina: nutriente orgánico hidrosoluble o liposoluble, necesario en pequeñas cantidades para el crecimiento, la prevención de algunas enfermedades y para la regulación de las funciones corporales. (pág. 135)

voltaje: medida de la cantidad de energía eléctrica potencial transferida por una carga eléctrica a medida que se mueve de un punto a otro en un circuito. (pág. 573)

volumen (m^3): la cantidad de espacio que ocupa un cuerpo, medido en metros cúbicos. (pág. 418)

músculo voluntario: músculo, como el músculo de una pierna o de un brazo, que se puede controlar a voluntad. (pág. 101)

* **water cycle:** never-ending cycle in which water circulates between Earth's surface and the atmosphere through the processes of evaporation, transpiration, precipitation, and condensation. (p. 295)

water table: upper surface of the zone of saturation; drops during a drought. (p. 364)

wave: a disturbance that transfers energy but not matter. (p. 594)

* **wavelength:** for a transverse wave, the distance between two adjacent crests or two adjacent troughs; for a compressional wave, the distance from the centers of adjacent rarefactions or adjacent compressions. (p. 600)

weather: current condition of the atmosphere including cloud cover, temperature, wind speed and direction, humidity, and air pressure. (p. 296)

weathering: mechanical or chemical surface processes that break rock into smaller and smaller pieces. (p. 324)

weight: a measurement of force that depends on gravity; measured in newtons. (p. 419)

wetland: a land region that is wet most or all of the year. (p. 241)

wind farm: area where many windmills use wind to generate electricity. (p. 267)

ciclo del agua: ciclo interminable en que el agua circula entre la superficie terrestre y la atmósfera a través de los procesos de evaporación, precipitación y condensación. (pág. 295)

capa freática: parte superior de la zona de saturación; baja durante las sequías. (pág. 364)

onda: perturbación rítmica que transfiere energía pero no materia. (pág. 594)

longitud de onda: en una onda transversal, es la distancia entre dos crestas adyacentes o entre dos valles adyacentes; en una onda de compresión es la distancia entre los centros de dos rarefacciones adyacentes o compresiones adyacentes. (pág. 600)

tiempo: condición actual de la atmósfera que incluye la capa de nubes, la temperatura, la velocidad y dirección del viento, la humedad y la presión atmosférica. (pág. 296)

meteorización: proceso superficial químico o mecánico que fragmenta las rocas en trozos cada vez más pequeños. (pág. 324)

peso: medida de fuerza que depende de la gravedad y que se mide en Newtons. (pág. 419)

humedad: cantidad de vapor de agua en la atmósfera. (pág. 298)

finca de energía eólica: área en donde muchos molinos usan el viento para generar electricidad. (pág. 267)

Index

A

Abdominal thrust(s), 143, *144*
Abiotic factor(s), *202,* **202**–204, *203;* soil, *202,* 202–203, *lab* 203; sunlight, 204, *204;* temperature, 203; water, 204, *204*
Abrasive(s), 275
Acari Marmoset, 30, *30*
Acceleration, 510
Accessory organ(s), 129
Accuracy, 426; and precision, 426
Acetylcholine, 111
Acid(s), and weathering, 327–328, 327, *331*
Acid rain, 339, 367
Acquired Immune Deficiency Syndrome. *See* AIDS
Active immunity, 175
Activities, Applying Math, 33, 47, 75, 81, 99, 108, 151, 184, 211, 221, 229, 242, 265, 283, 301, 303, 310, 317, 334, 337, 344, 347, 351, 365, 372, 379, 390, 420, 424, 439, 453, 460, 485, 497, 508, 510, 517, 529, 551, 557, 575, 576, 583, 603, 647, 666, 672, 679, 685; Applying Science, 150, 180, 210, 211, 276, 394, 459, 489, 545, 609, 637; Applying Skills, 13, 18, 21, 26, 43, 49, 57, 205, 215, 237, 245, 329, 336, 341, 426, 432; FCAT Test Practice, 124–125, 409–410, 468–469; Integrate, 17, 21, 39, 41, 47, 57, 69, 73, 82, 97, 108, 111, 132, 136, 145, 165, 170, 178, 209, 214, 236, 241, 244, 257, 267, 274, 292, 297, 301, 325, 333, 339, 344, 353, 367, 389, 399, 400, 416, 451, 455, 473, 478, 490, 491, 508, 523, 535, 548, 554, 566, 567, 579, 598, 600, 602, 626, 642, 643, 646, 650, 659, 668; Science Online, 8,

23, 39, 49, 54, 69, 83, 134, 145, 154, 163, 172, 201, 209, 227, 243, 269, 298, 305, 309, 314, 327, 328, 329, 332, 356, 360, 385, 394, 428, 445, 446, 476, 481, 490, 521, 567, 570, 603, 609, 612, 628, 633, 670, 675, 677, 682
Adaptation, 207
Addition, and subtraction, 423
Aerosol(s), 291, *291*
Africa, savannas of, 237, *237*
Aggregate, 276
Agriculture, and contour farming, 341, *341;* and deposition of sediment, *334, 362;* on grasslands, 237; and no-till farming, 340, *340;* and soil erosion, 338, 340–341, *341;* and terracing, 341
AIDS (Acquired Immune Deficiency Syndrome), 181
Air, 290; effects of temperature on, *lab* 289; temperature of, *lab* 289, 296, *296,* 297; weight of, 290, *290*
Air mass, 304, *304, act* 305
Air Quality Engineer, 57
Air temperature, 548
Alcohol, 116
Alcohol, energy from, 270, *270*
Aldrin, Edwin, 672
Algae, 43, **53,** 54; observing, *lab* 44
Algae cell(s), *19*
Algal cell(s), *19*
Allele(s), dominant, 79, *79;* multiple, 82, *82;* recessive, 79; in sex cells, *act* 81
Allergen(s), 182
Allergies. *See* Allergy
Allergy, 182
Alligator(s), 218, *218*
Alluvial fan, 334, 362
Alternative resource(s), biomass energy, 269–271, *270, 271;* geothermal energy, 268, *269;*

hydroelectric power, 268, *268;* nuclear energy, *263,* 263–265, *264, 265;* solar energy, *266,* 266–267, *lab* 272; wind energy, 267, *267*
Altitude, and skin, 97
Altocumulus cloud(s), 299, *299*
Altostratus cloud(s), 299, *299*
Aluminum, 273
Alveoli, 142, *142,* 145
Amazon, 30
Amino acid(s), 133–134
Ammonia, 21
Ampere (unit for electric current), 569, 575
Amplitude, *599,* **599**–600
Analyzing, data, *lab* 9
Anemia, 166
Anemometer, 301
Animal(s), classifying, 22, *22;* in desert, 236, *236;* endangered, 218, *218;* in grasslands, 237, *237;* habitats of, 211; identifying, 451, 453, *453;* migration of, *209, act* 209; protecting from severe weather, 314, *314;* on taiga, 232, *232;* in temperate deciduous forest, *232,* 233; in temperate rain forest, 233, *233;* and temperature, 297; in tropical rain forest, 234, *235;* on tundra, 231, *231;* and weathering, 325, *325*
Animal cell(s), *39, 40*
Annually Assessed Benchmark Checks, 10, 11, 17, 78, 111, 129, 181, 214, 215, 227, 235, 241, 264, 276, 340, 393, 417, 447, 448, 513, 516, 540, 541, 542, 595, 601, 633, 635, 676
Antibiotic(s), 52, 178, 180, 182
Antibody, 174; in blood, 165
Antigen(s), 165, **174**
Antihistamine(s), 182

Index

Index

Index

Index

Index

Index

Index

Index

Index

Index

Index

Magnification Key: Magnifications listed are the magnifications at which images were originally photographed.
LM–Light Microscope
SEM–Scanning Electron Microscope
TEM–Transmission Electron Microscope

Acknowledgments: Glencoe would like to acknowledge the artists and agencies who participated in illustrating this program: Absolute Science Illustration; Andrew Evansen; Argosy; Articulate Graphics; Craig Attebery represented by Frank & Jeff Lavaty; CHK America; Decode; Digital Art; John Edwards and Associates; Gagliano Graphics; JTH Illustration; Laurie O'Keefe; Morgan Cain & Associates; Matthew Pippin represented by Beranbaum Artist's Representative; Precision Graphics; Rolin Graphics, Inc.; WILDlife ART; Zoo Botanica.

Photo Credits

cover (t)Claudine Laabs/Photo Researchers, Inc., (c)CORBIS, (b)Warren Bolster/Getty Images; **vi** Raymond Gehman/CORBIS; **viii** Lawson Wood/CORBIS; **ix** Meckes/Ottawa/Photo Researchers; **x** Stephen Frink/CORBIS; **xi** Steve Starr/CORBIS; **xii** Ralph White/CORBIS; **xiii** NASA; **xiv** John Lund/Getty Images; **xv** NASA; **xvi** Rosemary Calvert; **xvii** Gary C. Will/Visuals Unlimited; **xviii** Dwight Kuhn; **xx** Burhan Ozbilici/AP/Wide World Photos; **xxi** Joseph Nettis/Photo Researchers; **xxii** Chad Ehlers/Stone; **xxiii** Randy Faris/CORBIS; **xxiv** Getty Images; **lv** CORBIS; **lvi–lvii** Arthur C. Smith III/Grant Heilman Photography; **lviii** Getty Images; **lix** John Evans; **lx** (l)John Evans, (r)PhotoDisc; **lxi** (l r)John Evans, (inset)PhotoDisc; **lxii** John Evans; **1** Brad Armstrong/AP/Wide World Photos; **2–3** Diane Scullion Littler; **3** (l)Jonathan Eisenback/ PhotoTake, NYC/ PictureQuest, (r)Janice M. Sheldon/Picture 20-20/ PictureQuest; **4–5** A. Witte/C. Mahaney/Getty Images; **6** Kjell B. Sandved/Visuals Unlimited; **8–9** Mark Burnett; **11** Tek Image/Science Photo Library/Photo Researchers; **12** (l b) Mark Burnett, (r)unknown; **13** Mark Burnett; **14** (t)Michael Abbey/Science Source/Photo Researchers, (bl)Aaron Haupt, (br)Michael Delannoy/Visuals Unlimited; **15** Mark Burnett; **16** (tl tcl bcl)Dwight Kuhn, (tcr)A. Glauberman/Photo Researchers, (tr)Mark Burnett, (others)Runk/Schoenberger from Grant Heilman; **17** (t)Bill Beaty/Animals Animals, (bl)Tom & Therisa Stack/Tom Stack & Assoc., (br)Michael Fogden/Earth Scenes; **18** Aaron Haupt; **19** Geoff Butler; **20** Johnny Autrey; **22** (t)Arthur C. Smith III from Grant Heilman, (bl)Hal Beral/Visuals Unlimited, (br)Larry L. Miller/Photo Researchers; **23** Lawson Wood/ CORBIS; **24** (l)Brandon D. Cole, (r)Gregory Ochocki/Photo Researchers; **25** (l)Zig Leszczynski/Animals Animals, (r)R. Andrew Odum/Peter Arnold, Inc.; **26** Alvin E. Staffan; **27** Geoff Butler; **28** (t)Jan Hinsch/Science Photo Library/ Photo Researchers, (b)Mark Burnett; **29** Mark Burnett; **30** Marc Von Roosmalen/AP; **31** (l)Mark Burnett, (r)Will & Deni McIntyre/ Photo Researchers; **32** KS Studios/Mullenix; **33** Jeff Greenberg/Rainbow; **36** Dave G. Houser/CORBIS; **37** Matt Meadows; **38** The Science Museum, London; **39** (l)Michael Keller/CORBIS, (c)David M. Phillips/Visuals Unlimited, (r)Richard Shiell/Earth Scenes; **43** Palmer/Kane, Inc. CORBIS; **44** Matt Meadows; **46** (tl)R. Kessel/G. Shih/Visuals Unlimited, (tc)Doug Martin, (tr)Carolina Biological Supply Co./Earth Scenes, (b)Bruce Iverson; **50** CNRI/Phototake, NYC; **51** (l)David M. Phillips/Visuals Unlimited, (c)Stone/

Getty Images, (r)PDS-3/Visuals Unlimited; **52** David M. Phillips/Visuals Unlimited; **53** Francois Gohier/Photo Researchers; **54** Lennart Nilsson/Albert Bonniers Forlag AB; **55** (c)Fred Habegger from Grant Heilman, (others)Mark Steinmetz; **56** (r)Dwight Kuhn, (others)John Shaw/Bruce Coleman, Inc; **58** (t)Envision/George Mattei, (b)Doug Martin; **59** Morrison Photography; **60** Custom Medical Stock Photo; **66–67** Inga Spence/Tom Stack & Assoc.; **68** (l)Gary Meszaros/Visuals Unlimited, (c r)Zig Leszczynski/Animals Animals; **71** Betty Barford/Photo Researchers; **72** (t)Inga Spence/Visuals Unlimited, (bl)Prof. P. Motta/Department of Anatomy/ University "La Sapienza", Rome/Science Photo Library/Photo Researchers, (br)David M. Phillips/Visuals Unlimited; **73** Biophoto Associates/Science Source/Photo Researchers; **74** (tl tr)Jane Hurd, (tcr)CNRI/PhotoTake, NYC, (br)Paul Hirata/Stock Connection, (others)Dr. Dennis Kunkel/ PhotoTake, NYC; **75** (l)Mark Burnett/Photo Researchers, (c)William J. Weber/Visuals Unlimited, (r)Inga Spence/ Visuals Unlimited, (br)John D. Cunningham/Visuals Unlimited; **76** Timothy Fuller; **77** Ariel Skelley/The Stock Market/CORBIS; **78** Bayard H. Brattstrom/Visuals Unlimited; **79** Bruce Berg/Visuals Unlimited; **80** Nigel Cattlin, Holt Studios International/Photo Researchers; **82** (l)Ken Chernus/ FPG/Getty Images, (r)Stephen Simpson/FPG/Getty Images; **83** Inga Spence/Tom Stack & Assoc.; **84** (t)Tom Rosenthal/ SuperStock, (others)The Photo Works/Photo Researchers; **85** Jeff Smith/Fotosmith; **86** Arnold Zann/Black Star; **87** Robert F. Myers/Visuals Unlimited; **88** Richard Sheill/ Earth Scenes; **89** Alan & Linda Detrick/Photo Researchers; **92–93** Birgid Allig/Stone/Getty Images; **93** (inset)Don Mason/The Stock Market/CORBIS; **94–95** Michael Pasdzior/ Getty Images; **95** Matt Meadows; **97** (tl)Clyde H. Smith/Peter Arnold, Inc., (tcl)Erik Sampers/Photo Researchers, (tcr)Dean Conger/CORBIS, (tr)Michael A. Keller/The Stock Market, (bl)Ed Bock/The Stock Market, (bcl)Joe McDonald/Visuals Unlimited, (bcr)Art Stein/Photo Researchers, (br)Peter Turnley/CORBIS; **99** Jim Grace/Photo Researchers; **100** Mark Burnett; **101** Aaron Haupt; **102** (l)Breck P. Kent, (c)Runk/ Schoenberger from Grant Heilman, (r)PhotoTake, NYC/ Carolina Biological Supply Company; **107** Geoff Butler; **109** (t)C Squared Studios/PhotoDisc, (b)M. McCarron; **110** KS Studios; **113** KS Studios; **117** Michael Newman/ PhotoEdit; **118** (t)Jeff Greenberg/PhotoEdit, (b)Amanita Pictures; **120** Sara Davis/The Herald-Sun; **126–127** Chris Trotman/ NewSport/CORBIS; **129** Geoff Butler; **133–134** KS Studios; **135** Visuals Unlimited; **137** KS Studios; **140** Dominic Oldershaw; **141** Bob Daemmrich; **144** Richard T. Nowitz; **146** Renee Lynn/Photo Researchers; **151** Richard Hutchings/ Photo Researchers; **152** KS Studios; **153** Matt Meadows; **154** (t)Eising/Stock Food, (b)Goldwater/Network/Saba Press Photos; **155** (l)Ed Beck/The Stock Market, (r)Tom & DeeAnn McCarthy/The Stock Market; **160–161** Julian Calder/ CORBIS; **163** National Cancer Institute/Science Photo Library/Photo Researchers; **166** Meckes/Ottawa/Photo Researchers; **167** Aaron Haupt; **170** (r)StudiOhio, (l)Matt Meadows; **171** Aaron Haupt; **173** Runk/Schoenberger from Grant Heilman; **175** CC Studio/Science Photo Library/Photo Researchers; **178** Holt Studios International (Nigel Cattlin)/ Photo Researchers; **179** (tr bl)Jack Bostrack/Visuals Unlimited, (tl br)Visuals Unlimited, (cl)Cytographics Inc./ Visuals Unlimited, (cr)Cabisco/Visuals Unlimited; **181** Oliver Meckes/E.O.S/Gelderblom/Photo Researchers; **182** Andrew Syred/Science Photo Library/Photo Researchers; **186** (t)Wyman IRA/CORBIS, (b)Matt Meadows/Peter Arnold,

Inc.; **187** Matt Meadows; **189** (tl)Manfred Kage/Peter Arnold, Inc., (tr)K.G. Murti/Visuals Unlimited, (bl)Don W. Fawcett/ Visuals Unlimited; **194–195** (bkgd)Jodi Jacobson, (inset) Andrew A. Wagner; **195** L. Fritz/H. Armstrong Roberts; **196–197** Joe McDonald/CORBIS; **198** (l)David M. Dennis/ Tom Stack & Assoc., (r)Todd Gipstein/Photo Researchers; **198–199** (bkgd)Carr Clifton/Minden Pictures; **199** (l)Colin Milkins/OSF/Animals Animals, (tr)Harold R. Hungerford/ Photo Researchers, (br)Ed Reschke/Peter Arnold, Inc.; **200** SSEC/University of Wisconsin at Madison; **202** (l)Charlie Ott/Photo Researchers, (r)Terry Donnelly/Tom Stack & Assoc.; **203** (l)F. Stuart Westmorland/Photo Researchers, (r)Jim Zipp/Photo Researchers; **204** Francois Gohier/Photo Researchers; **205** (t)Wendell Metzen/Index Stock Imagery, (b)Joshua Rodas/Getty Images; **207** Stephen Frink/CORBIS; **208** Stephen Frink/CORBIS; **209** Glencoe photo; **211** Matt Meadows; **215** Tom McGuire; **216** Matt Meadows; **217** Doug Martin; **218** Rosemary Calvert; **219** (l)David Woodfall/ENP Images, (r)David M. Dennis; **224–225** William Campbell/ CORBIS Sygma; **226** Darrell Gulin/CORBIS; **227** David Muench/CORBIS; **228** (bkgd)Craig Fujii/Seattle Times, (t)Jeff Henry, (c)Kevin R. Morris/CORBIS, (b)Jeff Henry; **229** Rod Planck/Photo Researchers; **231** (t)Steve McCutcheon/Visuals Unlimited, (bl)Pat O'Hara/DRK Photo, (br)Erwin & Peggy Bauer/Tom Stack & Assoc.; **232** (t)Peter Ziminski/Visuals Unlimited, (c)Leonard Rue III/Visuals Unlimited, (bl)C.C. Lockwood/DRK Photo, (br)Larry Ulrich/DRK Photo; **233** (t)Fritz Polking/Visuals Unlimited, (b)William Grenfell/ Visuals Unlimited; **234** Lynn M. Stone/DRK Photo; **236** (l)Joe McDonald/DRK Photo, (r)Steve Solum/Bruce Coleman, Inc.; **237** Kevin Schafer; **239** W. Banaszewski/ Visuals Unlimited; **240** CORBIS; **241** James R. Fisher/DRK Photo; **242** D. Foster/ WHOI/ Visuals Unlimited; **243** (l)Stephen Frink/CORBIS, (r)The Image Bank/Getty Images; **244** (tl)Dwight Kuhn, (tr)Glenn Oliver/Visuals Unlimited, (b)Stephen J. Krasemann/DRK Photo; **245** (l)David Muench/CORBIS, (r)Jerry Sarapochiello/Bruce Coleman, Inc.; **246** (t)Dwight Kuhn, (b)John Gerlach/DRK Photo; **247** Fritz Polking/Bruce Coleman, Inc.; **248** Courtesy Albuquerque Public Schools; **249** (l)James P. Rowan/DRK Photo, (r)John Shaw/Tom Stack & Assoc.; **254–255** Bill Ross/ CORBIS; **257** Visuals Unlimited; **260** (l)George Lepp/ CORBIS, (r)Carson Baldwin Jr./Earth Scenes; **261** Paul A. Souders/CORBIS; **262** (bkgd)Ian R. MacDonald/Texas A&M University, (l)Emory Kristof, (r)National Energy Technology Laboratory; **263** Hal Beral/ Visuals Unlimited; **265** Roger Ressmeyer/CORBIS; **266** Steven C. Spencer, Florida Solar Energy Center; **267** Inga Spence/Visuals Unlimited; **268** Robert Cameron/ Stone/Getty Images; **269** Vince Streano/ CORBIS; **270** (t)David Young-Wolff/PhotoEdit, Inc., (b)Earl Young/Archive Photos; **271** Peter Holden/Visuals Unlimited; **273** Aaron Haupt; **274** Joseph Nettis/Photo Researchers; **275** (t)Mark Joseph/ Stone/Getty Images, (bl)Aaron Haupt, (br)Wyoming Mining Association; **278** (t)Aaron Haupt, (b)Joel W. Rogers/CORBIS; **279** Aaron Haupt; **280** (t)Ed Clark, (bl)Brown Brothers, (br)Shell Oil Co.; **281** (l)Andrew J. Martinez/Photo Researchers, (r)Coco McCoy/Rainbow; **286** Stephen Dalton/Animals Animals; **286–287** A.T. Willett/ Image Bank/Getty Images; **288–289** National Oceanic & Atmospheric Administration; **289** Mark Burnett; **291** Pat & Tom Leeson/Photo Researchers; **294** (bkgd)Picture Perfect, (tl bl br)CORBIS, (tr)Ellis Herwig/Stock Boston/ PictureQuest; **297** Miles Ertman/Masterfile; **303** Timothy Fuller; **308** Jim Zuckerman/CORBIS; **309** NOAA/NESDIS/ Science Source/Photo Researchers; **311** (l)Steve Starr/ CORBIS, (r)Jay Reeves/AP Wide World; **312** Howard Bluestein/Photo Researchers; **313** AFP/CORBIS; **314** Doug Martin; **315** (t)Timothy Fuller, (b)Mark Burnett; **316** Ron Magill/Miami Metrozoo; **317** Roger Ressmeyer/CORBIS; **322–323** Andrew Brown, Ecoscene/CORBIS; **325** (l)Studiohio, (r)Tom Bean/DRK Photo; **326** W. Perry Conway/CORBIS; **327** Hans Strand/Stone; **328** (tl)Craig Kramer, (tr)A.J. Copley/Visuals Unlimited, (bl br)John Evans; **329** (l)Runk/Schoenberger from Grant Heilman, (r)William Johnson/Stock Boston; **331** (t)James D. Balog, (c)Martin Miller, (b)Kenneth H. Thomas/Photo Researchers, (bkgd)Stephen R. Wagner; **332** (l)Bonnie Heidel/Visuals Unlimited, (r)John Bova/Photo Researchers; **338** (l)Gary Braasch/CORBIS, (r)Donna Ikenberry/Earth Scenes; **339** Chip & Jill Isenhart/Tom Stack & Associates; **340** (t)Dr. Russ Utgard, (b)Denny Eilers from Grant Heilman; **341** Georg Gerster/Photo Researchers; **342** (t)George H. Harrison from Grant Heilman, (b)Bob Daemmrich; **343** KS Studios; **345** (l)Tom Bean/DRK Photo, (r)David M. Dennis/Earth Scenes; **347** Matt Meadows; **348** Georg Gerster/Photo Researchers; **350–351** William Manning/The Stock Market/CORBIS; **351** Aaron Haupt; **352** (l)Michael Busselle/Stone, (r)David Woodfall/DRK Photo; **353** Tim Davis/Stone/Getty Images; **354** (t)Grant Heilman Photography, (b)KS Studios; **356** Mel Allen/ICL/Panoramic Images; **358** CORBIS/PictureQuest; **359** (l)Harald Sund/The Image Bank/Getty Images, (r)Loren McIntyre; **360** C. Davidson/Comstock; **361** James L. Amos/CORBIS; **362** (l)Wolfgang Kaehler, (r)Nigel Press/Tony Stone Images; **363** First Image; **365** CORBIS; **366** file photo; **367** Barbara Filet; **368** Chad Ehlers/Stone; **370** Macduff Everton/The Image Bank/Getty Images; **371** (tl)David Muench/CORBIS, (tr)SuperStock, (bl)Robert Holmes/ CORBIS, (br)Breck P. Kent/Earth Scenes; **372** Alan Schein Photography/CORBIS; **374** KS Studios; **375** KS Studios; **376** Gary Bogdon/CORBIS Sygma; **377** (l)Todd Powell/Index Stock, (r)J. Wengle/DRK Photo; **382–383** Bourseiller/ Durieux/Photo Researchers; **386** Martin Land/Science Source/Photo Researchers; **389** Ralph White/CORBIS; **395** Davis Meltzer; **396** Craig Aurness/CORBIS; **398** Craig Brown/Index Stock; **400** Roger Ressmeyer/CORBIS; **402** Burhan Ozbilici/AP/ Wide World Photos; **404** L. Lauber/ Earth Scenes; **410–411** (bkgd)Wolfgang Kaehler, (inset)PhotoDisc; **412–413** Buck Miller/SuperStock; **414** Paul Almasy/CORBIS; **415** (t)Jerry Lampen/Reuters, (b)David Young-Wolff/ PhotoEdit; **417** Gary W. Carter/CORBIS; **418** Image Bank/Getty Images; **419** (t)Micael Dalton/ Fundamental Photographs, (cl)David Young-Wolff/ PhotoEdit, Inc., (cr)Dennis Potokar/Photo Researchers, (b)Matt Meadows; **421** Mark Burnett; **422** (l)David Young-Wolff/PhotoEdit, (r)Dennis MacDonald; **423** Glencoe photo; **425** Photo by Richard T. Nowitz, imaging by Janet Dell Russell Johnson; **427** John Cancalosi/Stock Boston; **434** CORBIS; **436** (t)Fletcher & Baylis/Photo Researchers, (b)Charles O'Rear/CORBIS; **437** Mark Burnett; **438** Chuck Liddy/AP/ Wide World Photos; **442–443** AFP/CORBIS; **444** Matt Meadows; **445** Getty Images; **446** (tl)Paul A. Souders/ CORBIS, (tc)Getty Images, (tr)Bibi Eng/Getty Images, (b)SuperStock; **447** Matt Meadows; **450** David Taylor/ Science Photo Library/Photo Researchers; **451** Amanita Pictures; **452** (l)Steve Kaufman/CORBIS, (tr)Tom McHugh/ Photo Researchers, (br)Fred Bavendam/Minden Pictures; **453** Don Tremain/Getty Images; **454** (l)Richard Megna/ Fundamental Photographs, (cl)John Lund/Stone/Getty

Images, (cr)Richard Pasley/Stock Boston, (r)T.J. Florian/Rainbow/PictureQuest; **455** (l)Philippe Colombi/PhotoDisc, (c)Michael Newman/PhotoEdit, Inc., (r)Roger K. Burnard; **456** Matt Meadows; **457** (t)Ralph Cowan, (bl)Aaron Haupt, (br)Aaron Haupt; **459** Jeff J. Daly/Visuals Unlimited; **460** Timothy Fuller; **463** Photo Researchers; **464** (t)Denso/Rex Features, (b)Alexander Tsiaras/Photo Researchers; **465** (l)John Evans, (r)Siede Preis/PhotoDisc; **467** Elaine Shay; **470–471** Russell Dohrman/Index Stock Imagery; **472** (l)Gary C. Will/Visuals Unlimited, (c)Mark Burnett/Stock Boston, (r)CORBIS; **474** Mark Burnett; **475** (l)Mark Burnett, (r)NASA; **476** Van Bucher/Photo Researchers; **480** Fermi National Accelerator Laboratory/Science Photo Library/Photo Researchers; **481** Tom Stewart/The Stock Market/CORBIS; **482** (bkgd)Bettmann/CORBIS, (t)Bettmann/CORBIS, (bl)Bettmann/CORBIS, (br)New York Public Library, General Research Division, Astor, Lenox, and Tilden Foundations; **484** Emmanuel Scorcelletti/Liaison Agency/Getty Images; **486** Bettman CORBIS; **487** NASA; **488** Mark Burnett; **489** Klaus Guldbrandsen/Science Photo Library/Photo Researchers; **490** (tl)Mark Thayer, (tr)CORBIS, (bl)Kenneth Mengay/Liaison Agency/Getty Images, (bc)Arthur Hill/ Visuals Unlimited, (br)RMIP/Richard Haynes; **490–491** KS Studios; **492** (t)Mark Burnett, (b)Michael Newman/ PhotoEdit; **494** (tl)Robert Essel/The Stock Market/CORBIS, (tr)John Eastcott & Yva Momatiuk/DRK Photo, (bl)Ame Hodalic/CORBIS, (cr)Diaphor Agency/Index Stock Imagery; **500** Layne Kennedy/CORBIS; **500–501** Richard Pasley/Stock Boston/PictureQuest; **501** (inset)Mark Burnett; **502–503** Mike Powell/Getty Images; **504** Doug Martin Photography; **506** Stephen R. Wagner; **510** SuperStock; **511** (l)Tom Pantages, (r)Jodi Jacobson/Peter Arnold, Inc.; **512** Bob Daemmrich; **513** (t)Bob Daemmrich, (b)Lew Long/ CORBIS; **514** Bob Daemmrich; **515** Mark Burnett; **517** Jose Luis Pelaez/CORBIS; **518** Matt Meadows; **519** Doug Martin; **521** (l)Tom Pantages, (c)Mark Burnett, (r)Bob Daemmrich/ Stock Boston/PictureQuest; **522** Bob Daemmrich; **523** (t)Tom McHugh/Photo Researchers, (b)R.J. Erwin/Photo Researchers; **524** Larry Prosor SuperStock; **525** Matt Meadows; **526** (tl)Daniel J. Cox/Stone, (tr)Adam Woolfitt/CORBIS, (cl)Walter Geiersperger/IndexStock/ PictureQuest, (bl)Tom Brakefield/CORBIS; **527** (t)Ryan McVay/Getty Images, (b)David Young-Wolff/PhotoEdit; **532–533** Larry Prosor/SuperStock; **534** Kennan Ward/The Stock Market/CORBIS; **535** Alan Thornton/Stone/Getty Images; **536** (tr)W. Cody/CORBIS, (bl)Duomo/CORBIS, (cr)William Swartz/Index Stock/PictureQuest, (br)CORBIS; **539** (t)Getty Images, (c)Alfred Pasieka/Photo Researchers, (b)Stone/Getty Images; **540** Digital Vision; **541** Randy Faris/CORBIS; **543** Matt Meadows; **547** (t)Mark Burnett, (b)Paul Barton/The Stock Market/CORBIS; **548** David Higgs/CORBIS; **549** Thinsulate is a trademark of 3M. Photo courtesy 3M; **552** Matt Meadows; **560–561** Alfred Pasieka/ Photo Researchers; **563** Roger Ressmeyer/CORBIS; **564** Aaron Haupt; **567** John A. Ey III/Photo Researchers; **568** John Lund/Getty Images; **570** Matt Meadows; **572** PhotoDisc; **573** Matt Meadows; **576** Doug Martin; **577** Matt Meadows; **579** Richard Megna/Fundamental Photographs; **580** PhotoDisc; **584–585** Matt Meadows; **586** (t)Giraudon/Art Resource, NY, (c)Najlah Feanny/CORBIS, (bl)Hemera Technologies, Inc., (br)Science Museum, London/Topham-HIP/The Image Works; **592–593** Douglas Peebles/CORBIS; **594** (l)file photo, (r)David Young-Wolff/PhotoEdit; **595** Stan Osolinski/ CORBIS; **605** Mark Burnett; **607** David Parker/Photo Researchers; **608** Peter Beattie/Liaison Agency/Getty Images; **610** (bkgd)Stephen R. Wagner, (inset)D. Boone/CORBIS; **612** Mark Clarke/Science Photo Library; **614** (t)Roger Ressmeyer/CORBIS, (b)SuperStock; **620–621** Werner H. Muller/Peter Arnold, Inc.; **621** CORBIS/PictureQuest; **622–623** Aaron Horowitz/CORBIS; **627** Lick Observatory; **628** Francois Gohier/Photo Researchers; **629** Jerry Lodriguss/ Photo Researchers; **631** Doug Martin; **634** (l)USGS/Science Photo Library/Photo Researchers, (r)NASA/Science Source/ Photo Researchers; **635** (t)CORBIS, (bl)NASA, (br)USGS/ TSADO/Tom Stack & Associates; **636** (t)JPL/TSADO/Tom Stack & Associates, (b)CORBIS; **637** (t)ASP/Science Source/ Photo Researchers, (b)NASA/JPL/Tom Stack and Associates; **638** (t)NASA/JPL, (b)Dr. R. Albrecht, ESA/ESO Space Telescope European Coordinating Facility/NASA; **639** AP/Wide World Photos; **641** Dominic Oldershaw; **643** European Southern Observatory/Photo Researchers; **644** (bl)Royal Observatory, Edinburgh/Science Photo Library/ Photo Researchers, (others)Anglo-Australian Observatory; **645** Frank Zullo/Photo Researchers; **647** R. Williams (ST Scl)/NASA; **648** (t)Movie Still Archives, (b)NASA; **649** Mark Burnett; **650** Kevin Morris/CORBIS; **651** (l)NASA, (r)National Optical Astronomy Observatories; **652** Royalty-Free/CORBIS; **656–657** TSADO/NASA/Tom Stack & Assoc.; **658** (l)Myrleen Ferguson Cate/PhotoEdit, (r)Michael Porsche/CORBIS; **659** (l)PhotoEdit, Inc., (r)Brand X Pictures; **660** Chuck Place/Stock Boston; **661** (t)Simon Fraser/Science Photo Library/Photo Researchers, (b)SAGEM/European Southern Observatory; **662** (t)Getty Images, (b)NASA; **663** Raphael Gaillarde/Liaison Agency/Getty Images; **664** (t)Icon Images, (b)Diane Graham-Henry & Kathleen Culbert-Aguilar; **665** NASA; **666** NASA/Science Photo Library/Photo Researchers; **667** NASA; **668** (t tc)NASA/ Science Source/ Photo Researchers, (bc)M. Salaber/Liaison Agency/Getty Images, (b)Julian Baum/Science Photo Library/ Photo Researchers; **669** (bkgd)NASA, (1)Dorling Kindersley Images, (2)TASS from Sovfoto, (3 7 10)NASA, (4 8)NASA/JPL, (5 6)NASA/JPL/Caltech; **670** AFP/CORBIS; **671** NASA; **672** NASA/Science Source/Photo Researchers; **673** NASA/Liaison Agency/Getty Images; **674** (t)NASA, (b)NASA/Liaison Agency/Getty Images; **675** NASA/Science Source/Photo Researchers; **676** NASA/JPL/Liaison Agency; **677** NASA/JPL/ Cornell, NASA/JPL/Malin Space Science Systems; **678** (t)David Ducros/Science Photo Library/Photo Researchers; (b)NASA/JPL/Space Science Institute; **679** The Cover Story/CORBIS; **680** NASA; **681** CORBIS; **682** Robert McCall; **683** (l)Novosti/ Science Photo Library/Photo Researchers, (c)Roger K. Burnard, (r)NASA; **687** NASA/Science Photo Library/Photo Researchers; **688** PhotoDisc; **690** Tom Pantages; **694** Michell D. Bridwell/PhotoEdit; **695** (t)Mark Burnett, (b)Dominic Oldershaw; **696** StudiOhio; **697** Timothy Fuller; **698** Aaron Haupt; **700** KS Studios; **701** Matt Meadows; **702** Amanita Pictures; **704** KS Studios; **706** Doug Martin; **710** Dominic Oldershaw; **713** (l)Brad Armstrong/AP/Wide World Photos, (r)file photo; **715** Stuart Ramson/AP/Wide World Photos; **732** Comstock Images; **736** (t)NIBSC/Science Photo Library/Photo Researchers, (bl)Dr. Richard Kessel, (br)David John/Visuals Unlimited; **737** (t)Runk/Schoenberger from Grant Heilman, (bl)Andrew Syred/Science Photo Library/Photo Researchers, (br)Rich Brommer; **738** (t)G.R. Roberts, (bl)Ralph Reinhold/Earth Scenes, (br)Scott Johnson/Animals Animals; **739** Martin Harvey/DRK Photo; **740** Matt Meadows.

Credits

PERIODIC TABLE OF THE ELEMENTS

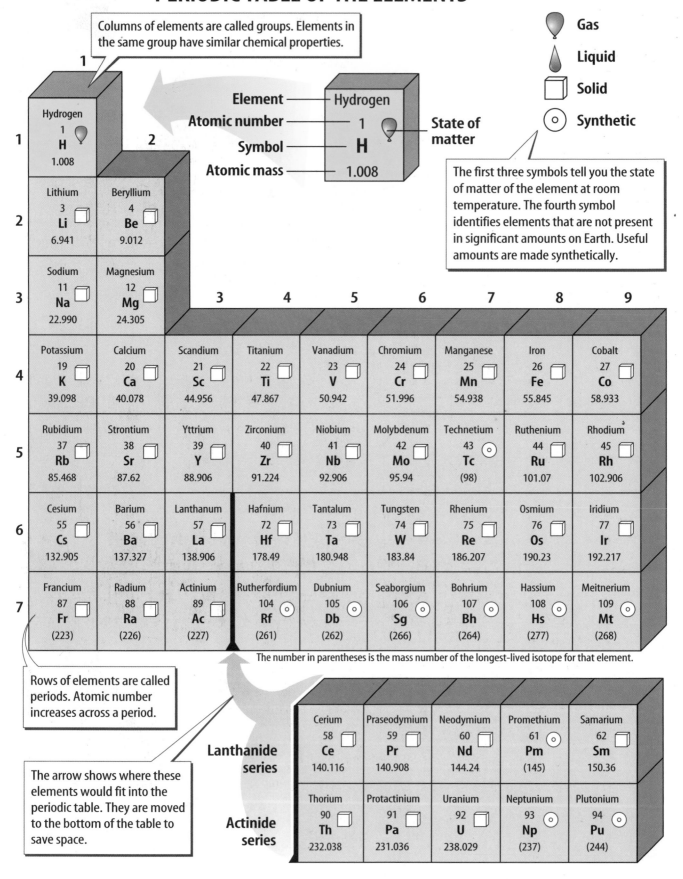

Columns of elements are called groups. Elements in the same group have similar chemical properties.

- Gas
- Liquid
- Solid
- Synthetic

Element — Hydrogen
Atomic number — 1
Symbol — H
Atomic mass — 1.008

State of matter

The first three symbols tell you the state of matter of the element at room temperature. The fourth symbol identifies elements that are not present in significant amounts on Earth. Useful amounts are made synthetically.

The number in parentheses is the mass number of the longest-lived isotope for that element.

Rows of elements are called periods. Atomic number increases across a period.

The arrow shows where these elements would fit into the periodic table. They are moved to the bottom of the table to save space.

Lanthanide series

Cerium	Praseodymium	Neodymium	Promethium	Samarium
58 Ce 140.116	59 Pr 140.908	60 Nd 144.24	61 Pm (145)	62 Sm 150.36

Actinide series

Thorium	Protactinium	Uranium	Neptunium	Plutonium
90 Th 232.038	91 Pa 231.036	92 U 238.029	93 Np (237)	94 Pu (244)